Symbol	Chapter Introduced	Meaning
P^e	18	expected price level
$P(z)$	19	price level in market z
PPI	1	producer price index
PPP	16	purchasing power parity
r	7	real interest rate
r^e	7	expected real interest rate
$\bar{r}$	14	real discount rate for people with poor collateral
$\overline{R}$	3	nominal interest rate
R^d	17	nominal interest rate on deposits
s	11	job-separation rate
$(\cdot)^s$	5	quantity supplied
S	15	nominal amount of national saving
$t\,(T)$	12	individual's (aggregate) nominal taxes
$(\cdot)_t$	2	price or quantity in period t
u	11	unemployment rate
$u(\cdot)$	2	utility function
U	11	number of persons unemployed
$v\,(V)$	8	individual's (aggregate) nominal transfers
w	6	nominal wage rate
$\overline{w}$	11	reservation wage rate
w^u	11	income received while unemployed
x	3	real present value of consumption
$y\,(Y)$	2	individual's (aggregate) real output
z	19	index of markets
α	12	substitution of public services for private consumption
β	12	marginal product of public services
γ	4	nominal transactions cost
δ	9	depreciation rate
Δ	2	change of some price or quantity
ε	16	exchange rate
η	11	job-finding rate
λ	20	rate of price adjustment
μ	8	growth rate of money
ν	20	marginal propensity to consume (or to spend)
π	7	inflation rate
π^e	7	expected inflation rate
$\hat{\pi}$	19	choice of inflation under discretionary policy
π^*	20	rate of change of market-clearing price level
ρ	10	rate of time preference in utility function
τ	13	marginal tax rate
ϕ	4	interval between withdrawals of money
$\psi(\cdot)$	19	function for policymaker's choice of inflation

MACROECONOMICS

MACROECONOMICS

ROBERT J. BARRO

Harvard University

THIRD EDITION

WILEY INTERNATIONAL EDITION

WILEY

JOHN WILEY & SONS, INC.

New York • Chichester • Brisbane • Toronto • Singapore

Cover art   Marjory Dressler
Cover design   Sheila Granda

Library of Congress Cataloging in Publication Data:
Barro, Robert J.
Macroeconomics/Robert Barro. — 3rd ed. p. cm.
Includes bibliographical references.
ISBN 0-471-50282-0
1. Macroeconomics.   I. Title.
HB172.5.B36   1990
339—dc20
                                                                89-22654
                                                                CIP

10 9 8 7 6 5 4

To Judy, with love.

PREFACE

Macroeconomics is in a state of flux. The Keynesian model, which was almost universally accepted as the basic paradigm until the late 1960s, has become increasingly less popular. This loss in popularity reflects embarrassments over past economic events, especially the failure of the model to deal satisfactorily with inflation and supply shocks. It also reflects the theoretical and empirical progress of an alternative "market-clearing approach," which is more closely related to the microeconomics that economists use successfully to study the behavior of individual households and businesses. Although some important problems remain, this approach provides a much more satisfactory macroeconomics than the one we had before. By more satisfactory, I mean that the approach avoids internal inconsistencies and also provides a better understanding of the real world.

Although the Keynesian model has been subject to increasing skepticism by economists, it has nevertheless continued to reign supreme in most textbooks. As a result, it has continued to organize the way the subject has been taught to the majority of students. Many textbooks present aspects of market-clearing models but these models have not been taken seriously in the study of real-world events or policy proposals. This gap between textbook material and the knowledge gained in the last 20 years motivated me to write the first edition of this book.

My purpose is to present the market-clearing approach as a general method for analyzing real-world macroeconomic problems. The stress on this approach means that the book is not a "balanced" treatment of alternative macroeconomic models. There is no book—and probably could be none of substance—that is balanced in this respect. Although I deal in a serious manner with the Keynesian model—and show carefully how it relates to the market-clearing approach—I do not use the Keynesian framework for most of the analyses of economic events or policies. In any case, whatever one's ultimate judgment about the value of the Keynesian model, there is a very good reason not to begin the study of macroeconomics with it. The Keynesian theory is an advanced topic that makes specific assumptions about the ways that private markets malfunction. The nature of these malfunctions and the special features of the Keynesian model cannot be fully understood and appreciated until the market-clearing analysis has been worked out.

I have been very encouraged by the market's reception of previous editions. This favorable reception shows up directly in the large and growing usage of the book in undergraduate courses at many colleges. The book has also received a lot of attention in the national press. Positive reviews appeared in *Newsweek, Fortune*, the *Wall Street Journal, Newsday*, the *Boston Globe*, the *Washington Times*, the

Rochester Democrat and Chronicle, and the *Financial Times*. Reviews of textbooks in the media are rare, and these were a pleasant surprise to me (and my publisher).

I think that the favorable reception reflects the widespread eagerness for a macroeconomic framework that outperforms the Keynesian model. Although the Keynesian model can be appealing as a teaching device, it tends to leave students with a poor understanding of how the economy works and how governmental policies can help—or hinder—it. In addition, I have found that many instructors have become convinced, after some initial skepticism, that the more satisfactory market-clearing approach really is accessible to undergraduates.

This third edition maintains the theme of previous editions but makes a number of improvements. The most important is the expanded treatment of the international economy. Partly because of the concern over recent economic events—such as the U.S. current-account deficit, the fluctuations of exchange rates, and the international debt crisis—most teachers of intermediate macroeconomics now desire to include a substantial discussion of the world economy. Chapters 15 and 16 (which significantly extend the previous Chapter 20) are new; they show how the market-clearing approach with stress on intertemporal considerations applies readily to international topics. The coverage includes international borrowing and lending, the current-account balance, shifts in the terms of trade, flexible and fixed exchange rates (including the gold standard and the European Monetary System), and the recent behavior of real exchange rates. A new section explores the role of fiscal policy in the world economy, with stress on the linkage between budget and current-account deficits.

Another addition worth highlighting is the discussion in Chapter 19 of rules versus discretion in the government's policy choices. This section discusses an application of game-theoretic reasoning to the study of policy formation. The analysis shows why monetary growth and inflation tend to be excessive, why credible rules can improve outcomes, and why such rules are difficult to enforce. This discussion approaches the frontiers of macroeconomic research by dealing with recent discoveries that have already proved to be of great importance for policy evaluation. Fortunately the key points can be explained in a way that is comprehensible for undergraduates.

As with previous editions, I discuss the material in as simple a fashion as I have found possible so that the book can be used for undergraduate courses in intermediate macroeconomics. Six years of experience have demonstrated that the book works well for these courses. However, the feedback from users has helped me to simplify the exposition in many places. Therefore, I am confident that students will find this third edition even more accessible than the earlier ones.

In writing this book, I have benefited from an unusual amount of excellent advice, as well as encouragement to carry out the project. Since regular revision is a part of textbook writing, I appreciate suggestions from readers. I am particularly grateful to Mark Rush, who provided valuable and detailed comments on several versions of all three editions. I also acknowledge the helpful comments of Ken Chapman, Marty Eichenbaum, Mark Fisher, Roger Goldberg, John Haltiwanger, Barry Ickes, Jim Kahn, Evan Koenig, Prakash Loungani, and James McGibbany.

Robert Barro

BRIEF CONTENTS

CONTENTS

CHAPTER 1

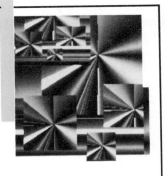

THE APPROACH TO MACROECONOMICS

n macroeconomics we study the overall or aggregate performance of an economy. For example, we consider the total output of goods and services as measured by the **gross national product (GNP).** We look also at the aggregates of employment and unemployment and at the breakdown of GNP into consumer expenditures, investment (which are purchases of new capital goods), government purchases of goods and services, and net exports.

The above terms refer to the quantities of goods or work effort. We shall also be interested in the prices that relate to these quantities. For example, we consider the dollar prices of the goods and services that the economy produces. When we look at the price of the typical or average item, we refer to the **general price level.** But we are also interested in the **wage rate,** which is the price of labor services, the **interest rate,** which determines the cost of borrowing and the return to lending, and the **exchange rates** between the currencies of different countries.

We shall want to know how the economy determines the various quantities and prices and how government policies affect these variables. Specifically, we shall consider monetary policy, which involves the determination of the quantity of money and the design of monetary institutions, and fiscal policy, which pertains to the government's expenditures, taxes, and budget deficits.

The performance of the overall economy is a substantial concern for everyone because it influences job prospects, incomes, and prices. Thus, it is important for us—and even more important for our government policymakers—to understand how the macroeconomy works. Unfortunately, as is obvious from reading the newspapers, the theory of macroeconomics is not a settled scientific field. There is much controversy among economists about what is a useful basic approach, as well as about the detailed analyses of particular economic events and policy proposals. There has, however, been a great deal of progress in recent years in designing a more satisfactory macroeconomic theory. The main objective of this book is to convey that progress to students in an accessible form.

THE BEHAVIOR OF OUTPUT, UNEMPLOYMENT, AND THE PRICE LEVEL IN THE UNITED STATES

To get an overview of the subject matter, consider the historical record on some of the major macroeconomic variables for the United States. Figure 1.1 shows the total output of goods and services in the United States from 1869 to 1988. (The starting date is determined by the available data.) The measure of aggregate output is the gross national product, expressed in terms of values for a base year, which happens to be 1982. This measure, which we discuss in a later section on national-income accounting, is called **real GNP.**[1]

Notice from Figure 1.1 the general upward trend of real GNP, which reflects the long-term growth or economic development of the U.S. economy. The average growth rate of real GNP from 1869 to 1988 was 3.3% per year. Consequently, over 119 years, the total output increased fifty-three-fold. If we divide through by population to determine real per capita GNP, we find that the average growth rate was 1.8% per year—the 3.3% average growth rate of real GNP less the 1.5% average growth rate of population. Hence, over 119 years, output per person increased by a factor of eight.

Figure 1.2 shows the growth rate of real GNP for each year. Notice in this figure the recurring ups and downs in real GNP. These movements are called aggregate business fluctuations or the business cycle.[2] When real GNP falls toward a low point or trough, the economy is in a **recession,** or an economic contraction. Conversely, when real GNP expands toward a high point or peak, the economy is in a **boom** or an economic expansion. The dates indicated in Figure 1.2 show the major U.S. recessions since 1869. Note especially the **Great Depression** of 1930 to 1933, where output fell 30% below the peak value reached in 1929. The other major economic contractions before World War II occurred in 1893–94, 1907–8, 1914, 1920–21, and 1937–38. For the post–World War II period, the most significant recessions were those for 1958, 1974–75, and 1980–82.

---

[1]The figure uses a proportionate scale, so that each unit on the vertical axis corresponds to an equal percentage change in real GNP.

[2]The term *business cycle* is somewhat misleading since it suggests a more regular pattern of ups and down in economic activity than actually appears in the data. But the term is too entrenched in the economics literature to avoid entirely.

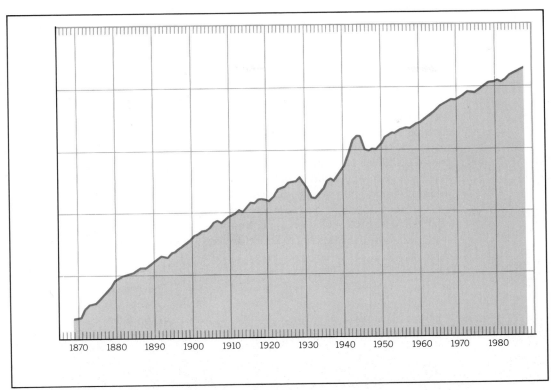

FIGURE 1.1 *The Behavior of Output in the United States, 1869–1988*
The figure shows real gross national product on a proportionate scale.
Sources for Figures 1.1–1.5:
For real GNP and the GNP deflator: Recent values are from the U.S. Commerce Department, U.S. Survey of Current Business, March 1989 and July 1988. Figures back to 1929 are from the U.S. Department of Commerce (1986). For 1869–1928, the values are from Christina Romer (1987, 1988).

For the unemployment rate: The figures are the number unemployed divided by the total labor force, which includes military personnel. Data since 1930 are from Citibase data bank and from Economic Report of the President, 1988, Table B-32; 1983, Table B-29; 1970, Table C-22. The data for 1933–43 are adjusted to classify federal emergency workers as employed, as discussed in Michael Darby (1976). Values for 1890–1929 are based on Christina Romer (1986, Table 9).

On the up side, notice first the high rates of growth in output during World Wars I and II and the Korean War. Other periods of economic boom—in the sense of unusually high growth rates of real GNP—were 1982–84, 1975–79, 1961–73 (except for the brief recession in 1970), the recovery from the Great Depression from 1933 to 1940 (aside from the recession of 1937–38), much of the 1920s, the period from 1896 to 1906, and the years from 1875 to 1880.

Figure 1.3, which reports the unemployment rate for each year, provides another way to look at recessions and booms. The unemployment rate is the fraction of the total labor force that has no job. (We discuss the precise meaning of this variable in Chapter 11.) Over the period 1890 to 1988, for which data are available, the median unemployment rate was 5.4%. (The mean was 6.4%.) But during recessions, the unemployment rate rises above the median. The extreme is the Great Depression, where unemployment reached 22% of the labor force in 1932. But also noteworthy are the average rates of 18% for 1931–35, 12% for 1938–39, 11% for 1894–98, 9% for 1982–83 and 1921, and 8% for 1975–76.

Figures 1.2 and 1.3 show the turbulence of the economy during the two world wars and the 1930s. But suppose that we abstract from these episodes and compare the post–World War II performance with that from before World War I. Then the major message from the data is the similarity between the post–World War II and pre–World War I experiences. For example, the average growth rate of real GNP was 3.2% per year from 1947 to 1988 and 3.8% from 1869 to 1914. The median unemployment rate was 5.4% from 1947 to 1988 and 5.2% from 1890 to 1914 (the means were 5.5% and 6.4%, respectively). The extent of fluctuations—in terms of the severity of recessions and booms—was only slightly greater in the earlier period than in the later one.[3] Therefore, although the economy has changed greatly

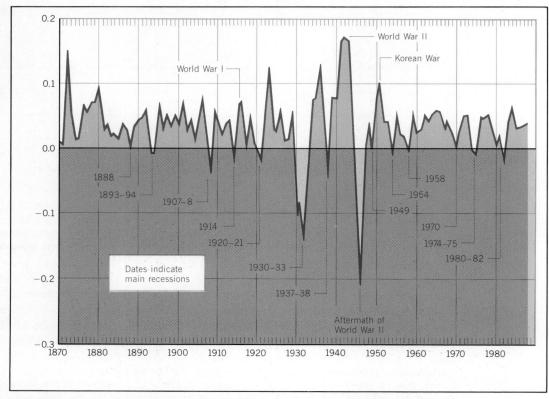

FIGURE 1.2 *Growth Rates of Output in the United States, 1870–1988*
The figure shows the annual growth rate of real gross national product.

[3]For a detailed comparison of real GNP and unemployment rates over the different periods, see Christina Romer (1986, 1987, 1988).

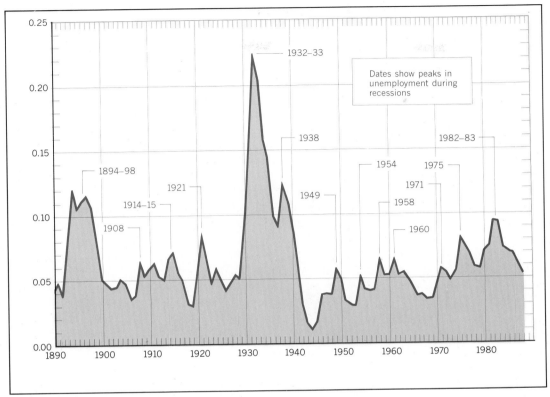

Dates show peaks in unemployment during recessions

1932–33

1938

1982–83

1954   1975

1894–98   1921   1971

1914–15   1949   1958

1908   1960

FIGURE 1.3 *U.S. Unemployment Rate, 1890–1988*

over a century—including a much larger role for government, a diminished share of agriculture in the GNP, and dramatic alterations in the monetary system—the data suggest no major change in the intensity of business fluctuations.[4]

Overall, when looking at Figures 1.1–1.3, we should recall the two main features that we would like to use economic analysis to understand. One is the long-term growth, and the other is the short-term pattern of business fluctuations. As we develop the macroeconomic model in subsequent chapters, we shall frequently compare the theoretical propositions about these phenomena with the patterns that appear in the real-world data.

Figure 1.4 shows an index of the general level of prices in the United States from 1870 to 1988. (We discuss the details of the particular measure—the deflator

[4]Until recently, economists believed that the post–World War II period exhibited milder business fluctuations than the pre–World War I period. (For example, Chapter 1 of the first edition of this book accepted this viewpoint.) This comparison depended, however, on data for the earlier period that were constructed differently from those for the later period. Christina Romer's research (see note 3 above) demonstrated that these data problems were crucial. She constructed estimates since the late nineteenth century on a consistent basis for real GNP, the unemployment rate, and industrial production. Her measures show little change in the volatility of these variables from before World War I to after World War II. We used her estimates in the construction of Figures 1.1–1.3.

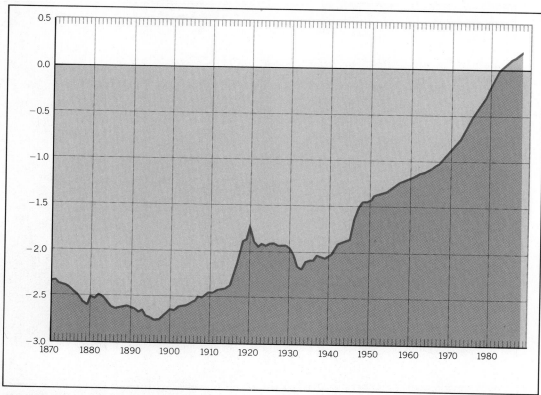

FIGURE 1.4 *U.S. Price Level, 1870–1988*
The figure shows the GNP deflator on a proportionate scale.

for the gross national product—toward the end of this chapter.) One striking observation is the persistent rise in prices since World War II, as contrasted with the movements up and down before the war. There are long periods in the earlier history—1869–92 and 1920–33—during which prices fell persistently.

Figure 1.5 looks at the year-to-year growth rate of the general price level, that is, the **inflation rate.** As already suggested, almost all of the inflation rates since World War II were positive, as contrasted with a mixture of positive and negative values from earlier periods. Note also that the inflation rate fell sharply from a peak of nearly 10% in 1980–81 to about 3% for 1983–88.

In subsequent chapters we shall relate the behavior of the general price level to monetary developments, especially to changes in the quantity of money. This monetary behavior depends, in turn, on the nature of monetary institutions, such as whether the United States was on the **gold standard** (as it was from 1879 until World War I and, to some extent, from World War I until 1933), on the presence of the Federal Reserve System (which began in 1914), and on the characteristics of the banking sector.

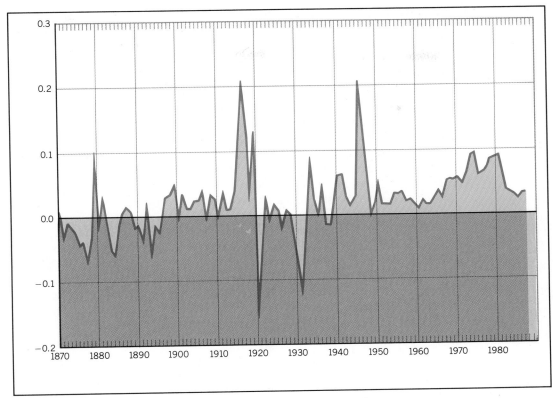

FIGURE 1.5 *U.S. Inflation Rate, 1870–1988*
The figure shows the annual rate of change of the GNP deflator.

THE APPROACH TO MACROECONOMICS

This section describes the basic theoretical approach that this book uses to design a useful macroeconomic model. In setting up this model, we shall spend a good deal of time on economic theory. In this context we worry about whether the theory seems sensible, whether it is internally consistent, and so on. But we should always remember that the main test of the model will be its ability to explain the behavior of macroeconomic variables in the real world. Therefore, especially after the basic theoretical framework is complete, we devote considerable space to comparisons of the theory with the real world, that is, with empirical evidence.

MICROECONOMIC FOUNDATIONS OF MACROECONOMICS

We begin by developing the basic price theory—or **microeconomic foundations**—that underlies the macroeconomic analysis of the aggregate variables in an economy. Much of this microeconomics will be familiar to students from previous courses in economics. In that sense, the macroeconomic approach in this book is a continuation of the economic reasoning used to explain the behavior of individual households and businesses. Here we apply this same economic science to understand the workings of the overall economy—that is, to study real GNP, employment and unemployment, the general price level and inflation, the wage rate, the interest rate, the exchange rate, and so on. Unfortunately, many basic textbooks in economics do not follow this general approach when dealing with macroeconomics. In fact, students could easily reach the conclusion that macroeconomics and microeconomics are two entirely distinct fields. A central theme of this book is that a more satisfactory macroeconomics emerges when it is linked to the underlying microeconomics. The term *more satisfactory* means, first, that the macroeconomic theory avoids internal inconsistencies, and second, that it provides a better understanding of the real world.

In Chapter 2 we examine the choice problems of an isolated individual, Robinson Crusoe. Naturally we assume that Crusoe's choices are guided by enlightened self-interest—that is, we exploit the central economic postulate of optimizing behavior. In the initial framework, the only choice problem concerns the level of work effort, which then determines the quantities of production and consumption. But by studying Crusoe's behavior, we can understand the trade-off between leisure and consumption that applies in complicated market economies. Also, by looking at an isolated individual, we bring out the role of a resource or **budget constraint** in its simplest form. When goods cannot be stored over time, Crusoe's budget constraint dictates that his consumption equal his production. As we shall see, extensions of this simple constraint are central to correct macroeconomic analyses in economies that include many consumers and producers, as well as a government.

We can use the model of Robinson Crusoe to predict his responses to changes in production opportunities—for example, to harvest failures or to discoveries of new goods or methods of production. Many of these results carry over to the predictions for aggregate output and employment in more realistic settings. In particular, when we consider the economy's responses to changes in production opportunities—such as the oil crises of 1973–74 and 1979—we usually get the right answer by thinking of the parallel situation for Robinson Crusoe.

Chapter 3 develops the microeconomic foundations needed to go from an analysis of Robinson Crusoe to a study of many persons who interact on various marketplaces. Once again we exploit the postulate of optimizing behavior, subject to budget constraints, to assess the responses of individuals to different circumstances.

To simplify matters, we start with only two markets. On the first market, households buy and sell goods in exchange for money. The dollar cost on this market is the theoretical counterpart of the general price level. On the other market, households can borrow and lend. This credit or loan market establishes an interest rate, which borrowers must pay to lenders.

The introduction of the goods market allows people to specialize in production activities, a setup that adds to the economy's productivity. (Robinson Crusoe did not have this option.) The existence of the credit market means that a household's expenditure during any period can diverge from its income during that period. Thus, unlike Robinson Crusoe, a household with a given income has choices about consuming now versus later. Similarly, households can choose between working now versus later. We discuss these choices by considering incentives to save, that is, to accumulate assets that pay interest income. We stress the idea that a higher interest rate motivates people to save more; thereby, they consume less today and plan to consume more later. Similarly, we show that various forces can induce people to rearrange their work and production from one period to another.

In a later chapter (Chapter 6), we introduce a labor market on which labor services are bought and sold at an established wage rate. But to simplify the basic model, we do not include this market at the outset. Rather, we pretend that households work only on their own production processes—that is, each household owns its own business and provides the labor input for this business. For many purposes—such as studying the main determinants of aggregate output and work effort, the general price level, and the interest rate—this simplification will be satisfactory. But to explore some other topics—such as the behavior of unemployment and the determination of wage rates—we have to deal explicitly with the labor market.

The analysis stresses the role of budget constraints, which ensure a balance between each household's sources and uses of funds. Although these budget conditions may seem tedious at times, it is important to keep these matters straight. Many serious errors in macroeconomic reasoning occur when economic theorists forget to impose the appropriate budget constraints in their models. We shall see that these conditions are especially important in evaluating temporary versus permanent changes in income, in studying the effects of interest rates on lenders and borrowers, and in evaluating the effects of money holdings. Also, when we introduce government policies in later chapters, we shall find it crucial to impose the government's budget constraint. Many errors in analyses of the government's expenditures and budget deficits result from a failure to impose this budget constraint.

Chapter 4 completes the discussion of microfoundations by exploring the incentives to hold non-interest-bearing paper money rather than financial assets that bear interest. The **demand for money** arises out of the process of carrying out transactions, which use money as a **medium of exchange.** Since households use money when they buy or sell goods or financial assets, it would require a great deal of planning and effort to hold little or no money. We then discuss how the quantity of money demanded depends on the price level, the interest rate, the level of income, and other variables.

MARKET-CLEARING CONDITIONS

We note in Chapter 5 that certain conditions must hold when we add up the actions of all households. For example, the total of goods sold by suppliers must equal the total bought by demanders. Similarly, the total amount loaned on the credit market must equal the total borrowed. We refer to conditions such as these as **aggregate-consistency conditions.** These conditions tell us something about how aggregate quantities must behave for the analysis to be internally consistent. Any reasonable macromodel must satisfy these conditions.

One way to ensure that the aggregate-consistency conditions hold is to assume that the various markets—say, for goods and credit—always clear. Clearing means that the price level and the interest rate adjust simultaneously so that the aggregate demand for goods equals the aggregate supply, and the aggregate of desired lending equals the aggregate of desired borrowing. We use this **market-clearing approach** for satisfying the aggregate-consistency conditions in the basic model.

The idea that markets clear is closely related to the notion that private markets function efficiently. With cleared markets, it is impossible to improve on any outcomes by matching potential borrowers and lenders or by bringing together potential buyers and sellers of goods. Cleared markets already accomplish all of these mutually advantageous trades. We can see that market clearing is reminiscent of the optimizing behavior of individuals. On the one hand, people determine their individual choices of work, consumption, and so on to make themselves as well off as possible. On the other hand, market clearing means that the people who participate in and organize markets—and are guided by the pursuit of their own interests—do not waste resources and thereby end up achieving efficient outcomes. Thus, market clearing is the natural macrocomplement to the microfoundations that underlie the model.

It is possible to satisfy the aggregate-consistency conditions without imposing market clearing in the sense described above. One important idea is that imperfect information makes it impossible to make the best decisions about production and work at all times. We shall explore later some macroeconomic models that incorporate incomplete information (particularly in Chapter 19). But it is best to explore the workings of the economy under full information before going on to this advanced topic. Thus, we do not introduce incomplete information into the model at the outset.

Another alternative to market clearing is the **Keynesian model.** This model assumes that some prices (usually of labor services or commodities) are sticky and that some rationing of quantities bought or sold comes into play. It turns out that outcomes are generally inefficient in the Keynesian model. Notably, some mutually advantageous trades do not take place. As a reflection of this "market failure," there tends to be chronic unemployment and underproduction. These conclusions from the Keynesian model have led many economists to advocate "corrective" policy actions by the government.

The Keynesian model depends crucially on the assumption that prices are sticky. Thus, not surprisingly, the rationale for price stickiness has been a subject of substantial debate, which is still unresolved. In any event, just as in the case of models with incomplete information, the Keynesian theory is an advanced topic that cannot be appreciated without first working through the logic of a market-clearing model. Thus, we take up the Keynesian model (in Chapter 20) after the market-clearing analysis is completed.

To summarize, the basic model relies on two key elements for making predictions about the behavior of quantities and prices in the real world. First, we use the microfoundations of the model, which stem from the optimizing behavior of individuals subject to budget constraints. Second, we exploit the notion of market clearing. As mentioned, this idea reflects the smooth operation of markets, that is, the efficient matching of potential buyers and sellers of goods, credit, labor services, and so on.

USING THE MARKET-CLEARING MODEL

Chapter 5 lays out the central theoretical apparatus used throughout the remainder of the book. After this point, the discussion amounts to extensions of the basic model to apply the reasoning to various topics in macroeconomics. The list of applications eventually includes supply shocks, inflation, business fluctuations, long-term economic growth, government purchases and public services, monetary and fiscal policies, international borrowing and lending, exchange rates, financial intermediation, incomplete information and rational expectations, and the Keynesian model.

We first use the model in Chapter 5 to study various disturbances that affect opportunities for production. Specifically, we assess the effects of supply shocks on output, employment, the price level, and the interest rate.

Chapter 6 brings in a labor market and allows for business firms as distinct economic units. With this extension of the model, we show how the clearing of the labor market determines the wage rate and the quantity of employment. For most purposes, however, the extended model yields results that coincide with those in Chapter 5. Therefore, for most of the subsequent analysis, we return to the setting that neglects the labor market and considers only one type of economic unit. We can think of this unit as a combination of a household and a firm. That is, this unit merges the consumption and working activities of households with the production and hiring activities of businesses. The main reason we proceed in this way is that it greatly simplifies the analysis without causing any mistakes.

Chapters 7 and 8 introduce the possibility of chronic rises in the general price level, that is, inflation. We look at inflation as primarily a monetary phenomenon. One of the major themes is that inflation and monetary growth can be largely independent of the variations in output and employment, which are examples of "real" variables. The interaction of monetary phenomena with output, employment, and other real variables is a major issue in macroeconomics but one that is not fully resolved. In this book we deal first with simple models where the interaction between monetary forces and the real variables is unimportant. Then we extend the analysis (in Chapters 17–20) to bring in more interesting possibilities for this interaction.

Chapters 9–11 apply the theory to business fluctuations and economic growth. Chapter 9 introduces investment, which is the accumulation of capital goods. By looking at actual recessions in the United States, we find that aggregate business fluctuations involve mainly variations in investment rather than consumption. The theory can explain this pattern and other features of real-world business fluctuations as responses to shocks that affect technology or preferences. These types of disturbances have been the focus of a recent area of research called **real business cycle theory.** (The approach contrasts with monetary theories, which stress the effects of monetary disturbances on the economy.)

Chapter 10 studies how investment shows up over the longer term as an increase in the stock of capital and thereby in economic growth. By allowing also for growth in population and for improvements in technology, we can apply the theory to a country's long-term economic development. Accordingly, we can use the model to study the behavior of the major macroeconomic variables in the United States over the past century. In addition, we apply the theory to a comparison of the growth experiences of a large number of countries since World War II.

Chapter 11 expands the model to allow for unemployment. We view unemployment as arising from the problem of matching workers to jobs. Specifically, we relate the average level and dynamics of unemployment to the rates at which people find and lose jobs. Then we show how various economic forces influence the rates of job finding and job separation. In particular, we show why unemployment rises during a recession.

Chapters 12–14 bring in government expenditures, taxes, and public debt and thereby allow us to consider fiscal policies. First, we introduce government purchases of goods and services, which we assume are used to provide public services to consumers and producers. Then we consider how households react to income taxes and to transfer programs, such as social security. Finally, by introducing the public debt, we can evaluate the economic consequences of the government's financing its spending by budget deficits rather than taxes.

Chapters 15 and 16 extend the theory from the economy of one country to that of many countries, which interact on international markets for goods and credit. Chapter 15 simplifies the analysis by assuming that all countries use the same currency and quote prices in units of this currency. We can then readily apply our previous framework to analyze a country's **balance of international payments.** In particular, we consider how shocks to technology and fiscal policies influence a country's incentive to borrow or lend internationally.

Chapter 16 allows for different currencies and considers the determination of exchange rates. We explore the distinction between fixed and flexible exchange rates and discuss how exchange rates interact with the balance of international payments.

Chapters 17–20 deal with interactions between monetary forces and real economic activity. Chapter 17 introduces financial intermediaries and studies the creation of deposits and the lending operations of banks and other institutions. The analysis stresses the role of intermediaries in promoting economic efficiency. Thus, a contraction in the amount of financial intermediation—such as that during the Great Depression and in other periods of financial crisis—tends to reduce the levels of production and employment. In addition, there are important effects of changes in financial intermediation on the general price level.

Chapter 18 explores the main pieces of empirical evidence that concern the interaction between monetary variables and the real economy. The theory can explain much of the evidence but not all of it. Specifically, using the model that we have developed up to this point, we cannot rationalize significant effects of purely monetary shocks on real economic activity. These effects seem to apply at least since World War II.

Chapter 19 extends the market-clearing model to account for the observed economic effects of monetary disturbances. The new feature is that individuals have incomplete information about prices in various markets and about the overall monetary picture. When people do not observe something directly—such as the general price level—they are motivated to use their available information to forecast the unobserved variables as accurately as possible. This type of expectation is called *rational,* and hence, the approach is often called *rational-expectations macroeconomics.* In this setting monetary disturbances can affect real economic activity more or less as appears in the U.S. data on business fluctuations. However, some empirical puzzles remain.

The theory in Chapter 19 has some intriguing implications for monetary policy. Namely, there are effects on real variables only from the erratic part of this policy, and the effects tend to be adverse. Thus, the main message is that monetary policy should be predictable rather than erratic.

Chapter 20 develops the model of business fluctuations that was stimulated by the research during the 1930s of the British economist, John Maynard Keynes. This theory departs from the previous analysis by assuming that some prices do not adjust instantaneously to clear all markets. That is, the prices of goods or wages of labor are assumed to be sticky rather than perfectly flexible. We begin with a simple version of the Keynesian model, a version that brings out the idea that shocks to the economy can have multiplicative effects on output. Then we work out the **IS/ LM model,** which is a popular extended version of this theory.

A basic conclusion from the Keynesian model is that recessions can result when monetary contractions or other disturbances lead to decreases in the aggregate demand for goods. There is more scope for active monetary and fiscal policies in this model than there was in the market-clearing framework.

For many years, the Keynesian model was the most popular tool of macroeconomic analysis. The popularity of this model has diminished since the late 1960s, however, especially at the frontiers of macroeconomic research. There are two main reasons for this decreased popularity. First, the Keynesian model does not deal very well with inflation or supply shocks, two problems that have been important since the late 1960s. Second, despite many attempts, economists have not found satisfactory ways to provide the Keynesian macromodel with internally consistent microfoundations. In any event, there is another good reason to postpone the consideration of the Keynesian model until late in the book. Namely, the model cannot be fully understood—and the distinctive features of it cannot be appreciated—until the market-clearing analysis has been worked out. Thus, whatever one's ultimate judgment about the usefulness of the Keynesian model, it is a great mistake to begin a study of macroeconomics with this model.

A NOTE ON MATHEMATICS AND ECONOMIC REASONING

This book does not use any advanced mathematics. Rather it relies on graphical methods and occasional algebraic derivations. Although calculus would speed up the presentation in some places, this higher mathematics is unnecessary for the main economic arguments. Therefore, students should not find the book difficult on technical grounds.

What will be demanding from time to time is the economic reasoning. It is this aspect of economics that is the most difficult—as well as the most rewarding. Unfortunately, not all of this difficulty can be avoided if we wish to understand the economic events that take place in the real world. The feature that should help students to master the material is the use of a single, consistent model, which is then successively refined and applied to a variety of macroeconomic problems. Anyone who invests enough effort to understand the basic model will eventually see the simplicity of the approach, as well as the applicability to a wide variety of real-world issues. Conversely, anyone who fails to master the basic model will be in serious trouble later on.

ELEMENTS OF NATIONAL-INCOME ACCOUNTING

Up to this point, we have used terms such as *gross national product (GNP), consumer expenditure, investment,* the *general price level,* and so on without defining them precisely. Now, by looking at the **national-income accounts,** we develop the meanings of these terms. There are many difficult issues that arise in the construction of these accounts. Here, we consider only the basic concepts, which will be adequate for the subsequent analysis.

NOMINAL AND REAL GNP

We begin with the GNP. Nominal GNP measures the dollar value of all the goods and services that an economy produces during a specified time period. For example, in 1988,.the nominal GNP in the United States was $4,862 billion.

Consider the definition of nominal GNP one step at a time. The word *nominal* means that the GNP is measured in units of dollars—or, more generally, in units of some currency, such as pounds, marks, yen, and so on. For most goods and services—pencils, automobiles, haircuts, and so on—the dollar value is the price for which these items sell in the marketplace. However, governmental services—which include national defense, the justice system, and police services—are not exchanged on markets. These items enter into nominal GNP at their dollar cost of production.

It is important to understand that the GNP includes only the goods and services that an economy produces during a given time period. In other words, current GNP measures only current production. For example, the construction and sale of a new house counts in GNP, but the sale of a second-hand house (which was produced earlier) does not count.

The nominal GNP can be misleading as a measure of production. That is because this measure depends on the overall level of prices, as well as on the physical amounts of output. The top part of Table 1.1 illustrates this problem. Think about a simple economy that produces only butter and golf balls. We show the hypothetical quantities and prices of these goods for 1988 in the first columns of the table. Notice that the nominal GNP for 1988 is $500. The columns labeled 1989A and 1989B show two possibilities for prices and outputs in 1989. In both cases nominal GNP rises by 10% to $550. In case A, however, the production of both goods has declined, while in case B the production of both has increased. Thus, identical figures on nominal GNP can conceal very different underlying movements in production.

Economists construct a measure of real GNP to solve the problem of changing price levels. Real GNP uses prices from only one year, which is called the *base year*. For example, if the base year is 1982, we refer to real GNP as "GNP in 1982 dollars" or as "GNP in constant dollars," since we use a set of constant (1982) prices. Similarly, we refer to nominal GNP as "GNP in current dollars," since it uses the prices of the current period.

We compute real GNP by multiplying the current quantity of output of each good by the price of that good in the base year. Then we sum up over all these multiples to get the economy's aggregate real GNP. Because the prices used in this

TABLE 1.1 *The Calculation of Nominal and Real GNP*

	1988			1989A			1989B		
	P_{1988}	Q_{1988}	Market Value at 1988 Prices	P_{1989A}	Q_{1989A}	Market Value at 1989A Prices	P_{1989B}	Q_{1989B}	Market Value at 1989B Prices
Butter	$2.00/lb.	50 lb.	$100.00	$2.30/lb.	44 lb.	$101.20	$1.80/lb.	70 lb.	$126.00
Golf balls	$1.00/ball	400 balls	$400.00	$1.20/ball	374 balls	$448.80	$0.80/ball	530 balls	$424.00
Nominal GNP			$500.00			$550.00			$550.00
	P_{1988}	Q_{1988}	Market Value at 1988 Prices	P_{1988}	P_{1989A}	Market Value at 1988 Prices	P_{1988}	Q_{1989B}	Market Value at 1988 Prices
Butter	$2.00/lb.	50 lb.	$100.00	$2.00/lb.	44 lb.	$ 88.00	$2.00/lb.	70 lb.	$140.00
Golf balls	$1.00/ball	400 balls	$400.00	$1.00/ball	374 balls	$374.00	$1.00/ball	530 balls	$530.00
Real GNP (1988 base)			$500.00			$462.00			$670.00

Note: P and Q refer to price and quantity, respectively, for the year indicated by the subscript.

calculation do not vary from year to year, we end up with a reasonable measure for the changes over time in the overall level of production.

The bottom portion of Table 1.1 illustrates this calculation, using 1988 as the base year. Consider the values of real GNP for the cases labeled 1989A and 1989B. These values differ substantially, although the values of nominal GNP are the same. In the 1989A example, real GNP falls below the 1988 level by 7.6%. This figure is a weighted average of the fall in butter production by 12% and that in golf ball production by 6.5%. Thus, real GNP gives a more accurate picture of the change in output than does the 10% increase in nominal GNP. Similarly, for the 1989B case, real GNP rises by 34% (a remarkable achievement for one year!). This figure is a weighted average of the rise in butter production by 40% and that in golf ball production by 32%.

Notice that the proportional change in real GNP is a weighted average of the proportional changes in production for the various goods, which are butter and golf balls in the example. Generally, there would be many ways to define the weights in this calculation. It turns out that the standard method for computing real GNP— which we employed in Table 1.1—uses as weights the shares of each good (butter or golf balls) in GNP for the base year. That is, as seems reasonable, this calculation gives more weight to the goods that account for a larger share of the economy's output (in the base year). But as we move away from the base year, these shares can change significantly. For that reason, the U.S. Commerce Department changes the designation of the base year from time to time. (For example, in 1986, it shifted from 1972 to 1982).

Although it reveals a lot about the economy's overall performance, the real GNP is not a perfect measure of welfare. Some of the problems with using real GNP as a measure of well-being are the following:

- Aggregate GNP does not consider changes in the distribution of income across households.
- The calculated GNP excludes a variety of nonmarket goods, among them legal and illegal transactions in the "underground economy," as well as services that people perform in their homes. For example, if someone mows his or her own lawn, GNP does not increase—but if the person hires someone to mow the lawn (and the transaction is reported to the government), GNP increases.
- The GNP assigns no value to leisure time.

Despite these shortcomings, we typically learn a great deal about an economy—in terms of short-run fluctuations and in the context of long-term development—by studying the changes in aggregate real GNP.

THE GROSS NATIONAL PRODUCT—EXPENDITURE, PRODUCTION, AND INCOME

We can think about GNP in three different ways. First, we can consider the expenditures on goods and services by different groups—households, businesses, all levels of government, and foreigners. Second, we can measure the production of goods by various industries—agriculture, manufacturing, wholesale and retail trade, and so on. Finally, we can calculate the incomes earned in the production of goods—compensation of employees, rental income, corporate profits, and so on. The important point is that all three approaches will end up with the same total for GNP. To see this, we take up each approach in turn, beginning with a breakdown by type of expenditure.

Measuring GNP by Expenditures The national accounts divide GNP into four parts, depending upon who or what buys the goods or services. The four sectors are households, businesses, all levels of government, and foreigners. Table 1.2 shows the details of this breakdown for 1988. The first column lists values in current dollars, while the second refers to real dollars—that is, values for the base year, 1982.

The purchases of goods and services by households for their own use is called **personal consumption expenditure.** This spending accounts for the bulk of GNP—for example, for $2592 billion out of a total $3996 billion or 65% of real GNP in 1988 (see Table 1.2).

The national accounts distinguish between purchases of consumer goods that will be used fairly quickly, such as toothpaste and various services, and those that will last for a substantial time, such as automobiles and appliances. The first group is called **consumer nondurables and services,** and the second is called **consumer durables.** The important point is that consumer durables yield a flow of

TABLE 1.2 *Expenditure Components of the Gross National Product for 1988*

Category of Expenditures	Billions of Dollars	Billions of 1982 Dollars
Gross national product	4864	3996
Personal consumption expenditure	3228	2592
Durable goods	451	410
Nondurable goods	1047	900
Services	1730	1283
Gross private domestic investment	766	722
Fixed investment	718	679
Nonresidential	488	488
Residential	230	192
Change in business inventories	48	42
Government purchases of goods and services	965	782
Federal	381	329
State and local	584	454
Net exports of goods and services	−95	−100
Exports	520	505
Imports	614	605

Source: Citibase data bank.

services in future periods, as well as currently. Table 1.2 shows the division of consumer expenditures among durable goods, nondurable goods, and services.

The second major category of GNP is **gross private domestic investment,** which is the purchase of goods and services by businesses. The "fixed" part of these investments comprises firms' purchases of new capital goods, such as factories and machines. Note that business's capital goods are durables, which serve as inputs to production over many years. Thus, investment goods are similar to the consumer durables that we mentioned before. In fact, in the national accounts, an individual's purchase of a new home—which might be considered the ultimate consumer durable—is counted as a part of fixed business investment rather than personal consumer expenditure. For many purposes, we should add the other purchases of consumer durables to the national accounts' measure of gross investment to get a broader concept of investment.

Total investment is the sum of fixed investment and the net change in business's inventories of goods. In 1988 this total investment equaled 18% of real GNP, or 28% if we include the purchases of consumer durables (see Table 1.2).

The third component of GNP is **government purchases of goods and services.** This category combines governmental consumption expenditures with public investment. It is possible, however, to get a rough breakdown into the two components. There are two points about the government sector that sometimes cause confusion. First, it includes all levels of government, whether federal, state, or local. Second, it includes purchases of goods and services but excludes the government's **transfer payments.** (Examples of transfer payments are social security benefits and welfare payments.) The idea is that transfers do not represent payments to individuals in exchange for currently produced goods or services. Hence, these expenditures should not appear in GNP. In 1988 government purchases of goods and services accounted for 20% of real GNP (see Table 1.2).

Some of the goods and services produced in an economy are exported to foreign users. **Exports** must be added to domestic purchases to compute the economy's total production (GNP). But in addition to buying goods and services that are produced domestically, foreigners also produce goods and services that are imported into the domestic country. **Imports** must be subtracted from domestic purchases to calculate GNP. So the foreign component appears in GNP as **net exports**—that is, the spending by foreigners on domestic production (exports) less the spending by domestic residents on foreign production (imports). Notice that net exports may be either positive or negative. In 1988 this component was negative and equal to −2.5% of real GNP. (Real exports were 12.6% of real GNP while real imports were 15.1%.)

Economists often omit net exports when they construct a macroeconomic model for a single economy. Then the model applies to a **closed economy** rather than an **open economy,** which includes the foreign sector. The rationale for assuming a closed economy is, first, to simplify the theory, and, second, at least for the United States, that exports and imports are small relative to GNP. (However, the share of foreign trade is much higher now in the United States than it was twenty years ago.) We follow the closed-economy tradition of macroeconomics until Chapter 15, where we allow for foreign trade. When we omit the foreign sector, we get the familiar division of GNP into three parts:

GNP = consumer expenditure + gross investment + government purchases.

One common error about national accounting arises because the spending on new physical capital is called "investment." This terminology differs from the concept of investment in ordinary conversation, which refers to the allocation of saving among different financial assets, such as stocks, bonds, savings accounts, and so on. When we speak of a firm's investment, we refer to the purchase of physical goods, such as a factory. Do not be confused by these two different meanings of investment.

Another point about investment concerns **depreciation.** During any period, some of the existing stock of capital tends to wear out or depreciate. Thus, a part of gross investment merely replaces the old capital that has depreciated. The difference between gross investment and depreciation—called **net investment**—is the net change in the stock of capital goods. We shall discuss the difference between gross and net investment in Chapter 9. For now, note that the sum of consumption expenditures, *net* investment, government purchases of goods and services, and net exports is called **net national product (NNP).** The difference between GNP and NNP reflects the difference between gross and net investment, which is the amount of depreciation. Hence, we have the condition.

NNP = GNP − depreciation.

The NNP concept is useful because it measures output net of the amount needed to replace worn-out goods.

MEASURING GNP BY PRODUCTION

Instead of breaking down GNP into the sectors that do the spending, we can look at a breakdown by the sectors that do the producing (and selling). Table 1.3 shows such a breakdown for 1987. In terms of shares of real GNP, the breakdown was 22% in manufacturing, 17% in wholesale and retail trade, 16% in services, 15% in finance, insurance and real estate, 11% in production by government and government enterprises, 9% in transportation and public utilities, 5% in construction, 3% in mining, and 2% in agriculture.

In many cases a firm produces **intermediate goods,** which another business uses as an input. In order not to double-count intermediate goods in GNP, the national accounts give each business credit only for its **value added** to production. The value added by a firm is the difference between its revenues and the cost of goods that it buys from other firms. An example of an intermediate good is flour that a baker uses to make bread. The baker's value added is the market value of the bread less the value of the flour used to produce the bread. The amounts shown in Table 1.3 are the value added to production by each industry.

The last item shown in Table 1.3 refers to the rest of the world. This amount is the value added to production by the U.S. labor and capital that is used in other countries, net of the contribution of foreign labor and capital to domestic production.

TABLE 1.3 *Production Components of the Gross National Product for 1987*

Category of Production	Billions of Dollars	Billions of 1982 Dollars
Gross national product	4527	3847
Domestic industries (gross domestic product)	4497	3821
Agriculture	95	96
Mining	85	118
Construction	218	176
Manufacturing	854	840
Transportation and public utilities	408	349
Wholesale and retail trade	740	660
Finance, insurance, real estate	775	559
Services	794	611
Government	535	416
Statistical discrepancy	−8	−3
Rest of the world	30	26

Source: U.S. Survey of Current Business (July 1988), Tables 6.1, 6.2.

(The item is also called the *net factor income from abroad.*) The difference between GNP and this term is the production by domestic industries. This total is called **gross domestic product (GDP).**

INCOME

The third way to look at GNP is in terms of the income earned in production. This income is called **national income.** To make clear the relation between production and income, think of a simple economy that has one firm producing bread as the only final product and another firm producing flour as the only intermediate good. Suppose that the miller uses only labor to produce flour, while the baker uses labor and flour to produce bread. Sample income statements for these firms appear in Table 1.4. In this table the only sources of income are labor income and profits. Total nominal GNP, which is the market value of the bread, is $600. This amount also equals the total revenue of the baker. The income statement shows that this

TABLE 1.4 *Data for Calculation of Gross National Product and National Income*

Baker				Miller			
Revenue		Costs and Profits		Revenue		Costs and Profits	
Total revenue from sale of bread	$600	Labor	$200	Total revenue from sale of flour	$350	Labor	$250
		Flour	$350			Profit	$100
		Profit	$ 50				

revenue divides up into $350 for the cost of flour, $200 for payments to labor (or, from the workers' standpoint, $200 of labor income), and $50 of profits (or return on capital). For the miller, the revenue of $350 goes for $250 of labor costs (or labor income) and $100 of profits. Thus, in this simple case, national income equals the total labor income of $450 plus total profits (return on capital) of $150, which equals the $600 of GNP.

Table 1.5 shows the breakdown of national income in the United States for 1988: 73% of the total is compensation of employees, 8% is income of proprietors (owners of farms and small businesses), less than 1% is personal rental income (net of estimated depreciation on rental property), 8% is corporate profits, and 10% is net interest income.

Two complications disturb the equality between GNP and national income in the real world. First, suppose that the baker uses some capital goods in the production process. As the capital wears out, the baker subtracts depreciation charges from profits. Hence, the total income for labor and profit equals the baker's total revenue, which equals GNP, less the depreciation charges. That is, national income equals NNP, which is GNP less depreciation.

A second adjustment arises because of sales and excise taxes, which are called "indirect taxes." These levies create a gap between the market price of a good—which includes the tax—and the revenue received by the producer. (The gap shows up as revenue for the government.) In the example from Table 1.4, if there had been a 5% sales tax on bread, the consumer would have paid $630 for the bread, while the baker's total revenue would have remained at $600. As a result, national income would still be $600, while GNP (calculated at market prices) would be $630. Generally, national income equals GNP less depreciation and less these indirect taxes. Table 1.6 demonstrates this calculation using U.S. data for 1988.

Recall that the definition of national income includes only the amounts earned in the production of output. Economists also calculate the amount of income that people actually receive, which is called **personal income**. This concept differs from national income for several reasons. First, only a portion of firms' profits are paid out as dividends to individuals. Second, personal income excludes the contributions paid for social insurance, since households do not receive these amounts directly as income. Next there are a series of adjustments to ensure that the amount of

TABLE 1.5 *Breakdown of National Income in 1988*

Category of Income	Billions of Dollars
National income	3968
Compensation of employees	2905
Proprietors' income	325
Rental income of persons	19
Corporate profits	328
Net Interest	392

Source: Citibase data bank.

TABLE 1.6 *Data for Calculation of Net National Product, National Income, Personal Income, and Disposable Personal Income in 1988 (billions of dollars)*

Gross national product (GNP)	$4864
Less	
Depreciation	506
Equals	
Net national product (NNP)	458
Less	
Indirect business taxes (and related items)	390
Equals	
National income	3968
Less	
Corporate profits	328
Contributions for social insurance	445
Plus	
Government transfer payments	555
Net adjustment for interest income	184
Personal dividend income	96
Business transfer payments	31
Equals	
Personal income	4062
Less	
Personal tax and nontax payments	590
Equals	
Disposable personal income	3472

Source: Citibase data bank.

interest income in personal income corresponds to the amount that individuals receive. Finally, various transfer payments appear in personal income but not in national income. All of these adjustments are detailed in Table 1.6.

Economists also calculate the amount of income that households have left after paying personal taxes, which is called **disposable personal income.** Table 1.6 shows the calculation of disposable personal income from personal income.

PRICES

One objective of macroeconomic theory is to explain the general level of prices and the changes in the price level over time. To use the theory, we need an empirical measure (or measures) of the general price level. The analysis of real and nominal GNP provides one such measure. The **implicit GNP price deflator** (or, more compactly, the GNP deflator) can be calculated as

$$\text{implicit GNP price deflator} = \left(\frac{\text{nominal GNP}}{\text{real GNP}}\right) \times 100.$$

It is conventional to multiply by 100 to obtain an index number that takes on the value 100 for the base year (for which nominal GNP equals real GNP).

For a concrete example, consider again the data from Table 1.1. For the 1989A case, the GNP deflator is (nominal GNP/real GNP) · 100 = (550/462) · 100 = 119. In other words, the price of the "average item" increased by 19% from 1988 to 1989. This number is a weighted average of the percentage increase in the price of butter, which is 15%, and that of golf balls, which is 20%. It turns out that the weights used to compute the average percentage change are the shares of the two goods in the real GNP for 1989. Thus, by using the GNP deflator to measure the general level of prices, we give more weight to the items that are currently more important in the economy's market basket of produced goods.[5]

The formula for the implicit price deflator can be rearranged to see why we call it a price deflator. The rearranged equation is

$$\text{real GNP} = \left(\frac{\text{nominal GNP}}{\text{implicit GNP price deflator}} \right) \times 100.$$

Thus, we effectively divide or deflate the nominal GNP by the price deflator to compute the real GNP.

This implicit GNP price deflator is called "implicit" because it is not directly or explicitly calculated. Real GNP and nominal GNP are computed directly, and the GNP deflator is calculated by dividing the two as we have done. There are also explicit indexes of the general price level. Two important examples are the **consumer price index (CPI)** and the **producer price index (PPI)**, which is also called a wholesale price index. These are explicit indexes since they are calculated directly.

The CPI is based on a fixed market basket of consumer goods. Every few years the government takes a statistical survey to compile the base-year prices and expenditures on about 400 goods that are consumed by typical individuals. The expenditure shares serve as fixed weights until the next survey is taken. To calculate the CPI we first compute the ratio of the current market price of each good to its base-year price. Then we sum up over the ratios, weighting each by the share of the good in base-year expenditures. Typically, we also multiply the result by 100 so that the CPI for the base year is 100.

The PPI is computed in a similar manner. This index measures prices at an early stage of production, so the "basket" in the PPI consists of about 2800 items sold at wholesale. These goods are primarily raw materials and semifinished goods.[6]

It is possible to calculate inflation rates based on the CPI or the PPI, as well as on the GNP deflator (as shown in Figure 1.5). In fact, the inflation rates reported in the newspapers usually refer to the changes in the CPI or PPI. In our discussion of the general price level and inflation, we shall refer primarily to the GNP deflator. There are several reasons for this choice. First, the PPI is too narrow a concept to reflect the general level of prices. Second, the GNP deflator reflects the importance

---

[5]The GNP deflator, which weights by the importance of goods in current market baskets, is an example of a Paasche index of prices. For a discussion, see Edwin Mansfield (1985, pp. 105ff).

[6]The CPI and PPI, which weight by the importance of goods in the base year, are examples of Laspeyres indexes of prices. See ibid. for a discussion.

of the various items in current market baskets of produced goods, whereas the CPI refers to base-year market baskets, which can become less relevant over time. Third, the GNP deflator contains only the prices of goods that are produced domestically, whereas the CPI includes prices of imported goods. Our attempt to understand the domestic forces that contribute to changes in the domestic price level can be confused if we use the CPI. Finally, until recently, the inappropriate treatment of housing costs in the CPI caused the index to be unduly responsive to changes in mortgage interest rates.

IMPORTANT TERMS AND CONCEPTS

gross national product (GNP)	consumer nondurables and services
general price level	consumer durables
wage rate	gross private domestic investment
interest rate	government purchases of goods and services
exchange rate	transfer payments
real GNP	transfer payments
recession	exports
boom	imports
Great Depression	net exports
gold standard	closed economy
inflation rate	open economy
microeconomic foundations	depreciation
budget constraint	net investment
demand for money	net national product (NNP)
medium of exchange	intermediate goods
aggregate-consistency conditions	value added
market-clearing approach	gross domestic product (GDP)
Keynesian model	national income
real business cycle theory	personal income
balance of international payments	disposable personal income
IS/LM model	implicit GNP price deflator
national-income accounts	consumer price index (CPI)
personal consumption expenditure	producer price index (PPI)

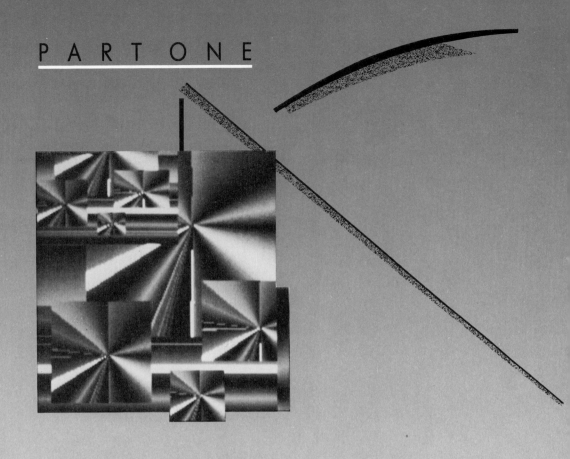

MICROECONOMIC FOUNDATIONS AND THE BASIC MARKET CLEARING MODEL

CHAPTER

WORK EFFORT, PRODUCTION, AND CONSUMPTION—THE ECONOMICS OF ROBINSON CRUSOE

n any economic analysis, the determination of work effort, production, and consumption depends on opportunities for production and on preferences about working and consuming. This basic interaction between opportunities and preferences shows up even in the simplest possible economy, which consists of isolated individuals, each of whom resembles Robinson Crusoe. In this setting, which we develop in this chapter, we can readily analyze the economy's responses to changed opportunities in terms of **wealth effects** and **substitution effects.** It turns out that the primitive environment of Robinson Crusoe contains the essence of choice problems that arise in complicated market economies. Therefore, the principal findings from this chapter remain valid when we extend the analysis in later chapters to settings that look more like modern industrialized economies.

We begin with a simple **production function,** which relates the quantity of output to the amount of work effort. This function determines the productivity of labor, which is the amount of extra output generated from more work. Next, we discuss preferences for consumption and leisure. Basically, people increase their work effort and accept less leisure only if they receive a sufficient addition to consumption.

PRODUCTION TECHNOLOGY

The basic theoretical model contains one type of economic unit, which we can think of as a combination of a household and a firm. Thus, this single unit combines the consuming and working activities of households with the producing and hiring activities of businesses. For most purposes, this abstraction will be satisfactory because some households ultimately own the private businesses. Further, by merging the functions of households and businesses, we achieve some major simplifications of the analysis. From now on we refer to this composite unit as simply a household.

Each household uses its labor effort as an input to production. Note that, to simplify matters, we do not yet consider stocks of capital as inputs to the production processes. This chapter concentrates on the economic incentives that make people work more or less in order to produce and consume more or fewer goods.

Formally, the quantity of a household's commodity output per period, denoted by y, is a function of the quantity of labor input, n. We write this relation as

$$y_t = f(n_t), \tag{2.1}$$

where f is the household's production function, which specifies the relation between the amount of work and the quantity of goods produced. The subscript t, which denotes the time period, is omitted when no ambiguity results.

Since the model contains a single physical type of commodity, there is no problem in measuring each household's output. The real-world counterpart of this output, when added up over all producers, is the gross national product (GNP). Many practical problems arise in using price indexes to add up goods that are physically different, but these difficulties do not arise in our simplified theoretical framework.

We assume in the basic model that people cannot store commodities from one period to the next, and thus, we neglect inventories of goods. We can think of the commodities as perishable consumer goods. Examples include personal services, restaurant meals, and so on.

Work is productive in the sense that more work effort, n, yields more output, y. The extra output produced by one more unit of work is called the **marginal (physical) product of labor,** henceforth designated MPL. We assume **diminishing marginal productivity,** which means that each successive unit of work effort generates progressively smaller, but still positive, responses of output.

Figure 2.1, which is the graphical representation of equation 2.1, shows the relation of output to the quantity of labor input. Note that the curve goes through the origin, which means that output is zero when labor effort is nil. The positive slope of the curve (that is, of a straight line that is tangent to the curve) at any point indicates the additional output that results from extra labor input, which is the marginal product of labor. For example, at the employment level n_1, the MPL equals the slope of the straight line that is tangent to the production function at point A.

The shape of the production function in Figure 2.1 implies that the slope becomes less steep as work effort increases. This property reflects the diminishing marginal productivity of labor. For example, at the employment level n_2, which

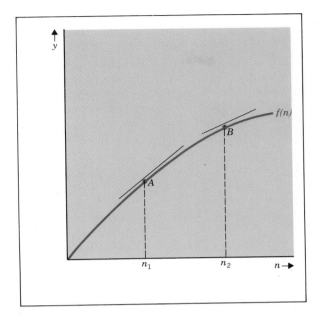

FIGURE 2.1 *Graph of Production Function*
The curve shows the level of output as a function of the quantity of labor input. At point A, the slope of the tangent straight line equals the marginal product of labor when n *= n_1. The same is true for point B where* n *= n_2.*

exceeds n_1, the slope of the tangent straight line at point *B* is smaller than that at point *A*. The full relation of the marginal product of labor, MPL, to the amount of work, *n*, appears in Figure 2.2. Note that the marginal product declines as work effort increases. We refer to the graph of MPL versus *n* as the *schedule* for the marginal product of labor. By a schedule, we mean the entire functional relation between MPL and *n*.

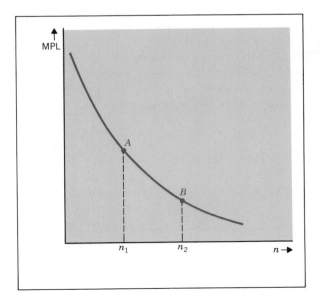

FIGURE 2.2 *Relation of Marginal Product of Labor to Level of Work*
Since $n_1 < n_2$, *the marginal product of labor at point A exceeds that at point B. That is, the marginal product of labor falls as work effort rises.*

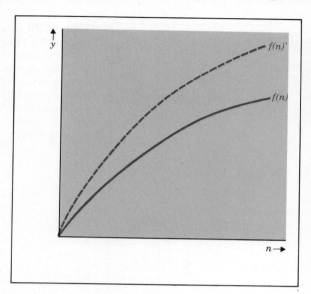

FIGURE 2.3 *Effect of an Improvement in Technology on the Level of Production*
The curve f(n)′ *corresponds to an improved technology, relative to the one labeled* f(n)*. This improvement raises the level of output for a given amount of labor input.*

The curves in Figures 2.1 and 2.2 apply at some initial level of technology, that is, for a given production function $f(n)$. We show this production function again as the solid curve in Figure 2.3. The dashed curve in the figure shows the level of output for an improved technology, denoted by $f(n)'$. The level of output is now higher at any given level of labor input.

What is the effect of an improvement in technology on the marginal product of labor? In general, a technological improvement may either raise or lower labor's marginal product. For our purposes, we would like to capture the typical or average response. Studies of production functions at an economy-wide level suggest that, in the usual situation, an improvement in technology raises the marginal product of labor at any given level of work effort.

The construction of the curves in Figure 2.3 reflects the assumption that an improvement in technology raises the marginal product of labor. Namely, the curve labeled $f(n)'$—which corresponds to the improved technology—is steeper than the initial curve at any level of work effort. Recall that the slopes of the curves measure the marginal product of labor, MPL, at each point. In Figure 2.4 we show explicitly that the technological advance leads to an upward shift in the schedule for the MPL.

TASTES FOR CONSUMPTION AND LEISURE

Suppose for now that, as with Robinson Crusoe, each person has no opportunity to exchange commodities or anything else with other households. In this case, each

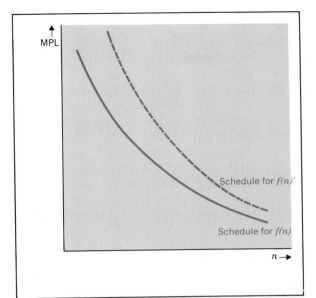

FIGURE 2.4 *Effect of an Improvement in Technology on the Marginal Product of Labor The dashed curve corresponds to an improved technology, f(n)', relative to the initial one, f(n). The technological advance shifts upward the schedule for the marginal product of labor.*

household's only option is to consume all the goods that it produces in each period. (Remember, there are no possibilities for storing commodities.) Then in the world of Robinson Crusoe we have

$$c_t = y_t = f(n_t), \qquad (2.2)$$

where c_t is the amount of consumption in physical units. The equation says that each household's consumption equals its production, which depends on its quantity of work effort.

Consumption in each period is a source of happiness or **utility** for households. (Henceforth, we use the economist's standard jargon, *utility*.) Equation 2.2 implies that someone can consume more only if he or she raises production. Further, for a given technology, the quantity of goods produced, y_t, depends on the level of work effort, n_t. So the amount of work is the key decision that households make in this model.

In the real world, households have a lot of flexibility in their choices of work effort. For example, someone might work four hours per day or eight hours. A person can pick a job that requires lots of hard work or one that does not. Someone might work for only part of the year, as is often the case for construction workers and professional sports figures. From the perspective of a family, there is a decision on how many members participate in the labor force. For example, there has been a strong increase over the last 40 years in the number of families with two full-time workers. One evidence of this trend is the growing rate of participation of women in the civilian labor force. This participation rate rose from 28% in 1940 to 56%

in 1987 (while that for males declined from 84% to 77%).[1] In a longer time perspective, the amount of time spent at work depends also on the typical lengths of schooling and retirement.

We model this real-world flexibility on work effort by allowing people freely to choose their hours of work in each period. Thus, we neglect any constraints that, for example, permit people to work on some jobs for eight hours per day or four hours but not seven or two. This abstraction will be satisfactory when we think about the overall behavior of work effort for a large number of households. In this context the constraints tend to average out.

Households have a fixed amount of time in each period, which they can divide between work and leisure. By the term *leisure,* we mean to capture the full array of activities—other than work to produce goods—on which people spend their time. We assume that leisure time is intrinsically more enjoyable than time at work. In other words, in the jargon introduced before, leisure is a source of utility for households.

Suppose that we can define a function to measure the amount of utility that derives each period from consumption and leisure. The form of this **utility function** is

$$u_t = u(c_t, n_t),$$
$$(+) \, (-)$$

(2.3)

where u_t is the amount of utility (in units of happiness, which are sometimes called *utils*) that someone obtains for period t.[2] We assume that the form of the utility function, u, is the same for all periods. The positive sign under the quantity of consumption, c_t, indicates that utility rises with consumption. The negative sign under work effort, n_t, signifies the negative effect on utility of more work (that is, of less leisure). For convenience, we now drop the time subscripts and refer to period t's consumption and work as c and n, respectively.

We analyze a household's decisions on working and consuming by exploiting the central economic postulate of optimizing behavior. Each household opts for the levels of work and consumption that maximize utility in equation 2.3. Note, however, that this maximization is subject to the constraint from equation 2.2, which says that each household's consumption in any period equals its production for the same period. We want to use these facts to understand the household's selection of work and consumption.

To make progress in analyzing the household's choices, we must characterize further the utility function, which expresses people's tastes for consumption and leisure. A basic assumption is that the utility gained from an extra unit of leisure, relative to that from an extra unit of consumption, diminishes as the ratio of leisure to consumption rises. In other words, if someone has a lot of leisure but relatively

---

[1]These figures, obtained from the *Citibase* data bank, refer to persons aged 16 years or more (14 years or more for 1940) who are neither full-time students nor members of the military.

[2]It is not really necessary to measure utility in units such as utils. The important idea is that households have a *preference ordering* over pairs of consumption and work, (c_t, n_t). Equation 2.3 says that a pair that has a higher value for the utility index, u_t, is preferred to one with a lower value.

little consumption, he or she is more concerned with adding to consumption rather than leisure. Consider the amount of extra consumption needed to compensate for the loss of a unit of leisure time. If a person starts with little consumption and a lot of leisure, it is important to add to consumption. Therefore, he or she is willing to work a lot more to get additional consumption. If the person is already working quite a bit and has a high level of consumption, leisure becomes more significant. Therefore, he or she is less willing to work more and give up leisure to obtain extra consumption.

The curve in Figure 2.5 summarizes this discussion. At zero work effort, $n = 0$, the curve specifies a level of consumption, c^0, on the vertical axis. This amount of consumption, together with full-time leisure (that is, $n = 0$), determines some level of utility from equation 2.3. Denote this level of utility by u^1. Then we construct the curve in the figure to show all other possible combinations of work and consumption that provide the same level of utility, u^1, as that from the first pair, where $n = 0$ and $c = c^0$.

Suppose that the person works a positive amount, so that leisure becomes less than a full-time activity. For concreteness, assume that work is one hour per day, as represented by $n = 1$ in Figure 2.5. By itself, this reduction in leisure lowers utility. But we want to know how much additional consumption would restore the

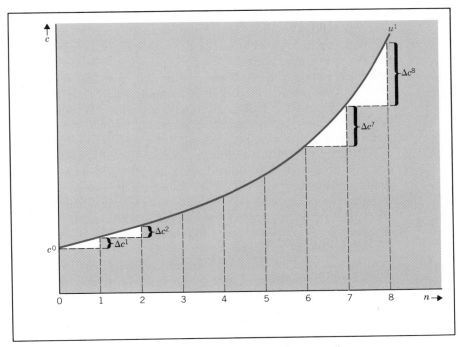

FIGURE 2.5 *An Indifference Curve for Work and Consumption*
All points, (n, c), on the curve yield the same level of utility, u¹. Hence, the household is indifferent among these pairs of work effort and consumption.

original level of utility. Denote by Δc^1 the required amount of extra consumption. Then the new combination of work and consumption, where $n = 1$ and $c = c^0 + \Delta c^1$, yields the same utility as the initial pair, where $n = 0$ and $c = c^0$. Hence, the person is indifferent between these two pairs of work and consumption. We show that these two points yield the same level of utility, u^1, by connecting them with the curve shown in the figure.

If the person works another hour—that is, chooses $n = 2$—some additional consumption is again needed to maintain the level of utility. Figure 2.5 assumes that the required extra consumption is the amount Δc^2. Therefore, the position where $n = 2$ and $c = c^0 + \Delta c^1 + \Delta c^2$ again provides the same utility as the initial pair, where $n = 0$ and $c = c^0$.

We can continue this exercise as the amount of work rises. The result is the curve in Figure 2.5, which shows all pairs, (n, c), that yield the same level of utility. Since people are indifferent among these pairs of work and consumption, the curve is called an **indifference curve.**

The previous discussion tells us something about the shape of an indifference curve. As someone works more, each additional unit of work requires a greater amount of extra consumption to maintain utility. Therefore, the size of each addition to consumption, Δc, is larger the higher is the associated number of work hours. In particular, note that $\Delta c^1 < \Delta c^2 < \ldots < \Delta c^7 < \Delta c^8$ in Figure 2.5.

At any point along the indifference curve, the slope of a tangent straight line indicates the increment in consumption that a person requires to make up for the loss of a unit of leisure. Each of the additions to consumption, Δc, that appear in Figure 2.5 approximates this slope in the vicinity of the corresponding level of work. For example, the amount Δc^2 is a good measure of the slope when the level of work lies between one and two hours per day. The previous results imply that the slope of the indifference curve rises as the amount of work, n, increases.

The slope of the indifference curve in Figure 2.5 indicates the amount of consumption that someone needs to make up for the loss of a unit of leisure. Put alternatively, if a worker receives more than this amount of consumption, he or she would be better off. For example, when someone is already working seven hours per day, he or she is willing to work an additional hour if consumption thereby rises by at least the amount Δc^8 in the figure. If it turns out that the extra hour of work increases consumption by an amount greater than Δc^8, economic reasoning predicts that the worker will work that extra hour. This viewpoint allows us to determine the number of hours that people actually work.

All points on the curve in Figure 2.5 yield the same level of utility u^1. But suppose that we look along the vertical axis and raise the consumption level above c^0; then utility increases. Corresponding to this higher level of utility, say u^2, we can construct another indifference curve. The new curve is similar to the one shown in the figure, but it lies wholly above this curve. That is, for any level of work, n, the amount of consumption, c, is higher. That is why the new indifference curve corresponds to a higher level of utility. (We can also say that for any level of consumption, c, the amount of work effort, n, is smaller along the new curve.)

Similarly, we could lower the level of consumption below c^0 along the vertical axis. In this case, we can start the construction of an indifference curve for a lower

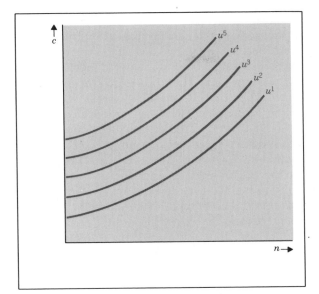

FIGURE 2.6 *A Family of Indifference Curves for Work and Consumption*
The level of utility rises as the household moves from the curve labeled u[1] *to that labeled* u[2], *and so on.*

level of utility. As a general matter, we can define a whole "family" or "map" of indifference curves, each of which corresponds to a different level of utility. Figure 2.6 shows five of these curves, labeled by their levels of utility, where $u^1 < u^2 \ldots < u^5$. Along any curve the level of utility is constant. But as a person moves vertically from one curve to others—thereby raising consumption while keeping work fixed—the level of utility increases. We have already mentioned the central idea that the household wants to achieve the highest possible level of utility. Therefore, we can also say that the household's objective is to reach the highest possible indifference curve among the family of curves in Figure 2.6.

DECIDING HOW MUCH TO WORK

Suppose that a household begins from a particular combination of work and consumption, (n, c). Then we can consult Figure 2.6 to find the indifference curve to which this point corresponds. The slope of the indifference curve at this point indicates how much extra consumption, Δc, someone insists on to work an additional unit of time. To determine how much someone actually works, we combine the indifference curves with a description of people's opportunities for raising consumption when work effort rises. In the model, these opportunities come from the production function, which appears in Figure 2.1. The marginal product of labor, MPL, is the amount of extra output generated by an extra unit of work. Further, we know from equation 2.2 that each addition to output corresponds to an equal addition to consumption.

The MPL is the addition to production—and therefore to consumption—that results from an extra unit or work. The slope of the indifference curve is the amount of extra consumption that a person needs to make up for less leisure time. Therefore, if the MPL exceeds the slope of the indifference curve, the person will be better off if he or she works more and uses the added output to expand consumption. However, as work rises, the MPL declines, and the slope of the indifference curve rises. Therefore, the increase in work lessens the initial excess of the MPL over the slope of the indifference curve. When the gap vanishes—that is, when the marginal product equals the slope of the indifference curve—it no longer pays to work more.

The results are in Figure 2.7. Consider the intersection of the production function, $y = f(n)$, with indifference curve u^1 at point D. At this position, the slope of the production function—which is the MPL—exceeds the slope of the indifference curve. Therefore, an increase in work expands output—and thereby consumption—by more than enough to maintain the level of utility. Graphically, by raising work and moving along the production function beyond point D, a household intersects higher indifference curves and thereby raises utility.

Assume that work rises enough to reach point E in Figure 2.7. At this point the slope of the production function equals the slope of the indifference curve. We show this graphically by drawing the production function, $f(n)$, as tangent to indifference curve u^3 at point E. Then we designate the associated levels of work and consumption as n^* and c^*. Notice that, at this point, a movement along the production function beyond point E intersects lower indifference curves. In other words, the extra output and consumption are now insufficient to make up for the loss of utility from extra work. Therefore, utility declines if work rises above the amount n^*.

To summarize, each household chooses the combination of work and con-

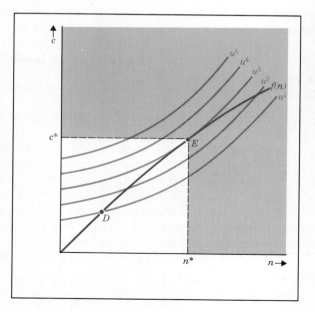

FIGURE 2.7 *Combining the Indifference Curves with the Production Function*
The household moves along the production function, f(n), *to reach the highest possible indifference curve. This occurs at point* E, *where the production function is tangent to indifference curve* u³.

sumption that maximizes utility. Therefore, the household selects the pair, (n^*, c^*), at which the production function is tangent to an indifference curve.

SHIFTS IN THE PRODUCTION FUNCTION

We want to understand how people alter their work effort and consumption when there are changes in the opportunities for production. Here, we represent these changes by shifts of the production function, $f(n)$. Remember that we are examining the choices of work and consumption for a single period. So think here of changes in the production function that apply for that same period.

There are many examples of economic disturbances that alter production opportunities. For instance, the drought of 1988 reduced U.S. agricultural output and thereby amounted to a downward shift in the production function. The oil crises of 1973–74 and 1979 led to increases in the price of oil, which meant that users of energy had to give up more resources to carry out their production. From the standpoint of these users, the disturbance again looks like a downward shift in the production function, $f(n)$. On the other hand, discoveries of new technology—such as practical uses of electricity, nuclear energy, computer chips, and fiber optics—amount to upward shifts of the production function.

In analyzing the reaction of households to economic changes, we shall find it useful to place the responses into two categories:

- wealth effects
- substitution effects

Briefly, a wealth effect (which economists also call an **income effect**) concerns the overall scale of opportunities. If a change allows people to obtain more of the things that provide utility, wealth increases. On the other hand, a substitution effect refers to the relative ease or cost with which people can obtain the various items that provide utility. For example, we might have a change in the possibilities for transforming more work (and, hence, less leisure) into more consumption. More generally, we could have a change in the relative costs of obtaining any two goods, such as bread and television sets.

We shall use the concepts of wealth and substitution effects extensively throughout this book. Here, we start with the details of wealth effects for the model that we have been analyzing. Throughout this discussion we assume that people have a given pattern of tastes for consumption and leisure. Specifically, people's indifference curves, which appear in Figures 2.6 and 2.7, do not move around when the production function shifts.

WEALTH EFFECTS

As a general definition, some change raises wealth if it enables people to reach a higher level of utility. On the other hand, wealth declines if the change forces people to a lower level of utility.[3] Unfortunately, this definition may be difficult to apply in some circumstances. We want to use the notions of wealth and substitution effects to assist in analyses of various economic changes, such as a harvest failure. In some cases, we do not know at the start whether a particular change will end up raising or lowering utility, so if we have to solve the whole problem to determine what happens to wealth, there may not be much point in using the concept.

We can usually test for the sign of the change in wealth by the following method. Start with a household's initial choices of work and consumption at the position (n^*, c^*) in Figure 2.7. Then see how the economic change alters opportunities in the vicinity of this initial point.[4] For example, the initial quantity of work effort, n^*, may allow the household to consume at a higher level than before. Then wealth surely increases (because the household can attain a higher level of utility). On the other hand, the initial level of work effort, n^*, may allow only a smaller quantity of consumption than before. In this case wealth probably declines.

Let's be more concrete about this method for the case of a shift to the production function. An increase in wealth arises if households can produce and consume more goods for the same amount of work effort. In the simplest case of a pure wealth effect, the production function shifts upward in a parallel manner. This shift means more output for a given amount of input but no change in the slope of the production function at each level of work. That is, the marginal product of labor does not change at a given level of work. We show this case in Figure 2.8. Here, the initial production function, $f(n)'$, parallels the old one, $f(n)$.

Recall that our previous case of a shift to the production function, as shown in Figure 2.3, involved changes in the slope of the function. For the moment we neglect this type of change because it brings in substitution effects. The parallel shift shown in Figure 2.8 is easier because it involves only a wealth effect.

How do people respond to an increase in wealth? We find the answer in Figure 2.9 by combining the change to the production function with two of the indifference curves. Initially, the production function is tangent to an indifference curve at the point (n^*, c^*). Then, as mentioned before, the upward shift of the production function enables a household to reach a higher indifference curve. The new production function, $f(n)'$, is tangent to a higher indifference curve at the point $[(n^*)', (c^*)']$. The figure indicates that consumption increases—$(c^*)' > c^*$—while work effort decreases—$(n^*)' < n^*$. In other words, households respond to the increase in wealth by raising the quantities of both things that provide utility—here, consumption and leisure. We say that consumption and leisure are **superior goods** because the quantities of both rise in response to an increase in wealth. (Sometimes economists use the term **normal goods** instead of superior goods.) Alternatively, we can say that the wealth effect is positive for consumption and negative for work.

Generally, when there are many types of goods, we cannot be sure that the wealth effect is positive for all of them. Some goods may be **"inferior,"** which means

[3]This viewpoint comes from John Hicks (1946, Chap. 2).

[4]This general approach derives from the work of the Russian economist, Eugen Slutsky. For a discussion (in the context of markets for goods), see Hal Varian (1987, pp. 147–150).

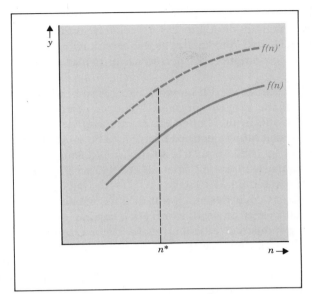

FIGURE 2.8 *A Parallel Upward Shift of the Production Function*
The new production function, f(n)′, lies everywhere above the old one, f(n). With this type of parallel shift, the two functions have the same slope at any given level of work effort.

that people desire less of them when wealth rises. (Often, economists pick on potatoes and margarine as candidates.) But when thinking of only two broad categories of things that provide utility—consumption and leisure—we can be pretty sure that both goods are superior. That is, some reasonable assumptions about the nature of preferences guarantee this result. Hence, from now on, we assume that consumption and leisure are superior goods.

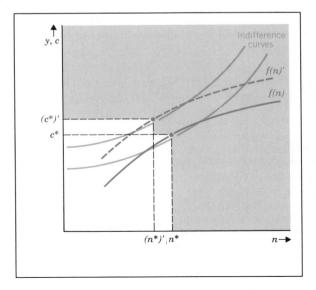

FIGURE 2.9 *The Response of Work and Consumption to an Increase in Wealth*
The parallel upward shift of the production function motivates the household to consume more and work less.

It is not surprising that the wealth effect on consumption is positive. Casual observation across families or countries immediately supports this proposition. Similarly, we can look at the United States as the economy has developed over time. It is no surprise that consumption per person has grown along with the rise in output per capita.

The negative effect of wealth on work effort is somewhat harder to verify. But it does show up in the long-run negative influence of economic development on average hours of work. In the United States, the average hours worked per week for workers in manufacturing declined from 55 to 60 in 1890 to about 50 in 1914, 44 in 1929, and 41 in 1987.[5] Similarly, in the United Kingdom the average weekly hours of male manual workers fell from 60 in 1850 to 55 in 1890, 54 in 1910, 48 in 1938, 47 in 1965, and 44 in 1986.[6]

If we look across countries at a point in time, we get some further indication of a negative wealth effect on work effort. For example, over the period 1953–60, the mean over ten industrialized countries for the average weekly hours in manufacturing was 43.9. (The ten are the United States, Canada, Switzerland, Sweden, New Zealand, the United Kingdom, Norway, France, West Germany, and the Netherlands.) But the mean over ten less-developed countries was 47.4. (These ten are Yugoslavia, Colombia, the Philippines, El Salvador, Ecuador, Guatemala, Peru, Taiwan, Egypt, and Ceylon.)[7]

On the other hand, the negative effect of economic development on average hours of work seems to weaken at high levels of development. In the United States the long-term downward trend in average hours worked per week in manufacturing apparently ended around World War II—the figure of 40.4 average hours per week for 1947 is nearly equal to that of 41.0 for 1987.[8] For male manual workers in the United Kingdom, the value of 47.0 average hours for 1965 is nearly equal to that of 47.6 for 1946. But the value did decline to 44.5 in 1986.

We have to go further with our economic analysis to explain the observations for the recent period. As mentioned before, we want to bring in substitution effects as influences on the choices of work and consumption.

---

[5] The data are from U.S. Department of Commerce (1975, pp. 168, 169) and *Economic Report of the President,* 1988, Table B-44. For a full analysis, we should also consider changes in labor-force participation. See problem 2.10 at the end of the chapter.

[6] The earlier data are rough averages from M. A. Bienefeld (1972, Chaps. 4, 5). Figures for 1938 and 1965 are from B. R. Mitchell and H. G. Jones (1971, p. 148). The value for 1986 is from Central Statistical Office, *Annual Abstract of Statistics,* 1988 edition, Table 6.15.

[7] The data are in Gordon Winston (1966, Table 1). His study deals also with cross-county differences in labor-force participation.

[8] The available statistics refer, however, to hours paid by employers. The decline in hours worked may be greater than the data indicate because of the increasing importance of vacations and sick days. Also, more of a decline shows up when we look at the total private, nonagricultural economy. Here, average weekly hours worked in the United States fell from 40.3 in 1947 to 34.8 in 1987. But these data reflect partly the changing composition of the labor force, especially toward more female workers.

SUBSTITUTION EFFECTS FOR WORK
VERSUS CONSUMPTION

We started with a pure wealth effect where the production function shifted upward in a parallel manner, as shown in Figure 2.8. This change in technology allows people to produce more goods for a given amount of work. However, there is no change in the schedule for the marginal product of labor, MPL. This last condition is unrealistic, since technological advances tend to raise the MPL at each level of work.

Suppose that we want to understand the effects on households' choices from the type of upward shift to the production function that appears in Figure 2.10. The new function, $f(n)'$, is proportionately higher than the initial one, $f(n)$, at each level of work. Therefore, the slope of the new curve exceeds that of the initial one at each level of work. This change in slope brings in a substitution effect, which we now have to consider.

The proportional shift in Figure 2.10 combines the parallel shift in Figure 2.8 with a counterclockwise twist of the new function, $f(n)'$. Recall that we already understand the pure wealth effects from the parallel shift; therefore, we need only to study the consequences of a counterclockwise twist of the production function to assess the type of proportional shift that appears in Figure 2.10. Therefore, we now isolate this twist in Figure 2.11. Note that the new production function, $f(n)'$, is more steeply sloped than the old one, $f(n)$, at each level of work. Hence, the twist raises the marginal product of labor at any level of work.

Figure 2.12 shows the household's response to a twist of the production function. The initial function, $f(n)$, is tangent to an indifference curve at the point (n^*,

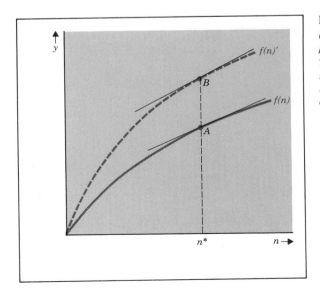

FIGURE 2.10 *A Proportional Upward Shift of the Production Function*
The new production function, f(n)', is higher and more steeply sloped than the old one, f(n), at each level of work.

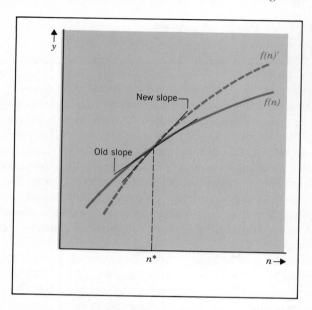

FIGURE 2.11 *A Twist of the Production Function*
At n^* *the level of output is the same for the two production functions. However, the new function,* $f(n)'$, *is more steeply sloped than the old one,* $f(n)$, *at any level of work.*

c^*). Since the new function, $f(n)'$, passes through this point, it would still be possible to work the amount n^* and consume the amount c^*. Initially households were happy to stay at this point because the MPL equaled the slope of the indifference curve, but the MPL is now higher. Therefore, more work now generates enough additional output (and consumption) to raise utility. That is, a move along the new production function, $f(n)'$, in Figure 2.12, reaches higher indifference curves. Eventually, the

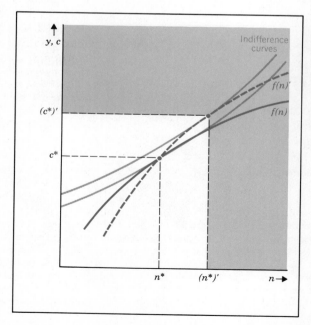

FIGURE 2.12 *Response of Work and Consumption to a Substitution Effect*
The schedule for the marginal product of labor shifts upward when the production function shifts from $f(n)$ *to* $f(n)'$. *The response is an increase in work—from* n^* *to* $(n^*)'$—*and a rise in consumption—from* c^* *to* $(c^*)'$.

household gets to one that is tangent to the new production function at the point $(n^{*\prime}, c^{*\prime})$. Then any more work would lower utility.

We have shown that a rise in the schedule for the marginal product of labor induces more work, $(n^*)^\prime > n^*$, and more consumption, $(c^*)^\prime > c^*$. Recall that a household always has the opportunity to work one more unit of time and use the additional MPL units of output to raise consumption. In terms of the two things that provide utility—leisure and consumption—households have the option to give up one unit of leisure in exchange for MPL extra units of consumption. When the schedule for labor's marginal product shifts upward, this deal becomes more favorable. That is, households now get more consumption, MPL, when they give up a unit of leisure. Or, to put this another way, consumption has become less costly relative to leisure. A rational person who wants to maximize utility finds it desirable to substitute toward the items that have become cheaper. In our example, this substitution effect motivates more consumption and less leisure (which means more work).[9]

COMBINING THE WEALTH AND SUBSTITUTION EFFECTS

We can now work out the full effects from a proportional upward shift of the production function, as shown in Figure 2.10. This change combines an increase in wealth with a substitution effect from the rise in the schedule for the marginal product of labor.

Figure 2.13 shows the effects on the household's choices. Notice that consumption increases, $c^{*\prime} > c^*$. However, the effect on work effort is ambiguous. Let's consider the nature of this ambiguity. The positive wealth effect leads to more consumption and more leisure, which means *less* work. However, the substitution effect from the higher schedule for the MPL implies more consumption and less leisure, which means *more* work. Notice that the wealth and substitution effects reinforce themselves with respect to consumption but oppose each other with respect to work and leisure. The proportional shift of the production function leads to less work and more leisure only if the wealth effect dominates the substitution effect. We cannot say in general which force will be more important.

Let's use the perspective of wealth and substitution effects to reconsider the facts on work hours that we looked at before. Recall that over the last 40 years or so, there has been no strong trend in average hours worked per week in industry

---

[9]Figure 2.12 shows that the household reaches a higher indifference curve. Therefore, the disturbance involves an increase in wealth as well as a substitution effect. However, it turns out that the wealth effect is relatively unimportant, which means that the example provides a close approximation to a pure substitution effect. To isolate the substitution effect exactly, we would have to include a small, parallel downward shift of the production function along with the twist shown in the figure. If this small shift were of the right size, the household would remain on the initial indifference curve. But this minor modification would still leave people with higher levels of work effort and consumption. Thus, the elimination of the small wealth effect would not change any qualitative results.

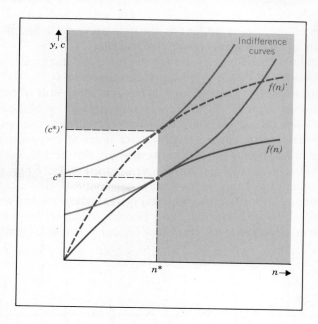

FIGURE 2.13 *Response of Work and Consumption to Combined Wealth and Substitution Effects When the production function shifts upward proportionately, there is an increase in consumption but an ambiguous change in work effort.*[*]

for the United States. However, there was a major decline in average hours worked at earlier stages of economic development.

Suppose that we think of economic development as represented by a series of proportional upward shifts to production functions. Figure 2.14 picks out three stages of economic development: a low level where the production function (for the typical producer) is $f(n)^I$, a middle level at $f(n)^{II}$, and a high level at $f(n)^{III}$. We can think of the first curve as applying to the United States before World War I, the second curve as applying at the end of World War II, and the third as applying in 1989.

Consider the patterns for households' tastes that would be consistent with the data on average work hours. Imagine first an economy at a low level of development; that is, a situation where the production function allows the typical person to reach only a low indifference curve. In this circumstance, people are likely to be willing to work long hours to maintain their consumption levels, even if their marginal products are low and although they are already working a lot. Diagrammatically, the indifference curve marked *low* in Figure 2.14 is extremely flat up to a high level of work effort. The flat slope means that people are willing to work a lot to gain a small amount of extra consumption. Notice that the first production function is tangent to the low indifference curve at the point $[(n^*)^I, (c^*)^I]$. Here, people work many hours but produce and consume relatively little because of the low level of the production function.

When production opportunities improve to the second level, $f(n)^{II}$, the production function is tangent to the indifference curve labeled *middle* at the point, $[(n^*)^{II}, (c^*)^{II}]$, in Figure 2.14. The figure shows this middle indifference curve with a slope that is higher and more steeply rising than that for the low indifference

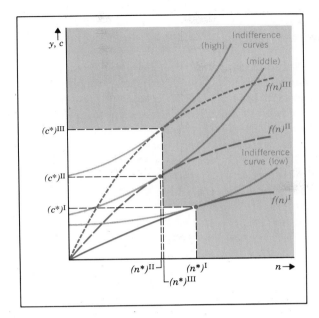

FIGURE 2.14 *Effect of Long-Term Economic Development on Average Work Hours*
The figure shows three levels of the production function as the economy develops from f(n)^I *to* f(n)^{II} *to* f(n)^{III}. *The indifference curves in the corresponding regions are labeled "low," "middle," and "high." Notice that work effort falls at early stages of economic development but changes little at more advanced stages.*

curve. This shape means that extra leisure has become more important relative to additional consumption. For this reason a reduction in hours worked, $(n^*)^{II} < (n^*)^I$, accompanies the rise in consumption, $(c^*)^{II} > (c^*)^I$. In this range of economic development, the negative wealth effect on work effort dominates the substitution effect.

Finally, the move from the second production function, $f(n)^{II}$, to the third, $f(n)^{III}$, corresponds to the case that we explored before in Figure 2.13. Here, the wealth and substitution effects roughly cancel to yield little change in work hours. But consumption again increases, $(c^*)^{III} > (c^*)^{II}$.

SUMMARY

In this chapter, households are isolated from each other and therefore behave like Robinson Crusoes. There are no markets on which people can trade, and each household uses its own labor to produce goods via a production function. Since we treat goods as nonstorable, each household consumes what it produces.

We can express people's preferences in terms of their utility for consumption and leisure. Then we can translate these preferences into indifference curves for work and consumption. Basically, people work more only if they receive a sufficient addition to their consumption.

The combination of households' preferences with their opportunities for production determines the choices of work, production, and consumption. For convenience we analyze these choices in terms of wealth and substitution effects. An improvement in the production function increases wealth, which motivates less work and more consumption. That is, the wealth effect is positive for consumption and leisure.

The only substitution effect in the model involves the productivity of labor. If the schedule for labor's marginal product shifts upward, households can obtain more consumption for an extra hour of work. Since consumption becomes cheaper relative to leisure, households work more to raise their consumption. In other words, they substitute away from leisure and toward consumption.

Toward the end, we use the apparatus to analyze the long-term behavior of work hours. Initially, as an economy develops, the increase in wealth motivates people to consume more and to work fewer hours per week. As the economy develops further, the substitution effect from labor's higher productivity tends roughly to offset the wealth effect. Hence, there is little change in work hours, but consumption continues to rise.

IMPORTANT TERMS AND CONCEPTS

wealth effect	utility
substitution effect	utility function
production function	indifference curve
marginal product of labor (MPL)	superior goods (or normal goods)
diminishing marginal productivity	inferior goods

QUESTIONS AND PROBLEMS

Mainly for Review

2.1 What is a production function? How does it represent a trade-off that the individual *has* to make between work (and consumption) and leisure?

2.2 Distinguish between total product and marginal product. What are the implications for total product if marginal product is (a) positive and increasing, (b) positive and diminishing, and (c) negative?

2.3 What is a utility function? Show how to represent different levels of utility by a family of indifference curves. Can these curves shift in the way that the production function can?

2.4 Show how the slope of each indifference curve indicates the trade-off that the individual is willing to make between work (and consumption) and leisure. Explain why it may not be equal to the trade-off represented by the slope of the production function.

2.5 Suppose that to remain at the same level of utility, an individual would have to receive one additional unit of consumption as compensation for one less unit of leisure. Would it be utility maximizing for the individual to work more if at that point the additional output obtained is more than one? if it is less than one? Restate your answer using the concepts of indifference curves and the production function.

2.6 Suppose there is an improvement in the production function. Assume that the improvement includes an upward shift in the schedule for the marginal product of labor. Will the individual work more to obtain more output; or work less, obtain the same or a greater amount of output, and enjoy more leisure than before? Explain your answer in terms of wealth and substitution effects. How does your answer change if either consumption or leisure is an inferior good?

PROBLEMS FOR DISCUSSION

2.7 *Properties of a Specific Production Function*
Suppose that the production function has the form,

$$y = A \cdot \sqrt{n} + B$$

where y is output, n is labor input, A is a positive constant, and B is another constant, which may be positive, negative, or zero.

a. Graph the level of output, y, versus the quantity of labor input, n.
b. Is the marginal product of labor positive? Is it diminishing in n?
c. Describe the wealth and substitution effects from an increase in the coefficient A.
d. Describe the wealth and substitution effects from an increase in the coefficient B.

2.8 *Effects of Shifts in the Production Function on the Choice of Work Effort*
Assume again that the production function is $y = A \cdot \sqrt{n} + B$. What are the effects on a household's work effort, n, output, y, and consumption, c, from:

a. an increase in the coefficient A?
b. an increase in the coefficient B?

2.9 *Temporary versus Permanent Changes in the Production Function*
Suppose that the production function shifts upward. Assume, as in Figure 2.8, that the shift is parallel, so that no change occurs in the schedule for labor's marginal product. Recall that we showed in Figure 2.9 that people respond by raising consumption and reducing work.

The improvement in the production function could be permanent—as in the case of a discovery of some new technology—or it might be temporary—as in the case of good weather for this period. What difference does it make for the results whether the change is permanent or temporary? That is, do we predict different responses of consumption and work effort in the two cases?

2.10 *Changes in Labor-Force Participation*

In the text we mentioned some variations over time in average hours worked per week. But we also see important changes in aggregate work effort that reflect shifts in labor-force participation. For example, people may alter their time spent at school or in retirement. Also, especially for married women in recent years, people may choose to work in the market rather than at home. Overall we can assess the changes in labor-force participation from the following table, which shows the ratio of the total labor force (including the military) to the adult population aged less than 65.[10]

Total Labor Force ÷ Population Aged 16–64	(%)
1980	76
1960	69
1940	64
1920	63
1900	63

Notice that labor-force participation rose sharply during the post–World II period. Most of this change reflected the increased activity of women, especially married women, in the market sector.

What does our analysis of wealth and substitution effects say about this behavior of labor-force participation? (Think here of the effects on a family that includes more than one potential worker.) Can we reconcile the rising rate of labor-force participation with the tendency of average hours worked per worker to stay constant or fall slowly? (Note: This question does not have a clear-cut answer!)

2.11 *Productivity*

A popular measure of productivity is the ratio of output (say, real GNP) to employment (say, worker hours). In the graph of the production function below, this concept of productivity at the employment level n^1 is given by the ratio, y^1/n^1. Productivity at this point equals the slope of the dashed line that is drawn from the origin to intersect the production function at the employment level n^1.

a. For the production function shown and for any employment level n, show graphically that productivity, y/n, always exceeds the marginal product of labor, MPL.

b. Consider a technological change that shifts the production function upward proportionately at all levels of n (as shown in Figure 2.10). What happens to the choices of work effort, n, and output, y? What happens to productivity, y/n?

[10]The data are from U.S. Department of Commerce (1975, pp. 10, 128) and the *Citibase* data bank.

(Empirically, long-run economic development is associated with a sustained rise in output per worker hour.)

c. Assume now that the form of the production function does not change. But suppose that people shift their tastes and become more willing to work. That is, at the initial levels of work and consumption, each person requires a smaller addition in consumption to give up a unit of leisure. What happens here to the choices of work effort, n, and output, y? What happens to productivity, y/n?

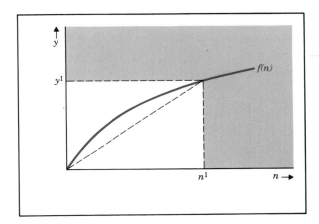

CHAPTER 3

THE BEHAVIOR OF HOUSEHOLDS WITH MARKETS FOR COMMODITIES AND CREDIT

*I*n the previous chapter, households were Robinson Crusoe–like producers and consumers. Hence, there were no possibilities for trade between one household and another. This chapter introduces two types of opportunities for exchange. First, there is a commodity market where people can sell their outputs and buy those of others. On this market, the price level is the amount of money that exchanges for a unit of commodities. One important aspect of this market is that it allows people to specialize in their type of production. This specialization is a major element in efficient economic organization.

Second, there is a credit market on which households can borrow and lend. The interest rate determines the cost of borrowing and the return to lending. By using the credit market, people can avoid substantial fluctuations in their consumption even if their incomes vary a great deal from period to period. The effect of the interest rate on the time pattern of consumption and work is one of the key relations in this chapter.

THE COMMODITY MARKET

In the real world, people consume very little of most of the goods that they help to produce in the marketplace. For example, an auto worker's contribution to the output of cars is much greater than that worker's expenditure on cars. Typically, a person works on one or a few products and receives income from the sale of these products or from the sale of labor services, which help to create the products. Then this income is spent on a wide range of consumer goods. As Adam Smith observed over two centuries ago, people tend to specialize with respect to occupations and production activities. This specialization aids efficiency—in fact, the national output would be many times smaller if everyone participated in the production of all goods. In this case, people would learn each job badly and would spend most of their time shifting from task to task.

In the theoretical model, we want to capture the feature that individuals consume little of what they produce. To keep things workable, it is convenient to go to the extreme and assume that producers sell their entire output on a market where people buy and sell commodities. Then sellers use their proceeds to buy other goods for consumption purposes.

The model would become unmanageable if we tried to keep track of the physical differences among many kinds of goods. Therefore, we continue to pretend that there is a single physical type of good, which households produce by one type of production process. As before, the production function is

$$y_t = f(n_t). \tag{3.1}$$

MONEY

Consider the sales and purchases of goods on the commodity market. We assume that it is inconvenient to trade one type of good directly for another. As economists have noted for hundreds of years, this form of **barter** exchange would require a person to find someone who wants exactly the goods that he or she has and has exactly the goods that he or she wants. Therefore, we assume that society has settled on a **medium of exchange,** called money. People sell their outputs for money and use money to buy other goods for consumption purposes. The use of money facilitates the exchange of one good for another.

The money in our model is analogous to paper **currency** issued by a government. At the present time, almost all governments issue currency. (Two exceptions are Panama and Liberia, which use U.S. currency. Some others that lack their own paper money are Andorra, Greenland, Guadalupe, Liechtenstein, and Luxembourg.) Money takes a paper form in the model, with no backing by gold or other commodities. The monetary roles of gold and silver were important historically but are much less significant under present-day arrangements.

Money is denominated in an arbitrary unit, such as a "dollar." We shall often refer to dollar amounts as **nominal** magnitudes. One important property is that, unlike some assets that we introduce later, money does not bear interest.[1]

---

[1]Historically, it is rare for currency to pay interest. Some early forms of U.S. Treasury notes, such as those issued from 1812 to 1815, paid interest and also had some limited use as media of exchange. However, because no denominations below $100 were issued, these notes were used mostly as bank reserves. For a discussion, see Richard Timberlake (1978, pp. 13–17).

Denote the dollar quantity of money that someone holds during period t by m_t. The aggregate quantity of money, denoted by M_t, equals the sum of the holdings by all individuals. (We adopt the convention of using a capital letter to represent an aggregate quantity.) For now, we assume that the aggregate quantity of money does not change over time.

THE PRICE LEVEL

Since goods are physically the same, we expect that all can be sold for the same number of dollars on the commodity market. The number of dollars that people receive for each unit of goods sold is the dollar *price* of the good. We denote the price by P and measure it in units of dollars per good. Often, we refer to P as the **general price level.**

For a seller of commodities, the price P is the number of dollars obtained for each unit of goods sold. For a buyer, the price is the number of dollars paid per unit of goods. Since P dollars buy 1 unit of goods, \$1 would buy $1/P$ units of goods. Therefore, the expression $1/P$ is the value of \$1 in units of the commodities that it buys. Similarly, \$$m$ exchanges for $(m) \times 1/P$ units of commodities. Whereas the quantity m is the value of money in terms of dollars, the quantity m/P measures the value of this money in terms of the quantity of commodities that it buys. Expressions like m/P are in units of commodities or in **real terms.** By contrast, a quantity like m is in dollar or nominal terms.

In the present chapter, we assume that people perceive the price level to be constant over time. (We drop this unrealistic assumption in Chapter 7, which begins the study of inflation.) Throughout the analysis, we assume that each household views itself as sufficiently small that it can buy or sell any amount of goods in the commodity market without influencing the established price. Economists call this **perfect competition.**

THE CREDIT MARKET

In the Robinson Crusoe model of Chapter 2, people had no way to shift resources over time. Goods could not be stored, and individuals could not borrow from others and repay these loans later. For now, we retain the assumption that goods cannot be stored, but we introduce possibilities for borrowing and lending on a credit market.

A person who makes a loan receives a piece of paper that indicates the terms of the contract. In our model we call this piece of paper a **bond.** The holder of a bond—the lender—has a claim to the amount owed by the borrower. Bonds in the model come in units of dollars. When someone buys 1 unit of bonds with \$1 of money, he or she lends \$1 on the credit market. If a person issues 1 unit of bonds in exchange for \$1 of money, he or she borrows \$1.

To simplify matters, pretend that all bonds have a maturity of one period. Each dollar unit of these bonds commits the borrower to pay the lender the **principal**, \$1, plus interest, \$R, in the next period. The variable R is the **interest rate**—that is, the ratio of the interest payment, \$R, to the amount borrowed, which is \$1. For the buyer of a bond, the interest rate is the return per period to lending; for the issuer of the bond, the interest rate is the cost per period of borrowing.

We assume that the credit market treats all bonds alike, regardless of the issuer. That is, to keep things manageable, we do not differentiate among persons with respect to their credit-worthiness, the type of collateral that they put up for a loan, and so on. Accordingly, the interest rate, R, must be the same for all bonds. Further, any household is small enough to be able to buy or sell any amount of bonds without affecting the interest rate. Again, this is an assumption of perfect competition. We can modify this framework later to bring in various real-world complications, such as limitations on individuals' access to borrowing and the existence of bonds with various maturities.

Let b_t represent the number of bonds in dollar units that a household holds during period t. The amount of bonds may be positive or negative for an individual household. Notice, however, that for any dollar borrowed by one person, there must be a corresponding dollar lent by someone else. Hence, the *total* of positive bond holdings for lenders must exactly match the *aggregate* of negative bond holdings for borrowers. In the model we allow only one type of economic unit, households, to borrow and lend. In particular, we do not yet deal with governments, foreigners, financial institutions, or corporations as participants in the credit market. (We shall see later that the essential ideas do not change when we make these additions.) Therefore, in the model the *total* of bonds held by all households, denoted by B_t, must always be zero.

As noted before, b_{t-1} is the dollar amount of bonds that someone holds during period $t - 1$. In period t these bonds pay the interest, Rb_{t-1}, and principal, b_{t-1}. (Notice that the bonds bought or sold in period $t - 1$ do not bear interest until period t.) Thus, the receipts from bonds are positive for lenders—for whom b_{t-1} is positive—and negative for borrowers. Recall that the aggregate stock of bonds for period $t - 1$, B_{t-1}, is zero. Therefore, the aggregates of interest and principal payments for period t must also be zero. The total of interest receipts always balances the total of interest expenses.

We measure **saving** in the form of bonds as the net change in someone's asset position, $b_t - b_{t-1}$. Note that this saving is a *flow*, which determines the *change* over one period in someone's *stock* of bonds. This saving is positive for some persons and negative for others. However, when we sum up across households, we know that $B_t = B_{t-1} = 0$. Therefore, the aggregate of saving in bonds, $B_t - B_{t-1}$, must also be zero in each period. In the aggregate, the additions to loans balance the additions to debts.

An individual's total of financial assets equals the sum of money and bonds, $m_t + b_t$. Recall that money holdings are nonnegative for all persons—that is, $m_t \geq 0$. (Only the government can issue money!) In the aggregate, since $B_t = 0$, the stock of financial assets equals the total money stock, M_t.

The change in an individual's financial assets, $(m_t + b_t) - (m_{t-1} + b_{t-1})$, is the total amount that an individual saves during period t. When summing up across all households, we know that $M_t - M_{t-1} = 0$ (because we are assuming that the total stock of money is constant), and $B_t - B_{t-1} = 0$. Therefore, the aggregate of total saving is zero at all points in time in the present model. (When we introduce investment in Chapter 9, this result will change.)

BUDGET CONSTRAINTS

BUDGET CONSTRAINTS FOR ONE PERIOD

Each household receives income from sales of output, y_t, on the commodity market. The quantity of output depends on the amount of labor input, n_t, through the production function, $y_t = f(n_t)$. Since the price of goods is P, the dollar income from selling output is Py_t. Recall that interest income from the bond market, Rb_{t-1}, is positive for lenders and negative for borrowers. Also, remember that people receive no interest income from their holdings of money.

Each household purchases the quantity of consumable goods, c_t, from the commodity market. Since the price of goods is P, the amount of consumption expenditure in dollars is Pc_t.

For a given total of financial assets, a household can use the credit market to exchange money for bonds, or vice-versa, and thereby achieve the desired composition of assets between bonds and money. The amount held as bonds, b_{t-1}, determines the interest income or expense for period t. The motivation for holding money, which does not bear interest, derives from money's convenience in carrying out exchanges. For expositional purposes, we shall not deal explicitly with the demand for money until Chapter 4. For now, we just assume that people hold part of their assets as money.

We can express the equality between a household's total sources and uses of funds in the form of a budget constraint. The condition for period t is

$$Py_t + b_{t-1}(1 + R) + m_{t-1} = Pc_t + b_t + m_t. \qquad (3.2)$$

The left side of equation 3.2 contains sources of funds, which include income from the commodity market, Py_t, the principal received on last period's bonds, b_{t-1}, the interest receipts from these bonds, Rb_{t-1}, and the amount of money held over from the previous period, m_{t-1}. The right side of the equation comprises uses of funds, which are consumption expenditures, Pc_t, holdings of bonds, b_t, and holdings of money, m_t. Since we treat the price level and interest rate as constants, these variables appear without time subscripts in the equation.

Rearrangement of equation 3.2 yields an expression for a household's nominal saving, which is the change over time in the dollar value of financial assets,

$$\text{nominal saving} = (b_t + m_t) - (b_{t-1} + m_{t-1}) = Py_t + Rb_{t-1} - Pc_t. \quad (3.3)$$

Nominal saving equals the income from producing and selling output plus interest receipts less consumption expenditures.

Households can leave saving intact by making simultaneous changes in income and consumption. For example, suppose that someone works more in period t and raises income, Py_t, by \$1000. Then if he or she also raises consumption spending, Pc_t, by \$1000, saving does not change. Therefore, the budget constraint allows people to work more and raise consumption during any period, without altering the amounts of assets that they carry over to the following period. This trade-off between consumption and leisure in a single period was the only choice available to Robinson Crusoe in the model from Chapter 2. The expanded model retains this option but also introduces possibilities that exploit the credit market. Specifically, individuals can vary current saving, which is the difference between income and expenditure. Thereby, people alter the amount of assets that they carry over to the future.

Recall that equation 3.3 specifies the saving for one household. As mentioned before, the total of this saving across households is zero. When we add up the right side of equation 3.3 over all households, we find that aggregate income equals aggregate spending, $PY_t = PC_t$. (Remember that the aggregate stock of bonds, B_{t-1}, is zero.) For Robinson Crusoe, the equality between production and consumption holds individually at every point in time. Now, because of the credit market, *some* people can consume more than their income (dissave), while others consume less (save). But it is still true for *the economy as a whole* that total output cannot depart from total consumption. Consumption is the only use for commodities in the present model.

BUDGET CONSTRAINTS FOR TWO PERIODS

The previous discussion brought out the effects of current consumption and work on the assets that a household carried over to the future. We can clarify this process by studying choices over two periods.

The budget constraint from equation 3.2 holds for any period. For example, for period 1, the condition is

$$Py_1 + b_0(1 + R) + m_0 = Pc_1 + b_1 + m_1. \tag{3.4}$$

Now we shall find it convenient to assume that each household's money holdings are constant over time—that is, $m_1 = m_0$. Anyone who maintains a constant quantity of money carries out any saving or dissaving in the form of bonds. By making this assumption, we avoid a clutter of minor terms in the household's budget constraint over more than one period. But we shall return later (in Chapter 4) to reconsider the case where money holdings change over time.

Using the condition, $m_1 = m_0$, the budget constraint from equation 3.4 simplifies to

$$Py_1 + b_0(1 + R) = Pc_1 + b_1. \tag{3.5}$$

There is a similar one-period budget constraint for period 2,

$$Py_2 + b_1(1 + R) = Pc_2 + b_2. \tag{3.6}$$

The two budget constraints are not independent because b_1 appears as a use of funds in period 1 and as a source of funds in period 2.

We can combine the two one-period budget constraints into a single two-period budget constraint. First, solve equation 3.6 for b_1 to get

$$b_1 = \frac{Pc_2}{(1 + R)} + \frac{b_2}{(1 + R)} - \frac{Py_2}{(1 + R)}.$$

Next, substitute for b_1 in equation 3.5 and collect terms into sources and uses of funds to get

$$Py_1 + \frac{Py_2}{(1 + R)} + b_0(1 + R) = Pc_1 + \frac{Pc_2}{(1 + R)} + \frac{b_2}{(1 + R)}. \quad (3.7)$$

The sources of funds on the left side of equation 3.7 include the income from the commodity market for periods 1 and 2, Py_1 and Py_2, and the initial stock of bonds, b_0. The uses of funds on the right side involve the consumption expenditures over the two periods, Pc_1 and Pc_2, and the stock of bonds held at the end of the second period, b_2.

Observe how the incomes, Py_1 and Py_2, appear in equation 3.7. We divide next period's amount, Py_2, by the term $(1 + R)$ before adding it to this period's, Py_1. It is important to understand why incomes from the two periods, Py_1 and Py_2, are not just added together in the household's two-period budget constraint. Similarly, on the right side of equation 3.7, we divide next period's expenditure, Pc_2, by the term $(1 + R)$ before adding it to this period's, Pc_1. Again, we want to understand why we combine expenditures from different dates in this manner.

PRESENT VALUES

If the interest rate is positive—that is, $R > 0$—a given dollar amount of today's bonds translates into a larger number of dollars next period. Accordingly, individuals who can buy or sell bonds on the economy-wide credit market (that is, people who can lend or borrow) regard a dollar's worth of income or expenses differently depending on when it arises. Specifically, $1 received or spent earlier is equivalent to more than $1 later. Or, viewed in reverse, dollars received or spent in the future must be discounted to express them in terms that are comparable to dollars in the present.

Suppose, for example, that $R = 10\%$ per year. Assume that someone has $100 of income today but plans to spend these funds in the future. Then he or she can buy $100 of bonds now and have $110 available next year. Hence, $100 today is worth just as much as $110 next year. Equivalently, the $110 is discounted to correspond to the amount of today's income needed to generate $110 next year. We find this amount by solving the following equation:

$$(\text{Income needed today}) \times (1 + 10\%) = \$110.$$

The required amount of current income is $\$110/(1.1) = \$100$.

More generally, if we substitute any value of the interest rate, R, for 10%, the income for next period, Py_2, is divided by the term $(1 + R)$ to find the equivalent amount for this period. The result, $Py_2/(1 + R)$, is the **present value** of the future income. Economists call the term $(1 + R)$ the **discount factor.** When we discount by this factor—that is, when we divide by the term $1 + R$—we determine the present value of next period's income.

Equation 3.7 shows that we express the second period's income as a present value, $Py_2/(1 + R)$, before combining it with the first period's income, Py_1. Thus, the sum, $Py_1 + Py_2/(1 + R)$, is the total present value of income from the production (and sales) of goods over periods 1 and 2. Similarly, we express next period's expenditure as the present value, $Pc_2/(1 + R)$, before adding it to this period's spending, Pc_1. The sum, $Pc_1 + Pc_2/(1 + R)$, is the total present value of consumption expenditures over periods 1 and 2.

THE HOUSEHOLD'S BUDGET LINE

The two-period budget constraint in equation 3.7 brings out the choices that a credit market allows to a household. Assume, for example, that a household raises today's spending, Pc_1, by \$1000, and thereby cuts today's saving by \$1000. This change reduces assets at the end of the first period, b_1, by \$1000 (see equation 3.5). For the second period, the household loses \$1000 in receipts of principal from bonds and \$100 in receipts of interest (assuming that $R = 10\%$). With \$1100 less during the second period, the household can decrease next period's spending, Pc_2, by this amount to keep the final asset position, b_2, intact. Therefore, the increase in today's spending by \$1000 balances against a decrease in next period's spending by \$1100. More generally, the required decrease in spending for the next period, Pc_2, equals the increase in this period's spending, Pc_1, multiplied by the discount factor, $(1 + R)$.

To study the choices of c_1 and c_2 it is convenient to express everything in real terms by dividing through equation 3.7 by the price level, P. If we rearrange terms to place those involving consumption on the left side, we get

$$c_1 + \frac{c_2}{(1 + R)} = y_1 + \frac{y_2}{(1 + R)} + \frac{b_0(1 + R)}{P} - \frac{b_2}{P(1 + R)}. \qquad (3.8)$$

Note that each term in equation 3.8 is in real terms. For example, y_1 is period 1's real income from the commodity market, in the sense of indicating the number of commodity units that someone can buy during period 1 with the dollar income of Py_1.

Suppose that we fix the total of the items on the right side of equation 3.8 at some amount, which we can call x. So we can think of fixing the starting real value of bonds, $b_0(1 + R)/P$, the real present value of bonds carried over to period 3, $b_2/P(1 + R)$, and the total present value of real income from the commodity market, $y_1 + y_2/(1 + R)$. Then we can rewrite equation 3.8 as

$$c_1 + \frac{c_2}{(1 + R)} = x, \qquad (3.9)$$

where $x = b_0(1 + R)/P - b_2/P(1 + R) + y_1 + y_2/(1 + R)$. Equation 3.9 makes clear that for a given quantity x, a household can change today's consumption, c_1, by making the appropriate adjustment in next period's consumption, c_2.

The straight line in Figure 3.1 shows the possibilities. If the household consumes nothing in the second period, so that $c_2 = 0$ (which would probably cause starvation and therefore be undesirable), equation 3.9 says that today's consumption, c_1, equals x. Hence, the line in the figure intersects the horizontal axis at this point. Alternatively, if the household consumes nothing today, so that $c_1 = 0$, the real present value of next period's consumption, $c_2/(1 + R)$, equals x. In this case, next period's consumption is given by $c_2 = x(1 + R)$. Therefore, the line in the figure intersects the vertical axis at this point.

The straight line in Figure 3.1 connects the value x on the horizontal axis to the value $x(1 + R)$ on the vertical. This **budget line** shows all the combinations of consumptions, c_1 and c_2, that satisfy the household's budget condition from equation 3.9. The important point is that the budget line shows the attainable pairs of consumption, c_1 and c_2, for a given real present value of spending over the two periods.

The slope of the budget line in Figure 3.1 is $-(1 + R)$. (The magnitude of the slope is the ratio of the vertical intercept, $x[1 + R]$, to the horizontal, x.) Along this line, a decrease by 1 unit in today's real spending, c_1, is matched by an increase of $(1 + R)$ units in next period's real spending, c_2. To put it another way, the interest rate R is the premium in future consumption for saving today rather than consuming.

So far, the analysis describes a household's opportunities for consuming in one period versus another. But we have not yet studied people's preferences for consumption at different dates. When we combine the opportunities with the prefer-

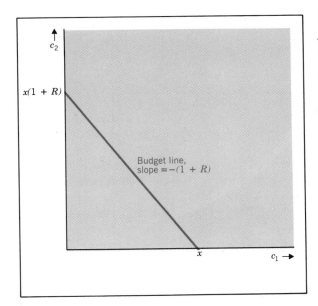

FIGURE 3.1 *The Possibilities for Consuming Now versus Later The budget line with slope* $-(1 + R)$ *shows the attainable combinations of consumption levels, c_1 and c_2. Along this line, the total real present value of expenditures over the two periods equals the fixed amount, x.*

ences, we shall determine the actual choices of consumption over time. Thus, we now turn our attention to these preferences.

PREFERENCES FOR CONSUMING NOW VERSUS LATER

In Chapter 2 we derived indifference curves for consumption and work in each period. Now we want to think about choices over time—specifically, about consumption in period 1 versus consumption in period 2 and about work in period 1 versus work in period 2. To begin, suppose that the two work efforts, n_1 and n_2, are given. Then we want to construct indifference curves to show the household's attitude toward different combinations of the two consumption levels, c_1 and c_2. Figure 3.2 shows such a curve. For high levels of c_1 relative to c_2, such as at point A in the figure, a household is more interested in next period's consumption than this period's. Hence, a small increase in c_2 makes up for the loss of a unit of c_1. Thus, the curve in the figure has a relatively flat slope at point A. Similarly, the curve has a steep slope when c_1 is relatively low, as at point B in the figure. At any point, the slope of the indifference curve reveals the amount of next period's consumption needed to make up for the loss of a unit of current consumption.

As in Chapter 2, we can define a family of indifference curves, each applying to a different level of utility. Figure 3.3 shows three of these curves, labeled by their levels of total utility, where $U^1 < U^2 < U^3$.

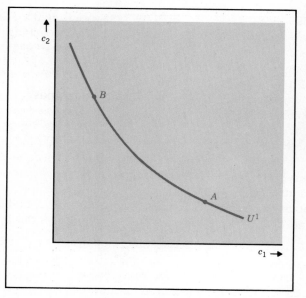

FIGURE 3.2 *An Indifference Curve for Consumption Now versus Consumption Next Period The household is equally happy with any combination of consumptions, c_1 and c_2, that lie along the curve. Today's consumption is high relative to next period's at point A and low relative to next period's at point B. Hence, the curve is steeper at point B than at point A.*

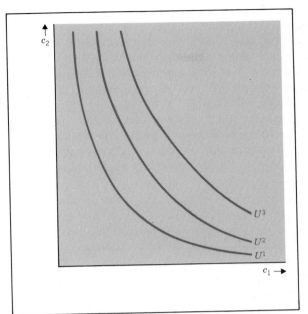

FIGURE 3.3 *A Family of Indifference Curves for Consumption Now versus Consumption Next Period* Along each curve, the level of utility is constant. Utility increases as the household moves from the curve labeled U^1 to that labeled U^2, and so on.

CHOOSING CONSUMPTION OVER TWO PERIODS

The budget line in Figure 3.1 describes how households can use the credit market to shift between consumption now and consumption in the next period. The family of indifference curves shown in Figure 3.3 describes people's willingness to exchange consumption now for consumption in the next period. If we combine the market opportunities from Figure 3.1 with the indifference map from Figure 3.3, we can determine the choices of consumption over the two periods.[2]

Figure 3.4 combines the budget line from Figure 3.1 with the indifference curves shown in Figure 3.3. Notice that the household moves along the budget line to reach the highest possible indifference curve. This occurs at the point of tangency, shown in the figure, where the slope of the budget line equals the slope of an indifference curve. We label the corresponding levels of consumption for the two periods as c_1^* and c_2^*.

Recall that the slope of an indifference curve measures the bonus in next period's consumption needed to compensate for the loss of a unit of this period's consump-

---

[2]This method comes from Irving Fisher (1930, especially Chap. 10). Interestingly, Fisher—who did his main work at Yale University—is one of the few macroeconomists who is popular today at both Yale and Chicago.

tion. On the other hand, the slope of the budget line is $-(1 + R)$, which determines the premium, R, for saving more. At the point of tangency shown in Figure 3.4 the premium from saving more just balances the willingness to defer consumption. For this reason, any choice along the budget line other than the point (c_1^*, c_2^*) leads to lower utility. This result is clear geometrically from Figure 3.4.

To sum up, we combined people's opportunities (the budget line) with their preferences (the indifference curves) to determine the choices of consumption over two periods. At the same time, we determined how much people save today. We can use this analysis to see how the time pattern of consumption and saving changes when there are shifts in the interest rate or other variables. The effects of changes in the interest rate turn out to be especially important for our subsequent macroeconomic analysis.

WEALTH AND SUBSTITUTION EFFECTS

As in Chapter 2, we can use the notions of wealth and substitution effects to analyze people's choices. In the present setting, wealth effects relate to the quantity previously denoted as x, which is the total present value of real consumption expenditures for periods 1 and 2. The important substitution variable for consuming now versus later, or for how much to save, is the interest rate, R.

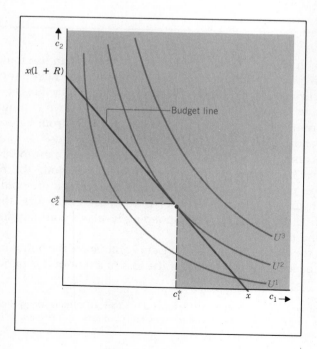

FIGURE 3.4 *Choosing Consumption Today and Next Period*
The choice of consumption levels, c_1^* and c_2^*, occurs where the budget line is tangent to an indifference curve.

WEALTH EFFECTS ON CONSUMPTION

Before, we found that parallel shifts of the production function implied pure wealth effects. These wealth effects shown up here as shifts in the total real present value of expenditures, x, which is given by

$$x = c_1 + \frac{c_2}{(1 + R)} = y_1 + \frac{y_2}{(1 + R)} + \frac{b_0(1 + R)}{P} - \frac{b_2}{P(1 + R)}. \quad (3.10)$$

Also, recall that the amounts of real income from the commodity market come from the production function as $y_1 = f(n_1)$ and $y_2 = f(n_2)$.

Assume that the production function shifts upward for periods 1 and 2. Think of parallel shifts that do not change the schedule for labor's marginal product. Assuming for the moment that work efforts, n_1 and n_2, do not change, there are increases in the amounts of real income, y_1 and y_2. Now suppose that we hold constant the initial and final stocks of bonds, b_0 and b_2. Then the increases in y_1 and y_2 raise the total real present value of spending, x, from equation 3.10.

Figure 3.5 shows that the increase in the total real present value of spending generates a parallel outward shift of the budget line. (The slope stays the same because the interest rate does not change.) The new budget line allows the household to reach a higher indifference curve than before. Note that the new point of tangency between the budget line and an indifference curve occurs at higher levels of consumption for each period. Hence, the wealth effect is positive for c_1 and c_2—or equivalently, c_1 and c_2 are both superior goods.

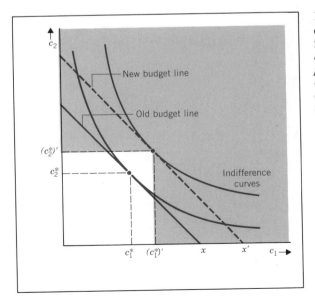

FIGURE 3.5 *Wealth Effects on Consumption*
The total real present value of consumption expenditures for periods 1 and 2 rises from x to x'. Consumption increases from c_1^* to $(c_1^*)'$ in period 1 and from c_2^* to $(c_2^*)'$ in period 2.

THE INTEREST RATE AND
INTERTEMPORAL SUBSTITUTION

If the interest rate is R, each household faces the budget line that we label as "old" in Figure 3.6. Given the total real present value of spending for periods 1 and 2, the household selects the consumption pair, (c_1^*, c_2^*). If the interest rate rises to R', the new budget line is steeper than the old one. There are, however, many places that we could draw this new line in Figure 3.6. For present purposes, we want to isolate the substitution effect from a higher interest rate. If we held fixed the overall real present value of spending, x, the new budget line would start from the value x on the horizontal axis but otherwise would lie to the right of the old budget line. But then the new budget line would allow the household to consume the same amount today, c_1^*, and more next period. Since wealth increases in this case, the shift would not be a pure substitution effect.

We can approximate a pure substitution effect by rotating the budget line around the point where the household initially chose the levels of consumption. When drawn this way, the new budget line shown in Figure 3.6 intersects the old one at the point (c_1^*, c_2^*). Thus the household still has the option to buy this initial pair of consumptions. But the household cannot increase either quantity without giving up some of the other.

Although the new budget line passes through the point (c_1^*, c_2^*) in Figure 3.6, the line is not tangent to an indifference curve at this point. Since the new budget line is steeper than the indifference curve, the premium to saving more, R', exceeds

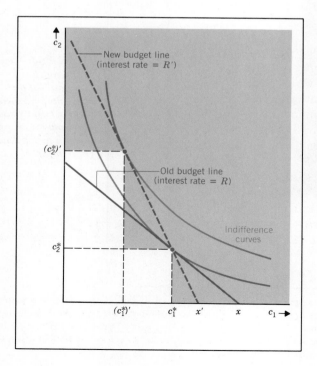

FIGURE 3.6 *Effect on Consumption from an Increase in the Interest Rate*
When the interest rate is R on the old budget line, the household chooses the consumption pair (c_1^*, c_2^*). If the interest rate rises, to R' on the new budget line, the household opts for the pair [(c_1^*)', (c_2^*)']. Notice that the increase in the interest rate motivates people to choose a higher ratio of consumption next period to consumption this period.

EMPIRICAL EVIDENCE ON INTERTEMPORAL SUBSTITUTION OF CONSUMPTION

O ur theoretical analysis predicts that a higher interest rate motivates people to defer consumption from the present to the future. A recent empirical study by David Runkle (1988) has isolated this effect by examining the behavior of food consumption over time (1973–82) for a sample of 1100 U.S. households. (The data come from the Panel Study on Income Dynamics, which is constructed at the University of Michigan.) Runkle found that an increase in the annual interest rate by one percentage point raised the typical family's growth rate of consumption by about one-half percentage point per year. (Runkle's estimates adjust the interest rate for inflation and taxes in ways that we shall explore in Chapters 7 and 13, respectively.) The response of consumption growth to the interest rate turned out to be larger for households that had substantial liquid assets (such as stocks, bonds, and bank deposits) than for those without such assets. Economists have been less successful at finding these types of effects in aggregate consumption data. For a discussion of this evidence, see Robert Hall (1989).

the amount needed to motivate more saving. It follows that the household would raise saving—that is, c_1 falls and c_2 rises. The new choices, labeled $[(c_1^*)', (c_2^*)']$ in the figure, are where the new budget line is tangent to an indifference curve.[3] The important point is that the increase in the interest rate motivates people to raise future consumption, c_2, relative to current consumption, c_1. Equivalently, the rise in the interest rate induces households to save a larger fraction of current income.

Recall that the total real present value of spending over periods 1 and 2 is $c_1 + c_2/(1 + R)$. Note again that we divide c_2 by the discount factor, $(1 + R)$, before adding it to c_1. A rise in R lowers the cost of next period's consumption relative to that of current consumption because a person can obtain more units of consumption next period for each unit of current consumption foregone. It is this change in relative costs that motivates people to substitute future goods, c_2, for current ones, c_1. Economists call this mechanism an **intertemporal-substitution effect**.

---

[3]Note that the household reaches a higher indifference curve. Hence, wealth increases, even though we rotated the budget line through the point where the household initially chose consumption, (c_1^*, c_2^*). But it turns out that this wealth effect becomes negligible, relative to the substitution effect, when we look at smaller and smaller changes in the interest rate. So at least for small changes, we can neglect the wealth effect as a satisfactory approximation.

CHOOSING WORK EFFORT AT DIFFERENT DATES

In Chapter 2 we studied the choice of work and consumption for a single period. There we stressed substitution effects from changes in the schedule for labor's marginal product. Also, we explored wealth effects from shifts in the position of the production function.

In this chapter, we have examined an individual's choices of consumption over time. But so far we have not considered the choices of work effort. If we combine the previous analysis of work and consumption with the present analysis of consumption over time, we shall understand how households choose work effort over time.

WEALTH EFFECTS ON WORK EFFORT

We can write the household's budget constraint for two periods as

$$f(n_1) + \frac{f(n_2)}{(1 + R)} + \frac{b_0(1 + R)}{P} = c_1 + \frac{c_2}{(1 + R)} + \frac{b_2}{P(1 + R)}. \quad (3.11)$$

Note the substitutions, $y_1 = f(n_1)$ and $y_2 = f(n_2)$, in the expression for the real sources of funds on the left side. Suppose that the production function shifts up in a parallel fashion for periods 1 and 2. For given amounts of work, n_1 and n_2, the real sources of funds increase on the left side of equation 3.11. As we saw before, households respond by raising c_1 and c_2.

Recall from Chapter 2 that people also react to more wealth by taking more leisure. Hence, the levels of work, n_1 and n_2, tend to decline rather than stay fixed. Macroeconomists usually stress the positive wealth effect on consumption but neglect the effect on leisure. However, the evidence on hours of work, which we reviewed in Chapter 2, indicates that this effect on leisure is important. For example, at early stages of economic development, the wealth effect is strong enough that average hours worked tend to diminish as an economy develops.

THE INTEREST RATE AND CHOICES OF WORK EFFORT

Figure 3.6 shows that an increase in the interest rate motivates households to reduce current consumption, c_1, and raise next period's consumption, c_2. Notice from the right side of equation 3.11 that an increase in R makes next period's consumption, c_2, cheaper relative to this period's, c_1. That is why people substitute toward c_2 and away from c_1 when R rises. But the same argument holds for leisure in the two periods. If someone takes leisure in period 2, he or she discount the loss in output, $f(n_2)$, by the factor $(1 + R)$. Therefore, when R rises, the leisure from period 2 becomes cheaper relative to that in period 1. That is, the future output lost by working less in period 2 has a smaller present value than before. The conclusion is

EMPIRICAL EVIDENCE ON INTERTEMPORAL SUBSTITUTION OF WORK EFFORT

*T*ypically macroeconomists stress the effect on saving that results from intertemporal substitution of consumption but neglect the effect from changes in work effort. However, there is some evidence that intertemporal substitution of work effort is also important. For example, George Alogoskoufis (1987b) found for U.S. data from 1948 to 1982 that an increase in the annual interest rate by one percentage point lowered the growth rate of work by about 0.6 percentage point per year. For British data from 1950 to 1982, the corresponding estimate (Alogoskoufis, 1987a) was about 0.2. These results applied if aggregate work effort was measured by the total number of employees. If work effort was measured instead as hours worked per person, the results were not statistically significant. Thus, these findings suggest that intertemporal substitution of work effort is more important for the number of workers than for hours worked per person. Thomas MaCurdy (1981) reports additional evidence that supports the importance of intertemporal substitution of work effort.

that an increase in the interest rate motivates people to substitute toward next period's leisure and away from this period's. Or, equivalently, this period's work, n_1, rises relative to next period's, n_2. Note also that the increase in n_1 reinforces the decrease in c_1 in the sense of raising current saving.

Overall, an increase in the interest rate has two types of intertemporal-substitution effects. First, today's consumption, c_1, declines relative to next period's, c_2. Second, today's work, n_1, rises relative to next period's, n_2. Both effects—the reduction in current spending and the increase in current income—show up as an increase in current saving. Thus, both responses reflect the positive response of an individual's desired saving to the return from saving, which is the interest rate.

BUDGET CONSTRAINTS OVER MANY PERIODS

Thus far, we have examined the behavior of households over two periods. To carry out this analysis, we had to hold fixed the amount of bonds that someone carries over to later periods. In fact, this amount is not a given, since it depends on people's plans for consuming and earning income in the future. Now, we make this connection explicit by dealing with households' plans over many periods.

BUDGET CONSTRAINTS FOR ANY NUMBER OF PERIODS

Start with the two-period budget constraint from equation 3.7:

$$Py_1 + \frac{Py_2}{(1 + R)} + b_0(1 + R) = Pc_1 + \frac{Pc_2}{(1 + R)} + \frac{b_2}{(1 + R)}.$$

The final stock of bonds from the second period, b_2, determines the initial stock for period 3. Specifically, for period 3 the budget constraint is

$$Py_3 + b_2(1 + R) = Pc_3 + b_3.$$

We can use this equation to solve out for the stock of bonds, b_2, and substitute the result into the two-period budget constraint. Then we find that the three-period budget constraint is

$$Py_1 + \frac{Py_2}{(1 + R)} + \frac{Py_3}{(1 + R)^2} + b_0(1 + R)$$

$$= Pc_1 + \frac{Pc_2}{(1 + R)} + \frac{Pc_3}{(1 + R)^2} + \frac{b_3}{(1 + R)^2}. \tag{3.12}$$

By now we see how to construct a budget constraint for any number of periods. For example, the budget constraint for j periods is

$$Py_1 + \frac{Py_2}{(1 + R)} + \frac{Py_3}{(1 + R)^2} + \cdots + \frac{Py_j}{(1 + R)^{j-1}} + b_0(1 + R)$$

$$= Pc_1 + \frac{Pc_2}{(1 + R)} + \frac{Pc_3}{(1 + R)^2} + \cdots + \frac{Pc_j}{(1 + R)^{j-1}} + \frac{b_j}{(1 + R)^{j-1}}. \tag{3.13}$$

Notice that the previous examples of budget constraints are special cases of equation 3.13. For $j = 2$ we get the two-period budget constraint in equation 3.7, while for $j = 3$ we get the three-period constraint in equation 3.12.

Notice two things about the budget constraint for j periods in equation 3.13. First, the right side involves the stock of bonds, b_j, held at the end of period j. Second, we calculate the present value of income or expense for any period t by dividing by the factor $(1 + R)^{t-1}$. This factor represents the accumulation of interest between period 1 and period t—that is, over $t - 1$ periods.

THE HOUSEHOLD'S PLANNING HORIZON

Suppose that a household is choosing today's consumption and work effort, c_1 and n_1. Typically, households make these choices in the context of a long-term plan that considers future levels of consumption and income. These future values relate to the current choices through the j-period budget constraint in equation 3.13. We can refer to the number, j, as the household's **planning horizon.**

How long is the horizon that people consider in making current decisions? Because we are dealing with households that have access to a credit market, a long planning horizon is appropriate. That is, by borrowing or lending, people can effectively use future income to finance current spending, or current income to pay for future spending. When expressed as a present value, prospective incomes and expenses from the distant future are as pertinent for current decisions as are today's incomes and expenses.

Economists often assume that the planning horizon is long but finite. For example, in a class of theories called **life-cycle models,**[4] the horizon, j, represents an individual's expected remaining lifetime. If people do not care about things that occur after their death, they have no reason to carry assets beyond period j. Accordingly, they set to zero the final asset stock, b_j, which appears on the right side of the budget constraint in equation 3.13. (We also have to rule out the possibility of dying in debt, which would correspond to $b_j < 0$.)

Usually researchers who use life-cycle models assume that the working span, which is the interval where $n_t > 0$, is shorter than the length of life. In this case, people have retirement periods during which consumption must be financed either from savings accumulated during working years or from transfer payments. These transfers could come from the government (**social security**) or from children.

It is straightforward to define the anticipated lifetime—and thereby the finite planning horizon—for an isolated individual who has no concern for descendants. However, the appropriate horizon is not obvious for a family in which the parents care about their children. (The children may also care about their parents!) In this context, the applicable horizon extends beyond someone's expected lifetime, and people would give some weight to the expected future incomes and expenses of their children. Further, since children care about the welfare of their children— should they have any—and so on for each subsequent generation, there is no clear point at which to terminate the planning period. Of course, this argument does not imply that anticipated incomes and expenses for the distant future count as much as those for a few years off. But by using present values, we already place a large discount on incomes and expenses from the distant future.

Instead of imposing a finite horizon, we can think of the household's plan as having an **infinite horizon.** There are two good reasons for proceeding in this way:

- First, if we think of the typical person as part of a family that has concerns about the members of future generations—children, grandchildren, and so on—into the indefinite future, this setup is the correct one. In particular, it would be inappropriate to identify the horizon with the typical person's expected lifetime.

- Second, although it is not obvious at this point, an infinite horizon is the easiest to work with.

[4]See Franco Modigliani and Richard Brumberg (1954) and Albert Ando and Franco Modigliani (1963).

BUDGET CONSTRAINTS FOR AN INFINITE HORIZON

When the planning horizon is infinite, the budget constraint includes the present values of incomes and expenses for the indefinite future. Then, using equation 3.13, we have

$$Py_1 + \frac{Py_2}{(1 + R)} + \frac{Py_3}{(1 + R)^2} + \cdots + b_0(1 + R)$$

$$= Pc_1 + \frac{Pc_2}{(1 + R)} + \frac{Pc_3}{(1 + R)^2} + \cdots . \qquad (3.14)$$

We no longer terminate the sums for incomes and expenses at some finite date, j, as we did in equation 3.13. Notice also that the final stock of bonds, b_j, does not appear in the budget constraint. In effect, there is no "final" period to consider here.

For most purposes, we prefer to deal with the budget constraint when expressed in real terms. If we divide through equation 3.14 by the price level, P, we get.

$$y_1 + \frac{y_2}{(1 + R)} + \frac{y_3}{(1 + R)^2} + \cdots + \frac{b_0(1 + R)}{P}$$

$$= c_1 + \frac{c_2}{(1 + R)} + \frac{c_3}{(1 + R)^2} + \cdots . \qquad (3.15)$$

Equation 3.15 says that the present value of real income from sales to the commodity market over an infinite horizon, plus the real value of the receipts from the initial stock of bonds, equals the present value of real consumption expenditure over an infinite horizon. We shall use this form of the budget constraint when studying households' choices over many periods.

CHOICES OVER MANY PERIODS

Before, we discussed the choices of consumption over two periods, c_1 and c_2. Now we consider the entire path of consumption, $c_1, c_2, c_3, \ldots$. In some of our previous discussion, we thought about a given total present value of real spending over two periods, $x = c_1 + c_2/(1 + R)$. Here we proceed analogously by looking at the total present value of real spending over an infinite horizon. Using the budget constraint in equation 3.15, we have

$$x = c_1 + \frac{c_2}{(1 + R)} + \frac{c_3}{(1 + R)^2} + \cdots$$

$$= y_1 + \frac{y_2}{(1 + R)} + \frac{y_3}{(1 + R)^2} + \cdots + b_0(1 + R)/P. \qquad (3.16)$$

THE INTEREST RATE AND
INTERTEMPORAL SUBSTITUTION

Given the total present value of real spending over an infinite horizon, a household can still substitute between c_1 and c_2. Just as before, for each unit of c_1 foregone, a household can obtain $(1 + R)$ additional units of c_2. But there is nothing special about periods 1 and 2. People can substitute in a similar manner between c_2 and c_3, c_3 and c_4, and so on. In general, if someone gives up 1 unit of c_t, the credit market allows him or her to raise c_{t+1} by $(1 + R)$ units.

Consider an increase in the interest rate, R. As before, we want to abstract from wealth effects to isolate the substitution effect from this change. In the two-period case, we know that an increase in R motivates people to reduce c_1 relative to c_2. That is because the higher interest rate makes today's consumption more expensive relative to the next period's. But the same reasoning applies to any pair of consumptions, c_t and c_{t+1}. An increase in R lowers c_t relative to c_{t+1}.

When we allow for variable work effort, we find that changes in the interest rate also have intertemporal-substitution effects on work and leisure. The generalization from the two-period model is that an increase in R motivates people to take less leisure in one period relative to that in the next period. That is, n_t rises relative to n_{t+1}.

Finally, note that the decrease in c_1 and increase in n_1 both imply an increase in current saving. Thus, as in the two-period case, a higher interest rate motivates people to save more.

WEALTH EFFECTS

As before, wealth effects involve changes in the total present value of real spending, x, which is given in equation 3.16. Remember that the aggregate value of the initial stock of bonds, B_0, is zero. Therefore, if we think about the typical or average household, for which $b_0 = 0$, wealth effects will arise only from changes in the present value of real income from the commodity market, $y_1 + y_2/(1 + R) + \ldots$. For a given amount of work effort in each period, these changes must involve shifts in the production function.

Permanent Shifts of the Production Function   Consider first the case where the production function, $f(n_t)$, shifts upward in a parallel fashion for all periods. As examples, we can think of discoveries of new technology or natural resources— that is, changes that create permanent improvements in productive capacity. Given each period's amount of work, n_t, each period's level of output, y_t, rises. Hence, the total real present value of spending, x, increases in equation 3.16.

As a generalization of the results for two periods, we find that the increase in the present value of real spending, x, leads to increases in consumption, c_t, for each period. Consumption in any period is a superior good, which means that the wealth effect is positive. Similarly, we find that more wealth leads to more leisure in each period. Therefore, an increase in wealth implies less work effort, n_t, at each date.

The Marginal Propensities to Consume and Save   Suppose that real income, y_t, rises by one unit in each period. One possibility is that consumption, c_t, also increases by one unit in each period. (This response would satisfy the budget constraint in equation 3.16.) If someone does respond in this way, economists say that his or her **marginal propensity to consume**—defined as the change in consumption during a period relative to the change in that period's income—is one. Since consumption and income change by equal amounts in all periods, there is no change in saving for any period. In other words, the **marginal propensity to save**—defined as the change in saving for a period relative to the change in income for that period—is zero.

If income, y_t, changes by one unit in each period, as before, but a household increases current consumption, c_1, by less than one unit, the current marginal propensity to consume is less than one. Correspondingly, the current marginal propensity to save is positive. Households must, however, use this extra saving to expand some future level of consumption. Hence there must be at least one subsequent period during which consumption, c_t, rises by even more than one unit.

Suppose that a household planned initially for a constant amount of consumption. Then the increase in period t's consumption, c_t, by more than one unit means that this consumption increases relative to today's, c_1. That is, consumption shifts away from the present and toward the future. We know that this type of shift is appropriate if the interest rate increases. But since the interest rate does not change here, the household would tend to maintain the relative amounts of consumption at different dates. For the case at hand, this balance results only if the household increases consumption in every period by one unit. Hence, if the improvement in the production function is permanent, we predict that the marginal propensity to consume would be close to one. Correspondingly, the marginal propensity to save would be near zero.

Temporary Shifts of the Production Function   Suppose now that the parallel upward shift of the production function lasts only for the current period. So instead of discoveries of new technologies or resources, we can think of the effects of weather, temporary changes in the supply of raw materials, strikes, and so on.

If work efforts do not change, the increase in real income occurs only in the current period. Households would like to spread this extra income over consumption in all periods. But to raise future consumption, households now have to raise current saving. Hence, current consumption, c_1, rises by much less than the increase in current real income, y_1. In other words, if the improvement of the production function is temporary, the marginal propensity to consume is small, and the marginal propensity to save is positive and nearly equal to one.[5]

---

[5]Our findings about permanent and temporary changes of the production function correspond to Milton Friedman's (1957, Chaps. 2, 3) concept of **permanent income.** The general idea is that consumption depends on a long-term average of incomes—called permanent income—rather than just current income. If the change in income is temporary, permanent income and hence consumption rise relatively little. Hence, as in our earlier discussion, the marginal propensity to consume out of temporary income is small.

EMPIRICAL EVIDENCE ON THE MARGINAL PROPENSITY TO CONSUME

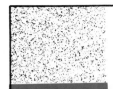

*E*mpirical research provides strong evidence that the marginal propensity to consume out of permanent changes in income is much greater than that for temporary changes. Some of the clearest evidence comes from special circumstances where there are windfalls of income, which people surely regard as temporary. One example is the receipt by Israeli citizens of lump-sum, nonrecurring restitution payments from Germany in 1957–58 (see Mordechai Kreinin, 1961, and Michael Landsberger, 1970). The payments were large, with a value that roughly equaled the average family's annual income. For this case, the data indicate that the typical family's consumption expenditure during the year of the windfall rose by no more than 20% of the amount received. Further, the measure of consumer spending includes purchases of consumer durables. Since these goods last for many years, we should view these purchases as partly saving rather than consumption. Therefore, the true marginal propensity to consume out of the windfall was much less than 20%.

Another example is the payment in 1950 to U.S. World War II veterans of an unanticipated, one-time life insurance dividend of about $175. At the time, this amount represented about 4% of the average family's annual income. In this case, the statistical estimates indicate that consumption rose by 30 to 40% of the windfall (see Roger Bird and Ronald Bodkin, 1965). But since the data again include purchases of consumer durables, the true marginal propensity to consume would be much lower than 30%.

More generally, statistical studies of consumer behavior indicate that the marginal propensity to consume out of permanent changes in income is large and not much different from one. By contrast, the marginal propensity to consume out of temporary income is only about 20 to 30% (see Robert Hall, 1989). Although this response to temporary changes is somewhat greater than that predicted by our theory, the important point for our analysis is that the response of consumer demand to permanent changes in income is much greater than that to temporary changes.

Wealth Effects from Changes in the Interest Rate   Thus far, we have looked only at intertemporal-substitution effects from changes in the interest rate. Now let's see whether a change in the interest rate leads to a wealth effect.

We can test for the effect on wealth by using the budget constraint, which is again

$$y_1 + \frac{y_2}{(1 + R)} + \cdots + \frac{b_0(1 + R)}{P} = c_1 + \frac{c_2}{(1 + R)} + \cdots .$$

Abstract from the term that involves the initial stock of bonds, $b_0(1 + R)/P$, because this term will equal zero when we sum up over all households.

Suppose that we hypothetically hold fixed the paths of real incomes, y_1, y_2, ..., and expenditures, c_1, c_2, ... Then consider the separate effects of an increase in R on the left and right sides of the budget constraint. The rise in R reduces the present values of real income, $y_1 + y_2/(1 + R) + \ldots$, and real spending, $c_1 + c_2/(1 + R) \ldots$. But the important question is which sum falls by the greater amount. If the present value of real spending falls by more, the given path of real income would be sufficient to continue purchasing these goods and still have something left over. Then the household could increase consumption for some periods without necessarily decreasing it for others. Hence, wealth increases. However, the opposite conclusion applies if the present value of real spending falls by less than that of real income.

The budget constraint indicates that the terms that decline most with the rise in R are those that are most distant into the future. That is, the discount factor for period t is $1/(1 + R)^{t-1}$, which is more sensitive to changes in R the higher the value of t. When R rises, the present value of real spending declines by more than that of real income if the path of spending is more heavily concentrated in the future than is the path of income. For the case where the initial bonds, b_0, equal zero, this property applies for someone who has positive saving in most of the earlier years and negative saving in most of the later years. In other words, people who plan usually to be lenders experience an increase in wealth when the interest rate rises. Conversely, those who plan usually to be borrowers have a decline in wealth.

Although either situation may hold for an individual, neither case can apply for the average person. Since the aggregate stock of bonds is always zero in our model, we know that the average household is neither typically a lender nor typically a borrower. Therefore, in the aggregate, the wealth effect from a change in the interest rate is nil.[6] This result is important. It says that for aggregate purposes we can neglect wealth effects from changes in the interest rate, and we should focus on the inter-temporal-substitution effects from these changes.

SHIFTS IN THE SCHEDULE FOR LABOR'S MARGINAL PRODUCT

Usually a rise in the schedule for labor's marginal product accompanies an improvement in the production function. As we know, a higher schedule for labor's marginal product motivates people to work more. If the change is the same for each period,

---

[6]For further discussion of this result, see Martin J. Bailey (1971, pp. 106–8).

work and hence real income rise by roughly equal amounts in each period. In this case the marginal propensity to consume would be close to one, so that each period's consumption would increase by roughly the same amount as income. In other words, saving would not change.

A permanent improvement in labor's productivity means that consumption becomes cheaper relative to leisure at each date. Therefore, people work and consume more in every period. Since there are no changes in the relative costs of consumption or leisure for different periods, the responses in work and consumption tend to be the same in each period; hence, there are no effects on saving.

We should be careful to distinguish the substitution between consumption and leisure from the intertemporal-substitution effect. The intertemporal effect involves the cost of taking consumption or leisure in one period rather than another. For example, an increase in the interest rate motivates people to reduce today's consumption and leisure relative to future consumption and leisure. In contrast, the schedule for labor's marginal product determines the relative cost of consumption and leisure at a point in time. Therefore, a shift in this schedule induces changes in the relative amounts of consumption and leisure. But if the change in labor's productivity is permanent, there are no intertemporal-substitution effects.

The results are different if the change in productivity is temporary. As an example, think of a gold rush or other temporary profit opportunity, which makes the reward for today's effort unusually high. We can represent this case by shifting the schedule for labor's marginal product only for the current period. Then the new element is that today's leisure becomes more expensive relative to future leisure or consumption. Therefore, people have an incentive to expand today's work to increase future consumption and leisure. Thus, a temporary improvement of productivity stimulates saving. That is, today's output rises by more than today's consumption.

SUMMARY

We introduced a commodity market on which people buy and sell goods at the price P. The existence of this market promotes economic efficiency because it allows producers to specialize.

We also introduced a credit market on which people borrow and lend at the interest rate R. By using this market, individuals can choose a time pattern for consumption that differs from that for income.

We began with a budget constraint over two periods but then extended the analysis to any number of periods. For most purposes, we can think of the behavior of households over an infinite horizon. We motivated the infinite planning period by thinking about a family in which parents care about their children, who care about their children, and so on.

An increase in the interest rate motivates households to shift away from consumption over the near term and toward that in the future. The opposite responses apply to work effort. These intertemporal-substitution effects mean that a higher interest rate motivates people to save more.

Improvements in the production function have wealth effects that are positive on consumption and negative on work for each period. If the shift is permanent, the marginal propensity to consume is near one, and the marginal propensity to save is near zero. If the shift is temporary, the marginal propensity to consume is small, and the marginal propensity to save is almost one. We also showed that a change in the interest rate has no aggregate wealth effect.

A permanent upward shift in the schedule for labor's marginal product raises work and consumption in each period but does not affect saving. In contrast, a temporary upward shift in the schedule raises current output by more than current consumption and thereby raises saving.

IMPORTANT TERMS AND CONCEPTS

barter	present value
medium of exchange	discount factor
currency	budget line
nominal	intertemporal-substitution effect
general price level	planning horizon
real terms	life-cycle model
perfect competition	social security
bond	infinite horizon
principal of bond	marginal propensity to consume
interest rate	marginal propensity to save
saving	permanent income

QUESTIONS AND PROBLEMS

Mainly for Review

3.1 Why would individuals be interested only in the real value of consumption expenditures, income, and assets such as money and bonds? Would a fall in the dollar amount of consumption spending leave the individual worse off when it is accompanied by an equiproportionate fall in the price level?

3.2 Distinguish clearly between an individual's initial asset position and the change in that position. Which is affected by current consumption and saving decisions? Is an individual who is undertaking negative saving necessarily a borrower in the sense of having a negative position in bonds?

3.3 Derive the two-period budget constraint, and draw a graph of it. Why are there no terms involving money holdings on the side of sources of funds?

3.4 Show how taking a present value involves giving different weights to dollar values in different periods. Why is income in the present more "valuable" than income in the future? Why is consumption in the future "cheaper" than consumption in the present?

3.5 Review the factors that determine an individual's choice of consumption over two periods, c_1 and c_2, and show this choice graphically. Why is the individual best off where the budget line is tangent to an indifference curve?

3.6 What factors determine whether the marginal propensity to consume is less than one or equal to one? Can the marginal propensity to consume be greater than one?

3.7 Review the effects of the following changes on current consumption and work, distinguishing clearly between wealth effects and substitution effects:

a. A permanent parallel shift of the production function.
b. A change in the interest rate.
c. A temporary change in the marginal product of labor.

PROBLEMS FOR DISCUSSION

3.8 *Discount Bonds*
The one-period bonds in our model pay a single interest payment or "coupon" of $R and a principal of $1. Alternatively, we could consider a one-period discount bond like a U.S. Treasury bill. This type of asset has no coupons but pays a principal of $1 (or, more realistically, $10,000) next period. Let P^B be the dollar price for each unit of discount bonds, where each unit is a claim to $1 next period.

a. Is P^B greater or less than $1?
b. What is the one-period rate of interest on discount bonds?
c. How does the price, P^B, relate to this one-period rate of interest?
d. Suppose that instead of coming due next period, the discount bond comes due (matures) two periods from now. What is the interest rate *per period* on this bond? How do the results generalize if the bond matures j periods from now?

3.9 *Financial Intermediaries*
Consider a financial intermediary, such as a bank or savings and loan association, that enters the credit market. This intermediary borrows from some people and lends the proceeds to others. (The loan to a bank from its customers often takes the form of a *deposit.*)

a. How does the existence of intermediaries affect the result that the aggregate amount of loans is zero?
b. What interest rate would the intermediary charge to its borrowers and pay to its lenders? Why must there be some spread between these two rates?
c. Can you give some reasons to explain why intermediaries might be useful?

3.10 *Wealth Effects*

Consider the household's budget constraint in real terms over an infinite horizon, $y_1 + y_2/(1 + R) + \ldots + b_0(1 + R)/P = c_1 + c_2/(1 + R) + \ldots$ Using this condition, evaluate the wealth effect of the following:

a. An increase in the price level, P, for a household that has a positive value of initial bonds, b_0. (The result has implications for the effects of unexpected price changes on the wealth of nominal creditors and nominal debtors.)

b. An increase in the interest rate, R, for a household that has $b_0 = 0$ and $c_t = y_t$ in each period.

c. An increase in the interest rate, R, for a household that has $b_0 = 0$, $c_t > y_t$ for $t \geq T$, and $c_t < y_t$ for $t < T$, where T is some date in the future.

3.11 *Short-Term and Long-Term Interest Rates*

Assume that \$1 worth of one-period bonds issued at the end of period 0 pays out $\$(1 + R_1)$ during period 1—that is, the principal of \$1 plus the interest payment of $\$R_1$. Assume that \$1 worth of one-period bonds issued at the end of period 1 will pay out $\$(1 + R_2)$ during period 2. Suppose that people also market a two-period bond at the end of period 0. \$1 worth of this asset pays out $\$(1 + 2R)$ during period 2. Lenders from date 0 to date 2 have the option of holding a two-period bond or a succession of one-period bonds. Borrowers have a similar choice between negotiating a two-period loan or two successive one-period loans.

a. What must be the relation of R to R_1 and R_2? Explain the answer from the standpoint of borrowers and lenders.

b. If $R_2 > R_1$, what is the relation between R (the current *long-term interest rate*) and R_1 (the current *short-term interest rate*)? The answer is an important result about the *term structure of interest rates*. (Greg Mankiw and Jeff Miron, 1986, studied this relation by looking at assets with three- and six-month maturities. They found that the U.S. data from before 1914 were more in line with the theory than were the data after 1914.)

3.12 *The Household's Budget Constraint with a Finite Horizon*

Consider the household's budget constraint for j periods from equation (3.13):

$$Py_1 + \frac{Py_2}{(1 + R)} + \cdots + \frac{Py_j}{(1 + R)^{j-1}} + b_0(1 + R)$$

$$= Pc_1 + \frac{Pc_2}{(1 + R)} + \cdots + \frac{Pc_j}{(1 + R)^{j-1}} + \frac{b_j}{(1 + R)^{j-1}}.$$

Assume that $y_t = 0$ for $t > T_1$, and $c_t = 0$ for $t > T_2$. Here, T_2 might represent the expected lifetime and T_1 the anticipated working span for an individual.

a. Assume that the household uses the planning horizon $j = T_2$. Why might the household do this? What value would the household select for b_j? What does the j-period budget constraint look like in this case?

b. Discuss the pattern of saving, $b_t - b_{t-1}$, for the "retirement period," where $T_1 < t \leq T_2$. What can be said about saving for the typical working year where $0 < t \leq T_1$? (This result concerns the *life-cycle* motivation for household saving.)

   c. Suppose that the government forces people to retire earlier than they would otherwise choose. How would this action affect the choices of work effort, consumption, and desired saving for people who are still working but anticipating an earlier retirement?

   d. Given that individuals care about their children (and parents), what difficulties arise in specifying a value for the finite planning horizon, $j = T_2$?

3.13 **Permanent Income (optional)**

   The idea of permanent income is that consumption depends on a long-run measure of income rather than just on current income. Operationally, we can define permanent income to be the hypothetical, constant flow of income that has the same present value as a household's actual sources of funds.

   a. Use the budget constraint in equation 3.15 to obtain a formula for permanent income. Explain the various terms in the formula.

   b. What is the marginal propensity to consume out of permanent income?

   c. If consumption is constant over time, what is the value of permanent income?

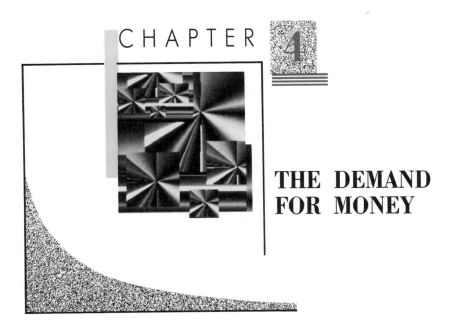

CHAPTER 4

THE DEMAND FOR MONEY

he model contains two forms of financial assets, money and bonds. But so far, we have not analyzed how much money people hold or how these holdings change over time. Thus, we carried out the analysis in the previous chapter under the assumption that each household maintained a constant stock of money. Whenever households changed their saving, they altered their holdings of bonds but not their holdings of money.

Now we provide the remaining building block in the model by explaining people's willingness to place part of their assets into money; that is, we explain the demand for money. We shall see later that this demand is a crucial determinant of the price level.

THE NATURE OF A MONETARY ECONOMY

We assume that money is the sole medium of exchange in the economy. Trades occur between money and commodities and between money and bonds but not directly between bonds and commodities or between the commodities that different households produce. The direct exchange of goods for goods, which is called barter, is inefficient for many types of transactions.[1] Barter requires a **double coincidence of wants,** which is a situation where one person has the goods that someone else desires and vice-versa. A general means of payments, such as money, avoids this problem. Buyers use money to purchase goods or bonds, while sellers receive money in exchange for goods or bonds. The sellers accept money in payment because they know they can use it later to buy goods or bonds from someone else. Thus, the problem of double coincidence of wants does not arise.

Historically, commodities such as gold and silver served as money. These precious metals possess attractive physical characteristics, which classical economists enumerated as portability, indestructibility, homogeneity, divisibility, and cognizability.[2] But when paper money—such as U.S. dollar bills—replaces commodity money, these physical characteristics no longer enter into the analysis. In our model we think of money as this kind of paper currency rather than gold, silver, or other commodities.

We assume that the interest-bearing bonds in the model are not money; that is, these paper claims do not function as media of exchange. There are several reasons for this. First, the government may impose legal restrictions that prevent private parties, such as General Motors, from issuing small-size, interest-bearing notes that could serve conveniently as hand-to-hand currency. Further, the government may enact statutes that reinforce the use of its money. As an example, there is the proclamation that the U.S. dollar is "**legal tender** for all debts public and private."[3] Also, U.S. courts are more willing to enforce contracts that are denominated in U.S. dollars rather than in some other unit. Second, there are costs of establishing one's money as reliable and convenient. These costs include the prevention of counterfeiting, the replacement of worn-out notes, the willingness to convert notes into different denominations and possibly into other assets, and so on. Because of these costs, money would tend to bear interest at a rate lower than bonds. In fact, because of the inconvenience of paying interest on hand-to-hand currency, the interest rate on currency is typically zero.

Let's consider the relation of our abstract concept of money to conventional measures of the money stock. The theoretical construct corresponds closely to currency held outside commercial banks. At the end of 1988, the amount of this currency in the United States was $212 billion, which amounted to 4.4% of the nominal gross national product (GNP). That is, people held a little more than two weeks' worth of the GNP as currency in 1988.

The term *money* typically refers to a monetary aggregate that is broader than currency. The standard definition, called **M1,** attempts to classify as money the assets that serve regularly as media of exchange. Specifically, this concept includes the checkable deposits that people hold at banks and some other financial institutions.

---

[1]The classic discussion of the difficulties with barter exchange is W. Stanley Jevons (1896, Chaps. 1–3). An interesting model of the evolution of specialized media of exchange appears in Robert Jones (1976).

[2]See Jevons (1896, Chap. 5) and—for an earlier discussion—John Law (1966, Chap. 1).

[3]Notice that this provision does not determine the price at which currency exchanges for goods. If the price level were infinite, what would the legal-tender property mean?

The amount of these checkable deposits in the United States at the end of 1988 was $578 billion, or 12% of annual GNP. Therefore, M1—the sum of currency and checkable deposits—equaled $790 billion at the end of 1988, or 16% of GNP. Put alternatively, M1 amounted to a bit more than eight weeks' worth of the GNP in 1988.

Table 4.1 shows comparable data for 1987 on money in the major industrialized countries. The ratio of currency to annual GNP ranged from lows of 2% for Finland and New Zealand to highs of 11% for Switzerland and 8% for Japan. The definition of M1 is less homogeneous because the decision of which deposits to include and which to exclude is somewhat arbitrary. For instance, in the United States, some interest-bearing deposits at commercial banks are deemed to be checkable and are therefore included in M1, whereas others are excluded (but included in still broader monetary aggregates, such as M2). In any event, the ratio of M1 to annual GNP ranged from lows of 8% for Finland and 11% for New Zealand to highs of 38% for Italy and 35% for Denmark.

As mentioned, we can readily identify the money in the theoretical model with currency, but the concept does not correspond precisely to a broader monetary

TABLE 4.1 *Ratios of Money to GNP for Industrialized Countries in 1987*

Country	Currency	Checkable Deposits	M1
Australia	.041	.076	.117
Austria	.063	.082	.145
Belgium	.078	.128	.206
Canada	.031	.127	.158
Denmark	.031	.323	.354
Finland	.018	.059	.077
France	.043	.206	.249
Germany	.061	.120	.181
Italy	.055	.320	.375
Japan	.083	.216	.299
Netherlands	.076	.163	.239
New Zealand	.018	.095	.113
Norway	.051	.228	.279
Spain[a]	.076	.162	.238
Sweden	.056	.059	.115
Switzerland	.113	.216	.329
United Kingdom	.034	.189	.223
United States	.044	.127	.171

[a]Data are for 1986.

Note: The ratio is the value of the monetary aggregate at the end of 1987 divided by the GNP (or in some cases, GDP) for 1987.

Source: International Monetary Fund, *International Financial Statistics,* June 1989, and *Yearbook,* 1988.

aggregate, such as M1. When we expand the theoretical framework to incorporate financial institutions, such as banks (in Chapter 17), we can deal with checkable deposits or other types of deposits. For now, however, we should think of money as being currency. We also assume that the government has a monopoly in the issue of money (that is, currency) and that the interest rate on money is zero.

Given that people use money to transact, how much money should they hold? Suppose that everyone synchronized each sale of goods or bonds with an equal-sized purchase of some other good or bond. Then although people used money for all exchanges, they would end up holding virtually zero cash. But to hold this low average money balance, each person would have to spend a lot of effort on financial planning. He or she would have to synchronize the timing of sales and purchases and would have to carry out a large number of transactions. Typically it is more convenient to allow receipts to accumulate for awhile as cash before spending these funds or converting them into bonds. As Milton Friedman put it, money serves as a *temporary abode of purchasing power.* As a general statement, people can reduce their average holdings of cash only by incurring more costs. These costs are often called **transaction costs,** which refer to the expenses of carrying out trades, as well as the costs of making financial decisions.

Given the total of financial assets, a lower average cash balance means a higher average stock of bonds. Hence, by economizing on money, people earn more interest (or pay less interest if they are borrowing). The demand for money reflects this trade-off between transaction costs and interest earnings. In the next section we illustrate this trade-off and show how it determines the demand for money.

A MODEL OF OPTIMAL
CASH MANAGEMENT

Consider a retired person, who is living off previously accumulated assets. This person keeps financial assets primarily in bonds but holds some money to facilitate the purchases of consumer goods. For simplicity, assume that consumption expenditure is constant at the amount Pc dollars per year. (We still pretend that the price level, P, does not change over time.) The retiree makes occasional withdrawals of funds from the stock of interest-bearing assets. Suppose that these withdrawals occur at the interval ϕ (ϕ is the Greek letter *phi*). For example, if an exchange occurs every month, $\phi = \frac{1}{12}$ of a year. Equivalently, the frequency of exchange is 12 per year. Note that this frequency is the reciprocal of the period between withdrawals, $1/\phi$.

Each exchange of interest-bearing assets for money involves a transaction cost. There may be explicit brokerage changes, but, more likely, the main expense is the time and trouble for carrying out the transfer. If a person spends more time trans-acting, he or she has less time remaining for work or leisure. Suppose that each exchange costs $\$\gamma$ (where γ is the Greek letter *gamma*). (This cost includes the dollar value that a person attaches to the time needed for the exchange.) We assume a lump-sum transaction cost, which means that the charge is independent of the number of dollars withdrawn. If the retiree transacts at the frequency $1/\phi$ per year, the total of transaction costs per year is the dollar amount $\gamma \cdot (1/\phi)$. Dividing by the price level, P, we find that the real transaction cost per year is

$$\text{real transaction cost} = \left(\frac{\gamma}{P}\right) \cdot (1/\phi). \tag{4.1}$$

The term, γ/P, is the real cost per transaction.

When the retiree makes a withdrawal, he or she obtains the amount of money needed to meet expenses until the next withdrawal. In the present case, the money must cover the expenditures over an interval of length ϕ. Since the person spends at the rate $\$Pc$ per year, the amount needed is $Pc \cdot \phi$. The retiree spends these funds gradually to buy goods, running out of money when the time ϕ has elapsed. At that point, he or she replenishes cash by making the next withdrawal from the stock of interest-bearing assets.

Figure 4.1 shows the time pattern of money holdings. Notice that a withdrawal of $\$Pc \cdot \phi$ occurs at date 0. The retiree spends gradually at the rate $\$Pc$ per year and thereby just exhausts the stock of money at time ϕ. Between dates 0 and ϕ, the level of money is shown by the downward-sloping line in the figure. At date ϕ there is another withdrawal of size $\$Pc \cdot \phi$. Hence, money jumps upward—along the dashed line in the figure—to the level $Pc \cdot \phi$. Then the money balance declines steadily again until the time for a new withdrawal at 2ϕ. This sawtooth pattern for money holdings keeps repeating with the peaks spaced at interval ϕ.

Given the form of cash management from Figure 4.1, the average money balance is half the vertical distance to the peak, which is

$$\overline{m} = \tfrac{1}{2}Pc \cdot \phi, \tag{4.2}$$

where $\overline{m}$ denotes the average holding of cash. If we divide by the price level, P,

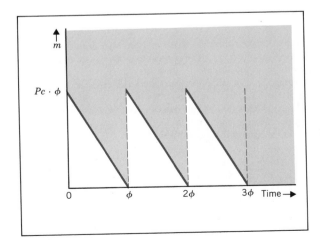

FIGURE 4.1 *Time Pattern of Money Holdings*
Money holdings reach a peak, Pc · φ, just after each withdrawal. Then money declines gradually, reaching zero when it is time to make the next withdrawal. Notice that the withdrawals occur at the interval φ.

we can express the average holdings of money in real terms as

$$\frac{\overline{m}}{P} = \frac{1}{2} c\phi. \tag{4.3}$$

Suppose that the retiree has already determined the amount of his or her total financial assets for each period. Then an increase in the average money balance must imply a reduction in the average holdings of bonds, and hence a decline in interest income. If the interest rate is R (per year), the dollar magnitude of interest earnings foregone per year is the quantity $R \cdot \overline{m} = R \cdot (\frac{1}{2})Pc\phi$. If all financial assets had been held as bonds, the interest income per year would have increased by this amount. As usual, we can divide through by the price level to express this dollar magnitude in real terms. Therefore, the real amount of interest income foregone per year is given by

$$\text{interest foregone in real terms} = R \cdot \frac{\overline{m}}{P} = R \cdot \frac{1}{2} c\phi. \tag{4.4}$$

There are two types of costs in our cash-management problem.[4] First, we can think of the interest foregone in real terms, $R \cdot \frac{1}{2}c\phi$, as a cost of holding money. We graph this cost versus the transaction interval, ϕ, in Figure 4.2. Note that this cost is a straight line from the origin with slope equal to $R \cdot \frac{1}{2}c$. Second, there is the real transaction cost, which is given in equation 4.1 as $(\gamma/P) \cdot (1/\phi)$. This cost appears as the rectangular hyperbola in Figure 4.2. Transaction costs approach zero as the interval between transactions tends toward infinity and approach infinity as the interval tends toward zero.

We show also the total of interest and transaction costs in Figure 4.2. This curve is U shaped. Costs decline initially as the transaction interval rises above zero because transaction costs decline by more than interest costs increase. Eventually transaction costs do not fall as fast as interest costs rise. Therefore, total costs start to increase with increases in the interval, ϕ. There is some amount of time between trips, denoted by ϕ^* in the figure, which minimizes total costs.[5] Hence, a rational person chooses the interval ϕ^*.[6]

---

[4]The model is an example of the *inventory approach to money demand*, which was pioneered by William Baumol (1952) and James Tobin (1956). (The approach is often called the Baumol-Tobin model.) The two costs for holding money are analogous to those that arise when a firm holds an inventory of its product. The interest-foregone cost for money parallels the costs of foregone interest, storage, and depreciation, which apply to inventories of goods. The transaction cost for financial exchanges corresponds to the costs of restocking—that is, the transaction cost for ordering, shipping, and processing new goods from a supplier. More complicated models of inventories—whether of goods or money—stress the uncertainties in receipts and expenditures.

[5]The answer can also be found using calculus. We want the value of ϕ that minimizes total costs, $R \cdot \frac{1}{2}c\phi + (\gamma/P) \cdot (1/\phi)$. The result from calculus is $\phi^* = \sqrt{2(\gamma/P)/Rc}$. Since $\overline{m}/P = \frac{1}{2}c\phi$, the solution for ϕ^* implies $\overline{m}/P = \sqrt{c(\gamma/P)/2R}$. The last result is sometimes called the *square-root formula*, because it relates $\overline{m}/P$ positively to $\sqrt{c}$.

[6]In our example, the period ϕ^* turns out to equalize the two components of the total costs. That is, in Figure 4.2, the interest-foregone line intersects the curve for transaction costs at the point ϕ^*. This property depends on the details of our example; it does not hold more generally.

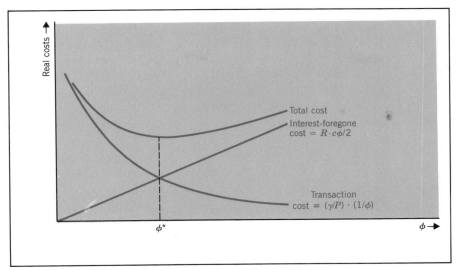

FIGURE 4.2 *Costs of Cash Management*
The interest foregone by holding money, R · ½cϕ, *increases with the period between withdrawals,* ϕ. *Transaction costs,* (γ/P) · (1/ϕ), *decline as the period rises. Total costs reach a minimum at the point* ϕ*.

For later purposes, the important point is that the choice of transaction interval, ϕ, determines the average holding of real cash from equation 4.3 as the amount, $\overline{m}/P = (\frac{1}{2})c\phi$. Therefore, a person's choice of transaction interval translates into that person's choice of an average holding of real money. Our main concern now is how various changes in the economy affect the transaction interval and thereby a person's average holding of real money.

There are three variables that determine the transaction interval, ϕ^*, in the model: (1) the interest rate, R, (2) the real flow of expenditures, c, and (3) the real cost per transaction, γ/P. We can use graphical methods to study the effects of changes in any of these variables.

Figure 4.3 assumes an increase in the interest rate from R to R'. This change steepens the slope of the line that describes interest-foregone costs. In calculating total costs we find that the interest component has become more important relative to the transaction-cost component. Hence, we reach sooner the position where increasing interest costs dominate over falling transaction costs. It follows that the minimum of total costs occurs at a shorter interval between withdrawals—that is, $(\phi^*)' < \phi^*$ in the figure.

We can interpret the result as follows. An increase in the interest rate makes it more important to economize on cash in order to avoid large amounts of foregone interest income. In our simple model, people can reduce average holdings of money only by transacting more frequently—that is, by shortening the period between financial exchanges, ϕ. Although this process entails a higher transaction cost, people are motivated by the rise in the interest rate to incur these costs. Hence,

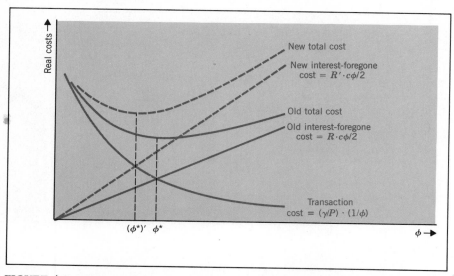

FIGURE 4.3 *Effect on the Transaction Interval of an Increase in the Interest Rate*
An increase in the interest rate from R to R' steepens the line that describes interest-foregone costs. People respond by lowering the period between withdrawals from ϕ^* to $(\phi^*)'$.

the rise in the interest rate, R, leads to a decline in the interval between transactions.

Recall from equation 4.3 that the average real money balance equals $\frac{1}{2}c\phi$. Since the increase in the interest rate lowers the period, ϕ, it follows that average real money holdings decline. In other words, a higher cost of holding money—that is, a rise in the interest rate—reduces the real demand for money. We shall use this important result many times in the subsequent analysis.

We can use a similar method to assess changes in the real flow of spending, c. A rise in the spending flow shifts the interest-foregone cost exactly as shown in Figure 4.3. Hence, someone with a greater annual flow of real expenditure chooses a shorter interval between withdrawals, ϕ. This result follows because an increase in the real volume of spending, c, makes the interest-foregone cost more important relative to the transaction cost. Households with more real spending—typically, households with higher income—find it worthwhile to devote more effort to financial planning in order to economize on their cash.

Average real money balances equal the quantity, $\frac{1}{2}c\phi$. For a given choice of transaction interval, ϕ, a rise in real spending, c, increases average real money balances proportionately. But we have just shown that the period, ϕ, declines as the volume of spending increases. This response means that a rise in real spending leads to a less-than-proportionate increase in the average holding of real money.[7]

---

[7]We can show that the decline in the transaction interval, ϕ, is by a smaller proportion than the increase in real spending, c. Therefore, the average real money balance does rise on net. See note 5 above for an exact result using calculus.

Sometimes economists refer to this result as **economies of scale** in cash holding. This property means that households with a larger scale of spending hold less money when expressed as a ratio to their expenditures.

Finally, we can consider an increase in the real cost of transacting, γ/P. We can show graphically that this change leads to a lengthening of the period between exchanges, ϕ. People transact less frequently when the cost of each exchange rises. Because the period, ϕ, lengthens, average real money balances, $\frac{1}{2}c\phi$, increase.

PROPERTIES OF THE DEMAND FOR MONEY

The results tell us the effects on average real money balances from changes in the interest rate, R, the real volume of spending, c, and the real cost of transacting, γ/P. We can summarize these findings in the form of a function, ℓ, for average real money demanded,

$$\frac{\overline{m}}{P} = \ell\left(R, c, \frac{\gamma}{P}\right).$$
$$(-)\ (+)(+)$$

(4.5)

Again the signs indicate the effect of each independent variable on the dependent variable, $\overline{m}/P$.

To find the average money balance in nominal terms, we can multiply through equation 4.5 by the price level. Then we get

$$\overline{m} = P \cdot \ell\left(R, c, \frac{\gamma}{P}\right).$$
$$(-)\ (+)(+)$$

(4.6)

Consider what happens if we double the price level, P, but hold fixed R, c, and γ/P. (Note that nominal spending, Pc, and the dollar cost of transacting, γ, both double along with the doubling of the general price level.) These changes leave unaltered the curves in Figure 4.2, which describe the real cost of transacting and the real value of interest income foregone. Therefore, people do not change their choice of transaction interval, ϕ. It follows that average *real* balances, $\overline{m}/P = \frac{1}{2}c \cdot \phi$, do not change in equation 4.5. But average *nominal* balances, $\overline{m} = \frac{1}{2}Pc \cdot \phi$, double along with the doubling of the price level, as shown in equation 4.6.

THE AGGREGATE DEMAND FOR MONEY

For an individual household in our model, the level of real money follows a sawtooth pattern and varies between zero and the amount $c \cdot \phi$. Equation 4.5 determines the average level of real money, $\overline{m}/P = \frac{1}{2}c \cdot \phi$. Suppose that we sum up over many households, each of which has the same average real balance. Then, unless the timing of transactions is synchronized across households, this aggregation smooths out the sawtooth pattern. In particular, aggregate real money balances at any date look like an individual's average amount, $\overline{m}/P$, multiplied by the number of households.

We can write out a function, L, for aggregate real money demanded as

$$M/P = L\left(R, C, \frac{\gamma}{P}\right).$$

$$(-)\ (+)(+)$$

(4.7)

The function L looks like the individual's function ℓ in equation 4.5 but magnified to incorporate the adding up across many households. Similarly, the aggregate version of equation 4.6 for nominal money demand is

$$M = P \cdot L\left(R, C, \frac{\gamma}{P}\right).$$

$$(-)\ (+)(+)$$

(4.8)

GENERALIZATIONS OF THE SIMPLE MODEL

Although we can complicate the theory of money demand in many ways, the properties that we derived from the simple model still tend to hold. That is because the simple model captures the basic trade-off that determines the demand for money. Namely, if people put more effort into transacting and financial planning, they can lower their average holding of money. A lower money balance means, in turn, a greater amount of interest earnings. Someone engages in various aspects of cash management up to the point where the gain in interest income just compensates for the added transaction costs. Consequently, an increase in the interest rate motivates people to incur more costs in order to economize on money.

An increase in the volume of expenditures raises the benefits from financial planning. Therefore, although a higher level of spending means more money held, we predict that money balances rise less than proportionately with the scale of spending.

The theory relates the demand for money in real terms to a set of real variables, which include the real flow of spending, the real costs of transacting and financial planning, and the interest rate. A change in the general price level—with all the real variables held fixed—does not change the demand for money in real terms. Therefore, the nominal demand for money rises by the same proportion as the price level if all real variables do not change. For example, an increase in the price level by 10% raises the demand for nominal money, M, by 10%, so as to leave the real amount, M/P, unchanged.

In our simple model, the real transaction costs incurred per year, $(\gamma/P) \cdot (1/\phi)$, pertain to transfers from interest-bearing assets to money. More generally, transaction costs apply also to other forms of exchanges, such as the costs of buying commodities with money and the costs of making wage payments to workers.

THE PAYMENTS PERIOD AND THE DEMAND FOR MONEY

I rving Fisher (1971, pp. 83–85) stressed the dependence of the demand for money on the period between payments of wages. The effects of this period are analogous to those for the interval between withdrawals from a financial asset. In particular, a shorter payments period reduces the average holding of real money balances. This effect is important during extreme inflations—for example, during the German hyperinflation after World War I. In such situations the cost of holding money becomes very high. Therefore, people incur more transaction costs—such as the costs of making more frequent wage payments—to reduce their average holdings of real money. For 1923, the final year of the German hyperinflation, an observer reported, "It became the custom to make an advance of wages on Tuesday, the balance being paid on Friday. Later, some firms used to pay wages three times a week or even daily" (Costantino Bresciani-Turroni, 1937, p. 303). Similarly, during the Austrian hyperinflation after World War I, "The salaries of the state officials, which used to be issued at the end of the month, were paid to them during 1922 in installments three times per month" (J. van Walre de Bordes, 1927, p. 163).

We would want also to bring in the costs of financial planning and decision making. Typically, people who do more calculating manage to maintain a smaller average money balance and thereby achieve a greater amount of interest earnings. But this broader view of transaction costs does not alter the main conclusions with respect to the form of the functions for aggregate money demand in equations 4.7 and 4.8.

The costs of transacting change when there are technological innovations in the financial sector. For example, the use of computers by financial institutions makes it easier for customers to shift between money (defined as currency or checkable deposits) and alternative assets. These improvements tend to lower the demand for money. Similarly, the development of convenient checkable deposits in the late nineteenth and early twentieth centuries in the United States had a negative effect on the demand for currency (and a positive effect on the holdings of demand deposits).

The possibilities for economizing on money holdings are influenced also by the use of credit. It is easier to synchronize receipts and payments—and thereby easier to achieve a lower average money balance—when people buy with credit rather than cash. In any case, credit favors the use of checks rather than currency.

A broader model would bring in uncertainties associated with the timing and size of receipts and expenditures. An increase in these uncertainties tends to raise the average holding of money because people hold cash partly to guard against unexpected delays in receipts or unanticipated opportunities for purchases. While it adds some new effects, the introduction of uncertainty does not eliminate the types of influences on aggregate money demand that we summarize in equations 4.7 and 4.8, and which we shall use later on.

THE VELOCITY OF MONEY

Economists often think of the relation between the average amount of money that someone holds, $\overline{m}$, and the amount of transactions carried out by that money. In our simple model, the dollar volume of transactions equals the amount of consumption expenditure, Pc. The ratio of transactions to the average money balance, $Pc/\overline{m}$, is called the **velocity of money.** The velocity is the number of times per unit of time, such as a year, that the typical piece of money turns over.

In our model, a person's average real balance is given from equation 4.3 by $\overline{m}/P = \frac{1}{2}c\phi$. Therefore, velocity is $c/[\overline{m}/P] = 2 \cdot (1/\phi)$. Notice that the velocity of money depends directly on the frequency of exchange, $1/\phi$, between alternative financial assets and money. One variable that has an important effect on velocity is the interest rate, R. An increase in R motivates a higher frequency of financial exchanges, $1/\phi$, and therefore a higher velocity.

THE VELOCITY OF MONEY IN THE UNITED STATES

Figure 4.4 shows the velocity of money in the United States from 1889 to 1987. Velocity is defined here as the ratio of aggregate personal consumption expenditures for the year, *PC*, to the annual average of the money stock.[8] For the upper curve in the figure, we define money as the public's holding of currency. It is more common, however, to use the broader monetary aggregate, M1, which includes checkable

---

[8]More often, economists use gross national product (GNP) rather than consumer spending to measure aggregate velocity. However, the pattern of results is similar if we use GNP. Although GNP is broader than consumer spending, it still covers only the final goods that an economy produces. Total transactions include intermediate exchanges, such as sales from suppliers to producers, from wholesalers to retailers, and so on. These trades are netted out in GNP. Also, a large and rapidly increasing volume of monetary exchange involves financial trades—such as purchases or sales of stocks and bonds. We do not have data on the total volume of transactions. However, we do know the quantity of expenditures that are made by checks, which are called *debits* to demand deposits. For 1987, these debits totaled $220 trillion, which was 49 times the GNP of $4.5 trillion! The ratio of debits to GNP has increased dramatically in recent years—it was 31 in 1985, 16 in 1975, 11 in 1970, 8 in 1965, and between 5 and 7 from 1945 to 1960. The main reason for this change was the explosion of various types of financial transactions. (The data on debits are in issues of the *Federal Reserve Bulletin.*)

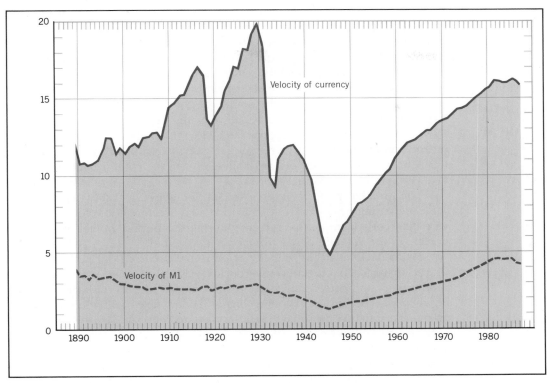

FIGURE 4.4 *Velocity of Money in the United States, 1889–1987*
The upper curve is the ratio of consumption expenditure for the year to the annual average of currency held by the public. The lower curve uses M1 rather than currency. (Prior to 1915, the numbers are based on the broader monetary aggregate, M2, which includes all deposits at commercial banks.) Sources: The data on currency and M1 are from Milton Friedman and Anna Schwartz (1970, Table 2), Board of Governors of the Federal Reserve System (1976, 1981), and the Federal Reserve Bulletin, *various issues.*

deposits. Since these checkable deposits are an alternative to currency as a medium of exchange, we can readily apply our theory of the demand for money to the broader concept, M1. The lower curve in the figure uses the M1 definition of money.

Notice in Figure 4.4 the tendency for velocity to rise since the end of World War II. This pattern appears whether we define money as currency or as M1. However, from 1985 to 1987, the trend reversed, and the velocity of M1 fell from 4.4 to 4.0, while that of currency declined from 15.9 to 15.7.

Two main factors account for the post–World War II behavior of velocity. First, interest rates tended to rise from 1945 until the early 1980s. For example, the interest rate paid on three-month maturity U.S. Treasury bills rose from 0.4% in 1945 to 2.9% in 1960, 6.5% in 1970, and a peak of 14.0% in 1981 but then declined to 7.5% in 1985 and 5.8% in 1987. The rise in interest rates until the early 1980s motivated a reduction in real money balances relative to the volume of real spending, which meant an increase in velocity. But the decline in interest rates from the early 1980s until 1987 tended to reverse this pattern.

The second factor is technological advances in financial management, which enabled people to economize more easily on their money.[9] In our simple model, these developments appear as reductions in the real cost of financial exchanges, γ/P. Such changes induce people to switch from holdings of money to holdings of alternative financial instruments, which again implies a higher velocity of money.

The velocity of currency rose over most of the period from 1889 to 1930. The important element here was the spread of checkable deposits as a convenient alternative to currency. It is interesting that the peak of currency velocity around 1930 actually exceeded the peak in 1985. Although there has been much talk recently about the economy's learning to dispense with currency, we see that there was actually less currency outstanding relative to the volume of consumer spending in 1930 than there was in 1985.

The broader monetary aggregate, M1, includes checkable deposits, which became increasingly popular from 1889 to 1930. Therefore, the velocity of M1 behaved very differently from that of currency during this period. In fact, there was a small decline in the velocity of M1 from 1889 to 1930.

Major declines in the velocity of currency occurred during World Wars I and II. The demand for currency rises during wartime because there are more transactions with strangers, reduced desires to leave records of transactions from checking accounts (because of rationing, higher income taxes, and other legal restrictions on private activities), and increased demand for currency by foreigners (for a discussion, see Phillip Cagan, 1958). There was also a sharp decrease in the velocity of currency during the Great Depression. In this case, the major financial collapse lessened the attractiveness of alternatives to currency, including demand deposits. Therefore, the velocity of currency fell dramatically from 1930 to 1935.

The influences of the Great Depression and World War II led also to declines in the velocity of M1. There was, however, no noticeable effect during World War I.

EMPIRICAL EVIDENCE ON THE DEMAND FOR MONEY

Our simple model provides a number of conclusions about the factors that influence the demand for money. We can summarize the main results as follows:

- An increase in the interest rate, R, reduces the real demand for money.

- An increase in real consumer spending, C, say, by 10%, raises the real demand for money but by less than 10%—that is, there are economies of scale in the holding of money. More generally, the real demand for money depends positively on real income, Y (measured, say, by real GNP), as well as on real consumer spending.

---

[9]Some of these advances—particularly the ready availability of money-market funds—were triggered by the rise in interest rates. Therefore, the second factor for explaining the rise in velocity is partly related to the first one.

- An increase in the price level, *P*, say again by 10%, raises the nominal demand for money by 10%—hence, the real demand for money does not change.

- An increase in real transaction costs, γ/P, raises the real demand for money.

We want to know how these propositions accord with the facts. Over the past 30 years, there have been many statistical studies of the demand for money, so that a good deal of empirical evidence is available.[10]

The negative effect of interest rates on the demand for money is confirmed by investigators whether they measure money by M1 or currency. For example, Steven Goldfeld (1973, 1976) found for the United States from 1952 to 1973 that a 10% increase in interest rates (say, a rise from 10 to 11%) on time deposits and on commercial paper reduced the real demand for M1 in the long run by about 3%. The reduction in M1 reflected roughly the same proportionate declines in currency and in checkable deposits.[11]

There is strong evidence for a positive effect of real spending on the real demand for money and weaker evidence of economies of scale in this relation. For example, Goldfeld found that an increase by 10% in real GNP led in the long run to an increase by 6 to 7% in the real demand for M1. (A somewhat larger response of M1 shows up if we consider a 10% increase in real consumer expenditure rather than real GNP.) The appearance of economies of scale—that is, a less than 10% response of real M1—turns out to reflect the behavior of checkable deposits. An increase by 10% in real GNP implies a long-run expansion of real currency by roughly 10% but a rise in real checkable deposits by only about 6%.

Our model predicts that an increase in the price level raises the nominal demand for money by the same proportion. This proposition receives strong empirical support. For example, Goldfeld found that an increase of the price level by 10% led to a 10% increase in the nominal demand for M1.

Finally, our theory predicts that a decrease in transaction costs lowers the demand for money. This effect has been important since the early 1970s because a variety of financial innovations have made it easier for people to hold less currency and checkable deposits. The innovations include automatic-teller machines, the spread of credit cards, and various accounts that allow inexpensive computerized transfers between checkable and noncheckable deposits.

Most economists, when trying to estimate the demand for money, ignored these financial innovations. Until about the mid-1970s, the estimated equations seemed to work well in that their predictions about the demand for money were fairly accurate. However, most of the developments that substantially reduced transaction costs have occurred only since the mid-1970s. It is in this period that the estimates that ignored financial innovations started to fail. In particular, the actual amount of money that people held was substantially less than the amount predicted by earlier evidence. (This result has sometimes been referred to as "missing money.")

Michael Dotsey (1985) found that the volume of electronic funds transfers was a good proxy for the state of financial innovation. Thereby he showed that recent

[10]For surveys of the evidence see David Laidler (1985, Chap. 4), and John Judd and John Scadding (1982).
[11]For the effects on currency, see Jack Ochs and Mark Rush (1983).

financial innovations had a strong downward effect on holdings of checkable deposits.[12] Further, by including his measure of financial innovation, he derived a money-demand equation that looked stable before the early 1970s and since. His fitted equation showed effects from interest rates and real spending that were similar to those, such as Goldfeld's, that included data only up to the early 1970s.

MONEY AND HOUSEHOLDS' BUDGET CONSTRAINTS

We want now to incorporate the discussion of money demand into our treatment of households' budget constraints. Recall the form of the budget condition for period t,

$$Py_t + (1 + R)b_{t-1} + m_{t-1} = Pc_t + b_t + m_t. \tag{4.9}$$

Before, we simplified the analysis by pretending that each household's money balance was constant over time—that is, $m_t = m_{t-1}$. Then the money-balance terms on each side of equation 4.9 canceled, and terms involving money did not appear in the budget constraint over an infinite horizon. Now we want to reconsider this analysis when households can alter their holdings of money.

In our model of the demand for money, the cash position moved up and down during a period in accordance with the sawtooth pattern shown in Figure 4.1. But for the purpose of constructing a budget constraint over an infinite horizon, it is satisfactory to neglect these ups and downs of money within a period. Hence we now pretend that a household's money holding is constant during a period, although it can change from one period to the next.

As before, we can use the one-period budget constraint from equation 4.9 to derive a budget condition that applies for any number of periods. When we consider an infinite horizon, the results are[13]

$$y_1 + \frac{y_2}{(1 + R)} + \cdots + \frac{b_0(1 + R)}{P} + \frac{m_0}{P}$$

$$= c_1 + \frac{c_2}{(1 + R)} + \cdots + \frac{R\left(\frac{m_1}{P}\right)}{(1 + R)} + \frac{R\left(\frac{m_2}{P}\right)}{(1 + R)^2} + \cdots. \tag{4.10}$$

---

[12]Differences in financial sophistication are also important when considering the demand for money across countries. For some empirical estimates over the long term, see Michael Bordo and Lars Jonung (1981).

[13]Equation 4.9 for period 1 implies

$$Py_1 + (1 + R)b_0 + m_0 = Pc_1 + b_1 + m_1.$$

Use equation 4.9 for period 2 to solve out for b_1 as

$$b_1 = \frac{1}{(1 + R)} \cdot [Pc_2 + b_2 + m_2 - Py_2 - m_1].$$

Consider the role of the monetary terms in equation 4.10. First, the sources of funds on the left side include the initial real money balance, m_0/P. This term makes sense because households can use their initial money to pay for goods, just as they can use their initial bonds, $b_0/(1 + R)/P$. Second, the uses of funds on the right side include a series of terms that reflect the interest foregone by holding money rather than bonds. The first term is $R(m_1/P)/(1 + R)$. The household could have held the real quantity of assets, m_1/P, as bonds rather than money during period 1. If the assets had been held as bonds, the real interest income during period 2 would have increased by the amount $R(m_1/P)$. Thus, by holding money in period 1, the household loses $R(m_1/P)$ of real interest income in period 2. The term $R(m_1/P)/(1 + R)$ is the real present value of this foregone interest. Similarly, the expression $R(m_2/P)/(1 + R)^2$ is the real present value of the interest foregone during period 3. Overall, the series of monetary terms on the right side of equation 4.10 equals the real present value of interest income that is lost by holding money.

Consider the effect of the monetary terms on the sources of funds, which appear on the left side of equation 4.10, net of that on the uses of funds, which appear on the right side. This net effect equals the difference between the initial real money balance and the present-value sum of interest foregone. That is, the net effect is

$$\frac{m_0}{P} - \left[\frac{R}{(1 + R)}\right]\left[\frac{m_1}{P} + \frac{\left(\frac{m_2}{P}\right)}{(1 + R)} + \frac{\left(\frac{m_3}{P}\right)}{(1 + R)^2} + \cdots\right]. \tag{4.11}$$

Recall that all of the terms within the brackets relate to planned holdings of real money, $m_1/P, m_2/P, \ldots$ To understand the nature of expression 4.11, suppose that these planned amounts were all the same—that is, $m_1/P = m_2/P = \ldots$ Then we can evaluate the sum within the brackets in expression 4.11 as

$$\left(\frac{m_1}{P}\right)\left[1 + \frac{1}{(1 + R)} + \frac{1}{(1 + R)^2} + \cdots\right] = \left(\frac{m_2}{P}\right)\left[\frac{(1 + R)}{R}\right].^{14}$$

After substituting into the equation above and putting the term involving y_2 on the left side, the result is

$$Py_1 + \frac{Py_2}{(1 + R)} + (1 + R)b_0 + m_0 = Pc_1 + \frac{Pc_2}{(1 + R)} + m_1 + \frac{m_2}{(1 + R)} - \frac{m_1}{(1 + R)}.$$

Dividing through by P and combining the two terms on the right containing m_1 leads to

$$y_1 + \frac{y_2}{(1 + R)} + \frac{b_0(1 + R)}{P} + \frac{m_0}{P} = c_1 + \frac{c_2}{(1 + R)} + \frac{R\left(\frac{m_1}{P}\right)}{(1 + R)} + \frac{\left(\frac{m_2}{P}\right)}{(1 + R)} + \frac{b_2}{(1 + R)}.$$

Continuing to substitute out for $b_2, b_3, \ldots$, using equation 4.9 leads to equation (4.10).

[14]We use here a result about *geometric progressions*. Consider the sum, $1 + z + z^2 + \ldots$ If $-1 < z < 1$, this sum equals $1/(1 - z)$. We can verify this answer by multiplying the expression $(1 + z + z^2 + \ldots)$ by the term $(1 - z)$. Then we get $1 - z + z - z^2 + z^2 - \ldots = 1$. (If the magnitude of z is one or greater, the sum is unbounded.) In the present case, $z = 1/(1 + R)$, which is between 0 and 1. Therefore, $1 + 1/(1 + R) + 1/(1 + R)^2 + \ldots = 1/[1 - 1/(1 + R)] = (1 + R)/R$.

Substituting back into expression 4.11, we find that the net monetary term is $m_0/P - m_1/P$. The net of sources and uses of funds depends on the difference between the initial real money balance, m_0/P, and the real balance that the household plans to hold in future periods, m_1/P. To get this answer, we assumed that all future real balances equaled the amount m_1/P. But more generally, some average of planned future holdings would appear rather than just the amount for period 1.

We see now what happens when we include the monetary terms in the household's budget constraint, as we do in equation 4.10. The sources of funds on the left side rise relative to the uses of funds on the right side if the initial real money balance, m_0/P, exceeds the amount m_1/P that the household plans to hold on average in the future. Thus, if $m_0/P > m_1/P$ applies for a household, we predict—as in the cases of increased wealth that we considered before—that the household's consumption and leisure in various periods would be higher than otherwise. Similarly, if $m_0/P < m_1/P$ applies for a household, consumption and leisure in various periods would be lower than otherwise. On the other hand, for a household that plans to maintain a constant real money balance—that is, $m_0/P = m_1/P$—the net effect is nil. Because the typical person will end up in this position (in the analysis of Chapter 5), it turns out that this last result will be especially important.

THE REAL-BALANCE EFFECT

Let's calculate the wealth effect from a change in the price level, P. Look at the household's budget condition in real terms from equation 4.10. Suppose that we hold fixed the levels of output, $y_1, y_2, \ldots$, and consumption, $c_1, c_2, \ldots$. Also, hold constant the interest rate, R, the planned levels of *real* money balances, m_1/P, $m_2/P, \ldots$, and the initial *nominal* money holding, m_0. Finally, consider the average person, for whom the initial bonds, b_0, equal zero.

Consider the effects on the left and right sides of equation 4.10 from a decline in the price level. Given our assumptions, nothing changes on the right side, which measures the uses of funds in real terms. The only effect on the left side (since $b_0 = 0$) is an increase in the real value of the initial money balance, m_0/P. Thus, wealth increases because people can use these higher initial real balances to raise some levels of consumption or leisure.[15] The increase in wealth from a decline in the price level is often called the **real-balance effect.**[16] As with other wealth effects, we predict that this one leads to increased consumption and reduced work effort (that is, increased leisure) at all dates.

The real-balance effect operates only when there is a change in initial real money, m_0/P, relative to the average of planned holdings, $m_1/P, m_2/P \ldots$. In most of our subsequent analysis, we shall look at situations where the aggregates of actual

---

[15]We can modify these results to accommodate a nonzero value for the initial level of bonds, b_0. Lenders, for whom $b_0 > 0$, benefit from a decline in the price level. Borrowers lose out by a corresponding amount. In the aggregate, since $B_0 = 0$, the only effect comes from the change in real money balances, M_0/P.

[16]The effect has been stressed by many economists. See, for example, Gottfried Haberler (1939, especially Chaps. 8, 11), A. C. Pigou (1947), Don Patinkin (1948), and Robert Mundell (1971).

and planned real money balances move by equal amounts. Then, as mentioned before, there are equal changes to the left and right sides of the aggregate form of the budget constraint in equation 4.10. In these cases, the change in real balances will not involve net wealth effects on the aggregates of consumption and work effort.

WEALTH EFFECTS FROM TRANSACTION COSTS

In our simple model of the demand for money, we considered transaction costs and interest-foregone costs. The interest foregone from holding money appears on the right side of the budget constraint in equation 4.10. We have, however, not yet incorporated any transaction costs.

Recall from our simple model that each household picks a frequency of transacting, $1/\phi$. Suppose that the chosen frequency for period t is $(1/\phi_t)$. Then, if the real cost of each transaction is (γ/P), the total of transaction costs incurred during period t is $(\gamma/P)(1/\phi_t)$. In terms of the household's budget constraint, these transaction costs are just like the real expenditure on consumption, c_t. Therefore, we should augment the right side of equation 4.10 to include the present value of real transaction costs. Assuming that the real cost per transaction, γ/P, is constant over time, this present value equals

$$\left(\frac{\gamma}{P}\right)\left[\left(\frac{1}{\phi_1}\right) + \frac{\left(\frac{1}{\phi_2}\right)}{(1 + R)} + \ldots\right].$$

Other things equal, an increase in the present value of real transaction costs reduces wealth. In normal times, however, these costs are small relative to a household's total present value of real expenditure. Therefore, economists usually neglect changes in transaction costs when analyzing the determination of work effort, consumption, and saving. For most purposes, we shall follow this practice.

SUMMARY

In this chapter, we explained why people hold part of their financial assets as money rather than interest-bearing bonds. The explanation involves, first, the role of money (but not bonds) as a medium of exchange and, second, the extra transaction costs that arise when people economize more on their holdings of money. We showed that the average amount of real money held involves a trade-off between transaction costs and interest-income foregone. A higher interest rate motivates people to incur more transaction costs in order to achieve a lower average real money balance.

Our theoretical model has the following major implications for the aggregate demand for money:

- An increase in the interest rate reduces the real demand for money.

- An increase in the volume of real consumer spending and real income raises the real demand for money but by a smaller proportion.

■ An increase in the price level raises the nominal demand for money by the same proportion.

■ An increase in real transaction costs raises the real demand for money.

The empirical evidence generally supports these propositions.

We incorporated the holdings of money into households' budget constraints over an infinite horizon. If the average of planned future holdings of real money equals the initial holding, there is no impact on the sources of funds net of the uses of these funds. Therefore, in these cases, we do not have to worry about net wealth effects from real money balances on the aggregates of consumer demand and work effort. On the other hand, an increase in the present value of real transaction costs reduces wealth. But in most instances, we assume that this wealth effect is small enough to neglect.

IMPORTANT TERMS AND CONCEPTS

double coincidence of wants

legal tender

M1

transaction costs

economies of scale in the demand for money

velocity of money

real-balance effect

QUESTIONS AND PROBLEMS

Mainly for Review

4.1 What are the costs of transacting between money and financial assets? (You may want to make a list and include such items as the cost of a trip to the bank and the time spent waiting in line.) How would the development of electronic teller services affect this cost?

4.2 Suppose that an individual's consumption expenditure is $6000 per year and that it is financed by monthly withdrawals of money from a saving account.

a. Depict on a graph the pattern of the person's money holdings over a period of one year. What is the average money balance?

b. Graph the pattern of money holdings when withdrawals of money are made only once in two months. Show that the average money balance is higher.

4.3 Refer to question 4.2. If consumption expenditure rises to $9000 per year and withdrawals continue to be made monthly, what is the average money holding? Is it optimal for the frequency of withdrawals to remain the same when consumption increases? Explain.

4.4 What is the definition of the aggregate velocity of money? Use the concept of velocity to explain how a given aggregate quantity of money balances can be used to pay for a relatively large volume of consumption expenditures over a year.

4.5 Consider the following changes and state whether their effect on the real demand for money is an increase, a decrease, or uncertain:

a. A decrease in the interest rate.
b. An increase in real transaction costs.
c. An increase in real consumption.
d. An increase in the price level.

4.6 Consider again the changes listed in question 4.5, and describe their effect on velocity.

PROBLEMS FOR DISCUSSION

4.7 ***Transaction Costs and Households' Budget Constraints***
Assume that the real cost of transacting between bonds and money, γ/P, rises.

a. How does this change show up in households' budget constraints? What is the effect on wealth?
b. We neglected transaction costs when considering households' choices of work effort, consumption, and saving. Suppose now that we bring in the wealth effect from part (a). What then is the effect of an increase in the real cost of transacting, γ/P, on households' work effort, consumption, and saving?
c. Have we left out a new substitution effect in part (b)? Think about the choice between consumption and leisure. Consumption involves market exchange, which requires the use of money. But people can "buy" leisure without using money! So what substitution effect arises for consumption versus leisure when the real cost of transacting, γ/P, rises? How does this affect the answer to part (b)?

4.8 ***Further Aspects of Transaction Costs***
In problem 4.7 we considered the effects of transaction costs on households' budget constraints. These costs might show up as purchases of financial services—for example, as brokerage fees or service charges by banks. Alternatively, transaction costs might just represent the time that it takes to go to the bank or to make a decision.

a. How do these two different views of transaction costs affect the way that the costs appear in households' budget constraints?
b. Do these differences affect our other answers to problem 4.7?
c. How should we think about the production of financial services? That is, how can we incorporate this "good" into the model?

4.9 ***Effects of the Payment Interval on the Demand for Money***
Think of a worker with an annual income of $12,000. Suppose that he or she receives wage payments once per month. Consumption spending is constant at $12,000 per year. Assume that the worker holds no bonds—that is, he or she holds all financial assets in the form of money.

a. What is the worker's average money balance?
b. What would the average money balance be if the worker were paid twice per month instead of once per month?

c. What is the general relation between the average money balance and the interval between wage payments?

4.10 *Effects of Shopping Trips on the Demand for Money*

Assume again the conditions of problem 4.9 with workers paid once per month. But instead of carrying out consumption expenditures in a uniform flow, the worker now makes periodic shopping trips. At each trip he or she buys enough goods (for example, groceries) to last until the next trip.

a. If the worker shops four times each month, what is the average money balance? Why is the answer different from that in part (a) of problem 4.9?

b. What happens if he or she shops only twice each month?

c. What is the general effect on the average money balance of the interval between shopping trips? Compare the answer with that for part (c) of problem 4.9.

d. Suppose that the cost of making shopping trips rises—for example, because of an increase in the cost of gasoline. How would this change affect the frequency of shopping trips? What does the result imply about the effect of an increase in the cost of shopping trips on the average real holding of money? How does this effect compare with the impact of financial transaction costs, γ/P, which we explored in the text?

4.11 *Expenditures and the Demand for Money*

a. Consider an increase in the aggregate of real spending, C. What is the effect on the aggregate demand for real cash balances, M/P? Notice that aggregate real spending can rise for two reasons. First, there could be an increase in everyone's real spending, with no change in the number of people. Second, there could be an increase in the number of people, with no change in each person's level of real spending. How does the response of aggregate real money, M/P, depend on which case applies?

b. What should happen to the velocity of money as an economy develops? (Take a look at Figure 4.4 to see the history of velocity in the United States.) In answering, be sure to specify what happens to the interest rate, R, and the real cost of transacting between money and interest-bearing assets, γ/P.

4.12 *Effects of Other Variables on the Demand for Money*

For given values of real income and spending, the interest rate, and real transaction costs, would you say that the following statements are true, false, or uncertain?

a. An agricultural society has lower real money demand than an industrial society.

b. Real money demand is higher in dictatorships than in democracies.

c. A country with a large fraction of elderly people has higher real money demand than a country with a small fraction of elderly.

d. A country with a higher literacy rate has lower real money demand. (For evidence on these kinds of effects on money demand, see Lawrence Kenny, 1988.)

4.13 *The Denominations of Currency (optional)*

Consider how people divide their holdings of currency between large bills (say, of $100 and over) versus small ones. How would the fraction of the value of currency that someone holds as large bills change with:

a. an increase in the price level?
b. an increase in a person's real income?
c. an increase in the interest rate?
d. a greater incentive to avoid records of payments (for example, to evade taxes or to engage in criminal transactions)?

Given the results above, the facts for the United States are not so easy to explain. The fraction of currency held as large bills (denominations of $100 and over) stayed nearly constant—between 20 and 22%—from 1944 to 1970. Then the fraction rose steadily to over 48% in 1988. What do you think explains these numbers?

CHAPTER 5

THE BASIC MARKET CLEARING MODEL

n Chapter 2, we discussed households' choices of work efforts, which determined their production of commodities. In this Robinson Crusoe environment with no possibilities for storing goods, production was equal to consumption for each household. In Chapter 3, we allowed people to buy and sell goods at the price P and to borrow and lend at the interest rate R. With these market opportunities, a household could save or dissave, so that consumption and production need not be equal in every period. The accumulation of saving over time determined a household's stock of financial assets, which could be held as money or bonds. Finally, by studying the demand for money in Chapter 4, we saw how people divided their assets between money and bonds.

During the discussion of a market economy in Chapter 3, we mentioned three conditions that must hold when we sum up over all households. First, since consumption is the only use for output in the model, total production, Y_t, equals total consumption, C_t. Second, because each dollar lent by someone on the credit market corresponds to a dollar borrowed by someone else, the aggregate stock of bonds, B_t, equals zero in every period. Finally, since the stock of money does not change over time, the total that people hold in each period, M_t, equals the given quantity, M_0. We shall refer to these three conditions as aggregate-consistency conditions.

AGGREGATE-CONSISTENCY CONDITIONS AND THE CLEARING OF MARKETS

How do we know that the totals of individuals' choices satisfy the three aggregate-consistency conditions? For example, on the commodity market, individuals think that they can sell, or *supply,* a desired quantity of goods, and also buy, or *demand,* a desired quantity. We need something to guarantee that the total of commodities supplied equals the total demanded.

Similarly, on the credit market, each person thinks that he or she can borrow or lend any amount at the going interest rate, R. For a particular interest rate, there is no reason to think that the total of desired holding of bonds, B_t, would be zero. But then we have an inconsistency because the total that people want to borrow does not equal the total that others want to lend. One way or another, the credit market has to operate to balance the overall amounts of borrowing and lending.

Finally, with respect to money, each person believes that he or she can hold the quantity that he or she demands. Yet somehow the total of these demands must equal the given aggregate quantity of money.

The classical solution is that the interest rate, R, and the price of commodities, P, adjust to ensure that

- the total of commodities supplied equals the total demanded,
- the total of desired holdings of bonds is zero, and
- the total of money demanded equals the aggregate quantity of money.

This viewpoint is called the *market-clearing approach*. In this approach the various prices, which are R and P in our model, adjust so that each market clears. By clearing we mean that the quantity supplied of each good—bonds, money, or commodities—equals the quantity demanded. When this condition holds simultaneously for every good, **general market clearing** applies.

When all markets clear, no one is unable to buy or sell commodities at the going price or unable to extend or receive credit at the going interest rate. When markets clear, everyone can buy and sell as much as they want of each good at the market-clearing prices.

Recall that each household regards the interest rate, R, and the price level, P, as given. However, the aggregates of households' choices determine R and P to satisfy the market-clearing conditions. Hence, R and P cannot be independent of the aggregate of people's choices about bonds, money and commodities. But any individual's transactions are assumed to be a small fraction of the totals on any market. Therefore, as a good approximation, each person can disregard the effects of his or her behavior on the market-clearing values of R and P. So we can continue to use the analyses of individual choices worked out in Chapters 3 and 4.

As mentioned before, we need to ensure that the three aggregate-consistency conditions hold. But why do we use market clearing to ensure these conditions? This device amounts to assuming that private markets function to allocate resources efficiently. When the markets clear, it is impossible to improve on any outcomes by matching potential borrowers and lenders or by bringing together potential buyers and sellers of commodities. Cleared markets already accomplish all of these *mutually advantageous trades*. Thus, the assumption that markets clear is tied closely to the view that the individuals who participate in and organize markets—and who are guided by the pursuit of their own interests—end up generating efficient outcomes.

We could use some concept other than market clearing to ensure that the aggregate-consistency conditions hold. One alternative is the Keynesian model, where some markets do not clear in the sense of our concept of cleared markets. Rather, some prices are sticky, and some rationing of quantities comes into play. For example, households may be unable to sell all of the goods or labor services that they desire at the going price. We shall explore this viewpoint in detail in Chapter 20. But the subtleties of Keynesian arguments cannot be appreciated without first understanding the workings of a market-clearing model. Therefore, it is best to begin by studying a framework where markets clear.

Economists often use the term *equilibrium* to signify market clearing. But because the concept of an equilibrium has been used in so many different ways in the economics literature, its meaning has become unclear. For example, some economists think of the Keynesian model as a *disequilibrium* framework, and others view it as a different concept of equilibrium. We shall avoid the terms *equilibrium* and *disequilibrium* in this discussion. But let's emphasize two basic ideas central to our thinking about markets. First, we have some aggregate-consistency conditions, which must be satisfied by any reasonable model. Second, we assume in most of the analysis that the interest rate and price level adjust to clear the markets. That is how we satisfy the aggregate-consistency conditions in the market-clearing model. We shall see later how the Keynesian model modifies the second idea but not the first one.

WALRAS' LAW OF MARKETS

Consider again a household that faces a given price level, P, and interest rate, R. Denote by y_1^s the quantity of goods that the household decides to produce and *supply* to the commodity market during period 1. By the amount supplied, we mean the quantity offered for sale at a particular price. Similarly, let c_1^d represent the quantity of goods that a household offers to buy—or *demands*—from the commodity market. Finally, let b_1^d and m_1^d denote the household's planned stocks of financial assets for period 1—that is, b_1^d is the demand for bonds and m_1^d is the demand for money.

Suppose that a household carries over from period 0 the stocks of financial assets, b_0 and m_0. Then the household's budget constraint in real terms for period 1 is

$$y_1^s + \frac{b_0(1 + R)}{P} + \frac{m_0}{P} = c_1^d + \frac{b_1^d}{P} + \frac{m_1^d}{P}. \tag{5.1}$$

Summing up equation 5.1 over all households gives the aggregate form of the budget constraint for period 1:

$$Y_1^s + \frac{B_0(1 + R)}{P} + \frac{M_0}{P} = C_1^d + \frac{B_1^d}{P} + \frac{M_1^d}{P}. \tag{5.2}$$

During period zero, every dollar lent must correspond to a dollar borrowed, so that $B_0 = 0$. Using this condition and rearranging terms, equation 5.2 simplifies to

$$(C_1^d - Y_1^s) + \left(\frac{B_1^d}{P}\right) + \left(\frac{M_1^d}{P} - \frac{M_0}{P}\right) = 0. \tag{5.3}$$

Equation 5.3 shows how the market-clearing model deals with the three aggregate-consistency conditions that we mentioned before. For period 1, these conditions are:

- $C_1^d = Y_1^s$—the total demand for commodities equals the total supply.
- $B_1^d = 0$—any dollar that someone wants to lend corresponds to a dollar that someone else wants to borrow.
- $M_1^d = M_0$—people willingly hold the outstanding stock of money, M_0.

But look at equation 5.3. Suppose that the first two aggregate-consistency conditions hold—that is, $C_1^d = Y_1^s$ and $B_1^d = 0$. Then equation 5.3 guarantees that the third condition, $M_1^d = M_0$, holds also. In fact, if any two of the three conditions hold, the third one must hold. Thus, we have to worry about satisfying only two of the three conditions for aggregate consistency. The third follows automatically from the aggregate form of households' budget constraints in equation 5.3. This result is called **Walras' Law of Markets,** in honor of the nineteenth-century French economist, Leon Walras, who pioneered the study of models under conditions of general market clearing. (Economists refer to his analysis as *general equilibrium theory.*)

We shall obtain the same results regardless of which pair of aggregate-consistency conditions that we examine. Usually macroeconomists look at the condition for clearing the commodity market, $C_1^d = Y_1^s$, and at the one for money to be willingly held, $M_1^d = M_0$. We shall find it convenient to follow this practice. Remember, however, that the results would not change if we substituted for one of these conditions the condition that the credit market clear, $B_1^d = 0$.

CLEARING THE COMMODITY MARKET

We want to ensure that the aggregate quantity of commodities supplied, Y_1^s, equals the aggregate quantity demanded, C_1^d. We refer here to quantities for the current period, which is period 1, but it is convenient now to drop the time subscripts.

The previous analysis pinpoints several variables that influence the aggregate supply and demand for commodities, including the following:

- The interest rate, R: A higher rate implies intertemporal-substitution effects, which reduce current demand, C^d, and raise current supply, Y^s (by raising current work).

- Wealth effects from changes in the position of the production function: An increase in wealth raises demand, C^d, but lowers work effort. (This decline in work partially offsets the direct effect from an improvement in the production function on the supply of goods, Y^s.)

- Substitution effects from changes in the schedule for the marginal product of labor: An upward shift leads to an increase in supply, Y^s (because people work more), and an increase in demand, C^d.

We can write out the condition for clearing the commodity market during the current period as

$$Y^s(R, \ \cdots) = C^d(R, \ \cdots).$$
$$(+) \qquad\qquad (-)$$

$$(5.4)$$

The function Y^s refers to the aggregate supply of commodities, while the function C^d refers to the aggregate demand. We indicate explicitly only the effects of the interest rate in these functions. The omitted variables in the functions, denoted by $\ldots$, include the wealth and substitution effects that arise from changes in the production function.

Equation 5.4 deals with the summation over a large number of households. We would like to use this analysis even when households are not identical—for example, when they differ by productivity, age, tastes, initial assets, and so on. In some cases, the aggregation over different types of people will not cause major problems. For example, a change in the interest rate implies the same type of intertemporal-substitution effect for everyone. We can also handle shifts in production functions when these shifts are similar for all producers. However, some changes benefit some people and harm others. For instance, we discussed before how movements in the price level or the interest rate have positive or negative effects on wealth, depending on someone's status in the credit market. These types of changes shift the distribution of resources across households without changing the aggregate value of these resources. Economists call these kinds of changes **distributional effects.** Typically, we have no presumption about how distributional effects influence the aggregates of commodities supplied or demanded. So, as is customary in macroeconomics, we assume (hope) that we can neglect the distributional effects for the purpose of aggregate analysis.

Recall some variables that do not influence aggregate supply and demand in equation 5.4. The aggregate quantity of bonds, B_0, is zero and therefore does not appear. We discussed in Chapter 4 the role of initial real money balances, M_0/P. We showed there that, as long as we consider only positions where $M_0/P = M_1^d/P$—which will hold when we have general market clearing—the level of real money balances has no net wealth effect on consumption demand and labor supply. It follows that M_0/P—and the price level P itself—do not appear in equation 5.4.

WHY DOES THE PRICE LEVEL NOT AFFECT COMMODITIES SUPPLIED AND DEMANDED?

*I*t seems odd that the price level, P, does not appear in the condition for clearing the commodity market, equation 5.4. Intuitively, we would expect a higher price of commodities to discourage demand and encourage supply. Let's think about what happens when P goes up. The production function, $f(n)$, does not change. Therefore, given n, a household's nominal income from sales of commodities, $P \cdot f(n)$, goes up along with P. But real income, $f(n)$ (obtained by dividing the nominal income by P), does not change. Since real income from production is the same, it is reasonable on this count that consumption demand and labor supply would not change.

We are also holding fixed the interest rate, R. Therefore, a once-and-for-all increase in the price level, P, does not affect the relative costs of consumption or leisure in different periods. That is, the change in P has no intertemporal-substitution effects.

For a given amount of nominal bonds, b_0, an increase in P would reduce the real amount, b_0/P. This effect is bad for someone with positive bond holdings but correspondingly good for someone with negative bond holdings. The effect is nil in the aggregate because the total of bond holdings, B_0, is zero and because we neglect distributional effects.

Finally, the increase in P lowers M_0/P. Real wealth falls on this count, and households would respond by lowering consumer demand and raising labor supply. In Chapter 4 we called this mechanism the *real-balance effect*. We know, however, that in a position of general market clearing, households will be motivated to hold the existing money—that is, M_1^d/P will end up being the same as M_0/P. In this situation, we know from Chapter 4 that there will be no net wealth effect on consumption demand and labor supply. That is why we can ignore the real-balance effect when we think about positions of general market clearing. That is also why the price level, P, does not appear in equation 5.4.

We discussed some types of transaction costs in Chapter 4. There are wealth and substitution effects associated with these transaction costs, but we assumed before that these effects were small enough to neglect. Hence, these effects are also absent from equation 5.4.

Finally, we demonstrated in Chapter 3 that a change in the interest rate, R, has no aggregate wealth effect. (A rise in R is good for people who are usually lenders but correspondingly bad for those who are usually borrowers.) Therefore, the effects of R shown in equation 5.4 refer only to intertemporal-substitution effects. For this reason, we know that a rise in R lowers current consumer demand, C^d, and raises current commodity supply, Y^s.

Because the interest rate has important influences on commodities supplied and demanded, we shall find it convenient to depict equation 5.4 graphically with R on the vertical axis. Figure 5.1 shows that the interest rate has a positive effect on aggregate supply, Y^s, and a negative effect on aggregate demand, C^d. When R changes, the responses of supply and demand show up as *movements along the curves* in the figure. (We show the curves as straight lines only for convenience.)

The positions of the supply and demand curves in Figure 5.1 depend on the omitted elements, denoted by . . . , in equation 5.4. When any of these elements change—for example, because of a shift in the production function—the effects on commodity supply and demand show up as *shifts of the curves* in the figure. For given values of these elements, we can read off from the figure the value of the interest rate, R^*, which corresponds to the clearing of the commodity market, $Y^s = C^d$. Generally we use an asterisk to signal that the value of a variable, such as $R = R^*$, derives from a market-clearing condition. Notice from the figure that the market-clearing level of output is the quantity $Y^* = C^*$.

Remember that each household's quantity of output, y, depends on the level of work, n, through the production function, $y = f(n)$. We assume that we can use an aggregate form of this relation:

$$Y = F(N). \tag{5.5}$$

The aggregate production function connects the aggregate amount of work, N, to the aggregate quantity of output, Y. Once we know the market-clearing level of

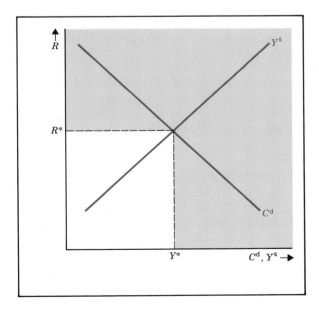

FIGURE 5.1 *Clearing the Commodity Market*
Clearing of the commodity market, $C^d = Y^s$, *occurs at the interest rate,* R^*. *At this point the level of aggregate output is* $Y^* = C^*$.

output Y^* from Figure 5.1, we can use equation 5.5 to compute the corresponding level of aggregate work effort, N^*.

The market-clearing diagram in Figure 5.1 is the central graphical tool for the subsequent study of macroeconomic disturbances. Even when we complicate the model, we shall be able to use a version of this diagram to derive the main results. Therefore, let's stress the basic ideas behind this diagram. First, a higher interest rate stimulates the desire to produce and sell goods today but deters the desire to buy goods. These forces underlie the upward slope of the supply curve and the downward slope of the demand curve. Second, we determine the market-clearing values of the interest rate and the quantity of output by equating aggregate supply to aggregate demand.

THE QUANTITY OF MONEY EQUALS THE QUANTITY DEMANDED

The second aggregate-consistency condition requires the stock of money, M_0, to equal the aggregate quantity demanded during period 1, M_1^d. For convenience, we again drop the time subscripts.

In Chapter 4 we derived a function for the aggregate demand for money. When expressed in real terms—that is, as M^d/P—this demand depends negatively on the interest rate, R, and positively on the real amounts of spending, C, and income, Y. Therefore, we can write the condition for money to be willingly held as

$$M = P \cdot L(\underset{(-)}{R}, \ \underset{(+)}{Y}, \ \cdots).$$

(5.6)

Note that the function, L, on the right side of equation 5.6 determines the demand for money in real terms, M^d/P. Therefore, $P \cdot L(R, Y, \ldots)$ is the nominal demand for money, M^d. For convenience, we include aggregate output, Y, as the measure of real transactions in the money-demand function. (Recall that $C = Y$ will apply in any case in this model.) The omitted terms, denoted by $\ldots$, include any effects on real money demanded other than the interest rate and the level of output. For example, transaction costs would enter here.

Figure 5.2 shows graphically the equality between the quantity of money and the quantity demanded. We shall find it convenient to put the price level, P, on the vertical axis. Then the quantity of money is the constant M, which appears as a vertical line in the figure. The nominal demand for money is $M^d = P \cdot L(R, Y, \ldots)$. For given values of R and Y, this demand is directly proportional to P. Hence, we show it in the figure as a positively sloped straight line, starting from the origin. Notice that the quantity of money equals the quantity demanded when the price level is the value P^*.

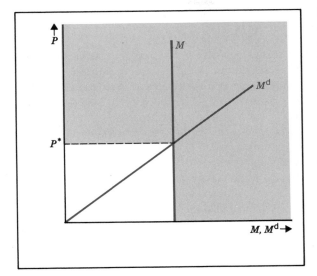

FIGURE 5.2 *The Demand for Money Equals the Quantity of Money*
The nominal demand for money is $M^d = P \cdot L(L, Y, \ldots)$. *For given values of Y and R, this demand is a straight line starting from the origin. The nominal quantity of money is the constant M. The amount of money demanded equals the quantity of money when the price level is the value* P*.

GENERAL MARKET CLEARING

We want to determine the values of the interest rate, R^*, and the price level, P^*, that are consistent with the two aggregate-consistency conditions:

- the commodity market clears, as in Figure 5.1, and
- the quantity of money equals the quantity demanded, as in Figure 5.2.

Remember, from Walras' Law, that these two conditions ensure that the credit market clears; that is, $B^d = 0$. So we can refer to R^* and P^* as the general-market-clearing values of the interest rate and the price level.

We can readily see the basic workings of the model. The market-clearing diagram from Figure 5.1 determines the interest rate, R^*, and the level of aggregate output, Y^*. We can substitute the values for R^* and Y^* into the money-demand function on the right side of equation 5.6. Then for a given quantity of money, M, Figure 5.2 determines the general-market-clearing value of the price level, P^*.

The procedure for solving the model is this simple because the price level does not appear in equation 5.4, which is the condition for clearing the commodity market. To put it another way, changes in P do not shift the curves in Figure 5.1. For this reason, we do not have to know the general-market-clearing value of the price level, P^*, when we determine the interest rate, R^*. We can just look at Figure 5.1 to determine R^*. Then, conditional on this result, we can use equation 5.6 and Figure 5.2 to solve out for P^*. The best way to clarify the workings of the model is to work through some examples, which are of substantial interest for their own sake.

SUPPLY SHOCKS

Economists use the term **supply shocks** to refer to sudden changes in the conditions of production. Adverse effects include harvest failures, strikes, natural disasters, epidemics, and political disruptions. The most important recent examples of supply shocks are the oil crises of 1973–74 and 1979. In fact, most economists became interested in supply shocks only after these dramatic changes in the market for oil.

For some reason, the term *supply shock* always refers to a negative effect on the supply of goods. But there can also be positive developments, such as technical innovations, bountiful harvests, or the sharp reduction in the price of oil in 1986. Our analysis applies to either favorable or unfavorable changes in productive conditions. However, as in some previous discussion, we shall find it important to distinguish temporary from permanent changes.

A TEMPORARY SHIFT OF THE PRODUCTION FUNCTION

Start with a temporary change to the production function, say a shift that lasts for only the current period. As examples, we can think of the drought of 1988 that limited U.S. agricultural output and coal strikes that lowered production in Great Britain.

Consider first a purely parallel downward shift of the production function, as shown in Figure 5.3. This case is the simplest example of a supply shock because it does not alter the schedule for the marginal product of labor. Hence, there are no substitution effects from changes in the relative costs of consumption and leisure.

Effects on the Interest Rate and Output. One effect of the supply shock is that output decreases for a given level of work effort. On this count, the supply of goods, Y^s, falls.

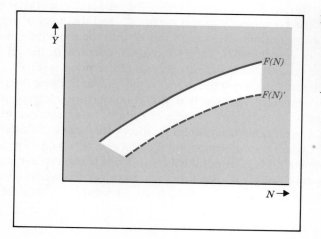

FIGURE 5.3 *A Parallel Downward Shift of the Production Function*
We examine here a parallel downward shift of the production function from F(N) to F(N)'.

Second, the disturbance reduces wealth. However, because the change is short-lived, the wealth effects are small. So we predict a small negative response of aggregate consumer demand, C^d, and a small positive response of aggregate work effort. The increase in work implies a rise in goods supplied, Y^s. But since the wealth effect is weak, this increase offsets only a small part of the initial cutback in supply. Thus, there is a net decrease in aggregate supply, Y^s, which exceeds the small decline in aggregate demand, C^d.

Figure 5.4 shows the changes to the commodity market. Before the shift, the market cleared at the interest rate R^*. Then the disturbance causes the aggregate supply curve to shift leftward from the one labeled Y^s to that labeled $(Y^s)'$. Also, the aggregate demand curve shifts leftward from the one marked C^d to that marked $(C^d)'$. As discussed before, the shift of the supply curve is larger than that of the demand curve. Hence, there is **excess demand** for commodities—$(C^d)' > (Y^s)'$—at the initial interest rate R^*. (In the opposite situation—where there is a temporary favorable shift of the production function—there would be an **excess supply** of commodities.)

The excess of goods demanded over those supplied means that—at the going interest rate—everybody would like to reduce their saving or borrow more. That is because the worsening of the production function is temporary. Instead of cutting their consumption, individuals would like to absorb most of their temporarily depressed income by reducing current saving or by increasing current borrowing. People plan to repay their debts or build up their assets later when income is higher. But we know that everybody cannot reduce their saving or increase borrowing because aggregate saving must end up being zero. The interest rate has to adjust to make the aggregate of desired saving conform to the economy's possibilities—

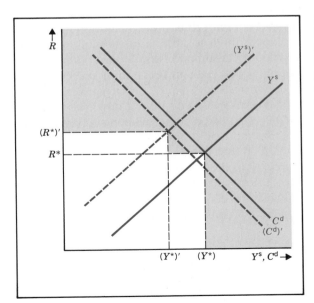

FIGURE 5.4 *Effect of a Supply Shock on the Commodity Market*
The temporary worsening of the production function lowers aggregate supply by more than demand. Therefore, clearing of the commodity market requires the interest rate to rise.

namely, zero total saving. To put this point another way, the interest rate must change to clear the commodity market.

Figure 5.4 shows that the new interest rate, $(R^*)'$, exceeds the initial one, R^*. This rise in the interest rate eliminates people's desires to carry out negative aggregate saving. Equivalently, the increase in the interest rate lowers the quantity of goods demanded along the curve $(C^d)'$ and raises the quantity supplied along the curve $(Y^s)'$. At the new interest rate, $(R^*)'$, the commodity market again clears—that is, $(Y^s)' = (C^d)'$.

The new level of output, $(Y^*)'$, can be read off the intersection of the new supply and demand curves in Figure 5.4. Notice that the disturbance—the temporary worsening of the production function—leads to a fall in output. From the perspective of commodity demand, $(C^d)'$, it is clear that output must be lower. First, the decrease in wealth shifts the demand curve leftward. Second, the increase in the interest rate reduces the quantity demanded along the new curve, $(C^d)'$. So aggregate demand—and hence output, which equals the quantity demanded—must decline overall.

From the standpoint of commodity supply, $(Y^s)'$, there is the initial leftward shift of the curve. Then the rise in the interest rate raises the amount supplied along the curve $(Y^s)'$. However, this increase in quantity supplied only partially offsets the initial decrease. This result follows since supply and demand are again equal at the new interest rate, $(R^*)'$, and we have just shown that demand is lower.

Effects on Work Effort. The forces that operate on work effort are closely related to those that affect consumer demand. First, the decline in wealth leads to more work and less leisure. Second, the rise in the interest rate reinforces these effects on current work and leisure, so aggregate work effort rises, while aggregate leisure falls. This result makes sense because the disturbance does not change the terms on which people can transform leisure into consumption—that is, the schedule for labor's marginal product does not shift. If the quantities of consumption and leisure change, we would expect them to change in the same direction. In the present example, the aggregates of consumption and leisure both decrease.

Overall, the supply shock leads to less output and consumption but to more work. Recall from the analysis in Chapter 2 that we reached similar conclusions when we confronted Robinson Crusoe with a downward shift of the production function. We might have expected some differences because people can use the credit market to borrow and lend in the present model, whereas Robinson Crusoe could not borrow and lend. But the interest rate adjusts in the market economy to ensure that the aggregate of desired saving is zero. Therefore, the typical person ends up saving zero, just like Robinson Crusoe. For this reason, we end up with similar predictions about the effects of a worsening of the production function on work effort, production, and consumption.

Effects on the Price Level. To determine the price level, we use the condition that all money be willingly held. Recall that this condition is

$$M = P \cdot L(R, \quad Y, \cdots).$$
$$(-)(+)$$

We know that the disturbance lowers aggregate output and raises the interest rate. Both of these changes reduce the real demand for money, which appears on the right side of the equation. Therefore, Figure 5.5 shows that the demand for money shifts leftward from the line labeled M^d to that labeled $(M^d)'$. Notice that the price level rises from the initial value P^* to the higher value $(P^*)'$. This change is necessary to restore equality between the amount of money demanded and the fixed quantity of money, M.

We can use this analysis to understand the effects on the U.S. price level from the oil crises of the 1970s. Sharp increases in the price of oil, relative to that of other goods, occurred in 1973–74 and 1979–81. For two reasons, this disturbance resembles an adverse shock to production functions. First, oil is an important input to production. Therefore, a cutback in the supply of oil—as reflected in an increase in its relative price—tends to deter the production of other goods. Second, an increase in oil's relative price means that oil importers, such as the United States, pay out more of their income to foreigners per unit of oil purchased. Therefore, for a given amount of work effort and production, oil importers end up with less income to spend on consumption.

Overall, the oil crises created adverse shifts of the type shown in Figure 5.4. (At least, these changes apply if people perceived the increase in oil's relative price to be temporary.) Then we find that output falls, the interest rate rises, and the real demand for money declines. Hence, for a given quantity of money, the general price level increases. By similar reasoning, we find that the reductions in the relative price of oil in 1983–84, and especially in 1986, helped to hold down the overall level of prices in the United States.

We should not conclude that an increase in the relative price of any commodity leads to a rise in the general price level. By the general price level, we mean the number of dollars that it takes to buy a typical market basket of goods. This general level of prices can move up or down while some relative prices increase and some

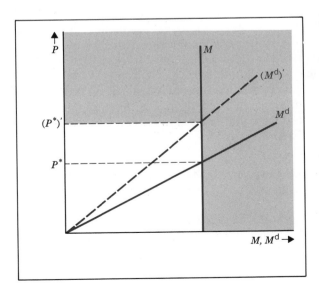

FIGURE 5.5 *Effect of a Supply Shock on the Price Level*
The increase in the interest rate and the fall in output imply a leftward shift to money demand. The price level rises from P* to (P*)' to restore equality between the amount of money demanded and the fixed quantity of money, M.

decrease. As an example, consider a poor harvest of grain that affects foreign countries but not the United States. The price of grain rises relative to the price of other goods. From the standpoint of the United States as an exporter of grain, the disturbance amounts to a temporary upward shift of the production function. Hence, there is an increase in real money demanded, which leads to a decline of the overall price level in the United States.

The Dynamics of Changes in the Interest Rate and the Price Level. We have figured out how a particular disturbance, such as a temporary worsening of the production function, changes the general-market-clearing values of the interest rate and the price level. We know that the aggregate-consistency conditions will not be satisfied unless we get to the new position of general market clearing. But we have not really explained how R and P move from one position of market clearing to another.

We mentioned before that a temporary worsening of the production function makes everyone want to save less at the initial interest rate. This decline in offers to lend funds relative to the offers to borrow tends to bid up the interest rate on loans. This reaction is consistent with the increase in the market-clearing value of the interest rate.

We noted also that the disturbance creates excess demand for commodities. It seems reasonable that suppliers would react to this excess demand by raising the price, P, at which they are willing to sell. This response accords with the increase in the market-clearing value of the price level.

The above sketch suggests that some plausible stories about market pressures would lead the economy toward the new position of general market clearing. Economists have, in fact, constructed some elaborate models of these dynamics. But it remains true that economists do not understand these processes very well. For one thing, it is difficult to explain how people behave along the way while the aggregate-consistency conditions do not hold.[1] But if we look only at positions where these conditions hold, we limit our attention to situations of general market clearing.

In the subsequent analysis, we focus on the characteristics of market-clearing positions. Along the way, we sometimes provide dynamic stories to motivate the changes in the price level and the interest rate. But these stories should be treated with caution since they do not correspond to fully worked-out models. Our main propositions about the real world come from seeing how particular disturbances influence the conditions for general market clearing. Often this method provides answers that accord well with real-world observations. So from an empirical standpoint, the lack of a formal dynamic theory of price changes may not be that much of a shortcoming.

Summarizing the Results. Let's review our findings for a temporary worsening of the production function. We found that this disturbance leads to cutbacks in

---

[1] Walras thought of an auctioneer who adjusted various prices along the lines of our dynamic sketch, but no trades were concluded until all markets cleared. In this case, we would not have to worry much about how people behaved in situations where markets did not clear. Of course, the device of an auctioneer who adjusts prices should not be taken literally for most markets. The idea is that buyers and sellers will manage quickly to establish prices that accord with the market-clearing conditions.

output and consumption but to a rise in work effort. The interest rate and the price level both rise.

Consider why the interest rate rises. Because everyone regards the fall in output as temporary, they would like to borrow funds to maintain their levels of consumption. Since not everyone can borrow at once, the interest rate increases to restore the balance between desired borrowing and lending. Anyone who lends funds in this depressed situation receives a premium in terms of a high rate of interest.

Consider why the price level rises. The decline in current consumption and output, combined with the rise in the interest rate, reduce the real demand for money. Since the quantity of money is fixed, the price level must rise for the amount of money demanded to equal this fixed quantity.

Including a Shift to the Schedule for the Marginal Product of Labor. We have just studied an example where the production function shifted downward in a parallel fashion. But we are usually interested in situations where the cutback in the production function involves also a worsening in the schedule for labor's marginal product. There may, for example, be a proportional downward shift of the production function, as shown in Figure 5.6. Here the marginal product of labor falls at any given level of work effort. But we assume again that the change to the production function applies only for the current period—that is, people still perceive the disturbance to be temporary.

We again have the effects on the commodity market that appear in Figure 5.4. We have to add some new effects, however, which concern the decrease in labor's marginal product. Because of this lower productivity, people want to work less now to shift from consumption to leisure. Also, because the worsening in production opportunities is temporary, people want to shift toward current leisure and away from future leisure and consumption. That is, an intertemporal-substitution effect applies. Overall, there is an incentive to cut current work, *N,* and a weaker incentive

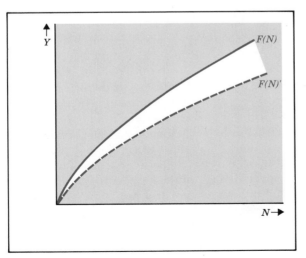

FIGURE 5.6 *Proportional Downward Shift of the Production Function*
We examine here a proportional downward shift of the production function from F(N) *to* F(N)'.

to reduce current demand for goods, C^d. Note that the decrease in current work means a cutback in the current supply of goods, Y^s.

To incorporate the new effects, we have to make modifications to Figure 5.4. First, we add a leftward shift to the supply curve, $(Y^s)'$. Second, we add a smaller leftward shift to the demand curve, $(C^d)'$. Notice that these changes do not alter the general configuration of the curves shown in Figure 5.4. Hence, we still conclude that output and consumption decrease, while the interest rate rises. But because of the fall in the schedule for labor's marginal product, these effects are all larger than before.

The only qualitative difference in the results concerns the behavior of work effort. We found before that work effort increased. Recall that this response reflected the decrease in wealth and the increase in the interest rate. But now people want to work less because of the fall in the marginal product of labor (MPL). Hence, it is now uncertain whether work effort rises or falls on net.

Think of this last result again in terms of a harvest failure. People want to work a lot today because output is low (the wealth effect) and because the interest rate is high (an intertemporal-substitution effect). But if the harvest failure makes additional labor today relatively unproductive, people prefer to take leisure instead of work. Overall, it is unclear whether the net of these forces leads people to work more or less.

When we look at the condition that money be willingly held, as shown in equation 5.6 and Figure 5.5, we again find that the disturbance raises the price level. However, because output and the interest rate move by more than before, we also conclude that the increase in the price level is greater than previously.

SUPPLY SHOCKS AND THE INTEREST RATE IN NINETEENTH CENTURY FRANCE

David Denslow and Mark Rush (1989) studied the effects of agricultural harvests on French interest rates over the period 1828 to 1869. This sample was attractive for several reasons: agriculture was a major part of output (roughly 50%), short-term fluctuations in agricultural output reflect mainly the influence of weather (which is a force from outside the economy and is therefore easy to interpret), the French economy had some aspects of an economy without international trade (as in our theoretical model), and good data are available. Denslow and Rush found that a temporary shortfall of wheat production had a statistically significant, inverse effect on the long-term interest rate in France. In particular, a 10% decline in the output of wheat raised the interest rate by 0.1 percentage point above the comparable interest rate in England. Thus, these results are consistent with our theoretical analysis.

A PERMANENT SHIFT OF THE PRODUCTION FUNCTION

Return to the case of a parallel downward shift of the production function, where labor's marginal product does not change. But suppose now that this change is permanent rather than lasting for just one period.

The difference from the previous case concerns the size of the wealth effects. Now there is a strong negative effect on consumer demand. Also, there is a strong positive effect on work effort, so that the supply of goods falls by less than before. Recall that our analysis in Chapter 3 showed that a permanent shift in the production function had little effect on desired saving. In particular, people do not want to borrow more today because future income will be just as low as current income. It follows, for a given interest rate, that the decreases in commodities supplied and demanded would be roughly equal. We use the market-clearing diagram in Figure 5.7 to illustrate this case. Notice that the leftward shifts to the supply and demand curves are the same. Commodity supply still equals commodity demand at the initial interest rate, R^*, and the new market-clearing interest rate, $(R^*)'$, equals R^*.

Output and consumption again decline. Since the interest rate does not change, the reduction in consumer demand now reflects only the decrease in wealth. Similarly, the fall in wealth implies an increase in work effort.

Since output declines and the interest rate does not change, we know that real money demanded declines. Therefore, we can still use Figure 5.5 to see that the price level rises. Overall, the results for output and the price level resemble those that we found before when the change in the production function was temporary.

The major difference in results is the rise in the interest rate when the worsening

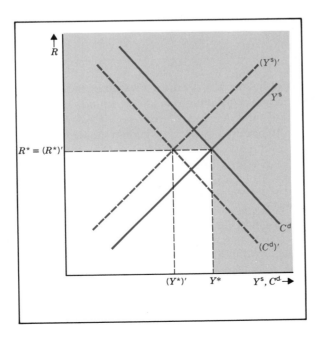

FIGURE 5.7 *Effect of a Permanent Downward Shift of the Production Function on the Commodity Market*
The permanent worsening of the production function reduces aggregate supply and demand by comparable amounts. Therefore, the interest rate does not change.

of the production function is temporary but no change when the worsening is permanent. The interest rate is a signal that tells people the cost of using resources now rather than later. Specifically, a high interest rate attaches a high cost to current consumption and leisure, relative to future consumption and leisure. When the production function worsens temporarily, there is a scarcity of goods today relative to the future. A high interest rate makes sense in this situation because it makes people take today's relative scarcity into account when they decide how much to consume and work. Conversely, a permanent worsening of the production function means that fewer goods are available at all times; there is no shift in today's position relative to tomorrow's. The interest rate stays the same because there is no change in the cost of using resources today rather than tomorrow.

The results tell us something important about movements in interest rates. Interest rates change when there are economic disturbances that alter present conditions relative to prospective ones. Harvest failures, natural disasters, and major strikes fall into this category. As we stress in a later chapter, war may be empirically the most important example of a disturbance that has a temporary effect on the overall economy. On the other hand, for disturbances that have permanent effects, we do not predict large changes in interest rates. (*Warning:* The analysis has so far left out the important influence of inflation on interest rates. We cover this topic in Chapters 7 and 8.)

As before, we can also include a downward shift to the schedule for the marginal product of labor. This extension does not change most of the results. We still predict that a permanent worsening of the production function has no effect on the interest rate. However, as in the analysis of a temporary shift, the response of work effort is ambiguous. That is because the reduction in wealth motivates more work, while the fall in labor's marginal product motivates less work.

CHANGES IN THE STOCK OF MONEY

In the previous examples, we deduced the change in the price level by examining the condition that money be willingly held. We found that changes in output and the interest rate altered the demand for real money balances. Then the price level changed to equate the nominal quantity of money demanded to the given nominal quantity of money. Essentially, we have dealt with changes in the demand for money while holding fixed the aggregate supply of nominal money, M.

Many economists have argued that changes in the quantity of money, M, are empirically the major source of variations in the price level. To study this linkage, we have to allow for changes in the stock of money. Therefore, we now construct a simple device that enables us to study these changes.

Think of a case where the initial stock of money, M_0, and all subsequent stocks, M_t for $t > 0$, rise by the same amount. In this case there is a once-and-for-all increase in the quantity of money, which might arise by the government's printing up the extra money and giving it to people. In Chapters 7 and 17 we shall examine further how new money gets into the economy. For now, we assume that the government will never repeat this odd business of printing money and giving it away, so nobody expects to receive any more money later.

The condition for clearing the commodity market, $Y^s(R, \ldots) = C^d(R, \ldots)$, does not involve the level of the money stock, M. Therefore, we know right away that the change in the number of dollar bills outstanding does not alter the market-clearing value of the interest rate, R^*, or the levels of output and consumption, $Y^* = C^*$.

Consider again the condition that the money stock be willingly held,

$$M = P \cdot L(R, \quad Y, \cdots).$$
$$(-)(+)$$

Since the interest rate and the level of output do not change, there is no change in the real demand for money, $L(R, Y, \ldots)$, which appears on the right side of the equation. Therefore, the line labeled M^d in Figure 5.8 does not shift. The figure shows, however, that the nominal quantity of money increases from M to M'. It follows that the price level rises from P^* to $(P^*)'$. In order for the change in the nominal amount of money demanded, M^d, to equal the change in the quantity of money, the price level must rise by the same proportion as the money stock. In other words, the real quantity of money, M/P, does not change. This result makes sense because the real amount of money demanded, $L(R, Y, \ldots)$, also does not change.

As before, we can outline a dynamic story that makes plausible the increase in the price level. At the initial level of prices, households have more money than they wish to hold, so everyone tries to spend their excess money, partly on goods and leisure and partly on bonds. The positive effect on goods and leisure is the real-balance effect. Remember that this effect operates when—as in the present case—

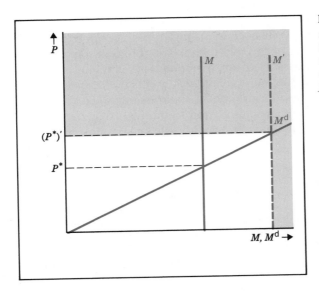

FIGURE 5.8 *Effect of a Change in the Stock of Money*
The quantity of money rises from M *to* M'. *In order for this money to be willingly held, the price level rises from* P* *to* (P*)'.

households have more money than they plan to hold in the future. Since the real-balance effect raises the aggregate demand for goods above the supply, there is upward pressure on the price level.[2] Further, this increase in prices continues until the outstanding amount of money is willingly held. At this point, households no longer have excess money that they wish to spend, and there is no further pressure for the price level to rise.

THE NEUTRALITY OF MONEY

The results exhibit an important property that is called the **neutrality of money.** Once-and-for-all changes in the aggregate quantity of money affect nominal variables but leave real variables unchanged. For example, if the money stock doubles, the price level doubles, as does the nominal value of production and consumption, $PY = PC$. But no changes occur in the real variables, which include output and consumption, $Y = C$, real money balances, M/P, and the quantity of work, N. The interest rate, R, also does not change. We should think of the interest rate as a real variable, which signals the cost of buying consumption or leisure today rather than tomorrow. In later chapters, we explore further aspects of monetary neutrality.

THE QUANTITY THEORY OF MONEY AND MONETARISM

The **quantity theory of money** refers to a body of thinking about the relation between money and prices. This viewpoint goes back hundreds of years, with some of the most interesting statements coming from David Hume, Henry Thornton, and Irving Fisher.[3] There are two common elements in these analyses. First, changes in the quantity of money have a positive effect on the general price level. Second, as an empirical matter, movements in the money stock account for the major longer-run movements in the price level.

Some writers refined the quantity theory to apply to changes in the stock of money relative to changes in the quantity of goods on which people could spend their money. The last element corresponds in our model to the total output of goods, Y. But output is only one variable that affects the demand for real money balances. To go further, some quantity theorists stress that the price level increases when the quantity of money rises in relation to the real balances that people want to hold. Hence, most movements in prices would reflect movements in money if the vari-

---

[2] We noted that households attempt to spend some of their excess money on bonds. This increase in the demand for bonds tends to drive down the interest rate. A lower interest rate causes excess demand for commodities and thereby reinforces the pressure toward higher prices. As the price level rises, the increase in the nominal demand for money reverses the pressure on the bond market and causes the interest rate to rise. At the new position of general market clearing—where the quantity of money, the price level, and the nominal demand for money have all risen in the same proportion—the net change in the interest rate is nil.

[3] See Eugene Rotwein (1970), H. Thornton (1978), and I. Fisher (1963, Chaps. 2, 8).

ations in the nominal quantity of money are much greater than the fluctuations in the demand for real money balances.[4]

Sometimes economists identify the quantity theory of money with the statement that monetary changes are neutral. Then we have our previous proposition that shifts in the stock of money have proportional effects on the price level but no effects on real variables. Many quantity theorists regard this hypothesis as accurate in the long run but not for short-run variations in money. The quantity theory allows for the possibility that fluctuations in money have temporary effects on real economic activity. At this point, our model does not admit these short-run real effects of money, but we shall reexamine this matter in later chapters.

More recently, economists and journalists have used the term **monetarism** to describe a school of thought that is similar to modern versions of the quantity theory of money. As with most other terms common in the popular press, this one has been used in contradictory ways. But it is clear that monetarists regard the quantity of money as the major determinant of the price level, especially over the long run. Thus, monetarists stress control of the money supply as the central requirement for price stability. Also, monetarism allows for important short-term effects of monetary fluctuations on real economic activity. But monetarists typically regard these effects as unpredictable. Therefore, they argue that stable money is the best policy for avoiding erratic movements of the real variables.[5]

CHANGES IN THE DEMAND FOR MONEY

As mentioned, we can determine the price level by looking at the condition that money be willingly held:

$$M = P \cdot L(\, R, \quad Y, \cdots).$$
$$(-)\,(+)$$

We have just studied changes in the money stock. Shifts in the quantity of money change the price level in the same direction. Earlier, we examined disturbances to the production function, which ended up changing output, Y, or the interest rate, R. With the money stock held constant, these changes affect the price level by shifting the real demand for money. Notice that the price level moves in the direction opposite to changes in the real demand for money.

An economy may experience changes in the demand for money that do not reflect movements in output or the interest rate. For example, in our model of the

[4]Milton Friedman stresses the stability of the demand for money as the hallmark of a modern quantity theorist. See Friedman (1956, p. 16).

[5]The term *monetarism* apparently originates with Karl Brunner (1968). Brunner (p. 9) stresses three major features of the monetarist position: "First, monetary impulses are a major factor accounting for variations in output, employment, and prices. Second, movements in the money stock are the most reliable measure of the thrust of monetary impulses. Third, the behavior of the monetary authorities dominates movements in the money stock over business cycles."

demand for money from Chapter 4, there may be changes in the cost of transacting between interest-bearing assets and money. These costs have declined significantly in recent years with the development of money-market funds, automated bank tellers, and other financial innovations. We predict that these types of changes reduce the demand for real money balances.

To represent this type of change, suppose that the real demand function for money, $L(R, Y, \ldots)$, shifts leftward, as shown in Figure 5.9. The result is that the price level must rise for the nominal amount of money demanded to remain equal to the given nominal quantity, M. Hence, we predict that the financial innovations of recent years—which reduced the demand for real money balances—raise the price level for a given behavior of the nominal quantity of money. Notice also that these innovations lead to a lower level of real balances, M/P.

In our model the change in the real demand for money—and the resulting change in real balances—do not influence the condition for clearing the commodity market, $Y^s(R, \ldots) = C^d(R, \ldots)$. Therefore, these changes do not affect the market-clearing values of output or the interest rate.

SUMMARY

Any macroeconomic model must satisfy some conditions for aggregate consistency. In our context these are, first, total output equals total consumption; second, any dollar that someone lends corresponds to a dollar that someone else borrows; and third, people hold the outstanding stock of money. We use the idea of market clearing to satisfy these conditions. Specifically, we require that the supply of commodities equals the demand, the aggregate demand for bonds is zero, and the amount of

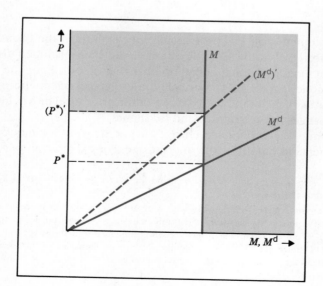

FIGURE 5.9 *Effect of a Decrease in the Demand for Money on the Price Level*
The demand for money shifts leftward from M^d *to* $(M^d)'$. *The price level rises from* P^* *to* $(P^*)'$ *to restore equality between the amount of money demanded and the fixed quantity of money,* M.

money demanded equals the quantity outstanding. Because of the budget constraints of households, these three conditions are not independent. Walras' Law says that we can use any two of the three conditions. We focus on the condition for clearing the commodity market—that the supply of commodities equals the demand—and on the condition that the stock of money be willingly held.

We constructed a market-clearing diagram to show how the condition for clearing the commodity market determines the interest rate and the level of output. Then the condition that money be willingly held determines the price level for a given nominal quantity of money.

We use the market-clearing apparatus to analyze supply shocks, which we represent as shifts to the production function. A temporary adverse shock lowers output, raises the interest rate and price level, and has an ambiguous effect on work effort. When the unfavorable shift to the production function is permanent rather than temporary, the main difference is that the interest rate does not increase. That is because a higher interest rate signals the scarcity of goods today relative to later. When things get permanently worse, there is no reason for the interest rate to change.

Shifts in the nominal quantity of money are neutral in the model. Specifically, the price level changes in the same proportion as money, but no real variables change. If we neglect transaction costs, shifts to the demand for money do not influence any real variables except for the quantity of real money balances. But the price level falls when the real demand for money increases.

IMPORTANT TERMS AND CONCEPTS

general market clearing

Walras' Law of Markets

distributional effects

supply shock

excess demand

excess supply

neutrality of money

quantity theory of money

monetarism

QUESTIONS AND PROBLEMS

Mainly for Review

5.1 How are transactions in different markets, such as consumption and borrowing, linked in individual budget constraints? How does Walras' Law show that this linkage carries over to the markets as a whole?

5.2 How does a change in (a) the interest rate, (b) wealth, and (c) the production function affect the aggregate demand and supply of commodities? Describe the effects graphically, making sure to distinguish between *shifts in* and *movements along* the demand and supply curves.

5.3 Why is a change in the price level not effective in reducing excess demand or supply in the commodity market? Explain how a change in the price level can ensure that the outstanding quantity of money is held willingly.

5.4 Consider a parallel upward shift of the production function, which raises the aggregate supply of commodities. Use a graph to convince yourself that:

   a. If consumption demand shifts by an equal amount, the interest rate does not change.

   b. If consumption demand shifts by a smaller amount, the interest rate declines.

5.5 Describe your results in question 5.4 in terms of the marginal propensity to consume. Which of the two possibilities is likely to hold when the shift in the production function is temporary?

5.6 What is meant by the neutrality of money? Explain its implications for the popular notion that an increase in the quantity of money reduces the interest rate.

5.7 Consider a decline in the transaction cost of converting financial assets into money. Describe its effect on (a) the price level, (b) the real quantity of money, and (c) velocity. Do these effects contradict the neutrality of monetary changes?

PROBLEMS FOR DISCUSSION

5.8 *Walras' Law of Markets*

   a. Show how to derive Walras' Law of Markets (equation 5.3) by using the household's budget constraints.

   b. We seem to have three independent conditions for aggregate consistency: zero aggregate demand for bonds, $B_1^d = 0$; the money stock is willingly held, $M_0 = M_1^d$; and equality between commodities supplied and demanded, $Y_1^s = C_1^d$. Walras' Law says that only two of these conditions are independent. Explain this result.

   c. How do the number of independent conditions for aggregate consistency compare with the number of market prices that we have to determine in the model? By the term *market prices*, we mean to include both the price level, P, and the interest rate, R. That is, the interest rate is the price of credit.

5.9 *Effects of a Change in Population*

Assume a one-time decrease in population, possibly caused by an onset of plague or a sudden out-migration. The people who left are the same as those who remain in terms of productivity and tastes. The aggregate quantity of money does not change.

   What happens to aggregate output, Y, work effort, N, the interest rate, R, and the price level, P?

5.10 *Effects of a Change in the Willingness to Work*

Suppose (in a magical, unexplained fashion) that all households change their preferences to favor consumption over leisure. That is, people raise their willingness to work. Assume that no change occurs in preferences for expenditures now versus later, so that aggregate desired saving does not change at the initial interest rate.

What happens to aggregate output, Y, work effort, N, the interest rate, R, and the price level, P?

Can you think of some real-world events that might raise everybody's willingness to work?

(*Note:* We will be in trouble if we permit unrestricted fluctuations in preferences. A basic strength of the economic approach—and the basis for forming hypotheses that we can conceivably reject from observed data—is the assumption of stable tastes. Then we can analyze changes to production possibilities and other disturbances in terms of wealth and substitution effects, as we did in the text. In this manner, we end up with predictable influences on observable variables, such as output and the price level. But if tastes are unstable, we can reconcile any observed behavior by invoking the appropriate shift in unobservable preferences. This capacity for explaining all data means that the model has no predictive value. Also, unaccountable shifts in preferences are more plausible for an individual than for the aggregate of households. Usually there is no good reason for everyone to become more eager to work precisely at the same time.)

5.11 *Effects of a Shift in Desired Saving*

Suppose that all households increase their preference for current expenditures over future expenditures. In particular, desired saving declines at a given value of the interest rate.

What happens to aggregate output, Y, work effort, N, the interest rate, R, and the price level, P?

(The note attached to problem 5.10 applies also to the change in tastes assumed in this problem.)

5.12 *Temporary Changes in the Price Level*

Consider again the analysis of a temporary worsening of the production function (Figures 5.4 and 5.5). We showed that the price level rises from its initial value, P^*, to a higher value, $(P^*)'$. But since the disturbance is temporary, the price level would return in later periods to the initial value, P^*. At least, this would happen if nothing else changes, including the quantity of money.

So far, the analysis assumes that people expect the price level to remain constant over time. But we just showed that the current price level is above its expected future values when there is a temporary worsening of the production function. Think about how to modify the analysis to take account of expected future changes in the price level. (Do not spend too much time on this problem, since we shall study this topic in detail in Chapters 7 and 8.)

5.13 *Consumption, Saving, and the Interest Rate* (optional)

According to the theory, an increase in the interest rate motivates people to reduce current consumption relative to current income. Correspondingly, people increase current saving. Yet although a temporary downward shift of the production function leads to an increase in the interest rate, it does not lead to any change in the ratio of aggregate consumption to aggregate income (which equals one in this model). Also, there is no change in aggregate saving, which equals zero.

a. Explain these results.

b. Researchers often attempt to estimate the effects of a change in the interest rate on an individual's choices of consumption and saving. Many studies look at the relation between the interest rate and either the ratio of aggregate consumption to aggregate income or the amount of aggregate saving. What does the theory predict for this relation? Why does it not reveal the effect of a change in the interest rate on an individual's desire to consume and save?

c. The theory says that an increase in the interest rate motivates people to raise next period's consumption, c_2, relative to this period's, c_1. Suppose that we look at the relation of the interest rate, R_1, to the ratio of aggregate consumptions, C_2/C_1. Does this relation reveal something about the behavior of individuals?

d. Suppose that we want to use aggregate data to figure out the effects of the interest rate on an individual's choices of consumption and saving. What do the answers to this question suggest that we should look at?

5.14 *The Dynamics of Changes in the Price Level*

In the text, we examined a case where the real demand for money declined. Then the price level increased, but the interest rate did not change.

a. Outline a dynamic story that describes the pressures for the price level to rise.

b. Does the interest rate stay fixed or move around while the price level adjusts in part (a)?

c. Can you tell a story where the price level jumps immediately to its new market-clearing position rather than adjusting gradually in accordance with the sketch in part (a)?

5.15 *A Currency Reform*

Suppose that the government replaces the existing monetary unit with a new one. For example, the United States might shift from the old dollar to the Reagan dollar, which equals 10 old dollars. People can exchange their old currency for the new one at a ratio of 10 to 1. Also, any contracts that were written in terms of old dollars are converted at the ratio of 10 to 1 into Reagan dollars.

a. What happens to the price level and the interest rate?

b. What happens to the quantities of output, consumption, and work effort?

c. Do the results exhibit the neutrality of money?

5.16 *Temporary versus Permanent Changes of the Production Function (optional)*

Consider the parallel downward shift of the production function in Figure 5.3. This type of change does not affect the schedule for labor's marginal product. Suppose first that this change is permanent.

a. We dealt with this type of disturbance for an isolated individual, Robinson Crusoe, in Chapter 2. We found that Crusoe reduced output and consumption but raised work effort. How do these results compare with those we obtained in the present chapter, which includes markets for commodities and credit? Think of the typical or representative household. Does that household's responses of output, consumption, and work effort differ from those of Robinson Crusoe?

b. Suppose now that the change to the production function is temporary. Compare again Robinson Crusoe's responses of output, consumption, and work effort with those of the typical household in the model from the present chapter.

c. For Robinson Crusoe, how do the responses of output, consumption, and work effort depend on whether the improvement to the production function is temporary or permanent? (Problem 2.9 in Chapter 2 deals with this matter.)

d. Put together the results from parts (a), (b), and (c). They tell us how to compare temporary and permanent changes in the production function for the model in the present chapter, which includes markets for commodities and credit. How do the responses of output, consumption, and work effort for the typical household depend on whether the change in the production function is permanent or temporary?

CHAPTER 6

THE LABOR MARKET

o simplify matters, we pretended that households used only their own labor to produce goods. Now we make things more realistic by introducing a market where people exchange labor services. The people who buy labor services are the firms or employers in the economy. Those who sell services are the employees.

Think of the labor market as a place where people supply and demand labor services. Then the clearing of this market—along with those for commodities and credit—determines the aggregates of work and output. One objective of this chapter is to see how the presence of the labor market and the existence of firms change the way that work and output are determined. For most macroeconomic questions, it turns out that the answer is, "Not much." Our previous simplified setting where people work only on their own production processes is satisfactory for most purposes. However, the extensions in this chapter do allow us to explore the determination of wage rates and the manner in which a labor market promotes economic efficiency. Also, the extended framework will be essential later when we study unemployment (in Chapter 11).

SETUP OF THE LABOR MARKET

Suppose, for simplicity, that everyone's labor services are physically the same. But instead of working on one's own production process, people now sell their labor services on the labor market. This market establishes a single wage rate, which we denote by w and measure in units of dollars per person-hour. (For convenience, we omit time subscripts here.) By the wage rate we mean that buyers of labor services pay w dollars for each hour that someone works for them. Correspondingly, sellers of labor services receive w dollars for each hour of work. As in our treatment of the commodity market, we assume that each individual buyer and seller regards the wage rate, w, as a given.

Denote by n^s the number of person-hours of labor services that a household supplies to the labor market during a period. Correspondingly, this household receives the dollar quantity, $w \cdot n^s$, of labor income.

Suppose that some of the households—who are inclined to be entrepreneurs—set themselves up as **firms**. These firms hire other people as workers. Let n^d denote the number of person-hours of labor services that a firm demands from the labor market. Correspondingly, the firm pays the dollar amount, $w \cdot n^d$, as wage payments to its workers.

Each firm uses its input of labor services, n^d, to product commodities. The quantity produced and supplied to the commodity market is

$$y^s = f(n^d), \tag{6.1}$$

where f is again the production function. Since the goods sell at the price P, the firm's gross revenue from sales is $P \cdot y^s$. The firm's **profit** (or earnings) equals gross revenue less wage payments—that is,

$$\text{profit} = P \cdot y^s - w \cdot n^d = P \cdot f(n^d) - w \cdot n^d. \tag{6.2}$$

Note that firms do not issue or hold bonds at this stage of our analysis. The potential to borrow becomes important in Chapter 9 when we allow for investment.

The profit from a firm goes to the household or households that own the firm. We could introduce a **stock market,** where poeple buy and sell the ownership rights in businesses. Then the profits would go to the current shareholders in the form of dividend payments. To keep things simple, we do not introduce a stock market and assume that the ownership rights in firms are distributed in some manner among the households.[1] In any event, it is important to note that all firms must be owned 100% by some households. Each household's total income now includes its share of profits from firms, as well as wage income, $w \cdot n^s$, and interest income.

THE DEMAND FOR LABOR

Think about a household that owns all or part of a firm. The household's utility depends on its consumption, c^d, and work, n^s. Hence, the demand for labor, n^d,

---

[1]The ability to buy and sell stocks in various businesses becomes more interesting if we allow for uncertainties about each firm's earnings. Then households have an incentive to diversify their holdings of stock across many types of businesses. Since we have not introduced these uncertainties, a stock market would not add much to the analysis.

matters to the household only through its effect on the firm's profit, which appears in equation 6.2. If the firm acts to benefit its owners—which we assume—it sets its demand for labor, n^d, to maximize profit in each period.

An increase in labor input, n^d, has two effects on profit. First, an extra hour of work means that output, $f(n^d)$, increases by the marginal product of labor, *MPL*. Hence, gross sales revenue rises by the dollar amount, $P \cdot MPL$. Second, the wage bill increases by the dollar wage rate, w. Therefore, profit rises with an increase in labor input if the value of labor's marginal product, $P \cdot MPL$, exceeds w. To maximize profit a firm expands employment, n^d, up to the point where the value of the marginal product just equals the wage rate—that is, until $P \cdot MPL = w$. If we divide through by the price level, the condition that each firm satisfies in every period is

$$MPL = \frac{w}{P}. \tag{6.3}$$

Notice that the right side of equation 6.3 is the **real wage rate**, w/P. This variable is the quantity of commodities that someone can buy with the dollar amount w. Equation 6.3 says that a producer chooses the quantity of labor input, n^d, so that the marginal product, *MPL*, equals the real wage rate. At that point, the last unit of labor contributes just enough to output, *MPL*, so as to cover the extra cost of this labor in units of commodities, which is the real wage rate.

Figure 6.1 illustrates the results. The curve shows the negative effect of more labor input on the marginal product, *MPL*. Notice that firms set their demand for labor, n^d, at the point where the marginal product equals the real wage rate, w/P.

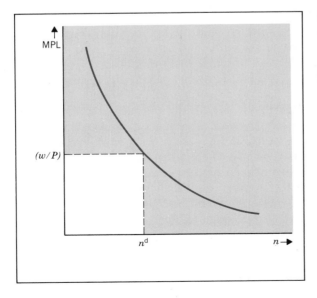

FIGURE 6.1 *Demand for Labor* *Labor's marginal product, MPL, declines as the quantity of labor increases. Producers set the demand for labor, n^d, at the point where the* marginal product equals the real wage rate, w/P.

THE GAINS FROM EQUALIZING LABOR'S MARGINAL PRODUCT ACROSS FIRMS

At a point in time, each worker receives the same real wage rate since we assume that all labor services are identical. Hence, labor's marginal product ends up being the same on all production processes. This result holds even if there are differences across firms in production functions or across households in their willingness to work. It is efficient to equalize these marginal products. Otherwise the economy's total output could rise, without changing total work effort, by shifting workers from one production process to another. In particular, this increase in output would result if a worker moved from an activity where his or her marginal product was low to one where it was high. But it is only the existence of the labor market that ensures the equality in marginal products. In our earlier model, where people worked only on their own production processes, workers might end up with large differences in marginal products. Since one person could not work on another's production activity, there was no mechanism to equalize the marginal products.

Consider two isolated regions, A and B. The technology in A is primitive, so that workers end up with the low marginal product and real wage rate, $MPL^A = (w/P)^A$. Region B is more advanced and ends up with a higher marginal product and real wage rate, $MPL^B = (w/P)^B$. Now suppose that an economy-wide labor market develops, and this market allows people from region A to work in region B and vice-versa. As we set things up, the workers from the low-wage region A would migrate to region B. Then, by working with the better technology, these workers can produce more goods without working any harder. The movement of workers out of A and into B continues until the marginal products and real wage rates are equalized in the two regions. This equalization results partly through a higher marginal product in A (where work declines) and partly through a lower marginal product in B (where work increases). But for our purposes, the important point is that the opening up of the economy-wide labor market allows for an expansion of aggregate output without requiring an increase in total work effort. In that sense the economy operates more efficiently when the labor market exists.

As with the commodity and credit markets, we find that the existence of the labor market aids economic efficiency. Specifically, this market exhausts all the potential gains from movements of workers from one place to another. Because everyone's marginal product and real wage rate end up being the same, there are no gains of this type that remain unexploited.

PROPERTIES OF THE DEMAND FOR LABOR

We can use Figure 6.1 to see how various changes affect the demand for labor. It follows at once that a decrease in the real wage rate, w/P, means a higher quantity of labor demanded. When the real cost of hiring workers decreases, firms expand employment until labor's marginal product falls by as much as the decrease in w/P.

An upward shift in the schedule for labor's marginal product—that is, an upward shift of the curve in Figure 6.1—leads to a greater quantity of labor demanded for any given real wage rate. Specifically, employment expands until the marginal product again equals w/P.

We can summarize the results by writing down a function for the aggregate demand for labor. This function takes the form

$$N^d = N^d \left(\underset{(-)}{\frac{w}{P}}, \cdots \right), \tag{6.4}$$

where the expression . . . again refers to characteristics of the production function.

Recall that each firm's choice of labor input determines its supply of goods through the production function, $y^s = f(n^d)$. Since labor demanded decreases with the real wage rate, we can write the function for the aggregate supply of goods as

$$Y^s = Y^s \left(\underset{(-)}{\frac{w}{P}}, \cdots \right). \tag{6.5}$$

LABOR SUPPLY AND CONSUMPTION DEMAND

The introduction of the labor market does not greatly alter our earlier analysis of work effort and consumption demand. The main modification concerns the household's choice between consumption and leisure at a point in time. In our previous model the schedule for labor's marginal product, *MPL,* tells people the terms on which they can substitute consumption for leisure. When someone works an extra hour on his or her own production process, he or she can use the additional output (of *MPL* units) to raise consumption. Now households sell their labor services at the real wage rate, w/P, rather than working on their own production. So the real wage rate indicates the terms on which people can substitute consumption for leisure. Someone who works an extra hour can use the additional w/P units of real income to expand consumption.

For a household, the real wage rate now appears where previously the schedule for labor's marginal product appeared. Specifically, an increase in the real wage rate motivates households to increase labor supply and consumption demand. But recall that the choice of labor demand by firms guarantees that the real wage rate equals the economy-wide marginal product of labor. Therefore, the effects from the real wage amount, ultimately, to corresponding effects from the schedule for labor's marginal product.

As before, wealth effects can arise from shifts in production functions. These effects show up first on firms' profits (and on stock prices if we had introduced a stock market). But it is important to remember that the profits go to the households that own the firms. Therefore, the shifts in production functions ultimately have wealth effects on households, as in our earlier model that ignored firms.

One new consideration is the wealth effect from a change in the real wage rate, given the position of the production function. An increase in w/P benefits the households that sell labor services. But this benefit is matched by an extra cost for the firms, which buy labor services. Since the firms are owned by households, the overall wealth effect on households from a change in w/P is nil. (There would be distributional effects if households differ by their relative amounts of wage and profit income. But we follow our usual practice of neglecting distributional effects on the aggregates of labor supply and consumption demand.)

The interest rate, R, has the same intertemporal-substitution effects as before. An increase in R motivates households to save more by reducing current consumption demand and raising current labor supply. An additional intertemporal-substitution effect arises if people anticipate variations over time in the real wage rate. Suppose, for example, that workers regard the current real wage rate as high relative to future values. Then they increase current labor supply and plan to reduce labor supply in the future. Before, we found similar effects if people anticipated changes in the schedule for labor's marginal product.

EMPIRICAL EVIDENCE ON THE RESPONSE OF LABOR SUPPLY TO TIME VARIATIONS IN REAL WAGE RATES

We discussed in Chapter 3 the estimates of George Alogoskoufis (1987a, 1987b) for intertemporal-substitution effects on labor supply. Aside from the influence of interest rates, which we mentioned before, these studies also consider the response of labor supply to anticipated variations in real wage rates. For the United States, an increase by one percentage point per year in the expected growth rate of real wages raised the growth rate of the number of workers by about one percentage point per year. For the United Kingdom, the results showed less sensitivity of work effort to variations in real wages; an increase by one percentage point per year in the expected growth rate of real wages raised the growth rate of the number of workers by only about 0.4 percentage point per year. For both countries, the results were weaker if work effort was measured by hours worked per person rather than the number of workers. In particular, there was no statistically significant relation between the expected growth rate of real wages and the growth rate of hours worked per capita. Thus, the evidence suggests that intertemporal substitution of labor supply in response to time variations of wages is more important for the number of people working than for hours worked per person.

We can summarize the results in this section by writing down functions for the aggregates of labor supply and consumption demand. These functions take the forms

$$N^s = N^s \left(\frac{w}{P}, R, \cdots \right)$$
$$(+)(+)$$

$$(6.6)$$

and

$$C^d = C^d \left(\frac{w}{P}, R, \cdots \right).$$
$$(+)(-)$$

$$(6.7)$$

The omitted terms, denoted by . . . , include characteristics of the production function, as well as any elements that generate departures of expected future real wage rates from the current value.

CLEARING OF THE LABOR MARKET

The labor market clears when the aggregate supply of labor, N^s, equals the aggregate demand, N^d. Therefore, using equations 6.4 and 6.6, the condition for clearing the labor market is

$$N^d \left(\frac{w}{P}, \cdots \right) = N^s \left(\frac{w}{P}, R, \cdots \right).$$
$$(-) \qquad\qquad (+)(+)$$

$$(6.8)$$

Recall that the terms denoted by . . . include characteristics of the production function.

As before, there are also conditions for clearing the commodity market and for ensuring that all money is willingly held. These conditions must hold along with equation 6.8 to ensure the clearing of all markets. When we take these conditions together, we shall be able to determine the nominal wage rate, w, as well as the interest rate, R, and the price level, P. In other words, we add one new market-clearing condition, equation 6.8, and thereby determine one more "price"—the price of labor services, w. For now, we focus on the new condition for clearing the labor market.

Figure 6.2 shows the clearing of the labor market. For convenience, we place the real wage rate, w/P, on the vertical axis and labor demand and supply on the horizontal. Notice that the quantity of labor demanded by firms falls as w/P rises. On the other hand, the quantity of labor supplied by households increases with w/P.

Notice from Figure 6.2 that the aggregates of labor demand and supply are equal when the real wage rate is $(w/P)^*$ and the level of work is N^*. We can think of this overall level of work effort as corresponding to aggregate **employment** (number of persons working) or to total hours worked by all persons. Figure 6.2 allows us to relate the market-clearing values of the real wage rate and employment (or total hours worked) to variables that shift either the labor-demand curve or the labor-supply curve. These variables include the interest rate, R, the forms of production functions, and prospective changes in the real wage rate. For example, an increase in the interest rate shifts the labor-supply curve rightward in Figure 6.2. Hence employment, N^*, rises, while the real wage rate, $(w/P)^*$, declines.

CLEARING OF THE COMMODITY MARKET

Using equations 6.5 and 6.7, we can write the condition for clearing the commodity market as

$$C^d \left(\frac{w}{P}, R, \cdots\right) = Y^s \left(\frac{w}{P}, \cdots\right).$$
$$(+)\,(-) \qquad\qquad (-)$$

$$(6.9)$$

We want to show that this condition is essentially the same as the one for clearing the commodity market in Chapter 5. That is, we want to demonstrate that the introduction of the labor market and firms leaves intact our previous analysis of the commodity market. This finding is important because it means that our results from Chapter 5 carry through to the extended model that includes a labor market.

Recall that the condition for clearing the labor market in equation 6.8 (and Figure 6.2) determines w/P. This condition implies that an increase in the interest rate, R, shifts the labor-supply curve rightward in Figure 6.2. Hence, w/P falls when R rises. We can use this result to substitute out for the real wage rate, w/P, in the condition for clearing the commodity market, equation 6.9. In particular, we have shown that w/P varies inversely with R. Therefore, after substituting for w/P in terms of R, we get the simplified condition for clearing the commodity market,

$$C^d (R, \cdots) = Y^s (R, \cdots).$$
$$(-) \qquad\qquad (+)$$

$$(6.10)$$

As usual, the expression ... includes characteristics of the production function.

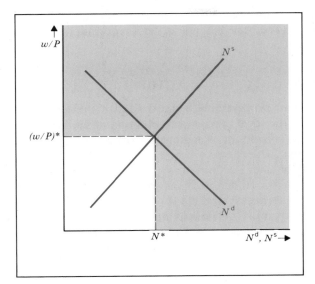

FIGURE 6.2 *Clearing of the Labor Market*
For a given value of the interest rate, R, and for a given form of the production function, the labor market clears when the real wage rate is $(w/P)^*$ and the quantity of work is N^*.

Notice that w/P does not appear in equation 6.10 because we have replaced it by the various elements, including R, that determine the real wage rate. In particular, since Y^s depends on w/P in equation 6.9 and since w/P depends on R, Y^s depends indirectly on R. Therefore, when we solve out for w/P, Y^s depends directly on R in equation 6.10.

Let's examine in detail how the interest rate enters into the condition for clearing the commodity market in equation 6.10. Recall that an increase in R shifts the labor-supply curve rightward in Figure 6.2, which leads to a decline in w/P. This decline in w/P leads, as shown in equation 6.9, to an expansion of goods supply, Y^s. Therefore, the positive effect of R on Y^s in equation 6.10 picks up this channel of effects.

On the demand side, the change in the interest rate has two effects. First, from equation 6.9, an increase in R lowers consumer demand, C^d, for a given value of w/P. Second, because an increase in R leads to a lower value of w/P, there is a further decline in consumer demand. Therefore, the negative effect of R on C^d in equation 6.10 picks up both channels of effect.

The important point is that equation 6.10 looks just like the condition for clearing the commodity market that we used in Chapter 5.[2] Since the condition for clearing the commodity market looks as it did before, we can still use our previous

[2]The only difference is that the labor market ensures that everyone's marginal product of labor, which equals the real wage rate, is the same. The equality of real wage rates arises only because we assumed, first, that everyone's labor services were physically identical and, second, that all jobs had similar working conditions. We could expand the analysis to deal with different levels of skills and different characteristics of jobs. Then we would find that real wage rates were higher for people who were more productive and on jobs that were less pleasant. But these considerations would not change the major macroeconomic results.

analysis to determine the interest rate and the quantities of output and work effort for each period. To see how this works, let's reconsider the example of a shift in the production function.

AN IMPROVEMENT IN THE PRODUCTION FUNCTION

Assume a permanent proportional upward shift of the production function. This change means that the level of aggregate output and the marginal product of labor increase for any given amount of aggregate work effort.

Figure 6.3 shows the effects on the labor market. Since the disturbance raises wealth, the supply of labor declines for a given value of w/P. Because of the upward shift to the schedule for labor's marginal product, the demand for labor rises for a given value of w/P. Hence, Figure 6.3 shows that the real wage rate increases, but the change in the quantity of work is uncertain. As in some previous cases, the wealth effect suggests less work, but the improvement in productivity suggests more work.

Figure 6.4 shows the effect on the commodity market. We use the market-clearing condition from equation 6.10, which takes account of the determination of the real wage rate from the labor market. Notice first the rightward shift in consumer demand. This shift reflects partly the wealth effect from the improvement in the production function and partly the substitution effect (toward consumption and away from leisure) from the rise in the real wage rate.

The supply of goods rises with the improvement in the production function but falls because of the increase in the real wage rate. Recall, however, that the shift in the production function and the resulting change in w/P are permanent in this example. Therefore, the aggregate of desired saving would change little, if at all, at

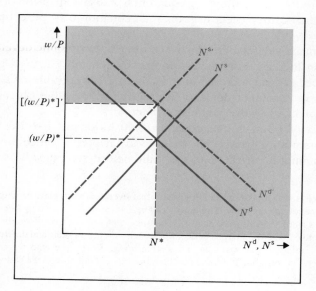

FIGURE 6.3 *Effect of an Improvement in the Production Function on the Labor Market The permanent upward shift of the production function raises the demand for labor but lowers the supply. Therefore, the real wage rate increases, but the change in work is uncertain.*

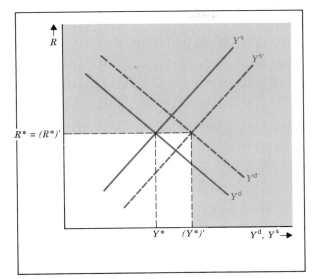

FIGURE 6.4 *Effect of an Improvement in the Production Function on the Commodity Market*
The permanent upward shift of the production function raises the demand and supply of commodities by roughly equal amounts. Hence, output increases, but the interest rate does not change.

the initial interest rate. This result means that goods supply, Y^s, shifts rightward on net by roughly the same amount as C^d. We conclude from Figure 6.4 that output increases, but the interest rate does not change.[3]

An important observation is that the results coincide with those that we reached earlier, when people worked on only their own production processes. A permanent improvement in production opportunities raises aggregate output but has an ambiguous effect on work effort. Further, because the shift in the production function is permanent, there is no change in the interest rate.

The introduction of the labor market does deliver an important result about the behavior of the real wage rate. Economic development involves a series of permanent improvements to the production function of the sort that we considered in Figures 6.3 and 6.4. Hence, our analysis shows that economic development leads to continuing increases in the real wage rate. This proposition accords with data for a large number of countries. For example, in the United States, the average hourly real wage rate rose at an average rate of 1.0% per year from 1948 to 1987.[4]

NOMINAL WAGE RATES

To determine nominal wage rates and other nominal variables, we again consider the condition for money to be willingly held. This condition looks as it did in Chap-

---

[3]Since the interest rate does not change, we do not have to modify the analysis of the labor market in Figure 6.3. Recall that this diagram applies for a given value of the interest rate.

[4]The wage rate refers to average hourly earnings (adjusted for overtime and interindustry shifts) in the total private nonagricultural economy. The real wage rate is the ratio of the nominal wage to the GNP deflator. For the data, see *Economic Report of the President,* 1988, Tables B-44, B-3.

ter 5:

$$M = P \cdot L(\underset{(-)}{R}, \underset{(+)}{Y}, \cdots).$$ (6.11)

The aggregate real demand for money, $L(\cdot)$, now includes money held by firms as well as households. However, the form of this function does not differ greatly from that in our earlier analysis. In particular, the amount of real money demanded still falls with an increase in the interest rate, R, and rises with an increase in real transactions as measured by real output, Y.

The full market-clearing model now consists of equation 6.11 plus the conditions derived earlier for clearing the labor and commodity markets:

$$N^d \left(\underset{(-)}{\frac{w}{P}}, \cdots \right) = N^s \left(\underset{(+)}{\frac{w}{P}}, \underset{(+)}{R}, \cdots \right)$$ (6.12)

and

$$C^d \left(\underset{(+)}{\frac{w}{P}}, \underset{(-)}{R}, \cdots \right) = Y^s \left(\underset{(-)}{\frac{w}{P}}, \cdots \right).$$ (6.13)

We have already seen that equations 6.12 and 6.13 determine the real wage rate, w/P, the interest rate, R, and the levels of output, Y, and employment, N.

We showed in Chapter 5 that an increase in the quantity of money, M, was neutral. The price level, P, rose in the same proportion, but all real variables—including output, Y; work effort, N; the interest rate, R; and real money balances, M/P—were unchanged. This property of monetary neutrality still holds in the model that includes a labor market. However, we have to add the real wage rate, w/P, to the list of real variables that do not change. Then we have to include the nominal wage rate, w, along with the nominal variables that rise in the same proportion as the quantity of money.

To verify these results, remember that equations 6.12 and 6.13 determine R and Y. These variables then determine the real demand for money, $L(\cdot)$. Given this real demand, equation 6.11 implies that an increase in M raises P in the same proportion. Therefore, real money balances, M/P, do not change when there is a once-and-for-all shift in the nominal quantity of money.

Recall that equations 6.12 and 6.13 determine w/P and N. In fact, the real wage rate equals the marginal product of labor at this value of N. We can find the nominal wage rate, w, by multiplying the real wage rate, w/P, by the price level, P, which we have already determined. Notice that an increase in M raises P in the same proportion but does not change w/P. Therefore, an increase in M must raise the nominal wage rate w (as well as P) in the same proportion.

THE LABOR MARKET IN THE MACROECONOMIC MODEL

Consider how the introduction of the labor market and firms affects our analysis. We have shown that these new features do not change the way that shifts to the production function affect the interest rate and the aggregate quantities of output and work effort. We also found that the extensions did not change the interaction between money and prices. In other words, our earlier simplification—which neglected the labor market and the existence of firms—allows us to get reasonable answers to many important questions. Therefore, for most of the subsequent analysis, we shall find it satisfactory to return to the simpler framework, which does not deal explicitly with the labor market or firms. The main place where we reintroduce firms and the labor market is in Chapter 11, where we study unemployment.

SUMMARY

We introduced a labor market in which firms demand labor and households supply labor at a going wage rate. This market clears when the aggregate demand for labor equals the aggregate supply. One important aspect of a cleared labor market is that it equates each worker's marginal product to the real wage rate. Thereby, this market exhausts all the gains in output that can result by shifting workers from one production activity to another.

The requirements for general market clearing are that the labor market clear along with the markets for commodities and credit. In comparison with our previous analysis, we have added one new condition—that the labor market clear—and one new "price," which is the wage rate for labor services.

The conditions for determining the aggregate quantities of output and work, as well as the interest rate and the price level, turn out to be similar to those from before. Therefore, for many purposes, we can carry out the analysis by pretending, as before, that households work on only their own production processes. (We have to consider firms and a labor market later when we study unemployment.) In addition, the inclusion of the labor market enables us to determine the wage rate. The theory predicts that the real wage rate will increase as an economy develops, a proposition that accords with empirical evidence.

IMPORTANT TERMS AND CONCEPTS

firm

profit

stock market

real wage rate

employment

QUESTIONS AND PROBLEMS

Mainly for Review

6.1 How does an increase in the real wage rate affect the demand for labor? Where does the assumption of diminishing marginal productivity of labor come in?

6.2 Consider two individuals, *A* and *B*; they have the same production function, but *A* has a greater willingness to work. If each individual is isolated on an island, who will work more? Who will have the higher marginal product? Show how total output can increase, with no increase in total labor, by exchanging labor services for goods between the two islands—that is, by opening up a labor market.

6.3 Suppose that the interest rate increases. How does this change affect the supply of labor and hence the real wage rate?

6.4 Explain why economic development tends to raise the real wage rate.

6.5 Suppose that the quantity of money, *M*, increases.
   a. The increase in the nominal wage rate suggests that workers will be better off. Why is this not so?
   b. The increase in the price level suggests that workers will be worse off. Is this correct?

PROBLEMS FOR DISCUSSION

6.6 *The Labor Market and Efficiency*
   In the text we considered two isolated regions, *A* and *B*. The technology in *A* was inferior to that in *B*. Therefore, we found that the opening up of an economy-wide labor market led to higher aggregate output without requiring an increase in aggregate work effort. In this sense the new market improved the economy's efficiency.
   a. Does the result mean that everyone is better off? In answering, consider the position of workers and firms (and the owners of firms) in both regions.
   b. Does your answer suggest that some groups might oppose moves to free up markets, even when there would be gains in the aggregate? Can you think of any real-world examples of this phenomenon?

6.7 *Walras' Law*
   a. When we introduce the labor market, what new aggregate-consistency condition arises?
   b. Use the aggregate form of households' budget constraints to derive Walras' Law of Markets. How does the law differ from that in Chapter 5?

6.8 *Wealth Effects from Changes in the Real Wage Rate*
   Suppose that the real wage rate, w/P, increases.

a. Why are there offsetting effects on wealth? What would you predict for the wealth effect on aggregate consumption demand and labor supply?

b. Suppose that most suppliers of labor own relatively little of the ownership rights in firms. What would you predict for the wealth effect on aggregate labor supply?

6.9 *Temporary Shifts of the Production Function*
Consider a temporary, parallel downward shift of the production function.

a. What are the effects on the interest rate, the real wage rate, and the quantities of output and employment?

b. Do the results differ from those in Chapter 5, where people worked only on their own production processes?

c. How do the answers change if the shift of the production function is proportional rather than parallel?

6.10 *Short-Run Movements of the Real Wage Rate* (*optional*)
Consider again a temporary, parallel downward shift of the production function.

a. Using the results from problem 6.9, what is the pattern of association between changes in the real wage rate and changes in the quantities of employment and output?

b. Assume, more realistically, that the schedule for labor's marginal product shifts downward. In particular, assume that this shift is large enough so that work effort declines. In this case, what is the pattern of association between changes in the real wage rate and changes in the quantities of employment and output?

c. Suppose that business fluctuations result from temporary shifts of the production function. What do you predict for the "cyclical" behavior of real wage rates? That is, do real wage rates move together with or inversely to output and employment? (There is much empirical debate about the cyclical behavior of real wage rates. However, most researchers find a weak "procyclical" pattern; that is, real wage rates tend to be high when output and employment are high.)

6.11 *The Short-Run Behavior of Productivity* (*optional*)
Suppose that we use the popular definition of labor productivity as the ratio of output to employment, Y/N.

a. How does this measure of productivity relate to the marginal product of labor?

b. Assume, as in problem 6.10, that business fluctuations result from shifts of the production function. How would productivity behave? In particular, is productivity high or low when output is high?

6.12 *Determination of Stock Prices* (*optional*)
Suppose that there are a fixed number of firms in the economy, each with access to the same production function, $f(n)$. Assume that the owner of a firm prints up and sells 100 ownership certificates (shares), each of which entitles the holder to 1% of the firm's profits. What would be the price of each share?

PART TWO

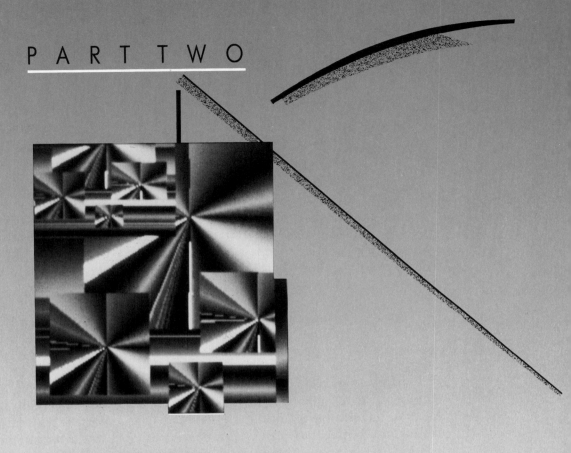

INFLATION

*T*hus far, we have simplified the analysis by holding fixed the general price level. Although this assumption was convenient, it conflicts dramatically with real-world experience, especially in recent years. These days prices tend to rise over time—that is, there tends to be inflation. Therefore, it is important to modify the model to allow for the effects of changing price levels.

Chapter 7 begins by noting the empirical association between inflation and monetary growth. Then we discuss the important distinctions between expected and unexpected inflation and between nominal and real interest rates.

Chapter 8 incorporates the new tools into the market-clearing model. With these extensions we can study the effects of monetary growth on inflation, interest rates, and other variables. One important finding is that fluctuations in monetary growth can be the principal source of variations in inflation. Nevertheless, these movements in monetary growth and inflation may have little to do with the behavior of real variables. That is, money can still be approximately neutral in the model.

CHAPTER

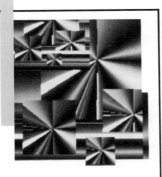

INFLATION AND INTEREST RATES

n this chapter we begin the study of **inflation.** By inflation, we mean a continuing upward movement in the general price level. The theoretical analysis suggests some possible sources of inflation. To sort out the possibilities, we shall find it convenient to think about the condition that all money be willingly held:

$$M = P \cdot L(R, \ Y, \ \cdots).$$
$$(-)(+)$$

(7.1)

One way for the price level to increase is through a downward movement in the real demand for money. For example, a permanent downward shift in the production function would lower aggregate output, Y, and thereby decrease the real quantity of money demanded. But notice that a single disturbance of this type creates a single increase in the price level rather than a continuing series of increases in prices. To generate inflation along this line, we would need a succession of downward shifts to the production function. There is no doubt that adverse shocks to the production function—such as oil crises, harvest failures, and strikes—can influence the general level of prices over short periods. But there is no evidence that these forces can account for inflation in the sense of persistent rises in prices. In fact, the typical pattern in most countries is one of growing output. Since this growth raises the real demand for money, we predict that prices would fall over time if the nominal stock of money, M, did not change.

There can also be reductions in the real demand for money that reflect increasing financial sophistication. For example, in recent years many countries have developed financial instruments and procedures that make it easier for people to economize on money. In the United States in the post–World War II period, this factor has led to a downward trend in the real demand for money. This element can account, however, for only a small amount of inflation; something like 1 to 2% per year is a reasonable estimate. Therefore, we cannot use this idea to explain the persistently high rates of inflation that have prevailed in many countries since the late 1960s.

The remaining suggestion from the previous analysis is a link between inflation and increases in the quantity of paper money, M. At an empirical level it is clear, first, that the quantity of money often grows at a high rate over long periods of time and, second, that **rates of monetary growth** differ substantially across countries and over time for a single country. Therefore, monetary growth is a good candidate as a source of inflation.

CROSS COUNTRY DATA ON INFLATION AND MONETARY GROWTH

To assess the role of money as a determinant of inflation, let's examine some data. Table 7.1 shows the experiences of 83 countries during the post–World War II period. The table reports the average growth rates of an index of consumer prices and of money, defined as hand-to-hand currency. (The results are similar for the broader monetary aggregate, M1, which includes checkable deposits. However, because of differences in the nature of financial institutions, the meaning of M1 varies more across countries than does that of currency.) The table arranges the countries in descending order with respect to their average rates of inflation. Note the following:

- The average growth rates of prices and money are positive for all countries since World War II.

- The average growth rates are typically high. For example, the median inflation rate for the 83 countries is 7.4% per year, with 21 of them exceeding 10%. For the average growth rate of currency, the median is 11.4% per year, with 57 of the countries above 10%.

- There is a broad cross-sectional range for the average growth rates of prices and money. The average inflation rates vary from 94% for Argentina, 68% for Chile, and 54% for Bolivia to about 3% for Switzerland and West Germany. The rate for the United States is 4.2%. Notice that the growth rates of currency have a comparable range, varying from 92% for Argentina, 73% for Chile, and 52% for Bolivia to 4% for Belgium, 5% for Switzerland, and 6% for the United States.

- The average growth rate of currency exceeds that of prices in almost all cases. That is, growing real money balances are typical in the post–World War II

TABLE 7.1 *Annual Growth Rates of Prices, Money, and Output for 83 Countries in the Post–World War II Period (arranged by decreasing order of the inflation rate)*

Country	ΔP	ΔM	$\Delta M - \Delta P$	ΔY	Time Span
Argentina	93.9	91.6	−2.3	1.4	1979–86
Chile	67.9	73.3	5.4	1.5	1960–84
Bolivia	54.4	51.6	−2.8	3.2	1962–87
Brazil	44.8	46.6	1.8	6.6	1963–85
Uruguay	42.1	41.0	−1.0	1.4	1960–86
Israel	30.8	31.4	0.6	7.0	1950–86
Zaire	30.0	29.8	−0.2	2.4	1963–86
Peru	28.1	31.7	3.6	3.5	1960–85
Yugoslavia	20.9	24.7	3.8	4.9	1960–86
Iceland	18.8	19.0	0.2	4.1[b]	1950–87
Ghana	18.7	16.9	−1.8	0.2[a]	1950–85
Turkey	18.5	21.2	2.6	5.7[a]	1955–86
Mexico	15.3	19.2	4.0	5.4	1950–86
Somalia	15.3	18.0	2.8	—	1960–86
Korea (South)	13.4	22.6	9.3	7.4	1953–87
Colombia	13.3	17.1	3.8	5.0	1950–85
Paraguay	12.2	16.7	4.5	4.8	1952–87
Sierra Leone	12.1	13.6	1.5	3.8	1963–83
Jamaica	11.4	14.9	3.6	1.6	1960–86
Costa Rica	11.2	16.0	4.8	4.6	1960–87
Portugal	10.3	11.1	0.8	4.7	1953–85
Gambia	9.8	11.5	1.7	3.2[a]	1964–86
Spain	9.6	12.7	3.2	4.4	1954–86
Greece	9.5	14.9	5.4	4.7	1953–87
Madagascar	9.5	8.8	−0.7	1.5[a]	1964–86
Nigeria	9.2	12.9	3.8	3.4	1955–86
Sudan	9.0	11.6	2.6	3.0[a]	1951–83
Guyana	8.9	12.9	3.9	0.1[a]	1960–87
Ecuador	8.8	13.6	4.8	5.4	1951–86
Senegal	8.6	11.9	3.3	0.8[a]	1967–84
Iran	8.4	20.0	11.6	6.2	1959–83
Trinidad and Tobago	8.4	12.1	3.7	2.6	1960–85
Central African Republic	8.4	12.3	3.9	—	1963–87
Mauritius	8.3	12.0	3.7	3.6	1963–87
Gabon	8.0	11.4	3.4	7.8[a]	1962–85
Philippines	8.0	10.7	2.7	4.8	1950–87
Nepal	7.9	14.3	6.4	2.6	1964–87
Cameroon	7.8	11.8	4.0	6.9[a]	1963–84
Ireland	7.6	7.9	0.4	3.1	1950–86
Niger	7.5	10.7	3.2	3.1[a]	1963–85
Italy	7.4	10.5	3.1	4.4	1950–87
New Zealand	7.4	6.1	−1.2	3.1	1954–85
Egypt	7.4	12.3	5.0	4.3[a]	1955–87
Ivory Coast	7.3	12.0	4.7	5.0[a]	1962–86
India	7.3	10.0	2.8	3.9	1960–86

TABLE 7.1 *(continued)*

Country	ΔP	ΔM	$\Delta M - \Delta P$	ΔY	Time Span
Syria	7.2	15.0	7.8	5.7	1957–86
South Africa	7.0	9.6	2.6	3.8	1950–87
Finland	6.9	8.4	1.5	4.3	1950–86
Congo	6.8	10.7	3.9	—	1960–86
Togo	6.8	13.2	6.4	3.6[a]	1963–84
Pakistan	6.7	10.3	3.7	4.7	1955–87
El Salvador	6.6	7.8	1.2	3.1	1951–87
United Kingdom	6.5	6.4	0.0	2.4	1951–87
France	6.4	7.1	0.7	4.1	1950–87
Australia	6.3	8.4	2.1	3.9	1950–87
Saudi Arabia	6.3	18.3	12.0	6.0	1968–86
Denmark	6.2	6.8	0.7	3.1	1950–87
Norway	6.1	6.8	0.6	4.1	1950–87
Sweden	6.1	7.5	1.4	3.0	1950–86
Burkina Faso	5.9	10.1	4.2	3.6[a]	1962–85
Dominican Republic	5.8	10.8	5.0	5.0	1950–86
Chad	5.8	7.2	1.4	—	1960–77
Morocco	5.7	11.1	5.4	3.7	1958–86
Tunisia	5.4	10.9	5.5	6.4[a]	1960–87
Libya	5.4	25.0	19.7	5.7[a]	1964–79
Haiti	5.3	8.4	3.0	1.9	1953–86
Sri Lanka	5.2	10.1	4.9	5.4[a]	1950–87
Japan	5.0	11.4	6.4	6.9[b]	1953–87
Guatemala	4.9	8.4	3.5	3.9	1950–86
Thailand	4.8	8.8	4.0	6.3	1955–87
Venezuela	4.8	8.8	4.0	4.6	1950–86
Iraq	4.7	14.1	9.4	6.6	1965–75
Austria	4.7	7.3	2.6	3.9	1950–87
Canada	4.6	7.1	2.5	4.3	1950–87
Cyprus	4.5	10.7	6.2	5.0	1960–87
Netherlands	4.4	6.5	2.0	3.8[b]	1950–87
Honduras	4.3	8.7	4.3	3.6	1950–87
Belgium	4.2	4.2	−0.1	3.3[b]	1950–87
United States	4.2	5.6	1.4	3.1[b]	1950–87
Malta	3.8	9.8	6.0	6.2	1960–86
Singapore	3.6	10.8	7.3	8.0	1963–87
Switzerland	3.3	4.8	1.6	3.1	1950–86
Germany (West)	3.1	6.8	3.7	4.1[b]	1953–87

Note: All growth rates are annual averages for the sample periods shown in the right column. ΔP is the growth rate of consumer prices. ΔM is the growth rate of the stock of currency. ΔY is the growth rate of real gross domestic product.

[a]Data on real domestic product were unavailable for these countries. ΔY was calculated by subtracting the average growth rate of consumer prices, ΔP, from the average growth rate of nominal gross domestic product.

[b]Real gross national product was used instead of real gross domestic product.

Source: All data are from issues of *International Financial Statistics.*

period. The median growth rate of real currency across the countries is 3.6% per year.

- Most significant, there is a strong positive association across countries between the average rates of price change and the average rates of monetary growth.

Figure 7.1 brings out the nature of the association between inflation and monetary growth. The graph shows the positive correlation between inflation and the growth rate of currency. Further, each increase by one percentage point per year in the rate of monetary growth is associated with an increase by roughly one percentage point per year in the rate of inflation. This relation is closer, however, for the more extreme cases than for the moderate ones. For example, the association is less dramatic for countries where the average rate of monetary growth is between 5% and 15% per year.

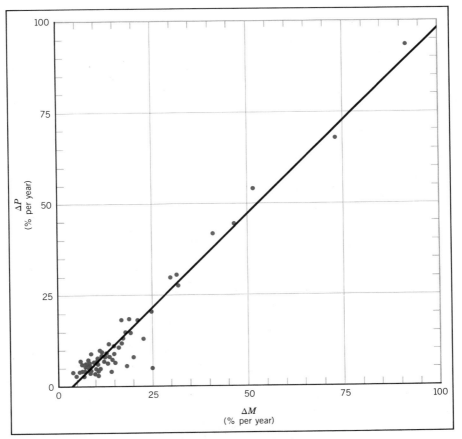

FIGURE 7.1 *Graph of the Inflation Rate versus the Growth Rate of Currency for 83 Countries*
We show here the positive relation between inflation and the growth rate of currency.

If the growth rate of money exceeds the growth rate of prices, real money balances, *M/P*, increase over time. Since money is willingly held at each date, the growth rate of real balances must equal the growth rate of real money demanded. Recall that our previous analysis of the demand for money suggested several factors that could lead to increases over time in the quantity of real money demanded. The most important is the growth rate of output. Table 7.1 shows the average growth rate of output for 79 countries (those for which data are available), and Figure 7.2 graphs these growth rates along with the average growth rate of real money balances. Notice the positive association between the growth rate of output and the growth rate of real balances. In addition, the median growth rate of output, 4.1% per year, is close to the median growth rate of real money balances, 3.6% per year. These findings imply that a country with a higher growth rate of output tends to have a lower rate of inflation for a given rate of monetary growth. Therefore, differences

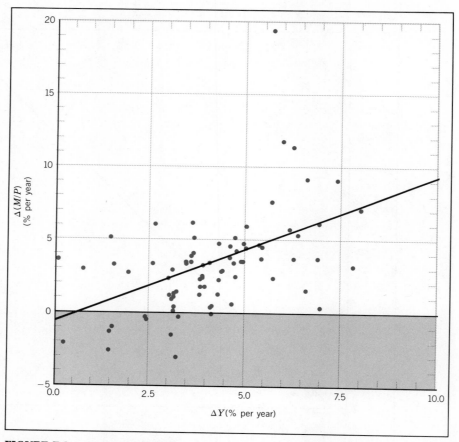

FIGURE 7.2 *Graph of the Growth Rate of Real Cash Balances versus the Growth Rate of Output for 79 Countries*
We show here the positive relation between the growth rate of real currency and the growth rate of output.

in the growth rates of output explain some of the imperfect association between monetary growth and inflation, as shown in Figure 7.1.

Another variable that influences the demand for money is the interest rate, R, which determines the cost of holding money. Other things equal, we predict that the average growth rate of real money balances will be lower for countries in which the interest rate has increased, and vice-versa. Notice that the change in the interest rate, rather than the average level of the interest rate, matters here. Although researchers have verified this proposition for industrialized countries, we cannot demonstrate it for the substantial number of countries that lack organized securities markets on which interest rates are quoted. We shall see, however, in this and the next chapter that interest rates and inflation rates are closely related. In particular, increases in the rate of inflation also mean greater costs of holding money—that is, a higher rate of inflation means that money depreciates in real terms at a faster rate. It follows that an increase in the rate of inflation tends to reduce the real demand for money. Therefore, we predict that the average growth rate of real money balances will be lower for countries in which the inflation rate has increased. (Notice again that what matters here is the change in the inflation rate rather than the average level of the rate.) As examples, the sharp rises in inflation rates explain the negative growth rates of real money balances that show up in Table 7.1 for Argentina, Bolivia, and Zaire.

Overall, the cross-country data suggest a significant, positive association between monetary growth and inflation. Further, this relation is closer than it first appears if we consider additional variables, such as the growth rate of output and changes in interest rates and inflation rates, which affect the real demand for money.

U.S. TIME SERIES DATA ON INFLATION AND MONETARY GROWTH

Table 7.2 reports data for the United States on average rates of inflation and monetary growth over 20-year periods from 1860 to 1980. Over the entire 120-year span, the average inflation rate was 2.1% per year, while the average growth rate of currency was 4.8% per year. Correspondingly, the average growth rate of real money balances was 2.7% per year. Notice that this figure accords with the average growth rate of output, which was 3.3% per year. (Again, the results are similar if we look at the broader monetary aggregate, M1, rather than currency.)

Although the time-series data for the United States do not provide the range of experience that appears in the cross-country sample, there are substantial differences in the various 20-year periods. For example, the average inflation rate was negative over two intervals: −1.6% for 1920−40 (which includes the Great Depression) and −0.6% for 1880−1900. But the rate exceeded 4% in three of the cases: 4.8% for 1960−80, 4.6% for 1900−20, and 4.3% for 1940−60. The world wars strongly influence the observations for the last two subperiods. For currency, the range of growth rates was from 2.4% for 1920−40 to 6.9% for 1960−80.

There is a positive, though imperfect, association between monetary growth

TABLE 7.2 *U.S. Time Series Data on Inflation and Monetary Growth: Averages for 20-Year Periods (average growth rates in % per year)*

	ΔP	ΔM (Currency)	$\Delta M - \Delta P$	ΔY
1860–1880	1.1	3.4	2.3	4.3
1880–1900	−0.6	3.2	3.8	3.0
1900–1920	4.6	6.5	1.9	2.8
1920–1940	−1.6	2.4	4.0	2.4
1940–1960	4.3	6.8	2.5	3.8
1960–1980	4.8	6.9	2.1	3.5
1860–1980	2.1	4.9	2.8	3.3

Note: All growth rates are annual averages for the period shown in the first column. ΔP is the growth rate of the deflator for the gross national product. ΔM is the growth rate of currency. ΔY is the growth rate of real gross national product.

Sources: For the price level and real GNP, see Figures 1.1 and 1.4. For money, see Friedman and Schwartz (1970, Tables 1 and 13) and *Federal Reserve Bulletin,* various issues.

and inflation over the different 20-year periods. As in our previous analysis, we can explain some of the divergences between monetary growth and inflation by considering variables that alter the demand for money. These include the growth rate of output, changes in interest rates, and the development of financial institutions.

INFLATION AS A MONETARY PHENOMENON

Casual observation of two types of data—across countries and over time for the United States—suggests that we should consider seriously Milton Friedman's (1968b, p. 29) famous statement, "Inflation is always and everywhere a monetary phenomenon." We should, however, remember some important points. First, the analysis will not rule out effects of real disturbances, such as supply shocks, on the price level. But we expect that these effects will be more important for isolated episodes of price changes than for chronic inflation. Second, we should view the expression *monetary phenomenon* as incorporating variables that influence the real demand for money, as well as the nominal supply of money. Third, we would eventually like to know why monetary growth behaves differently in different countries and at different times. This question would require us to explore a number of new subjects, including governmental incentives to print more or less money. We sidestep the theory of money supply in this and the next chapter. Here, we look at the consequences for inflation and other variables of a given—unexplained—time path of money. This type of analysis is crucial for an understanding of inflation, although it does not constitute a full study of the topic.

ACTUAL AND EXPECTED INFLATION

Here we begin the process of incorporating inflation into the theoretical model. The inflation rate between periods t and $t + 1$ is

$$\pi_t = \frac{(P_{t+1} - P_t)}{P_t}, \tag{7.2}$$

where π is the Greek letter pi. Notice that the inflation rate equals the rate of change of the price level between periods t and $t + 1$. By rearranging equation 7.2, we can solve out for the next period's price level as

$$P_{t+1} = (1 + \pi_t)P_t. \tag{7.3}$$

Hence, prices rise over one period by the factor $1 + \pi_t$. Although we focus on rising prices—that is, positive rates of inflation—we can also consider declining prices. These cases are called **deflations.**

In making various decisions, such as the choice between consuming now or later, people want to know how prices will change over time. Therefore, people form forecasts or **expectations of inflation.** We use the symbol π_t^e to denote an expectation for the inflation rate π_t. Usually we think of someone as forming this expectation during period t. Since people already know the current price level, P_t, the expectation of inflation, π_t^e, corresponds to a forecast of the next period's price level, P_{t+1}.

In general, forecasts of inflation are imperfect. That is, the actual rate of inflation is typically higher or lower than the average person's expectation. Hence, the forecast error—or **unexpected inflation**—is usually nonzero. However, people have incentives to form their expectations *rationally*—making efficient use of the available information on past inflation and other variables—to avoid systematic mistakes. Therefore, we should not find that unexpected inflation is either typically positive or typically negative. Further, there ought not to be a systematic pattern of errors over time. For example, if unexpected inflation is positive this period, it may be either positive or negative in the next period.

REAL AND NOMINAL INTEREST RATES

As before, let R_t be the interest rate on bonds. If a person buys \$1 of a bond (with a maturity of one period) during period t, he or she gets \$$(1 + R_t)$ as receipts of principal plus interest during period $t + 1$. Hence the dollar value of assets held as bonds rises over one period by the factor $1 + R_t$. Accordingly, we can think of the rate R_t as the dollar or **nominal interest rate.**

What happens over time to the real value of assets that people hold as bonds? If the price level is constant, as in previous chapters, the real value of these assets also grows at the rate R_t. Thus, in a world of constant prices, the nominal interest rate, R_t, is also the **real interest rate**—that is, the rate that determines the growth over time in the real value of assets.

If the inflation rate, π_t, is nonzero, the real and nominal interest rates will differ.

In particular, if the inflation rate is positive, goods next period will cost more than those this period. Equation 7.3 indicates that the price level rises over one period by the factor $1 + \pi_t$. Hence, if the dollar value of assets rises over one period by the factor $1 + R_t$, the real value of assets rises by the proportion $(1 + R_t)/(1 + \pi_t)$. Here, we consider that the dollars available next period—which grow by the factor $1 + R_t$—face a price level that is higher by the factor $1 + \pi_t$.

If households hold assets in the form of bonds, the real value of these assets rises over one period by the factor $(1 + R_t)/(1 + \pi_t)$. Let's define the real interest rate, r_t, to be the rate at which assets held as bonds grow in real terms. Then the real interest rate satisfies the condition

$$(1 + r_t) = \frac{(1 + R_t)}{(1 + \pi_t)}. \tag{7.4}$$

It is the real interest rate, rather than the nominal rate, that determines the amount of extra consumption that someone can get in period $t + 1$ if he or she foregoes a unit of consumption in period t. For example, if someone lowers c_t by one unit, he or she saves P_t extra dollars (in the form of bonds) and thereby has an additional $P_t \cdot (1 + R_t)$ dollars to spend in period $t + 1$. This amount buys $P_t \cdot (1 + R_t)/P_{t+1}$ units of additional consumption in period $t + 1$. This term equals $(1 + R_t)/(1 + \pi_t)$, which is the same as $1 + r_t$ from equation 7.4.

The results imply that, in deciding how much to consume (or work) in one period versus another—that is, in deciding how much to save—households will look at the real interest rate rather than the nominal rate. For this reason we want to explore further the meaning and measurement of the real interest rate.

We can obtain a more useful expression for the real interest rate, r_t, if we manipulate equation 7.4. Multiply through on both sides by the term $1 + \pi_t$, and simplify the result to get the condition

$$r_t + \pi_t + r_t\pi_t = R_t. \tag{7.5}$$

Recall that we measure each variable—R_t, π_t and r_t—as a growth rate per period. Suppose that a period is a month. Then think of nominal interest rates and inflation rates that are no larger than, say, 10 or 20% per year. In this case, the various rates per month—R_t, π_t, and r_t—will be no greater than 1 or 2%. It follows that the interaction term, $r_t\pi_t$, will be very small in equation 7.5. In particular, it will be smaller than the amount $0.02 \cdot 0.02 = 0.0004$. Therefore, we can neglect this term and satisfactorily approximate the real interest rate as

$$r_t \simeq R_t - \pi_t, \tag{7.6}$$

where the symbol, $\simeq$, means approximately equal to.[1]

Recall that the nominal interest rate, R_t, tells people how the dollar value of assets held as bonds grows over time. By contrast, the real interest rate, r_t, determines

---

[1] The approximation becomes better the shorter the length of the period. In fact, the length of the period plays no economic role in the model. Rather, we carry out the analysis in terms of periods—which economists call *discrete time*—solely for convenience. Therefore, we can reasonably assume that a period is extremely brief. Then equation 7.6 is a very accurate approximation.

how fast these assets grow in real terms. Equation 7.6 says that the real interest rate, r_t, equals the nominal rate, R_t, less the rate of inflation, π_t. Thus, the real rate is lower than the nominal rate if the inflation rate is positive. Further, the real rate is positive only if the nominal rate exceeds the inflation rate. Otherwise—that is, when the nominal rate is less than the inflation rate—the real interest rate is negative. In this case the rise in dollar value at the rate R_t does not cover the rise in prices at the rate π_t.

ACTUAL AND EXPECTED REAL INTEREST RATES

Usually we think of situations where people observe the nominal interest rate on bonds, R_t. To calculate the **expected real interest rate** between periods t and $t + 1$, people have to subtract from R_t their expectation of inflation, π_t^e. The expected real interest rate, denoted by r_t^e, is

$$r_t^e \simeq R_t - \pi_t^e. \tag{7.7}$$

Recall that the actual inflation rate, π_t, can be above or below its expectation, π_t^e. If inflation turns out to be surprisingly high—that is, $\pi_t > \pi_t^e$—the real interest rate, r_t is less than its expectation, r_t^e. In other words, if we combine equations 7.6 and 7.7, the unexpected part of the real interest rate, $r_t - r_t^e$, is

$$r_t - r_t^e \simeq -(\pi_t - \pi_t^e). \tag{7.8}$$

Errors in forecasts of inflation, $\pi_t - \pi_t^e$, generate errors of the opposite sign in forecasts of the real interest rate.

It is possible to have different institutional arrangements where borrowers and lenders specify in advance the real interest rate, r_t, rather than the nominal rate, R_t. In this case the nominal payments for principal and interest adjust to compensate for inflation. These adjustments ensure that the actual real interest rate equals the prespecified value. Therefore, people would know the real interest rate in advance but would be uncertain about the nominal interest rate.

The financial arrangements where people contract in advance for real interest rates are called **indexation** or **inflation correction.** These systems tend to exist in countries, such as Brazil and Israel, in which extreme inflation is chronic. Recently, as we discuss below, the British government issued a long-term indexed bond of this type. But the U.S. government has thus far resisted economists' suggestions to issue this kind of security. Economists do not know why private parties and governments typically prefer to borrow and lend at prespecified nominal interest rates rather than real rates.[2]

[2]There have been some suggestions: (1) People use and hold money—an asset that is denominated in nominal units—which makes it desirable to borrow and lend in the same units. (2) The government enforces contracts in nominal units more diligently than contracts in other units. (3) The tax treatment of indexed bonds is unclear. (4) It is hard to agree on a price index to use in making inflation corrections. Huston McCulloch (1980) suggested another reason: U.S. courts were unwilling to enforce indexing provisions on bonds after 1933. In that year Congress resolved not to honor the "gold clauses" that appeared in some previously issued bonds. These clauses—which were a form of indexing—committed borrowers to repay in a stated amount of gold rather than U.S. dollars. When the Congress voided these gold clauses, the courts interpreted the restriction as applying to all types of indexed bonds. However, Congress rescinded this resolution in 1977, so the ban on indexed bonds no longer applies.

***Nominal and Real Interest Rates in the Post–World War II United
States*** Table 7.3 shows the relation between nominal and real interest rates for
the United States over the post–World War II period. The nominal rate, R_t, is the
average for each year on three-month maturity U.S. Treasury bills (short-term U.S.
government securities). The inflation rate for each year, π_t, is the rate of change of
the general price level, as measured by the consumer price index (CPI). The real
interest rate for each year comes from the formula $r_t = R_t - \pi_t$.

The actual rate of inflation, π_t, may diverge substantially from the rate that
people expected, π_t^e. In that case the real interest rate, r_t, differs from the expected
rate, r_t^e. Since the expected real interest rate will be important for the subsequent
analysis, we should make some effort to measure expected inflation.

Measures of Expected Inflation Economists have employed at least three methods to measure expectations of a variable like inflation or the real interest rate.

1. Ask a sample of people about their beliefs.
2. Use the hypothesis of **rational expectations,** which says that people's beliefs
   correspond to optimal predictions, given the available information. Then
   use statistical techniques to figure out these optimal predictions.

TABLE 7.3 *Inflation Rates, Nominal Interest Rates,
and Real Interest Rates for Recent U.S.
Experience (% per year)*

Year	R_t	π_t	r_t	π_t^e	r_t^e
1948	1.0	0.4	0.6	1.2	−0.2
1949	1.1	−2.8	3.9	−4.0	5.1
1950	1.2	8.0	−6.8	−0.2	1.4
1951	1.6	4.3	−2.7	3.1	−1.5
1952	1.8	0.4	1.4	1.1	0.7
1953	1.9	0.7	1.2	−0.6	2.5
1954	1.0	−1.4	2.4	−0.9	1.9
1955	1.8	0.0	1.8	0.3	1.5
1956	2.7	3.5	−0.8	0.5	2.2
1957	3.3	3.4	−0.1	1.3	2.0
1958	1.8	1.3	0.5	0.1	1.7
1959	3.4	1.3	2.1	0.6	2.8
1960	2.9	1.6	1.3	0.7	2.2
1961	2.4	0.6	1.8	0.6	1.8
1962	2.8	1.3	1.5	1.0	1.8
1963	3.2	1.5	1.7	1.0	2.2
1964	3.6	0.9	2.7	1.0	2.6
1965	4.0	2.1	1.9	1.1	2.9
1966	4.9	3.2	1.7	1.7	3.2
1967	4.3	3.4	0.9	2.1	2.2
1968	5.3	3.8	1.5	2.8	2.5
1969	6.7	5.5	1.2	2.9	3.8

TABLE 7.3 *Continued*

Year	R_t	π_t	r_t	π_t^e	r_t^e
1970	6.5	4.5	2.0	3.6	2.9
1971	4.4	3.3	1.1	3.8	0.6
1972	4.1	3.7	0.4	3.3	0.8
1973	7.0	9.5	−2.5	3.6	3.4
1974	7.9	11.3	−3.4	6.2	2.7
1975	5.8	6.4	−0.6	6.7	−0.9
1976	5.0	5.2	−0.2	5.6	−0.6
1977	5.3	5.9	−0.6	5.6	−0.3
1978	7.2	8.1	−0.9	6.2	1.0
1979	10.1	11.4	−1.3	7.6	2.5
1980	11.4	10.2	1.2	10.4	1.0
1981	14.0	7.6	6.4	9.7	4.3
1982	10.7	4.1	6.6	6.1	4.6
1983	8.6	4.0	4.6	4.5	4.1
1984	9.6	3.1	6.5	5.3	4.3
1985	7.5	3.2	4.3	4.2	3.3
1986	6.0	0.6	5.4	3.5	2.5
1987	5.8	3.7	2.1	3.5	2.3
1988	6.7	4.7	2.0	4.2	2.5

Note: The inflation rate, π_t, refers to the change in the CPI from January of each year to January of the next year. We use the figures that exclude the shelter component to avoid some problems of measuring mortgage interest costs. The nominal interest rate, R_t, is the average annual rate on secondary markets for U.S. Treasury bills with a three-month maturity. The real interest rate, r_t, equals $R_t - \pi_t$.

Source: The data are from the *Citibase* data tape. The variable π_t^e, from the Livingston survey, comes from the Federal Reserve Bank of Philadelphia. The figures are an average for each year of the six-month forecasts (from December of the previous year and June of the current year).

3. Use market data, such as interest rates or prices of financial contracts, to infer what people believe.

The main shortcoming of the first approach is that the sample may not be representative of the whole economy. Also, economists have a better theory of how people take actions than of how they answer questions on surveys. Unlike in a market where the participants back up their statements with money, it is less clear what it means when someone just expresses opinions about inflation or other variables.

The second approach, based on rational expectations, has produced some successes and some difficulties.[3] One problem arises in figuring out what information

---

[3] For uses of this approach to measure expected inflation, see, for example, James Hamilton (1985).

people have when they form expectations. Another concerns the choice among statistical models. In any event, the results about expected inflation from some of these studies do not differ in many respects from the survey findings that we consider below.

The third approach, which relies on market data, has had limited success thus far for measuring expected inflation.[4] One interesting source of data is the futures contract based on the CPI that was traded on the Coffee, Sugar & Cocoa Exchange. Traders in this market essentially bet on the value of the CPI in future periods. Then these traders win or lose money depending on the value that the CPI actually takes later on. By looking at the current bets, we can infer traders' expectations of future changes in the price level. For example, in February 1986, people anticipated an inflation rate of 4.5% for the remainder of 1986, 7.3% for 1987, and 8.1% for 1988. However, by June 1986, the expected inflation rates had fallen to 4.4% for 1987 and 6.6% for 1988. (Note that the actual inflation rates—far below expectations as revealed by the CPI futures market—were 0.6% for 1986, 3.7% for 1987, and 4.7% for 1988.) Unfortunately, it is impossible to bring these data up to date because insufficient trader interest has prevented this market from operating.

Let's return now to the first approach, which uses survey data to measure expected inflation. Joseph Livingston, a Philadelphia journalist, began in 1946 to survey about 50 economists (fewer in the early years of the sample) for their forecasts of the CPI 6 to 12 months in the future. The variable denoted π_t^e in Table 7.3 is the average of the two 6-month-ahead forecasts for each year, when expressed as the implied prediction for the annual rate of inflation.[5] The last column in Table 7.3 shows the corresponding value of the expected real interest rate, $r_t^e = R_t - \pi_t^e$.

Interest Rates and Expected Inflation in the Post–World War II Period One point to notice in Table 7.3 is that the nominal interest rate rose dramatically in the post–World War II period. This rate increased from 1% per year in 1948 to about 3% in the early 1960s, 5 to 6% in the late 1960s, 10% in 1979, and 14% in 1981, but then fell to 6% in 1987–88. The increase was not steady; the interest rate declined from 3.3% in 1957 to 1.8% in 1958, from 6.5% in 1970 to 4.1% in 1972, from 7.9% in 1974 to 5.0% in 1976, and from 14.0% in 1981 to 5.8% in 1987. Further, despite the appearance of a generally upward drift in interest rates, it would not have been easy to forecast this "trend." In any event, someone who foresaw this pattern could have made a fortune by speculating on bond prices.

Figure 7.3 plots the data from Table 7.3 on the nominal interest rate, R_t, the expected inflation rate, π_t^e, and the expected real interest rate, r_t^e. A striking feature of the graph is the tendency for the nominal interest rate and the expected inflation rate to move together. Especially from the early 1950s until 1980, expected inflation increased roughly in parallel with the nominal interest rate. The same is true for actual inflation, although it showed more fluctuation from year to year. In the

---

[4]Eugene Fama (1975) suggested that nominal interest rates were good measures of expected inflation. But his estimated relationships broke down after the early 1970s. For some discussion of this topic, see Charles Nelson and William Schwert (1977).

[5]For a discussion of the Livingston survey, see John Carlson (1977).

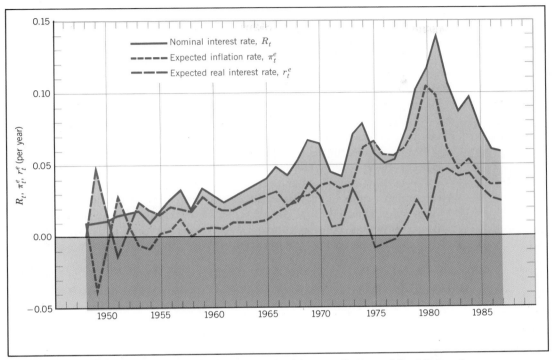

FIGURE 7.3 *Behavior of the Inflation Rate, Nominal Interest Rate, and Real Interest Rate in the United States*
The expected inflation rate and the nominal interest rate rose over much of the post–World War II period but fell after 1981. Expected real interest rates were unusually high from 1981 to 1984.

subsequent analysis (in Chapter 8), we shall want to understand why nominal interest rates and inflation rates tend to move together on roughly a one-to-one basis.

The behavior of expected real interest rates differs markedly from that of nominal rates. Since expected inflation and nominal interest rates moved together nearly one-for-one, there was no regular pattern for expected real interest rates, r_t^e. For example, from 1948 to 1964 the average value of r_t^e was 1.8%, while that from 1965 to 1980 was 1.7%.

From 1981 to 1988 the average value of r_t^e was 3.5%, or 1.7 percentage points above the average from 1948 to 1980. The rate fell, however, from above 4% from 1981 to 1984 to an average of 2.4% from 1986 to 1988. This value is only 0.6 percentage point above the average from 1948 to 1980.

Another fact to note from Table 7.3 is that deviations of actual from expected inflation, $\pi_t - \pi_t^e$, explain some of the behavior of actual real interest rates, r_t. Remember that, for a given value of r_t^e, the inflation surprise, $\pi_t - \pi_t^e$, reduces r_t one-to-one.

As an example, surprise inflation—where $\pi_t > \pi_t^e$—accounts for some of the smallest real interest rates. In 1950, the inflation rate of 8.0%—as compared to the expected rate of -0.2%—was a surprise associated with the start of the Korean War. Therefore, the real interest rate of -6.8% was well below the anticipated rate

(1.4%). Similarly, for 1973–74, the inflation rates of 9.5% and 11.3%—as compared to expectations of 3.6% and 6.2%—were surprises related to the first oil crisis. Thus, the real interest rates, -2.5% and -3.4%, were again well below expectations.

In a longer-run context, the average of the Livingston survey's measure of expected inflation from 1948 to 1980 was 2.4%, as compared to an average for actual inflation of 3.7%. Correspondingly, the average expected real interest rate, r_t^e, of 1.8% was well above the average of the actual rate, r_t, of 0.5%. In other words, the persisting tendency—through 1980—to underpredict inflation is a partial explanation for why r_t averaged only slightly above zero.[6]

Finally, to use inflation surprises to explain high real interest rates, we have to search for unexpectedly low inflation. Mainly we find this pattern in the period from 1981 to 1986. The actual inflation rates for 1981, 1982, and 1984 were each about 2 percentage points below the expected values, while the actual for 1986 was about 3 percentage points below the expected. For this reason, the average of r_t from 1981 to 1986 was 5.6%, as compared to an average for r_t^e of 3.8%. In other words, unexpectedly low inflation accounts for 1.8 percentage points of the high average for r_t from 1981 to 1986.

INDEXED BONDS IN THE UNITED KINGDOM

We mentioned before that indexed bonds adjust their nominal payments to provide a known real interest rate. Therefore we do not have to measure expected inflation to compute expected real interest rates (which equal the actual rates in this case). Although indexed bonds do not exist currently in the United States,[7] it is worthwhile to study the British experience.

The British government in March 1981 began to issue marketable bonds ("gilts") that linked the nominal interest payments and principal to a broad index of retail

---

[6]Conceivably the chronic tendency to underpredict inflation means that the respondents to the Livingston survey were irrational. But this assessment depends heavily on hindsight. In fact, as we mentioned in Chapter 1 and showed in Table 7.2, the high average inflation of the post–World War II period was a dramatic departure from the U.S. history during peacetime. Statistical models that forecast a lot better than the Livingston survey might not have been used by people who had access only to historical data. For a discussion of the rationality of the Livingston survey, see John Carlson (1977) and John Caskey (1985).

[7]The famous economist, Irving Fisher, had his company, Cardex Rand, issue an indexed bond in the 1920s, but it was not very popular.

TABLE 7.4 *Real Interest Rates on Indexed Bonds in the United Kingdom*

Period	Real Interest Rate[a] (%)
1981 (April–December)	2.4
1982	2.8
1983	2.9
1984	3.3
1985	3.3
1986	3.5
1987	3.7
1988	3.8

Source: For 1981–83, Buckmaster & Moore, *Index-Linked Gilt Book*, May 1985; for 1984–88 Bank of England.

[a]The rate applies to bonds with roughly a 25-year maturity. From April 1981 to March 1982, the values are estimated from the yield on bonds due in 1996.

prices.[8] Table 7.4 shows that real interest rates on British indexed bonds rose from 2.4% in 1981 to 3.3% in 1984–85 and 3.8% in 1988. From 1982 to 1988 the average value of 3.3% coincides with the average for expected real interest rates, r_t^e, in the United States (see Table 7.3). However, the British real yields were lower in the earlier part of the period (3.1% for Britain versus 4.1% for the United States from 1982 to 1985) and higher in the later part (3.7% versus 2.3% from 1986 to 1988).

Since there are participants in the financial markets who can move readily between U.K. indexed bonds and U.S. nominal bonds, we would anticipate that the expected real interest rates on these assets would be similar. Otherwise, some people would switch to the bond that promised the higher real yield. This process of switching would continue until the prices of the bonds adjusted to keep the expected real interest rates close to each other.[9] In any event, the data shown in Table 7.4 give us another measure of expected real interest rates in the 1980s.

[8]Because the index linking involves a lag of eight months, the real yield varies somewhat with actual inflation. But as a first approximation, we can treat the real interest rate as known in advance.

[9]There are some elements that would allow the real interest rate on the British government's indexed bonds to differ from the expected real interest rate on U.S. government bonds. First, the returns on U.S. bonds are riskier because of the uncertainty of inflation. Second, the British bonds have a more favorable tax treatment because only the earnings corresponding to the real interest rate are taxable. Third, the British bonds are tied to an index of British prices, which may behave differently from U.S. prices. Finally, the debt studied in Table 7.4 has a maturity of about 25 years, whereas the U.S. Treasury bills considered in Table 7.3 have a maturity of 3 months.

INTEREST RATES ON MONEY

We have discussed the nominal and real interest rates on bonds. But the same analysis applies to money once we specify that the nominal interest rate on money is zero rather than R_t. Recall that the real interest rate on any asset equals the nominal rate less the rate of inflation, π_t. Therefore, for bonds, the real rate is $r_t = R_t - \pi_t$. Since money (currency) has a nominal interest rate of zero, the real interest rate is $-\pi_t$. Positive inflation means that the purchasing power of money erodes over time.

As with bonds, we can distinguish the expected real interest rate on money from the actual rate. The expected real interest rate on money is the negative of the expected inflation rate, $-\pi_t^e$. Given the persistent increase in U.S. inflation rates over the post–World War II period, as shown in Table 7.3, it follows that the expected real interest rate on money is much lower than it used to be.

Remember that the money in our model is like currency, which pays a zero nominal interest rate. Recently most forms of checkable deposits have started to pay interest. For these types of "moneys," we would calculate the real interest rate just as we do for bonds. That is, the real rate on these deposits equals the nominal interest rate less the rate of inflation.

SUMMARY

We began by examining data on monetary growth and inflation across countries and over time for the United States. These data suggest that variations in monetary growth account for a good deal of the variations in inflation rates.

The real interest rate on bonds, r_t, equals the nominal rate, R_t, less the inflation rate, π_t. If a bond specifies the nominal interest rate in advance, the expected real interest rate, r_t^e, depends inversely on the expected inflation rate, π_t^e. We examined the U.S. data since World War II on U.S. Treasury bills and on the Livingston survey of inflationary expectations. Until the early 1980s the nominal interest rate and the expected rate of inflation rose dramatically and by roughly equal amounts. From 1981 to 1987 the nominal interest rate and the expected inflation rate declined substantially. The expected real interest rate averaged 1.8% from 1948 to 1980, rose to above 4% from 1981 to 1984, and then fell to 2.3% from 1986 to 1988.

IMPORTANT TERMS AND CONCEPTS

inflation

rate of monetary growth

deflation

expectation of inflation

unexpected inflation

nominal interest rate

real interest rate

expected real interest rate

indexation

inflation correction

rational expectations

QUESTIONS AND PROBLEMS

Mainly for Review

7.1 Monetarists hold that changes in the price level are primarily the results of changes in the quantity of money. Can this conclusion be based solely on theoretical reasoning? Explain.

7.2 Define the real interest rate. Why does it differ from the nominal interest rate in the presence of inflation?

7.3 Why does the actual real interest rate generally differ from the expected rate? How does this relation depend on whether bonds prescribe the nominal interest rate or the real interest rate?

7.4 Consider the Livingston survey of inflationary expectations. What are the pluses and minuses of using this type of information to measure expected rates of inflation?

PROBLEMS FOR DISCUSSION

7.5 *Monetary Growth and Inflation*
Suppose that the money-demand function takes the form

$$\left(\frac{M}{P}\right)^d = L(Y, \; R, \ldots) = Y \cdot H(R),$$
$$(+)(-)$$

where H is some function. This form says that an increase in real output by, say, 10% raises the real demand for money by 10%.

a. Is it possible that this form of the demand for money accords with our theory of money demand from Chapter 4?

b. Consider the relation across countries between the average growth rates of money and prices. If the functional form shown above for money demand applies, how does the average growth rate of real output affect the relation between the growth rates of money and prices?

c. What is the relation between the average growth rates of money and prices for a country where the nominal interest rate, R, has increased?

d. If the expected real interest rate is constant, what is the relation between the average growth rates of money and prices for a country where the expected inflation rate, π^e, has increased? How does this result apply to countries for which we do not observe the nominal interest rate, R, on an organized credit market?

7.6 *Statistical Relations between Monetary Growth and Inflation (optional)*
Students who have studied econometrics and who have access to a statistical package on a computer should do the following exercise.

a. Use the data in Table 7.1 to run a regression of the inflation rate, ΔP, on a constant and the growth rate of money, ΔM. What is the estimated coefficient on money growth, and how should we interpret it? What is the meaning of the constant term?

b. Run a regression of the growth rate of real money balances, $\Delta M - \Delta P$, on the growth rate of real output, ΔY, and a constant. Interpret the coefficient on ΔY.

c. Suppose that we add the variable, ΔY, to the regression run in part a. What is the estimated coefficient on ΔY, and how should it be interpreted?

7.7 *Prepayments of Mortgages and Callability of Bonds*

Mortgages typically allow the borrower to make early payments of principal, which are called *prepayments*. Sometimes the mortgage contract specifies a penalty for prepayments, while sometimes there is no penalty. In recent years many state governments have prohibited prepayment penalties on mortgages. (However, there are generally some fees for negotiating a new mortgage.) Similarly, most long-term bonds—although not those of the U.S. government—allow the issuer to prepay the principal after a prescribed date and with a specified penalty. When the bond issuer exercises this option to prepay, he or she is said to "call" the bond. Bonds that allow this option are said to be *callable* or to have a *call provision*.

a. When would a borrower want to prepay (or call) his or her mortgage or bond? Would we see more prepayments when nominal interest rates had unexpectedly increased or decreased?

b. From the late 1970s until 1982, banks and savings and loans were especially eager for their customers to prepay their mortgages. Why was this the case?

c. Suppose that there is an increase in the year-to-year fluctuations of nominal interest rates. (These fluctuations were particularly great from the mid-1970s through the early 1980s.) From the standpoint of a borrower, how does this change affect the value of having a prepayment option—that is, callability—in his or her mortgage or bond?

7.8 *Rational Expectations and Measures of Expected Inflation*

How would the hypothesis of rational expectations help us to measure inflationary expectations? What seem to be the pluses and minuses of this approach?

7.9 *Indexed Bonds*

Consider a bond that costs $1000. Suppose that the bond pays a year later the principal of $1000 plus interest of $100.

a. What is the nominal interest rate on the bond? What are the actual and expected real interest rates? Why is the nominal rate known, but the real rate uncertain?

Suppose that someone issues an indexed bond, which adjusts the payments to compensate for inflation. For example, assume that the total amount paid a year later is the quantity $1100 \cdot (1 + \pi)$, where π is the inflation rate over the year.

b. What is the real interest rate on the indexed bond? Why is the real rate known but the nominal rate uncertain?

c. Can you think of other types of indexed bonds? Are the real and nominal interest rates both uncertain in some cases?

CHAPTER 8

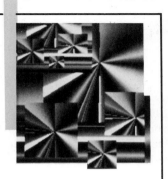

MONEY, INFLATION, AND INTEREST RATES IN THE MARKET CLEARING MODEL

n this chapter, we use the market-clearing model to study inflation and nominal interest rates. For the main analysis we return to the setting from Chapter 5 that does not deal explicitly with a labor market or firms. As we saw in Chapter 6, this simplification will be satisfactory for most purposes. The basic approach will be to specify a given time path of the money stock, M_t. Then we figure out what time path of the price level, P_t—hence, of the inflation rate, π_t—and of the nominal and real interest rates, R_t and r_t, satisfy the conditions for general market clearing.

We will focus on the consequences of different rates of anticipated inflation and monetary growth. Even when the inflation rate, π_t, varies over time, we assume that people forecast these changes accurately. Put another way, people have **perfect foresight** about future price levels, so that there is always equality between the actual and expected inflation rates, $\pi_t = \pi_t^e$. Accordingly, if people know the nominal interest rate, R_t, there is also equality between actual and expected real interest rates, $r_t = r_t^e$.

The analysis is limited since it does not address unanticipated inflation and monetary growth. (We shall explore these matters later.) But it is useful to study anticipated inflation as a separate topic. In particular, the changes in anticipated inflation explain the principal longer-term movements in U.S. nominal interest rates since World War II.

INCORPORATION OF INFLATION AND MONETARY GROWTH INTO THE MODEL

We want to incorporate into the model the various new elements from Chapter 7. These include inflation and the distinction between real and nominal interest rates. Also, to analyze the link between monetary growth and inflation, we have to extend the model to allow for changes in the stock of money.

For simplicity, we begin with situations where the nominal interest rate, R, and the inflation rate, π, are constant over time. Therefore, the real interest rate, $r = R - \pi$, is also constant. Since we assumed equality between actual and expected inflation, $\pi = \pi^e$, there is also equality between actual and expected real interest rates, $r = r^e$.

MONETARY GROWTH AND TRANSFER PAYMENTS

We choose the simplest possible way to introduce monetary growth into the model: We assume that new money shows up as transfers from the government to households. (Later we shall see that the main results still hold for other, more realistic methods of introducing new money into the economy.)

Denote by v_t the dollar amount of transfer that a household receives during period t. This amount need not be the same for everyone. The government finances the total of transfers, V_t, by printing and distributing new money. Therefore, the change in the aggregate quantity of money, $M_t - M_{t-1}$, equals the aggregate amount of transfers:

$$V_t = M_t - M_{t-1}. \tag{8.1}$$

Equation 8.1 is a simple version of a **governmental budget constraint.** The left side is total government expenditures, all of which take the form of transfers at this point. The right side shows government revenues. At present, this revenue derives solely from the printing of new paper money.

We can think of transfer payments as arising via a "helicopter drop" of cash.[1] Our public officials effectively stuff a helicopter full of paper currency and fly around dropping money randomly over the countryside. The transfer payments occur when people pick up the money. Despite the unrealistic flavor of this story, the only important aspect of it is that each person's transfer is independent of his or her level of income, previous amount of money holdings, and so on. Economists refer to these kinds of transfers as **lump-sum transfers,** which means that the amount someone receives is independent of his or her level of work effort, holdings of money, or other activities. Since the transfers are lump sum, an individual understands that changes in his or her holdings of money, m_t and m_{t-1}, have no impact on the size of his or her transfer, v_t.[2]

---

[1] I think that the original source of this popular story is Milton Friedman (1969, pp. 4–5).

[2] The discussion assumes positive transfers, although we could deal with negative ones. Negative transfers are taxes, which can also be lump sum—that is, independent of individuals' levels of income, amount of money holdings, and so on. While we view transfers as financed by a helicopter drop of cash, we can view taxes as collected by a giant vacuum cleaner.

We have to modify households' budget constraints to include the transfer payments. Each household's budget constraint for period t is

$$P_t y_t + b_{t-1}(1 + R) + m_{t-1} + v_t = P_t c_t + b_t + m_t. \tag{8.2}$$

As before, the sources of funds on the left side include the dollar receipts from the commodity market, $P_t y_t$, plus the values of the bonds and money that were held last period, $b_{t-1}(1 + R) + m_{t-1}$. The new element is the dollar amount of transfer, v_t, which is an additional source of funds for a household. The right side of equation 8.2 contains the same uses of funds as before. These are the nominal purchases of commodities, $P_t c_t$, plus this period's holdings of bonds and money, $b_t + m_t$. Notice that we date the price level, P_t, since it will no longer be constant over time. Since we assume that the nominal interest rate, R, is constant, we do not have to date it.

BUDGET CONSTRAINTS OVER AN INFINITE HORIZON

We have to make some adjustments to incorporate inflation into households' budget constraints over an infinite horizon. Let's put aside the various monetary terms, which include the initial stock of real money balances, the transfers received from the government, and the interest foregone by holding money. (The appendix to this chapter shows that this omission is satisfactory.) Then, when written in terms of nominal present values, the budget constraint over an infinite horizon looks basically like it did before. Since we assume that the nominal interest rate R is constant, the condition is

$$P_1 y_1 + \frac{P_2 y_2}{(1 + R)} + \frac{P_3 y_3}{(1 + R)^2} + \cdots + b_0(1 + R)$$
$$= P_1 c_1 + \frac{P_2 c_2}{(1 + R)} + \frac{P_3 c_3}{(1 + R)^2} + \cdots. \tag{8.3}$$

The only new element in equation 8.3 is the dating of the price level.

Recall that we assume a constant rate of inflation, π. Therefore the price levels for any two adjacent periods satisfy the condition, $P_t = (1 + \pi)P_{t-1}$. We can use this condition repeatedly to express each future level of prices in terms of the current price, P_1, and the constant inflation rate π. Then we get the sequence

$$P_2 = (1 + \pi)P_1,$$
$$P_3 = (1 + \pi)^2 P_1,$$
$$\vdots$$

If we substitute these results into the budget constraint from equation 8.3, we get the revised condition

$$P_1 \left[y_1 + y_2 \cdot \frac{(1 + \pi)}{(1 + R)} + y_3 \cdot \frac{(1 + \pi)^2}{(1 + R)^2} + \cdots \right] + b_0(1 + R)$$
$$= P_1 \left[c_1 + c_2 \cdot \frac{(1 + \pi)}{(1 + R)} + c_3 \cdot \frac{(1 + \pi)^2}{(1 + R)^2} + \cdots \right]. \tag{8.4}$$

Notice that the next period's real income and spending, y_2 and c_2, enter multiplicatively with the factor $(1 + \pi)/(1 + R)$. But recall from Chapter 7 that the relation between real and nominal interest rates is $(1 + r) = (1 + R)/(1 + \pi)$. Therefore, the term in equation 8.4, $(1 + \pi)/(1 + R)$, is equal to $1/(1 + r)$. Hence, to express the next period's real income and spending, y_2 and c_2, as present values, we divide by the discount factor, $1 + r$. This result makes sense since the real interest rate tells people how they can exchange goods of one period for those of another. In particular, it is the *real* interest rate, rather than the *nominal* rate, that matters here.

The same idea applies for any future period. For example, the real income and spending for period 3, y_3 and c_3, enter into equation 8.4 as a multiple of the factor $(1 + \pi)^2/(1 + R)^2$, which equals $1/(1 + r)^2$. If we make all these substitutions into equation 8.4—and also divide through by the current price level, P_1—we end up with a simplified form of the budget constraint:

$$y_1 + \frac{y_2}{(1 + r)} + \frac{y_3}{(1 + r)^2} + \cdots + \frac{b_0(1 + R)}{P_1}$$

$$= c_1 + \frac{c_2}{(1 + r)} + \frac{c_3}{(1 + r)^2} + \cdots. \tag{8.5}$$

(The nominal interest rate appears in the term $b_0(1 + R)$ because this term is the nominal value of the bonds carried over to period 1.)

Equation 8.5 is the budget constraint in real terms over an infinite horizon. The new element is that the real interest rate, r, appears instead of the nominal rate, R, in the various discount factors.

INTERTEMPORAL-SUBSTITUTION EFFECTS

We discussed before how the interest rate has intertemporal-substitution effects on consumption, leisure, and saving. These effects involve the relative costs of taking consumption or leisure at one date rather than another. In making these comparisons an individual wants to know, for example, how much extra consumption he or she can get next period by reducing consumption this period. As we worked out before, an individual can save and thus transform each unit of consumption foregone this period into $1 + r$ units of added consumption for the next period. An increase in the real interest rate, r, motivates people to reduce current consumption and leisure to raise future consumption and leisure. In other words, a higher r motivates people to save more today. The important point is that the real interest rate matters here rather than the nominal rate. Thus, our previous discussions of intertemporal-substitution effects remain valid as long as we replace the nominal interest rate by the real rate.

Recall that in this chapter we treat the real interest rate, r, as a known quantity. More generally, the expected real interest rate, $r^e = R - \pi^e$, is what matters for intertemporal-substitution effects. No one shifts their planned time paths of consumption and leisure, and hence their saving, unless they anticipate that the real interest rate will be either higher or lower. For intertemporal-substitution effects to arise, there must be a change in the nominal interest rate, R, relative to the expected rate of inflation, π^e.

INTEREST RATES AND THE DEMAND FOR MONEY

Recall that the demand for money involves a trade-off between transaction costs and interest foregone. Further, the interest foregone depends on the differential between the interest rate on bonds and that on money. Since the nominal interest rate on money is zero, this differential equals the *nominal* interest rate, R (and not the *real* interest rate, r). It follows that the demand-for-money function involves the nominal interest rate, R. Therefore, as in our previous analysis that neglected inflation, the function for the aggregate real demand for money takes the form

$$\left(\frac{M_t}{P_t}\right)^d = \underset{(+)\ (-)}{L(Y_t,\ R, \cdots)}.\tag{8.6}$$

Notice an important point. It is the (expected) real interest rate, r, that exerts intertemporal-substitution effects on consumption and work. But it is the nominal interest rate, R, that influences the real demand for money.

MARKET-CLEARING CONDITIONS

We know from Chapter 5 how to express the conditions for general market clearing. First, the aggregate supply of goods, Y_t^s, equals the demand, C_t^d. Here we write this condition as

$$\underset{(+)}{Y^s(r_t, \cdots)} = \underset{(-)}{C^d(r_t, \cdots)}.\tag{8.7}$$

Equation 8.7 shows the intertemporal-substitution effects from the real interest rate, r_t. As usual, this effect is positive on the supply of goods for period t and negative on the demand. The omitted terms, denoted by . . . , include various aspects of the production function.

Second, we have the condition that all money be willingly held. We can write this condition for period t as

$$M_t = P_t \cdot \underset{(+)\ (-)}{L(Y_t,\ R_t, \cdots)}.\tag{8.8}$$

On the left is the actual quantity of money. On the right is the nominal demand for money, which depends positively on the price level, P_t, and aggregate output, Y_t, and negatively on the nominal interest rate, R_t. Any other factors that influence money demand, such as transaction costs, are denoted by the expression . . . in equation 8.8. Here, we assume that these factors do not change over time.

THE SUPERNEUTRALITY OF MONEY

Before we explore the details of the link between monetary behavior and inflation, we can already see an important property from the condition for clearing the commodity market. Consider the underlying real factors in the model, which include the forms of production functions, population, and the preferences of households. These elements enter into the demand and supply of commodities through the omitted terms, which we denote by . . . in equation 8.7. For given values of these elements, equation 8.7 determines the real interest rate, r_t, and the level of aggregate output, $Y_t = C_t$, at each date. If the underlying real elements do not change over time, the market-clearing values of the real interest rate and output are constants.

The important point is that the real interest rate and output are determined independently of the path of money. Although changes in money will end up affecting the paths of the price level and the nominal interest rate, these monetary changes will not affect at least some of the real variables in the model. If all real variables are invariant with the behavior of money, economists say that money is **superneutral.** Note that this term suggests an extension of another concept, the neutrality of money, which we discussed before. Neutrality of money means that once-and-for-all changes in the quantity of money affect nominal variables but not real variables. Superneutrality extends this idea from one-time changes in the stock of money to arbitrary variations in the entire path of money.

We know from before that money is neutral in the model. One point we want to consider in this chapter is whether money is superneutral. To the extent that money is not superneutral, we shall find some effects of money and inflation on real variables.

MONETARY GROWTH, INFLATION, AND THE NOMINAL INTEREST RATE

We want now to examine the details of the linkages among monetary growth, inflation, and the nominal interest rate. We carry out this analysis for given values of the real interest rate, r, and output, Y. By holding these variables fixed, we are making two types of assumptions. First, we use the property that anticipated variations in money and prices do not affect the real interest rate and output. Second, we assume that no other shifts occur over time to the functions for aggregate commodity demand or supply. Generally these types of changes could lead to movements in the real interest rate and output.

More specifically, the analysis neglects any systematic growth of output. Recall from Chapter 7 that countries with higher average growth rates of output tend to have less inflation for a given average growth rate of money. Although it is not hard to incorporate this feature into the analysis, we assume that output is constant to bring out the major points in the easiest possible way.

We can illustrate the main results by assuming a constant rate of monetary growth. In this case we have

$$M_t = (1 + \mu)M_{t-1}, \tag{8.9}$$

where μ (the Greek letter mu) is the monetary growth rate. Assume that equation 8.9 governs the behavior of money from the current date, $t = 1$, into the indefinite future.

We want to calculate the price level at each date, given that money grows at a constant rate. Generally the model determines the time path of prices from the market-clearing conditions that we mentioned before. But we already determined the real interest rate and output to equate aggregate commodity supply and demand in equation 8.7. Further, if the supply and demand functions do not shift over time, the real interest rate, r, and output, Y, are constants. Given these results, the price level, P_t, must satisfy the condition that money be willingly held. Writing this condition in real terms, we have

$$\frac{M_t}{P_t} = L(Y, \quad R_t, \quad \cdots). \tag{8.10}$$
$$\quad\quad (+)(-)$$

In Chapter 5 we found that once-and-for-all increases in the quantity of money raised the price level in the same proportion. Therefore, it is reasonable to consider the possibility that the price level, P_t, grows at the same rate as the money stock, M_t. In this case the inflation rate, π, is constant and equal to the rate of monetary growth, μ. So let's make this guess and see whether it accords with the condition from equation 8.10 that all money be willingly held.

If money and prices grow at the same rate, the ratio of these two, which is the level of real money balances, M_t/P_t, does not change over time. Therefore, the amount of real money, which appears on the left side of equation 8.10, is constant.

Recall that the nominal interest rate, R_t, equals the quantity $r_t + \pi_t$. But we already know that the real interest rate is constant. Therefore, if the inflation rate is constant, the nominal interest rate is also constant. This result means that the real demand for money, $L(\cdot)$, which appears on the right side of equation 8.10, is constant. (Remember that output, Y, does not change over time.)

Since real money balances and the real amount of money demanded are each constant, we have only to be sure that the two constants are the same. This condition holds if we determine the current price level, P_1, to equate the amount of real money balances, M_1/P_1, to the real quantity demanded, $L(\cdot)$. Then, since actual and desired real money do not vary over time, we can be sure that all money will be willingly held at each date. That is, equation 8.10 holds in every period.

We have now verified that our guess—where prices grow at the same rate as money—satisfies the conditions for general market clearing. Therefore, this path of prices is the one that will prevail. To summarize, the results are as follows:

- Prices grow at the same rate as the money stock—that is, $\pi = \mu$.
- Aggregate real money balances, M_t/P_t, are constant.
- The nominal interest rate, R, is constant and equal to $r + \pi$.

▪ The aggregate demand for real balances, $L(Y, R, \ldots)$, is constant.

▪ The current price level, P_1, equates the quantity of real money balances, M_1/P_1, to the real amount demanded, $L(Y, R)$.

The results imply that the growth rate of money, μ, shows up one-for-one in the inflation rate, π, and in the nominal interest rate, $R = r + \pi$. But recall that a higher nominal interest rate means a lower level of real money demanded. Therefore, a higher growth rate of money corresponds to a lower level of aggregate real money balances, M_t/P_t.

A SHIFT IN THE MONETARY GROWTH RATE

We can better understand the results by studying a change in the monetary growth rate. Suppose that the money stock has been growing for a long time at the constant rate, μ. Further, assume that everyone expects this behavior to persist indefinitely. Hence, the inflation rate is the constant, $\pi = \mu$, and the nominal interest rate is given by

$$R = r + \pi = r + \mu.$$

We show this initial situation on the left side of Figure 8.1.

Consider how the quantity of money, M_t, behaves over time. We have the sequence

$$M_1 = (1 + \mu)M_0$$

$$M_2 = (1 + \mu)M_1 = (1 + \mu)^2 M_0$$

$$\vdots$$

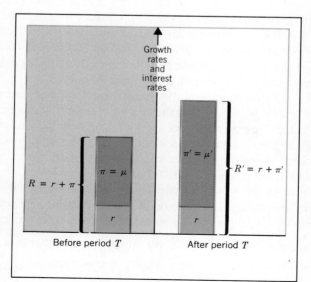

FIGURE 8.1 *Growth Rates of Money and Prices and Levels of Interest Rates: Effects of an Increase in the Monetary Growth Rate*

Before period T, *the growth rate of money is* μ. *Hence, the left side of the figure shows that the inflation rate is* π = μ, *and the nominal interest rate is* R = r + π = r + μ. *After period* T, *the growth rate of money is the higher value* μ'. *Consequently, the new inflation rate is* π' = μ', *and the new nominal interest rate is* R' = r + π' = r + μ'.

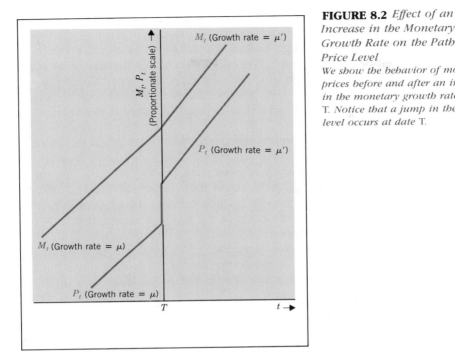

FIGURE 8.2 *Effect of an Increase in the Monetary Growth Rate on the Path of the Price Level*
We show the behavior of money and prices before and after an increase in the monetary growth rate at date T. Notice that a jump in the price level occurs at date T.

Therefore, for any period t, the quantity of money is given by

$$M_t = (1 + \mu)^t M_0. \tag{8.11}$$

We shall find it convenient to graph the quantity of money, M_t, on a proportionate or logarithmic scale. Then each unit on the vertical axis corresponds to an equal proportional change in a variable—say, a 1% change in the stock of money. Since money grows at the constant proportionate rate μ, the graph of money versus time is a straight line on a proportionate scale. Further, the slope of the line equals the growth rate, μ. Accordingly, on the left side of Figure 8.2, the quantity of money, M_t, is a straight line with slope μ.[3]

We found before that the price level grows also at the constant rate, $\pi = \mu$—that is,

$$P_t = (1 + \pi)^t P_0 = (1 + \mu)^t P_0. \tag{8.12}$$

Therefore, the graph of the price level, P_t, on the left side of Figure 8.2 is also a straight line with slope μ. This line parallels the one for the stock of money, M_t.

Assume now that the growth rate of money rises from μ to μ' at some date T. Here, we think of this change as a surprise—that is, before date T, no one anticipated the acceleration of money. But once it happens, we assume that everyone expects

---

[3]We ignore the discrete length of periods in this graph. In effect, we treat this length as being extremely brief.

the new monetary growth rate, μ', to persist indefinitely. Hence, we study here the consequences of a once-and-for-all increase in the rate of monetary expansion.

After the change in the monetary growth rate, the economy is in the same type of situation as before. The only difference is that the growth rate of money is μ' rather than μ. Therefore, we show on the right side of Figure 8.1 that the new inflation rate is $\pi' = \mu'$. Also, we know that the change in monetary behavior does not affect the real interest rate, which remains at the value r. Therefore, the new nominal interest rate is $R' = r + \pi' = r + \mu'$. In other words, the inflation rate and the nominal interest rate each rise by as much as the increase in the monetary growth rate.

We show the levels of money and prices after date T on the right side of Figure 8.2. Because the growth rate of money rises after date T, the line for the money stock, M_t, has the slope μ', which exceeds the original slope. Note, however, that there is no immediate jump in the stock of money at date T; money just starts to grow faster at this point.

Since prices grow at the rate $\pi' = \mu'$ after date T, we again show the line for the price level, P_t, as parallel to that for the money stock. But notice an important complication in the graph of P_t in Figure 8.2: There is a jump in P_t at date T. Let's see why this jump occurs.

The acceleration of money at date T raises the nominal interest rate from the value $R = r + \mu$ to the higher value $R' = r + \mu'$. Recall that an increase in the nominal interest rate reduces the real demand for money. Hence, the existing amount of money will be willingly held at date T only if the actual real balances, M_T/P_T, fall by as much as the real demand. But there is no sudden change in the nominal quantity of money at date T—only an increase in the rate of growth. Therefore, real balances can fall to equal the smaller amount demanded only if there is an upward jump in the price level at date T.

We can say something about the size of the jump in the price level. The proportionate rise in the price level equals the proportionate fall in real money balances, which equals the proportionate decline in the real demand for money. Further, the magnitude of the decline in money demand depends on two things: first, the change in the nominal interest rate, which is $\mu' - \mu$, and second, the sensitivity of real money demanded to changes in the nominal interest rate. Therefore, the jump in the price level is greater the larger is the acceleration of money, $\mu' - \mu$, and the greater is the sensitivity of money demand to changes in the nominal interest rate.

The Increase in the Nominal Interest Rate   Let's think about why the acceleration of money at date T leads to a rise in the nominal interest rate. At date T, people learn that henceforth the government will pursue a more expansionary monetary policy. They know also that this policy means a rate of inflation, $\pi' = \mu'$, which exceeds the initial rate, $\pi = \mu$. Consider what the higher expected rate of inflation does at date T in the credit market. Borrowers now regard the old nominal interest rate, R, as a better deal. That is because the real interest rate that they must pay has fallen from the value $R - \mu$ to a lower value, $R - \mu'$. Hence, if the nominal interest rate did not change, borrowers would raise their demand for loans. On the other side, lenders see that their real rate of return has deteriorated. Therefore, if the nominal interest rate did not change, lenders would decrease their supply of loans. A balance between the demand and supply for loans prevails—that is, the credit market clears—only if the nominal interest rate rises.

The new nominal interest rate, R', exceeds the old one, R, by the amount of the increase in the inflation rate, $\mu' - \mu$. Lenders view this rise in the nominal rate as just sufficient to compensate them for the loss of purchasing power over time because of the higher inflation rate. Similarly, borrowers are willing to pay the higher nominal interest rate because they expect to repay their loans with more heavily deflated dollars. In other words, the increase in the nominal interest rate incorporates fully the change in expected inflation. Thereby, the acceleration of money and prices does not change the real interest rate, r.

The Jump in the Price Level   Consider now the intuition for why the price level jumps upward at date T. The sudden prospect of higher inflation and the consequent rise in the nominal interest rate lead to a fall in the real demand for money at date T. If the price level did not adjust, people's actual real balances, M_T/P_T, would exceed their desired amount. Consequently, everyone would attempt to spend their excess money by buying either goods or bonds. The rise in the demand for goods puts upward pressure on the price level, and the economy returns to a position of general market clearing only when the price level rises enough to equate actual and desired real money. This condition is the one that we used to determine the size of the jump in the price level in Figure 8.2.

Wage Rates   If we added a labor market to the model, we would find again that the real wage rate, w/P, and the quantity of employment, N, were independent of money. Therefore, the path of nominal wage rates must parallel the path of prices, which appears in Figure 8.2. This result means that nominal wages grow at the rate μ up to date T and at the higher rate μ' after date T. Further, the nominal wage rate would jump upward at date T.

Summarizing the Results for an Acceleration of Money   Let's summarize the results for a once-and-for-all increase in the growth rate of money (a decrease in the growth rate of money just reverses the signs of all effects):

- There are no changes in the real interest rate, the real wage rate, or the levels of output and employment.
- The inflation rate and the nominal interest rate (and the growth rate of nominal wages) rise by as much as the increase in the growth rate of money.
- The real demand for money and the actual quantity of real money balances decrease.
- The price level jumps upward to equate actual real money balances to the smaller quantity demanded.

Let's use these results to see whether money is superneutral—that is, whether the path of money matters for real variables. Recall that the path of money does not affect the real interest rate, the real wage rate, and the quantities of output and employment. However, because the acceleration of money raises the inflation rate, it also raises the nominal interest rate and thereby lowers the amount of real money demanded. The resulting fall in real money balances is one real effect of the change in monetary behavior. Therefore, money is not quite superneutral in the model.

Underlying the decline in real money demanded is an increase in the transaction costs that people incur to economize on money. These costs absorb resources; therefore, the increase in these costs is an adverse real effect from the increase in monetary growth. Our analysis neglected any effects of transaction costs on house-holds' choices of work effort, consumption, and saving. If we took account of these effects, we would find that an acceleration of money might have some effect on the real interest rate, the real wage rate, and the quantities of output and employment. Therefore, the independence of these real variables from the path of money is only an approximation, which is satisfactory when transaction costs are small.

Remember that the present analysis assumes perfect foresight about future price levels (except for the jump in prices that accompanies the surprise acceleration of money at date T). Hence (except at date T), there is equality between actual and expected inflation and thereby between actual and expected real interest rates. We saw in Chapter 7 that unexpected inflation has important effects on realized real interest rates. If inflation and, hence, future real interest rates are uncertain, there are a variety of real effects that would arise (some of which we shall explore in Chapter 19). At this point we have considered only the effects from anticipated variations in money and prices.

THE DYNAMICS OF INFLATION

Consider again the case where monetary growth rises at date T from the initial value, μ, to the higher value, μ'. Let's think further about the transition from the initial rate of inflation, $\pi = \mu$, to the subsequent rate, $\pi' = \mu'$. Because the nominal interest rate increases, the level of real money balances decreases. For real money to fall, there must be a transition period during which prices rise by proportionately more than money. So far our analysis says that this transition occurs in an instant at date T by an upward jump in the price level. But in the real world there are a number of considerations that stretch out the transition. Here, we introduce some of these features to study some aspects of the dynamics of inflation.

GRADUAL ADJUSTMENT OF THE DEMAND FOR MONEY

Return to the case where people first learn at date T that money will be growing at a higher rate. Recall that the size of the jump in the price level at date T depends on the extent of the fall in real money demanded. Suppose now that people reduce their demand for money only gradually when the nominal interest rate increases.

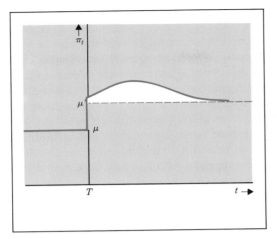

FIGURE 8.3 *Effect of Higher Monetary Growth on Inflation, including Gradual Adjustment of the Demand for Money*
The growth rate of money rises from μ to μ' at date T. The solid line shows that the inflation rate, μ', stays above μ' for awhile but eventually approaches μ'.

Then we may find only a small jump in the price level at date T. Most of the extra upward kick to the price level shows up only gradually as people reduce their real demand for money.

Recall that a person's real demand for money reflects some underlying decisions about the frequency of transactions, financial planning, and so on. If the nominal interest rate rises, it is reasonable that people would take some time to modify these aspects of their behavior. Hence, in the aggregate, the real demand for money would decline gradually in response to an increase in the nominal interest rate.

Slow adjustment in the demand for money effectively spreads out the jump in the price level over a transition interval. When money accelerates at time T, the inflation rate reacts something like the solid line shown in Figure 8.3. The figure shows that the inflation rate, π_t, exceeds the new growth rate of money, μ', over an extended interval.[4] Throughout this period, real money balances fall gradually as the real demand for money declines. Eventually the inflation rate approaches its new long-term value, μ'. Then the quantity of real money again remains constant but at a lower level than initially.

ANTICIPATED CHANGES IN MONETARY GROWTH

Our analysis can deal with situations where the growth rate of money either rises or falls. But so far, we have looked only at cases where the change in actual monetary growth coincides with the change in perceptions about future monetary growth. That is, two things happen at date T in the previous examples. First, money accelerates or decelerates permanently. Second, people first learn at date T that this acceleration or deceleration will occur.

Sometimes people receive information in advance that allows them to forecast increases or decreases in the rate of monetary growth. For example, if the end of

[4]The figure shows that the inflation rate rises after date T and later falls toward the value μ'. The details of this path depend on the precise specification of gradual adjustment in the demand for money.

a war is imminent, people would project a likely decline in the growth rate of money. Alternatively, during an extreme inflation, there may be promises of a change to a stable monetary regime. For instance, toward the end of the post–World War I **hyperinflation** in Germany, people apparently anticipated that a **monetary reform** was coming.[5] It is also possible that political events—such as the outcomes of elections—signal that the government plans to shift to a more or less expansionary monetary policy. For example, William Jennings Bryan campaigned for president in the 1890s on a program of easy money (free coinage of silver). His defeat probably lowered expectations of future monetary growth and inflation; presumably these expectations would have increased if he had been elected. Similarly, it may be that the election of Ronald Reagan, rather than Jimmy Carter, in 1980 lowered expectations of future monetary growth and inflation.

If people forecast an acceleration or deceleration of money, the path of inflation differs from those already discussed. To avoid a good deal of complicated details, the subsequent discussion just sketches the types of effects that arise.

Suppose that people learn currently that an acceleration of money is coming at the future date T. Then they know also that inflation rates and nominal interest rates will be higher in the future. When people know that the cost of holding money will rise after date T, they tend to reduce their demand for money even before date T. Otherwise they will get caught holding money at date T when the big increase in prices occurs. Thus, the expectation of future inflation has a negative effect on people's willingness to hold money today. This reduction in today's demand for money means that today's price level must rise. In other words, although the acceleration of money has not yet occurred, the expectation of the future monetary acceleration leads to a higher current rate of inflation. Finally, since this higher rate of inflation becomes anticipated, the nominal interest rate also rises before the acceleration of money.

The precise path of inflation depends on when people learn about the acceleration of money. But, as mentioned, one general point is that changes in expectations about future money can generate variations in inflation and the nominal interest rate that precede the changes in monetary growth. Thus, although the analysis stresses monetary factors as the source of inflation, significant divergences can arise in the short run between the growth rates of money and prices. Also, these divergences are likely to be important in an environment—such as those present today in the industrialized countries—where a volatile monetary policy induces frequent revisions in people's forecasts of monetary behavior. Such an environment would also be marked by volatility in inflation rates and nominal interest rates.

THE TRANSITION FROM ONE INFLATION RATE TO ANOTHER

Let's stress a basic feature of the results concerning changes from one long-term inflation rate to another. Although jumps in the price level need not occur, an acceleration of money must involve a transition during which prices rise by pro-

---

[5]Robert Flood and Peter Garber (1980) and Laura Lahaye (1985) provide quantitative estimates for these expectations of impending monetary reform.

portionately more than money. This conclusion follows inevitably from the eventual decline in real money balances.

We can turn the results around to deal with the case where money decelerates. Although a downward jump in the price level need not occur, we find that the transition must involve a period where prices grow by proportionately less than money. This result holds because the lower nominal interest rate raises the real demand for money.

As an example, suppose that the government reduces monetary growth permanently from 10% per year to 5%. Presumably the objective of this policy is to reduce inflation. Our analysis implies that there is a transition period during which the inflation rate is even less than 5% per year. In fact, there may be deflation—that is, falling prices—for awhile. Thus, when contemplating a monetary policy to end inflation, we have to think about the potential for very low or negative rates of inflation as a temporary side effect.

MONEY AND PRICES DURING THE GERMAN HYPERINFLATION

We can assess some of the theoretical results by examining the data on the post–World War I German hyperinflation. Here, we have something close to a laboratory experiment for studying the consequences of high and variable rates of monetary growth and inflation.[6] Over the period from 1921 to 1923, the rates of inflation ranged from near zero to over 500% per month! Further, the available data suggest that relatively small changes occurred in aggregate real variables, such as total output and employment. Hence aggregate real money demanded would not be affected very much by changes in real income or real spending.

When inflation rates are volatile, it is impossible to predict accurately the real interest rate on loans that prescribe nominal interest rates. Therefore, this type of lending tends to disappear during hyperinflations, such as the one in Germany. For this reason, when analyzing the demand for money during the German hyperinflation, we have no useful measures of the nominal interest rate. In this environment the best indicator of the cost of holding money comes directly from the expected rate of inflation, π^e. This rate tells people how much they lose by holding money rather than consuming or holding a durable good that maintains its value in real terms.

Table 8.1 summarizes the behavior of the monetary growth rate, μ, the inflation

---

[6]Not surprisingly, the topic has fascinated many economists. Two of the more important studies are Costantino Bresciani-Turroni (1937) and Phillip Cagan (1956).

TABLE 8.1 *Monetary Growth, Inflation, and Real Money Balances during the German Hyperinflation*

Period	μ	π	M/P (End of Period) (1913 = 1.0)
	(% per Month)		
2/20– 6/20	5.7	6.0	1.01
6/20–12/20	3.0	1.1	1.13
12/20– 6/21	0.8	0.1	1.18
6/21–12/21	5.5	8.4	0.99
12/21– 6/22	6.5	12.8	0.68
6/22–12/22	29.4	46.7	0.24
12/22– 6/23	40.0	40.0	0.24
6/23–10/23	233	286	0.03
Reform Period			
12/23– 6/24	5.9	−0.6	0.44
6/24–12/24	5.3	1.4	0.56
12/24– 6/25	2.0	1.6	0.57
6/25–12/25	1.2	0.4	0.60

Note: M is an estimate of the total circulation of currency. Until late 1923 the figures refer to total legal tender, most of which consists of notes issued by the Reichsbank. Later, the data include issues of the Rentenbank, private bank notes, and various "emergency moneys." However, especially in late 1923, many unofficial emergency currencies, as well as circulating foreign currencies are not counted. The numbers are standardized so that the quantity outstanding in 1913 is 1.0. P is an index of the cost of living, based on 1913 = 1.0.

Source: Sonderhefte zur Wirtschaft und Statistik, Berlin, 1925.

rate, π, and real money balances, M/P, in Germany from 1920 until 1925. In most cases the table indicates the average growth rates of money and prices over six-month intervals. The level of real money balances pertains to the ends of each of these intervals.

At the beginning of 1920 the growth rates of money and prices were already at the very high rate of about 6% per month. (Typically, when talking about hyperinflations, economists measure these rates per month rather than per year!) Then there was a deceleration of money to an average rate of less than 1% per month for the first half of 1921. Notice that, as the theory predicts, the growth rate of prices, π, fell by more than the growth rate of money, μ, when money decelerated. Correspondingly, real money balances increased by about 20% from early 1920 to early 1921. (The level of real money in early 1920 was roughly equal to that from before the war in 1913.)

In 1922 money accelerated dramatically to an average growth rate of nearly

30% per month toward the end of the year. During this period the growth rate of prices, π, exceeded that of money, μ. Hence, by late 1922 real money balances fell to about a quarter of the level prevailing in early 1920.

During the first half of 1923 there was some let-up in the acceleration of money, and money and prices grew together at the extraordinary average rate of 40% per month. Correspondingly, although the rate of inflation was enormous, the level of real money remained fairly stable. But late in 1923 the hyperinflation built to its climax with rates of monetary expansion of 300 to 600% per month for October–November. Again, the acceleration of money led to rates of inflation that exceeded the growth rates of money. Therefore, real money balances reached their low point in October 1923 at about 3% of the level for early 1920. If we neglect variations in aggregate real income from 1920 to 1923—which is satisfactory as a first-order approximation—the reduction in real money implies a rise in velocity by over thirty-fold. In other words, if in 1920 people held the typical piece of currency for two weeks before spending it, in October 1923 they held it for about half a day.

A major monetary reform occurred in Germany during November 1923. This reform included the introduction of a new type of currency, a promise not to print new money beyond a specified limit to finance government expenditures or for other purposes, some changes in government spending and taxes, and a commitment to back the new currency by gold.[7] In any event, there was a sharp curtailment in monetary growth and inflation after December 1923. For example, during 1924 monetary growth averaged 5–6% per month. But because of the deceleration of money after November 1923, the average inflation rate was even less—below 1% per month for 1924. Most dramatically, the quantity of real money balances rose from 3% of the early 1920 level in October 1923 to 56% of that level by December 1924.[8] (Much of the increase in real money arose as an infusion of new types of currency during the reform months of November and December 1923.)

Finally, in 1925 the growth rate of money fell to 1–2% per month, while the inflation rate remained at roughly 1% per month. Correspondingly, there was a slow rise in real money, which reached 60% of the early 1920 level by late 1925. Interestingly, although the inflation rate remained low for the remainder of the 1920s, the level of real money did not reattain the early 1920 level. Perhaps this discrepancy reflects a long-lasting negative influence of the hyperinflation on people's willingness to hold money.

[7]For discussions of the reform, see Bresciani-Turroni (1937), Thomas Sargent (1982), and Peter Garber (1982). Sargent's analysis deals also with the ends of hyperinflations in Austria, Hungary, and Poland in the early 1920s. He stresses the rapidity with which inflations can be ended once governments make a credible commitment to limiting money creation in the long run.

[8]The biggest hyperinflation on record occurred in Hungary after World War II: the price level rose by a factor of 3×10^{25} over the 13 months from July 1945 to August 1946. In the stabilization period from August 1946 to December 1947, the inflation rate declined to about 15% per year, and real money balances rose by a factor of 14. For a discussion, see William Bomberger and Gail Makinen (1983).

REAL EFFECTS OF INFLATION

SOME EFFECTS FROM UNANTICIPATED INFLATION

Our analysis in this chapter focuses on anticipated inflation. But let's note briefly some real effects that arise from unexpected inflation. During the German hyperinflation, one effect of this type was a substantial redistribution of wealth. Before the extreme inflation began, some households and businesses had nominal debts (including mortgages and other loans), while others held nominal assets. The hyperinflation—which was not anticipated at the time when people acquired these nominal debts and assets—wiped out most of the real value of claims that had a predetermined nominal value. Therefore, debtors gained while creditors lost. The general point is that unexpected inflation can have significant effects on the distribution of wealth.

The unpredictability of inflation reduces the willingness of people to enter into contracts that specify nominal values in advance. Thus, as we already noted, the usual types of bond and loan markets tended to disappear during the German hyperinflation and other extreme inflations. Although other kinds of markets may still function (such as a stock market and transactions denominated in foreign currencies in hyperinflation Germany or indexed bond markets in modern inflations), the loss of the traditional types of bonds and loans is an adverse real effect from unpredictable inflation.

EFFECTS OF ANTICIPATED INFLATION ON REAL MONEY BALANCES AND TRANSACTION COSTS

In the discussion of superneutrality of money, we mentioned that some real variables, such as aggregate output, were at least approximately independent of anticipated variations in money and the general price level. But even in the case where aggregate output changes little, one real effect from an increase in expected inflation is the reduction of real money balances. During the German hyperinflation, this response was dramatic, with aggregate real money falling to about 3% of its initial level.

Corresponding to the increase in expected inflation and the reduction in real money, people expend more resources on transaction costs. Although we regard these costs as small in normal times, we cannot neglect them during extreme circumstances, such as the German hyperinflation. For example, people spent a significant portion of their time on the process of receiving wage and other payments once or twice per day and in searching rapidly to find outlets for their cash. Given these magnitudes, we would also predict that extreme inflation would have significant effects on aggregate output. For the German case, there is some evidence that the process of dealing with the severe inflation in late 1923 had adverse effects on aggregate output and employment.

THE REVENUE FROM MONEY CREATION

A different real effect from inflation concerns the **government's revenue from printing money.** In our theory thus far, the government uses this income solely to finance transfers. More realistically, governments use the printing press to pay for a variety of expenditures.

Recall that the real amount of revenue for period t is the quantity $(M_t - M_{t-1})/P_t$. Using the condition $M_t = (1 + \mu)M_{t-1}$, we can rewrite this expression as

$$\text{real revenue from printing money} = \frac{(M_t - M_{t-1})}{P_t} = \mu \cdot M_{t-1}/P_t. \quad (8.13)$$

Economists often refer to the government's revenue from money creation as the **inflation tax.** A higher value of μ implies a higher value of the inflation rate, π, which implies a higher value for the nominal interest rate, $R = r + \pi$. Therefore, a higher growth rate of money generates a higher rate of tax on the holding of money; people must forego interest at a higher rate to hold money. We can also say that the higher value of π means that the real value of money declines at a faster rate.

Note from equation 8.13 that the real revenue from money creation is the product of the growth rate of money, μ, and a term that approximates the level of aggregate real money held, M_{t-1}/P_t. Recall that an increase in μ leads to a reduction in real money balances. Hence, if μ rises by, say, 10%, real revenue increases only if the magnitude of the proportionate decline in real money is by less than 10%. Empirically this condition holds except for the most extreme cases. For example, during the German hyperinflation, the condition was apparently not violated until the growth rate of money approached 100% per month between July and August 1923. Until then, the government successfully extracted more real income by printing money at higher rates.

In normal times for most countries, the government obtains only a small portion of its revenue from printing money. For example, in 1987, the Federal Reserve obtained about $17 billion from this source. This amount corresponded to about 2% of total U.S. government revenues and to 0.4% of GNP. More broadly, for 14 industrialized countries over the period 1960–78, the revenue from money creation averaged about 1% of GNP (see Stanley Fischer, 1982, Table A2).

In a few high-inflation countries, the revenue from money creation is more important. As an extreme example, for Argentina over 1960–75, money creation accounted for nearly half of government revenues and for about 6% of GNP. Some other countries where the revenue from printing money is important are Chile (5% of GNP over 1960–77), Libya (3% of GNP over 1960–77), and Brazil (3% of GNP over 1960–78).

During the German hyperinflation and in some other hyperinflations (such as Austria, Hungary, Poland, and Russia after World War I), money creation became the primary source of government revenue. Eventually the amounts obtained approached 10 to 15% of GNP, which appears to be about the maximum obtainable from printing money. Also, there was a close month-to-month connection in Germany between the volume of real government spending and the growth rate of the money supply. That is, the variations in monetary growth—and hence, inflation—were driven in this case by shifts in real government spending (see Zvi Hercowitz, 1981). Interestingly, much of the government spending over this period went to reparations payments associated with World War I. Therefore, the reduction in these payments after November 1923 was probably a major factor in the success of the German monetary reform.

SUMMARY

We introduced monetary growth into the model by allowing for governmental transfer payments. By considering the government's budget constraint, we found that the aggregate of these transfers equals the change in the stock of money.

We modified the households' budget constraints to include inflation. The main result is that these constraints involve the real interest rate rather than the nominal rate. Similarly, the intertemporal-substitution effects on consumption and leisure depend on the real interest rate. When there is uncertainty about inflation, it is the expected real interest rate that matters in the budget constraints and for intertemporal-substitution effects.

The nominal interest rate, R, still determines the cost of holding money rather than bonds. Therefore, although the real interest rate matters for choices of consumption and work, it is the nominal rate that appears in the demand-for-money function.

We used the market-clearing model to analyze the interactions among monetary growth, inflation, and nominal and real interest rates. An important result is that the real interest rate, the real wage rate, and the aggregates of output and employment are invariant with anticipated variations in the quantity of money. However, money is not superneutral in the model. (By superneutral, we mean that variations in the path of money have no real effects.) The behavior of money influences the level of real money balances, the nominal interest rate, and the volume of transaction costs. Further, the invariance of the real interest rate and aggregate output holds only as an approximation.

An increase in the growth rate of money shows up in the long run as equal increases in the inflation rate, the nominal interest rate, and the growth rate of nominal wages. However, because the higher nominal interest rate reduces the real demand for money, there must be a transition interval during which the rate of inflation exceeds the growth rate of money. In a simple case the transition occurs in an instant by an upward jump in the price level. But if we bring in some realistic extensions of the model—such as gradual adjustment of money demand and foreknowledge of the acceleration of money—we find a richer dynamics of prices during the transition. Here the inflation rate exceeds the growth rate of money for awhile.

Similar results apply to a decrease in the growth rate of money. In this case the process of reducing inflation involves a transition period with unusually low rates of inflation, which may even be negative.

We illustrated some of the results by observing the dynamics of monetary growth and inflation during the post–World War I German hyperinflation. The data show that higher rates of monetary growth led to lower levels of real money balances, while reductions in monetary growth had the opposite effect. We also discussed the effects of inflation on transaction costs and on the real revenue that the government obtains from printing money.

APPENDIX (OPTIONAL)
THE WEALTH EFFECTS FROM THE MONETARY TERMS

We neglected in the text any wealth effects associated with money. These effects involve the initial level of real money balances, transaction costs, the interest foregone by holding money in future periods, and the transfers that households receive from the government. We argued in Chapter 4 that this procedure was satisfactory as an approximation in the simpler model that ignored inflation and transfer payments. This appendix reconsiders this issue in the context of inflation. The main result is that the approach is still satisfactory as an approximation.

Consider the right side of equation 8.5, which shows the real present value of a household's uses of funds over an infinite horizon. If we neglect transaction costs, we have to add the real present value of interest foregone from holding money. Thus, the new terms are

$$\frac{R \cdot m_1}{[P_2(1 + r)]} + \frac{R \cdot m_2}{[P_3(1 + r)^2]} + \cdots, \qquad (8.14)$$

where ... represents similar terms involving m_3, m_4, and so on. To understand this series of terms, let's consider the first one. The term Rm_1 is the dollar interest earnings that a household foregoes during period 2 by holding the quantity of money m_1 rather than bonds during period 1. Since the foregone interest income applies to period 2, we divide by period 2's price level, P_2, to convert to real terms. Then we divide by the discount factor, $(1 + r)$, to express the result as a present value. Notice that the subsequent terms in expression 8.14 are similar except for the discount factor.

For subsequent purposes, it is convenient to modify expression 8.14. The first part of the expression involves the term $P_2(1 + r)$. But the price level for period 2, P_2, equals the quantity $(1 + \pi)P_1$, where π is the constant rate of inflation. Therefore we have

$$P_2(1 + r) = P_1(1 + \pi)(1 + r) = P_1(1 + R).$$

If we make this type of substitution for the price level in each term of expression

8.14, we obtain the simplified formula

$$\left[\frac{R}{(1 + R)}\right] \cdot \left[\frac{m_1}{P_1} + \left(\frac{m_2}{P_2}\right)\bigg/(1 + r) + \cdots\right]. \qquad (8.15)$$

Now consider the left side of equation 8.5, which shows the real present value of a household's sources of funds. To these terms we have to add the initial real money balance plus the present value of real transfers received from the government. Thus, the additional terms are

$$\frac{m_0}{P_1} + \left(\frac{v_1}{P_1}\right) + \left(\frac{v_2}{P_2}\right)\bigg/(1 + r) + \left(\frac{v_3}{P_3}\right)\bigg/(1 + r)^2 + \cdots. \qquad (8.16)$$

We can sum up across households in expression 8.16 to determine the aggregate real present value of the new sources of funds. Then we get the expression

$$\frac{M_0}{P_1} + \left(\frac{V_1}{P_1}\right) + \left(\frac{V_2}{P_2}\right)\bigg/(1 + r) + \left(\frac{V_3}{P_3}\right)\bigg/(1 + r)^2 + \cdots.$$

But recall from the government's budget constraint that the aggregate transfer for each period, V_t, equals the change in the stock of money, $M_t - M_{t-1}$. If we make this substitution above, we obtain the revised form,

$$\left(\frac{M_0}{P_1}\right) + \left\{\frac{(M_1 - M_0)}{P_1} + \frac{(M_2 - M_1)}{[P_2(1 + r)]} + \frac{(M_3 - M_2)}{[P_3(1 + r)^2]} + \cdots\right\}.$$

Observe that the first term, M_0/P_1, cancels with one of the terms inside the brackets. Hence we can rewrite the expression as

$$\frac{M_1}{P_1} - \frac{M_1}{[P_2(1 + r)]} + \frac{M_2}{[P_2(1 + r)]} - \frac{M_2}{[P_3(1 + r)^2]}$$

$$+ \text{ terms that involve } M_3, M_4, \cdots.$$

Recall that we can make the substitution

$$P_2(1 + r) = P_1(1 + \pi)(1 + r) = P_1(1 + R).$$

Therefore, we can combine the terms that involve M_1 in the above expression to get

$$\left(\frac{M_1}{P_1}\right)\left[1 - \frac{1}{(1 + R)}\right] = \left(\frac{M_1}{P_1}\right) \cdot \frac{R}{(1 + R)}.$$

Similarly, the terms that involve M_2 simplify to

$$\left(\frac{M_2}{P_2}\right) \cdot \left[\frac{R}{(1 + R)}\right]\bigg/(1 + r).$$

If we put this all together, the expression for the aggregate real present value of the new sources of funds becomes

$$\left[\frac{R}{(1 + R)}\right] \cdot \left[\frac{M_1}{P_1} + \left(\frac{M_2}{P_2}\right)\middle/ (1 + r)\right.$$

$$\left. + \text{ similar terms that involve } M_3, M_4, \cdots\right] \quad (8.17)$$

But look at expression 8.15, which shows the real present value of a household's new uses of funds. The aggregate of these new uses coincides with the aggregate of the new sources, which appears in expression 8.17. Hence, the monetary terms have no impact in the aggregate on the sources net of the uses. Accordingly, we do not have to consider wealth effects on the aggregates of consumption and leisure from the combination of, first, initial real money balances; second, the present value of real transfers; and third, the interest foregone from future holdings of money.

Finally, recall that aggregate wealth effects do arise when we consider the present value of real transaction costs. But as before, we assume as an approximation that we can neglect these effects.

IMPORTANT TERMS AND CONCEPTS

perfect foresight

governmental budget constraint

lump-sum transfer

superneutrality of money

hyperinflation

monetary reform

government's revenue from printing money

inflation tax

QUESTIONS AND PROBLEMS

Mainly for Review

8.1 Consider an individual who lives for two periods, earns a nominal income of $1000 in each period, and has zero initial and terminal assets. The nominal interest rate, R, on dollar loans is 15%, and the expected rate of inflation, π^e, between the two periods is 10%. Assume that the price level in the first period is 1.

a. What is the real value of period 1 income?

b. What is the maximum amount of dollars that could be borrowed in period 1? Find the real value of this amount, and add it to the real value of period 1 income to see the maximum amount of (real) consumption possible in period 1.

c. What is the price level in period 2? What is the real value of period 2 income?

d. What is the maximum amount of dollars that can be obtained in period 2 by saving in period 1? Find the real value (in period 2) of this amount, and add it to the real value of period 2 income to see the maximum amount of (real) consumption possible in period 2.

e. As in question 3.3 of Chapter 3, plot a graph showing the consumption possibilities in the two periods.

f. What is the slope of the budget line that you drew in part e? Show that it is equal to $-(1 + R)/(1 + \pi^e)$.

8.2 Based on your answer to question 8.1, explain why $(1 + R)/(1 + \pi^e)$, rather than $1 + R$, is the correct measure of the trade-off between real consumption in the two periods. In what situation would it be appropriate to use the nominal interest rate?

8.3 Suppose that the commodity market clears at a real interest rate of 4%.

a. If the inflation rate is zero, what is the nominal interest rate? If the inflation rate is 10%, what is the nominal interest rate?

b. If the nominal interest rate did not go up by the same amount as the inflation rate, what would happen to the commodity market—that is, would there be excess supply or excess demand?

8.4 Which of the following statements is correct?

a. A constant rate of increase in the price level will lead to a continuous rise in the nominal interest rate.

b. A continuous increase in the inflation rate will lead to a continuous rise in the nominal interest rate.

8.5 What would be the effect on the nominal interest rate of each of the following events?

a. The announcement of a one-time increase in the money stock.

b. The announcement of a planned increase in the rate of monetary growth.

Why does the price level jump in both instances? Does the velocity of money increase in both cases?

8.6 Critically review the following statement: "The quantity theory of money predicts that the rate of inflation must equal the rate of monetary growth. In fact, the two are not equal; therefore the theory is wrong." How do factors such as an anticipated increase in inflation or gradual adjustment in the demand for money alter the prediction? What about factors considered in Chapter 7, such as growth in output?

8.7 Can the government always increase its revenue by raising the rate of monetary growth? How does the answer depend on the response of real money demanded to the nominal interest rate?

PROBLEMS FOR DISCUSSION

8.8 *Inflation and the Demand for Money*

Suppose that households hold stocks of goods—for example, groceries—as well as money and bonds. Assume that these goods depreciate in a physical sense at the rate δ per year (δ is the Greek letter delta).

   a. What is the "nominal interest rate" on holdings of these goods? Does this interest rate affect the demands for stocks of goods and money?

   b. Assume that the nominal interest rate on bonds, R, does not change, but the expected inflation rate, π^e, rises. What happens to the demand for money?

     Note: This problem shows that the demand for money can involve substitution between money and goods, as well as between money and bonds. Therefore, the demand for money may change with a shift in the expected inflation rate, even if the nominal interest rate on bonds does not change.

  8.9   ***Wealth and Substitution Effects from Inflation (optional)***

Suppose that the expected inflation rate, π^e, and the nominal interest rate, R, each increase by 1 percentage point. Thus, the expected real interest rate on bonds does not change.

   a. What happens to the real demand for money?

   b. Underlying this change in the demand for money, what happens to the real amount of transaction costs that people incur?

Assume now that we do not neglect the role of transaction costs in households' budget constraints.

   c. What is the effect of higher inflation on people's wealth? How do consumption and leisure respond?

   d. Does higher expected inflation also exert substitution effects on consumption and leisure? (Note that, unlike consumption, leisure does not require people to use money.) Therefore, what is the overall effect of higher expected inflation on consumption and leisure?

 8.10   ***The Superneutrality of Money***

   a. What is the meaning of the term *superneutrality of money?*

   b. Is money superneutral in the model? In particular, if the behavior of money changes, which real variables change and which do not change? Explain the factors that underlie these results.

 8.11   ***Inflation and Saving (optional)***

   a. Suppose that we define a household's real saving to be the change in the real value of its assets, bonds and money. Use the household's budget constraint from equation 8.2 to derive an expression for real saving. Does real saving equal real income less real consumer expenditure? In the expression for real income, how do we measure the real interest income on bonds? In particular, does it involve the nominal interest rate, R, or the real interest rate, $R - \pi$? Is there also a term for real "interest income" on money?

   b. Nominal saving equals real saving multiplied by the price level P_t. What is the formula for nominal saving?

   c. Suppose as an alternative that we define nominal saving to be the change in the nominal value of a household's assets held as bonds or money. (The standard national accounts follow this practice.) Compare the results with those from part **b**. What differences arise in the measurement of interest income on bonds and money?

d. Suppose that we define real saving to be nominal saving divided by the price level, P_t, where nominal saving is defined as in part **c**. Does this concept of real saving measure the change in the real value of assets?

Compare the result with that from part **a**, which does measure the change in the real value of assets.

8.12 *A Case of Counterfeiting*

In 1925 a group of swindlers induced the Waterlow Company, a British manufacturer of bank notes, to print up and deliver to them 3 million pounds worth of Portuguese currency (escudos). Since the company also printed the legitimate notes for the Bank of Portugal, the counterfeit notes were indistinguishable from the real thing (except that the serial numbers turned out to be duplicates of those from a previous series of legitimate notes). Before the fraud was discovered, 1 million pounds worth of the "counterfeit" notes had been introduced into circulation in Portugal. After the scheme unraveled (because the duplication of serial numbers was discovered), the Bank of Portugal made good on the fraudulent notes by exchanging them for newly printed, valid notes. The bank subsequently sued the Waterlow Company for damages. The company was found liable, but the key question was the amount of the damage award. The bank argued that the damages were 1 million pounds (less funds collected from the swindlers). The other side contended that the bank suffered only negligible real costs in having to issue an additional 1 million pounds worth of new money to redeem the fraudulent notes. (Note that the currency was a purely paper issue, with no promise of convertibility into gold or anything else.) Thus, the argument was that the only true costs to the bank were the expenses for the paper and printing itself. Which side do you think was correct? (The House of Lords determined in 1932 that 1 million pounds was the right measure. For discussions of this fascinating episode in monetary economics, see R. G. Hawtrey, 1932, and Murray Bloom, 1966.)

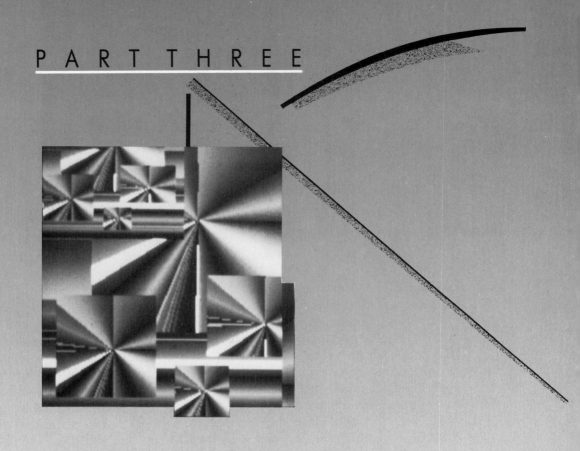

BUSINESS FLUCTUATIONS,
ECONOMIC GROWTH,
AND UNEMPLOYMENT

*T*his part of the book considers the important problems of business fluctuations, economic growth, and unemployment. Chapter 9 extends the model to incorporate investment, which plays a key role in the short-term fluctuations of an economy. We then consider the extent to which the model can explain some observed features of business cycles.

At this stage our model does not include the government's spending, taxes, and debt (which we take up in Chapters 12–14). Also, we do not allow any role for monetary disturbances as sources of changes in real economic activity. (We consider this topic in Chapters 17–20). Thus, business fluctuations can arise in the model only because of supply shocks—that is, shifts in the production function—and perhaps from changes in preferences. Models that rely on these kinds of disturbances to explain economic fluctuations are called *real business cycle theories*. (Economists who use these models should perhaps be called "realists," as opposed to monetarists.) Such theories have been receiving a lot of attention recently from economists.[1] Later we shall build on the form of the analysis that we carry out here to understand business fluctuations that originate from movements in the government's spending, taxes, and debt or from monetary changes.

In Chapter 10, we take up the longer-term aspect of investment—namely, its manifestation over time as the accumulation of productive capital. This accumulation plays a central role in the process of long-term economic growth.

In Chapter 11 we show that fluctuations in economic activity involve variations in unemployment. As a related matter we discuss the average or "natural" rate of unemployment and show why it will be positive.

---

[1]The term *real business cycles* originates with John Long and Charles Plosser (1983). For a general discussion and an extension to include monetary disturbances, see Robert King and Charles Plosser (1984).

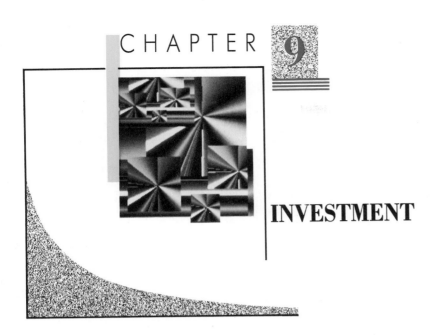

CHAPTER 9

INVESTMENT

o far we have simplified matters by pretending that labor services were the only variable input to the production process. Now we want to be more realistic by including capital services as well. We shall think primarily of **physical capital,** such as machines and buildings used by producers. In the national accounts this category is called **producer's durable equipment and structures.** But we can broaden this concept of capital to include the goods held as **inventories** by businesses. We might also add consumer durables, such as homes (called residential structures in the national accounts), automobiles, and appliances. In fact, we could usefully go further to include **human capital,** which measures the effects of education and training on the skills of workers. But while the general economic reasoning applies also to human capital, we shall confine most of our analysis here to physical capital.

THE CAPITAL STOCK AND INVESTMENT IN THE UNITED STATES

Let's start with an overview of the U.S. capital stock. Figure 9.1 shows how a standard concept of physical capital evolved from 1925 until 1987. This concept, called **private fixed capital,** includes business's durable equipment and structures, plus

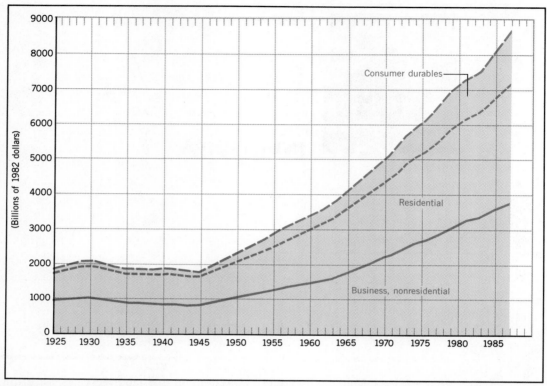

FIGURE 9.1 *Private Fixed Capital in the United States, 1925–1987*
The solid line is real business, nonresidential capital. The dotted line adds real residential capital. The dashed line adds to the dotted line the real stock of consumer durables.

residential structures.[1] The data are in real terms; that is, they express the quantity of capital in terms of dollar values for the base year, 1982.

Figure 9.1 shows the total of private fixed capital, as well as the breakdown between nonresidential and residential components. The residential part accounts for about half the total throughout the period. Note that private fixed capital excludes business inventories (which are not part of "fixed" capital), capital stocks owned by governments, and consumer durables other than homes. The figure shows separately the capital stocks held by households in the form of consumer durables (other than homes). The sum of these durables and the standard measure of fixed capital gives a broader measure of private fixed capital.

The various components of the capital stock grew throughout the post–World War II period. From 1946 to 1987, the average growth rate for the broad concept of private fixed capital was 3.8% per year. For the components, the average annual

[1] The data are from U.S. Department of Commerce (1987) and *U.S. Survey of Current Business* (August 1988).

growth rates were 3.6% for business, nonresidential capital, 3.4% for residential capital, and 5.7% for consumer durables. Thus, the rapid growth in consumer durables is noteworthy.

The capital stock behaved very differently before 1946. After growing for most of the 1920s (only partially shown in the figure), the overall stock and its components declined during the depressed years of the 1930s. Then, after some growth from the late 1930s until 1941, the capital stock declined again during World War II.

Changes in the capital stock correspond to fixed investment expenditures by firms or households. Figure 9.2 shows various categories of real fixed investment, expressed as ratios to real GNP. The categories correspond to those for the capital stock in Figure 9.1. The investment numbers refer to actual expenditures (called gross investment) and do not adjust for estimated depreciation of capital stocks. (We shall discuss depreciation later in this chapter.) An allowance for the usual estimates of depreciation, which come from mechanical formulas, would not disturb the general nature of the time patterns shown in Figure 9.2.

The behavior of investment will be a particular concern in our study of business

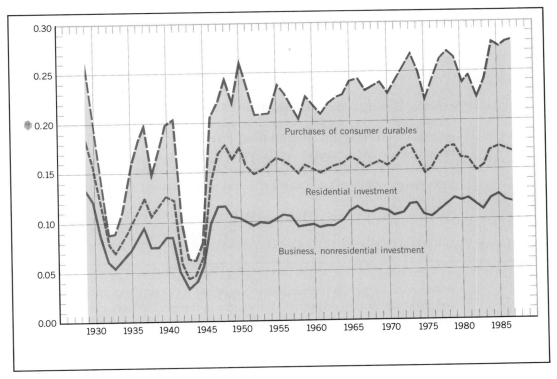

FIGURE 9.2 *Ratios of Fixed Investment to GNP*
The solid line shows the ratio of real business, nonresidential investment to real GNP. The dotted line adds the ratio of real residential investment to real GNP. The dashed line adds to the dotted line the ratio of real purchases of consumer durables to real GNP.

fluctuations. The ratio to GNP of private fixed investment (business, nonresidential plus residential) averaged 16.0% from 1947 to 1987. But the values ranged from 14.6% in 1952 to 17.7% in 1948. Aside from the Korean War, the lowest values of this ratio pick out most of the principal recessions since World War II: 14.6% in 1958, 14.7% in 1975 and 1961, and 14.9% in 1982.

For the broader category of fixed investment, which includes purchases of consumer durables, the ratio averaged 23.7% from 1947 to 1987. Here the values ranged from 20.0% in 1958 to 28.2% in 1987. As with the narrower concept of fixed investment, the troughs in this broader measure pick out the main recessions. Because of the strength in consumer durables, the broader definition of fixed investment shows a more pronounced investment boom in recent years. The broad ratio averaged 27.9% from 1984 to 1987, or 4.2 percentage points above the mean of 23.7% from 1947 to 1987. (With consumer durables excluded, the ratio of fixed investment to GNP from 1984 to 1987 averaged 17.1%, as compared to the mean of 16.0% from 1947 to 1987.)

We see a stronger pattern of fluctuation in investment spending before World War II. The ratio for fixed investment exclusive of consumer durables reached a low point of 6.7% at the trough of the Great Depression in 1933. After some recovery, the dip to a low point of 10.4% in 1938 corresponds to another recession. The lowest ratios of all—3.9% in 1943 and 4.5% in 1944—occurred during World War II. But we shall postpone our consideration of this wartime behavior until we study government expenditure in Chapter 12.

Aside from fixed investment, business's investment spending also includes additions to stock of goods held as inventories of finished product or of goods-in-process. This inventory accumulation can be either positive or negative. Figure 9.3 shows the ratio of business's real inventory investment to real GNP. This ratio is extremely volatile, and, as with fixed investment, the low points tend to pick out the recessions. For example, real inventory investment was negative in the recession years of 1982–83, 1980, 1975, 1958, 1954, and 1949. Before World War II, inventory investment was negative during the recession years of 1938 and 1930–34.

REAL GNP AND ITS COMPONENTS DURING RECESSIONS

In this section we explore the behavior of real GNP, and especially of its investment components, during economic downturns in the United States. If we examined times of economic upturn, we would reach similar conclusions, except that all signs would be reversed.

Table 9.1 shows how real GNP behaved during recent recessions. Consider, for example, the recession of 1957–58. Real GNP for 1958 (on a 1982 base) was $1539 billion. Using real GNP for 1956 as a benchmark, we can calculate the real GNP that would have resulted in 1958 if output had grown at the annual rate of 2.9% (the average rate from 1929 to 1987). This value is $1617 billion. The gap between

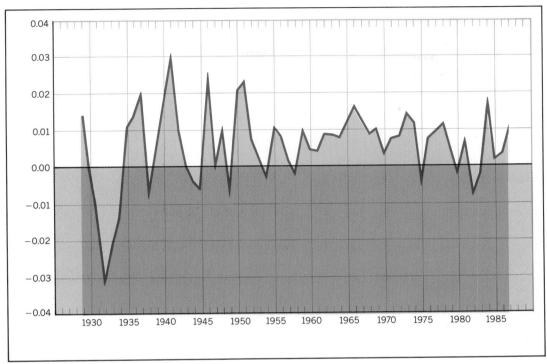

FIGURE 9.3 *Inventory Investment as a Ratio to GNP*
The graph shows the ratio of real business inventory investment to real GNP.

this value and actual real GNP is $78 billion, which constitutes a shortfall in output of 4.8%. These last two numbers appear in the first two lines of Table 9.1. This measure of a shortfall in output gives us a reasonable way to gauge the magnitude of a recession.

Table 9.1 shows the results of this calculation for the six main U.S. recessions since World War II and for the Great Depression of 1929–33. The table excludes the 1961 recession, which showed a shortfall for real GNP of only 1.0%. (On the other hand, Richard Nixon thought that this contraction was large enough to cost him the presidential election of 1960.) The sharpest postwar contractions were the ones for 1982[2] and 1975, where the shortfalls in output were by 9.1% and 7.3%, respectively. On average for the six post–World War II recessions, the shortfall in real GNP was 5.2%. By contrast, for 1933, the estimated shortfall was a remarkable 37%.

---

[2]There is some controversy as to whether to treat 1980 and 1982 as the final years of two distinct recessions or to consider 1980–82 as one prolonged contraction. Since the intervening recovery in late 1980 and early 1981 was so brief, we treat 1980–82 as a single recession.

TABLE 9.1 *Consumption and Investment during Recessions*

Final Year of Recession Benchmark Year for Comparison	1933 1929	1949 1948	1954 1953	1958 1956	1970 1969	1975 1973	1982 1979	Mean for Six Postwar Recessions
Shortfall of real GNP (billions of 1982 dollars)	298	32	61	78	78	213	317	—
Shortfall as % of Trend Real GNP	37.4	2.8	4.1	4.8	3.1	7.3	9.1	5.2
% of shortfall in real GNP accounted for by:								
Personal consumption expenditures	50	20	5	27	10	37	43	24
Durables	8	−13	2	15	13	13	12	7
Nondurables and services	42	33	4	12	−4	24	31	17
Gross fixed investment	37	72	4	45	30	53	44	41
Nonresidential	26	51	11	34	17	26	18	26
Residential	10	22	−6	11	12	27	26	15
Change in business inventories	8	69	13	22	23	26	13	28
Government purchases	2	−64	86	−13	46	9	7	12
Net exports	2	3	−9	19	−7	−25	−7	−4
Total investment[a]	53	128	19	82	66	92	69	76

[a]Purchases of consumer durables plus gross fixed investment plus change in business inventories.

Note: The method for calculating the shortfall in each component is discussed in the text.

Source: U.S. Department of Commerce (1986) and *Citibase* data bank.

We use the same method in Table 9.1 to compute the shortfalls in the main components of real GNP.[3] For the six postwar recessions, the mean shares for the shortfall in real GNP were 24% in personal consumption expenditures, 41% in gross fixed investment, 28% in changes in business inventories, 12% in government purchases of goods and services, and −4% in net exports.

One important finding is the relatively small contribution from consumption expenditures. Although this component constituted 61% of GNP on average since World War II, the fluctuations in consumer expenditures accounted on average for only 24% of the fall in output during the six postwar recessions. The reason is that consumption spending fluctuates proportionately much less than total output.

Personal consumption expenditures include purchases of consumer durables (except for residences). As mentioned before, we should think of this spending as a form of investment carried out by households. Table 9.1 shows that consumer

---

[3]The calculated shortfall in any component is the difference of a trend value from the actual. The trend value assumes 2.9% annual growth from the benchmark year.

expenditures for nondurables and services accounted on average for only 17% of the shortfall in output during the six postwar recessions (although these expenditures averaged 54% of GNP since World War II). Thus, consumer spending on nondurables and services is far more stable than aggregate GNP.

Table 9.1 shows that a broad measure of investment spending—fixed investment plus changes in business inventories plus purchases of consumer durables—accounted on average for 76% of the fall in output during the six postwar recessions. In contrast, this spending constituted only 24% of GNP on average since World War II. Thus, investment spending is far more volatile than overall GNP. In fact, as a first approximation, explaining recessions amounts to explaining the sharp contractions in the investment components.

Two other components of GNP—government purchases of goods and services and net exports—do not bear a very regular relationship to recessions and booms. On average for the six postwar recessions, these two components accounted for 12% and −4%, respectively, of the shortfall in real GNP.[4] We shall discuss government purchases in Chapter 12 and net exports in Chapter 15.

Finally, notice the figures in Table 9.1 for the Great Depression of 1929–33. In this case the consumption of nondurables and services accounted for 42% of the shortfall in real GNP, while the total of the investment components accounted for 53%. (Neither government purchases nor net exports were important here.) Thus, the cutback in consumption was relatively more important during the Depression than it was for the milder contractions since World War II.

Overall, there are several features of the data that we would like our theory to explain. We want to know why

- Investment is far more volatile than consumption.

- The ratio of investment to GNP is low during recessions and high in booms.

- Consumption expenditures, especially on nondurables and services, decline little in proportional terms during mild recessions, but fall significantly during a severe contraction.

CAPITAL IN THE PRODUCTION FUNCTION

We now begin to incorporate capital into the theoretical model. To keep things manageable, imagine that there is a single type of capital, which we can measure in physical units—for example, as a number of standard-type machines. Denote by k_{t-1} the quantity of capital that a producer has at the end of period $t - 1$. Because it takes time to make new capital operational, we assume that the stock from period

---

[4]For the 1954 and 1970 recessions, the large contribution from government purchases reflects the sharp cutbacks in military spending after the Korean and Vietnam wars, respectively. For the 1949 recession, there was a substantial increase in government purchases. Therefore, government purchases showed a large negative contribution to the shortfall of real GNP.

$t - 1$ is available for use in production during period t. In other words, it takes one period for newly acquired capital to come on line.

The production function is now

$$y_t = f(k_{t-1}, \; n_t),$$
$$(+) \quad (+)$$

(9.1)

where the variable, k_{t-1}, is capital input and the variable, n_t, is labor input. In the real world there are variations in the **utilization rate** of capital. By the utilization rate we mean the fraction of total time that a piece of capital is used. For example, a factory may operate for one shift per day or two or could be open or closed on weekends. But we neglect these possible changes in utilization for the production function shown in equation 9.1. Here, we can think of the quantity of capital, k_{t-1}, as always operating for one standard-length shift per day.

The plus signs under the two inputs in equation 9.1 signify that each is productive at the margin. That is, an increase in either input, with the other held fixed, leads to more output. Remember that the marginal product of labor for period t, MPL_t, is the effect on output, y_t, from an extra unit of work, n_t. Note that we hold fixed the quantity of capital, k_{t-1}, when we measure the marginal product of labor. We define the **marginal product of capital** in a similar manner. This marginal product, MPK_{t-1}, is the response of output, y_t, when capital, k_{t-1}, increases by one unit, while the amount of work, n_t, does not change. Notice that the dating on this marginal product shows that it relates to the quantity of capital, k_{t-1}, from the end of period $t - 1$. However, because of the lag in making new capital operational, this marginal product refers to the effect on output for period t.

We have discussed the diminishing marginal productivity of labor. Labor's marginal product, MPL_t, falls as the amount of work increases, at least if the quantity of capital does not change. Now we make a parallel assumption about the marginal product of capital. This marginal product, MPK_{t-1}, declines as the quantity of capital, k_{t-1}, increases, at least if the amount of labor does not change.

Figure 9.4 shows how output responds as a producer uses more capital. Here, we hold fixed the quantity of labor. Notice that the curve goes through the origin, which means that a producer gets no output if the capital stock is zero. The slope of the curve is the marginal product of capital, MPK_{t-1}. The slope is positive throughout but declines as the amount of capital increases. To stress this relationship, we show it explicitly in Figure 9.5.

INVESTMENT GOODS AND CONSUMER GOODS

Investment is the purchase of capital goods—for example, machines or buildings—from the commodity market. In the real world, most physical investment is carried out by businesses. But, as before, we shall find it simpler not to distinguish firms from households. We can think of households in their role of producers as carrying out investment.

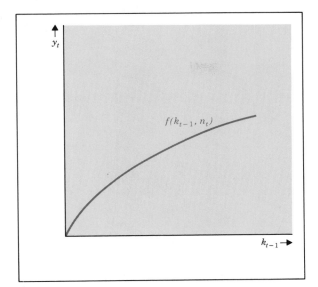

FIGURE 9.4 *Response of Output to Quantity of Capital Input* The graph shows the effect on output, y_t, from a change in capital input, k_{t-1}. Here, the quantity of labor input, n_t, does not change.

Generally capital goods differ physically from consumer goods. But to keep things simple, we assume that there is only one physical good that people produce and exchange on the commodity market. One household buys this good for consumption purposes, while another (perhaps a business) buys it to accumulate more capital—that is, for investment purposes.[5]

As before, producers sell all of their output, y_t, on the commodity market at the price P_t. Households or firms buy these goods either for consumption, c_t, or investment, which we denote by i_t. Therefore, if we think of households as doing the investment, a household's total demand for goods, y_t^d, equals the sum of consumption demand, c_t^d, and investment demand, i_t^d. Because all goods sell at the same price, suppliers do not care whether their goods are labeled as consumer goods or investment goods. Therefore, we shall focus on a producer's total supply of goods, y_t^s.

DEPRECIATION

Capital goods do not last forever, but rather tend to depreciate—or wear out—over time. We model this process in a simple form, where the amount of depreciation during period t is a constant fraction of the stock of capital, k_{t-1}, that is carried

---

[5]This setup is called a *one-sector production technology*. This specification, which appears in most macroanalyses, has only one process that allows producers to use inputs to produce goods. Some economists use a *two-sector production model*. Then there is one process for producing consumer goods and another for capital goods. (However, there is still only one physical type of capital and only one physical type of consumable.) For an example of a model with a two-sector production technology, see Duncan Foley and Miguel Sidrauski (1971, especially Chapter 2).

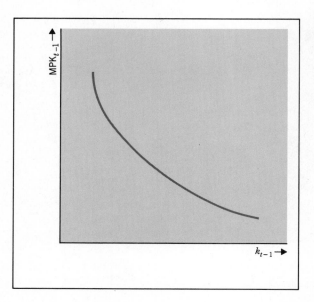

FIGURE 9.5 *Relation of the Marginal Product of Capital to the Quantity of Capital*
The graph shows that the marginal product of capital, MPK_{t-1}, declines as the amount of capital, k_{t-1}, increases.

over from period $t - 1$ and used during period t. In other words, if d_t denotes the amount of depreciation in units of commodities, then

$$d_t = \delta k_{t-1}, \tag{9.2}$$

where δ (the Greek letter delta) is the constant rate of depreciation per period. To calculate the stock of capital, k_t, that is available for use in period $t + 1$, we have to start with k_{t-1}, then add investment, i_t, and subtract depreciation, d_t; that is,

$$k_t = k_{t-1} + i_t - \delta k_{t-1}. \tag{9.3}$$

There are two concepts of investment:

1. Gross investment is the quantity of capital goods purchased, i_t.
2. Net investment is the change in the capital stock, $k_t - k_{t-1}$, which equals gross investment, i_t, less the amount of depreciation, δk_{t-1}.

In thinking about the current demand for goods, gross investment will matter. But, in analyzing how the capital stock changes, net investment will be what counts.

Correspondingly, there are also two concepts of output:

1. Gross product is the total amount produced, y_t.
2. Net product equals gross product less depreciation, $y_t - \delta k_{t-1}$. That is, net product is the quantity of goods produced less the amount of capital goods worn out during the process of production.

In considering the total amount of commodities supplied and demanded, gross output will be relevant. But, in assessing the quantity of goods available for consumption or net investment, net output will be the important variable.

CHARACTERISTICS OF EXISTING CAPITAL

Remember that producers can call their output consumables or capital. But once a purchaser has put capital into place—for example, as a factory—it would be unrealistic to assume that these goods can be reclassified as consumables and then eaten up. Hence, we assume that the initial labeling choice as consumables or capital is irreversible. In other words, producers cannot consume their capital at a later date. However, they can allow capital to depreciate and not replace it.

A second issue concerns the possibilities for moving capital goods from one production activity to another. Here we simplify the analysis by assuming that these movements are possible at negligible cost. This mobility of capital ensures that producers place all existing stocks in their most favorable use. Otherwise, someone could be better by shifting capital to another location. Recall also that we treat all units of capital as physically identical. Therefore, each unit must end up with the same physical marginal product.

Sometimes we shall find it convenient to think of resales of used capital. Then if a piece of capital has a low marginal product for one person, he or she will find it advantageous to sell the capital to someone else. But since old and new capital are identical, the price of a unit of old capital during period t must equal that for new capital, which is P_t. Given this result, we can think of old capital goods as being sold along with new ones on the commodity market. Hence, we do not have to worry about a separate market for resales.

INVESTMENT DEMAND

Consider a producer's incentive to invest during period t. Recall that the stock of capital that will be available for production next period is the quantity

$$k_t = k_{t-1} + i_t - \delta k_{t-1}.$$

At date t, the previous stock, k_{t-1}, and the amount of depreciation, δk_{t-1}, have already been determined by previous decisions. Therefore, an increase by one unit in gross investment, i_t, means an increase by one unit in net investment, $i_t - \delta k_{t-1}$, and also an increase by one unit in the stock of capital, k_t. Hence, each producer decides how much to invest during period t by weighing the cost of this investment against the return from having more capital, k_t.

To raise investment by one unit, a producer must purchase an additional unit of goods from the commodity market at the price P_t. Hence, P_t is the dollar cost of an extra unit of investment.

There are two components of the return to investment. First, an additional unit of investment raises capital, k_t, by one unit. If we hold fixed the quantity of work for the next period, n_{t+1}, next period's output, y_{t+1}, rises by the marginal product of capital, MPK_t. Since producers sell this output at the price P_{t+1}, the additional dollar sales revenue is the amount $P_{t+1} \cdot MPK_t$.

Remember that the fraction, δ, of each unit of capital disappears after one period because of depreciation. But the remaining fraction, $1 - \delta$, is still around. We can simplify the analysis by pretending that producers sell their old capital on the commodity market at date $t + 1$. (If they like, they can "buy back" this capital during period $t + 1$ to use for production at date $t + 2$.) Since goods sell at price P_{t+1} during period $t + 1$, the dollar revenue from the sale of used capital is $(1 - \delta)P_{t+1}$. Hence, this term is the second part of the return to investment.

Overall, an additional unit of investment costs P_t during period t and yields the amount $P_{t+1}(MPK_t + 1 - \delta)$ in period $t + 1$. Therefore the dollar return on the investment is the difference, $P_{t+1}(MPK_t + 1 - \delta) - P_t$. If we divide by the number of dollars invested, P_t, we determine the nominal rate of return to investment, which is

$$\frac{P_{t+1}(MPK_t + 1 - \delta) - P_t}{P_t} = (1 + \pi_t)(MPK_t + 1 - \delta) - 1.$$

In the calculation above we used the condition $P_{t+1} = (1 + \pi_t)P_t$, where π_t is the inflation rate for period t.

The nominal rate of return from investment looks good or bad depending on how it relates to other available returns. Specifically, households can earn the nominal interest rate, R_t, on bonds. Also, a household or firm that borrows to finance investment has to pay the rate R_t on its debt. If the nominal rate of return from investment exceeds the nominal interest rate, R_t, it pays to raise investment—that is, to buy more capital goods. But as the capital stock rises, diminishing marginal productivity implies that capital's marginal product, MPK_t, falls. Eventually this decline in the marginal product reduces the nominal rate of return to investment enough to equal the nominal interest rate, R_t. Then producers have no further incentive to expand investment.

Algebraically, investors act to satisfy the condition

$$(1 + \pi_t)(MPK_t + 1 - \delta) - 1 = R_t,$$

where the left side is the nominal rate of return from investment. Recall, however, that the real rate of return on bonds, r_t, satisfies the relation $(1 + r_t) = (1 + R_t)/(1 + \pi_t)$. Using this condition, we can simplify the above result to the form

$$MPK_t - \delta = r_t. \tag{9.4}$$

The left side of equation 9.4 is the **real rate of return from investment**—the gross return, MPK_t, less the rate of depreciation, δ. Investors act to equate this return to the real rate of return on bonds, r_t. Any difference between these two rates makes it profitable to select either a higher or lower amount of investment. Therefore, the amount of investment that households or firms choose generates a marginal product, MPK_t, that equates the two real rates of return.

Figure 9.6 shows the results graphically. As the quantity of capital k_t rises, the marginal product MPK_t declines, as shown in the upper curve in the figure. The real rate of return from investment is the amount, $MPK_t - \delta$, as shown by the lower

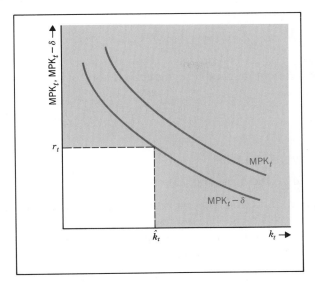

FIGURE 9.6 *Choice of Capital Stock*
Producers aim for the quantity of capital, $\hat{k}_t$, where the real rate of return from investment, $MPK_t - \delta$, equals the real interest rate on bonds, r_t.

curve in the figure. A producer chooses the quantity of capital, denoted by $\hat{k}_t$, where the real rate of return from investment, $MPK_t - \delta$, equals the real interest rate, r_t.

Given the schedule for capital's marginal product, the **desired stock of capital,** $\hat{k}_t$, depends on the real interest rate, r_t, and the depreciation rate, δ. Hence, we can write the desired stock of capital as the function

$$\hat{k}_t = \hat{k}(r_t, \quad \delta, \cdots).$$
$$\;\;\;\;\;(-)\,(-)$$

(9.5)

The expression ... represents the characteristics of the production function that affect the schedule for capital's marginal product. Note that an increase in r_t or δ means that the marginal product of capital, MPK_t, must be higher in equation 9.4. Therefore, for a given schedule of capital's marginal product, the desired stock of capital declines.

For given values of the real interest rate and the rate of depreciation, an upward shift in the schedule for capital's marginal product raises the desired stock of capital. We can show this result graphically by shifting the two curves upward in Figure 9.6.

Once we know the desired stock of capital $\hat{k}_t$, we know also the choice of gross investment, i_t. Specifically, to attain the stock $\hat{k}_t$, a producer demands for investment purposes the quantity of goods i_t^d, where

$$i_t^d = \hat{k}_t - (1 - \delta)k_{t-1}.$$

Notice that, for given values of the starting capital stock, k_{t-1}, and depreciation, δk_{t-1}, gross **investment demand** varies one-to-one with changes in the desired stock of capital, $\hat{k}_t$. Using equation 9.5, we can write out a function for gross investment demand as

$$i_t^d = \hat{k}(r_t,, \quad \delta, \cdots) - (1 - \delta)k_{t-1} = i^d(r_t, \quad \delta, \quad k_{t-1}, \cdots).$$
$$(-)\,(-) \qquad\qquad\qquad\qquad (-)\,(?)\,(-)$$

(9.6)

Given gross investment demand, the implied amount of net investment demand is

$$i_t^d - \delta k_{t-1} = \hat{k}(r_t, \quad \delta, \cdots) - k_{t-1}.$$
$$(-)\,(-)$$

(9.7)

PROPERTIES OF INVESTMENT DEMAND

Here, we summarize the main implications of the analysis for investment demand:

- A reduction in the real interest rate, r_t, raises the desired stock of capital, $\hat{k}_t$. Therefore, investment demand rises.

- Given r_t, an upward shift in the schedule for capital's marginal product, MPK_t, raises the desired stock of capital, $\hat{k}_t$. Hence, investment demand increases.

- Other things equal, investment demand declines if the previous stock of capital, k_{t-1}, rises. By "other things equal," we mean to include the various elements that determine the desired stock of capital, $\hat{k}_t$. Recall that net investment demand equals the quantity $\hat{k}_t - k_{t-1}$. Therefore, this demand falls with a rise in the initial stock, k_{t-1}. Gross investment demand equals the quantity $\hat{k}_t - (1 - \delta)k_{t-1}$. As long as the depreciation rate, δ, is less than 100%, a rise in the initial stock, k_{t-1}, means less gross investment demand, i_t^d.

- An increase in the rate of depreciation, δ, lowers the desired stock of capital, $\hat{k}_t$. Therefore, net investment demand, $\hat{k}_t - k_{t-1}$, declines. However, recall again that gross investment demand equals the quantity $\hat{k}_t - (1 - \delta)k_{t-1}$. Because the desired capital stock declines while depreciation rises, the overall effect on gross investment demand is ambiguous.

- Gross investment demand is positive as long as the desired stock, $\hat{k}_t$, exceeds the fraction, $1 - \delta$, of the initial stock, k_{t-1}. For an individual producer, negative gross investment means that someone's sales of old capital goods exceed his or her purchases of new ones.

We assumed before that capital goods cannot be converted back into consumables; that is, we assumed **irreversible investment**.[6] Therefore, one person's negative gross investment (sales of capital goods) must correspond to someone else's positive gross investment. Hence, when we aggregate over all producers, we cannot

---

[6]If producers are uncertain about future conditions—such as the future state of technology—the irreversible nature of investment becomes especially important. Basically, people are motivated to defer irreversible decisions, such as the initiation of investment projects, until the uncertainties are resolved. If the degree of uncertainty rises, investment demand tends to fall. This element seems to underlie Keynes's (1935, chap. 22) belief that investment demand is volatile and therefore causes variability of aggregate economic activity. For a discussion of irreversible investment, see Ben Bernanke (1983a).

ABSENCE OF A RESALE MARKET (OPTIONAL)

*I*n determining the choice of investment, we pretended that producers resell the undepreciated portion of their capital, $(1 - \delta)k_{t-1}$, on the commodity market during period t. Then, if they desire, producers can again buy investment goods in period $t + 1$, resell them in period $t + 2$, and so on. By pretending that producers resell their old capital, we can easily calculate the rate of return to investment over one period. But this device is artificial. Typically a firm or household keeps a piece of capital for many years. In fact, the sale of used capital goods is unusual for most types of producers' equipment and structures, although it is common for residences and automobiles.

In most cases our analysis of investment goes through even if resales are impossible. In the previous setup, a producer resells the quantity of capital, $(1 - \delta)k_{t-1}$, during period t, and then buys back the desired stock, $\hat{k}_t$. The difference between purchases and sales is the quantity $\hat{k}_t - (1 - \delta)k_{t-1}$, which equals gross investment demand, i_t^d. If we look only at producers who always have positive gross investment demand, the potential for resale is irrelevant. That is because someone with positive gross investment does not have to resell any capital. The producer just keeps the existing capital, and then buys new goods in the amount i_t^d. In this case, there are no changes if we eliminate the possibility for resale.[7]

Remember that gross investment demand, i_t^d, equals net investment demand, $\hat{k}_t - k_{t-1}$, plus depreciation, δk_{t-1}. Therefore, for the previous results to hold, we do not need net investment demand to be positive for the typical producer. Rather, we need only to rule out net investment demand being so negative that it outweighs the positive amount of depreciation, δk_{t-1}.

For subsequent purposes, we assume that the previous analysis of investment demand is satisfactory. Recall that this analysis works either if we allow resale of capital or if gross investment demand is always positive for every producer. But, of course, we shall also do okay as an approximation if—as seems plausible—gross investment demand is positive at most times for most producers.

---

[7]For a discussion of this issue and some related topics on investment, see Robert Hall (1977, especially pp. 71–74).

GRADUAL ADJUSTMENT OF INVESTMENT DEMAND

*I*n our analysis we assume that producers purchase enough goods in a single period—which might be a year—to attain their desired stock of capital. That is, firms or households invest enough to close the gap between the capital carried over from the previous period, $(1 - \delta)k_{t-1}$, and the desired stock, $\hat{k}_t$.

We have ignored a variety of costs that arise when producers install new capital goods. For example, to place new plant and equipment into operation, a business normally goes through a phase of planning and decision making, then a time of building and delivery, and finally an interval where managers and workers familiarize themselves with the new facilities. Producers can speed up parts of this process but only by incurring extra costs. As examples, quicker decisions mean more mistakes, and faster construction requires larger payments to workers and suppliers.

Because there are costs in adjusting the levels of capital, we predict two types of lags in the investment process. First, a gap between the starting stock of capital, $(1 - \delta)k_{t-1}$, and the desired level, $\hat{k}_t$, stimulates higher investment over an extended interval. That is, since it takes time to build and install new plant and equipment, investors stretch out their purchases of new capital goods over an interval of time. Second, the higher capacity for production becomes available only after the investment project is completed. (Note that we capture some of this element by assuming that this period's capital stock affects production for the next period.)

Although adjustment costs for investment are quantitatively important, we continue to ignore these costs as a simplification.[8] Fortunately, the main features of our analysis would not change if we brought in these complications.

have negative gross investment, I_t. To put this result another way, the aggregate stock of capital, K_t, cannot fall below the initial stock, K_{t-1}, by more than the amount of depreciation, δK_{t-1}. Correspondingly, aggregate net investment, $K_t - K_{t-1} = I_t - \delta K_{t-1}$, can be negative only up to the magnitude of depreciation, δK_{t-1}.

Recall from Figure 9.1 that the capital stock declined during the Great Depression and World War II. At these times, private fixed net investment was negative. Our interpretation is that the aggregate desired stock of capital, $\hat{K}_t$, fell below the initial stock, K_{t-1}, during these years.

[8]For discussions of adjustment costs in investment demand, see Robert Eisner and Robert Strotz (1963) and Robert Lucas (1967).

Quantitative Effects on Investment Demand   Let's think about the quantitative behavior of net investment demand. Since World War II, fixed net investment (exclusive of purchases of consumer durables) has averaged about 4% of the capital stock, K_{t-1}. Consider changes in the real interest rate, r_t, or in the schedule for capital's marginal product, MPK_t. These changes affect the aggregate desired stock of capital, $\hat{K}_t$. Suppose, as an example, that some change occurs that reduces this desired stock by 1%. Then the aggregate of net investment demand—over a period of, say, a year—declines by about 1% of the capital stock. If net investment demand were initially equal to 4% of the capital stock, this change would lower it to 3% of the stock. Thus, a decline by 1% in the desired stock of capital translates into a fall by roughly 25% in one year's net investment demand. Because one year's net investment is a small fraction—on the average about 4%—of the existing capital stock, small percentage changes in the desired stock generate large percentage changes in net investment demand. Therefore, we should not be surprised by two features of the U.S. data that we noticed before. First, because net investment demand is volatile, the share of investment spending in GNP fluctuates substantially from year to year. Second, the desired stock of capital is sometimes low enough—namely, during the Great Depression and World War II—so that aggregate net investment is negative.

INVESTMENT AND HOUSEHOLDS' BUDGET CONSTRAINTS

Remember that we can think of households, in their role as producers, as carrying out investment expenditures. When we include investment as another use of funds in a household's budget constraint, we get the condition

$$P_t y_t + b_{t-1}(1 + R) + m_{t-1} + v_t = P_t c_t + P_t i_t + b_t + m_t. \qquad (9.8)$$

As before, the left side shows the sources of funds, and the right side shows the uses. The new term is the expenditure for investment, $P_t i_t$, on the right side.

Before, we defined saving to be the change in the value of a household's assets, which could be held as either bonds or money. In the presence of inflation, we have to distinguish the change in the real value of assets from the change in the nominal value. Generally households would care about how the *real* value of their assets varies over time. Therefore, we should define **real saving** to be the change in the real value of assets; in particular, the change in real bond holdings plus the change in real money balances. (**Nominal saving** can then be calculated by multiplying real saving by the price level.)

Aside from bonds and money, households now have another store of value—physical capital goods. (Remember that we can think of households as owning the capital goods.) Therefore, a household's total real saving is the change in the real value of bonds and money plus the change in the quantity of capital,

$$\text{real saving} = \frac{(b_t + m_t)}{P_t} - \frac{(b_{t-1} + m_{t-1})}{P_{t-1}} + k_t - k_{t-1}. \quad (9.9)$$

Notice that the last term in equation 9.9 is net investment. Hence, net investment is one component of real saving.

One way for a household to finance more net investment, $k_t - k_{t-1}$, is to raise real saving, which requires either a cut in consumption or an increase in work effort (which would raise real income). But households can also finance investment by running down the real value of financial assets, bonds, and money. For example, a household (or business) can borrow to pay for additional capital goods. (A firm might borrow to finance a factory, or a household might borrow to purchase a new home.) Hence, a household's or firm's decision to raise investment does not require a corresponding increase in that household's or firm's real saving.

From the standpoint of a single household or firm, there are substantially different forces that influence net investment and real saving. For example, net investment increases with an upward shift in the schedule for capital's marginal product but falls with a rise in the real interest rate, r_t. On the other hand, a household's real saving increases when income is temporarily high or when the real interest rate rises.

If it were impossible to borrow and lend, equation 9.9 would require each household's or firm's net investment to be financed only by that household's or firm's real saving. Then producers could exploit attractive investment opportunities only if they were willing to abstain from current consumption or leisure. The potential for running down financial assets or borrowing means that producers can undertake investments even if they are personally unwilling to save very much. In particular, the opportunities to borrow and lend ensure that all investment projects will be undertaken if the real rate of return to investment is at least as great as the real interest rate, r_t. Hence, the separation of individual decisions to invest from individual decisions to save promotes economic efficiency.[9]

What is the economy's aggregate of real saving? Since the total stock of bonds, B_t, is still zero in each period, we find from equation 9.9 that

$$\text{aggregate real saving} = \frac{M_t}{P_t} - \frac{M_{t-1}}{P_{t-1}} + K_t - K_{t-1}. \quad (9.10)$$

Let's ignore the part of aggregate real saving that consists of changes in aggregate real money balances. Typically that part is small relative to aggregate net investment. Then equation 9.10 says that aggregate real saving equals aggregate net investment, $K_t - K_{t-1}$. Recall that individuals can invest by running down bonds or borrowing. But then others must be expanding their holdings of bonds—that is, lending. So for society as a whole, greater net investment does require greater aggregate real saving.

Earlier we did not allow for possibilities of investment. Then, if we neglected changes in aggregate real money balances, we found that aggregate real saving must

---

[9]Irving Fisher (1930, especially chaps. 7, 11) stresses this feature of a market economy.

be zero. Without investment, there is no way for the whole economy to save—that is, to change its real assets. But when the capital stock can vary, we find that aggregate real saving can be nonzero. In other words, the economy can now adjust aggregate net investment to shift resources from one period to another. These possibilities for shifting resources over time were present before for an individual, who could borrow and lend on the credit market at the real interest rate, r_t. Once we add a variable amount of capital stock to the analysis, the total economy has opportunities for real saving that resemble those available to individuals on the credit market. These opportunities have important consequences for the analysis of market-clearing conditions.

CLEARING OF THE COMMODITY MARKET

There are still two aggregate-consistency conditions to satisfy—first, that the aggregate demand for commodities equal the supply, and, second, that all money be willingly held. The existence of investment has major implications for the first condition but not the second, so we focus here on the condition for clearing the commodity market.

Clearing of the commodity market requires the aggregate supply of goods to equal the demand—that is,

$$Y^s(r_t, \cdots) = C^d(r_t, \cdots) + I^d(r_t, \cdots).$$
$$(+) \qquad (-) \qquad (-) \qquad\qquad (9.11)$$

The left side of the equation shows the positive intertemporal-substitution effect from the real interest rate, r_t, on the aggregate supply of goods, Y_t^s. As before, this response reflects a positive effect on work effort, N_t. The omitted terms in the function, denoted by . . . , include various characteristics of the production function, as well as the quantity of capital from the previous period, K_{t-1}.

The right side of equation 9.11 contains the two components of aggregate demand, consumption and gross investment. As before, the real interest rate, r_t, has a negative intertemporal-substitution effect on consumer demand, C_t^d. In addition, the real interest rate has a negative effect on gross investment demand, I_t^d. Again, the omitted terms include the characteristics of the production function, as well as the quantity of capital, K_{t-1}, and the depreciation rate, δ.

In Chapter 10, which considers long-term economic growth, it will be important to keep track of how the aggregate capital stock changes over time. Then we have to detail the role of the capital stock, K_{t-1}, in the market-clearing condition from equation 9.11. But for now we assume a given value of this stock. That is, we carry out a short-run analysis in which changes in the stock of capital are small enough to neglect. It turns out that this setting is adequate to study the main role of investment during business fluctuations.

Following the approach developed in Chapter 5, Figure 9.7 graphs the aggregates of commodities supplied and demanded versus the real interest rate, r_t. As before, the supply curve, Y^s, slopes upward, while the demand curve, Y^d, slopes downward. Also the figure breaks down aggregate demand into its two components, which are consumption demand, C^d, and gross investment demand, I^d. Each of these curves slopes downward versus r_t. We discussed before why investment demand would be especially sensitive to variations in the real interest rate. Therefore, the figure shows the I^d curve with more of a negative slope than the C^d curve.

Figure 9.7 shows that the commodity market clears at the real interest rate r_t^*. Correspondingly, we label the level of output as Y_t^*. At this point, the uses of output break down between C_t^* of consumption and I_t^* of gross investment.

SUPPLY SHOCKS

We want to see how the presence of investment affects our analysis of supply shocks. As before, we distinguish temporary changes from permanent ones.

A TEMPORARY SHIFT OF THE PRODUCTION FUNCTION

Consider a temporary downward shift of the production function, such as that caused by a harvest failure. To keep things simple, assume to begin with a parallel downward shift of the production function for period t. Then there are no changes in the schedules for the marginal products of labor, MPL_t, or capital, MPK_{t-1}. Also, we assume that there is no change in the schedule for the prospective marginal product of capital, MPK_t.

The decline in the production function lowers the aggregate supply of goods, Y_t^s, on the left side of equation 9.11. Also, there is a negative effect on wealth, which

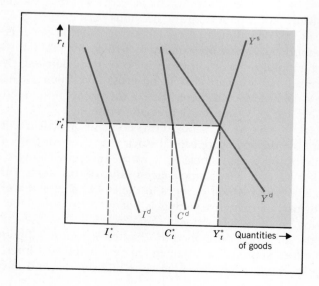

FIGURE 9.7 *Clearing of the Commodity Market*
The commodity market clears at the real interest rate, r_t^*. Here, the total output, Y_t^*, breaks down into C_t^* of consumption and I_t^* of gross investment.

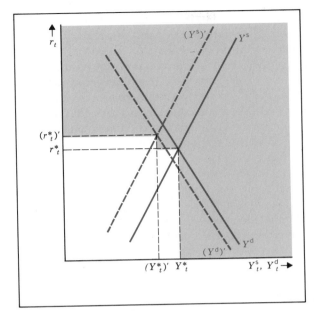

FIGURE 9.8 *Effects of a Temporary Downward Shift of the Production Function*
There is a leftward shift to aggregate supply, Y^s, which exceeds the leftward shift to demand, Y^d. Hence, the real interest rate rises, while aggregate output falls.

is small since the reduction in income is temporary. Therefore, there is a small decline in consumer demand, C_t^d, and a small increase in work effort, N_t. Note that this increase in work offsets part of the decline in the supply of goods. Finally, since the schedule for capital's marginal product, MPK_t, does not change, there is no shift to gross investment demand, I_t^d.

Figure 9.8 shows the shifts to aggregate supply and demand. There is a leftward shift in supply and a smaller leftward shift in demand. In the figure the real interest rate labeled r_t^* is the one that cleared the market in the absence of the shifts. Therefore, at this real interest rate, there is now an excess of goods demanded over those supplied—that is, $Y_t^d > Y_t^s$. This excess demand arises because people react to the temporary shortfall of production, and hence income, by lowering their desired real saving. Thus, we can also say that the disturbance creates an excess of net investment demand over desired real saving.

As in our previous analysis of this situation, the real interest rate must rise for the commodity market to clear. Therefore, in Figure 9.8, the new market-clearing real interest rate, $(r_t^*)'$, exceeds the initial value, r_t^*. We can think of this increase in the real interest rate as resulting from the excess of desired borrowing over desired lending.

How does the increase in the real interest rate compare with that in our earlier analysis, which did not consider investment? In the earlier analysis the real interest rate had to rise enough to make aggregate desired saving equal zero. Now the amount of aggregate real saving equals the quantity of aggregate net investment. Since the rise in the real interest rate reduces investment demand, we do not require as large an increase in the real interest rate as we did before.

Figure 9.8 shows that the new level of output, $(Y_t^*)'$, is below the initial amount, Y_t^*. Further, this drop in output reflects partly a decline in consumption, $(C_t^*)' < C_t^*$, and partly a decline in gross investment, $(I_t^*)' < I_t^*$. (Since depreciation is fixed at the amount δK_{t-1}, the fall in net investment equals that in gross investment.) Note that the rise in the real interest rate reduces consumption and investment demand. In addition, the decrease in wealth reinforces the decline in consumer demand. Finally, the higher real interest rate and the reduction in wealth imply that the quantity of work effort, $(N_t^*)'$, exceeds the initial amount, N_t^*.

Consider the quantitative responses of consumption and work effort. Because the wealth effect is weak, the changes in consumption and work will be large only if there is a substantial increase in the real interest rate, r_t. However, consider what happens if investment demand is highly responsive to r_t. (We discussed before why this is likely.) In this case a small increase in r_t is sufficient to equate desired real saving to net investment demand—that is, to clear the commodity market. Hence, most of the drop in output reflects a decline in investment, and there are only small changes in consumption and work effort.

The important conclusion is that fluctuations in investment partially insulate consumption and work from some types of temporary economic disturbances. Let's explain why this happens. When there is a temporary drop in supply—such as a harvest failure—everybody wants to maintain their previous levels of consumption and work by saving less or borrowing more at the initial real interest rate. But if there are no possibilities for investment, it is infeasible for everyone to save less or borrow more. In this case the real interest rate rises enough to make the total of desired real saving equal zero. Therefore, households must end up making substantial adjustments in their consumption and work. When we introduce investment, it becomes possible for aggregate real saving to change. By lowering aggregate net investment, the *economy* does what each individual would like to do at a given real interest rate. In fact, if investment demand is highly sensitive to the real interest rate, as we anticipate, the bulk of the decline in output shows up as a reduction in investment and real saving. By contrast, consumption and work change relatively little.

Notice that the results imply that investment fluctuates by more than consumption, at least in response to some temporary economic disturbances. In particular, adverse shocks—such as a harvest failure—lead to declines in output and to accompanying decreases in investment as a share of GNP. Conversely, favorable shocks lead to higher output and to increases in the ratio of investment to GNP. Therefore, the theoretical results accord in this respect with the observed behavior of investment during recessions and booms.

The Behavior of Employment

One feature of the results that conflicts with the U.S. data is the behavior of work effort. Recessions are invariably accompanied by declines in employment. But the analysis so far suggests that a temporary adverse shock to the production function leads to a small increase in work.

Work effort rises in our example because we omitted a likely adverse effect on labor's productivity. As mentioned in some earlier cases, a downward shift of the schedule for labor's marginal product, MPL_t, usually accompanies a downward shift of the production function. This change motivates people to reduce work effort, N_t. In fact, because the cutback in productivity is temporary, there is an intertemporal-substitution effect, which reinforces the tendency for work to decline.

The decrease in work effort implies additional leftward shifts to commodity supply and demand of the sort shown in Figure 9.8. Hence, there is a larger decline in output. There is also a larger increase in the real interest rate and a correspondingly sharper decline in investment. Overall, the main result is the tendency for a reduction in work to accompany the decline in output. We shall reexamine the behavior of employment during recessions in Chapter 11, which deals also with unemployment.

A PERMANENT SHIFT OF THE PRODUCTION FUNCTION

Previously we contrasted permanent shifts of the production function with the type of temporary change that we just examined. Now consider a permanent downward shift in the presence of investment. But assume again a parallel shift, which leaves unchanged the schedules for the various marginal products. In particular, since there is no change in capital's marginal product, MPK_t, there is again no shift to investment demand, I_t^d.

When the adverse shock is permanent, the wealth effects become important. There is a strong negative effect on consumer demand, C_t^d, and a strong positive effect on work effort, N_t. Recall from our previous discussions that this type of permanent change to the production function exerts little net effect on desired real saving. Therefore, in Figure 9.9, we show the leftward shift in demand as equal to that in supply. (This result still holds if we include a permanent downward shift of the schedule for labor's marginal product, although the curves shift by greater amounts.)

The main point is that the supply of goods equals the demand at the initial real interest rate, r_t^*. (Equivalently, net investment demand still equals desired real saving.) Since the real interest rate does not change, there is no effect on investment. Hence, in this case, all of the decline in output reflects a fall in consumption.

The main new result concerns the role of investment as a buffer for consumption. When there are temporary shocks to the production function, the sharp fluctuations in investment prevent large changes in consumption. But movements in investment cannot insulate consumption from permanent changes in production possibilities. Permanent shifts of the production function, which have substantial wealth effects, lead to large changes in consumption.

SHIFTS TO THE PRODUCTIVITY OF CAPITAL

The previous examples dealt with disturbances that left unchanged the schedule for capital's marginal product, MPK_t. In these cases, there were no shifts to investment demand. However, shifts in this component of demand can also be a source

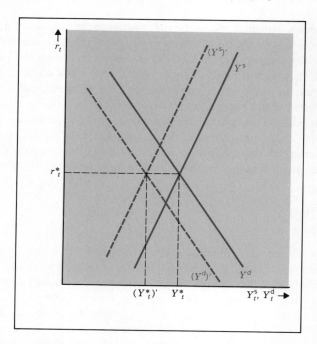

FIGURE 9.9 *Effects of a Permanent Downward Shift of the Production Function*
With a permanent downward shift of the production function, the leftward shifts of demand and supply are roughly equal. Therefore, output falls, but the real interest rate does not change.

of shocks to the economy. In fact, John Maynard Keynes (1936, chaps. 11, 12) stressed this element as a major reason for business fluctuations.

In thinking about supply shocks, which affect the production function, we mentioned the oil crises as important examples. There is some evidence (see Ernst Berndt and David Wood, 1979) that energy and capital are complementary inputs to production. That is, a cutback in the quantity of energy input—as in the oil crises—tends to reduce the marginal product of the complementary input, capital. Therefore, in addition to lowering the supply of goods, a supply shock related to energy would tend to lower investment demand. Aside from supply shocks, there are other circumstances where producers would change their assessments for the prospective marginal product of capital and hence for the likely returns from investment. One important example is where the government either raises or lowers the effective tax rate on the income from capital. (We explore the effects of taxes in Chapter 12.)

To assess the effects that arise in these kinds of examples, assume a downward shift of the schedule for capital's marginal product, MPK_t. Recall that this marginal product refers to the output for period $t + 1$. To keep things simple, assume that no changes occur to the production function for period t. That is, we neglect for the moment any direct negative effects on the current supply of goods. Also, abstract for now from any wealth effects.

Recall that the condition for clearing the commodity market is (with time subscripts now omitted)

$$Y^s(r, \cdots) = C^d(r, \cdots) + I^d(r, \cdots).$$
$$(+) \qquad\qquad (-) \qquad\qquad (-)$$

Given our assumptions, the only initial effect from the disturbance is a decline in gross investment demand, I^d, on the right side of the equation. Therefore, Figure 9.10 shows only a leftward shift of the aggregate demand curve, Y^d, which reflects the reduction in investment demand.

We see from the figure that the real interest rate and output decrease. Note that the fall in output reflects the negative effect of the lower real interest rate on work effort. Also, the lower real interest rate means that consumption rises. Therefore, investment falls by more than the decrease in total output.

Let's go back to the temporary supply shock that we considered before. As mentioned, this kind of disturbance—especially if it is related to energy supplies—tends to be accompanied by a downward shift in the schedule for capital's marginal product, MPK_t. Therefore we should combine the effects from Figure 9.10 with those that we found before in Figure 9.8. When we do this, we reinforce the downward effects on output and investment. However, the downward shift in investment demand tends to lower the real interest rate, which offsets the tendency for consumption to decline. In fact, the overall movement in consumption is now ambiguous.

An important new result concerns the short-run behavior of the real interest rate, r. In Figure 9.8 we found that a temporary adverse shock to the production function led to a higher real interest rate. This response reflects everyone's desire to save less in order to maintain their levels of consumption. But an opposing force arises if the shock also lowers the marginal product of capital. Then, as shown in Figure 9.10, the downward shift in investment demand tends to reduce the real interest rate. Thus, the overall effect on the real interest rate is uncertain. The net

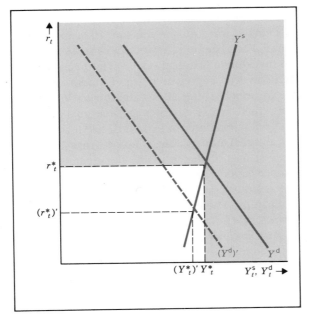

FIGURE 9.10 *Effects of a Decrease in the Marginal Product of Capital*
The decrease in the schedule for capital's marginal product reduces investment demand. Therefore, the real interest rate and the level of output decline.

change depends on whether the decrease in desired real saving is larger or smaller than the fall in net investment demand.

Empirically, real interest rates do not have a clear pattern of association with recessions and booms. That is, contrary to the reports that one often reads in the media, higher real interest rates are not necessarily a signal that the economy is doing badly, and lower real interest rates are not always an indicator that the economy is doing well. Therefore, we should not feel bad that our theory fails to generate an unambiguous prediction for the association between real interest rates and the state of the economy.

SUMMARY

Investment fluctuates proportionately by much more than total output, which fluctuates by more than consumption. Further, the ratio of investment to GNP is low during recessions and high in booms. For six recessions since World War II, the shortfall in total investment—which includes gross fixed investment, changes in business inventories, and purchases of consumer durables—accounted on average for 76% of the shortfall in real GNP. By contrast, consumer expenditures on nondurables and services declined relatively little during these recessions. The decline in consumption was, however, relatively more important during the Great Depression.

We began the theoretical analysis of investment by introducing the stock of capital as an input into the production function. The marginal product of capital is positive but diminishes as the quantity of capital rises.

Gross investment is the quantity of capital goods that a producer buys from the commodity market. Since we treat capital goods and consumables as physically identical, the total demand for goods is the sum of gross investment demand and consumption demand. The change in a producer's stock of capital—or net investment—equals gross investment less depreciation. In the aggregate, gross investment cannot be negative. However, aggregate net investment can be negative—and was in the United States for much of the 1930s and during World War II.

The real rate of return to investment is the marginal product of capital less the rate of depreciation. Producers determine their desired stocks of capital by equating this rate of return to the real interest rate. It follows that the desired stock of capital rises if the real interest falls, if the schedule for capital's marginal product shifts upward, or if the depreciation rate declines.

Given their initial stocks, producers invest enough during a period to achieve the desired stock of capital. Therefore, given the initial stock, investment demand rises if the desired stock of capital increases. Also, given the desired stock of capital, a smaller initial stock means a larger investment demand. Finally, we note that small percentage changes in the desired stock of capital translate into large percentage changes in net investment demand. This property explains why investment expenditure is volatile.

The existence of the credit market means that a household's or firm's decision to invest does not require that household or firm to save. In the aggregate, however, real saving equals net investment (plus the change in real money balances). Therefore, the existence of investment allows the whole economy to change its amount of real saving. This possibility has important implications for the characteristics of short-term business fluctuations.

Aggregate gross investment demand enters as a component of aggregate demand in the condition for clearing the commodity market. Because this component tends to be especially sensitive to variations in the real interest rate, investment absorbs the bulk of short-term fluctuations in output. Specifically, a temporary adverse shock to the production function leads to a major proportionate reduction in investment but to a relatively small decline in consumption. The effect of this kind of supply shock on the real interest rate is uncertain; it depends on whether the decline in desired real saving is larger or smaller than the decrease in net investment demand.

Finally, changes in investment cannot buffer consumption against permanent shifts to the production function. Here, an adverse shock leads to a strong downward response of consumption.

IMPORTANT TERMS AND CONCEPTS

physical capital	marginal product of capital (MPK)
producers' durable equipment and structures	real rate of return from investment
inventories	desired stock of capital
human capital	investment demand
private fixed capital	irreversible investment
utilization rate	real saving
	nominal saving

QUESTIONS AND PROBLEMS

Mainly for Review

9.1 What is meant by private domestic fixed investment? Does it include purchases of consumer durables? What about purchases of bonds?

9.2 Distinguish gross investment from net investment. When is net investment negative? Can gross investment be negative if capital goods cannot be resold?

9.3 Suppose producers expect inflation—that is, a higher price level in the next period. Will they want to increase their current purchases of capital goods? What if the nominal interest rate rises to reflect the higher expected inflation?

9.4 Does higher investment require higher saving on the part of an individual household or firm? For the economy as a whole, how do changes in the interest rate ensure that real saving rises to match an increase in investment?

9.5   Show graphically how the division of total output into consumption and investment is achieved through clearing of the commodity market. How does a temporary shift of the production function alter this division? Does your answer depend on the relative sensitivity of consumption demand and investment demand to changes in the interest rate?

9.6   Why does a decline in the productivity of capital reduce the interest rate? Could the interest rate fall so much as to leave the quantity of investment unchanged? Explain.

PROBLEMS FOR DISCUSSION

9.7   ***The One-Sector Production Function***

In our model, output can be labeled as either consumables or capital goods. Economists call this a one-sector production function.

a.   Why does the price of a unit of consumables always equal the price of a unit of capital in this model? What would happen if the price of consumables exceeded the price of capital goods, or vice-versa?

b.   Suppose that everyone wants to undertake negative gross investment—that is, everyone wants to resell old capital on the commodity market. Can the price of capital goods fall below the price of consumables in this case?

c.   **(optional)** Consider a "two-sector model," where different production functions apply to consumables and capital goods. Would the price of a unit of consumables always equal the price of a unit of capital goods in this model?

9.8   ***Inventory Investment***

Businesses hold inventories of goods, partly as finished products and partly as goods-in-process and raw materials. Suppose that we think of inventories as a type of capital, which enters into the production function. Then changes in these stocks represent investment in inventories. (Typically economists assume that the rate of depreciation on inventories is near zero.)

a.   How does an increase in the real interest rate affect the quantity of inventories that businesses want to hold? Therefore, what happens to inventory investment?

b.   Consider a temporary adverse shock to the production function. What happens to the amount of inventory investment? Therefore, what do we predict for the behavior of inventory investment during recessions?

(From 1947 to 1987, real inventory investment by businesses averaged only 0.7% of GNP. But inventory investment is highly volatile; in fact, during recessions, the change in inventories is often negative. Hence, Table 9.1 indicates that shortfalls in this component accounted, on average over six postwar recessions, for 28% of the shortfall in real GNP.)

9.9   ***The Investment Tax Credit***

For most years from 1962 to 1986, some types of investments qualified for a credit against income taxes. Assume that this governmental program effectively refunds the fraction, *a*, of investment expenditures. How does the size of the refund percentage, *a*, influence producers' desired stocks of capital and, hence, their investment demand? (Assume that someone who resells capital has to return the investment credit on the amount sold.)

9.10 *Capacity Utilization (optional)*

One way for a producer to generate extra output is to use capital more intensively. That is, a producer can run more shifts per day or allow less "downtime" for performing maintenance. Assume that more intensive utilization causes capital to depreciate faster.

a. How does a producer determine the best intensity of use for capital?

b. Show that an increase in the real interest rate, r_t, motivates producers to use their capital more intensively. What does this imply for the effect of the real interest rate on the supply of goods, y_t^s?

9.11 *The Ownership of Capital (optional)*

In our model, the people who use capital also own the capital. Suppose that these people print up certificates, each of which conveys ownership rights to one unit of capital. Then these certificates can be sold to others (on a stock market). But instead of using the capital themselves, the buyers of these certificates may allow other people ("businesses") to use the capital. Then the users pay a fee to holders of certificates. This fee may be either a fixed rental or a share of the profits.

a. Why might it be a good idea to separate the ownership of capital from the use of that capital? (Remember that households or firms can already finance the purchase of capital by borrowing.) Why might it be a bad idea?

b. What determines the nominal and real value of the ownership certificates when each is a claim to one unit of capital?

c. In the real world why is the future real value of a certificate subject to great uncertainty? Specifically, why does the value depend on the fortunes of the company that issued it?

9.12 *Temporary Shocks to the Production Function and Consumption*

Because of the strong response of investment, we found that temporary shocks to the production function had little effect on consumption. Suppose that we look at larger and larger—but still temporary—shocks. How does consumption react as the shocks get bigger? In particular, what happens to the division of the shortfall in output between consumption and investment? How does the answer relate to the Great Depression?

9.13 *Investment Opportunities for Robinson Crusoe*

In the market economy we found that investment takes the brunt of temporary shocks to the production function. Suppose that we introduce opportunities for investment into the model of Robinson Crusoe, which we constructed in Chapter 2. How would Robinson Crusoe's investment and consumption respond to temporary and permanent shifts to the production function? Are the results basically similar to those for the market economy?

9.14 *Saving, Investment, and the Real Interest Rate* (optional)

Suppose that shocks to the production function are sometimes favorable and sometimes unfavorable. Also, the shocks are sometimes temporary and sometimes permanent.

a. What pattern of association results between the real interest rate and the aggregate quantities of net investment and real saving?

b. Suppose that we try to deduce the effect of the real interest rate on an individual's desired real saving by examining the relation between the real interest rate and aggregate real saving. What do we find? What is the source of the problem?

c. Suppose that we try to estimate the effect of the real interest rate on investment demand from the relation between the real interest rate and aggregate net investment. What do we find? What is the source of the problem?

d. Suppose that we look at the relation of the real interest rate, r_t, to the ratio of aggregate consumptions, C_{t+1}/C_t. What will this tell us about an individual's saving behavior?

CHAPTER 10

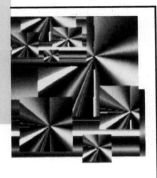

THE ACCUMULATION OF CAPITAL AND ECONOMIC GROWTH

hus far, we have studied investment in a short-run context, where changes in the stock of capital were small enough to neglect. In this context we focused on the role of investment as a component of the aggregate demand for goods. Now we want to allow for the effects of changing capital stocks on productive capacity—that is, on the aggregate supply of goods. Thereby, we bring in one of the central forces that influences a country's economic development over the long term.

There are some important elements that we hold constant initially while we study the process of capital accumulation. One of these is population, which is a major determinant of the aggregate labor force. Another is the accumulation of human capital—that is, education and training—which alters the quality of the labor force. In many respects, the economic forces that influence the accumulation of human capital are similar to those that affect physical capital. Therefore we can incorporate human capital by taking a broad view of capital in the model to include education and training along with buildings and machines.

Finally, we omit for the moment **technological change,** which we might model as shifts in the production function. We can think here of research and experience, which lead over time to better understanding about methods of production and types of goods. For some purposes, we can think of knowledge as another form of capital, which producers accumulate through expenditures on research and development. But there are some important differences: it is hard to maintain property rights to knowledge, and an awareness about how to produce things does not tend

229

to diminish as it spreads over more producers or a larger scale of operations. Hence, the possibilities for expanding knowledge mean that the aggregate economy may be able to grow for a long time without having to face diminishing returns.

EFFECTS OF THE CAPITAL STOCK ON PRODUCTION, WORK EFFORT, AND CONSUMPTION

Our previous analysis treated the aggregate stock of capital as constant. But since this stock will now change over time, we have to investigate how these changes affect the quantities of goods supplied and demanded. First we will consider how the quantity of capital input interacts with the quantity of labor input.

INTERACTIONS BETWEEN CAPITAL AND LABOR

How does an increase in capital affect the productivity of labor, and vice-versa? We could construct examples where an increase in one input, capital or labor, either raises or lowers the marginal product of the other. But for our purposes, we want to capture the typical pattern of interaction between capital and labor. Research on production functions at an economy-wide level indicates that cooperation between the inputs is the usual case. Therefore, we assume that an increase in one factor, capital or labor, raises the marginal product of the other.

Returns to Scale   What happens to output if a producer (a household or firm) doubles the quantities of both inputs—capital and labor? Does the producer get twice the output, or more or less than twice the output? If output exactly doubles, we say that the production function exhibits **constant returns to scale.** Alternatively, there are either **increasing or decreasing returns to scale** if output more or less than doubles, respectively. There may be increasing returns over some range of operations, constant returns over another range, and decreasing returns over a third range.

Usually the operation of a business requires some *fixed costs,* such as setting up an assembly line or learning about techniques of production. Since these fixed costs arise only once, there tends to be an interval of increasing returns to scale— in particular, the second unit produced requires fewer inputs than the first. Later, as the effect of the fixed cost becomes less important and the owner's span of attention and control becomes stretched, there may be a range of decreasing returns.[1] Until they reach this last range, firms in an industry tend to grow larger to exploit the economies of scale. For present purposes, we assume that firms (still owned by households) have already exploited their range of increasing returns and have be-

---

[1]For discussions of how this and related factors determine the sizes of firms, see Ronald Coase (1937) and Armen Alchian and Harold Demsetz (1972).

come large enough so that diminishing returns apply. That is, in the relevant range, a doubling of a producer's capital and labor leads to less than twice as much output.

THE CAPITAL STOCK AND HOUSEHOLDS' CHOICES

Remember that a producer's output for period t depends on the previous stock of capital, k_{t-1}, through the production function

$$y_t = f(k_{t-1}, n_t).$$

From the standpoint of a producer during period t, a greater amount of capital, k_{t-1}, is the same as an upward shift in the production function. In particular, given the amount of work effort, n_t, an increase in capital, k_{t-1}, means a larger supply of goods, y_t^s.

Other things equal, households are better off at date t if they own a greater amount of capital, k_{t-1}. To acquire this capital, households (or firms) had to make investments, which had to be paid for, possibly by borrowing on the credit market. But from the standpoint of society as a whole, the amounts borrowed and lent cancel. Therefore, the total stock of capital, K_{t-1}, must reflect previous acts of saving—that is, abstinence from either consumption or leisure. Once period t arrives, these costs associated with acquiring the aggregate stock of capital are bygones. Thus, households count the capital as wealth but make no subtraction in the aggregate for the past expenses that underlie the acquisition of the capital. (An individual household or firm subtracts its current debts that were incurred to finance investment. But in the aggregate, the stock of debt is zero.) Therefore, a larger stock of capital, K_{t-1}, means more aggregate consumer demand, C_t^d.

There are two effects from more capital, K_{t-1}, on aggregate work effort, N_t. First, the wealth effect motivates less work. But second, the increase in capital raises the schedule for labor's marginal product. Since this change stimulates work effort, the overall effect is ambiguous.

CAPITAL IN THE CONDITION FOR CLEARING THE COMMODITY MARKET

Putting the results together, the condition for clearing the commodity market at date t is now

$$Y^s(r_t, \ K_{t-1}, \ \cdots) = C^d(r_t, \ K_{t-1}, \ \cdots) + I^d(r_t, \ K_{t-1}, \ \cdots).$$
$$\begin{array}{ccc} (+)(+) & (-)(+) & (-)(-) \end{array} \qquad (10.1)$$

Notice the role of the capital stock, K_{t-1}, in this equation. An increase in this stock raises productive capacity and thereby increases goods supplied, Y_t^s. Because of the wealth effect, the higher stock of capital also raises consumer demand, C_t^d. However, given producers' desired stocks of capital for period t, an increase in the previous stock, K_{t-1}, reduces gross investment demand, I_t^d. Finally, there is also an ambiguous effect of the capital stock on work effort. This effect modifies the overall impact of the capital stock on Y_t^s and C_t^d.

For subsequent purposes, we shall find it convenient to subtract depreciation, δK_{t-1}, from both sides of equation 10.1. Then the market-clearing condition becomes

$$Y^s(r_t, \ K_{t-1}, \ \cdots) - \delta K_{t-1} = C^d(r_t, \ K_{t-1}, \ \cdots)$$
$$(+)(+) \qquad\qquad\qquad (-)(+)$$
$$+ \ I^d(r_t, \ K_{t-1}, \ \cdots) - \delta K_{t-1}. \qquad (10.2)$$
$$(-)(-)$$

The left side of the equation is the supply of net product, $Y^s_t - \delta K_{t-1}$. The right side is the sum of net investment demand, $I^d_t - \delta K_{t-1}$, and consumption demand, C^d_t.

The process of capital accumulation works as follows. Given the stock of capital, K_{t-1}, the market-clearing condition in equation 10.2 determines the real interest rate, r_t, and the quantities of net product, $Y_t - \delta K_{t-1}$, and net investment, $I_t - \delta K_{t-1}$. Hence the stock of capital for the next period comes from the condition

$$K_t = K_{t-1} + I_t - \delta K_{t-1}. \qquad (10.3)$$

That is, we add net investment, $I_t - \delta K_{t-1}$, to the previous stock of capital, K_{t-1}, to determine the next period's stock, K_t.

Once we know the capital stock, K_t, we can again use the market-clearing condition to determine the next period's values of the real interest rate, net product, and net investment. Thus, we determine a sequence of capital stocks, outputs, and so on. In this way we can use the model to chart out the path of economic development. (But remember that we do not allow yet for changes in population or technology.)

AN INCREASE IN THE CAPITAL STOCK OVER ONE PERIOD

Suppose that at some initial date, $t = 1$, the economy has the aggregate capital stock, K_0. Using equation 10.2, the market-clearing condition is

$$Y^s(r_1, \ K_0, \ \cdots) - \delta K_0 = C^d(r_1, \ K_0, \ \cdots) + I^d(r_1, \ K_0, \ \cdots) - \delta K_0.$$
$$(+)(+) \qquad\qquad (-)(+) \qquad\qquad (-)(-) \qquad\qquad (10.4)$$

In Figure 10.1 the upward-sloping line shows the supply of net product, $Y^s_1 - \delta K_0$, while the downward-sloping line shows the demand, $Y^d_1 - \delta K_0$. The market-clearing real interest rate is the value r^*_1, while the corresponding quantity of net product is the amount $Y^*_1 - \delta K_0$. Note that the figure shows also the two components of demand, which are consumption, C^d_1, and net investment, $I^d_1 - \delta K_0$. As before, the figure shows that investment demand is more responsive than consumption demand to variations in the real interest rate. We can use the figure to determine the breakdown of net product into consumption, C^*_1, and net investment, $I^*_1 - \delta K_0$.

Assume that aggregate net investment, $I^*_1 - \delta K_0$, is positive, as shown in Figure 10.1. Then the next period's stock of capital, K_1, would exceed the initial stock, K_0.

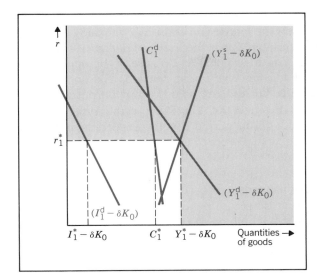

FIGURE 10.1 *Clearing of the Commodity Market*
At date 1 the commodity market clears at the real interest rate r_1^*. Net product is $Y_1^* - \delta K_1$, which breaks down into C_1^* of consumption and $I_1^* - \delta K_0$ of net investment.

Now we have to solve the following problem: How does the increase in the quantity of capital from K_0 to K_1 change the market-clearing condition? In particular, how does the next period's real interest rate, r_2^*, compare with the initial one, r_1^*? Note that in solving this problem we assume that the aggregate capital stock is the only thing that changes between periods 1 and 2.

Using equation 10.2, the market-clearing condition for period 2 is

$$Y^s(r_2, K_1, \cdots) - \delta K_1 = C^d(r_2, K_1, \cdots) + I^d(r_2, K_1, \cdots) - \delta K_1. \quad (10.5)$$
$$(+)(+) \qquad\qquad (-)(+) \qquad\quad (-)(-)$$

Consider how the increase in capital from K_0 to K_1 changes the various terms. For a given amount of work, an increase in capital stock makes the supply of net product, $Y_2^s - \delta K_1$, greater than before. In fact, an extra unit of capital raises this net supply by the amount $MPK_1 - \delta$, which is the real rate of return to investment.

The increase in capital also makes consumer demand, C_2^d, higher than before. Consider the magnitude of this response. If we neglect variations over time in capital's marginal product, an extra unit of capital provides a constant flow of additional real income in the amount $MPK_1 - \delta$. As in the case of a permanent improvement in the production function, we anticipate that the marginal propensity to consume would be close to one in this situation. Thus, if work did not change, consumer demand would also rise by approximately the amount $MPK_1 - \delta$. In other words, the rise in consumption demand roughly equals the increase in the supply of net product. Therefore, the increase in the stock of capital does not lead to a significant change in desired real saving.[2]

---

[2]The change in the amount of work effort is ambiguous. But whatever this change, there will still be little effect on desired real saving.

The increase in the supply of net product on the left side of equation 10.5 approximately equals the increase in consumer demand on the right side. However, we have not yet considered that the increase in capital from K_0 to K_1 reduces net investment demand on the right side. Because of the opposing movements in consumption demand and net investment demand, it is uncertain whether aggregate demand rises or falls. But the key point for our purposes is that aggregate supply must rise by more than demand. Therefore, at the initial real interest rate, r_1^*, the supply of net product during period 2 would exceed the demand—or, equivalently, desired real saving would exceed net investment demand. It follows that the real interest rate must fall to clear the commodity market in period 2—that is, $r_2^* < r_1^*$.

Consider what happens to the various quantities. First, consumption increases, so that $C_2^* > C_1^*$. That is because the direct effect from more capital and the decline in the real interest rate combine to raise consumer demand. However, the change in work is ambiguous. The decline in the real interest rate and the wealth effect from more capital motivate less work, but the positive effect of the extra capital on labor's marginal product motivates more work. Except in the unlikely case where work effort falls by a great deal, the increase in capital input means that gross and net product expand.

We know also that net investment declines—that is, $I_2^* - \delta K_1 < I_1^* - \delta K_0$. Otherwise the increase in net product would exceed the rise in consumption. But this outcome is impossible if the initial impacts to the supply of net product and consumer demand are roughly equal, as we assumed. Thus, an increase in the stock of capital leads to less net investment. It follows that net investment declines as a ratio to net or gross product.

INCREASES IN THE CAPITAL STOCK OVER MANY PERIODS

As long as net investment is positive, the process just described continues over time. The increase in the capital stock is accompanied by a declining real interest rate, rising consumption, and falling net investment. Also, there are probable increases in net and gross product but ambiguous changes in work effort.

Recall that the growth rate of capital declines over time. Remember also that the change in the capital stock generates the changes in the other variables. Therefore, the responses of the other quantities—in particular, consumption and total output—tend to become proportionately smaller over time. That is, there are declining growth rates of consumption and of gross and net product.

Consider why the real interest rate declines over time. At the start, date 1, the economy has a relatively low capital stock, K_0, and a correspondingly high marginal product of capital, MPK_1. The high real interest rate, r_1^*, signals the cost of using up resources during period 1 rather than later. This high cost reflects the favorable investment climate, in the sense of a high level of the investment demand function. Consuming at date 1 rather than later is justified only if people are willing to forego returns at the rate r_1^*, which equals the real rate of return to investment, $MPK_1 - \delta$.

As the economy matures, the capital stock rises, and the marginal product of capital declines. Because of the diminishing opportunities for investment, the real interest rate, r_t^*, declines, thereby signaling a decreasing return from deferring consumption.

THE STEADY-STATE CAPITAL STOCK AND REAL INTEREST RATE

How long does the process of capital accumulation go on?[3] (Recall again that, so far, we ask this question when population and technology are fixed.) The growth rate of capital tends to fall over time and eventually approaches zero. Therefore, the capital stock tends to some constant level, and net investment eventually becomes zero. Corresponding to the fixed quantity of capital, there are constant levels of output, consumption, gross investment (which equals depreciation here), and work effort. Economists refer to this situation as a **steady state,** defined as a position where a set of variables stays constant over time. In the model the growth rates of capital, output, consumption, and work effort are all zero in the steady state. (When we introduce growth of population and technology, we shall find that the steady-state growth rates can be positive.)

To determine the real interest rate in the steady state, we have to extend the analysis from Chapter 3 about households' choices over time. Suppose that we can express each household's overall utility, beginning from date 1 and extending into the indefinite future, in the form

$$U = u(c_1, n_1) + \frac{1}{(1 + \rho)} \, u(c_2, n_2) + \cdots. \qquad (10.6)$$

where ρ is a positive constant (ρ is the Greek letter rho). In effect, we calculate the present value of utility, but we use the number ρ, rather than the real interest rate r, to compute the present value. We shall call the number ρ the **rate of time preference.** The higher is the rate of time preference, the greater is the discount applied to future utility. Put another way, for each unit of utility that a household gives up today, it needs $1 + \rho$ extra units next period to maintain total utility, U. So a higher value of ρ signifies a greater preference for current utils over future ones.

In a steady state, each household picks the constant values, $c_1 = c_2 = \cdots =$

---

[3]This discussion draws on the classic treatment of the dynamics of saving and investment from Frank Ramsey (1928).

c, and $n_1 = n_2 = \cdots = n$. Hence overall utility is

$$U = u(c, n) + \frac{1}{(1 + \rho)} \cdot u(c, n) + \cdots.$$

But for this to be the right answer, it must be that households cannot do better by picking something other than constant values for consumption and work. (Otherwise, they would not, in fact, have chosen constant levels of consumption and work.)

If the steady-state real interest rate is r^*, a household can use the credit market to trade one unit of consumption at any date t for $(1 + r^*)$ units at date $t + 1$. Suppose, for example, that a decrease of c_t by one unit would lower period t's utility, $u(c, n)$, by the amount Δu. Then an increase of the quantity c_{t+1} by $(1 + r^*)$ units would raise period $t + 1$'s utility by the amount $(1 + r^*) \cdot \Delta u$.[4] We have to multiply this last change by the term, $1/(1 + \rho)$, to find the effect on overall utility. Therefore the full effect on overall utility is given by

$$\Delta u \left[-1 + \frac{1}{(1 + \rho)} \cdot (1 + r^*) \right].$$

Consider the term in square brackets in the above expression. If the term were positive, households could raise total utility by cutting consumption by one unit in period t and then using their extra saving to raise consumption by $1 + r^*$ units in period $t + 1$. Similarly, if the term were negative, households could raise total utility by raising consumption by one unit in period t and then balancing their diminished saving by lowering consumption by $1 + r^*$ units in period $t + 1$. Thus, the only way households could be satisfied with their initial choices is for the term in square brackets to be zero. This condition requires the steady-state real interest rate, r^*, to equal the rate of time preference, ρ. If this equality does not hold, households could raise their overall utility by either lowering or raising today's consumption and making the corresponding adjustment to future consumption.

The conclusion is that if $r^* = \rho$, households are happy with a constant level of consumption (and work). Since consumption is constant, the amount of consumption must equal the amount of net product. In other words, real saving is zero in the steady state. This result is consistent with the finding that net investment equals zero.

Recall that the process of increasing capital stocks involves reductions in the real interest rate, r_t^*. Now we know that the real interest rate eventually approaches the rate of time preference, ρ. Thus, the path of real interest rates looks like the one shown in Figure 10.2. Along the path, where $r_t^* > \rho$, net investment and real saving are positive. As the capital stock expands, net investment and real saving decline toward zero, while the real interest rate falls toward the value ρ.

What determines the level of the steady-state capital stock? Recall that, for any period, the real rate of return to investment, $MPK_t - \delta$, equals the real interest rate,

[4]This calculation works because we start from a position where $c_{t+1} = c_t$ and $n_{t+1} = n_t$. Otherwise we would have to worry about the relative amounts of consumption and work for the two periods.

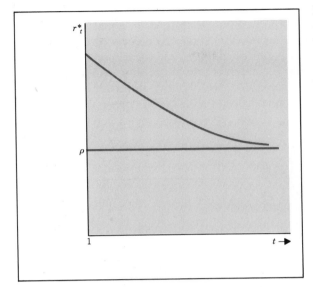

FIGURE 10.2 *Behavior of the Real Interest Rate over Time*
As the capital stock grows over time, the real interest rate declines and approaches the rate of time preference, ρ.

r_t^*. Since the steady-state real interest rate equals the rate of time preference, ρ, the condition for the steady state is

$$MPK - \delta = \rho. \tag{10.7}$$

We do not date the marginal product, *MPK*, since it remains constant in a steady state.

Let's sketch an example to illustrate the nature of the steady-state results. Suppose that at date 1 the economy is in a steady-state position where capital's marginal product, MPK_1, equals $\rho + \delta$. Call this steady-state level of capital K_0. Note that during period 1 the real interest rate is the value, $r_1^* = MPK_1 - \delta = \rho$. Further, the initial quantities of net investment and real saving are zero.

Now assume that there is a permanent improvement of the production function during period 2; hence, producers get more output for given inputs. Also, suppose that there are permanent upward shifts in the schedules for the marginal products of labor and capital. Because the changes are permanent, there are roughly equal increases in the supply of net product and in consumer demand. That is, desired real saving remains close to zero. However, because of the rise in capital's marginal product, net investment demand becomes positive. Therefore, at the initial real interest rate, $r_1^* = \rho$, there would be an excess of commodity demand over supply. Equivalently, net investment demand would exceed desired real saving. It follows that the real interest rate, r_2^*, rises above its initial value, $r_1^* = \rho$.

Now the economy is in the sort of position where we began our previous analysis of capital accumulation. Net investment is positive, and the real interest rate exceeds its steady-state value, ρ. Hence, the stock of capital rises over time, while the real interest rate falls. Eventually the economy approaches a new steady state, where the stock of capital exceeds the amount K_0 from the previous steady state. At that point the real interest rate again equals the steady-state value, ρ.

To summarize, a permanent improvement in the production function (which includes an upward shift to the schedule for capital's marginal product) raises net investment and the real interest rate in the short run. In the long run, the economy ends up with more capital—as well as more output and consumption—but no change in the real interest rate.

CHANGES IN POPULATION

A ONE-TIME INCREASE IN POPULATION

Suppose that at date 1 the economy is again in a steady state with the aggregate quantity of capital, K_0. Assume that during period 2 the population increases once and for all by, say, 10%. Think of a case where the number of households (and firms) rises as well by 10%, and assume that the new households are just like the old ones in terms of average age, tastes, and productivity. The new households might begin life with zero capital. Alternatively, the old households (parents) may provide the new ones (children) with a starting amount of capital. However, the main results are the same in both cases.

If the aggregate stock of capital does not change, the typical producer has less capital to work with than before. (Remember that the number of producers—households or firms—increased by 10%.) Therefore, the marginal product of capital exceeds its steady-state value, $\rho + \delta$. In the aggregate, the desired stock of capital increases, so that aggregate net investment demand becomes positive. There are also increases in the aggregates of work effort, goods supply, and consumer demand. However, these changes exert little influence on the aggregate of desired real saving. Therefore, at the initial real interest rate r_1^*, the demand for goods would exceed the supply by the amount of the increase in investment demand. It follows that the real interest rate increases—that is, $r_2^* > r_1^* = \rho$.

The one-time increase in population puts the economy in the familiar position where the real interest rate exceeds its steady-state value, ρ. We can understand this by noting that the rise in population effectively places the typical producer back in an earlier stage of economic development in which he or she has less capital to work with. In this situation the real interest rate exceeds its steady-state value.

Following the increase in the real interest rate for period 2, we can trace out the usual path where the aggregate capital stock increases, while the real interest rate declines toward its steady-state value, ρ. But what can we say about the various quantities in this new steady state? In particular, do the aggregates of capital, output, consumption, and work all rise by 10%—that is, by the same proportion as population?

The aggregate quantities would all be higher by 10% if production exhibited constant returns to scale. Then a 10% increase in the aggregates of capital and labor would produce 10% more goods. Also, the marginal product of capital would be the same as initially—equal to its steady-state value, $\rho + \delta$.

Since the number of producing units also increases by 10%, why would we expect something other than constant returns? There is some tendency for diminishing returns because there is no change in the aggregate of "land," by which we mean to include various types of natural resources and physical space. Probably there is a range of production over which constant returns is a reasonable approximation. That is, returns to scale are nearly constant until the fixed quantity of land becomes a significant constraint. Over the range where nearly constant returns applies, an expansion of population by 10% does lead in the long run to nearly 10% increases in the aggregates of capital, output, consumption, and work effort.

POPULATION GROWTH

We would like to study continuing growth in population. The details of this subject bring in some complications that would take the discussion far afield, so let's just sketch some results, which are only suggestive.

Continue to assume that returns to scale are roughly constant. But assume now that population grows at a steady rate rather than jumping all at once. For example, growth rates of population between 0 and 2% per year are typical of industrialized countries in the post–World War II period. For the United States, the rate was around 3% per year in the early nineteenth century but only 1.1% between 1960 and 1987.[5]

The growth in population has a continuing upward effect on the aggregates of capital, output, consumption, and work effort. Accordingly, the economy no longer approaches a steady state where these aggregates are constant. We have instead a situation that economists call **steady-state growth.** In this situation the aggregate quantities of capital, output, consumption, and work effort grow at the same rate as population. Although the levels of these variables change over time, certain ratios are constant in a position of steady-state growth. These ratios include the per capita amounts of capital, output, and consumption. Hence, the per capita growth rates of capital, output, and consumption are all zero in a position of steady-state growth.

Unlike our previous steady states, a position of steady-state growth has positive aggregate net investment and real saving. The net investment provides capital for the new members of society. Thereby, the quantities of capital per person and per worker can remain constant over time. We can think of parents as carrying out the saving to provide for their children—in effect, to establish their children in a business (or to provide them with education). Notice that, with a positive growth rate of population, it is not enough for people just to pass on capital to their descendants. There is more than one child per adult on average. Therefore, the typical adult must carry out positive real saving over his or her lifetime.

---

[5]Immigration accounted for roughly one-third of the growth in population from the mid-nineteenth century until the 1920s. Then immigration was relatively small from the 1930s through the 1960s. But the numbers rose in recent years. In 1986 the reported figures on immigration accounted for 26% of the increase in population. (See *Statistical Abstract of the U.S.,* 1988, p. 10.) If all illegal immigrants were included, this fraction would be much higher.

What is the real interest rate in a position of steady-state growth? Since consumption per person is constant, the previous results suggest that the real interest rate would still equal the rate of time preference, ρ. But remember that the typical parent carries out positive real saving here. The saving goes not to raise consumption per person but rather to provide for the growing population. For this analysis to work out, it must be that parents care about their children. That is, they care to the extent of discounting their children's utility (which comes in the future) by the rate of time preference, ρ.

Finally, we should mention that the discussion treats the path of population as a given. We should, however, be able to apply economic reasoning to determine population. Some classical economists, such as Malthus, Ricardo, and Marx, regarded this topic as a central element of economic analysis (although their theories did not stand up empirically). Recently, some economists have again been using economic analysis to study population growth.[6] So far, the empirical results are encouraging but cannot fully explain the behavior of population growth over time.

TECHNOLOGICAL CHANGE

We know that a permanent improvement of the production function leads in the long run to increases in the per capita quantities of capital, output, and consumption. Typically, the process of economic development involves a continuing series of these improvements through a process called technological progress. As in the case of population growth, we shall only sketch some effects from steadily improving technology.

Continuing technological improvements lead to persistent increases in the per capita quantities of capital, output, and consumption. In some cases, the economy approaches a position of **steady-state per capita growth,** in which the amounts per person of capital, output, and consumption grow at a constant rate. That is, the economy no longer tends toward per capita growth rates of zero.

What about the real interest rate in a position of steady-state per capita growth? Unlike our previous cases, there is now long-run growth in consumption per person. Therefore, the real interest rate in the steady state must be high enough to motivate people to defer consumption from early dates to later ones. This result means that the steady-state real interest rate exceeds the rate of time preference, ρ. (Recall that an interest rate equal to ρ would be just high enough to motivate constant consumption per person.)

Finally, as with population growth, our discussion does not use economic analysis to explain the changes in technology. We would like to explain producers' incentives to carry out the research and development that leads to new products and better methods of production. One interesting issue concerns the property rights that people have in their inventions, production techniques, and so on. We

---

[6]See, for example, Richard Easterlin (1968), Gary Becker (1981), and Gary Becker and Robert Barro (1988).

should also consider the eventual limitations on new ideas—that is, the likelihood that technology cannot advance forever. Theories about technological progress are a promising area of research in economics.

SUMMARIZING THE CONCLUSIONS ABOUT ECONOMIC DEVELOPMENT

Before we look at some evidence, let's summarize the main theoretical conclusions about the path of economic development. Suppose first that we abstract from growth in population and technology. Also, assume that the economy begins with a capital stock below its steady-state value. Then we predict positive but diminishing growth rates of the capital stock, output and consumption. These growth rates all approach steady-state values of zero. Correspondingly, the real interest rate falls toward its steady-state value, which is the rate of time preference, ρ. We also predict decreases over time in the ratio of net investment to net and gross product, with net investment equaling zero in the steady state.

When we introduce population growth, we find that the economy approaches a position of steady-state growth. The per capital growth rates of capital, output, and consumption are all zero, but net investment is positive in this situation. Otherwise the results are similar to those already summarized.

Finally, we can allow for continuing improvements in technology. Because of technological progress, the economy may exhibit steady-state per capita growth, where the growth rates of capital, output, and consumption per person all equal a positive constant. In this situation the steady-state real interest rate exceeds the rate of time preference, ρ.

LONG-TERM EVIDENCE FOR THE UNITED STATES

Let's see how the theory relates to the long-term performance of the U.S. economy. Table 10.1 contains data from the nineteenth and twentieth centuries on the growth rate of real gross national product (GNP), on a measure of the real interest rate, and on the ratios of gross and net investment to real GNP. The data are averages over 20-year periods, excluding the years around the three major wars (1861–66, 1917–19, 1941–46).

To get a long time series, we use the interest rate on prime commercial paper, which applies to short-term notes issued by established companies. (U.S. Treasury bills were first issued in 1929.) Recall that during most of the post–World War II period, real interest rates were low; the average for 1947–80 was only 0.6%. However, for 1981–88, the average was much higher—4.7%. Despite these relatively high real interest rates since 1981, the principal observation from Table 10.1 is the marked decline in real interest rates over the longer term. The average value of the real interest rate was 9.1% for 1840–60 and 1867–80, 6.3% for 1880–1900, 3.1% for 1900–16, 4.9% for 1920–40, −0.2% for 1947–60, and 1.2% for 1960–80. In comparison with the numbers from before World War II, the real interest rates for 1981–88 no longer seem dramatic. In any event, the longer-term pattern of real interest rates conforms to the theory, which predicts that capital's marginal product and the real interest rate will decline as an economy develops.

The ratios of gross and net fixed private investment to GNP show some decline over the long term. Specifically, the ratio for net investment decreased from 9–10% for 1869–1900 to 6% for 1947–80. The theory predicts that this decline would accompany the fall in real interest rates.

Table 10.1 shows average growth rates of real GNP, population, and real GNP per capita since 1840. (The figures on real GNP for the nineteenth century are rough estimates.) There is a pronounced decline in the growth rate of population—

TABLE 10.1 *Growth Rates, Interest Rates, and Investment Ratios for the United States since 1840*

| | Growth Rates (% per year) | | | Interest and Inflation Rates (% per year)[a] | | | Investment Ratios | |
| | | | | | | | Gross Private Fixed Investment | Net Private Fixed Investment |
	Real GNP	Population	Real GNP per Capita	R	π	$r = R - \pi$	GNP	GNP
1840–1860	4.9	3.1	1.8	8.6	−0.5	9.1	—	—
1867–1880	5.6[b]	2.3[b]	3.3[b]	6.7	−2.4	9.1	0.17[c]	0.09[c]
1880–1900	3.2	2.1	1.1	5.6	−0.7	6.3	0.19[d]	0.10[d]
1900–1916	3.7	1.8	1.9	5.5	2.4	3.1	0.17	0.07
1920–1940	2.2	1.1	1.1	3.3	−1.6	4.9	0.12	0.01
1947–1960	3.4	1.7	1.7	2.3	2.5	−0.2	0.14	0.06
1960–1980	3.2	1.2	2.0	5.9	4.7	1.2	0.14	0.06

Notes: The periods exclude the years around three major wars: 1861–66, 1917–19, and 1941–46.

For the data on real GNP, see Figure 1.1 of Chapter 1.

R is the nominal interest rate on four- to six-month prime commercial paper. For 1857–89, the variable refers to 60- to 90-day rates, as reported in Macaulay (1938, Table 10). For 1840–56 the rates are Bigelow's estimates for the "New York and Boston money markets," as reported by Macaulay in Table 25. Interest rates since 1890 are in U.S. Department of Commerce (1975, p. 1001), and *Federal Reserve Bulletin*, various issues.

The inflation rate, π, is based on the GNP deflator since 1869. For the data, see Figure 1.4 of Chapter 1. Data on the price level before 1869 refer to the consumer price index, as reported in U.S. Department of Commerce (1975, p. 211).

The investment ratios equal real fixed, private, domestic investment divided by real GNP. Data on investment for 1869–1928 are from Kendrick (1961, Tables A-I, A-III).

Data on all variables for recent years are from U.S. Department of Commerce (1986).

[a]Dates for the interst rate are 1840–59, 1867–79, 1880–99, 1900–15, 1920–39, 1947–59, and 1960–79. Thereby the periods correspond roughly to those for the inflation rate.

[b]1869–80 (data on real GNP for 1867–68 are unavailable).

[c]1869–78.

[d]1879–1900.

from about 3% per year in the mid-nineteenth century to a little over 1% for 1960–80. There is also some decline in the growth rate of real GNP—from about 5% per year in 1840–60 to 3.5% in 1960–80. But there is no indication of decline since 1880. Finally, there is no clear pattern over time in the growth rates of real GNP per capita. In fact, the value of 2.3% per year for 1960–80 is exceeded only by the value of 3.5% per year for 1869–80. This last finding conflicts with the theoretical prediction of declining per capita growth rates.

A CROSS SECTION OF COUNTRIES IN THE POST–WORLD WAR II PERIOD

Let's consider now the growth experiences of a cross section of countries in the post–World War II period. For this purpose we can use the data set that Robert Summers and Alan Heston (1988) have constructed (with the earlier help of Irving Kravis) for over 100 countries. Figure 10.3 plots for 113 countries the average growth rate of real per capita gross domestic product (GDP) from 1960 to 1985 against the level of real GDP per capita in 1960. The figure reveals a slightly positive relationship, but the main indication is that the per capita growth rate bears little relation to the starting level of per capita output. In other words, there is no tendency for the countries that started with low per capita product to grow relatively fast and thereby catch up with the countries that began with high per capita product.

If countries were similar with respect to conditions of technology and preferences, the theory would predict that countries that began with low output per person would tend to converge toward those that started with high values. This process would correspond to low-income countries growing for awhile at relatively high rates. But the behavior of per capita growth shown in Figure 10.3 does not support this proposition. In this respect the cross-country results are similar to the long-period evidence for the United States. Remember that we saw no tendency for per capita growth to slow down as the U.S. economy developed.

Figure 10.4 shows that there is a weak negative relation across countries between the growth rate of real GDP (rather than real GDP per capita) and the starting level of real GDP per capita. This association reflects the strong inverse relation between population growth and the starting value of real GDP per capita. That is, in the post–World War II period, the poorer countries tended to have higher growth rates of population. This result is again similar to the findings for the United States. Recall that U.S. population growth tended to decline as the economy developed.

Figures 10.5 and 10.6 give the results for the 41 countries that began in 1960 with a relatively high per capita income. (This sample consists of countries in which real GDP per person in 1960 exceeded $1500 in terms of 1980 prices.) For this group there is some negative relation between the growth rate of real GDP per capita and the starting level of real GDP per capita (Figure 10.5). There is also a strong negative relation between the growth rate of real GDP and the starting level of real GDP per capita (Figure 10.6). Thus, the data indicate some tendency for convergence among the countries that were reasonably well off by 1960.

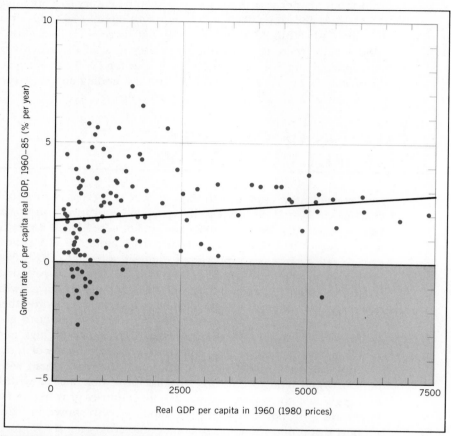

FIGURE 10.3 *Growth per Capita versus the Starting Level of Output per Capita (for 113 countries)*

Overall the cross-country data indicate two systematic patterns with regard to economic growth. First, there are countries that attained a level of relative prosperity by 1960. In these cases there is some tendency for the lower-income countries to grow faster and thereby to converge toward the higher-income countries. This behavior accords with the predictions from the theory in this chapter. Second, there are countries that began at low levels of income (say, less than $1000 per capita in 1980 prices) and did not tend to grow at the high rates needed to catch up with the wealthier countries. In this range, the data did not show any tendency toward convergence. Therefore, the theory would have to be expanded to match the existence of a "low-level trap" for the least developed countries.

While the theory in this chapter has some explanatory value, it cannot explain most of the differences in growth rates that show up along the vertical axes in Figures 10.3 and 10.4. That is, the theory cannot explain very well why countries grow at substantially different rates over long periods of time. There have, however, been some exciting recent developments in growth theory, which have promise for understanding more about the data. Some elements stressed in the recent theory are the determinants of technological progress, the influences on population growth, and the role of investments in human capital. The behavior of saving and investment, the role of free markets, and the effects of governmental services and taxation are central elements of this research. Some of the work brings out the potential for a low-level trap on economic development, a phenomenon that seems to characterize the data across countries. For a (technically demanding) survey of the recent research, see Paul Romer (1989).

SUMMARY

This chapter studies the process of capital accumulation over the long term. As the quantity of capital increases, the diminishing marginal product of capital implies

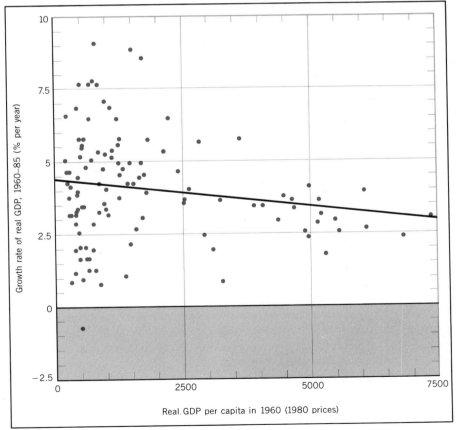

FIGURE 10.4 *Growth versus the Starting Level of Output per Capita (for 113 countries)*

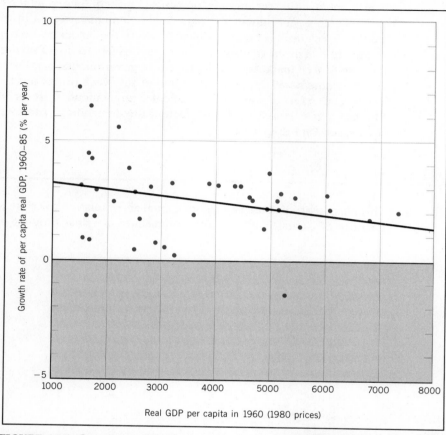

FIGURE 10.5 *Growth per Capita versus the Starting Level of Output per Capita (for 41 countries with starting levels above $1500)*

that the real interest rate falls. The path of economic development features rising consumption and output but declining net investment. Work effort may either rise or fall over time. The growth rates of capital, consumption, and output tend to decline, and the economy eventually approaches a steady state in which output and the quantity of capital do not change. In this situation, net investment and real saving are zero, and the real interest rate equals the rate of time preference.

Steadily growing population leads to persistent growth in output and the quantity of capital. Although the economy no longer approaches a position in which net investment and real saving are zero, the per capita growth rates of capital, consumption, and output tend to zero. If there is continuing technological progress, these per capita growth rates can be positive in the long run.

The U.S. data since 1840 reveal a long-term decline in the real interest rate and some decrease in the ratio of fixed investment to GNP. While there is some decline over time in the growth rate of output, there is no systematic decline in the growth rate of output per capita.

We also examined the growth experiences of over 100 countries from 1960 to 1985. There is little overall relation between the growth rate of real GDP per capita and the starting level of real GDP per capita. Therefore, the lower-income countries do not tend systematically to converge toward the higher-income countries. For countries that began in a position of relative prosperity, there is some tendency for the lower-income countries to grow at a faster rate. Therefore, the data indicate some tendency for convergence among the group of relatively prosperous countries.

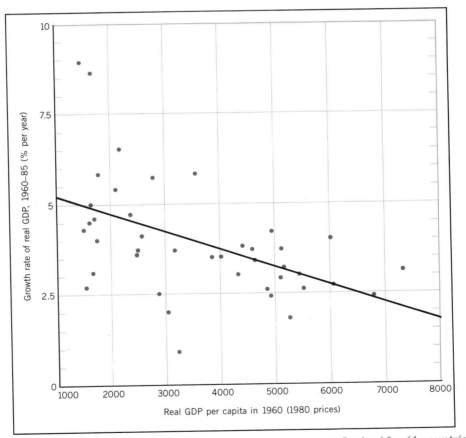

FIGURE 10.6 *Growth versus the Starting Level of Output per Capita (for 41 countries with starting levels above $1500)*

IMPORTANT TERMS AND CONCEPTS

technological change

constant returns to scale

increasing or decreasing returns to scale

steady state

rate of time preference

steady-state growth

steady-state per capita growth

QUESTIONS AND PROBLEMS

Mainly for Review

10.1 Why does an increase in the capital stock reduce the real interest rate?

10.2 Summarize the effect of a higher capital stock on the quantities of:

a. Consumption
b. Leisure
c. Net investment

Distinguish where necessary between wealth and substitution effects.

10.3 What is the immediate effect of a one-time, permanent improvement in the production function on the real interest rate and net investment? If the rise in the real interest rate were equal to the rise in the marginal product of capital, would net investment rise? Explain why this situation is unlikely to occur.

10.4 What are the long-run effects of the improvement in the production function considered in question 10.3? Why does net investment remain positive in future periods even though there are no more increases in *MPK*? Why does the economy eventually reach a steady state, in which net investment is zero?

10.5 Compare an economy in steady-state growth with one in a steady state. Explain why, in the former situation, there is positive net investment in every period.

PROBLEMS FOR DISCUSSION

10.6 *The Effects of More Capital on the Commodity Market*
Construct a diagram to show the effects of an increase in the capital stock from period 1 to period 2 on the commodity market.

a. What determines the direction and magnitude of the shift in the aggregate demand for net product?

b. Draw in the curve for net investment demand. After the capital stock increases, what is the quantity of net investment demanded when the real interest rate equals the value r_1^*?

    c. Consider the effect of more capital on the quantity of net investment. Why is this effect negative?

10.7 *Economic Development and the Real Wage Rate*

Suppose that we introduce a separate labor market into the model.

    a. Assume that population and technology are fixed but the economy starts with a capital stock below the steady-state amount. As the economy accumulates capital, what happens to the real wage rate?

    b. Suppose that at date 1 the economy is in a steady state. Then there is a once-and-for-all improvement of the production function. This improvement includes upward shifts to the schedules for the marginal products of labor and capital. What happens to the real wage rate in the short run and the long run?

10.8 *Population Growth (optional)*

Suppose that technology is fixed, but population grows at the constant rate η (the Greek letter eta). Assume that returns to scale in production are nearly constant. How does the value of η affect the following variables *in a position of steady-state growth:*

    a. the growth rates of aggregate capital, gross output, consumption, and work effort?

    b. the growth rates of capital, gross output, consumption, and work effort per capita?

Assume now that changes in η do not affect the ratio of aggregate capital to either aggregate gross output or aggregate work effort in a position of steady-state growth. Then, how does the value of η affect the following variables under steady-state growth:

    c. the ratio of aggregate net investment to the aggregates of capital and gross output?

    d. the ratio of aggregate consumption to aggregate gross output?

CHAPTER 11

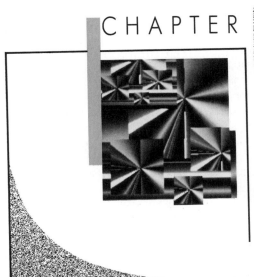

UNEMPLOYMENT

hus far we have focused on the model's predictions about fluctuations in aggregate output and in the composition of output between investment and consumption. An adverse supply shock can lead to a recession, where output falls and investment declines as a share of output. The model can also explain a decline in aggregate work effort during a recession. In a setting with firms and a separate labor market, as in Chapter 6, the changes in work show up as variations either in employment— that is, the number of persons with jobs—or in the amount of hours worked by those employed.

We have not yet discussed **unemployment,** which is the number of people who are looking for work but have no job. The sum of unemployment and employment is the **labor force.** People who neither have a job nor are looking for one are classed as being **outside of the labor force,** and the ratio of the number unemployed to the labor force is the **unemployment rate.** Finally, while unemployment refers to unsuccessful job seekers, the term *vacancies* describes the number of jobs that firms have been unable to fill.

In the labor market of Chapter 6, the wage rate adjusted to equate labor supply and demand. In this setting, anyone who sought work at the going wage was able to get a job. Similarly, firms managed to hire their desired number of workers. Thus, unemployment and vacancies were both zero, and employment equaled the labor force. Although this model of the labor market can account for some of the fluctuations in employment (that is, the labor force), it cannot explain why the quantities of unemployment and vacancies are nonzero. Therefore, the model also cannot tell us why unemployment and vacancies change over time. Given these deficiencies, it is also likely that the model is not yet satisfactory for understanding all of the movements in employment and production.

To explain unemployment and vacancies, we have to introduce some type of "friction" into the workings of the labor market. Specifically, we have to explain why people without jobs take some time to find and accept employment. Similarly, we have to see why businesses with unoccupied positions take some time to fill them. Thus, the key to unemployment and vacancies is the process of workers searching for jobs and businesses searching for workers.

In our earlier discussion we simplified matters by thinking of all workers as identical. Similarly, by thinking of only one type of production process, we assumed that all jobs were the same. But then the process of search among workers and firms would be trivial. To make the analysis meaningful, we have to allow for differences among workers and jobs. In fact, we can think of the labor market as operating to find good matches between jobs and workers. Because jobs and workers differ, this matching process is difficult and time-consuming. Unemployment and vacancies arise as aspects of this process.

The next section develops a simple model of job matching. But before getting into the model, let's stress two important objectives. First, we want to explain why the levels of unemployment and vacancies are positive. Second, we want to see how these variables change over time and how they interact with the determination of employment. In particular, we want to understand how unemployment and employment behave during recessions and booms.

A MODEL OF JOB FINDING

Consider a person who has just entered the labor force and is not yet employed—for example, a student who has just graduated from school and is seeking his or her first job or someone who is entering or reentering the labor force after raising a family. Suppose that this person searches for a position by visiting various firms. Each firm interviews job candidates to assess their likely qualifications for a position. As a result of each inspection, the firm estimates the value of the candidate's marginal product. To keep things simple, assume that the firm offers the person a job with a nominal wage, w, equal to this estimated value of marginal product. (We assume, only for simplicity, that the job entails a standard number of hours worked per week.)

The candidate must decide whether to accept an offer at the wage rate w. The alternative to taking a job is to remain unemployed and continue searching for another one.[1] More search pays off if a subsequent wage offer exceeds the initial

---

[1] We assume that it does not pay to accept a job and nevertheless keep searching. That is because the costs of getting set up in a job usually make it undesirable to take positions with short expected durations and because it may be easier to search while unemployed.

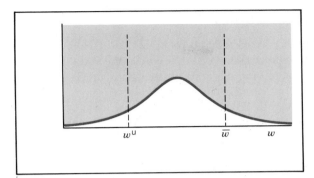

FIGURE 11.1 *Distribution of Wage Offers*
The curve shows the chances of receiving wage offers of different sizes. The higher the curve, the more likely that wages of that size will be offered. Note that w^u is the effective wage while unemployed, and $\overline{w}$ is the reservation wage. Wage offers are accepted if they are at least as good as $\overline{w}$ and rejected otherwise.

one. On the other hand, the cost of turning down an offer is the wage income foregone while not working. This income foregone must, however, be measured net of any income that people receive because they are unemployed. This income includes unemployment insurance, which we shall discuss later, and any value attached to time spent unemployed (and searching for a job) rather than working.[2]

In evaluating an offer, the first point to determine is how it compares with others that might be available. In making this comparison, a job seeker would have in mind a distribution of possible wages,[3] given the person's education, experience, locational preferences, and so on. Figure 11.1 shows a possible distribution of wage offers. For each value of wages on the horizontal axis, the height of the curve shows the relative chance or probability of receiving that wage offer. For the case shown, the offers usually fall in a middle range of values for w. There is, however, a small chance of getting either a very high wage offer (in the right tail of the distribution) or an offer near zero.

Figure 11.1 shows the value w^u, which is the effective wage received while unemployed. We know right away that a person would reject any offer that paid less than w^u. For the case shown in the figure, w^u lies toward the left end of the distribution of wage offers. This construction implies that most—but not all—wage offers would exceed w^u. Given the position of w^u, a job seeker's key decision is whether to accept a wage offer when $w > w^u$ applies.

As mentioned before, a person may refuse a wage that exceeds w^u to preserve the chance of getting a still better offer (see note 1). But there is a trade-off because the job seeker then foregoes the income $w - w^u$, while not working. The balancing of these forces involves what economists call a **reservation wage** (or sometimes an acceptance wage), which we denote by $\overline{w}$. Wage offers below $\overline{w}$ are refused, and those above $\overline{w}$ are accepted. If a person sets a high value of $\overline{w}$, he or she will probably

[2]Presumably the unemployed have more leisure, even after considering the time required to search for a job. However, the basic results would not change if people preferred time at work to time spent unemployed.

[3]We assume for simplicity that the attractiveness of different jobs depends only on the wage paid. However, we could expand the model to consider an effective wage, which took account of working conditions, hours, job location, and similar factors.

spend a long time (perhaps forever) unemployed and searching for an acceptable job. On the other hand, a low value of $\overline{w}$ (but still greater than w^u) means that the expected time unemployed will be relatively brief. However, the expected wage received while employed is lower the lower is the value of $\overline{w}$.

The optimal value of $\overline{w}$ depends on the shape of the wage-offer distribution in Figure 11.1, as well as on the value of w^u and the expected duration of jobs.[4] For our purposes we do not have to go through the details of the calculation of the optimal $\overline{w}$. We can, however, note some properties that would come out of this calculation.

First, since some wage offers would generally be unacceptable—that is, $w <$ $\overline{w}$ for some offers—it typically takes time for a job searcher to find an acceptable job. In the interim the person is "unemployed" (although engaged in job search). Therefore, incomplete information about where to find the best job can explain positive amounts of unemployment.

Second, an increase in the income while unemployed, w^u, motivates job seekers to raise their standards for job acceptance—that is, $\overline{w}$ increases. Given the distribution of wage offers in Figure 11.1, it becomes more likely that $w < \overline{w}$, which means that wage offers are more likely to be rejected. It follows that job searchers tend to take a longer time in finding a job when w^u increases. Hence, for a group of workers, the **job-finding rate** falls, and the expected **duration of unemployment** increases.

Third, suppose that the whole distribution of job offers becomes better. For example, a favorable shock to firms' production functions might mean that marginal products of labor were all 10% higher than before. Then the distribution of wage offers in Figure 11.1 would shift rightward. (The height of the curve at the old wage w is now the height at the wage $1.1w$.) For a given reservation wage $\overline{w}$, it follows that wage offers are more likely to be in the acceptable range, $w \geq \overline{w}$. Therefore, the job-finding rate rises, and the expected duration of unemployment falls.

Generally a better distribution of wage offers also motivates people to raise their reservation wage $\overline{w}$. However, if the wage while unemployed, w^u, does not change, the first effect tends to dominate.[5] A shift to a better distribution of wage offers—generated, for example, by a favorable shock to productivity—raises the job-finding rate and lowers the expected duration of unemployment.

SEARCH BY FIRMS

Thus far, we have taken an unrealistic view of how firms would contribute to the job-search process. Up to now, firms received job applications, evaluated candidates

---

[4] For a discussion of models of job search that involve an optimal reservation wage, see Belton Fleisher and Thomas Kniesner (1984, pp. 477–507).

[5] If w^u and all wage offers were higher by 10%, the trade-off between the benefits and costs of accepting a job would not change. Therefore, the job-finding rate and the expected duration of unemployment would also not change. If we instead hold w^u constant—as we did in the text—the net effect must be equivalent to a fall in w^u. Therefore, the net effect is an increase in the job-finding rate and a decrease in the expected duration of unemployment.

in terms of likely marginal products, and then expressed wage offers.[6] This process does not allow firms to utilize the information that they have about the characteristics of their jobs, the traits of workers who are usually productive on these jobs, and the wages that typically have to be paid for such workers. Firms communicate this information by advertising job openings that specify ranges of requirements for education, experience, and so on, and also indicate a salary range. Such advertisements appropriately screen out most potential applicants and tend to generate more rapid and better matches of workers to jobs.

Although search by firms is important in a well-functioning labor market, the inclusion of this search leaves unaltered our major conclusions. In particular,

- It still takes time for workers to be matched with acceptable jobs, so that the expected durations of unemployment and vacancies are positive.

- An increase in workers' wages while unemployed, w^u, lowers the job-finding rate and raises the anticipated duration of unemployment.

- A favorable shock to productivity raises the job-finding rate and reduces the expected duration of unemployment.

JOB SEPARATIONS

Workers search for jobs that offer high wages, relative to perceived opportunities elsewhere, while employers search for workers with high productivity, given the wages that must be paid. Although workers and firms evaluate their information as well as possible, they often find out later that they made mistakes. For example, an employer may learn that a worker is less productive than anticipated, or a worker may discover that he or she dislikes the job (or boss). When a job match looks significantly poorer later on than it did before, firms are motivated to discharge the worker, or the worker is motivated to quit. In either case there is a job separation, which typically reinstates a vacancy for the firm and unemployment for the worker. The main point is that a separation restarts the process of job search for firms and workers.

Separations also come about because of changed circumstances, even when firms and workers made accurate initial assessments of each other. For example, an adverse shock to a firm's production function could lower its evaluation of a worker's marginal product and thereby lead to a discharge (which tends to create unemployment but not a vacancy). If we distinguish the products of firms, we would get a similar effect from a decline in the relative demand for a firm's product. Also, jobs are sometimes known to be temporary at the outset, as in the case of seasonal workers in agriculture or at sports facilities.

---

[6]Since the marginal product of most people on most jobs would be negative (for example, of college professors as the chief executive officer of General Motors), we would have to allow wage offers to be negative. Usually these negative offers would be unacceptable, so we can just as well think of no job being offered in such cases.

On the other side of the labor market, workers may experience changed circumstances with respect to family status, schooling, location, and retirement, as well as alternative job prospects. (Some of these changes would be anticipated and others would not.) Shifts in these factors could induce a worker to quit a job (which may create a vacancy but not unemployment).

For a group of employed workers, we can identify factors that influence the **job-separation rate.** For example, the rate is higher for inexperienced workers who are harder to evaluate initially or for younger persons who are likely to experience changes in family size or job preferences. The separation rate would also be higher in industries subject to frequent shocks to technology or product demand.

If there were no separations (and no new persons entering the labor force), the process of job search would tend eventually to eliminate unemployment and vacancies. But the existence of separations means that the finding of new jobs is continually offset by the loss of old ones—that is, by the creation of new unemployment and vacancies. The level and change in unemployment and vacancies involves the interplay between job finding and job separation. We now illustrate this process with a simple example, which focuses on the number of people employed and unemployed.

JOB SEPARATIONS, JOB FINDING, AND THE NATURAL UNEMPLOYMENT RATE

Let N be the number of people employed, and U be the number unemployed. For now, we assume that the labor force, $N + U$, does not change over time. For example, we do not allow for retirements or entry of new persons into the labor force. Because of the reevaluation of jobs and workers, some fraction of those employed experience a job separation in each period. In Figure 11.2 the blue box labeled N denotes the number employed, while the white box labeled U shows those unemployed. The arrow from N to U represents the number of job separations. If the labor force is constant, and—also unrealistically—if no job loser finds a new job immediately, all those who lose jobs move from category N to category U. For the purpose of an

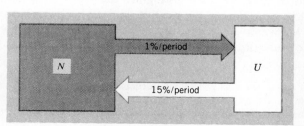

FIGURE 11.2 *Movements between Employment and Unemployment*
In this example, 1% of those employed (N) lose their jobs each period. Simultaneously, 15% of those unemployed (U) find jobs each period. Therefore, the net change in the number unemployed during a period is 15% · U − 1% · N. Also, the change in the number unemployed is the negative of the change in the number employed.

TABLE 11.1 *The Dynamics of Employment and Unemployment and the Natural Rate of Unemployment*

Period	Number Employed (N)	Number Unemployed (U)	Number Who Lose Jobs	Number Who Find Jobs	Net Change in Employment	Net Change in Unemployment
1	90.0	10.0	0.9	1.5	0.6	−0.6
2	90.6	9.4	0.9	1.4	0.5	−0.5
3	91.1	8.9	0.9	1.3	0.4	−0.4
4	91.5	8.5	0.9	1.3	0.4	−0.4
5	91.9	8.1	0.9	1.2	0.3	−0.3
6	92.2	7.8	0.9	1.2	0.3	−0.3
⋮	⋮	⋮	⋮	⋮	⋮	⋮
∞	93.8	6.2	0.9	0.9	0	0

Note: We assume that the economy starts with 90 million people employed (N) and 10 million unemployed (U). Then, from Figure 11.2, 1% of those employed lose their job each period, but 15% of those unemployed find jobs. Therefore, the net change in employment is $15\% \cdot U - 1\% \cdot N$. Also, the change in unemployment is the negative of the change in employment. When the number employed reaches 93.8 million and the number unemployed reaches 6.2 million, the net changes in employment and unemployment are zero. Thus, the natural unemployment rate in this example is 6.2%.

example, assume that 1% of those employed lose their jobs each period—that is, the job separation rate is 1% per period.

As discussed before, the other thing that happens each period is that some fraction of those unemployed find jobs. In Figure 11.2 the arrow pointing from U to N represents the number of unemployed persons who find jobs during a period. Here (for the example to generate roughly the right numbers later on), assume that 15% of those unemployed find work each period. In other words, the job-finding rate is 15% per period.

We can work through the process of job separation and job finding to determine the numbers of people employed and unemployed. Table 11.1 assumes that the labor force is fixed at 100 million people (the actual size of the total labor force in 1987 was 122 million), and the economy starts in period 1 with 90 million employed and 10 million unemployed. Thus, the unemployment rate is initially 10%. Then, of the 90 million workers, 1%—or 0.9 million people—lose their jobs in the first period. Simultaneously, 15% of those unemployed—or 1.5 million people—find jobs. Hence, the net change in employment during period 1 is 0.6 million. Correspondingly, unemployment falls by 0.6 million.

As the number of employed increases and the number of unemployed decreases, the quantity of job separations (1% of those employed) rises, while the quantity of job findings (15% of those unemployed) falls. Therefore, the increase in employment slows over time. Eventually the economy approaches levels of employment and unemployment at which the number of job separations and findings is equal. Then, as long as the rates of job separation and job finding do not change, employment and unemployment are constant. In our example the balance between job separations and job findings occurs when employment equals 93.8 million and unemployment equals 6.2 million—that is, when the unemployment rate is 6.2%.

Therefore, in this model, we can say that the **natural unemployment rate** is 6.2%. The economy tends toward this rate automatically, given the rates at which people lose and find jobs.

Let's observe some important points about the natural unemployment rate. First, although the unemployment rate eventually stays constant at this value, there is still a substantial amount of *job turnover*. Almost a million people lose and find jobs each period in the example when the unemployment rate is 6.2%. In this model—and in the real world—large flows from employment to unemployment, and vice-versa, are a normal part of the operation of the labor market.

Second, the dynamics of employment and unemployment, as well as the value of the natural employment rate, depend on the rates of job separation and job finding. In the example these rates per period were set at 1% and 15%, respectively. More generally, our earlier analysis showed how the rates of job separation and job finding depended on various factors, such as a person's age and experience, the income available while unemployed, and the variability of an industry's supply and demand conditions. To see how these factors influence employment and unemployment, we want to consider alternative values for the rates of job separation and job finding.

Let s be the job-separation rate and η (the Greek letter eta) the job-finding rate. Then the change in the number employed during a period, ΔN, is given by

$$\Delta N = \eta U - sN. \tag{11.1}$$

Note that the first term, ηU, is the number of unemployed who find jobs during a period, while the second term, sN, is the number of employed who lose jobs. Equation 11.1 says that the change in employment equals job findings less job separations.

Equation 11.1 implies that employment increases if job findings, ηU, exceed job separations, sN. In the reverse case, employment decreases. To determine the natural levels of employment and unemployment, we set the change in employment, ΔN, to zero in equation 11.1. Then, using the condition that the labor force, $N + U$, is fixed at 100 million, we find that

$$\eta U = sN = s(100 - U).$$

Solving this equation for the number unemployed, U, determines the natural values of unemployment and employment as

$$U = 100 \cdot \frac{s}{(s + \eta)}$$
$$N = 100 \cdot \frac{\eta}{(s + \eta)}. \tag{11.2}$$

Therefore, the natural employment rate is

$$u = \frac{U}{100} = \frac{s}{(s + \eta)}. \tag{11.3}$$

Recall that in our example, $s = 0.01$ per period and $\eta = 0.15$ per period. Thus, $u = 0.01/0.16 = 6.2\%$, as we found before.

Equation 11.3 relates the natural unemployment rate to the rates of job separation, s, and job finding, η.[7] A higher rate of separation, s, raises the natural unemployment rate, while a higher rate of finding, η, lowers it. Thus, when we examine differences in natural unemployment rates—either over groups of people or over time—we should look for differences in the rates of job separation and job finding. People who lose jobs more frequently or have more trouble in finding jobs will be unemployed a larger fraction of the time.

MOVEMENTS IN AND OUT OF THE LABOR FORCE

Before applying the theory to data on unemployment rates, we can usefully extend the analysis to include movements in and out of the labor force. Conceptually we classify people as outside of the labor force if they neither have a market job nor are currently looking for one. (Hence, the category includes full-time students and homemakers, who might reasonably think of themselves as "employed.") In practice, there are often difficulties in distinguishing those outside the labor force from those unemployed. That is because the distinction comes from people's answers to a survey question as to whether they are actively "looking for work" during a particular period. To some extent, the number classified as unemployed underestimates the true number, because some of those labeled as outside of the labor force would also like market jobs (at some wage rate!). But on the other hand, many of those who call themselves unemployed are not actually interested in accepting employment on terms that they could reasonably expect to receive.

For our purposes, the important new effects involve movements from inside the labor force to outside and vice-versa. There are many good reasons for these movements—for example, when people retire, when they leave or reenter school, when they have changes in marital status or in the number and ages of children, or when the nature of the available jobs changes.

Figure 11.3 shows the possible transitions among the three categories employment, unemployment, and outside of the labor force. (Notice that the flows labeled 2 and 3 are those that we studied before.) The list of possibilities is as follows:

1. A change in job, without becoming unemployed or leaving the labor force. (This type of shift is especially popular among sports figures and professors of economics—but, more generally, over half of all job changes do not involve any unemployment; see Kim Clark and Lawrence Summers, 1979, p. 43.)

2. A loss of a job with a move to unemployment.

3. The finding of a job from the ranks of the unemployed.

---

[7]For more thorough analyses of this type of model, see Robert Hall (1979), Chitra Ramaswami (1983), and Michael Darby, John Haltiwanger, and Mark Plant (1985).

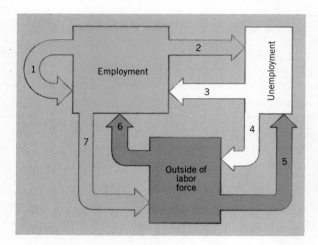

FIGURE 11.3 *Flows of People among Three Categories: Employment, Unemployment, and Outside of the Labor Force* The diagram shows the possible movements from one category to another.

4. A movement from unemployment to outside of the labor force—sometimes described as **discouraged workers.**

5. An entry or reentry to the labor force but initially unemployed.

6. An entry or reentry to the labor force with a job obtained at once (as in the case of most graduating majors in business and economics).

7. A loss of a job with a move outside of the labor force (which includes permanent retirements, as well as withdrawals from the labor market to raise a family or return to school).

Notice that total job separations are the sum of flows 1, 2 and 7, and total job findings are the sum of flows 1, 3 and 6. The difference between separations and findings is the change in employment. On the other hand, the change in unemployment is the sum of flows 2 and 5, less the sum of flows 3 and 4. Thus, because of the movements in and out of the labor force, the change in employment no longer coincides with the negative of the change in unemployment.

As before—but with greater complexity—people's tendencies to experience the various transitions shown in Figure 11.3 determine the levels of employment and unemployment over time. It is still true that employment tends to be lower the higher is the rate of job separation. Similarly, employment tends to be higher the greater is the rate of job finding. But the movements in and out of the labor force interact with these tendencies to lose and find jobs. For example, people who move frequently in and out of the labor force build up relatively little work experience. Hence, they tend to be the ones who are terminated first and hired last.

For unemployment, the new effects concern the possibilities for moving outside of the labor force. For example, the tendency for the unemployed to cease looking for work (flow 4 in Figure 11.3) reduces the number of persons counted as unemployed. But the tendency for people to shift from employment to outside of the labor force (flow 7) tends to raise unemployment. That is because, first, these people often become unemployed when they reenter the labor force (flow 5), and, second, they are more likely to lose a job later on (flows 2 and 7).

THE BEHAVIOR OF U.S. UNEMPLOYMENT RATES BY DEMOGRAPHIC GROUPS

Table 11.2 shows unemployment rates for all workers and for various categories of workers by age, sex, and race. The data are averages for 1948–87 and for various subperiods. The average unemployment rate for all civilian workers for 1948–87 was 5.7%. (The value for 1988 was 5.5%.) But the average unemployment rates vary substantially by demographic characteristics. For example, among persons 20 years and older, the average rate for females was 5.4%, while that for males was 4.6%. For both sexes, the average unemployment rate declines by age until people reach at least their 50s. But the sharpest distinction applies to teenagers, who had an average unemployment rate of 15.1%, as compared to 4.9% for those at least 20 years of age. Finally, the average rate for blacks and other minorities of 10.3% was roughly double that for whites of 5.1%.

Table 11.2 does not indicate much change over time in the relative unemployment rates for the various demographic groups. For example, the unemployment rate for teenagers averaged 2.6 times the overall rate, with no clear change in this relation over time. Similarly, the rate for blacks was reasonably stable at around 1.8 times the overall rate. The rate for females over 20 was typically close to the overall

TABLE 11.2 *Behavior of U.S. Unemployment Rates (% of civilian labor force within category)*

	All Civilian Workers	Males 20 years and Older	Females 20 years and Older	Teenagers (16–19)	White	Black and Other Minorities
1948–52	4.3	3.6	4.2	10.3	4.0	6.9
1953–57	4.3	3.6	4.2	10.8	3.8	7.9
1958–62	6.0	5.2	5.6	15.4	5.4	11.4
1963–67	4.6	3.3	4.6	14.8	4.1	8.6
1968–72	4.7	3.2	4.7	14.6	4.3	8.2
1973–77	6.7	5.0	6.6	17.5	6.1	11.8
1978–82	7.3	5.9	6.6	18.6	6.4	13.6
1983–87	7.5	6.6	6.6	19.0	6.5	14.1
1948–87	5.7	4.6	5.4	15.1	5.1	10.3

Note: The table shows the average unemployment rate over the period indicated for various categories of workers.

Source: Citibase data bank.

rate but was somewhat below the overall rate since the late 1970s. That is, the unemployment rate of females relative to males has declined somewhat over time.

Many economists thought that the unemployment rate had risen permanently after the mid-1970s (see Table 11.2). However, the rate of 5.5% for 1988 was actually below the average of 5.7% from 1948 to 1987.

We can think of the variations in average unemployment rates across demographic groups as differences in natural unemployment rates, where these differences reflect variations in the rates of job separation and job finding. To compare the rates of job separation for the various groups, we can look at data on the **duration of jobs.** Basically, people with high rates of job separation end up with short-term jobs, and vice-versa. Similarly, to get information about job-finding rates, we consider data on the duration of unemployment. Those who find jobs quickly end up with brief spells of unemployment, and vice-versa.

THE DURATION OF JOBS

The research by Robert Hall (1980a, 1982) on job separations allows us to understand some of the differences in unemployment rates by age, sex, and race. First, most new jobs that people get do not last very long. For example, using data for 1973, Hall estimated that 61% of new jobs last less than one year, while the average duration of a new job is four years. But as people get older and try a variety of jobs, most workers eventually find a good job match, which lasts for a long time. In particular (based on data from 1978), by age 50 over 70% of all workers have been on their present job for at least five years. Also, by age 40, about 40% of all workers are currently in a very long-term job, which will eventually last at least 20 years. These results mean that job separations (flows 1, 2, and 7 in Figure 11.3) are much more common for younger workers, most of whom have not yet found a long-lasting job match. Therefore, this element explains a good deal of the higher unemployment rate for younger persons, especially teenagers.

A lower average duration of jobs can also explain some of the higher average unemployment rate for women than for men. For example, Hall estimated for 1978 that about 50% of women who have jobs will eventually reach a tenure of at least five years on their job, while about 15% will reach at least 20 years. But the comparable figures for men are 64 and 37%, respectively. Basically, women move in and out of the labor force (flows 4, 5, 6, and 7 in Figure 11.3) over their lifetime more often than men do.

Surprisingly, Hall's figures suggest that blacks have roughly the same chance as whites to stay on a job for a long time. For example, for 1978, his estimate is that 63% of blacks who have jobs will have an eventual tenure of at least five years on their current job, and 26% will reach at least 20 years. The figures for whites—57 and 29%, respectively—are similar. On the other hand, some other data show that blacks are much more likely than whites to experience a job separation in any given month. Stephen Marston (1976, Table 4) estimates that this element accounts for about one-third of the higher average unemployment rate for blacks. If we put Marston's observations together with Hall's, the suggestion is that blacks have a strong tendency toward very short-term jobs although no less of a tendency to achieve jobs with a duration of at least five years.

THE DURATION OF UNEMPLOYMENT

The other main element that determines the average unemployment rate is the duration of a typical spell of unemployment. The longer it takes for an unemployed person to find a job or leave the labor force (flows 3 and 4 in Figure 11.3), the greater will be the measured number of unemployed at any point in time.

The research by Kim Clark and Lawrence Summers (1979) provides some interesting information about the duration of unemployment. One point is that a large fraction of spells end within one month—the percentages were 79% for 1969, 60% for 1974, and 55% for 1975. (Note that 1975 was a year of deep recession, 1974 was an early stage of a recession, and 1969 was a strong boom.) Correspondingly, the average length of a spell is not very long—1.4 months in 1969, 1.9 months in 1974, and 2.2 months in 1975. But Clark and Summers argue that the importance of the long-term unemployed is more significant than these figures suggest. First, in determining the average number of people unemployed at any date, we effectively weight the frequency of each spell by its length. Therefore, although the average length of a spell in 1974 was only two months, it also turns out that spells of more than two months accounted for 69% of the number unemployed. Similarly, spells of six months or more still accounted for 19% of unemployment in 1974.

Second, roughly half of all spells of unemployment end in withdrawal from the labor force (flow 4 in Figure 11.3) rather than in employment (flow 3 in the figure). Then many of those who leave the labor force soon reappear as job searchers (flow 5 in the figure) and thereby count as a new spell of unemployment in the data. Clark and Summers argue that these spells of unemployment and the intervening periods outside of the labor force should be counted as long periods of unemployment. But many of these people (as well as some who never leave the labor force) may not be serious job seekers and should not be counted as unemployed in the first place. This ambiguity points out the fundamental problem of defining and measuring the concept of unemployment. In general, it is easier to define and measure employment than unemployment.

Teenagers tend to find jobs or leave the labor force more quickly than do older persons. For example, in 1974, the average duration of unemployment for teenagers was 1.6 months, as compared with just over 2 months for those over 20. Therefore, the higher unemployment rate for teenagers reflects mostly the short duration of their jobs rather than a low rate of job finding.

The main difference by sex is the much higher tendency for unemployed females to leave the labor force (flow 4 in Figure 11.3). For example, in 1974, 58% of unemployed females over 20 eventually left the labor force, as contrasted with only 26% of males over 20.

For blacks, particularly those under 25, a greater difficulty in finding jobs accounts for a large part of their higher unemployment rate. For example, Marston (1976, Table 4) estimated that this element accounted for two-thirds of the higher average unemployment rate for blacks from 1967 to 1973.

FACTORS THAT INFLUENCE THE NATURAL UNEMPLOYMENT RATE

There is a long list of factors—especially government policies—that economists think influence the natural unemployment rate. We consider briefly some of the more important possibilities: unemployment insurance, the minimum wage, and labor unions.

UNEMPLOYMENT INSURANCE

The government's main program of **unemployment insurance** began in 1936. This program provides benefits to eligible persons who have lost their jobs and are currently "looking for work." Hence, those in the category labeled "unemployment" in Figure 11.3 are candidates for these benefits. While the federal government plays some role, the main rules for eligibility and levels of benefits are set by the various state governments. In general, a person's eligibility depends on a long enough work history in a covered job.[8] (In 1986, 92% of all civilian workers were in covered jobs—see *Economic Report of the President,* 1988, Tables B-32, B-42.) Also, an individual's benefits run out after a period, which typically lasts between 26 and 39 weeks. But in time of recession, such as 1982–83, the federal government typically extends the period of eligibility.

An employed person can compare his or her current wage with the unemployment benefits that he or she could get by not working. The ratio of the potential benefits to the wage is called the **replacement ratio.** There have not been dramatic changes in this ratio since World War II; the ratio of the average weekly check from unemployment insurance programs to average weekly earnings for all nonagricultural workers increased from 39% in 1947 to 45% in 1987 (*Economic Report of President,* 1988, Tables B-42, B-45). Over time, the main changes in the unemployment insurance program have been extensions of coverage (especially to small firms and to employees of state and local governments) and increases in the allowable duration of benefits.

Theoretically, the existence of unemployment insurance makes the unemployed who are receiving benefits less eager to accept jobs or leave the labor force (flows 3 and 4 in Figure 11.3). Also, the program makes the employed persons who will be eligible for benefits more willing to accept job separations (flow 2 in Figure 11.3).[9] In particular, unemployment insurance motivates **temporary layoffs**—that

---

[8]In some states people who quit their jobs or are fired for cause are eligible for benefits, while in others they are ineligible. Of course, it is often hard to tell who quits or is fired for cause and who loses a job for other reasons. For discussion of these and related issues, see Daniel Hamermesh (1977).

[9]This tendency diminishes if employers must pay for the average benefits given to their ex-employees through a process called **experience rating.** With experience rating, a business that has a lot of job separations pays a larger amount into the fund that finances the unemployment benefits. Hence this system motivates employers to hold down their rates of job separation. There is some experience rating in the unemployment insurance system for the United States but not in the systems of most other countries. For a discussion, see Robert Topel and Finis Welch (1980).

is, short-term job separations during a period of slack production. Overall, a more generous program of unemployment insurance leads to a higher natural rate of unemployment.

Most empirical estimates of the effects of unemployment insurance in the United States rely on differences across states in the levels of benefits and in criteria for eligibility. Using these data, some researchers report that unemployment insurance raises the natural unemployment rate by between $\frac{1}{2}$ and 1 percentage point.[10] In a recent study, Gary Solon (1985) notes that since 1979 unemployment insurance benefits have been taxable for high-income families. He estimates that the reduction in effective benefits lowered the duration of insured unemployment for high-income persons by about 10%.

Lawrence Katz and Bruce Meyer (1988) focused on the duration of benefits. They estimated that an extension of allowable benefits by 1 week raises the mean duration of unemployment by between .16 and .20 week. Therefore, an extension of benefits from 26 to 39 weeks—as in the 1982–83 recession—would raise the average duration of unemployment by more than 2 weeks.

Many economists think that the generous unemployment insurance programs in some Western European countries—especially the long period of eligibility for benefits—are responsible for the large amount of long-term unemployment. (For discussions, see Gary Burtless, 1987, and Michael Burda, 1988). For example, in the Netherlands, unemployed persons can receive benefits averaging 70% of wage earnings for up to $2\frac{1}{2}$ years, and in Denmark they can receive benefits averaging 90% of wage earnings for up to $2\frac{1}{2}$ years (see Michael Emerson, 1988, p. 90). Figure 11.4 plots for 13 industrialized countries the amount of long-term unemployment (those unemployed at least 6 months, expressed as a percentage of total unemployment) against a measure of the generosity of the unemployment insurance program. This measure considers the replacement ratio from the program, as well as the allowable duration of benefits.[11] (The countries turn out to differ more with respect to durations than with respect to replacement ratios.) The figure shows that the countries with more generous unemployment insurance programs have a greater incidence of long-term unemployment.

Although there is evidence that unemployment insurance raises the unemployment rate, there is not much indication in the United States that unemployment insurance programs have become significantly more generous over the last two decades. Therefore, it is not easy to blame this program for the high unemployment rates from the mid-1970s to the early 1980s (or for the decline in the unemployment rate from 1983 to 1988).

---

[10]See Daniel Hamermesh (1977, p. 52) and Kim Clark and Lawrence Summers (1982, Table 10). Hamermesh focuses on changes in the duration of unemployment. He also distinguishes the effects in a year of high unemployment from those in a year of low unemployment, but the reported differences are small. Clark and Summers's estimates refer to 1978, for which the overall unemployment rate was 5.9%.

[11]The data on the characteristics of the unemployment insurance programs come from Emerson (1988, p. 90) and "The Employer," Copenhagen, August 10, 1987, p. 6. The figures on long-term unemployment are from OECD (1987, p. 201).

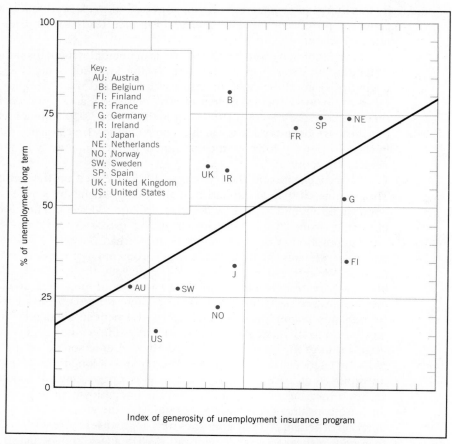

FIGURE 11.4 *Unemployment Insurance and Long-Term Unemployment in Industrialized Countries*

THE MINIMUM WAGE

When considering determinants of the natural unemployment rate, economists often mention the **minimum wage.** Since 1938, the federal government has set minimum wage rates in covered industries. In 1946 this regulation covered about 57% of all nonsupervisory employees. But changes in legislation raised the coverage to roughly 87% in 1986 (*Statistical Abstract of the U.S.,* 1988, p. 395).

Congress has changed the level of the basic hourly minimum wage numerous times since the initial choice of $0.25 in 1938. For example, the value was $0.75 in 1950, $1.25 in 1963, $1.60 in 1968, $2.30 in 1977, and $3.35 in 1981. However, at least through 1988, no change has occurred since 1981. The ratio of the minimum wage to average hourly nonfarm earnings ranged between 37 and 56% from 1950 to 1987. Although there is no clear trend, the ratio increased each time Congress enacted a new minimum but then declined gradually as average hourly earnings rose. For example, with no change in the minimum wage, the ratio fell from 46% in 1981 to 37% in 1987.

A higher minimum wage reduces the incentive of employers to hire low-productivity workers in sectors covered by the minimum. Empirically, researchers find that a higher minimum wage and greater coverage tend especially to reduce the employment of teenagers. Typical estimates suggest that an increase by 10% in the minimum wage lowers the quantity of teenagers employed by somewhat more than 1%.[12] There is also some indication of a negative effect on the employment of young adults aged 20–24 but no clear effect on older workers. In fact, since the minimum wage makes the labor of low-productivity workers artificially more expensive, it is likely that businesses would shift to more labor from high-productivity workers. Hence, labor unions tend to favor the minimum wage to protect their high-paid members from the competition of low-productivity, low-wage workers.

While the adverse effect of the minimum wage on teenage *employment* is clear, the effect on teenage *unemployment* depends also on the response of labor-force participation. Because a higher minimum wage reduces the chance of finding a job, it also reduces the number of teenagers who declare themselves as looking for work. This response lessens the tendency for a higher minimum wage to raise the measured unemployment rate of teenagers.

In any event, the behavior of the minimum wage cannot account for the high unemployment rate from the mid-1970s to the early 1980s. That is because, first, the minimum wage did not increase relative to average hourly earnings, and, second, the higher unemployment rates over this period applied as much to older workers as to teenagers and young adults.

LABOR UNIONS

People sometimes argue that labor unions cause unemployment. Mostly, unions can raise real wages and hold down the levels of employment in covered industries. Correspondingly, there is a higher supply of labor and lower real wage rates in uncovered sectors. Therefore, unions can create inefficiencies, which include the inappropriate distribution of work and production between covered and uncovered areas. Conceivably, more union power also leads to reductions in aggregate employment and output. But it is less clear that unions have anything to do with the amount of *unemployment*. That is because the adverse effects on total work may correspond mostly to reductions in the labor force.

In any event we should look for effects of unions by observing the changes in unionization over time. The fraction of the civilian labor force that is unionized declined from a peak of 27% in the mid-1950s to 21% in 1980 and about 15% in 1986 (*Statistical Abstract of the U.S.,* 1988, p. 402; 1982–83, pp. 408–9). Therefore, we cannot attribute the high unemployment rates from the mid-1970s to the early 1980s to an increase in unionization. (The principal increases in unionization were

---

[12]For a survey of the evidence, see Charles Brown, Curtis Gilroy, and Andrew Koehn (1982).

TABLE 11.3 *Behavior of U.S. Employment Ratios*

	Employment Ratio	
	% of Total Population	% of Population Aged 16–64
1948–52	40	63
1953–57	39	64
1958–62	37	64
1963–67	38	65
1968–72	39	66
1973–77	41	66
1978–82	44	69
1983–87	45	70
1948–87	40	66

Note: The table shows the ratio of total employment (including the military) to the total population and to the population aged 16–64.

Source: Economic Report of the President, 1988, Tables B-31, B-32; 1983, Table B-29.

the rise from less than 3% to 6% at the beginning of the twentieth century, the rise from 7% to 15% in the mid-1930s, and the increase from 6% to 26% during World War II.)

CHANGES IN EMPLOYMENT RATIOS

The high unemployment rates from the mid-1970s to the early 1980s contrasted with the behavior of employment when expressed relative to some measure of population. Table 11.3 shows the ratios of total employment (including the military) to total population and to the population aged 16–64. The first ratio varied between 37 and 41% until the mid-1970s but then increased to 47% in 1987. Similarly, the second ratio stayed between 61 and 66% until the mid-1970s but then rose to 72%.

The high employment ratios in recent years reflect mainly the increase in the labor-force participation rate of women. Because of this change, the fraction of the civilian labor force that is female rose from 29% in 1948 to 38% in 1969 and 45% in 1987. This development means that there are now many more families with more than one income earner. Accordingly, a given overall rate of unemployment does not have as much significance for the typical family's total earnings as it did previously. (The existence of unemployment insurance and other welfare programs also matters here.)

EMPLOYMENT AND UNEMPLOYMENT DURING RECESSIONS

In Chapter 9 we showed that supply shocks could account for some characteristics of real-world business fluctuations. In particular, adverse shifts of production functions could generate a recession that featured declines in real GNP and in the ratio of investment to GNP. Aggregate work effort might also decline, although this result depended on a balancing of substitution and wealth effects. Now we can use the apparatus from this chapter to see how supply shocks affect unemployment. We consider the case of a fixed labor force, so that changes in unemployment reflect inverse movements in employment.

Suppose that an adverse shock reduces the marginal product of labor for the typical worker and job. One effect, which we noted earlier, is that the job-finding rate, η, declines. That is because market opportunities—as determined by labor's marginal product—have become poorer relative to the income while unemployed, w^u. For the same reason, existing job matches become less mutually advantageous for firms and workers. Therefore, job separations tend to increase, especially in the form of layoffs or firings by firms. In any event, the job-separation rate, s, tends to rise.

To see the effects on unemployment and employment, return to the example where the labor force was fixed at 100 million persons and the job-finding rates were initially 15% and 1%, respectively. Table 11.4 assumes that the economy begins in period 1 at the natural employment rate—6.2% in this example. Then the adverse

TABLE 11.4 *The Dynamics of Employment and Unemployment during a Recession*

Period	Job-Separation Rate (s)	Job-Finding Rate (η)	Number Employed (N)	Number Unemployed (U)	Number Who Lose Jobs	Number Who Find Jobs	Net Change in Employment
1	0.015	0.10	93.8	6.2	1.4	0.6	−0.8
2	0.015	0.10	93.0	7.0	1.4	0.7	−0.7
3	0.015	0.10	92.3	7.7	1.4	0.8	−0.6
4	0.015	0.10	91.7	8.3	1.4	0.8	−0.6
5	0.015	0.10	91.1	8.9	1.4	0.9	−0.5
6	0.01	0.15	90.6	9.4	0.9	1.4	0.5
7	0.01	0.15	91.1	8.9	0.9	1.3	0.4
8	0.01	0.15	91.5	8.5	0.9	1.3	0.4
9	0.01	0.15	91.9	8.1	0.9	1.2	0.3
10	0.01	0.15	92.2	7.8	0.9	1.2	0.3
⋮	⋮	⋮	⋮	⋮	⋮	⋮	⋮
∞	0.01	0.15	93.8	6.2	0.9	0.9	0

Note: During the recession for periods 1 through 5, the job-separation rate is high—1.5% rather than 1%—and the job-finding rate is low—10% instead of 15%. Consequently, the unemployment rate rises from the natural rate, 6.2%, to 9.4% in period 6. When the job-separation and job-finding rates return to their normal values in period 6, the economy recovers gradually. In particular, the unemployment rate again approaches the natural rate of 6.2%.

shock to production functions—which we think of as initiating a recession—means that the job-separation rate rises from 1% to, say, 1.5%, while the job-finding rate falls from 15% to, say, 10%.

Although some people still find jobs, they are outnumbered by those who lose jobs. Hence, Table 11.4 shows that the unemployment rate rises steadily from 6.2% in period 1 to 9.4% in period 6. Correspondingly, the number employed falls from 93.8 million to 90.6 million.

Suppose that the temporary adverse shock to the production function lasts through period 5. As of period 6, the job-separation rate is again 1%, while the job-finding rate is 15%. Although some people still lose their jobs, they are now outnumbered by those who find jobs. Therefore, the unemployment rate falls gradually toward the natural rate of 6.2%. Correspondingly, employment rises back toward 93.8 million.

We should stress two realistic features of recessions that emerge from this example. First, the buildup of a recession involves a period of gradually rising unemployment and falling employment. Second, even after an economic recovery begins, it takes a substantial period for the unemployment rate to return to its prerecession level.

In this example, with a fixed labor force, the dynamics of employment is just the reverse of that of unemployment. Further, if we abstract from changes in the stock of capital, the movements in production would parallel those in employment. Although these patterns capture the broad features of business fluctuations, some elements are missing. First, hours worked per worker, especially *overtime* hours, are more flexible than numbers employed. Therefore, hours and output per worker tend to fall in a recession (or rise in a boom) before the corresponding changes in employment. Second, even without adjusting the number of hours worked, businesses can change their utilization of capital and hence the volume of production. With a given number of worker-hours, a decrease in utilization during a recession shows up as a reduction in output per hour worked.[13] Third, the labor force can vary. However, except for young persons—who tend to drop out of the labor force in bad times—there turns out to be little association of the labor force with the level of real economic activity (see problem 11.7).

UNEMPLOYMENT DURING RECENT U.S. RECESSIONS

Table 11.5 shows the behavior of output, employment, and unemployment during six U.S. recessions since World War II. The percentage shortfalls in real GNP are

---

[13] A decrease in capacity utilization generally implies that fewer worker-hours would suffice for current production. To the extent that worker-hours do not decline, firms are employing more labor input than is required for this production. Economists have speculated whether this "excess" labor is underutilized (with people working less intensively during recessions) or is used instead for activities that do not show up in measured output. By surveying 168 manufacturing firms, Jon Fay and James Medoff (1985) found that the typical firm reacted to a recession by assigning an additional 5% of work hours to maintenance and overhaul of equipment, training, and other activities that would not show up in current output. Thus, there seems to be a significant diversion of labor during recessions to these productive, but typically unmeasured, activities.

TABLE 11.5 *The Behavior of Output, Employment, and Unemployment during Recent U.S. Recessions*

Year of Recession	1949	1954	1958	1970	1975	1982	Average for Six Recessions
Benchmark Year for Comparison	1948	1953	1956	1969	1973	1979	
% shortfall in real GNP	2.8	4.1	4.8	3.1	7.3	9.1	5.2
Shortfall of employment	1.3	2.1	2.9	0.7	1.9	3.5	
Shortfall as % of trend	2.1	3.2	4.2	0.8	2.1	3.3	2.6
Shortfall of total hours	0.08	0.11	0.15	0.07	0.13	0.19	
Shorfall as % of trend	3.3	4.2	5.6	2.3	3.9	5.1	4.1
U	5.8%	5.3%	6.5%	4.8%	8.3%	9.5%	
$U - U^0$	2.1%	2.5%	2.5%	1.4%	3.6%	3.8%	2.6%

Note: The shortfall in real GNP comes from Table 9.1. The number employed is total employment (millions), including the armed forces. Total hours is total weekly hours (billions). U is the unemployment rate for the total labor force. The shortfall of employment is relative to benchmark year employment (adjusted for growth at 1.4% per year). The shortfall of total hours is relative to benchmark year hours (adjusted for growth at 1.2% per year). For the unemployment rate, U^0 is the value for the benchmark year.

Source: Economic Report of the President, 1988.

those that we calculated in Chapter 9 (Table 9.1). Now we make similar computations for employment. When using the total number employed (including the military), the average shortfall for the seven recessions was by 2.4%. These shortfalls ranged from less than 1% for 1970 to 4.2% for 1958. Notice that, for each recession, the percentage shortfall in employment was smaller than that in real GNP. As an average for the six recessions, the percentage shortfall in real GNP (5.2%) exceeded that of employment (2.6%) by 2.6 percentage points. Hence, the ratio of real GNP to the number of workers—which is one measure of labor productivity—fell on average by about $2\frac{1}{2}\%$ during these recessions.

From the standpoint of aggregate labor input, a measure of total hours is more pertinent than the number of persons employed. To get the figures for total hours, we multiply the values for numbers employed by an estimate of average weekly hours of persons employed. Since average weekly hours tend to decline during recessions, there are greater percentage shortfalls in total hours than in numbers employed. For the six recessions in Table 11.5, the average shortfall of 4.1% for total hours was only about one percentage point below that of 5.2% for real GNP. Hence, when measured as real GNP per worker-hour, labor productivity declined by about 1% during a typical recession. The two cases of substantial decline in this concept of labor productivity were those for 1975 and 1982.

Finally, Table 11.5 shows the behavior of the unemployment rate during the six recessions. On average, the unemployment rate increased by 2.6 percentage points. The 1980–82 recession was the worst with an increase by 3.8 percentage points, but 1974–75 was a close second with 3.6 percentage points.

SUPPLY SHOCKS, RECESSIONS, AND UNEMPLOYMENT

The theory shows how supply shocks could cause the high unemployment characteristic of recessions, such as those described in Table 11.5. We would like to know how much these recessions actually were the result of identifiable supply shocks. Although we cannot give a definite answer to this question, there are some suggestive findings from recent empirical research.

James Hamilton (1983) documents the important role of oil shocks. Most economists believe that the dramatic increases in oil prices in 1973–74 and 1979–80 were important factors in the recessions of 1974–75 and 1980–82, respectively. Hamilton supports this view, but he also makes the surprising observation that the tendency "for oil price increases to be followed by recessions has in fact characterized every recession in the United States since World War II, with the single exception of the recession of 1960–61" (p. 229). For example, the recession of 1957–58 followed the increase in oil prices that stemmed from the Suez crisis, and the downturn of 1954 came after a rise in oil prices because of the Iranian nationalization of facilities. Overall, Hamilton's statistical results suggest that oil shocks have been important sources of high unemployment and low growth of real GNP. Moreover, the magnitude of the shocks for 1973–74 and 1979–80 may explain why the two associated recessions—for 1974–75 and 1980–82—were the most severe of the post–World War II period.

Aside from oil, economists have not been very successful in pinpointing identifiable supply shocks as regular elements in U.S. business fluctuations. Of course, it is still possible that an array of disturbances to productive conditions—which macroeconomists cannot identify directly—accounted for the recessions and booms. David Lilien (1982) pursued this idea by focusing on the changing composition of U.S. production. This composition has moved away from traditional areas of manufacturing, such as steel and automobiles, and toward high-tech industries and services. (Earlier the dominant movement was from agriculture to manufacturing.) Lilien argues that the process of reallocating labor across sectors leads to high rates of job separation and therefore high rates of unemployment.[14] His empirical results (pp. 787–92) for the post–World War II United States show that periods of more rapidly changing industrial composition tend to be times of unusually high unemployment. Thus, the findings suggest that U.S. recessions derive in part from various

---

[14]Our simple theory, summarized in equation 11.3, says that the natural unemployment rate is $s/(s + \eta)$. Thus, we predict an increase in unemployment if the job-separation rate, s, rises proportionately more than the job-finding rate, η.

real shocks—such as technological innovations, changes in foreign competition, or variations in the relative prices of raw materials—that induce shifts in the composition of industry. However, a number of economists have questioned this conclusion. For example, Prakash Loungani (1986) shows that, once we hold fixed the behavior of oil prices, there is no longer much association in the U.S. data between changes in the composition of production and the unemployment rate.[15]

Most macroeconomists attempt to eliminate seasonal effects by using **seasonally adjusted data** (as provided by the U.S. Department of Commerce). The process of seasonal adjustment attempts to eliminate the normal fluctuations of a variable, such as real GNP, that occur from winter (the first quarter) to spring (the second quarter), and so on. However, Robert Barsky and Jeff Miron (1988) reached some interesting conclusions by focusing on the unadjusted numbers. First, the regular seasonal fluctuations in various quantities—such as the real values of GNP, consumption, and investment and the amounts of employment and unemployment—are of greater magnitude than the variations associated with typical recessions and booms. For example, on a quarterly basis from 1948 to 1985, over 80% of the overall fluctuations in real GNP and over 60% of those in the unemployment rate were due to systematic seasonals (Barsky and Miron, 1988, Table 1). Furthermore, the seasonal patterns of comovement among GNP and its major components and between GNP and employment look similar to the comovements associated with recessions and booms (ibid., Table 2). For example, in the seasonal pattern, investment and consumption tend to move along with GNP, but investment is far more volatile than consumption. Miron (1988) shows that the results about seasonal behavior for the United States typically apply also for a sample of 25 industrialized or semi-industrialized countries.

Presumably, the seasonal movements reflect the influences of weather and holidays. To some extent we can think of these movements as regular shifts to technology (such as the effect of weather on the construction industry) and to some extent as systematic effects on preferences (such as the positive impact of Christmas on consumer demand and the negative influence of summer vacations on labor supply). Thus, the seasonal effects are analogous to the disturbances stressed in real business cycle models—that is, real shocks to technology or preferences. The magnitude of the seasonal fluctuations shows that these types of real disturbances can be quantitatively significant in the short run. In particular, this evidence weakens the argument of some economists that shocks to technology and preferences cannot be large enough to account for the observed magnitude of recessions and booms. Furthermore, the similarity of seasonal comovements to those in recessions and booms suggests that similar kinds of disturbances may underlie all of the observed fluctuations. Therefore, the seasonal evidence supports the idea that real business cycle theory is a promising approach for understanding recessions and booms—and therefore for understanding the fluctuations in unemployment.

---

[15]For additional discussion see Katharine Abraham and Lawrence Katz (1986).

SUMMARY

When workers and jobs differ, it takes time for people to match up well with jobs. Workers search for positions with high wages (and other desirable characteristics), while businesses search for productive workers. During the process of search, some job seekers remain unemployed, and some positions remain vacant. The rate of job finding depends on such things as the income available while unemployed and the level and shape of the distribution of wage offers.

Because workers or firms make mistakes in their initial assessments and because circumstances change, existing jobs sometimes end. The job-separation rate depends on workers' characteristics—such as age and experience—and the variability of an industry's supply and demand conditions.

The dynamics of employment and unemployment depend on the rates of job separation and job finding. If these rates are constant, the economy tends automatically to a natural rate of unemployment. This natural rate rises with an increase in the job-separation rate but falls with an increase in the job-finding rate. Also movements in and out of the labor force influence the natural unemployment rate.

We use this framework to analyze differences in average unemployment rates by age, sex, and race. Specifically, we can relate these differences to underlying differences in the duration of jobs and of unemployment. For example, younger workers have much higher job-separation rates and therefore exhibit a higher average unemployment rate.

We found before that supply shocks can generate a recession in the sense that output declines. Now we show that this kind of shock also lowers the job-finding rate and raises the job-separation rate. Thereby unemployment rises and employment falls during a recession. Empirically, the main direct evidence for these effects from supply shocks concerns changes in oil prices. However, some results about seasonal fluctuations suggest that shifts in technology and preferences—the types of disturbances stressed in real business cycle theories—can be quantitatively important in the short run.

IMPORTANT TERMS AND CONCEPTS

unemployment

labor force

outside of the labor force

unemployment rate

vacancies

reservation wage

job-finding rate

duration of unemployment

job-separation rate

natural unemployment rate

discouraged workers

duration of jobs

unemployment insurance

replacement ratio (for unemployment insurance)

experience rating (for unemployment insurance)

temporary layoffs

minimum wage

seasonally adjusted data

QUESTIONS AND PROBLEMS

Mainly for Review

11.1 What is the definition of the unemployment rate? Since it does not include workers who moved from "unemployment" to "out of the labor force," is it an underestimate of the amount of unemployment in the economy? Can you think of any reason that the unemployment rate overstates unemployment?

11.2 Suppose that a job seeker receives a wage offer, w, that exceeds his or her wage while employed, w^u. Why might the person reject the offer?

11.3 Once a worker and a firm find a job match, why would they ever choose to end this match? List some elements that influence the rate of job separation.

11.4 What is the natural rate of unemployment? When would unemployment differ from the natural rate? Can the natural rate itself change over time?

PROBLEMS FOR DISCUSSION

11.5 *The Job-Finding Rate*
Discuss the effect on the job-finding rate and the expected duration of unemployment from the following:

a. an increase in unemployment-insurance benefits,
b. an increase in the minimum wage,
c. a technological shock that improves the available wage offers.

Consider a group of job seekers whose skills are hard to evaluate. For such people, the distribution of wage offers tends to have a wide dispersion. Would the job-finding rate be high or low for this group?

11.6 *The Job-Separation Rate, the Job-Finding Rate, and the Natural Rate of Unemployment*
Suppose that the labor force has 100 million people, of whom 92 million initially have jobs and 8 million are unemployed. Assume that the job-separation rate is 1% per period and the job-finding rate 20% per period. Also, suppose that we can neglect movements in and out of the labor force. Trace out the path of employment and unemployment. What is the natural unemployment rate?

11.7 *The Labor Force During Recessions*
The data show little systematic response of the overall civilian labor force to recessions and booms. What response would you predict on theoretical grounds? (*Hint:* Think first about people's incentives to leave the labor force—that is, to stop looking for work—during a recession. But are there also incentives for some people to enter the labor force during bad times?)

On the other hand, the teenaged labor force declines during recessions. How can we explain this observation?

11.8 *Women and Teenagers in the Labor Force*

The unemployment rate for women averages about one percentage point higher than that for men (see Table 11.2). Further, the fraction of the civilian labor force that is female rose from 29% in 1948 to 45% in 1987. How would this increased role of women in the labor force affect the overall value of the natural unemployment rate?

For teenagers (aged 16–19), the average unemployment rate is about 10 percentage points higher than that for adults. The fraction of the civilian labor force that is teenaged rose from 6.5% in the early 1950s to 9.5% in the late 1970s but then fell to 6.7% in 1987. What do these changes mean for the overall value of the natural unemployment rate?

11.9 *The Minimum Wage Rate*

How does an increase in the minimum wage rate affect the employment of:

a. high- and low-productivity workers in covered industries?
b. high- and low-productivity workers in uncovered industries?

What does a higher minimum wage rate mean for the employment rate of:

a. teenagers?
b. all workers?

11.10 *Okun's Law*

Okun's Law (named after the economist Arthur Okun) states that the ratio of the percentage shortfall in output during a recession to the percentage point increase in the unemployment rate is roughly equal to three.

Calculate these ratios for the six postwar recessions covered in Table 11.5. How does Okun's Law hold up?

How does Okun's Law relate to the behavior of labor productivity during a recession?

11.11 *Vacancies and Unemployment* (*optional*)

We considered in the text how an adverse shock to production functions could lead to higher unemployment (as well as lower employment and production).

a. What would this type of disturbance do to the number of job vacancies? Therefore, how would the number of vacancies relate to the level of real economic activity?

b. Consider a graph of unemployment versus vacancies. (Economists sometimes call such a graph a *Beveridge curve,* after the British economist William Beveridge.) What would you predict for the slope of this graph?

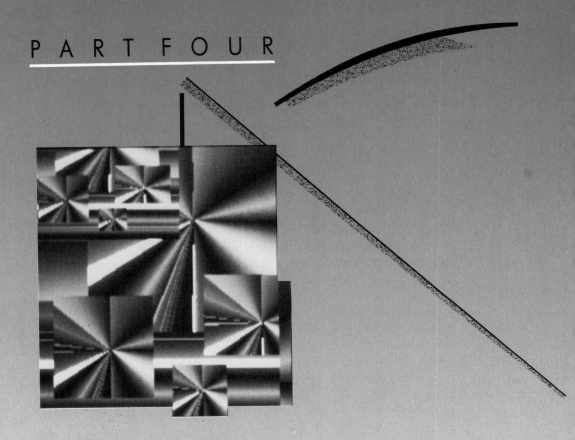

PART FOUR

GOVERNMENT BEHAVIOR

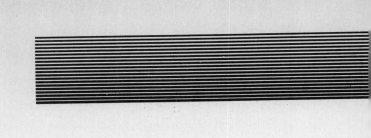

Up to this point the government has not played much of a role in the model. In fact, all the government does is print money and give away the proceeds as transfer payments. In the real world, governments have important influences on economic activity through their expenditures, taxes, transfer programs, regulations, and debt management. In this part of the book we consider the macroeconomic effects of these governmental activities.

Chapter 12 begins the study by considering government purchases of goods and services and a simple form of tax revenues. With this extension we can analyze how government purchases affect real interest rates, the level of real gross national product, and the split of GNP between private and public expenditures. For the United States, short-run changes in government purchases have played a major role during wartime but otherwise have not been a central element in business fluctuations. However, the longer-term increase in the size of government has crowded out private spending.

Chapter 13 introduces income taxes and transfer programs, which affect people's incentives to work, produce, and invest. Here we examine the possibility—stressed by "supply-side economists"—that changes in tax rates have major effects on the level of economic activity.

Chapter 14 discusses the public debt and the related concept of the government's budget deficit. Although these issues have attracted a lot of attention in recent years, the major conclusion is that budget deficits have exerted only minor influences on the U.S. economy.

CHAPTER 12

GOVERNMENT PURCHASES AND PUBLIC SERVICES

his chapter introduces government purchases of goods and services and a simple form of tax revenues. But before considering these extensions to the model, it is useful to get some background by looking at data on government spending for the United States and other countries.

DATA ON GOVERNMENT EXPENDITURES

Figures 12.1 and 12.2 show the evolution of government spending in the United States from 1929 to 1987. Excluding the wartime experiences, total dollar government expenditures when expressed as a ratio to nominal GNP rose from 0.10 in 1929 to 0.18 in 1940, 0.21 in 1950, 0.27 in 1960, 0.31 in 1970, 0.33 in 1980, and 0.35 in 1987 (a comparable figure for 1902 is 0.07).

The pattern of steady rise in the importance of total government expenditures conceals some different movements in the major underlying components. Figure 12.1 shows how purchases of goods and services have varied over time in the United States. Federal purchases rose from 0.01 relative to GNP in 1929 to 0.06 in 1940 and—after World War II—to 0.07 in 1950. Following a rise to 0.11 in 1960, the federal purchases' ratio declined to 0.07 in 1979, before rising to 0.09 in 1987.

Except during the Great Depression from 1933 to 1940, the dominant com-

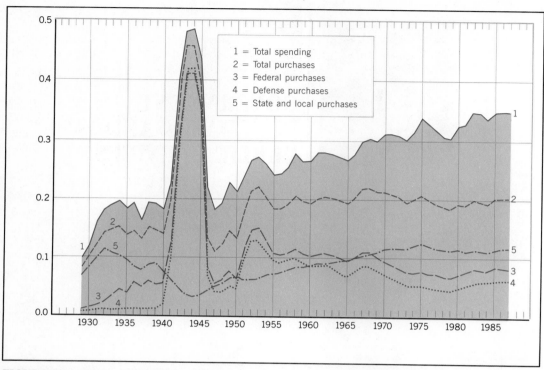

FIGURE 12.1 *Total Government Spending and Government Purchases, Expressed as Ratios to Nominal GNP*

ponent of federal purchases was defense spending. This spending was 0.02 relative to GNP in 1940 and 0.09 in 1960 but fell from there to a low point of less than 0.05 in 1979; then this ratio rose to 0.07 for 1987. (As a fraction of total government expenditure, military purchases declined from 33% in 1960 to 19% in 1987.) Figure 12.1 also shows the peaks in the defense purchases' ratio during wartime. These were 0.41 in 1943–44, 0.13 in 1952–53, and 0.09 in 1967–68.

State and local purchases relative to GNP were 0.07 in 1929 and 1950. Then this ratio rose to a peak of 0.13 in 1975 but subsequently remained relatively stable and equaled 0.12 in 1987. About half of the rise in this ratio from 1950 to 1975 took the form of increases in expenditures for education.

Figure 12.2 shows the behavior of transfers. Total transfer payments to persons rose from 0.01 relative to GNP in 1929 to 0.03 in 1940, 0.05 in 1950 and 1960, 0.08 in 1970, 0.11 in 1980, and 0.12 in 1987. The state and local part of these transfers (which includes aid to families with dependent children) rose from 0.013 relative to GNP in 1950 to 0.026 in 1987. But the main source of increase in the transfers' ratio derived from the federal government, in particular, from the growing benefits paid through social security. For example, the expenditures for old-age, survivors, and disability, the main social security program, increased from 0.003

relative to GNP in 1950 to 0.044 in 1987. Over the same period, medicare and medicaid expenses rose from zero to 0.018 relative to GNP.

We can summarize the movements in U.S. government expenditures relative to GNP since the 1950s in terms of three major developments: a sharp drop in spending for the military (which was reversed in part after 1979), a roughly compensating increase in social security benefits, and a substantial rise in state and local purchases (a major portion of which was for education) until the mid-1970s.

Table 12.1 shows the ratio of total government expenditures to gross domestic product (GDP) for 81 countries. The figures are averages from 1970 to 1985. The countries listed are those for which data are available on a broad concept of government expenditures. This concept is consolidated general government, which includes purchases of goods and services, transfer payments, and net interest payments by all levels of government. The ratios of government spending to GDP range from 11% for Paraguay and 12% for Guatemala to 77% for Israel and 54% for Sweden and the Netherlands. Aside from countries that have large defense expenditures, the ratios tend to be higher for the industrialized countries than for the less-developed countries. (Presumably, it is economic development that leads to big government rather than vice-versa!)

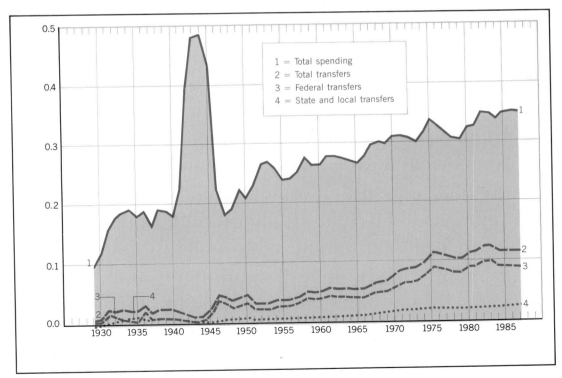

FIGURE 12.2 *Total Government Spending and Transfer Payments, Expressed as Ratios to Nominal GNP*

TABLE 12.1 *Government Expenditures in Various Countries*

Country	Spending Ratio (%)	Country	Spending Ratio (%)
Austria	46	Liberia	32
Argentina	27	Luxembourg	41
Australia	34	Malawi	27
Barbados	31	Malaysia	33
Belgium	50	Malta	40
Bolivia	13	Mauritius	29
Botswana	37	Mexico	22
Brazil	26	Morocco	32
Burkino Faso	14	Nepal	14
Burma	15	Netherlands	54
Cameroon	19	New Zealand	34
Canada	39	Nicaragua	21
Chile	32	Norway	51
Colombia	15	Oman	50
Costa Rica	22	Pakistan	24
Cyprus	27	Panama	34
Denmark	52	Papua New Guinea	34
Dominican Republic	16	Paraguay	11
Ecuador	26	Peru	18
Egypt	41	Philippines	13
El Salvador	15	Senegal	22
Fiji	26	Sierra Leone	23
Finland	39	Singapore	20
France	43	South Africa	28
Germany (West)	46	Spain	26
Ghana	17	Sri Lanka	31
Greece	36	Swaziland	25
Guatemala	12	Sweden	54
Guyana	53	Switzerland	34
Iceland	36	Syria	41
India	20	Thailand	17
Indonesia	21	Tunisia	31
Iran	35	Turkey	23
Ireland	48	Uganda	15
Israel	77	United Kingdom	44
Italy	44	United States	35
Japan	27	Uruguay	23
Jordan	51	Venezuela	24
Kenya	27	Yemen	35
Korea (South)	18	Zaire	35
		Zambia	34

Note: The table reports the ratio of government expenditure to gross domestic product. Government expenditure is total spending of consolidated general government. Data are averages from 1970 to 1985 from International Monetary Fund, *Government Finance Statistics* and *International Financial Statistics,* various issues.

THE GOVERNMENT'S BUDGET CONSTRAINT

Let G_t denote the government's demand for commodities during period t. In terms of the national accounts, G_t corresponds to real purchases of goods and services by the total of federal, state, and local governments. Total real government expenditure equals these purchases plus the real value of aggregate transfer payments, V_t/P_t. (We do not yet consider governmental interest payments.)

Thus far, we have assumed that the government's only revenue came from printing money. The real value of this revenue is the amount $(M_t - M_{t-1})/P_t$. Now we assume that the government also levies taxes on households. (The taxes could also apply to firms, but remember that the households own the firms in any event.) Let T_t be the aggregate dollar amount of taxes for period t. Then the real amount of tax revenues is T_t/P_t.

As before, the government's budget constraint equates total real expenditures to total real revenues.[1] Therefore, we have

$$G_t + \frac{V_t}{P_t} = \frac{T_t}{P_t} + \frac{(M_t - M_{t-1})}{P_t}. \qquad (12.1)$$

Our earlier formulation fits into equation 12.1 if we set real purchases, G_t, and taxes, T_t/P_t, to zero.

Earlier we assumed that transfer payments were lump sum. This specification means that a household's real transfer, v_t/P_t, does not depend on that household's level of income, effort at soliciting transfers, and so on. Now we assume also that the taxes are lump sum. Hence, a household's real tax liability, t_t/P_t, is independent of that household's level or type of income, effort at avoiding taxes, and so on.

In the real world, an elaborate tax law specifies the relation of someone's taxes to his or her income, business profits, sales, holdings of property, deductions from taxable income, and so on. Generally there are lots of things people can do—including hiring accountants, working less, underreporting income, and exploiting tax loopholes—to lower their obligations. These possibilities imply important substitution effects from the tax system on work effort, investment, relative demands for different goods (even including numbers of children), and so on. In general, people substitute in favor of the activities that lower their taxes.

In order to isolate the effects of government expenditures, we shall find it

---

[1] In the U.S. economy the revenue from printing money accrues directly to the Federal Reserve, which then turns most of its profits over to the U.S. Treasury. However, for historical reasons, the national accounts treat the Fed as though it were a private corporation rather than part of the central government. Therefore, the transfer of funds from the Fed to the Treasury appears in the national accounts as a tax on corporate profits. (We can almost feel sorry for the Fed, since its "profits" are taxed at nearly a 100% rate!) This quirk in the national accounts can cause trouble for unwary researchers since the Fed's payments to the Treasury amounted to 17% of the reported total for federal taxes on corporate profits in 1987 ($17.7 billion out of a total of $105.8 billion).

convenient initially to neglect these substitution effects from taxes. That is why we assume **lump-sum taxes,** which do not exert any substitution effects. (We bring in more realistic types of taxes and transfers in the next chapter.)

PUBLIC PRODUCTION

The government uses its purchases, G_t, to provide services to households and firms. We assume that the government provides these services free of charge to the users. In most countries public services include national defense, enforcement of laws and private contracts, police and fire protection, elementary education and some parts of higher education, highways, parks, and so on. The range of governmental activities has typically expanded over time, although this range varies significantly from one state or country to another.

We could model public services as the output from the government's production function. Then the inputs to this function would be the government-owned stock of capital, labor services from public employees, and materials that the government buys from the private sector. Instead, we simplify matters by neglecting production in the public sector. We do this—as do macromodels generally—by pretending that the government buys only final goods and services on the commodity market. In effect, the government subcontracts all of its production to the private sector. In this setup, public investment, publicly owned capital, and government employment are always zero. Ultimately the introduction of governmental production would affect the main results only if the public sector's technology or management capability differed from that of the private sector. Otherwise it will not matter whether the government buys final goods, as we assume, or instead buys capital and labor to produce things itself.

Before, we assumed that output could be labeled as either consumables or capital goods. Now we introduce a third function for output: the government can purchase goods to provide public services to households and firms. As before, the suppliers of goods and services do not care whether the buyers use the goods for consumption or investment or to provide public services. The demanders of commodities—which now include the government—determine its use.

PUBLIC SERVICES

In our model we allow for two types of public services. The first type provides utility to households. Examples are parks, libraries, school lunch programs, subsidized health care and transportation services, and the entertaining parts of the space program. An important feature of these services is that they may substitute closely for private consumer spending. (If the government buys someone's lunch at school, he or she does not buy his or her own lunch. But we have to be more subtle to find the private substitutes for the space program.)

The second type of service is an input to private production. Examples include the provision and enforcement of laws, aspects of national defense, government-sponsored research and development programs, fire and police services, and various regulatory activities. In some cases these services are close substitutes for private inputs of labor and capital. In other cases—such as "infrastructure" activities like the provision of a legal system, national defense, and perhaps highways and other transportation systems—the public services are likely to raise the marginal products of private factors.

In many situations a governmental program exhibits features of both types of services that we consider, but the mix varies across the range of programs. In our theory, however, we proceed as if there were only one type of governmental activity. This activity yields utility directly and also provides services to producers.

HOUSEHOLDS' BUDGET CONSTRAINTS

Before, we included real transfers, v_t/P_t, as a source of income for a household. Now we also have to subtract real taxes, t_t/P_t, to calculate real income after taxes. The budget constraint in real terms is now

$$y_t + b_{t-1}(1 + R_t)/P_t + m_{t-1}/P_t + (v_t - t_t)/P_t$$
$$= c_t + i_t + (b_t + m_t)/P_t. \quad (12.2)$$

In making decisions, each household cares about the present value of real transfers net of real taxes, as given by

$$\frac{(v_1 - t_1)}{P_1} + \left(\frac{1}{1 + r}\right) \cdot \left(\frac{v_2 - t_2}{P_2}\right) + \ldots$$

Consider the aggregate value of this expression. Each term involves the aggregate of real transfers net of real taxes $(V_t - T_t)/P_t$. But we know from the government's budget constraint in equation 12.1 that this term equals the real revenue from money creation less real government purchases—that is,

$$\frac{(V_t - T_t)}{P_t} = \left(\frac{M_t - M_{t-1}}{P_t}\right) - G_t. \quad (12.3)$$

If the money stock were constant, so that $M_t - M_{t-1} = 0$ holds in each period, equation 12.3 would imply that the aggregate real value of transfers net of taxes, $(V_t - T_t)/P_t$, equals the negative of real government purchases, $-G_t$. Therefore, in the aggregate, households include the present value of real government purchases, $[G_1 + G_2/(1 + r) + \ldots]$, as a negative item when computing the overall present value of their resources.[2] This result makes sense because the goods, G_t, that the government buys represents a part of the output stream that is not available for households.

---

[2] As in previous cases (discussed in Chapter 4 and the appendix to Chapter 8), the results do not change if the various monetary terms are also included.

TEMPORARY CHANGES IN GOVERNMENT PURCHASES

We want to explore the effects of government purchases on consumption, investment, and work effort. Consider an increase in the current level of purchases, G_1. We shall find that the effects differ depending on whether the change is temporary or permanent. To begin with, think about a temporary change—that is, G_1 rises, but households do not anticipate any changes in future values of G_t. Empirically, the most important example of this case is military spending during wars (if we think of the length of a period as corresponding to the expected duration of a war).

Recall that the government's budget constraint for period 1 is

$$G_1 + \frac{V_1}{P_1} = \frac{T_1}{P_1} + \frac{(M_1 - M_0)}{P_1}. \tag{12.4}$$

An increase in purchases, G_1, must involve some combination of an increase in real taxes, T_1/P_1, a decrease in real transfers, V_1/P_1, or an increase in the real revenue from money creation $(M_1 - M_0)/P_1$. Because we assume lump-sum taxes and transfers, our analysis of the real variables in the commodity market will be the same regardless of which combination we specify. For convenience, let's think of the extra government purchases as financed by more real taxes, T_1/P_1.

The higher current level of purchases, G_1, means more public services of the two types mentioned before. First, there is a positive effect on utility during the current period. That is because we assume that people like the services that the government provides. Suppose that the public services substitute for some private consumption but not for leisure.[3] For example, if the government provides free libraries, parks, school lunches, or transportation, households reduce their private spending in these areas. Let's use the parameter α (the Greek letter alpha) to measure the size of this effect. An increase in current purchases, G_1, by one unit motivates households to reduce aggregate private consumption demand, C_1^d, by α units.

It is possible for the parameter α to exceed one because an extra unit of government purchases may substitute for more than one unit of aggregate consumer spending. This outcome is possible if people benefit jointly from government projects, such as the Washington Monument. It is this characteristic of joint benefit that economists have in mind when they say that some governmental services are **public goods.** The more the government's services have this characteristic of publicness, the higher the parameter α tends to be.

It is plausible that the parameter α would decline as the quantity of government purchases rises. That is, as the amount of public services increases, the marginal unit substitutes less closely for private spending. Notice, however, that the value of the parameter α does not necessarily indicate how valuable an extra unit of public services is. People might like these services a lot even if they do not substitute much for private spending—that is, even if α is small.

---

[3] We follow here the general approach taken in Martin Bailey (1971, chapt. 9).

Some interesting empirical work provides estimates of the parameter α for the U.S. economy in the post–World War II period. The estimates suggest that α is between 0.2 and 0.4.[4] That is, an extra unit of government purchases substitutes for between 0.2 and 0.4 unit of aggregate private consumption. Thus, we are safe in assuming that α is positive but well below unity.

The second type of public service is an input to private production. Let's use the parameter β (the Greek letter beta) to measure the marginal product of public services. If the inputs of labor and capital do not change, an increase in current purchases, G_1, by one unit raises aggregate output, Y_1, by β units. Diminishing marginal productivity suggests that the parameter β would decline as the quantity of government purchases increases. Empirically, David Aschauer's (1988) results suggest important effects on output from the government's contributions to "infrastructure" but not from other types of government expenditure. The infrastructure components include highways, airports, electrical and gas facilities, mass transit, water systems, and sewers.

Changes in public services may also affect the schedules for the marginal products of labor (MPL) and capital (MPK). In some cases the public services substitute for private inputs. For example, free city police can replace private guards, and government housing or power plants can replace private projects. But more national defense and better enforcement of laws and improved infrastructure in the form of highways and airports may raise the marginal products of private factors, so there is no general presumption about the direction of these effects. For want of a better assumption, we consider the case where public services do not affect the schedules for the marginal products of labor and capital. In this case current government purchases, G_1, have no direct effect on work effort. Hence, for a given capital stock, an increase by one unit in government purchases, G_1, raises the aggregate supply of goods, Y_1^s, by β units.

Net investment demand (by households and firms) depends on the schedule for capital's marginal product, on the previous stock of capital, and on the real interest rate. Since we assume that public services do not affect the schedule for capital's marginal product, there is no direct impact of government purchases on investment demand. Any effects that arise must work through changes in the real interest rate.

Finally, recall that the present value of households' resources includes as a negative item the present value of government purchases. (This term corresponds to the present value of taxes net of transfers.) Since the increase in government purchases is temporary, the present value of these purchases rises but by only a small amount. Consequently there are small wealth effects, which show up as a reduction in consumer demand and an increase in labor supply. These changes would reinforce the effects on consumer demand and goods supply that we have already mentioned. To focus on the temporary nature of the change in government purchases, we shall find it convenient to neglect these small wealth effects. These effects will become important later when we consider permanent changes in government purchases.

[4] See Roger Kormendi (1983) and David Aschauer (1985).

CLEARING OF THE COMMODITY MARKET

Now we incorporate government purchases into the market-clearing conditions. Since the main new effects involve the demand and supply of commodities, we shall focus on the condition for clearing the commodity market. The new condition for period 1 is

$$C^d(r_1, \ G_1, \ldots) + I^d(r_1, \ldots) + G_1 = Y^s(r_1, \ G_1, \ldots).$$
$$(-)(-) \qquad\qquad (-) \qquad\qquad\quad (+)(+) \qquad\qquad (12.5)$$

The aggregate demand for commodities, Y_1^d, consists of consumption demand, C_1^d, gross investment demand, I_1^d, and government purchases, G_1. Hence if consumption and investment demand did not change, aggregate demand would increase one-to-one with an increase in government purchases. But an increase by one unit in purchases, G_1, reduces consumer demand, C_1^d, by α units. (This reduction would be slightly larger if we also included the wealth effect.) Since there is no effect on investment demand, an increase by one unit in government purchases raises aggregate demand by $1 - \alpha$ units. (Recall that we assume the condition $\alpha < 1$.)

Government purchases also influence the supply of commodities. An increase in purchases, G_1, by one unit raises the supply of goods, Y_1^s, by β units. (*Warning:* Our analysis assumes that taxes are lump sum. When we drop this unrealistic assumption in the next chapter, we introduce some important negative effects from governmental activity on the supply of goods.) Notice that if $\alpha + \beta < 1$, the increase in aggregate demand $(1 - \alpha)$ exceeds that in supply (β). This condition turns out to be important for figuring out the effects of a temporary increase in government purchases on the real interest rate.

Consider the inequality $\alpha + \beta < 1$. This condition says that if government purchases expand by one unit, households and firms get back less than one unit in the combined response from the substitution for consumer spending, α, and the increase in private output, β. One easy way to ensure this condition is to assume that public services are useless—that is, the government essentially buys up goods and throws them into the ocean. Although this assumption, where $\alpha = \beta = 0$, is popular (and appears implicitly in many macromodels), it may not be the most interesting way to model the functions of government!

But why does $\alpha + \beta < 1$ make sense? If $\alpha + \beta > 1$, the typical household would benefit from an increase in public services, paid for by an increase in taxes. That is because the amount that the typical household gets back—the value of the services that substitute for consumer spending (α) plus the value of the extra production (β)—exceeds the additional taxes. Hence, if $\alpha + \beta > 1$, it seems plausible that the government would grow larger, and this expansion tends to reduce the values of α and β. In particular, it would be popular for the government to expand until the condition, $\alpha + \beta < 1$, applied. (Note that the inequality, $\alpha + \beta < 1$, does not necessarily mean that a further expansion of the government is unpopular. Households might like public services a lot even if they substitute little for private spending—that is, even if the parameter α is small.)

Figure 12.3 shows the effects of a temporary increase in government purchases on the commodity market. Without this increase, the market clears at the real interest rate, r_1^*. Then the rise in purchases increases the aggregate quantities of goods demanded and supplied. But since $1 - \alpha > \beta$, the rightward shift of the aggregate demand curve exceeds that of the supply curve. Therefore, at the real interest rate, r_1^*, there is now excess demand for commodities. We conclude that the real interest rate increases to the value $(r_1^*)'$.

Figure 12.3 shows that output increases. There are two elements behind this increase. First, we assume that public services are productive. Second, the increase in the real interest rate motivates people to work more.

Consider now the composition of output. We know that government purchases rise. But private uses of output—for consumption and investment—decline. Consumption demand falls for two reasons. First, there is the substitution of public services for private spending. However, if we are talking about more military spending, this effect is likely to be weak—that is, the parameter α is small. Second, the higher real interest rate induces households to postpone their expenditures. This second effect accounts also for the drop in investment demand. Notice that the increase in government purchases **crowds out** private spending. Because of the higher real interest rate and the direct substitution of public services for consumer spending, the addition to government purchases induces consumers and investors to spend less.

We suggested before that investment demand is especially sensitive to variations in the real interest rate. Therefore, unless the direct substitution of public services for consumer spending is strong, we predict that the temporary increase in government purchases will mostly crowd out investment (including purchases of consumer durables) rather than consumption.

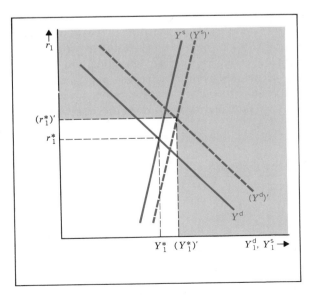

FIGURE 12.3 *Effect on the Commodity Market of a Temporary Rise in Government Purchases*
The temporary increase in purchases raises aggregate demand by more than supply. Therefore, the real interest rate and output rise.

Since consumption and investment decrease, it follows that total output rises by less than the increase in government purchases. That is, the ratio of the change in output to the change in purchases is positive but less than one. If the ratio were greater than one, we would say that a change in government purchases has a multiplicative effect on output. But we do not get this sort of **multiplier** in the model. That is because the economy typically operates to buffer shocks rather than to magnify them. In particular, the rise in government purchases leads to an increase in work effort and to decreases in private demands for consumption and investment. Each of these responses serves to alleviate the initial excess demand for goods. (When we study the Keynesian model in Chapter 20, we shall reexamine the potential for a multiplier.)

Consider why the temporary increase in government purchases raises the real interest rate. The increase in spending, financed by a temporary increase in taxes, implies a temporary decline in households' disposable income. Since the shortfall in income is temporary, the marginal propensity to consume is small. Therefore, households react mainly by reducing desired saving. As usual, when desired saving falls and investment demand does not shift, the real interest must increase. Note also that the higher real interest rate is the signal that indicates that a wartime emergency is the right time for households to work harder, to produce more goods, and to reduce demands for private consumption and investment. In other words, the market uses the real interest rate to achieve the appropriate allocations over time for work effort, production, consumption, and investment.[5]

Our discussion refers to wars as cases where government purchases are temporarily high. But we have ignored other aspects of major wars that can substantially affect the analysis. For one thing, we have neglected any negative effects of military reversals on productive capacity. These effects, an example of adverse supply shocks, would tend to reduce output. Another feature of wartime is the widespread use of rationing to hold down private demands for goods. Others are the military draft, confiscation of property, and appeals to patriotism to stimulate work and production. Essentially direct controls can be a rough substitute for a higher real interest rate as a mechanism for crowding out private spending and for stimulating work and production. These departures from free markets may not affect the general conclusions about the quantities of output, consumption, investment, and employment. But these controls may eliminate the increase in the real interest rate during wartime.

EVIDENCE FROM WARTIME EXPERIENCES

THE BEHAVIOR OF OUTPUT AND OTHER QUANTITIES

We can assess some effects of temporarily high government purchases by looking at the four most recent wars for the United States: World War I, World War II, Korea, and Vietnam. (For these cases we can reasonably neglect any direct effects of combat

[5]For some additional discussion of these effects, see Robert Hall (1980a).

on productive capacity in the United States.) Table 12. 2 describes the behavior of military spending, real gross national product (GNP), and the major components of GNP during these episodes.

The basic method of analysis is similar to one that we used before to examine recessions. For example, we contrast the peak year of the Korean War, 1952, with the benchmark year, 1950. Real military spending in 1952 was above its trend value by $146 billion, which was 11% of trend real GNP. On the other hand, real GNP was $102 billion, or 8% above its own trend.

Next, we calculate the ratio of excess real GNP and its various components to the excess of real military spending. For GNP the ratio in 1952 was 0.70. Hence— assuming that the boost in military spending was the major disturbance to the economy—this result supports the theory's predictions: a temporary increase in government purchases has a positive but less than one-to-one effect on output.

Since GNP rises by less than the increase in military spending, the nonmilitary components of GNP must decline overall. The figures shown for 1952 in Table 12.2 indicate that total investment (gross investment plus purchases of consumer durables) declined by the fraction, 0.35, of the increase in military spending. In contrast, consumer expenditures for nondurables and services were actually higher by the

TABLE 12.2 *The Behavior of Output and Its Components during Wartime*

Peak Year of War	1918	1944	1952	1968
Benchmark Year for Comparison	1915	1947	1950	1965
Excess real military spending (billions of 1982 dollars)	81.4	645.3	146.3	46.1
Excess as % of trend real GNP	16.8	66.2	11.4	2.0
Excess of real GNP (billions of 1982 dollars)	13.7	405.7	101.9	81.4
Excess as % of trend real GNP	2.8	41.6	8.0	3.6
Ratio to excess real military spending for the excess of:				
Real GNP	0.17	0.63	0.70	1.77
Real personal consumption expenditures	−0.45	−0.08	−0.05	1.15
Durables	—	−0.04	−0.09	0.31
Nondurables and services	—	−0.04	0.04	0.84
Real gross investment	−0.19	−0.16	−0.26	−0.21
Other[a]	−0.19	−0.13	0.01	−0.17
Excess of employment (millions)				
Total employment	2.1	8.4	1.5	2.5
Military personnel	2.7	9.9	1.9	0.7
Civilian employment	−0.6	−1.5	−0.4	1.8
Excess of total employment as % of trend value	5.3	14.8	2.4	3.2

[a]Nonmilitary government purchases and exports less imports.

Note: The method for calculating the excess or shortfall in each component is discussed in the text.

Sources: For World War II, the Korean War, and the Vietnam War, the data are from U.S Department of Commerce (1986). For 1915 and 1918, the data on real GNP are those shown in Figure 1.1. Estimates for the components of real GNP use the data from Kendrick (1961, Tables A-I, A-IIa). The shares of real GNP shown in each year from Kendrick's data are applied to the figures on total real GNP to estimate values for real military spending, real personal consumption expenditures, and real gross investment.

fraction 0.04. Thus, the temporary excess of military purchases crowded out only the investment part of private spending. Recall that the theory is consistent with this outcome, since military spending would have little direct substitution for consumer spending.

The final rows of the table show the effects on employment. Notice that total employment (numbers of persons working, including military personnel) in 1952 was above trend by 1.5 million, or 2.4% of the trend value. This total divided up between 1.9 million extra military personnel and 0.4 million fewer civilian workers. (We do not consider here the likely positive effects on hours and effort per worker.)

We apply a similar procedure for World War II. However, since the economy had not yet fully recovered in 1940 from the Great Depression, we use 1947 as the benchmark year. Basically the findings are similar to those from the Korean War except that the magnitudes are much larger. For example, the excess of real military spending in 1944 was $645 billion, or 66% of trend real GNP. Real GNP was $406 billion, or 42% above its own trend. Note that the ratio of excess GNP to excess military spending, 0.63, was similar to that for the Korean War.

For World War II, we find that the excess military spending crowded out total investment (gross investment plus purchases of consumer durables) by a fraction of 0.20 and consumer purchases of nondurables and services by a fraction of 0.04. Total employment for 1944 exceeded its trend value by 8.4 million, or 15%. This total broke down into 9.9 million extra military personnel and 1.5 million less civilian workers.

For World War I, the excess of real GNP above trend in 1918 was only 0.17 times the excess of real military spending. This value is well below those estimated for the Korean War and World War II. However, the computations for World War I are not so reliable because the underlying data on real GNP are subject to substantial uncertainty.

In any event, we lack the data during World War I to break down consumption into durable and nondurable components. The results shown in Table 12.2 indicate that the excess military spending in 1918 crowded out gross investment by the fraction 0.19 and personal consumer expenditure (which includes purchases of durables) by the fraction 0.45. The latter figure is much greater than that found for the Korean War and World War II. Finally, total employment in 1918 was above its trend by 2.1 million, or 5.3%. In this case there were 2.7 extra military personnel and 0.6 million fewer civilian workers.

The results for Vietnam differ sharply from those for the other wars. To begin, using 1965 as the benchmark year, the estimate for the excess of real military spending in 1968 was only $46 billion, or 2% of trend real GNP. Thus, unlike the other cases, it is doubtful that the increase in military spending was the overriding influence on the economy in the middle and late 1960s.

The estimated excess of real GNP for 1968 was $81 billion, or 4% of trend real GNP. Thus, the excess real GNP was 1.8 times the excess real military spending. Correspondingly, the total of the nonmilitary components of GNP was above trend in 1968. For example, the ratio to excess military spending was 0.10 for total investment (gross investment plus purchases of consumer durables) and 0.84 for the consumption of nondurables and services. Hence, the United States really was enjoying "guns and butter" at this time.

The most likely explanation for these results is that the economy was experiencing a boom in the 1960s that had little to do with the Vietnam War. This viewpoint is supported by the high growth rate of output in the period preceding the main increase in military spending. The average annual growth rate for real GNP was 5.1% from 1961 to 1965, as compared with 4.3% from 1965 to 1968.

Suppose that we focus on the results for the Korean War, World War II, and World War I. Then there is an interesting comparison between the behavior of the economy during wartime booms and during recessions. The contrast between wars and recessions concerns the relation between changes in total output and changes in private spending. Total output rises in wars but falls during recessions; however, private spending declines in both cases. The wartime experiences are also similar to recessions in that the major adjustments to private spending occur in the investment components. (World War I may be an exception here, although the data are too unreliable to be sure.) As with the six main postwar recessions that we studied in Chapter 9 (Table 9.1), there are relatively small reductions in consumer purchases of nondurables and services during the Korean War and World War II.

Finally, let's stress the finding that temporarily high government purchases raise total output and employment. But, as predicted, the ratio of the excess real GNP to the excess in purchases is less than one.

THE BEHAVIOR OF REAL INTEREST RATES

The theory predicts that temporarily high government purchases, as in wartime, raise the real interest rate. We have to be careful, however, when matching up this prediction with the wartime behavior of interest rates. Recall that the previous theoretical analysis assumes that government purchases are temporarily high only for the current period. But during wars, military expenditures tend to build up for awhile and then recede at the end of the war. Also, the length of the buildup and the timing of the war's concluson (or who wins) are unknown at the outset.

One implication from the theory is that the average real interest rate should be high over the period from the peak of a war until some time after the war finishes. In line with this viewpoint, Table 12.3 reports averages of interest rates over six-year intervals, beginning with the peak year of each war. Thereby, the figures include between one and five years of peacetime after each war. Notice that the table considers the four wars that we just studied, plus the Civil War. In each case we calculate the average for the nominal interest rate on prime commercial paper over six-year periods. Then we compute real interest rates by subtracting the average rate of change of the GNP deflator. (For the Civil War, we lack data on the GNP deflator and therefore use the consumer price index.)

For the Civil War, the average real interest rate over the period 1863–68 was 2.2%. This rate was substantially less than the averages for 1840–60 and 1867–80, which were each 9.1%. For World War I, the average real interest rate over the interval 1918–23 was 3.1%. This value equaled the average for 1900–16 but was

TABLE 12.3 *Interest Rates during Wartime*

Period	π_t	R_t	r_t
1863–68	4.8	7.0	2.2
1918–23	2.7	5.8	3.1
1944–49	6.2	1.0	−5.2
1952–57	2.2	2.6	0.4
1968–73	5.2	6.6	1.4

Note: All values are averages, expressed at annual percentage rates, for the periods indicated. π_t is the inflation rate, based on the consumer price index for the period 1863–68 and on the GNP deflator for the other periods. R_t is the interest rate on four- to six-month prime commercial paper. $r_t = R_t - \pi_t$.

Sources: See Table 10.1.

below that of 4.9% for 1920–40. For World War II, the average over the period 1944–49 was −5.2%, which was well below the averages of 4.9% for 1920–40 and −0.2% for 1947–60.

For the two most recent wars, Korea and Vietnam, the average real interest rates were 0.4% (for 1952–57) and 1.4% (for 1968–73), respectively. These values do not differ greatly from the average for 1947–80, which was 0.6%.

Overall, the results do not confirm a positive effect of wartime spending on real interest rates. In fact, the real interest rates were, if anything, below average during the wars.

For 1944–49 the substantially negative real interest rates reflect an overstatement of inflation because of the lifting of price controls. (General price controls did not apply to the earlier wars but were introduced to some extent during the Korean War.) The World War II controls kept the reported price levels below the "true" values from 1943 to 1945, so that inflation was understated for these years. As the controls were gradually eliminated from 1946 to 1948, the reported figures caught up with the true ones, and inflation was overstated. My estimate is that, without controls, the inflation rate from 1944 to 1949 would have averaged 1.1% per year rather than the official value of 6.2%.[6] If the controls merely obscured the behavior of the actual price level, the lower figure would be a reasonable estimate of the true inflation rate. Using this value, the average real interest rate for 1944–49 was −0.1% rather than −5.2%. Note that the adjusted value of −0.1% is close to the average of real interest rates for 1947–60 (−0.2%).

Even with this adjustment for price controls, we would not conclude that real

[6]These estimates, based on the behavior of money and other variables, are discussed in Barro (1978b, p. 572).

interest rates were especially high during wars in the United States. A possible explanation is the resort to aspects of a command economy, where governmental decrees on production, work, and expenditures substitute for free markets. Aside from the military draft, which applied to all the wars considered in Table 12.3, in the two world wars the government exerted direct pressures to work and produce and also rationed private consumption and investment. With few goods to buy and little option to take leisure, people would hold financial assets even if they paid low real interest rates. In other words, the command economy is in some respects a substitute for free markets with high real interest rates. While this argument may have some validity, it also implies that the data from U.S. wars may not be helpful for testing the theoretical link between temporary government purchases and real interest rates.

We can get around some of these difficulties by looking at the long-term relation between wartime spending and interest rates in the United Kingdom. From the standpoint of scientific inquiry, Britain was very cooperative by fighting numerous wars, especially before 1815. Prior to World War I, these wars were not accompanied by the introduction of aspects of a command economy. Thus, unlike the U.S. case, we can be confident of predicting a positive effect of temporary wartime expenditures on real interest rates.

The solid line in Figure 12.4 shows a measure of temporary real military spending expressed as a ratio to trend real GNP.[7] The peaks in this line correspond to the seven major wars for the United Kingdom over the period from 1730 to 1918. Notice that the high points for temporary spending were 50% of GNP in World War I (1916), 16% in the Seven-Years' War (1761), 9% during the War of American Independence (1782), and 7% during the Napoleonic Wars (1814).

The dashed line in the figure is the long-term nominal interest rate. The positive relation of this rate to temporary spending is clear visually and is also confirmed by statistical analysis.[8] Notably interest rates rose on average by 1.0 percentage point during the seven wars. This change is large relative to the average level of rates, which was 3.5% from 1730 to 1918.

For some additional evidence, David Denslow and Mark Rush (1987) looked at the relation between long-term interest rates and temporary government expenditures in France from 1828 to 1869. They observed a positive relationship, which resembles the one found for the long-term British history. Thus, as with the long-term evidence for the United Kingdom, these findings for France are more in line with the theory than are the recent results for the United States.

---

[7] The details of this variable and further results are in Barro (1987). For an earlier discussion of these data, see Daniel Benjamin and Levis Kochin (1984).

[8] The data are for British consols, which are government bonds that pay a perpetual stream of coupons but have no maturity date. (The confidence in the durability of the British empire used to be great.) The results refer to nominal interest rates, whereas the theory applies to real interest rates. Over the period of study, however, the long-term inflation rate in the United Kingdom was close to zero. It is therefore likely that the positive relation between temporary spending and nominal interest rates also reflects a positive relation with real interest rates.

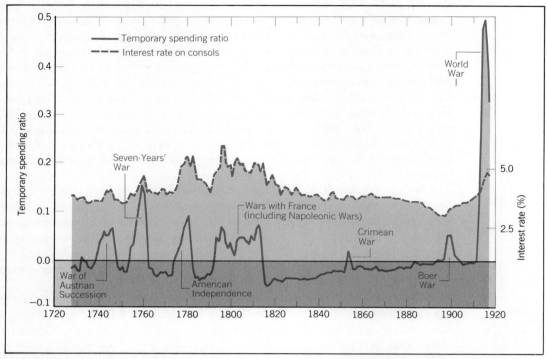

FIGURE 12.4 *Military Spending and the Interest Rate in the United Kingdom, 1730–1918*

PERMANENT CHANGES IN GOVERNMENT PURCHASES

The previous analysis applies to temporary changes in government purchases, such as in wartime. In other cases there are long-lasting shifts in the size of government. For example, the data that we looked at before for the United States showed permanent increases in the ratio of total government purchases to GNP during the 1930s and 1950s, but these ratios did not change a lot in the 1960s and 1970s.

We found before that a temporary increase in government purchases raised commodities demanded and supplied. But, as shown in Figure 12.3, the increase in demand exceeded that in supply. If the change in purchases is perceived to be permanent, the new element is that households anticipate a sizable increase in the present value of government purchases and, hence, in the present value of taxes net of transfers. Accordingly, there are now significant wealth effects, which reduce consumer demand and raise labor supply. These responses reduce the excess demand for goods. In fact, we shall find that an increase in government purchases now raises commodities demanded and supplied by roughly equal amounts—that is, a permanent change in government purchases does not disturb the equality between demand and supply. Let's see why this is the case.

Consider first a simplified setting where public services are useless ($\alpha = \beta = 0$) and labor supply is fixed. In this case, a permanent increase by one unit in government purchases effectively subtracts one unit from households' disposable income in each period. As with a permanent shift in the production function, the marginal propensity to consume is close to one in this situation. Therefore, consumer demand declines by about one unit—that is, one additional unit of public expenditure directly crowds out one unit of private consumer spending. Since government purchases are higher by one unit, the aggregate demand for goods does not change. With fixed labor supply and nonproductive public services ($\beta = 0$), the supply of goods also does not change. Therefore, as suggested before, a permanent increase in government purchases leaves the demand for goods equal to the supply. This last result turns out to follow even if government services are productive ($\alpha \neq 0$ or $\beta \neq 0$) or if labor supply varies. The argument that follows in the boxed section derives this result.

Figure 12.5 depicts the effects of a permanent increase in government purchases on the commodity market. Note that the demand and supply curves shift rightward by equal amounts. Therefore, aggregate demand still equals aggregate supply at the initial real interest rate, r_1^*. We conclude that a permanent expansion of government purchases has no effect on the real interest rate.

Figure 12.5 shows that output increases. This response reflects the productivity (β) of public services and a possible increase in labor supply. (Labor supply tends to rise because of the decline in wealth, as discussed in the boxed section. However, it is worth noting that the increase in work effort may not occur if government expenditures are financed by an income tax rather than a lump-sum tax. We consider more realistic types of taxes in the next chapter.)

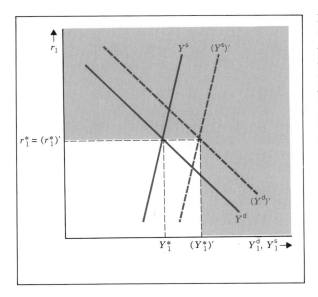

FIGURE 12.5 *Effects on the Commodity Market of a Permanent Rise in Government Purchases*
The permanent increase in purchases raises aggregate demand and supply by roughly equal amounts. Therefore, output increases, but the real interest rate does not change.

RESULTS WHEN PUBLIC SERVICES ARE PRODUCTIVE AND WHEN LABOR SUPPLY VARIES (OPTIONAL)

S uppose that public services substitute for private consumer spending—that is, $\alpha > 0$. We know from before that the direct substitution between public and private spending implies that consumer demand declines by α units when government purchases increase permanently by one unit. (This effect arises whether the change in government purchases is temporary or permanent.) However, if $\alpha > 0$, households effectively lose only $1 - \alpha$ units of disposable income in each period. The other α units provide services that households no longer have to buy on the market. Therefore, the wealth effect now implies that consumer demand falls by about $1 - \alpha$ units. (The marginal propensity to consume is still close to one here.) Adding this response to the decline of consumer demand by α units, we find that a one-unit increase in government purchases still leads to a decline by one unit overall in consumer demand. Therefore, as in the case where $\alpha = 0$, the demand for goods remains equal to the supply.

Assume now that public services are productive—that is, $\beta > 0$. If government purchases rise permanently by one unit, the supply of goods increases by β units in each period. Consequently, households' income from production rises by β units in each period. Since the marginal propensity to consume is close to unity here, consumer demand also increases by about β units. In other words, the aggregates of goods supplied and demanded are each higher by β units. Hence, excess demand is still zero.

Finally, if $\alpha + \beta < 1$, a permanent increase in government purchases reduces wealth and therefore motivates an increase in work effort. The higher work means an increase in the supply of goods and a corresponding rise in households' income from production. Since the marginal propensity to consume is again close to unity, consumer demand rises by roughly the same amount. Therefore, while the rise in work effort means that goods supplied and demanded are each higher, it still follows that excess demand is nil.

Consider next the composition of output. To begin, government purchases increase. But there are two forces that lower consumer demand. First, public services substitute for private spending, and, second, the reduction in wealth induces households to consume less. However, since the real interest rate does not change, there is no effect on investment. Notice that this last result differs from that when the change in government purchases was temporary. In that case the rise in the real interest rate crowded out both forms of private spending. Now, when the change in purchases is permanent, the extra government purchases crowd out only consumer spending.

Since consumption decreases while investment does not change, it follows that total output once more increases by less than the rise in government purchases. That is, the ratio of the change in output to the change in purchases is again positive but less than one. Thus, the model still does not have a multiplier.

Let's think about why the real interest rate increases when the rise in government purchases is temporary but does not change when the rise in purchases is permanent. Recall that a temporary increase in government purchases implies a temporary fall in households' disposable income, which leads to a decrease in desired saving. In contrast, if the increase in government purchases and taxes is permanent, the decline in households' disposable income is also permanent. In this case the marginal propensity to consume is close to one, and the effect on desired saving is small. For this reason, the real interest rate does not change.

Table 12.4 provides empirical estimates for the effects on real GNP from temporary and permanent changes in government purchases. For defense purchases, the results show a strong positive impact on output. Also, the estimated responses for temporary changes tend to exceed those for permanent changes. The estimates imply that output rises by between 50 and 120% of a temporary increase in defense purchases. These findings are broadly consistent with the less formal results that we derived from wartime experiences. There we found that the excesses of real GNP during World War II and the Korean War were 60–70% of the excesses of real military spending.

Table 12.4 indicates that real GNP rises by between 30 and 70% of a permanent increase in defense purchases. Since the response is again less than 100%, we find that a permanent rise in purchases must crowd out some private spending.

For nondefense purchases, the data did not provide much information about temporary changes, and the results apply only to permanent shifts. Unfortunately, the estimates are imprecise, covering the range of responses for output from −20% to +130% of the change in purchases. Therefore, although a positive effect is likely, we cannot pinpoint the magnitude.

One final point is that the empirical results suggested little role for government purchases in peacetime business fluctuations. The amount of peacetime variation in government purchases, combined with the estimated effects of these purchases on

TABLE 12.4 *Empirical Estimates of Effects of Government Purchases on Real GNP*

Change by One Unit in	Estimated Number of Units by Which Real GNP Increases
Temporary defense purchases	0.5 to 1.2
Permanent defense purchases	0.3 to 0.7
Permanent nondefense purchases	−0.2 to 1.3

Note: The results (from Barro, 1978b) apply to U.S. data over the period from 1946 to 1978, although the results are similar from 1942 to 1978.

real GNP, does not account for much of the observed booms and recessions. In particular, as we saw in Table 9.1, shifts in government purchases do not have a regular association with the six main U.S. recessions since World War II.

EFFECTS OF GOVERNMENT PURCHASES ON THE PRICE LEVEL

Economists often say that government spending is inflationary. Let's see what the model implies about the effects of government purchases on the price level.

Start, as usual, with the condition for all money to be willingly held. For period 1 we have

$$M_1 = P_1 \cdot L(Y_1, \quad R_1, \quad G_1, \cdots), \qquad (12.6)$$
$$(+)\,(-)\,(-)$$

where L is the function for real money demanded. We assume that total output, Y_1, measures real transactions, which have a positive effect on the real demand for money. As before, the nominal interest rate, R_1, has a negative effect on the real demand for money.

We also enter government purchases, G_1, in the money-demand function with a negative sign. Since public services are provided free of charge to users, there are fewer monetary transactions associated with government purchases than with private consumption or investment. Therefore, for a given level of total output, an increase in government purchases, G_1, means less money demanded.

Consider the consequences for the price level of an increase in government purchases, G_1. If the increase is permanent, there is an increase in output, Y_1, but no change in the real interest rate. Unless the direct negative effect of government purchases on real money demanded is substantial, real money demand would increase. Therefore, if the behavior of the nominal money stock does not change, an increase in government purchases tends to reduce the price level, P_1.

If the increase in government purchases is temporary, the real interest rate, r_1, tends to rise. Hence, for a given expected rate of inflation, π_1^e, the nominal interest rate, R_1, rises. This element lowers the real demand for money and thereby makes it more likely that the price level would rise.

Overall, for a given behavior of money, there is little basis to predict systematic effects of government purchases on the price level. Moreover, even if there were a positive effect, this channel would not account for chronic rises in prices—that is, for inflation. Rather, each increase in government purchases—relative to the scale of the economy—would generate a one-time rise in the price level. To explain inflation on this basis, we would need continuing expansions in the relative importance of government purchases. Yet as we saw before, government purchases have not changed much in relation to GNP in the 1960s and 1970s, which are the years when U.S. inflation became significant.

An increase in government purchases may also be inflationary because it stimulates money creation. That is, governments may resort to inflationary monetary growth to finance part of the higher level of purchases. Of course, this argument applies equally well to the government's transfer payments, which are another form of government spending. Notice that this mechanism connects a higher level of real spending to a faster growth rate of money and thereby to a higher rate of inflation. Hence, this route does show how higher real government spending can be inflationary.

Empirically there is not much evidence that changes in government purchases influence the price level, once we hold fixed the behavior of money. But for some countries, there are important linkages between real government spending and the rate of money creation. In other words, when some governments opt to raise real spending, they use the printing press to pay for part of it. For example, as discussed in Chapter 8, the connection between government spending and monetary growth was very close during the German hyperinflation from 1921 to 1923.

For the United States, there is no evidence that long-term changes in government spending as a ratio to GNP have led to higher rates of monetary growth. However, the sharp expansions of spending that occurred during wartime did trigger a lot of money creation. Like most other countries, the United States finances part of its wartime spending with the printing press. Hence, this mechanism accounts for some of the inflation that usually accompanies wars.

SUMMARY

We introduced government purchases of goods and services as another use of output. To finance these expenditures and its transfer payments, the government levies lump-sum taxes or prints money. The government uses its purchases to provide a flow of public services. An additional unit of these services substitutes for α units of aggregate consumer spending and also raises production by β units. We assume the condition $\alpha + \beta < 1$, which means that households and firms get back directly less than the cost of an additional unit of public services.

A temporary increase in government purchases, as in wartime, raises aggregate demand by more than supply. Hence, the real interest rate and output increase. However, the crowding out of investment and consumpton means that total output rises by less than the increase in government purchases. That is, there is no multiplier.

Empirically variations in government purchases play a major role during wartime but not in peacetime business fluctuations. The U.S. evidence from World War II and Korea supports the theory's predictions with respect to quantities. In particular, real GNP rises but by only 60–70% of the increase in real military spending. Thus, there is crowding out of private spending, especially investment. The U.S. data do not show a tendency for the real interest rate to rise during wartime. On the other hand, the long-period evidence for the United Kingdom and France reveals a positive effect of wartime spending on interest rates.

A permanent increase in government purchases increases goods supplied and demanded by roughly equal amounts. Therefore, output again increases, but there is no change in the real interest rate. In this case, the crowding out of private spending falls entirely on consumption.

Finally, we examined the connection between government purchases and inflation. For a given behavior of the money stock, the model does not predict any strong linkages. More government spending is inflationary if it induces the government to print money at a faster rate.

IMPORTANT TERMS AND CONCEPTS

lump-sum taxes
public goods

crowding out (from government purchases)
multiplier

QUESTIONS AND PROBLEMS

Mainly for Review

12.1   What are the channels by which government spending affects excess demand in the commodity market? How does it affect utility? Can you think of examples of public services that are not close substitutes for consumption ($\alpha = 0$) but nevertheless provide utility?

12.2   Could government services be a substitute for leisure? If so, what additional channel of effect arises in the commodity market?

12.3   Why does the real interest rate rise as a result of a temporary increase in government purchases?

12.4   What is crowding out? Does it involve an intertemporal substitution effect alone? Could there be direct substitution of government purchases for private investment purchases?

PROBLEMS FOR DISCUSSION

12.5   *Government Purchases in the National Accounts*
The national accounts treat all of government purchases as part of real GNP. But suppose that these purchases, G_t, are an input to private production—that is, $Y_t = F(K_{t-1}, N_t, G_t)$. Then public services are an intermediate product—that is, a good that enters as an input into a later stage of production. Hence, we ought not to include these services twice in real GNP—once when the government purchases them and again when the public services contribute to private production.

a.   Suppose that businesses initially hire private guards. But the government then provides free police protection, which substitutes for the guards. Assume that the private guards and police are equally efficient and receive the same incomes. How does the switch from private to public services affect measured real GNP?

b. How should we change the treatment of public services in the national accounts? Is the proposal practical?

These issues are discussed in Simon Kuznets (1948, pp. 156–57) and Richard Musgrave (1959, pp. 186–88).

12.6 *Public Ownership of Capital and the National Accounts*

When the government produces goods and services, the national accounts measure the contribution to GNP by the government's purchases from the private sector of labor, materials, and new capital goods. But the accounts neglect any contribution to output from the flow of services on government-owned capital. The accounts also do not subtract depreciation of this capital to calculate net product.

a. What happens to measured GNP if the government gives its capital to a private business and then buys the final goods from that business?

b. How should we change the treatment of government-owned capital in the national accounts? Is the proposal practical?

12.7 *The Role of Public Services*

We assume that an additional unit of public services has two direct effects: first, it substitutes for α units of private consumption, and second, it raises production by β units.

a. Consider various categories of government purchases, such as military spending, police, highways, public transit, research and development expenditures, and regulatory agencies. How do the parameters α and β vary across the categories? Are the parameters always positive?

b. Consider a permanent increase in government purchases. How do the sizes of the responses in output and consumption depend on the values of the parameters, α and β? Explain the results.

c. Repeat part b for the case of a temporary increase in government purchases.

12.8 *Prospective Changes in Government Purchases*

During the current period, date 1, people find out that government purchases will increase permanently in some future period. There is no change in current purchases or in the paths of the money stock and real transfers.

a. What happens currently to the real interest rate and the quantities of output, consumption, investment, and employment?

b. What happens to the current price level and nominal interest rate?

c. Can you think of some real-world cases where this question applies?

12.9 *Effects of Government Purchases on the Real Wage Rate*

Suppose that we include a labor market in the model.

a. What is the effect on the real wage rate from a temporary increase in government purchases?

b. What is the effect from a permanent increase in government purchases?

12.10 *Government Employment during Wartime* (*optional*)

In the model we assume that the government buys only final product from the commodity market. In particular, the government neither produces goods nor employs people. This assumption is basically satisfactory if the government's production function is similar to that of private producers. But the assumption is troublesome for wartime. For example, suppose that during World War II the government effectively removes 10 million people temporarily from the civilian labor force. But the government takes away no privately owned capital. Then, as before, assume that the government also temporarily raises its purchases of goods by a large amount.

a. Analyze the effects on the real interest rate and on the quantities of output, investment, and consumption. (How should we count the 10 million conscripts in the measure of output?) What happens to total and private employment?

b. If we include a labor market in the model, what happens to the real wage rate?

12.11 *The Price Level during the Korean War*

With the start of the Korean War, the price level (GNP deflator) rose at an annual rate of 10% from the second quarter of 1950 to the first quarter of 1951. By contrast, the inflation rate was negative for 1949, 1.4% from the first quarter of 1951 to the first quarter of 1952, and 2.0% from the first quarter of 1952 to the first quarter of 1953.

The table here shows over various periods the inflation rate, π_t, the monetary growth rates, μ_t, for currency and M1, the growth rate of real government purchases, ΔG_t, and the nominal interest rate on 3-month U.S. Treasury bills, R_t. Using these data, how can we account for the surge in the price level at the start of the Korean War? (This question does not have a definite answer!)

(*Hint*: Price controls were stringent during World War II. People may have expected a return to these controls under the Korean War in 1950).

		(M1)	(Currency)		
Year and Quarter	π_t	μ_t	μ_t	ΔG_t	R_t
1949.1 to 1950.2	−0.3	1.8	−1.6	2.7	1.1
Start of war					
1950.2 to 1951.1	10.0	4.0	−0.5	24.6	1.3
1951.1 to 1952.1	1.4	5.3	4.7	27.9	1.6
1952.1 to 1953.1	2.0	3.2	4.5	9.2	1.8

(Figures in % per Year)

12.12 *The Optimal Level of Public Services* (*optional*)

In the model a permanent increase in government purchases raises output but lowers consumption and leisure. Recall that we used the condition $\alpha + \beta < 1$, where α measures the substitution of public services for consumer spending, and β is the marginal product of public services. We assumed also that the parameters α and β declined as the quantity of government purchases rose.

a. What happens to the typical person's utility when the quantity of government purchases rises permanently by one unit?

b. If the government wants to maximize the typical person's utility, where should it set its level of purchases? What condition holds here for the parameters α and β?

c. Why is it not the right answer in part b to choose the level of government purchases that maximizes aggregate output (as measured by real GNP)?

d. Without working through the details, how does the analysis change if public services provide utility in other ways—that is, not only as a direct substitute for private consumer spending?

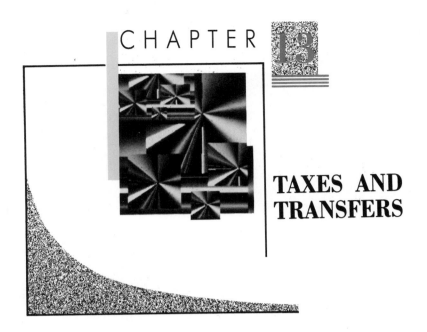

CHAPTER 13

TAXES AND TRANSFERS

hus far, we have taken an unrealistic view of governmental operations by assuming lump-sum taxes and transfers. In our model, the amount that a household or firm pays as taxes or receives as transfers has nothing to do with the household's or firm's income or other characteristics. In the real world governments levy a variety of taxes and pay out a lot of transfers, but none of them looks like the lump sums in our theory. Generally a household's or firm's taxes and transfers depend on its actions. But this dependence motivates changes in behavior. For example, income taxes deter people from working and discourage businesses from investing. Similarly, transfers to the unemployed or the poor may motivate people not to work. Overall, the system of taxes and transfers creates a variety of substitution effects on work effort, production, consumption, and investment. In this chapter we extend the theoretical analysis to incorporate some of these effects. But before considering the theory, it is useful to start with an overview of tax collections in the United States.

SOURCES OF GOVERNMENT REVENUES IN THE UNITED STATES

Figure 13.1 shows the breakdown of revenues by major types for the federal government since 1929. Individual income taxes were a reasonably stable share of total

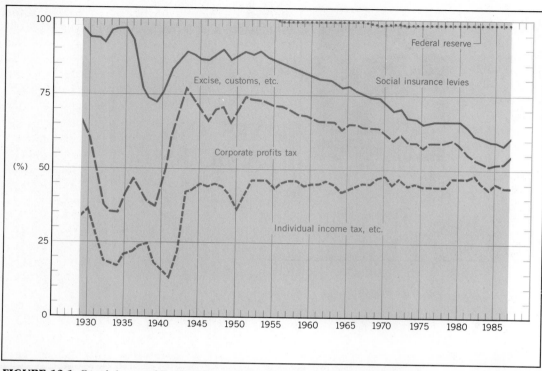

FIGURE 13.1 *Breakdown of Federal Revenue*
Figures are percentages of the total. Data are from U.S. Department of Commerce (1986) and U.S.
Survey of Current Business (*July 1988*).

federal revenues since World War II. For 1987, this share was 44%. The next component, corporate profits taxes, declined from about 25% of the total after World War II to 10% in 1987. Then there are levies for social insurance funds, which increased substantially since World War II. In 1987, 79% of these taxes were for social security (including health insurance). The rest were mainly for unemployment insurance and government employees' retirement. Notice that the total of payments into social insurance funds rose from 10% of all federal revenues in 1948 to 38% in 1987. Thus, in 1987, this category was almost as large as the federal income tax on individuals. Another part of federal revenues is excise taxes, customs duties, and so forth, which fell from about 20% of the total after World War II to 6% in 1987. Finally, the Federal Reserve's payments to the Treasury—which correspond to the government's revenue from printing money—amounted in 1987 to 2% of total federal receipts. These proceeds from money creation were near zero before the mid-1950s.

Before World War II, the excise taxes and customs duties were relatively more important. In fact, these items were the major source of federal revenues before World War I. Individual income taxes began in 1913, except for some levies around the Civil War and in 1895. Corporate taxes started in 1909. Notice also that the levies for social insurance funds were small until the beginning of the unemployment insurance program in 1936 and social security in 1937.

Figure 13.2 shows a breakdown for the revenues of state and local governments. Property taxes were traditionally the largest component, but the share of this component fell from about 60% in the early 1930s to less than 40% after World War II and to 19% in 1987. In the early period, the relative decline in property taxes corresponded to the growth in sales taxes. These increased from 6% of state and local revenues in 1929 to 20% in 1941 but maintained a roughly constant share since World War II. More recently, state and local governments have turned to individual income taxes. This category constituted 4% of state and local receipts in 1929 and 1948 but then increased to 14% in 1987. The other category of state and local revenues that became more important since World War II is federal grants-in-aid (transfers of funds from the federal government to state and local governments). These revenues climbed from 9% of the total in 1946 to 24% in 1978 but then fell to 17% in 1987. (Federal grants-in-aid are primarily for welfare, medical care, transportation, education, housing, training programs, and general revenue sharing.)

Figure 13.3 shows the federal share of total government revenues. (Federal grants-in-aid are excluded here from total revenues.) Notice that the federal share

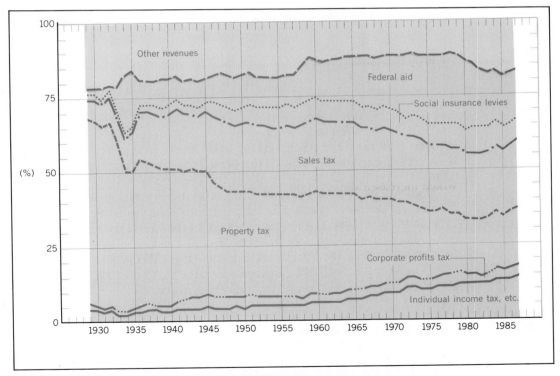

FIGURE 13.2 *Breakdown of State and Local Revenues*
Figures are percentages of the total. Data are from U.S. Department of Commerce (1986) and U.S. Survey of Current Business (July 1988).

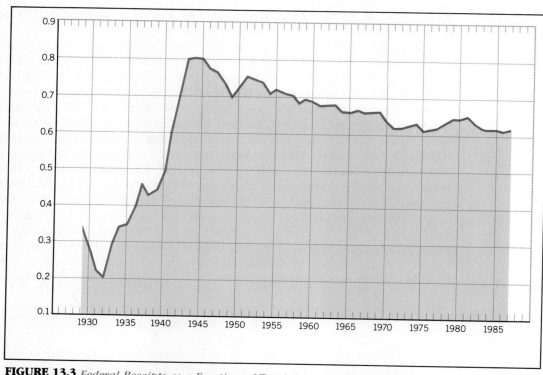

FIGURE 13.3 *Federal Receipts as a Fraction of Total Government Receipts*
Data are from U.S. Department of Commerce (1986) and U.S. Survey of Current Business (July 1988).

was 34% in 1929, fell to a low point of 19% in 1932, but subsequently rose during the New Deal period to reach 49% by 1940. After a peak of 80% during World War II, the share declined to 62% in the early 1970s. For 1987, the fraction was also 62%.

Figure 13.4 provides one measure of an overall tax rate—the ratio of total government revenues (excluding federal grants-in-aid) to GNP. The ratio rose from 11% in 1929 to 18% in 1940 and 25% in 1945. After a fall to 22% in 1949, the ratio increased slowly to 26% in 1956, 28% in 1960, 31% in 1969, and 32% from 1977 to 1982. With the Reagan tax cuts, the ratio fell (but by only one percentage point) to 31% for 1983–84, and then rose back to 32% in 1987. (It is not easy to detect the "Reagan revolution" from these figures!)

TYPES OF TAXES

Notice that some taxes fall on income (individual income taxes, corporate profits taxes, and contributions for social security, which are levied on wage earnings), others on expenditures (excise and sales taxes), and some on holdings of property.

But one way or another, the amount that someone pays depends on his or her economic activity. That is, none of these levies looks like the lump-sum taxes in our theory.

FEDERAL INDIVIDUAL INCOME TAX

Because it is the most important tax, let's look at how the federal individual income tax is calculated for households. First, subtract from someone's reported income the expenses for business purposes, deferred compensation through pension plans, and some other items to get **adjusted gross income.** Then take out either a standard deduction ($3000 for a single person, $5000 for a married couple in 1988) or the itemized deductions for medical care, some types of interest payments, certain taxes, and other categories. Then subtract the value of personal exemptions, which in 1988 was $1950 per dependent, including oneself, to get **taxable income.** Aside from any tax credits that apply, the law provides a schedule that relates the amount of tax to taxable income. (Marital status also matters here.) But it is important to note that the tax is not a constant fraction of taxable income—that is, it is not a **flat-rate tax.** Over most ranges of income, an increase in income (that is large

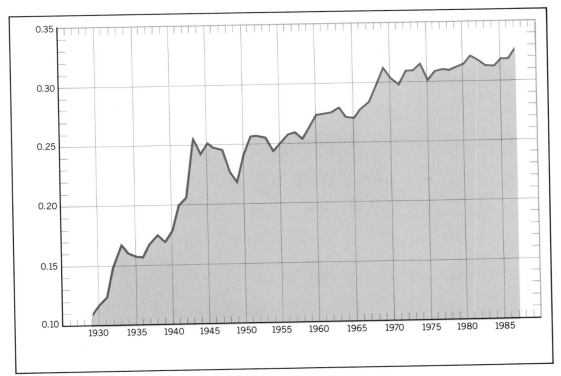

FIGURE 13.4 *Total Government Receipts as a Ratio to GNP*
Data are from U.S. Department of Commerce (1986) and U.S. Survey of Current Business (*July 1988*).

enough to move someone into the next tax bracket) raises the **marginal tax rate,** which is the tax rate on an additional dollar of income. This setup is called a **graduated-rate tax.** (Sometimes it is called a "progressive tax," which seems to express someone's opinion about its merits. In contrast, a "regressive tax" is one where the rate falls as income rises.)

Although the U.S. income tax in 1988 was graduated, the degree of graduation was substantially reduced by the tax reform of 1986 and by earlier tax legislation. (For a discussion of the 1986 reform, see Henry Aaron, 1987.) Figure 13.5 shows the relation of the marginal tax rate and the **average tax rate** (the ratio of taxes to adjusted gross income) to a family's adjusted gross income. The graph applies in 1988 to a married couple who have two children and do not itemize deductions. (This assumption is unrealistic at high incomes, where most people itemize deductions.) So the graph incorporates a standard deduction of $5000 and personal exemptions of $7800. Note that the marginal tax rate is 0 for adjusted gross incomes between $0 and $12,800, 15% for incomes between $12,800 and $42,550, and 28% for incomes between $42,550 and $84,400. For incomes between $84,400 and $205,430, the effective marginal tax rate is 33%. (Technically, the rate is 28% plus a surtax of 5%, corresponding to a phase-out of benefits from the 15% bracket and

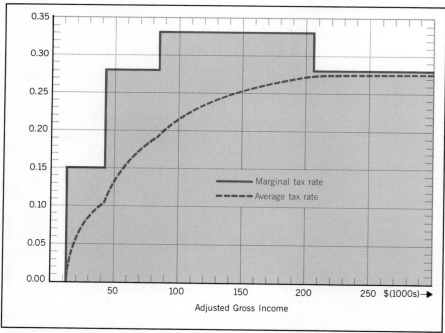

FIGURE 13.5 *Marginal and Average Tax Rates for the Federal Individual Income Tax in 1988*

The graph shows for 1988 the relation of marginal and average tax rates to adjusted gross income for a married couple with two children. We assume that the family uses the standard deduction.

the personal exemptions.) Then a peculiar feature of the 1986 tax law is that the marginal tax rate drops to 28% for adjusted gross incomes above $205,430.

Figure 13.5 also shows the average tax rate as a function of adjusted gross income. Note that the average tax rate rises steadily with income but approaches the constant value of 28% as income becomes very high. Recall that we ignored itemized deductions and various devices that make income nontaxable. These elements weaken the tendency for the average tax rate to rise as income increases.

The distinction between average and marginal tax rates is important for our analysis. *Average* tax rates indicate how much revenue the government collects as a fraction of income—that is, total revenue equals the average tax rate multiplied by the total amount of income. But the effects of the tax system on people's choices depend on *marginal* tax rates. These rates prescribe the fraction that the government takes from an additional dollar of income. So in deciding how much to work, produce, and invest, households and firms take account of these marginal tax rates.

STATE AND LOCAL INCOME TAXES

Many states and some cities impose individual income taxes. Some of these tax systems have a graduated structure that resembles the federal system. For example, in Nebraska, the tax is 19% of the federal levy and in California, a schedule of marginal rates rises from 0 to 11%. Other states have a flat rate of tax on income, except for a small exemption—for example, the rate is 2.5% in Illinois and 2.2% in Pennsylvania. Finally, there are a few states that have no income tax. For people who are looking for a place to move, these are Alaska, Florida, Nevada, South Dakota, Texas, Washington, and Wyoming. Connecticut, New Hampshire, and Tennessee tax only some forms of property income.

SOCIAL SECURITY TAX

Another important form of tax (which the government amusingly calls a "contribution") is the levy on wage earnings and income from self-employment to finance social security. At present, almost all workers are covered by social security. The main exceptions are some government employees.

The social security tax is much simpler than the individual income tax. For example, in 1988 covered employees paid 7.5% of earnings up to a ceiling of $45,000. Employers paid an equal amount. Thus, the combined marginal and average tax rates were 15.0% for labor earnings between 0 and $45,000. Then the marginal tax rate fell to zero, so that the average tax rate declined gradually as earnings increased.[1] Overall, except for the ceiling on earnings, the social security tax amounts

---

[1] In calculating effective marginal tax rates, we should deduct any extra benefits that someone gets *because they pay the tax.* Therefore, some parts of government revenue are not a tax at all—these include charges for school tuition and hospitals, contributions to government employee retirement funds, and some other items. This category accounted for 12% of total government revenues in 1987. For individual income taxes, we treat this extra benefit as nil. That is, even if people like public services, the amounts that they get do not depend on the individual taxes that they pay. For social security, there is some relation of an individual's benefits to that person's lifetime contributions to the program. However, Michael Boskin et al. (1987) argue that this effect is small for most people.

to a flat-rate levy on labor income. However, the tax rates and ceilings have increased substantially over time; for example, in 1960 the rates were only 3% for each employee and employer, with an earnings ceiling of $4800.

MARGINAL INCOME TAX RATES

The ratio of government receipts to GNP in Figure 13.4 is one measure of an average tax rate. But as mentioned before, we would like to measure marginal tax rates to assess the effect of the tax system on economic activity. Ideally, we would find the marginal tax rate for each family at each point in time. For personal income taxes we would do this by adding the marginal tax rates for each type of tax—the federal and state and local individual income taxes and the social security tax. Then we would average these marginal tax rates across families at each date.

Figure 13.6 shows the average marginal tax rate from the federal individual income tax and from the social security tax (on employees and employers) from 1916 to 1985. These values are averages over families' marginal tax rates, when weighted by the adjusted gross income of each family. Note that the average marginal tax rate went from 5% in 1920 to 2% in 1930, 6% in 1940, 20% in 1950, 25% in 1960, 27% in 1970, and 36% in 1980. After reaching an all-time peak of 38% in

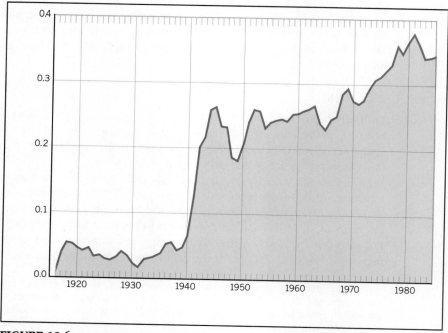

FIGURE 13.6 *Average Marginal Tax Rate from the Federal Individual Income Tax and Social Security*
The graph shows the average of marginal tax rates, when weighted by family incomes. The data are from Barro and Sahasakul (1986). updated with figures obtained from the Internal Revenue Service.

1981, the average marginal tax rate declined—because of the Reagan tax cuts—to 34% for 1983–85. As a rough statement, the time pattern of average marginal tax rates in Figure 13.6 parallels that for the ratio of government receipts to GNP in Figure 13.4.

CORPORATE PROFITS TAXES

Aside from taxing household income, governments also tax the net revenues of corporations. For large corporations in 1988, the federal marginal tax rate on taxable earnings was 34%. This rate had been close to 50% from the end of World War I! until the 1986 tax reform (but a complicated "excess profits tax" applied also during the Korean War and World War II). From 1918 to 1938, the tax rates were between 12 and 15%.

The relation of corporate taxes to corporate profits depends on various tax credits and on the rules for computing depreciation allowances and for valuing inventories. Figure 13.7 shows how the ratio of corporate taxes (federal plus state

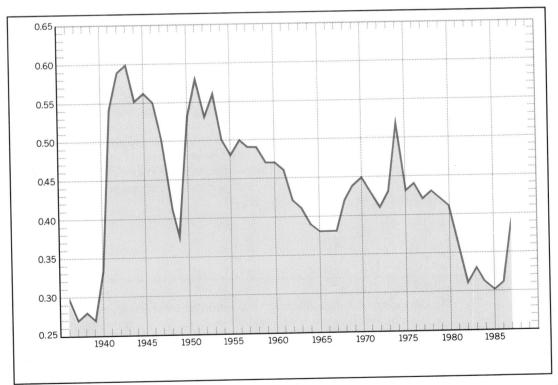

FIGURE 13.7 *Corporate Profits Taxes as a Ratio to Corporate Profits*
Corporate profits taxes are amounts paid to federal, state, and local governments. The earnings of the Fed are subtracted from corporate profits, and the Fed's transfers to the Treasury are subtracted from corporate taxes. Data are from U.S. Department of Commerce (1986) and U.S. Survey of Current Business (*July 1988*).

and local) to corporate profits changed over time. For 1946–81, this ratio varied between 39 and 59%, with no regular trend. The ratio fell, however, to about 30% for 1982–86 before rising back to 39% in 1987. This pattern reflected the more favorable depreciation allowances and some other changes in the 1981 tax law and the reversal of some of these changes in the 1986 law.

We can think of the corporate profits tax as a levy on the capital owned by corporations. But since households own the corporations, the tax amounts ultimately to another levy on household's income from capital. In fact, the government taxes the earnings of corporations directly and then taxes them a second time when people receive dividends or capital gains. (Economists call this *double taxation.*) For the purposes of our analysis, we can think of adding the tax on corporate profits to individual income taxes to calculate an overall tax on the income from capital.

PROPERTY TAXES

The various state and local governments use a wide array of procedures to determine the taxes on houses, factories, and other property. In a general way we can think of the property tax as another form of tax on capital. Therefore, for most purposes, we can combine this tax with the individual income taxes and the corporate profits tax to find the overall tax on the income from capital.

SALES AND EXCISE TAXES

Many states and localities have general sales taxes and also special levies on gasoline, alcohol, tobacco, and some other items. The federal government's excise taxes apply to gasoline, alcohol, tobacco, automobiles, tires, and telephone services.

An important feature of these taxes is that they apply to expenditures rather than to income or wealth.[2] In the subsequent theoretical analysis, we shall focus on income taxes. Thus, in a broad sense, the analysis encompasses the types of taxes discussed in previous categories. But we should remember that sales and excise taxes operate in a different manner.

AN INCOME TAX IN THE THEORETICAL MODEL

We can evaluate the main effects of taxation by examining a simple form of income tax. Assume that a household's real taxes, t_t/P_t, are a fraction, τ, of its real taxable income. (τ is the Greek letter tau.) Hence, for simplicity, we do not introduce a graduated-rated tax structure into the model but use instead a flat-rate tax. Also, we assume at this stage that the tax rate, τ, does not vary over time.

---

[2]Many other countries use a *value-added tax,* which amounts to a broad-based sales tax. Instead of applying to final sales, this levy depends on the value added to goods at various stages of production.

In the model—where the households are the producers as well as the workers—we assume that a household's real taxable income equals its real net product, $y_t - \delta k_{t-1}$, plus real interest income, less an amount of **tax-exempt real income, e_t.**[3] Notice that we treat governmental transfers as nontaxable, which is accurate in most cases. Finally, we assume initially that there is no inflation, so that the real and nominal interest rates on bonds are equal—that is, $r_t = R_t$. Therefore, a household's real taxes are given by

$$\frac{t_t}{P_t} = \tau\left(y_t - \delta k_{t-1} + \frac{r_{t-1}b_{t-1}}{P_t} - e_t\right). \tag{13.1}$$

If real taxable income is negative, we assume that taxes are negative rather than zero.[4] Also, we assume that the tax parameters, τ and e_t, are the same for all households. In particular, we neglect any actions that individuals can take to affect either their marginal tax rate, τ, or their quantity of tax-exempt income, e_t. Since each household's marginal tax rate is τ, the average of these rates across households—that is, the average marginal tax rate—is also τ.

Aggregate real income taxes follow from equation 13.1 as

$$\frac{T_t}{P_t} = \tau(Y_t - \delta K_{t-1} - E_t), \tag{13.2}$$

where E_t is the aggregate amount of tax-exempt income. (Remember that aggregate real interest payments, $r_{t-1}B_{t-1}/P_t$, equal zero.) Therefore, the government's budget constraint in real terms is now

$$G_t + \frac{V_t}{P_t} = \tau(Y_t - \delta K_{t-1} - E_t) + \frac{(M_t - M_{t-1})}{P_t}. \tag{13.3}$$

Here we measure aggregate real income taxes on the right side by the expression from equation 13.2.

Suppose that we take as given the amounts of real government purchases, G_t, aggregate real transfers, V_t/P_t, and the real revenue from money creation, $(M_t - M_{t-1})/P_t$. Then, for a given amount of aggregate net product, $Y_t - \delta K_{t-1}$, the two tax parameters, τ and E_t, must be set so as to satisfy the government's budget constraint. That is, the government has to generate enough income-tax receipts in each period to meet the expenditures that are not covered by printing money. Often we shall think about changing the marginal tax rate, τ, and then allowing the exempt amount, E_t, to vary in order for equation 13.3 to hold. In that way we can isolate the substitution effect from a change in the tax rate. Note that we do not allow the

---

[3]The formulation assumes that interest paid by borrowers reduces their taxable income one-to-one. This assumption was correct in most cases before the 1986 tax law for people who itemized deductions. However, the 1986 law placed more restrictions on the tax deductibility of interest payments.

[4]In the real world taxes can be negative because of the earned-income credit (a payment that the government gives to low-income families that have labor income) and because households and businesses can carry over some losses from one period to the next.

government to borrow and lend on the credit market. That is, we wait until the next chapter to allow for budget deficits or surpluses.

HOUSEHOLDS' BUDGET CONSTRAINTS

From our analysis in previous chapters, each household's budget constraint in real terms is

$$y_t - \delta k_{t-1} + \frac{b_{t-1}(1 + r_{t-1})}{P_t} + \frac{m_{t-1}}{P_t} + \frac{v_t}{P_t} - \frac{t_t}{P_t}$$

$$= c_t + i_t - \delta k_{t-1} + \frac{(b_t + m_t)}{P_t}. \quad (13.4)$$

Recall that we treat the households as carrying out the investment expenditures. We have also subtracted depreciation from both sides of equation 13.4 so that net product, $y_t - \delta k_{t-1}$, appears on the left, and net investment, $i_t - \delta k_{t-1}$, appears on the right. Notice that real taxes, t_t/P_t, subtract from the household's disposable funds on the left side.

Now substitute for real taxes from equation 13.1 into equation 13.4 and rearrange terms to get

$$(1 - \tau)(y_t - \delta k_{t-1}) + \frac{(1 - \tau)r_{t-1}b_{t-1}}{P_t} + \frac{(b_{t-1} + m_{t-1})}{P_t} + \frac{v_t}{P_t} + \tau e_t$$

$$= c_t + i_t - \delta k_{t-1} + \frac{(b_t + m_t)}{P_t}. \quad (13.5)$$

The first term on the left side equals net product or income, $y_t - \delta k_{t-1}$, less the tax on this income, $\tau(y_t - \delta k_{t-1})$. That is, the after-tax income, $(1 - \tau)(y_t - \delta k_{t-1})$, matters for the household. Similarly, the after-tax real interest income, $(1 - \tau)r_{t-1}b_{t-1}/P_t$, enters on the left side of equation 13.5.

Note that the uses of the household's funds on the right side of equation 13.5 do not involve the tax rate. This result follows because we assume no tax on the expenditures for consumption or net investment. More generally, any sales or excise taxes would enter here.

TAX RATES AND SUBSTITUTION EFFECTS

We want to see how the presence of an income tax alters the various substitution effects on households. For this purpose we have to reconsider our concepts of the real interest rate, the marginal product of labor (or real wage rate), and the return to investment.

After-Tax Real Interest Rate   Households receive real interest at the rate r_t, but they pay the fraction τ of their receipts to the government. Hence, when measured net of tax, households earn interest at the rate $(1 - \tau)r_t$. We refer to this variable as the **after-tax real interest rate.** Notice that this interest rate appears (for period $t - 1$) on the left side of equation 13.5.

In previous chapters we discussed the intertemporal-substitution effects that arise when the real interest rate changes. These effects still apply, but they refer now to the after-tax real interest rate. An increase in this interest rate, $(1 - \tau)r_t$, stimulates saving. The increase in saving reflects partly a reduction in current consumption demand and partly an increase in current work effort and the supply of goods.

After-Tax Marginal Product of Labor When someone works an additional hour, he or she raises output, y_t, and hence income by the marginal product of labor, MPL_t. But households keep only the fraction, $1 - \tau$, of their extra income. Hence, the **after-tax marginal product of labor,** $(1 - \tau)MPL_t$, matters for the choices of work and consumption. (With a separate labor market, the after-tax real wage rate, $(1 - \tau)w_t/P_t$, would matter.)

Suppose that there is a given schedule for labor's marginal product, MPL_t, when graphed versus the amount of work, n_t. An increase in the tax rate, τ, lowers the schedule when measured net of tax—that is, as $(1 - \tau)MPL_t$. Households respond just as they would to a decrease in the schedule for labor's marginal product: they reduce work effort, the supply of goods, and consumption demand.

After-Tax Rate of Return to Investment An increase in the stock of capital, k_t, by one unit raises next period's net product by the marginal product of capital less the rate of depreciation, $MPK_t - \delta$. Recall that this term is the real rate of return from an extra unit of investment. But owners of capital (households) now keep only the fraction, $1 - \tau$, of this return. Therefore, the **after-tax rate of return to investment** becomes $(1 - \tau)(MPK_t - \delta)$. Producers determine their desired stock of capital, $\hat{k}_t$, by equating this after-tax rate of return to the after-tax real interest rate on bonds, which is $(1 - \tau)r_t$. That is, the condition for the desired stock of capital is

$$(1 - \tau)(MPK_t - \delta) = (1 - \tau)r_t. \qquad (13.6)$$

We shall find it convenient not to cancel out the tax terms, $1 - \tau$, which appear on both sides of equation 13.6. Instead, we think of the desired stock of capital as depending separately on the after-tax real interest rate, $(1 - \tau)r_t$, and the tax rate τ. Then we can write the desired stock of capital, $\hat{k}_t$, as the function

$$\hat{k}_t = \hat{k}[(1 - \tau)r_t, \tau, \cdots]. \qquad (13.7)$$
$$(-) \quad (-)$$

As before, the term . . . represents characteristics of the production function that affect the schedule for capital's marginal product.

For a given tax rate τ, an increase in the *after-tax* real interest rate, $(1 - \tau)r_t$, on the right side of equation 13.6 raises the required after-tax return from investment. Hence, the desired capital stock falls. For a given value of $(1 - \tau)r_t$, a higher τ lowers the after-tax return from investment on the left side of equation 13.6.

Therefore, the desired capital stock again declines. Finally, as in earlier cases, the desired capital stock rises if there is an upward shift in the schedule for capital's marginal product, MPK_t.

As before, the desired stock of capital, $\hat{k}_t$, determines a producer's gross investment demand. Namely, the investment demand function is

$$i_t^d = \hat{k}[(1 - \tau)r_t, \tau, \cdots] - (1 - \delta)k_{t-1} \qquad (13.8)$$
$$\phantom{i_t^d = \hat{k}[}(-) \quad (-)$$
$$= i^d[(1 - \tau)r_t, \tau, k_{t-1}, \cdots].$$
$$(-) \quad (-)(-)$$

The new features concern the tax rate. First, for a given tax rate, it is the after-tax real interest rate, $(1 - \tau)r_t$, that has a negative effect on gross investment demand. Second, for a given value of $(1 - \tau)r_t$, the tax rate τ has a separate negative effect on investment demand.

A CHANGE IN THE TAX RATE

Suppose that the tax rate, τ, increases. Aggregate real tax revenues are given from the tax law in equation 13.2 by $T_t/P_t = \tau(Y_t - \delta K_{t-1} - E_t)$. If the exempt amount, E_t, did not change, real tax revenues would increase unless aggregate net product, $Y_t - \delta K_{t-1}$, fell by a great deal. Assume for the moment that this is not the case— that is, real tax receipts would rise if the exempt amount did not change.

Suppose that we hold constant the levels of government purchases, G_t, and aggregate real transfers, V_t/P_t, as well as the real revenue from money creation, $(M_t - M_{t-1})/P_t$. Then the government's budget constraint from equation 13.3 says that the amount of real taxes collected cannot change. So if we raise the tax rate, we have to increase the exempt amount, E_t, to keep real tax revenues the same. In effect, we can think of raising the *average marginal tax rate,* which is what the parameter τ represents in the model, without changing the *average tax rate.* For example, in the real world, the government might increase various exemptions in the income-tax law but then raise all of the tax rates on taxable income to maintain the level of real revenues. Alternatively, the government could switch from one type of tax, such as the social security tax on wage earnings, to another, such as the individual income tax. Because the social security tax has a low average marginal tax rate, compared to the revenue that it collects, this change tends to raise the average marginal tax rate while leaving unchanged the aggregate of real tax revenues.

The important point is that, conceptually, we want to keep separate the effects of changes in the average marginal tax rate, τ, from those of changes in government purchases, transfers, or money creation. That is why we want to consider first the case where the exempt amount varies along with the tax rate to keep fixed the volume of real tax revenues. Then we can also look at cases where tax revenues do change, along with some combination of shifts in government purchases, transfers, or money creation.

Finally, consider whether a change in the tax rate, τ, affects households' wealth. Remember that the aggregate of households' budget constraints involves the present value of aggregate real taxes net of transfers. This present value depends on the present value of government purchases. As long as we hold this present value fixed, a change in the tax rate does not affect the aggregate present value of taxes less transfers and therefore would not seem to affect wealth. In fact, this result turns out to be a satisfactory approximation in most cases. However, we shall see later that it is not exact. But for now, we neglect any effects on wealth from changes in the tax rate.

CLEARING OF THE COMMODITY MARKET

Now we incorporate the various effects from the tax rate into the condition for clearing the commodity market. The condition for period 1 is

$$C^d[r_1(1 - \tau), \tau, \cdots] + I^d[r_1(1 - \tau), \tau, \cdots] + G_1$$
$$\quad (-) \quad (-) \qquad\qquad (-) \quad (-)$$
$$= Y^s[r_1(1 - \tau), \tau, \cdots].$$
$$\quad (+) \quad (-)$$

(13.9)

To avoid a clutter of terms, we do not write out explicitly some of the variables that influence consumer demand, investment demand, and the supply of goods. These include the initial capital stock, K_0, and the amount of government purchases, G_1.

One new feature is that the after-tax real interest rate, $(1 - \tau)r_1$, appears where the real interest rate, r_1, used to appear. Given the value of $(1 - \tau)r_1$, the tax rate, τ, has some separate effects. First, a higher tax rate reduces the schedule for the after-tax marginal product of labor, $(1 - \tau)MPL_1$, and thereby reduces the incentive to work. Hence, there are reductions in the aggregates of goods supply, Y^s_1, and consumer demand, C^d_1. Second, a higher tax rate lowers the after-tax rate of return to investment, $(1 - \tau)(MPK_1 - \delta)$, and thereby reduces gross investment demand, I^d_1. Thus, in general, a higher tax rate tends to depress market activity—that is, it reduces the demands for consumption and gross investment, as well as the supply of goods. These results follow because a household's tax liability rises when it engages in more market activity. A higher tax rate motivates people to substitute away from market activities and toward untaxed areas, such as leisure or the **underground economy,** where income is not reported.

Figure 13.8 shows the clearing of the commodity market. It is convenient to place the after-tax real interest rate, $(1 - \tau)r_1$, on the vertical axis. The horizontal axis shows the levels of commodity demand and supply.

EFFECTS OF A HIGHER TAX RATE

Assume that the tax rate rises permanently from τ to τ' at date 1. Figure 13.9 shows the effects on the commodity market. First, there is a leftward shift of the demand curve, reflecting the decreases in consumption demand and gross investment de-

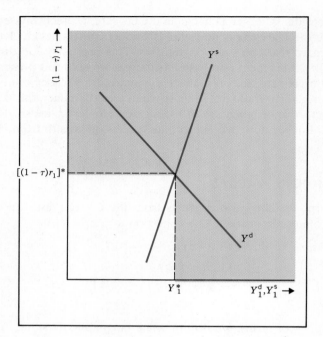

FIGURE 13.8 *Clearing of the Commodity Market*
We graph the demand and supply of commodities versus the after-tax real interest rate, $(1 - \tau)r_1$.

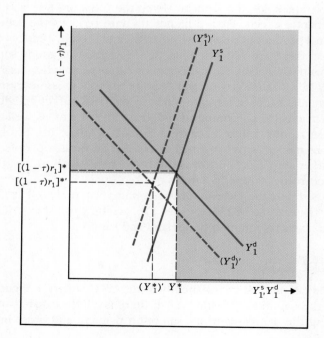

FIGURE 13.9 *Effects on the Commodity Market of a Higher Income-Tax Rate*
The increase in the income-tax rate from τ to τ' reduces the demand for commodities by more than the supply. Hence, output and the after-tax real interest rate fall.

mand. Second, there is a leftward shift of the supply curve. Since the increase in the tax rate is permanent, we predict little response of desired real saving. That is, at the initial value of the after-tax real interest rate, the cutback in goods supply is roughly equal to the fall in consumption demand.[5] Since investment demand also

THE WEALTH EFFECT FROM A CHANGE IN THE TAX RATE (OPTIONAL)

We carried out the analysis under the assumption that the change in the tax rate left wealth unchanged. This assumption seems reasonable since we varied the amount of tax-exempt income, E_1, to hold constant the quantity of real taxes collected, T_1/P_1. But let's consider more carefully whether wealth changes.

As we discussed in Chapter 2, the effect of a disturbance on a household's wealth is positive if it enables the household to achieve a higher level of utility. Similarly, the effect on wealth is negative if the attainable level of utility declines. The increase in the tax rate that we have just considered ends up reducing the utility of the typical household. Therefore, the effect on wealth is actually negative rather than zero.

To see why, note first that someone who produces the quantity of output y_1 gets to keep only the portion $(1 - \tau)y_1$; the remainder goes as taxes to the government. Therefore, a household's contribution to the economy's output, y_1, exceeds the contribution to that household's after-tax income, which is $(1 - \tau)y_1$. In deciding how much to work and invest, households consider only the fraction, $1 - \tau$, of the marginal products of their labor and capital. Hence, from a social perspective, people have insufficient incentives to work and invest.[6] In particular, the existence of the tax rate distorts private decisions, so that the aggregates of work, consumption, and investment end up below their desirable levels. Moreover, a higher tax rate means a greater distortion and therefore a lower level of utility for the typical household.

We could modify the previous analysis to include a negative effect on wealth from an increase in the tax rate; however, the general nature of the results would not change. Therefore, for most purposes, we can use the results that we already obtained while neglecting wealth effects.

[5]Recall that we hold constant aggregate real taxes. Therefore, the change in the aggregate of desired saving equals the change in goods supply, Y_1^s, less the change in consumer demand, C_1^d.

[6]The fraction τ that goes to taxes reduces the required payments of all other taxpayers (by a very small amount per person). No individual takes these benefits to others into account when deciding how much to work and invest. Economists call this an "external effect." This effect refers to the benefits that others get from one person's actions, when the person does not take these benefits into account.

declines, the overall fall in demand is greater than that in supply. Hence, Figure 13.9 shows that the increase in the tax rate creates an excess supply of commodities at the after-tax real interest rate that initially cleared the market.

Figure 13.9 shows that the after-tax real interest rate and the level of output decline. Since the initial capital stock, K_0, is given, the fall in output reflects a decrease in work effort. People work less in this situation because the government extracts a larger fraction of a marginal dollar of income.

Since government purchases do not change, the total of real private spending for consumption and investment must decline. Recall that the disturbance had no initial impact on desired real saving. Therefore, with the fall in the after-tax real interest rate, saving must fall in the end. Since real saving equals net investment, it follows that net investment decreases. (Gross investment also falls since depreciation is given.)

We can think of the drop in the after-tax real interest rate as signaling a diminished priority for using resources now—in order, specifically, to accumulate or maintain capital—rather than later. Notice that from the viewpoint of the private sector, the diminished priority for accumulating capital reflects the adverse effect of a higher tax rate on the after-tax rate of return to investment.

The effect on consumption is uncertain. That is because the decrease in the after-tax real interest rate motivates more consumption, while the higher tax rate motivates less consumption. In other words, although total output falls, the higher tax rate may crowd out enough investment to avoid a decline in consumption in the short run.

LONG-RUN EFFECTS OF A HIGHER TAX RATE

So far the analysis does not allow for changes in the capital stock. But since a higher tax rate reduces investment in the short run, we anticipate that the stock of capital will be lower in the long run. To explore this effect, we have to extend the analysis from Chapter 10 of steady-state situations. But we look here only at cases where population and technology do not change in the steady state.

In Chapter 10 we found that the rate of time preference, ρ, is the real rate of return that savers insist on in a steady state. If the real rate of return exceeds ρ, households save and increase their quantities of consumption over time. Alternatively, if the real rate of return is less than ρ, households dissave, so that consumption declines over time. In the steady state, where consumption is constant and real saving is zero, the real rate of return to saving equals ρ. But this real rate of return is now the after-tax real interest rate, $(1 - \tau)r$. Therefore, in the presence of taxation, it is the after-tax real interest rate that equals the rate of time preference, ρ, in the steady state.

The after-tax rate of return to investment, $(1 - \tau)(MPK - \delta)$, equals the after-tax real interest rate, $(1 - \tau)r$. Therefore, the full condition for the steady state is now

$$(1 - \tau)(MPK - \delta) = (1 - \tau)r = \rho. \qquad (13.10)$$

The condition, $(1 - \tau)(MPK - \delta) = \rho$, determines the level of the capital stock in the steady state. Namely, the level of capital corresponds to a marginal product for which the after-tax rate of return to investment, $(1 - \tau)(MPK - \delta)$, equals the rate of time preference, ρ. In this situation producers invest just enough to maintain the levels of their capital stocks—that is, aggregate net investment is zero.

What happens in the long run when the tax rate, τ, increases? From equation 13.10, the rate of time preference, ρ, pegs the after-tax rate of return to investment, $(1 - \tau)(MPK - \delta)$. An increase in the tax rate means that the before-tax rate of return to investment, $MPK - \delta$, must rise. But this change occurs only if the capital stock falls to generate a sufficient increase in the marginal product, MPK. Therefore, in the long run, a higher tax rate means a smaller stock of capital.

Suppose that we compare two steady states: one with the tax rate τ and another with the higher tax rate τ'. We know that the after-tax real interest rate is the same in both steady states, since $(1 - \tau)r$ equals the fixed number ρ. But the one with the higher tax rate has less capital. It also has lower gross and net output, as well as less consumption. However, the comparison for the levels of work effort is uncertain. (Why is that?)

EFFECTS OF A PERMANENT RISE IN GOVERNMENT PURCHASES UNDER INCOME TAXATION

In the previous chapter we studied the effects of a permanent increase in government purchases when financed by lump-sum taxes. We found that output increases partly because the public services are productive and partly because people work more (in response to a decrease in wealth). Also, consumption decreases, but there are no effects on the real interest rate and investment. The last result suggests that the steady-state stock of capital would not change when government purchases increase permanently.[7] That is, the long- and short-run responses coincide.

In the real world a permanent increase in government purchases typically requires a permanent increase in the average marginal tax rate, which we represent by the parameter τ. That is, the tax rate has to rise to generate more total real tax revenues. So in assessing the consequences of more government purchases, we want to combine the effects that we found under lump-sum taxes with those that arise when the tax rate increases.

Table 13.1 summarizes the results. Line 1 refers to a permanent increase in government purchases when financed by lump-sum taxes. The responses of the variables are those that we have already discussed. Line 2 deals with a permanent increase in the tax rate, τ. Here, we distinguish the short-run results—where the

---

[7]We are neglecting an effect from the increase in work on capital's marginal product. This effect tends to raise investment in the short run and the stock of capital in the long run.

TABLE 13.1 *Summary of Economic Effects from Permanent Changes in Government Purchases and the Tax Rate*

Nature of Disturbance	Response of								
	K	Y	$Y - \delta K$	N	C	I	$I - \delta K$	$(1 - \tau)r$	r
1. Permanent rise in government purchases, when financed by lump-sum taxes (short and long run)	0	+	+	+	−	0	0	0	0
2. Permanent increase in tax rate, τ									
Short run	0	−	−	−	?	−	−	−	+
Long run	−	−	−	?	−	−	0	0	+
3. Permanent rise in government purchases, with permanent increase in tax rate									
Short run	0	?	?	?	?	−	−	−	+
Long run	−	?	?	?	−	−	0	0	+

Note: We show the effects on the variables in each column from the disturbances shown in each row. The possible responses are positive (+), negative (−), zero (0), or uncertain (?).

capital stock does not change—from the long-run ones. The findings are those that we worked out earlier in this chapter.

Finally, line 3 combines the permanent rise in government purchases with a permanent increase in the tax rate. The short- and long-run effects on gross and net output are now ambiguous. That is because the negative effects from the higher tax rate offset the positive effects from more government purchases. Similarly, the effects on work effort are uncertain. We find, however, that the after-tax real interest rate, $(1 - \tau)r$, is pegged in the long run by the rate of time preference, ρ. Therefore, capital's marginal product, MPK, must still increase when the tax rate rises, and hence, the stock of capital declines in the long run. The counterpart of this result is the decrease in net investment in the short run.

Empirically, it is hard to separate the effects of more government purchases from the effects of a higher tax rate because the two variables tend to move together. We discussed before some empirical estimates for the effect on output of a permanent increase in government purchases. The results suggest a positive effect, although the estimates are imprecise for the case of nondefense purchases. We should interpret these findings as applying to the combined impact of more government purchases and a higher tax rate. Therefore, there is some evidence that this combined effect is positive, although the theory says that the response is ambiguous.

THE RELATION BETWEEN THE TAX RATE AND TAX REVENUES

We combined a permanent increase in government purchases with a rise in the tax rate, τ, to generate more real tax revenues for each period, T_t/P_t. But these revenues are given from the tax law as

$$\frac{T_t}{P_t} = \tau(Y_t - \delta K_{t-1} - E_t).$$

Therefore, if we hold the exempt amount E_t constant, real tax receipts increase with the tax rate only if the fall in output, Y_t, reduces real taxable income, $Y_t - \delta K_{t-1} - E_t$, by proportionately less than the increase in the tax rate.

We can view the long-run movements in aggregate output, Y, in terms of the changes in the two productive inputs, K and N. The long-run decline in the capital stock follows from the steady-state condition, $(1 - \tau)(MPK - \delta) = \rho$. When the tax rate rises, capital's marginal product must increase sufficiently in the long run to reestablish this equality. If the capital stock must fall by a lot to generate this increase in the marginal product—that is, if diminishing marginal productivity sets in slowly—the capital stock will fall a great deal in response to an increase in the tax rate.

The long-run response of work effort, N, is ambiguous. The main force that motivates a reduction in market work is the higher tax rate on labor income. This higher tax rate induces people to withdraw from the market to spend more time on leisure and other nonmarket (nontaxed) activities. If these alternative uses of time are close substitutes for the things that people can buy on the market, the negative effect on market work will be substantial.

The depressing effects of income taxation on capital and labor have to be very strong for tax revenues to fall when the tax rate rises. This outcome does, however, become more likely as the rate of tax, τ, increases. For example, when the tax rate is 10%, a 10% increase means that the new tax rate is 11%. Therefore, the fraction of extra income that people keep, $1 - \tau$, falls from 90 to 89%, or by a percentage of 1.1%. In other words, a 10% increase in the tax rate translates into a decline by only 1.1% in the term, $1 - \tau$, that influences capital and labor. Therefore, when we take account of the responses of capital and labor, we anticipate that a 10% increase in the tax rate would reduce real taxable income by much less than 10%.

Suppose that we consider higher starting values for the tax rate but continue to raise the rate each time by 10%. At a tax rate of 25%, a 10% increase (to a new rate of 27.5%) means that $1 - \tau$ falls from 75 to 72.5%, or by 3.3%. At a starting rate of 50%, a 10% increase lowers $1 - \tau$ from 50 to 45%, that is, by 10%. At the still higher rate of 75%, a 10% increase reduces $1 - \tau$ by 30%. Overall, the higher is the starting value of the tax rate, the greater is the proportional reduction of the term, $1 - \tau$, from a 10% increase in the tax rate. Table 13.2 summarizes these results.

The term $1 - \tau$ becomes proportionately more sensitive to a given percentage

TABLE 13.2 *Effects of a 10% Increase in the Tax Rate*

Old τ	New τ	Old $(1 - \tau)$	New $(1 - \tau)$	% Change in $(1 - \tau)$
1.0	1.1	99.0	98.9	− 0.1
10.0	11.0	90.0	89.0	− 1.1
25.0	27.5	75.0	72.5	− 3.3
50.0	55.0	50.0	45.0	− 10.0
75.0	82.5	25.0	17.5	− 30.0
90.0	99.0	10.0	1.0	− 90.0

Note: We show the effects of a 10% increase in the tax rate, τ, on the fraction of income that people keep, $1 - \tau$. Notice that the percentage decline of the term $1 - \tau$ becomes larger as the tax rate rises.

increase in the tax rate, τ, as the rate of tax increases. But recall that capital and labor—and therefore real taxable income—respond to the term $1 - \tau$. Therefore, we predict that the negative response of real taxable income to the tax rate becomes stronger as the rate of tax increases. At some point—but, surely, for a tax rate below 100%—we shall find that an increase in the tax rate reduces real taxable income by so much that real tax revenues fall.

Figure 13.10 shows the general form of the relationship between real tax receipts, T/P, and the tax rate, τ. (Think of this relation as applying in the long run, when capital and labor adjust fully to a change in the tax rate.) This relationship is often called a **Laffer curve,** in honor of the economist Arthur Laffer. (For a discussion, see Don Fullerton, 1982.) When the tax rate, τ, is zero, the government collects nothing. As the tax rate rises above zero, tax revenues become positive—hence, the curve has a positive slope. However, as the tax rate continues to increase, the negative response of real taxable income becomes stronger. Since this element reduces revenues, the slope of the curve becomes flatter as the tax rate rises. Eventually the tax rate becomes high enough so that a further increase in the tax rate reduces real taxable income by the same proportion as the increase in the tax

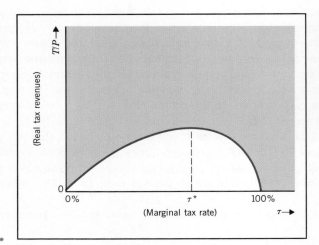

FIGURE 13.10 *The Relation of Tax Receipts to the Tax Rate (a Laffer curve)*

Real tax revenues, T/P, initially rise with the tax rate τ. However, revenues reach their peak when the rate is τ*. If the tax rate rises above τ*, revenues fall and approach zero as the tax rate approaches 100%.

rate. Therefore, real tax revenues do not change, and the curve in Figure 13.10 is flat. We label this tax rate as τ^* in the figure. If the government raises the tax rate above τ^*, real taxable income falls by proportionately more than the increase in the tax rate, and revenues start to decline. In fact, as the tax rate approaches 100%, tax receipts approach zero. If the government wishes to maximize its real revenues, it should not choose a tax rate of 100%. Rather, the value τ^* is the tax rate that maximizes receipts.

In 1980–81 some advocates of **supply-side economics** used a picture like that in Figure 13.10 to argue for an across-the-board cut in U.S. income-tax rates. These economists contended that the average marginal tax rate on income exceeded the value τ^*, so that a general cut in rates would yield a larger volume of real tax revenues. There is, however, no evidence that the United States has reached high enough tax rates for this result to apply.

A study for Sweden by Charles Stuart (1981) provides some perspective on the U.S. situation. Stuart estimated that the maximum of tax revenues occurs in Sweden when the average marginal tax rate is about 70%. That is, he estimated τ^* to be about 70%. The actual value of the average marginal tax rate in Sweden reached 70% in the early 1970s and rose subsequently to about 80%. (Here, Stuart took a broad view of taxes to go beyond the income-tax law.) Therefore, Sweden was operating on the falling portion of the Laffer curve during the 1970s.[8] In fact, Stuart attributed part of Sweden's relatively low growth rate of per capita real gross domestic product during the 1970s (1.7% per year) to this factor.

For the United States in 1985, the average marginal tax rate from the federal income tax and social security was 34% (see Figure 13.7). The rate would be higher, however, if we were able to include other taxes. Since we do not have these data, we can draw a rough comparison between the United States and Sweden by considering average tax rates.

For Sweden, the estimated value for τ^* of 70% corresponds to an average tax rate of about 50%. For the United States in 1987, a comparable figure for the tax rate, when calculated as the ratio of total government receipts to GNP, is 32%. So suppose that Sweden and the United States are roughly the same with respect to, first, the value of τ^*, and, second, the relation between marginal and average tax rates. Then we conclude that in 1987, the United States had a long way to go before reaching the average marginal tax rate, $\tau^* = 70\%$, at which tax revenues are maximized. We should, however, be cautious about this result for two reasons. First, the estimates for Sweden are rough. Second, we cannot be sure that the United States and Sweden have similar Laffer curves.

Lawrence Lindsey (1987) estimated the effect of the Reagan tax cuts from 1982 to 1984 on the tax payments by taxpayers in various income groups. He found that the reductions in tax rates lowered tax collections overall and for taxpayers with middle and low incomes. However, among taxpayers with the highest incomes

---

[8]A conceptually similar study by A. van Ravestein and H. Vijlbrief (1988) estimated that the value of τ^* for the Netherlands in 1970 was also about 70%. The actual value of τ (as estimated by the authors) rose steadily after 1970 to reach 67% in 1985. Thus, the conclusion was that the Netherlands was close to, but not yet beyond, the peak of the Laffer curve.

(adjusted gross incomes in excess of $200,000), the increase of reported taxable incomes was sufficient to more than offset the decrease in tax rates. Lindsey estimated that the tax-rate cuts raised collections in this group by 3% in 1982, 9% in 1983, and 23% in 1984. Therefore, while U.S. taxpayers as a whole were not on the falling portion of the Laffer curve, the taxpayers with the highest incomes appeared to be operating in this range.[9]

TRANSFER PAYMENTS

Suppose that the government raises the aggregate of real transfers, V/P, and finances these expenditures with more tax revenues, T/P. As in the case where government purchases increase, the rise in real taxes typically requires an increase in the average marginal tax rate, τ. Recall that we already discussed the adverse effects on work, production, and investment from an increase in the tax rate (see line 2 of Table 13.1). Note especially that an increase in transfers, when financed by an income tax, is no longer neutral in the model.

If transfer payments are lump sum, as we have been assuming, the analysis is finished. However, lump-sum transfers make little sense. Generally the point of transfer programs is to provide payments to persons in specified categories—for example, poor people, persons who have lost their jobs, old or sick people, farmers, college students, and others. But none of these transfers is lump sum—that is, the amount depends in some way on a person's status.

Think about a welfare program, where the payments depend on a family's current or long-run income. Typically individuals face a declining schedule of transfers—possibly subject to some discrete cutoff points—as a function of market income. The important point is that the negative effect of income on benefit payments looks just like a positive marginal tax rate. Since transfers are sometimes cut drastically when a family's income rises, these programs can imply high effective marginal tax rates on the earnings of low-income persons. For example, the Council of Economic Advisers (*Economic Report,* 1982, p. 29) estimated that "typical welfare recipients, namely single mothers with children, face marginal tax rates in excess of 75%." But unfortunately, we do not have estimates for the average marginal tax rate that is implied by the full array of transfer programs.

Suppose again that the government increases taxes to finance more welfare payments. We already noted the adverse effects on work, production, and investment that derive from the increase in the average marginal tax rate, τ. But the expansion of the welfare program means that low-income people stand to lose more benefits if they earn more market income. That is, there is also an increase in the effective marginal tax rate for potential welfare recipients. Hence, the negative influences of

---

[9]The 1986 tax law raised tax rates on income from long-term capital gains. Some economists think that this tax rate for 1988 is above the value that would maximize tax revenues—that is, a cut in the tax rate on capital gains might generate more tax receipts. While this outcome is plausible, the empirical evidence on this issue is not clear-cut.

this change on work and production reinforce the effects from the higher tax rate on market income.

In terms of dollar volume, the most important and rapidly growing transfer program in the United States and in most other countries is the payments to retirees and survivors under social security.[10] We have already discussed the financing of these programs in the United States. From this standpoint, an expansion of social security leads to a higher marginal tax rate on income, τ, which has the usual adverse effects on work and production.[11] If people received social security benefits without restrictions, except for age,[12] the distorting influences that arise from welfare programs would not apply. However, the U.S. system involves a test on earned income; persons (now below age 70) who earn income above a specified amount experience a partial or total cutoff of social security benefits. This income test works like an income standard for welfare—namely, it imposes a high effective marginal tax rate on the potential recipients. Not surprisingly, researchers (such as Michael Boskin, 1977) find that this income test motivates people to retire earlier than they would otherwise.

SUMMARY

In this chapter we expanded the model to include a simple form of income-tax law. The key parameters of this law are the marginal tax rate and the quantity of tax-exempt income. The term *marginal tax rate* refers to the extra tax that the government takes from an additional dollar of income. Households and firms take this marginal tax rate into account when deciding how much to work, produce, and invest. By·contrast, the government's tax receipts equal the product of the average tax rate (total taxes divided by total income) and the amount of income.

Intertemporal-substitution effects relate to the after-tax real interest rate. Similarly, the decisions to work and invest depend on the after-tax marginal products of labor and capital, respectively. For a given total of real taxes collected, an increase in the marginal tax rate motivates people to substitute away from market activities, which are taxed, and toward leisure (or the underground economy). Therefore, a higher tax rate leads in the short run to less work, output, and investment and in the long run to a smaller stock of capital and lower levels of production and consumption.

When we combine a permanent increase in government purchases with a rise in the marginal tax rate, we change some of the results from the previous chapter.

---

[10]One way to measure the size of this program is by the "replacement ratio." This measure equals the ratio of average benefits of retirees to their average earnings just before retirement. In 1983 this ratio equaled 48%, as compared to only 31% in 1965. (See Colin Campbell, 1984, p. xi.).

[11]However, the social security tax depends on labor income, not capital income. Therefore, the effects on investment are different.

[12]Before 1961, recipients had to be over 65. Since 1961, there is an opportunity to receive reduced benefits at age 62. The 1983 law will eventually raise the basic retirement age from 65 to 67.

Because of the adverse effects of higher taxation, the short-run effects on output and employment become ambiguous. Further, the higher tax rate leads in the long run to a lower stock of capital.

As the marginal tax rate rises, the quantity of real taxable income tends to fall. The sensitivity of this response becomes larger the higher is the tax rate. Therefore, we can draw a Laffer curve, which shows a diminishing effect of the tax rate on the quantity of real tax revenues. Eventually the economy reaches a tax rate for which revenues are at a maximum. At that point further increases in tax rates mean less real tax receipts. For Sweden, there is an estimate that this marginal tax rate is about 70%, which was reached and then surpassed in the early 1970s. The United States apparently has not yet reached this point.

Transfer payments have allocative effects that resemble those from taxation. First, tax rates rise to finance the program, and second, larger transfer payments mean that the potential recipients stand to lose more benefits by earning income. On both counts, an increase in transfers tends to contract real economic activity.

IMPORTANT TERMS AND CONCEPTS

adjusted gross income	after-tax real interest rate
taxable income	after-tax marginal product of labor
flat-rate tax	after-tax rate of return to investment
marginal tax rate	underground economy
graduated-rate tax	Laffer curve
average tax rate	supply-side economics
tax-exempt income	

QUESTIONS AND PROBLEMS

Mainly for Review

13.1 Distinguish between the average tax rate and the marginal tax rate. Must the two be equal for a flat-rate tax?

13.2 Why must we hold tax revenue constant when studying the effect of a change in the tax rate? What wealth effects would operate if we did not?

13.3 Explain briefly why a rise in the tax rate reduces the after-tax real interest rate in the short run but raises the before-tax real interest rate in the long run. How does the latter affect the capital stock?

13.4 Ignoring wealth effects from an increase in the tax rate, does the quantity of work decline in the long run? Explain why.

13.5 Could an increase in the tax rate reduce real tax revenues? How does the answer depend on the response of labor supply to changes in the (after-tax) marginal product of labor?

13.6 Define supply-side economics. How could the economy benefit from lowering the tax rate? Include in the answer a discussion of the wealth effects of taxes.

PROBLEMS FOR DISCUSSION

13.7 ***The Flat-Rate Tax***

Some economists advocate shifting from the graduated individual income tax to a flat-rate tax. Under the new system, there would be few deductions from taxable income, and the marginal tax rate would be constant. Because of the elimination of the deductions (sometimes referred to as loopholes), the average marginal tax rate would be lower than that under the current law.

a. What would this change do to the aggregate levels of output, employment, and investment?

b. How does the proposed flat-rate tax compare with the present social security tax?

c. How does the proposal relate to the changes in the 1986 tax law?

13.8 ***Subsidies***

Suppose that the average marginal tax rate, τ, is zero. We mentioned that an increase in the tax rate, τ, above zero—with total revenues, T/P, held fixed—reduces the utility of the typical household.

a. Explain this result.

b. Does the result mean that a reduction in the tax rate below zero would be desirable? (A negative value of τ means that the government subsidizes production.)

13.9 ***Consumption Taxes*** (*optional*)

Instead of an income tax, suppose that taxes are levied on the quantity of consumption during each period. A household's real tax payments for period t are then given by the formula $t_t/P_t = \tau(c_t - e_t)$. (A comprehensive sales tax on consumables might operate in this manner.)

a. Write down the budget constraints for the government and the representative household.

b. What is the after-tax real interest rate?

c. How does the tax rate, τ, now enter into the functions for consumption demand, C^d, gross investment demand, I^d, and goods supply, Y^s?

d. What is the short-run effect (while the capital stock is held fixed) of an increase in the tax rate, τ? Consider, in particular, the responses of the real interest rate and the quantities of output, work effort, consumption, and investment. Compare the results with those for an income tax.

13.10 *Effects of Inflation on a Graduated Income Tax*

In 1985 a married couple in the United States paid income taxes in accordance with the following graduated-rate table:

Range of Taxable Income	Tax Rate on an Extra Dollar of Taxable Income (Marginal Tax Rate) %
$3,540– 5,719	11
5,720– 7,909	12
7,910– 12,389	14
12,390– 16,649	16
16,650– 21,019	18
21,020– 25,599	22
25,600– 31,119	25
31,120– 36,629	28
36,630– 47,669	33
47,670– 62,449	38
62,450– 89,089	42
89,090–113,859	45
113,860–169,019	49
169,020–	50

a. Suppose that each person's real income stays constant over time, so that inflation steadily raises everyone's nominal income. If the tax law shown had remained unchanged, what would have happened over time to the average marginal tax rate and to total real tax collections?

b. Assume now that the dollar bracket limits that appear in the left column of the table are adjusted proportionately (or "indexed") over time for changes in the price level. What then is the effect of inflation on the average marginal tax rate and on total real tax collections? (This indexing rule applies in the United States as of 1985.)

13.11 *Taxes, Inflation, and Interest Rates (optional)*

Suppose that taxes are levied on nominal interest income and that the income-tax rate, τ, does not change over time.

a. What is the after-tax real interest rate on bonds?

Consider a permanent increase in the monetary growth rate from μ to μ'. The acceleration of money is a surprise, but people anticipate that the higher rate of monetary expansion, μ', will continue forever.

b. Given the presence of the income tax, what is the effect of the increase in monetary growth on the inflation rate, π, the nominal interest rate, R, and the aggregate level of real money balances, M/P? (Assume that the income-tax rate, τ, is unaffected by inflation.)

c. Discuss the implications of the answer to part b for the relation between R and π.

13.12 ***Effects of Transfer Programs on Work Effort***

Discuss the effects on people's incentives to work of the following governmental programs:

a. The food stamp program, which provides subsidized coupons for purchases of food. The allowable subsidies vary inversely with family income.

b. A negative income tax. This program would provide cash transfers to poor persons. The amount of transfers is reduced as some fraction of increases in family income.

c. Unemployment compensation. People who work for a specified interval and who lose their jobs receive cash payments while unemployed (and "looking for work"). The benefits can last for six months or sometimes for longer periods. What difference does it make if businesses with histories of more layoffs have to raise their contributions to the unemployment-insurance fund? (A program that has this feature is said to be "experience rated.")

d. Retirement benefits under social security. What is the consequence of the income test, which reduces benefits to persons (of age less than 70) who earn labor income in excess of a specified amount?

e. The earned-income credit. In 1988, for families that have no "unearned" income (basically income from assets), the credit is 14% of each dollar earned until income reaches $6225. Then the credit is constant at $874 until income hits $9850. Finally, the credit falls by 10% of each dollar earned, until the credit reaches zero at an income of $18,576.

CHAPTER 14

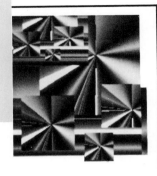

THE PUBLIC DEBT

n recent years, one of the hottest economic issues has been the **government's budget deficit** (which we shall define carefully later). At least from reading the newspapers, we might think that the economy suffers greatly when the government runs a large deficit. The most important task in this chapter will be to evaluate this view. As we shall see, the conclusions depart dramatically from those expressed in the newspapers.

Budget deficits arise when governments choose to finance part of their expenditures by issuing interest-bearing government bonds rather than levying taxes. The stock of government bonds outstanding is the interest-bearing part of the **public debt.** A budget deficit means that the quantity of public debt increases over time.

This chapter considers first the historical behavior of the public debt and government deficits. With these facts as a background, we extend the theoretical model to allow for public debt. Now the government can run budget deficits rather than levy taxes. We use the model to assess the effects of deficits on interest rates and other economic variables.

THE BEHAVIOR OF THE PUBLIC DEBT IN THE UNITED STATES AND THE UNITED KINGDOM

We can gauge the empirical significance of interest-bearing public debt by looking at the long-term history for the United States and the United Kingdom. Table 14.1 shows the behavior over the past two centuries of the central government's nominal interest-bearing public debt, denoted by B^g. The data for the United States are net of holdings of public debt by parts of the federal government, which include various agencies and trust funds. Also, we think of the monetary authority—that is, the Federal Reserve—as part of the central government. Therefore, the debt figures net out the Fed's holdings of U.S. government bonds.[1] The table reports also the ratio of the public debt to nominal GNP, $B^g/(PY)$. We show this ratio graphically for the United States from 1790 to 1987 in Figure 14.1, and for the United Kingdom from 1700 to 1986 in Figure 14.2.

For both countries the two main positive influences on the ratio of public debt to GNP are wartime and major economic contractions. Superimposed on these infrequent positive shocks is a regular pattern where the ratio declines over time.

Let's focus now on the United States. The major peaks in the ratio of public debt to annual GNP occur at the end of the Revolutionary War (the value for 1784 was 0.33), the end of the Civil War (0.25 in 1865), the end of World War I (0.31

TABLE 14.1 *Values for Public Debt in the United States and the United Kingdom*

	United States		United Kingdom	
	B^g ($ Billion)	$B^g/(PY)$	B^g (£ Billion)	$B^g/(PY)$
1700	—	—	0.015	0.22
1710	—	—	0.026	0.33
1720	—	—	0.039	0.57
1730	—	—	0.038	0.56
1740	—	—	0.033	0.44
1750	—	—	0.059	0.79
1760	—	—	0.074	0.91
1770	—	—	0.11	1.22
1780	—	—	0.12	1.01
1790	0.08	0.31	0.18	1.04
1800	0.08	0.18	0.28	0.78
1810	0.05	0.08	0.43	0.93
1820	0.09	0.11	0.57	1.32

[1]For example, at the end of 1987, the gross amount of interest-bearing debt of the U.S. Treasury was $2,432 billion. But $478 billion of this total was held by various U.S. government agencies and trust funds and $223 billion by the Federal Reserve. Therefore, the amount in private hands (including about $300 billion with state and local governments) was only $1745 billion.

TABLE 14.1 *(Continued)*

	United States		United Kingdom	
	B^g ($ Billion)	$B^g/(PY)$	B^g (£ Billion)	$B^g/(PY)$
1830	0.05	0.04	0.55	1.13
1840	0.00	0.00	0.56	1.01
1850	0.06	0.03	0.56	0.94
1860	0.06	0.01	0.59	0.69
1865	2.2	0.24	—	—
1870	2.0	0.25	0.59	0.51
1880	1.7	0.13	0.59	0.43
1890	0.7	0.05	0.58	0.37
1900	1.0	0.05	0.58	0.29
1910	0.9	0.03	0.70	0.29
1919	24.2	0.31	7.5	1.30
1920	23.3	0.27	7.9	1.21
1930	14.8	0.16	7.6	1.55
1940	41.2	0.41	9.1	1.18
1945	227.4	1.07	22.5	2.27
1950	198.6	0.69	27.0	2.03
1960	207.5	0.41	29.0	1.12
1970	229.1	0.23	34.1	0.66
1980	616.4	0.23	96.3	0.42
1987	1731.5	0.38	185.7	0.44
1988	1856.8	0.38	—	—

Note: For the United States: B^g is the end-of-year value (midyear value before 1916) of privately held, interest-bearing public debt of the U.S. federal government at nominal par value. The figures are net of holdings by the Federal Reserve and U.S. government agencies and trust funds. (They include holdings by some government-sponsored agencies and by state and local governments.) For the sources, see Barro (1978a, Table 1).

P since 1870 is the GNP deflator (1982 = 1.0; see Figure 1.4). Earlier data are based on wholesale price indexes, as reported in U.S. Department of Commerce (1975, p. 201).

Y is real GNP (see Figure 1.1). Estimates of real GNP for 1834–71 are unpublished data from Robert Gallman. Earlier figures are calculated from the growth rates of real output that are reported in Paul David (1967, Table 1) and Alice Jones (1980, Table 3.15).

For the United Kingdom: B^g since 1917 is the central government's interest-bearing public debt at nominal par value. Before 1917 the figures are the accumulation of the central government's budget deficit, starting with a benchmark stock of public debt in 1700.

P since 1830 is the GNP deflator (1980 = 1.0). Earlier data are wholesale price indexes.

PY since 1830 is nominal GNP. Earlier data are the product of *P* and an estimate of trend real GNP.

The sources for B^g are B. R. Mitchell and Phyllis Deane (1962), Mitchell and H. G. Jones (1971), and Central Statistical Office, *Annual Abstract of Statistics,* various issues. Data on *P* and *Y* are from the above and also from C. H. Feinstein (1972), Deane and W. A. Cole (1969), and *International Financial Statistics,* various issues.

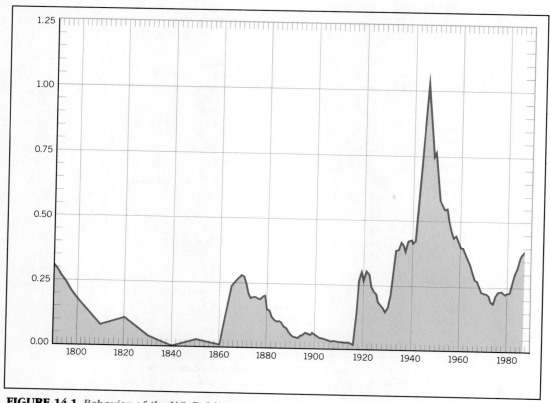

FIGURE 14.1 *Behavior of the U.S. Public Debt, 1790–1987*
The figure shows the ratio of the public debt to nominal GNP.

in 1919), and the end of World War II (1.07 in 1945). Smaller effects—which amount to pauses in the usual downward trend in the ratio rather than to actual increases—show up for the Spanish-American and Korean wars. However, little impact appears for the Vietnam War. (Recall from Chapter 12 that this war exhibited only a small excess of real military spending above trend.)

The positive effect of economic contraction on the ratio of public debt to GNP involves partly a negative effect on GNP and partly a positive effect on public debt. A dramatic response to an economic downturn shows up during the Great Depression, where the ratio of public debt to GNP rose from 0.14 in 1929 to 0.38 in 1933. Qualitatively similar behavior applies to less severe contractions; for example, the ratio rose from 0.23 in 1979 to 0.31 in 1983, from 0.20 in 1973 to 0.23 in 1975, and from 0.039 in 1892 to 0.047 in 1894.

During peacetime, nonrecession years, the ratio of public debt to GNP tends to decline. This pattern applies as much to the (mostly peaceful) post–World War II period from 1945 to 1987—when the ratio fell from 1.07 to 0.39—as to earlier times. For the previous peacetime periods aside from the Great Depression, the ratio fell from 0.31 to 0.14 between 1919 and 1929, from 0.24 to 0.02 between 1865 and 1916, from 0.11 to 0.01 between 1820 and 1860, and from 0.33 to 0.08 between 1784 and 1810. Notice also that the ratio for 1988, which is 0.38, is not high by historical standards and is well below the values for the 1950s.

The major element that distinguishes the behavior of the U.S. public debt since the late 1960s is the divergent patterns in nominal and real debt. The rapid inflation of recent years means that a declining ratio of the debt to GNP is consistent with a substantial run-up in the nominal debt. For example, the nominal debt for 1988 was $1857 billion, as compared with $228 billion in 1970. By contrast, the nominal debt changed very little between 1945 and 1970. These changes in the behavior of the nominal debt have not translated into dramatically different patterns for the debt when expressed either in real terms or as a ratio to GNP.

The experience for the United Kingdom is broadly similar to that for the United States. The major peaks in the ratio of public debt to annual GNP are again associated with wartime—1.3 at the end of the Seven-Years' War in 1764, 1.2 after the War of American Independence in 1785, 1.4 after the Napoleonic wars in 1816, 1.3 at the end of World War I in 1919, and 2.5 after World War II in 1946. It is noteworthy that the high points for the British debt in relation to GNP were more than twice as great as those for the United States. It is also interesting that the public debt amounted to more than 100% of annual GNP as long ago as the 1760s. Large amounts of public debt are not a modern invention!

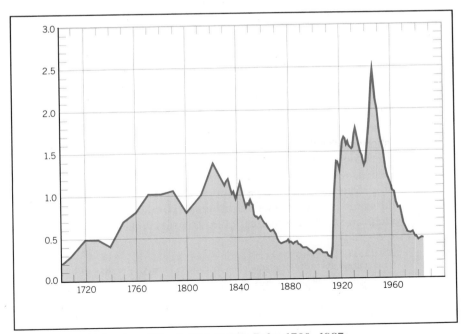

FIGURE 14.2 *Behavior of the British Public Debt, 1700–1987*
The figure shows the ratio of the public debt to nominal GNP.

Economic contractions again have a positive impact on the ratio of the debt to GNP. This response shows up especially for the United Kingdom during the depressed periods from 1920 to 1923 and from 1929 to 1933. The ratio of debt to GNP rose from 1.2 to 1.7 during the first interval and from 1.5 to 1.8 during the second.

Periods that involve neither war nor economic contraction typically display a declining pattern in the ratio of public debt to GNP. Again, this behavior applies as much to the post–World War II years as to earlier periods. In particular, the ratio declined from 1.47 in 1946 to 0.44 in 1987. The ratio for 1987 was not far above the low point over the past two centuries, which was 0.23 at the beginning of 1914.

CHARACTERISTICS OF GOVERNMENT BONDS

In the model the government can now borrow funds from households by selling interest-bearing bonds. We assume that these government bonds pay interest and principal in the same way as private bonds, which are already in the model. In particular, we continue to simplify matters by pretending that all bonds have a maturity of one period.[2] In the main analysis we assume also that bondholders regard public and private debts as equivalent. Specifically, we do not treat the government as more credit-worthy than private borrowers. In this case the government's bonds must pay the same nominal interest rate in each period, R_t, as that on privately issued bonds.

Our assumption about public and private bonds contrasts with our treatment of money. Since currency pays no interest, it seems that private enterprises would find it profitable to produce this stuff. In particular, the higher is the nominal interest rate, R_t, the greater is the gain from entering the business of creating currency. But because of legal restrictions or technical advantages for the government in providing a medium of exchange, we assume that the private sector does not issue currency.

With respect to bonds, we assume no legal restrictions on private issues and no technical advantages for the government in providing these types of securities. Hence, we do not allow the interest rate on government bonds to differ from that on private bonds. This assumption accords reasonably well with the U.S. data if we interpret private bonds as prime corporate obligations. For example, the market yield on six-month maturity U.S. Treasury bills averaged 6.4% from 1959 to 1987,

---

[2] The average maturity of marketable, interest-bearing public debt in the United States was around nine years in 1946. This figure declined fairly steadily to reach a low point of about two and a half years in 1976. During much of this period, the U.S. Treasury was prohibited from issuing long-term bonds at interest rates that would have made them marketable. With the ending of this restriction, the average maturity rose to about five years, nine months in 1987. *Economic Report of the President* (1975, Table C-73; 1988, Table B-85).

while that on four- to six-month maturity prime commercial paper averaged 6.9%.[3] A similar comparison applies to long-term bonds.

Denote by B_t^g the aggregate dollar amount of government bonds outstanding at the end of period t. We still use the symbol b for privately issued bonds. Therefore, an individual's total holdings of bonds for period t are now $b_t + b_t^g$. The aggregate of privately issued bonds is still zero—that is, $B_t = 0$. Hence, the aggregate quantity of bonds held by households now equals the public debt, B_t^g. Usually we think of cases where the government is a net debtor to the private sector, so that $B_t^g > 0$. However, the government may also become a creditor, where it holds net claims on the private sector.[4] We can represent this case by allowing for $B_t^g < 0$.

THE GOVERNMENT'S BUDGET CONSTRAINT

The presence of public debt alters the government's budget constraint in two respects. First, the dollar amount of net debt issue for period t, $B_t^g - B_{t-1}^g$, is a source of funds. (Notice that the simple rolling over or reissue of bonds as they come due is not a net source of funds. What counts is the difference between the stock outstanding at date t, B_t^g, and that outstanding in the previous period, B_{t-1}^g.) In this respect the printing of money and the printing of interest-bearing debt play the same role in the financing of the government's expenditures. Second, the government's nominal interest payments, $R_{t-1} \cdot B_{t-1}^g$, appear as an expenditure. Recall that this term is zero for money.

The government's budget constraint in dollar terms for period t is now

$$P_t G_t + V_t + R_{t-1} \cdot B_{t-1}^g = T_t + (M_t - M_{t-1}) + (B_t^g - B_{t-1}^g). \quad (14.1)$$

The two new terms are the government's interest payments on the left side, $R_{t-1} \cdot B_{t-1}^g$, and the net issue of debt on the right side, $(B_t^g - B_{t-1}^g)$. For simplicity, we return to the case where transfers, V_t, and taxes, T_t, are lump sum.

Figure 14.3 shows how the new item of expenditure—the government's net interest payments—has behaved since 1929. When expressed as a ratio to GNP, net federal interest payments were less than 1% until 1945, between 1.3% and 1.8% from 1945 to 1950, and between 0.9% and 1.2% from 1951 to 1978. For much of the latter period, the declining ratio of public debt to GNP (Figure 14.1) was offset by rising interest rates. Since 1978, the ratio of net federal interest payments to GNP

---

[3]At least some of the positive differential between the yields on commercial paper and U.S. Treasury bills reflects two advantages of the government's notes: first, the interest payments are exempt from state and local income taxes, and second, the Treasury bills satisfy the requirement that commercial banks hold some amount of government bonds as backing for the government's deposits in these banks.

[4]The last time this became a serious possibility for the United States was around 1835. A major concern was the outlet for further governmental revenues once the national debt was fully paid off. (We do not have this problem any more.) See the discussion in Davis Dewey (1931, p. 221).

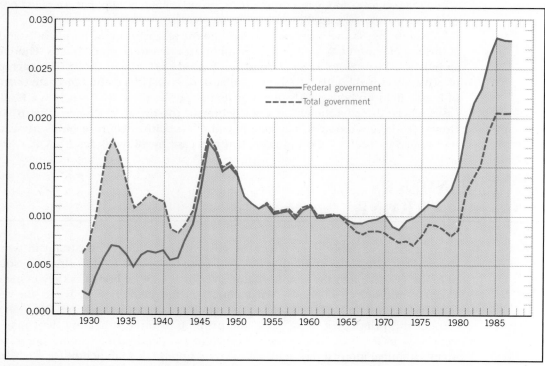

FIGURE 14.3 *Government Interest Payments as a Ratio to GNP*
The solid line is net federal interest payments as a ratio to GNP. (The figures are interest paid—net
of amounts paid by the federal government to the Federal Reserve—less interest received.) The
dashed line refers to total government. This line lies below the solid line since the mid-1960s
because state and local governments have been net recipients of interest income during this period.

has risen sharply, reaching 2.0% in 1981 and 2.8% from 1985 to 1987. Total government net interest payments behaved somewhat differently because state and local governments were net recipients of interest income in recent years. The ratio of total government net interest payments to GNP was only 2.1% from 1985 to 1987.

THE GOVERNMENT'S DEFICIT

We can think of the government's saving or dissaving in the same way as for households. The national accounts define the government's nominal saving to be the change in the dollar value of the government's holdings of money and bonds. (Recall that the government holds no capital in the model or in the national accounts.) Since we think of the government as issuing money and bonds—rather than holding them—an increase in money and bonds means that the government is dissaving. Economists use the term *surplus* to refer to positive saving by the government and the term *deficit* to refer to dissaving. (When saving is zero, the government has a **balanced budget**.)

Putting this terminology together, the nominal deficit, as measured in the standard national accounts, is

$$\text{nominal deficit (national accounts)} = (M_t + B_t^g) - (M_{t-1} + B_{t-1}^g). \quad (14.2)$$

Combining the definition from equation 14.2 with the government's budget constraint from equation 14.1 leads to the usual expression for the nominal deficit:

$$\text{nominal deficit (national accounts)} = P_t G_t + V_t + R_{t-1} B_{t-1}^g - T_t. \quad (14.3)$$

That is, the nominal deficit equals nominal expenditures—for purchases, transfers, and interest payments—less tax revenues. This concept of the budget deficit, amounting to $209 billion in 1986, $162 billion in 1987, and $142 billion in 1988 is the one that we often see in the newspapers.

The standard definition of the government's deficit in equation 14.2 does not take proper account of inflation.[5] Paralleling our treatment for households, we would define the government's real deficit—that is, its real dissaving—to be the change in the real value of its obligations in the forms of money and bonds. Therefore, the appropriate definition of the **real deficit** is

$$\text{real deficit} = \frac{(M_t + B_t^g)}{P_t} - \frac{(M_{t-1} + B_{t-1}^g)}{P_{t-1}}. \quad (14.4)$$

Multiplying through by the price level, P_t, the corresponding **nominal deficit** (which is simply the dollar value of the real deficit) is

$$\text{nominal deficit} = (M_t + B_t^g) - (1 + \pi_{t-1}) \cdot (M_{t-1} + B_{t-1}^g), \quad (14.5)$$

where $(1 + \pi_{t-1}) = (P_t/P_{t-1})$ was substituted on the right. Comparing equation 14.5 with the national accounts' concept of the nominal deficit in equation 14.2, the difference is the subtraction of the term $\pi_{t-1} \cdot (M_{t-1} + B_{t-1}^g)$. This term represents the reduction in the real value of the government's obligations due to inflation. If we want the real deficit (calculated by dividing the nominal deficit by the price level) to correspond to the change in the government's real obligations, we have to deduct this term from the standard measure of the nominal deficit.[6]

The differences between the two concepts of the deficit are large when the inflation rate is high. Therefore, the choice of definition matters especially for the high-inflation years from the late 1960s to the early 1980s. Table 14.2 compares the national accounts' concept of the deficit with the inflation-adjusted measure for the period 1965–88. For the years before 1965, where the inflation rate was typically small, the differences are much less significant. The national accounts' concept shows

---

[5]For a discussion of these effects from inflation, see Jeremy Siegel (1979).

[6]Note from equation 14.3 that the subtraction of $\pi_{t-1} B_{t-1}^g$ on the right side amounts to replacing the nominal interest rate, R_{t-1}, by the real rate, r_{t-1}. Similarly, the deduction of $\pi_{t-1} M_{t-1}$ corresponds to replacing the nominal interest rate on money, which is zero, by the real rate, which is $-\pi_{t-1}$. Thus, we effectively adjust for inflation by replacing nominal interest rates by real rates. Ideally we would also adjust the measurement of the government deficit for changes in the market value of government bonds because of changes in interest rates. Robert Eisner and Paul Pieper (1984) make these adjustments and also consider changes in the market value of government assets, such as land and gold.

TABLE 14.2 *Alternative Measures of the U.S. Government's Deficit, 1965–88*

	National Accounts' Basis		Inflation Adjusted	
	Nominal	Real	Nominal	Real
1965	1.1	3.3	−5.6	−16.6
1966	1.9	5.4	−8.1	−23.2
1967	7.5	20.9	−1.1	−3.0
1968	11.7	31.0	−2.1	−5.6
1969	−2.1	−5.3	−16.8	−42.2
1970	12.2	29.0	−2.7	−6.5
1971	23.7	53.4	9.0	20.2
1972	18.7	40.2	4.9	10.5
1973	7.4	14.9	−18.2	−36.8
1974	18.5	34.3	−15.2	−28.2
1975	82.4	139.0	53.3	90.0
1976	67.0	106.3	45.0	71.4
1977	60.0	89.2	27.5	40.9
1978	58.4	80.9	10.4	14.4
1979	49.1	62.5	−3.0	−3.9
1980	82.0	95.7	14.4	16.8
1981	85.6	91.1	17.6	18.8
1982	163.8	163.8	117.1	117.1
1983	186.1	179.2	146.5	141.1
1984	201.8	187.3	158.5	147.1
1985	224.0	201.5	177.8	160.0
1986	209.0	183.3	171.2	150.1
1987	161.7	137.7	99.5	84.7
1988	142.3	114.7	52.1	42.0

Note: For the national accounts' basis, the nominal deficit comes from equation 14.2 as $(M_t + B_t^g) - (M_{t-1} + B_{t-1}^g)$. The real deficit is the nominal one divided by the annual average of the GNP deflator. For the adjusted measure, the real deficit comes from equation 14.4 as $(M_t + B_t^g)/P_t - (M_{t-1} + B_{t-1}^g)/P_{t-1}$. Here, P_t is the seasonally adjusted value of the GNP deflator for the fourth quarter of year t. The nominal deficit is the real one multiplied by the annual average of the GNP deflator.

Sources (for the table and for Figure 14.4): The data for government bonds, B^g, are described in Table 14.1. M is the aggregate monetary liabilities of the Federal Reserve (the "monetary base"), which comprises currency outside the U.S. Treasury plus reserves held at the Federal Reserve. The data, which are values for December of each year, come from the *Federal Reserve Bulletin,* various issues. The data for the GNP deflator are from U.S. Department of Commerce (1986) and *U.S. Survey of Current Business,* various issues.

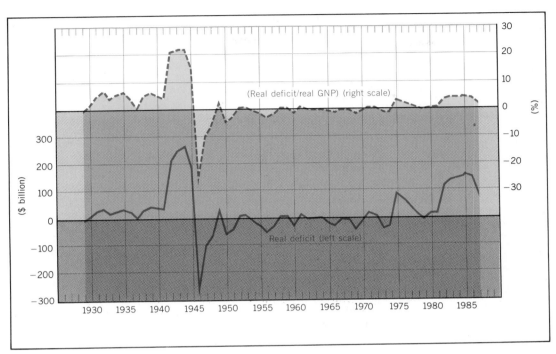

FIGURE 14.4 *Behavior of Real Federal Deficits*
The solid line shows the real deficit; the dashed line shows the ratio of the real deficit to real GNP.

a budget deficit for 23 of the 24 years since 1965, while the inflation-adjusted measure indicates one for only 15 of the years. With substantial inflation, increases in the government's nominal obligations often do not translate into increases in its real debt.

Figure 14.4 graphs the inflation-adjusted real deficit from 1929 to 1988. The solid line shows the level of the real deficit, and the dotted line expresses it as a ratio to real GNP. Note first the positive relation between the real deficit and wars. This relation stands out for World War II, where the real deficit exceeded 20% of real GNP from 1942 to 1944.[7] But there is also some effect during the Korean War for 1952–53 and perhaps during the Vietnam War for 1967–68.

The second important property is the positive relation between the real deficit and economic contraction. This pattern shows up strongly for the Great Depression, where the real deficit exceeded 7% of real GNP in 1932. Also, the real deficit tended to be positive during the post–World War II recessions—for example, in 1949,

---

[7]For 1946–47, the large negative real deficits reflect, first, decreases in the nominal debt and, second, large increases in the reported price level. Much of this increase in the price level arose from the removal of price controls. Probably the true price level rose more during World War II and less for 1946–47. (See the discussion in Chapter 12.) Hence, the true real deficits for 1946–47 were not as negative as those shown in the figure.

1958–59, 1971, 1975–76, and 1980–83. The ratio of the real deficit to real GNP was 3.3% in 1975 and 4.0% for 1982–83.

Table 14.3 quantifies the linkage between economic contraction and budget deficits. We begin with the estimated shortfall of real GNP in column 2 of the table; for example, the value for 1982 was 9.1%. The trend value of real federal receipts for 1982 was $716 billion (column 3 of the table). If real federal revenues fell below trend by the same fraction as the shortfall in real GNP, the real deficit for 1982 would have been 9.1% × 716 = $65 billion. In fact, the recession-induced deficit is larger for two reasons. First, the percentage shortfall of revenues tends to be greater than that of GNP. A major element here is the graduated-rate structure of the federal income tax, which puts households into lower tax-rate brackets when their incomes fall. Second, on the expenditure side, federal transfers tend to rise during recessions. Overall, I estimate (from Barro, 1979) that we should multiply the provisional estimate of $65 billion by 1.8 to account for these two factors. Then the estimated effect of the recession on 1982's real budget deficit becomes $117 billion (column 4 of the table), which happens to coincide with the actual real deficit in 1982.

Table 14.3 shows similar calculations for some other cases where recession was the major influence on the real deficit. (Significant movements in real federal expenditures would require separate attention.) This computation accounts for $75 billion of the real deficit of $90 billion for 1975. But for 1958, the actual real deficit of $9 billion was well below the projected figure of $26 billion. For 1933, the predicted real deficit of $20 billion compares to the actual value of $18 billion.

Over the U.S. history, wartime spending and recession explain the bulk of real federal budget deficits. This relation appears to break down, however, after 1983, when the Reagan tax cuts were not accompanied by comparable reductions in federal spending. From 1984 to 1986 the ratio of the real deficit to real GNP averaged 4.2%

TABLE 14.3 *Recession and Real Federal Deficits*

(1) Year of Recession	(2) Percentage Shortfall of Real GNP	(3) Trend Real Federal Receipts (Billions of 1982 Dollars)	(4) Predicted Real Deficit = 1.8 × col. 2 × col. 3	(5) Actual Real Deficit
1982	9.1	716	117	117
1975	7.3	572	75	90
1958	4.8	300	26	9
1933	37.4	30	20	18

Note: For each year of recession, column 4 shows the predicted real federal deficit. This value is 1.8 times the percentage shortfall in real GNP (col. 2) times the trend value of real federal taxes (col. 3). The trend assumes growth in real taxes at a rate of 3.6% per year (the average over 1948–87) from the benchmark year. Column 5 shows the actual real deficit for each year.

Sources: Column 2 comes from Table 9.1. The data on real federal receipts (nominal amounts divided by the GNP deflator) are from U.S. Department of Commerce (1986). The values from column 5 are those in Figure 14.4.

(see Figure 14.4) despite the strong economic recovery and the absence of wartime expenditure. But partly because of changes from the 1986 tax law, which particularly raised taxes paid by businesses, the ratio fell to 2.2% in 1987 and 1.1% in 1988.

PUBLIC SAVING, PRIVATE SAVING, AND NATIONAL SAVING

Real public saving is just the negative of the real budget deficit; that is, from equation 14.4,[8]

$$\text{real public saving} = -\frac{(M_t + B_t^g)}{P_t} + \frac{(M_{t-1} + B_{t-1}^g)}{P_{t-1}}. \qquad (14.6)$$

Real private saving—that is, real saving done by households—is given by

$$\text{real private saving} = \frac{(M_t + B_t^g)}{P_t} - \frac{(M_{t-1} + B_{t-1}^g)}{P_{t-1}} + K_t - K_{t-1}. \qquad (14.7)$$

This result extends the measure of real saving from Chapter 9 to include the change in households' holdings of real government bonds.

The sum of public and private saving is called **national saving.** Using equations 14.6 and 14.7, this real saving by the entire nation is given by

$$\text{real national saving} = K_t - K_{t-1}. \qquad (14.8)$$

Thus, the key result is that real saving for the overall economy must correspond to aggregate net investment.

PUBLIC DEBT AND HOUSEHOLDS' BUDGET CONSTRAINTS

As in Chapter 13, households care about the anticipated present value of real taxes. (Recall that we treat the taxes as lump sum at this stage.) Therefore, we want to know how the outstanding stock of public debt and the government's current and prospective deficits affect the present value of real taxes.

To illustrate the main results, let's start with a number of simplifications. First, assume that the price level and aggregate money stock do not change over time. In this case the government obtains no revenue from money creation. Second, take as given the quantity of government purchases, G_t, in each period. Third, suppose that aggregate transfers, V_t, are zero in each period. Finally, assume that the government starts with no interest-bearing debt—that is, $B_0^g = 0$. (Later we shall demonstrate that the conclusions do not depend on these unrealistic assumptions.)

[8]If the government owned capital, we would add the change in this public capital to the measure of real public saving. But we assume in the model that the government owns no capital.

Given our assumptions, the government's budget constraint in real terms for each period is

$$G_t + \frac{R \cdot B_{t-1}^g}{P} = \frac{T_t}{P} + \frac{(B_t^g - B_{t-1}^g)}{P}. \tag{14.9}$$

Recall that the government starts with no interest-bearing debt at date 0. Therefore, if the government balanced its budget from date 1 onward—that is, if $B_t^g - B_{t-1}^g = 0$ in every period—interest payments would always be nil. In this case, real purchases, G_t, would equal real taxes, T_t/P, at all times.

Suppose, instead of balancing its budget in period 1, that the government runs a deficit of \$1, so that $B_1^g = 1$. Since we hold fixed the quantity of government purchases, the budget constraint from equation 14.9 implies that this period's taxes, T_1, decline by \$1. That is, we are considering a *deficit-financed tax cut.* The cut in taxes by \$1 means that the aggregate of households' current disposable income rises by \$1.

Assume now that the government wants to restore the public debt to zero from date 2 onward—that is, $B_2^g = B_3^g = \ldots = 0$. Then in period 2, the government must raise taxes by enough to pay off the principal and interest on the \$1 of debt that it issued at date 1. Accordingly, the taxes for period 2, T_2, rise by $1 + R$ dollars. Since the extra debt is paid off in period 2, taxes in subsequent periods do not change.

Overall, taxes fall by \$1 during period 1 but rise by $1 + R$ dollars for period 2. The effect on the present value of real taxes is given by

$$\left(\frac{1}{P}\right) \cdot \left[-1 + \frac{(1 + R)}{(1 + R)} \right] = 0.$$

Note that we discount the increase in next period's taxes of $1 + R$ dollars by the discount factor, $1 + R$. Hence, the net effect on the present value of real taxes is nil. Since there is no change in the present value of real taxes, the government's deficit during period 1 has no aggregate wealth effect for households. Accordingly, the shift from current taxes to a deficit would not affect the aggregates of consumer demand and work effort. In this sense, households view as equivalent a current aggregate tax of \$1 and a current budget deficit of \$1. This finding is the simplest version of the **Ricardian Equivalence Theorem** on the public debt. (The theorem is named after the famous British economist David Ricardo, who first enunciated it.[9])

We can interpret the result as follows. Households receive \$1 of extra disposable income during period 1 because of the cut in taxes. But they also face $1 + R$ dollars of additional taxes during period 2. If households use the extra dollar of disposable income during period 1 to buy an extra dollar of bonds, they will have just enough additional funds—$1 + R$ dollars—to pay the extra taxes in period 2. The tax cut during period 1 provides enough resources, but no more, for households to pay the

---

[9]For discussions, see Ricardo (1957), James Buchanan (1958, pp. 43–46, 114–22), and Barro (1989). Gerald O'Driscoll (1977) points out Ricardo's own doubts about the empirical validity of his famous theorem.

higher taxes in the next period. That is why there is no aggregate wealth effect and no changes in consumer demand and work effort.

We can also interpret the results in terms of saving behavior. The budget deficit of $1 means that the government saves $1 less than before—that is, public saving falls by $1. Since households put all of their extra $1 of disposable income into bonds, private saving rises by $1. (In the case being considered, the marginal propensity to consume out of disposable income is zero and the marginal propensity to save is one.) Since the rise in private saving exactly offsets the decline in public saving, the sum of the two—that is, national saving—does not change.

To obtain the results, we assumed that the government paid off the entire public debt during period 2, but this assumption is unnecessary for the results. To see this, assume that the government *never* pays off the principal of $1 from the debt that it issued at date 1. Suppose instead that the government always balances its budget after the first period so that $B_t^g - B_{t-1}^g = 0$ holds from period 2 onward. In this case, the stock of debt stays constant over time, so that $B_1^g = B_2^g = \ldots = 1$. But then the government must finance its interest payments of R dollars in each period. (Remember that these payments would have been zero if the government had not run a deficit during period 1.) These extra expenses mean that taxes, T_t, are higher by R dollars for *every* period after the first.

Taxes fall by $1 during period 1 but rise by R dollars for each subsequent period. The change in the present value of real taxes is now given by the expression

$$\left(\frac{1}{P}\right) \cdot \left\{ -1 + R \cdot \left[\frac{1}{(1 + R)} + \frac{1}{(1 + R)^2} + \cdots \right] \right\}$$

$$= \left(\frac{1}{P}\right) + \left\{ -1 + \left[\frac{R}{(1 + R)} \right] \cdot \left[\frac{(1 + R)}{R} \right] \right\} = 0.\text{[10]}$$

Hence, the net change in the present value of real taxes is still zero.

We can think of this result as follows. Households receive $1 of extra disposable income during period 1 because of the cut in taxes. But they also face an additional R dollars of taxes in each subsequent period. If households use the extra dollar of disposable income during period 1 to buy an extra dollar of bonds, they receive $1 more of principal and R dollars more of interest in period 2. If they use the interest receipts to pay the higher taxes, households can again buy a bond for $1. Continuing in this manner, households can always use the interest income to meet the extra taxes in each period. The tax cut during period 1 provides enough resources, but no more, for households to pay the stream of higher future taxes. That is why the net change in the present value of real taxes is again equal to zero. Hence, we still predict no changes in the aggregates of consumer demand and work effort. Equivalently, we still predict that private saving rises to offset the decline in public saving so as to maintain the total of national saving.

The basic conclusion is that shifts between taxes and deficits do not generate aggregate wealth effects. This result still obtains if we drop many of the simplifying assumptions. For example, if the initial level of public debt is nonzero, the conclusion

---

[10]Use the condition, $(1 + z + z^2 + \cdots) = 1/(1 - z)$, where $z = 1/(1 + R)$. See the discussion of this geometric progression in n. 13, Chapter 4.

follows by considering the extra future interest payments and taxes that result from today's deficit. The results hold also if we superimpose an arbitrary pattern of transfers. Suppose, as an example, that the government reacts to higher future interest payments by reducing transfers rather than by raising taxes. Then we essentially add a new disturbance—equal decreases in future transfers and taxes—to the one that we already considered. Since this new disturbance has a zero aggregate wealth effect, the basic result remains valid.

We can also allow for money creation and inflation. As one possibility, the government may react to higher future interest payments by printing more money rather than increasing taxes. In this case economists say that the government **monetizes** part of the deficit or monetizes part of the stock of public debt. Then we essentially add another new disturbance—an increase in future money creation and a decrease in future taxes—to the one that we treated before. We know that changes in money, which finance a cut in taxes, have no aggregate wealth effect. Therefore, there is again no aggregate wealth effect from deficits. However, monetization of the public debt does have important implications for the behavior of prices. These effects work just like the increases in the quantity of money that we studied before. In particular, the monetization of deficits is inflationary.[11]

Finally, we can allow for nonzero deficits in future periods. As with a current deficit, these future ones do not generate any aggregate wealth effects. Therefore, the aggregate wealth effect is nil for any path of public debt. It follows that the aggregate of consumer demand does not react either to differences in the initial stock of real government bonds, B_0^g/P, or to variations in current or prospective government deficits.

Fundamentally, there is no aggregate wealth effect from budget deficits because they do not change the government's use of resources. The quantity of government purchases, G_t, is the amount of goods that the government buys during period t. Therefore, as before, aggregate wealth effects arise when there are changes in the present value of government purchases. But if we hold this present value constant, there are no aggregate wealth effects from shifts between taxes and deficits.

THE EFFECT OF A DEFICIT-FINANCED TAX CUT

Recall that with lump-sum taxes and transfers, the condition for clearing the commodity market is

$$C^d(r_1, \cdots) + I^d(r_1, \cdots) + G_1 = Y^s(r_1, \cdots).$$
$$(-) \qquad\qquad (-) \qquad\qquad\qquad (+)$$

(14.10)

[11]Aris Protopapadakis and Jeremy Siegel (1987) carried out an empirical study of the relation of money growth and inflation to budget deficits and the stock of public debt. For ten industrialized countries in the post–World War II period, there was little relation between budget deficits or public debt and the rates of growth of money or prices.

Here, we do not write out explicitly in the demand and supply functions the initial stock of capital, K_0, or the amount of government purchases, G_1. Also, recall that the previous analysis implies that the initial amount of real government bonds, B_0^g/P_1, does not matter for aggregate consumer demand, C^d, or goods supply, Y^s.

Suppose that the government cuts current taxes, T_1, and substitutes a corresponding increase in its interest-bearing debt, B_1^g. Assume that the government does not change either current or future purchases; thus, we are dealing with the pure effects from a budget deficit. Economists often refer to this type of action as stimulative **fiscal policy.** We found before that the replacement of current taxes by a deficit has no aggregate wealth effect. Hence, there are no effects on consumer demand or work effort. It follows that the tax cut has no impact on the condition for clearing the commodity market in equation 14.10. Accordingly, there is no effect on the real interest rate, r_1, or the quantities of output, Y_1, consumption, C_1, investment, I_1, and so on.

We can also think of the results in terms of desired saving and investment demand. Recall that the budget deficit stimulates an increase in desired private saving that exactly offsets the decrease in public saving. Therefore, the budget deficit has no effect on desired national saving. Since net investment demand also does not shift, it follows that no change in the real interest rate is needed to maintain the equality between desired national saving and net investment demand.

The condition that money be willingly held in period 1 is

$$M_1 = P_1 \cdot L(Y_1, \quad R_1, \cdots).$$
$$(+)(-)$$
$$(14.11)$$

Suppose that the government does not change either the current money stock, M_1, or the path of prospective money stocks. Then the deficit-financed cut in current taxes has no effect on equation 14.11. Hence, the price level, P_1, and the nominal interest rate, R_1, do not change. Notice also that the inflation rate, π_1, and all future price levels are unaffected by the tax cut.

We have found that a deficit-financed tax cut does not stimulate the economy or affect interest rates. Since these results are controversial and important, we shall want to see later whether modifications of the model change the conclusions.

OPEN-MARKET OPERATIONS

With public debt in the model, we can analyze **open-market operations.** An open-market purchase of securities occurs when the government—or a monetary authority like the Federal Reserve—buys government bonds with newly created money. In the opposite case there is an open-market sale of bonds for money. These open-market operations are the main way that the Federal Reserve actually affects the quantity of money in the United States. Therefore, we shall want to see whether this realistic way of changing the quantity of money leads to results that differ from the unrealistic "helicopter drops" of money that we studied in Chapter 8.

Consider an open-market purchase during period 1, whereby the stock of money,

M_1, increases by \$1 and the stock of government bonds, B_1^g, decreases by \$1. Assume that no subsequent changes in money occur; that is, there is a one-time increase in the quantity of money at date 1.

Table 14.4 shows that an open-market purchase of bonds amounts to the combination of two governmental policies that we have already examined. Suppose first that the government prints an extra dollar of money, M_1, and correspondingly reduces current taxes, T_1, by \$1. These changes are labeled as policy 1 in the table. Then suppose that the government raises taxes, T_1, back up by \$1 and uses the proceeds to pay off \$1 of the public debt, B_1^g. These changes are called policy 2 in the table. The net effect of combining these two policies is to raise money by \$1, leave taxes unchanged, and reduce government bonds by \$1. Thus, we end up with an open-market purchase of bonds, which is policy 3 in the table.

We know that policy 1 (more money and less taxes) raises the price level in the same proportion as the increase in the quantity of money. But except for a reduction in the real amount of government bonds, there are no changes in real variables. We know that policy 2 (the fiscal policy where taxes rise and public debt declines) has no effects except for another reduction in the real quantity of government bonds. By combining the two sets of responses, we find that an open-market purchase of bonds raises the price level and other nominal variables (aside from the quantity of public debt) in the same proportion as the increase in the stock of money. Aside from the fall in the real amount of government bonds, there are no changes in real variables. Thus, the previous results about the neutrality of money still apply to open-market purchases or sales of bonds.

WHY DOES THE PUBLIC DEBT MATTER?

The results suggest that the public debt and government deficits do not matter much for the economy. But think about the parallel with private debt. The aggregate quantity of private debt is always zero, which also seems uninteresting. Nevertheless, the possibilities for borrowing and lending are important because they eliminate the need for individuals to synchronize their incomes and expenditures. The public debt plays a similar role. Since the credit market exists, the government need not match its receipts from taxes and money creation to its expenditures in each period.

Using the government's budget constraint, the real amount of revenue from

TABLE 14.4 *Open-Market Purchases of Bonds and Other Government Policies*

Government Policy	Change in M_1	Change in B_1^g	Change in T_1
1. Print more money and reduce taxes	+ \$1	0	− \$1
2. Raise taxes and retire public debt	0	− \$1	+ \$1
3. Open-market purchase of bonds	+ \$1	− \$1	0

Note: An open-market purchase of bonds—policy 3—amounts to a combination of policies 1 and 2, which we have already studied.

taxation and money creation for period t is

$$\frac{T_t}{P_t} + \frac{(M_t - M_{t-1})}{P_t} = G_t + \frac{V_t}{P_t} + \frac{R_{t-1} \cdot B^g_{t-1}}{P_t} - \frac{(B^g_t - B^g_{t-1})}{P_t}. \quad (14.12)$$

Suppose that the paths for the government's real purchases and transfers are given. Also, assume for simplicity that the initial stock of interest-bearing debt, B^g_0, is zero. Then if the government never issues any bonds, its real receipts from taxes and money creation for period t must equal the given total of real expenditures for that period, $G_t + V_t/P_t$. The receipts have to be high whenever expenditures are high, and vice-versa. The potential to issue debt gives the government more flexibility. For example, by borrowing a lot when its expenditures are unusually large, the government can lessen the need for unusually high tax receipts or money creation at that time. The government can manage its issues of public debt to change its revenues for a period without changing the amount of expenditures for that period.

To bring out the main points, assume again that the stock of money is constant over time—that is, there is no revenue from money creation. Then the government's choices of public debt dictate the timing of its real tax collections, T_t/P_t. For a given present value of taxes, the economy will respond to differences in the timing of collections only if the taxes are not lump sum. To see the nature of this response, let's reintroduce the type of income tax that we studied in Chapter 13. In this setting the aggregate real taxes for period t are given by

$$\frac{T_t}{P_t} = \tau_t \left(Y_t + \frac{R_{t-1} \cdot B^g_{t-1}}{P_t} - E_t \right), \quad (14.13)$$

where τ_t is the marginal tax rate and E_t is the amount of tax-exempt real income for period t. (Note that the interest payments on the public debt—which are taxable—appear in the aggregate of households' real taxable income.)

By managing the public debt over time, the government determines the behavior of real tax revenues, T_t/P_t, which then determines the necessary values of the marginal tax rates, τ_t, in equation 14.13. Suppose, for example, that we start where the marginal tax rate is constant over time. Then consider the example where current taxes, T_1, fall by $1, while the public debt rises by $1. Further, assume that the government raises next period's taxes, T_2, by $(1 + R)$ to pay off the extra debt. Hence, in this example, the taxes collected change only for periods 1 and 2. Unless the government has gone beyond the point of maximum tax revenues on the Laffer curve, the changes in taxes collected show up as corresponding changes in marginal tax rates. Accordingly, today's marginal tax rate, τ_1, declines, while next period's tax rate, τ_2, rises. These changes motivate households to shift their income toward the current period and away from the next period. Specifically, households raise today's work but plan to reduce work in the next period. This response operates like some intertemporal-substitution effects that we considered before.[12]

Figure 14.5 shows the effect on the commodity market during period 1. The

---

[12]Since the tax law applies to income rather than spending, there is no intertemporal-substitution effect on consumer demand.

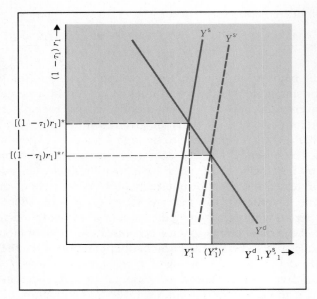

FIGURE 14.5 *Effect on the Commodity Market of a Deficit-Financed Cut in Today's Marginal Tax Rate*
The marginal tax rate falls at date 1. The increase in today's supply of goods leads to an increase in output and a fall in the after-tax real interest rate.

increase in today's work effort appears as a rightward shift of the supply curve. Since there is no direct stimulus to today's demand,[13] there is an excess supply of goods at the initial value of the after-tax real interest rate, $[(1 - \tau_1)r_1]^*$. Accordingly, Figure 14.5 shows that the after-tax real interest rate declines, while output increases. This extra output shows up partly as more consumption and partly as more investment.

The counterpart of this period's lower marginal tax rate is a higher tax rate for period 2. Figure 14.6 shows that the changes to the market-clearing diagram for period 2 are opposite to those found for period 1; in particular, the Y^s curve now shifts leftward. In comparison with the values that would have arisen in period 2 with no changes in taxes, there is an increase in the after-tax real interest rate and declines in output, work effort, consumption, and investment.

To summarize, when we consider income taxes, there are real effects from fiscal policy. A deficit-financed cut in today's marginal tax rate leads to increases in today's real economic activity. But the responses reverse later when the marginal tax rate is higher than otherwise. In our simple example, the higher future tax rate applies only to period 2. But more generally, the higher tax rate could be spread over many periods. Then the tendency for real economic activity to decline would also be spread out into the future. Overall, fiscal policy turns out to be an instrument that can influence the timing of real economic activity. But if the government uses this policy to stimulate output today, the side effect is a reduction in output in the future.

---

[13]There may be an effect on investment demand, but it depends on the change in the marginal tax rate for the time when the new capital stock is operational. If the changes in marginal tax rates are short-lived, the direct effect on investment demand will be minor. For simplicity, we neglect this effect.

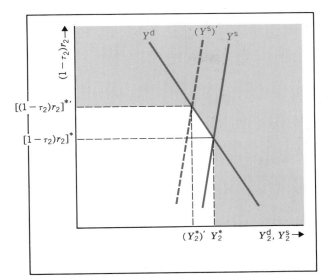

FIGURE 14.6 *Effect on the Commodity Market of a Temporary Increase in the Marginal Tax Rate*
During period 2, when the government pays off public debt, the marginal tax rate is higher. Therefore, output is lower and the after-tax real interest rate is higher.

THE TIMING OF TAXES

The government can manipulate its budget deficits to change the relative values of marginal tax rates for different periods and thereby influence the relative levels of output at different times. But it would not be a good idea for the government randomly to make tax rates high in some periods and low in others. These types of fluctuations in tax rates would cause unnecessary distortions because they would give people the wrong signals in determining how to allocate work and production over time. Fortunately, the U.S. government has not behaved in this erratic manner; rather, the public debt has typically been managed to maintain a pattern of reasonably stable tax rates over time.

One example of this behavior concerns income-tax rates during recessions. Typically, real government expenditures do not decline proportionately as much as aggregate output during a recession. (In fact, items such as unemployment compensation and welfare payments rise automatically.) To maintain a balanced budget, the government would have to raise tax rates when the economy contracts. But instead of raising taxes, the government typically runs a real deficit during recessions, as we saw in Figure 14.4.[14]

As another example, during wartime real government expenditures are much higher than normal, and real deficits are also especially high at these times. The government thereby avoids abnormally high tax rates during wars. In this way the necessary increases in tax rates are spread roughly evenly over time. Tax rates rise somewhat during wartime but also rise afterward along with the higher interest payments on the accumulated debt.

[14]Economists often estimate what the budget deficit would have been if the economy had been operating at a level of "full capacity" or "full employment." For discussions of the **full-employment deficit**, see E. Cary Brown (1956) and Council of Economic Advisers, *Economic Report* (1962, pp. 78–82).

"UNPLEASANT MONETARIST ARITHMETIC"

*T*homas Sargent and Neil Wallace (1981) analyzed the effects from changes in the timing of the inflation tax. Consider a country that obtains a significant fraction of its government revenue from money creation. (Thus, the analysis applies especially to hyperinflations and to countries such as Argentina and Brazil that typically have high inflation.) Suppose that the government cuts current monetary growth as an attempt to reduce inflation. Assume, however, that the government does not change the current or prospective values for its real expenditures and tax receipts. In this case, the decrease in the current real revenue from printing money must correspond to an increase in interest-bearing public debt. Moreover, the financing of this higher debt later on implies (with future real taxes and spending unchanged) that the future real revenue from money creation must rise. In other words, the government is just rearranging the timing of the inflation tax; less occurs now, and more occurs in the future. Since future monetary growth rises, the contractionary monetary policy will be unsuccessful in generating a long-term decline in the inflation rate. In fact, if people anticipate the increase in future monetary growth, inflation may not even decline in the short run. That is because, as discussed in Chapter 8, the expectation of higher monetary growth in the future tends to raise the current inflation rate. Sargent and Wallace conclude that a program to curb inflation by reducing monetary growth will be unsuccessful unless it is accompanied by a plan to offset today's lost real revenue from money creation by higher real taxes or lower real government expenditures.

THE STANDARD VIEW OF A DEFICIT-FINANCED TAX CUT

Our analysis of fiscal policy differs from that of most other macroeconomic models. To see why, return to the case of lump-sum taxes, which most macromodels assume. For our analysis, the key point is that households regard as equivalent a current tax of $1 or a government deficit of $1. In particular, if the behavior of government purchases does not change, shifts between taxes and deficits entail no aggregate wealth effects. In contrast, most macroeconomic models assume that a deficit-financed tax cut raises households' wealth even if there are no changes in government purchases. Let's look first at the results in this case and then examine briefly the arguments that some economists have made for a positive effect on aggregate wealth.

Suppose again that the government cuts current taxes by $1 and runs a deficit. If the tax cut makes people feel wealthier, aggregate consumer demand rises, but work effort and the supply of goods fall. The excess demand for goods leads to a higher real interest rate and thereby to lower investment. Thus, this analysis predicts that government deficits raise real interest rates and **crowd out** private investment.

Another way to look at the results is that the increase in households' current disposable income leads partly to more consumption and partly to more desired private saving. In particular, since the marginal propensity to consume is positive, the marginal propensity to save is less than one. It follows that the increase in desired private saving offsets only a portion of the reduction in public saving. Thus, desired national saving declines, and the resulting excess of investment demand over desired national saving leads to an increase in the real interest rate.

According to this analysis, the decrease in net investment shows up in the long run as a decrease in the stock of capital. Some economists refer to this negative effect on the capital stock as a **burden of the public debt.** Each generation "burdens" the next one by leaving behind a smaller aggregate stock of capital.[15]

THE EFFECT OF A TAX CUT ON WEALTH

To reach the standard conclusions mentioned above, we have to argue that a tax cut makes people feel wealthier, even if the behavior of government purchases does not change. Here, we consider two of the more interesting justifications for this assumption: one concerning the finiteness of life and the other the imperfections of private loan markets. It is worth exploring these matters in any case, since they come up in other areas, as well as in the context of public debt.

Finite Lives Suppose again that the government cuts current taxes by $1 and runs a deficit. We know that the government has higher interest payments and taxes in the future and that the present value of the extra future taxes equals $1. But assume that some of these taxes will show up after the typical person has already died. Then the present value of the extra future taxes that accrue during the typical person's lifetime falls short of $1. Hence, there is a positive effect on wealth when the government replaces current taxes by a deficit.

Why is there an increase in wealth when people have finite lives? The reason is that the increase in wealth for the aggregate of current taxpayers coincides with a decrease for the members of future generations. Individuals will be born with a liability for a portion of taxes to pay interest on the higher stock of public debt. But these people will not share in the benefits from the earlier tax cut. If these future liabilities on descendants were counted fully by present taxpayers, there would be no aggregate wealth effect.

Essentially government deficits enable members of current generations to die in a state of insolvency by leaving debts for their descendants. Current taxpayers experience an increase in wealth if they view this governmental shifting of incomes

---

[15]For some discussion, see James Ferguson (1964). Note especially in that volume the paper by Franco Modigliani, "Long-Run Implications of Alternative Fiscal Policies and the Burden of the National Debt."

across generations as desirable. But, in fact, most people already have private opportunities for intergenerational transfers, which they have chosen to exercise to a desired extent. As examples, parents make contributions to children in the form of educational investments, other expenses in the home, and bequests. In the other direction—and especially before the growth of social security—children provide support for their aged parents. To the extent that private transfers of this sort are operative, the shift from taxes to deficits does not offer the typical person a new opportunity to extract funds from his or her descendants. Rather, the response to higher deficits would be a shift in private transfers by an amount sufficient to restore the balance of income across generations that was previously deemed optimal. In this case, the shift from taxes to deficits again has no aggregate wealth effect.[16]

As a concrete example, assume that a couple plans to leave a bequest with a present value of $5000 for their children. Then suppose that the government runs a deficit, which cuts the present value of the couple's taxes by $1000 but raises the present value of their children's taxes by $1000. Our prediction is that the parents use the tax cut to raise the present value of their intergenerational transfers to $6000. Then the extra $1000 provides the children with the extra funds to pay their higher taxes. Thereby, parents and children end up with the same amounts of consumption and leisure as they enjoyed before the government ran its deficit.

Imperfect Loan Markets   The argument that taxes and deficits are equivalent assumes also that private and governmental interest rates are the same. However, the process of lending and borrowing involves transaction costs for loan evaluations, collections, defaults, and so on. It is relatively easy to borrow if a person has a house, car, or factory to put up as collateral. But it is much harder if someone, such as a student, just promises to repay a loan out of future labor earnings. Therefore, the interest rates for borrowing are especially high for those with poor collateral, who require large costs of supervision to ensure the repayment of loans.

Think of the world as divided into two groups. Group A consists of individuals or companies that lend or borrow at the same real interest rate, r, as the government. Group B comprises persons or businesses that would like to borrow at this interest rate but face higher borrowing rates. Let $\bar{r}$ be the real discount rate that someone from this group uses in calculating the present value of future incomes and expenses.[17] The rate $\bar{r}$ exceeds the real interest rate, r, for those from group A.

Suppose that the government cuts taxes and runs a deficit. The cut in taxes applies partly to group A and partly to group B. As before, the aggregate of future taxes increases. Let's assume that the division of these future taxes between those

---

[16]For a discussion of the interplay between public debt and private intergenerational transfers, see Barro (1974). A different view is that parents use bequests to control their children's behavior rather than purely for altruistic reasons. For a discussion of this "enforcement theory of giving," see Douglas Bernheim, Andrei Shleifer, and Lawrence Summers (1985).

[17]For someone who is borrowing at a high real interest rate, the discount rate $\bar{r}$ equals the borrowing rate. But if the borrowing rate is high enough (perhaps infinity), a person may end up borrowing nothing even though he or she would be willing to pay a rate that was well above r. For such a person, the discount rate $\bar{r}$ is the highest real interest rate that he or she would be willing to pay on a loan.

EMPIRICAL EVIDENCE ON THE MACROECONOMIC EFFECTS OF BUDGET DEFICITS

S ome important predictions from the standard analysis are that larger real government deficits lead to higher real interest rates, higher consumption, and lower national saving. There is little question that most government officials and news reporters, as well as many economists, believe that budget deficits raise interest rates. Nevertheless, this belief does not have much evidence to support it. For example, Charles Plosser (1982, 1987) and Paul Evans (1987a, 1987b) carried out detailed statistical analyses of government deficits and interest rates for the United States and other industrialized countries. Their major finding was that budget deficits had no significant effects on nominal or real interest rates. Thus, their evidence contradicts the standard theory in which deficit-financed tax cuts make people feel wealthier.

Despite many empirical studies for the United States and other countries, it has proved difficult to reach definitive conclusions about the effect of budget deficits on consumption and saving. One reason for statistical problems is that budget deficits often occur as responses to business fluctuations, government expenditures, and inflation. Since these variables themselves interact with consumption and saving, it is hard to distinguish the effects of budget deficits on the economy from the effects in the reverse direction.

One recent empirical study by Chris Carroll and Lawrence Summers (1987) avoids some of these problems by comparing the saving rates in the United States and Canada. The private saving rates were similar in the two countries until the early 1970s but have since diverged; for 1983–85 (the latest years in the study), the Canadian rate was higher by about six percentage points. After holding fixed some macroeconomic variables and aspects of the tax systems that influence saving, Carroll and Summers isolated a roughly one-to-one, positive effect of government budget deficits on private saving. This result accords with the Ricardian view.

Recent fiscal policy in Israel comes close to a natural experiment for studying the interplay between budget deficits and saving rates. Figure 14.7 shows the values from 1983 to 1987 for the national saving rate, the private saving rate, and the public saving rate. (In this case, real public saving equals public investment less the real budget deficit.) In 1983 the national saving rate of 13% corresponded to a private saving rate of 17% and a public saving rate of -4%. In 1984 the dramatic rise in the budget deficit led to a public saving rate of -11%. (A principal reason for the deficit was the strong adverse effect of the increase in the inflation rate on the collection of real tax revenues.) For present purposes, the interesting observation is that the private saving rate rose from 17% to 26%, so that the national saving

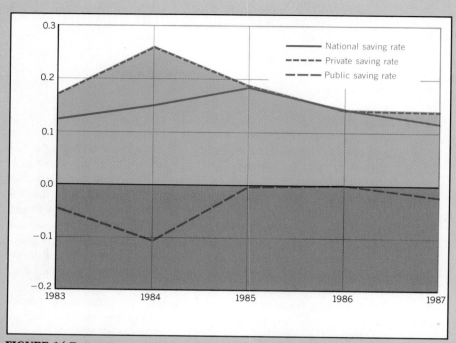

FIGURE 14.7 *Public and Private Saving Rates in Israel, 1983–1987*
Note that the pattern for the private saving rate roughly mirrors that for the public saving rate.
Therefore, the national saving rate is relatively smooth.

rate changed little, actually rising from 13% to 15%. Then the Israeli stabilization program in 1985 eliminated the budget deficit (along with eliminating most of the inflation), so that the public saving rate increased from −11% in 1984 to 0 in 1985–86 and −2% in 1987. The private saving rate decreased dramatically at the same time—from 26% in 1984 to 19% in 1985 and 14% in 1986–87. Therefore, the national saving rates were relatively stable, going from 15% in 1984 to 18% in 1985, 14% in 1986, and 12% in 1987. Although one episode cannot be decisive in verifying or refuting a theory, it is interesting that this dramatic example from Israel reveals the roughly one-to-one relationship between budget deficits and private saving that the Ricardian view predicts.

from group A and those from group B coincides with the division of the tax cut. (Otherwise there is a distributional effect, which would require separate attention.) For the members of group A, the present value of the higher future taxes again equals the amount of the tax cut. Therefore the wealth effect is nil. For group B, where the discount rate $\bar{r}$ exceeds r, the present value of the extra future taxes is less than their tax cut. Thus, the members of this group are wealthier; in effect, they are better off because the tax cut enables them to borrow at the lower real interest rate, r. This cut in the effective borrowing rate motivates the members of group B to raise current demands for consumption and investment.

We have shown that a deficit-financed tax cut leads to an increase in the aggregate demand for consumption and investment (the demands from group A do not change, while those from group B increase). The rise in consumer demand means that the aggregate of desired private saving rises by less than the budget deficit; that is, desired national saving declines. Since investment demand (which went up) exceeds desired national saving (which went down), the real interest rate, r, must rise. This higher real interest rate crowds out current consumption and investment by the members of group A. On the other hand, because of the initial stimulus to group B's demands, the consumption and investment of this group rise on net. Thus, the main effect is a diversion of current expenditures from group A to group B.

In the aggregate, investment may rise or fall, and the long-term effect on the capital stock is uncertain. The major change, however, is a better channeling of resources to their ultimate uses. Namely, the persons from group B—who started with the high borrowing rates—command a greater share of current output. Essentially the tax cut induces the type-A people to hold more than their share of the additional public debt so as effectively to lend to the type-B people at the real interest rate, r. This process works because the government implicitly guarantees the repayment of loans through its tax collections and debt payments. Thus loans between A and B take place even though such loans were not viable (because of "transaction costs") on the imperfect private loan market.

This much of the argument may be valid, although it credits the government with a lot of skill in the collection of taxes from people with poor collateral. Even if the government possesses this skill, the conclusions do not resemble those from the standard analysis. For example, in the model discussed above, budget deficits are a good idea because they effectively improve the functioning of loan markets. Moreover, with imperfect credit markets, budget deficits do not necessarily reduce aggregate investment.

SOCIAL SECURITY AND SAVING

Benefits paid through social security have expanded dramatically in the United States and most other countries. For example, the amounts paid out from 1984 to 1987 for old age, survivors, and disability averaged 4–5% of GNP, as compared to 3% in 1970, 2% in 1960, and less than 1% in 1950. Some economists, such as Martin Feldstein (1974), argued that this increase in social security reduced private saving. Since this effect could be quantitatively important, we want to examine it from the standpoint of our model.

The argument for an effect on saving applies when the social security system is not **fully funded.** In a funded setup, workers' payments accumulate in a trust fund, which provides later for retirement benefits. The alternative is a **pay-as-you-go system,** in which benefits to old persons are financed by taxes on the currently young. In this case, the people who are at or near retirement age when the program begins or expands receive benefits without paying a comparable present value of taxes. Correspondingly, the people from later generations pay taxes that exceed their expected benefits in present-value terms. (Unfortunately, most readers of this book are in this category.)

The U.S. system operates mainly on a pay-as-you-go basis. Although the plan in 1935 envisioned an important role for the social security trust fund, the system has evolved steadily since 1939 toward primarily a pay-as-you-go operation.[18] Retirees increasingly received benefits that—in present-value terms—exceeded their prior contributions.

Consider the effects of social security in a pay-as-you-go system. For this purpose, we neglect the substitution effects from the taxes and transfers since we already discussed these effects in the previous chapter. Now we look at possible wealth effects from an increase in retirement benefits, which are financed by higher taxes on workers.

The usual argument goes as follows. Old persons experience an increase in the present value of their social security benefits net of taxes. Therefore they respond to the increase in wealth by consuming more. Young persons face higher taxes, but these are offset partly by the expectation of higher retirement benefits. Since the decrease in wealth for the young is smaller in magnitude than the increase for the old, aggregate consumer demand tends to rise. In other words, more social security reduces the aggregate of desired saving. Therefore the real interest rate increases, and net investment decreases. In the long run, this decrease in investment shows up as a smaller stock of capital.

This argument for social security parallels the standard view of a deficit-financed tax cut. In both cases, the increase in aggregate consumer demand arises only if people neglect the adverse effects on descendants. Specifically an increase in the scale of the social-security program means that the typical person's descendants will be born with a tax liability that exceeds his or her prospective retirement benefits in present-value terms. If people take full account of these effects on their descendants,' the aggregate wealth effect from more social security is nil.

As in the case of a deficit-financed tax cut, more social security enables older persons to extract funds from their descendants. But as before, people value this change only if they give no transfers to their children and receive nothing from their children. Otherwise people respond to more social security by shifting private intergenerational transfers rather than by changing consumption. For example, in the United States, the growth of social security has strongly diminished the tendency of children to support their aged parents.

On an empirical level, there has been a great debate about the connection of social security to saving and investment. First, Martin Feldstein (1974) reported a dramatic negative effect of social security on capital accumulation in the United

---

[18]For a discussion of the institutional features, see Michael Boskin (1977) and Michael Boskin et al. (1987).

States. But subsequent investigators showed that this conclusion was unwarranted.[19] Neither the long-term evidence for the United States nor that from a cross-section of countries in recent years provides evidence that social security depresses saving and investment.

SUMMARY

The ability to issue and retire interest-bearing public debt allows government expenditures to diverge in the short run from the sum of tax receipts and the revenue from printing money. Shifts between taxes and budget deficits affect the timing of tax collections but not their overall present value. Hence, for a given path of government purchases, this type of fiscal policy has no aggregate wealth effect. In the case of lump-sum taxes, the absence of a wealth effect implies that budget deficits do not affect the real interest rate or the quantities of investment and output. This result is called the Ricardian Equivalence Theorem, which says that taxes and deficits have the same effect on the economy.

Budget deficits have some real effects in the presence of an income tax. These effects concern the timing of taxes, which exert intertemporal-substitution effects on work and production. It is desirable for the government to manage the public debt to avoid large random fluctuations in tax rates from period to period. This motivation accounts for the tendency of governments to run large real deficits during wars and recessions but to run real surpluses in "good times."

The standard view of deficit-financed tax cuts is that they make people feel wealthier. In this case, deficits would raise the real interest rate and crowd out investment. Sometimes economists rationalize the wealth effect from a tax cut by appealing to finite lives or imperfect capital markets. But an examination of these ideas suggests that they are unlikely to support the standard conclusions.

Finally, we note that social security is analogous to public debt. If debt-financed tax cuts have little effect on real interest rates and capital accumulation, the same conclusion holds for an increase in the scale of social-security programs.

IMPORTANT TERMS AND CONCEPTS

government's budget deficit (surplus)	nominal deficit
public debt	national saving
balanced budget	Ricardian Equivalence Theorem
nominal deficit (national accounts)	monetize the deficit
real deficit	fiscal policy

[19]For a summary of the debate, see Louis Esposito (1978), the papers in the May 1979 issue of the *Social Security Bulletin,* and Dean Leimer and Selig Lesnoy (1982).

open-market operations	fully funded system (for social security)
full-employment deficit	
crowding out (from government deficits)	pay-as-you-go system (for social security)
burden of the public debt	

QUESTIONS AND PROBLEMS

Mainly for Review

14.1 What is the real deficit? Does a rise in the inflation rate reduce the real deficit? Show how the real deficit is altered either by policy changes or by economic events such as recessions.

14.2 Suppose there is a temporary increase in lump-sum taxes. Is there any effect on households' wealth? Show how the typical household can use the credit market to offset the reduction in current disposable income.

14.3 Are government budget deficits inflationary? If so, do deficits affect the real interest rate? What about the nominal interest rate?

14.4 Why are open-market operations neutral?

14.5 Suppose the government announces a reduction in income-tax rates to take place in some future period. What intertemporal-substitution effect will this have on current work? What effect will it have on consumption?

14.6 Compare the effect of (a) government budget deficits and (b) social security on the tax liabilities of younger people. Why do the tax liabilities exceed expected future benefits in the case of social security?

PROBLEMS FOR DISCUSSION

14.7 *The Aggregate Wealth Effect from a Deficit*
Assume that taxes are lump sum. Suppose that the government cuts current taxes and runs a deficit. Then assume that the real public debt remains constant from period 2 onward. Also, the time paths of government purchases and real transfers do not change. Discuss the aggregate wealth effect that results from the government's current tax cut. In particular, how does this effect depend on the following considerations:

a. Finite lifetimes?
b. The existence of childless persons?
c. Uncertainty about who will pay the higher future taxes?

d. The possibility that the government will print more money in the future rather than raising taxes?

e. The imperfection of private loan markets?

14.8 *Effects of a Deficit-Financed Tax Cut*

Assume that taxes are lump sum. Suppose again that the government cuts current taxes and runs a deficit. Discuss the effects for the current period on, first, the real interest rate and the quantities of output and investment, and second, the price level and the nominal interest rate, assuming that

a. The paths of government purchases, real transfers, and money creation do not change.

b. The same as in part a, except that people expect the future growth rate of money to rise.

c. The same as in part a, except that people expect future real transfers to fall.

d. The same as in part a, except that people expect future government purchases to decline.

14.9 *The Reagan Tax Cut Plan for 1981*

President Reagan's initial proposal in 1981 for cutting U.S. federal income-tax rates involved roughly a 23% overall reduction in rates. The full cut was to be phased in over a three-year period ending in 1983. The plan involved also gradual reductions over time in real government expenditures when expressed as a fraction of real GNP.

Consider an alternative plan that yields the same present value of real tax revenues but that implemented the entire cut in tax rates in 1981. Assume that real government expenditures behave the same way as under Reagan's plan. Compare this plan with Reagan's with respect to the effects on work effort, production, and investment over the period 1981–83.

14.10 *Social Security and Capital Accumulation*

Suppose that the government introduces a new social security program, which will pay the real amount *s* to covered persons when they retire.

a. What long-run effects do you predict on the stock of capital?

b. How does the answer depend on whether the social security program is fully funded or pay-as-you-go?

14.11 *The Government's Stock of Gold*

The U.S. Treasury's gold stock is held at the Federal Reserve. Mostly because of changes in the price of gold, the market value of these holdings rose from $12 billion at the end of 1970 to $109 billion at the end of 1988. In terms of 1982 prices (using the GNP deflator), the increase was from $28 billion at the end of 1970 to $88 billion at the end of 1988.

a. How would you modify the measure of the government's deficit to include these changes in the value of gold holdings?

b. Apply this reasoning more generally to the government's holdings of other commodities, capital goods, and land.

(Amusingly, the Federal Reserve values its gold holdings at the official price of $42.22 per ounce rather than at the market price, which was $418 per ounce at the end of 1988.)

14.12 *Temporary Consumption Taxes (optional)*

Suppose that taxes are levied on consumption rather than income. An individual's real tax for period t is then $t_t/P_t = \tau_t c_t - e_t$. Assume that the government runs a deficit during period 1 and cuts the marginal tax rate on consumption, τ_1. For subsequent periods, the marginal tax rates are higher than otherwise.

a. What is the impact of the tax cut on the demand and supply of goods for period 1?

b. What is the effect during period 1 on the real interest rate, output, work effort, consumption, and investment?

PART FIVE

THE INTERNATIONAL ECONOMY

*T*hus far, we have dealt with the macroeconomic performance of a single, closed economy. In particular, we have neglected the interactions among countries on international markets. Most macroeconomists, especially those in the United States, focused until relatively recently on this closed-economy framework. The justifications for this practice were, first, that the U.S. economy represented a large share of the world economy; second, that a relatively small fraction of U.S. production and expenditure involved international trade; and finally, in a global context, that various restrictions inhibited the flow of goods and credit from one country to another. But, especially with the opening up of international markets over the last two decades, the practice of ignoring the rest of the world became increasingly unsatisfactory even for the large U.S. economy. For example, the ratio of U.S. exports to GNP averaged 5.9% from 1948 to 1971 but then increased to 10.1% from 1972 to 1987. (The ratios of imports to GNP were 4.7% and 10.1%, respectively.) Aside from this greater volume of international trade, recent economic events have included large increases in U.S. borrowing from foreigners, substantial fluctuations in exchange rates, and important effects from world supply shocks, such as those affecting the market for oil.

This chapter and the next extend the model to allow for trade in goods and credit across national borders. With these extensions we will be able to analyze the international economic issues that have become important in recent years. In particular, we will be able to discuss the U.S. current-account deficit, which has become almost as hot an issue as the U.S. budget deficit.

We shall find that our previous analysis of a closed economy applies to the macroeconomics of the world economy, whereas our earlier treatment of individuals carries over to the behavior of a small economy that operates on world markets. We can use this perspective to think about international borrowing and lending, changes in the prices of commodities such as oil, and the factors that determine a country's balance of international payments. Since the U.S. economy is so large, it is an intermediate case between the small economy and the entire world.

Aside from the parallels to the previous discussion, there are some entirely new issues that concern the determination of exchange rates among different currencies. As part of this analysis, we have to assess the linkages across countries of prices, interest rates, and monetary policies.

CHAPTER 15

WORLD MARKETS IN GOODS AND CREDIT

onsider a world economy, within which the United States is one of many countries. From the perspective of the United States, we want to allow for the possibilities of buying goods from abroad or of selling goods to foreigners. That is, we will extend the analysis of the commodity market to include imports and exports. To carry out this extension, we begin with a number of unrealistic assumptions, which we will later relax. Assume first that the goods produced in each country are physically identical. In addition, suppose that transport costs and barriers to trade across national borders are small enough to neglect. (In this sense, the analysis applies when international markets are relatively open, as is true in the main for the industrialized countries in recent years.) Finally, pretend at this stage that, instead of using their own currency, all countries use a **common currency,** such as the U.S. dollar. The residents of each country hold U.S. dollars and quote prices in units of U.S. dollars.

Given our assumptions, goods in all countries must sell at the same dollar price P_t. Otherwise households and firms would want to buy all goods at the lowest price and sell all goods at the highest price. This result is the simplest version of the **law of one price.** At this point, we also abstract from inflation, so that the dollar price level in all countries is the constant P.

Suppose that each country has a central bank and that this bank holds a quantity of **international currency.** This currency could be pieces of paper denominated in U.S. dollars or other national units or could be a commodity such as gold. The precise form of the international currency is unimportant for our purposes, except that we assume that the nominal interest rate on this currency is zero.

Let $\overline{H}_t$ denote period t's world quantity of international currency, denominated in units of U.S. dollars. (An overbar means that the variable pertains to the entire world.) For simplicity, we assume that $\overline{H}_t$ does not change over time; that is, $\overline{H}_t$ equals the constant $\overline{H}$. The domestic central bank demands the real quantity, H_t/P, of this international currency to facilitate transactions between domestic residents and foreigners. (In the next chapter, we shall discuss further this demand for international currency.)

Assume that a single credit market exists in the world. If we abstract from differences in credit-worthiness among borrowers, the real interest rate, r_t, on this world credit market must be the same for lenders and borrowers from every country. When measured in U.S. dollars—that is, as future dollars paid per current dollar per year—the nominal interest rate is R_t. Since we abstract from inflation, the real interest rate, r_t, equals the nominal rate.

THE UNITED STATES AS AN OPEN ECONOMY

Consider the situation from the standpoint of the residents of a single country, which might be the United States. We refer to this country as the domestic or home country, and we refer to other countries as the rest of the world. Let Y_t represent the total of goods and services produced domestically, which is the real gross domestic product (GDP). Correspondingly, the dollar income from this source is the amount PY_t.

For the residents of a single country, the total of funds lent need no longer equal the total borrowed. Rather, the total amount lent on net by domestic residents corresponds to the total borrowed on net from this country by foreigners. Let B_t^f represent the net holding of foreign bonds by domestic residents at the end of period t. (For simplicity, we think of B_t^f as held by households, although the results would not change if the government held foreign claims or borrowed from abroad.) If $B_t^f > 0$, the home country is a net creditor to the rest of the world, whereas if $B_t^f < 0$, the country is a net debtor. Correspondingly, the amount $R_{t-1}B_{t-1}^f$ is the net interest income (positive or negative) for period t to domestic residents from abroad.[1]

If we add up for the entire world, we must have that the total amount borrowed equals the total lent. Hence, the world aggregate for the net holding of foreign bonds, $\overline{B}_t^f$, is zero. This result for the world parallels the condition that we had before for a single country when we neglected foreigners. In our previous setting,

---

[1] More generally, the variable B_t^f includes not only interest-bearing securities but also any other net claims of domestic residents on the rest of the world. Specifically, it includes ownership of capital abroad, which arises from **direct investment** in foreign countries. The term $R_t B_t^f$ encompasses the income from this ownership of capital.

an isolated country had no place to borrow from. While this constraint no longer applies to an individual country, it still holds for the entire world (if we neglect the possibility of borrowing from Mars). Correspondingly, the world aggregate of net interest income from abroad, $R_{t-1}\overline{B^f_{t-1}}$, is also zero.

Suppose that the net interest income from abroad is the only source of income from the rest of the world.[2] Then the total dollar income of domestic residents during period t is the gross national product, which equals gross domestic product, PY_t, plus the net interest income from abroad, $R_{t-1}B^f_{t-1}$. This total income can be spent in the following ways:

- Personal consumption expenditures, PC_t, whether on goods and services produced domestically or abroad.
- Private domestic gross investment, PI_t, which is the expenditure on capital goods located at home.
- Government purchases of goods and services, PG_t.
- **Net foreign investment,** which is the name given to the net acquisition of interest-bearing claims from abroad, $B^f_t - B^f_{t-1}$, plus any accumulation of international currency, $H_t - H_{t-1}$. Typically the change in international currency is a small fraction of GNP.

Putting the results together yields the budget constraint for the home country,

$$PY_t + R_{t-1}B^f_{t-1} = P(C_t + I_t + G_t) + (B^f_t - B^f_{t-1}) + (H_t - H_{t-1}). \quad (15.1)$$

For a single economy in isolation (a closed economy), the gross domestic product, PY_t, must equal the total expenditure by domestic residents for goods and services, $P(C_t + I_t + G_t)$. When we open the economy to the rest of the world, we introduce some new items, which can create a divergence between the gross domestic product and the total of domestic expenditures on goods and services. The left side of equation 15.1 includes the net interest income from abroad, $R_{t-1}B^f_{t-1}$. The right side includes net foreign investment, which equals the net acquisition of interest-bearing claims, $B^f_t - B^f_{t-1}$, plus the accumulation of international currency, $H_t - H_{t-1}$.

The term $B^f_t - B^f_{t-1}$ is called the **balance on capital account** for the home country. If $B^f_t - B^f_{t-1}$ is positive, there is an **outflow of capital**. (If it is negative, there is an **inflow of capital**.) An outflow of capital means that the home country acquires interest-bearing claims on foreigners and thereby provides funds for the foreigners to purchase goods and services.

---

[2]Our formulation neglects transfer payments from one country to another and also ignores any net labor income from abroad. This net labor income equals the earnings of domestic residents working in foreign countries, less that of foreigners working in the home country. This category of income is unimportant for most countries. It is, however, a significant negative item for Germany, which imports many foreign workers as *gastarbeiter,* and a significant positive item for countries like Pakistan and Turkey, which export workers to other places. If we included this net labor income, we would add it to the net interest income to measure the overall **net factor income from abroad**. The term *factor income* means that the income flows to the factor labor or to the factor "capital," which corresponds here to the net claims, B^f, on assets abroad.

Domestic residents have a total income of $PY_t + R_{t-1}B^f_{t-1}$ (which equals GNP) and a total expenditure on goods and services of $P(C_t + I_t + G_t)$. The difference between income and expenditure corresponds to saving by domestic residents in the form of additional assets acquired from the rest of the world and is called the **current-account balance.** Notice from equation 15.1 that

$$\text{current-account balance} = PY_t + R_{t-1}B^f_{t-1} - P(C_t + I_t + G_t)$$
$$= \text{net foreign investment} \tag{15.2}$$
$$= B^f_t - B^f_{t-1} + H_t - H_{t-1}.$$

This expression is the basic identity for the balance of international payments. The equation says that the current-account balance equals net foreign investment, which is the sum of the net capital flow, $B_t - B^f_{t-1}$, and the change in international currency, $H_t - H_{t-1}$. If the current-account balance is positive (or negative), a country is said to have a **surplus** (or **deficit**) **on current account.** Notice that as an accounting identity, a surplus on current account must have an offsetting financial transaction in the form of an increase in interest-bearing claims, B^f, or international currency, H.

Now consider an alternative view of a country's position with respect to the rest of the world. The gross national product, $PY_t + R_{t-1}B^f_{t-1}$, is the total value of the goods and services produced this period by domestic residents. Therefore, the difference between GNP and domestic expenditures equals the value of goods and services produced by domestic residents less the value of goods and services used currently by these residents. If the difference is positive, the home country must be selling goods and services on net to the rest of the world; if negative, the home country must be buying goods and services on net. Exports are the goods and services produced by domestic residents that are sold to foreigners, and imports are the goods and services produced by foreigners that are bought by domestic residents. Hence, using equation 15.2 and defining net exports to be the value of exports less the value of imports,

$$\text{current-account balance} = PY_t + R_{t-1}B^f_{t-1} - P(C_t + I_t + G_t) \tag{15.3}$$
$$= \text{net exports.}$$

Rearranging equation 15.3 leads to the customary definition of the gross national product

$$\text{GNP} = PY_t + R_{t-1}B^f_{t-1} = P(C_t + I_t + G_t) + \text{net exports.} \tag{15.4}$$

We can get another perspective on international borrowing and lending by thinking about the home country's saving and investment. From equation 15.2, the current-account balance is $PY_t + R_{t-1}B^f_{t-1} - P(C_t + I_t + G_t)$. The expression $PY_t + R_{t-1}B^f_{t-1} - P(C_t + G_t)$ is national saving—that is, the part of GNP that is not spent on private consumption (C_t) or government purchases (G_t). It follows that the current-account balance is the difference between national saving and domestic investment—that is, if we denote national saving (in dollar terms) by S_t,

current-account balance

$$= PY_t + R_{t-1}B^f_{t-1} - P(C_t + I_t + G_t) = S_t - PI_t. \tag{15.5}$$

Thus a country runs a surplus on current account—and thereby lends funds abroad—when its national saving exceeds its domestic investment. Another way to think about equation 15.5 is that national saving, S_t, can be used either for domestic investment spending, PI_t, or for net foreign investment, which equals the current-account balance. (Recall from equation 15.2 that net foreign investment corresponds to saving in the form of additional claims on foreigners, $B_t^f - B_{t-1}^f$, or increments of international money, $H_t - H_{t-1}$.)

Figure 15.1 shows the ratio of the U.S. current-account balance to GNP from 1869 to 1987. Note that the current account was in deficit during the period from 1869 to 1896, except for 1894 and the years from 1876 to 1881. (The current account was also in deficit for most of the years from 1830 to 1868.) The deficit averaged 1.6% of GNP from 1869 to 1875 and 1.4% of GNP from 1886 to 1891.

The current account was in surplus for most years after 1896, averaging 0.8% of GNP from 1897 to 1914, 1.2% for the 1920s, and 0.5% for the 1930s. Because of World War I, the surplus on current account averaged 4.6% of GNP from 1915 to 1919. This surplus represented the substantial lending from the United States to

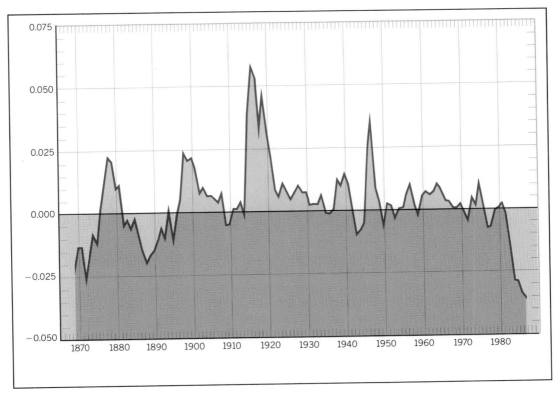

FIGURE 15.1 *U.S. Current-Account Balance, 1869–1988*
The figure shows the ratio to GNP of the current-account balance. The data are from U.S. Department of Commerce (1975, 1986) and U.S. Survey of Current Business, *various issues.*

its foreign allies. During World War II the account was in surplus in 1940–41 (averaging 1.3% of GNP) before the United States entered the war. After the United States entered, the account was in deficit from 1942 to 1945 (averaging −0.7% of GNP). For 1946–47, the current-account surplus averaged 3.1% of GNP.

From 1948 to 1976 the current account was typically in surplus but by an amount that averaged only 0.3% of GNP. Subsequently, there were deficits of 0.7% of GNP in 1977–78, followed by near balance in 1979–81, and a deficit of 0.3% of GNP in 1982. Then the current account shifted sharply toward deficit, reaching −1.4% of GNP in 1983 and averaging −3.2% of GNP from 1984 to 1987. For 1988, the value was −2.1%. We have to go back to the 1880s and 1870s to find U.S. current-account deficits that were comparable in relation to GNP. We shall consider later possible explanations for the recent surge in the U.S. current-account deficit.

THE ROLE OF THE INTERNATIONAL CREDIT MARKET

For an individual in a closed economy, the credit market allows for divergences between income and spending. For example, if a disturbance temporarily lowers someone's income, he or she can borrow—or spend out of accumulated assets—to avoid a temporary decline in consumption or investment. Similarly, an individual can save most of a windfall of income to spread it over extra consumption in many periods.

On the other hand, when a closed economy experiences an economy-wide disturbance—such as a temporary decline in everyone's production opportunities—it is impossible for everyone to borrow more. In this case, the real interest rate adjusts so that the aggregate of desired borrowing equals the aggregate of desired lending. Hence, in a closed economy, the credit market cannot cushion spending against an economy-wide disturbance, even if it is temporary. (It is possible, in the short run, for a closed economy to avoid a cutback in aggregate consumption by accepting a decline in aggregate investment.)

A single country functions in a world credit market much like an individual functions in the credit market of a closed economy. Assume that the home country initially has a zero balance on current account. Then suppose that a temporary supply shock, such as a harvest failure or a natural disaster, makes everyone in the home country desire to borrow more at the initial real interest rate. (The assumption here is that the disturbance has little effect on investment demand.) If the home country's economy is small, the world credit market can accommodate the increase in borrowing without significant changes in the world's real interest rate.

Now suppose that the supply shock applies to the entire world instead of just to the home country. Then the universal desire to borrow more cannot be satisfied. In these circumstances the real interest rate would rise on the international credit market to ensure that the world aggregate of desired borrowing equaled the world aggregate of desired lending.

Figure 15.2 illustrates the case of a temporary supply shock that applies only to the home country. The vertical axis plots the real interest rate, r_t, which prevails on the international credit market. For a small economy, which has access to the world credit market and exerts little effect on this market, it is appropriate to treat the real interest rate as a given. The downward-sloping solid curve in the figure shows the domestic residents' aggregate demand for goods, $Y_t^d = C_t^d + I_t^d + G_t$. As in our previous analysis of a closed economy, a lower real interest rate stimulates this demand.

The upward-sloping solid curve in the figure shows the domestic residents' aggregate supply of goods, $Y_t^s + R_{t-1}B_{t-1}/P$. Note that this concept corresponds to real GNP, which is the total of goods produced by domestic residents, including the real interest income from abroad. (We define supply in this way so that an equality between supply and demand for goods corresponds to a balance on the current account.) As in previous analyses, a higher real interest rate raises the quantity of goods supplied.

We draw the solid lines in the figure so that, at the given world real interest rate, the domestic residents' aggregate quantity of goods demanded, Y_t^d, is initially equal to the aggregate quantity supplied, $Y_t^s + R_{t-1}B_{t-1}/P$. Hence, real domestic expenditure on goods and services initially equals real GNP. It follows from equation 15.2 that the current account is in balance. Hence, if the home country's holding of international currency is constant ($H_t = H_{t-1}$), the capital account is initially in balance ($B_t^f = B_{t-1}^f$).

Now suppose that a temporary supply shock reduces the home country's supply of goods but has a negligible effect on demand. Then the new supply curve is the one shown by the dashed line in Figure 15.2. At the going world real interest rate,

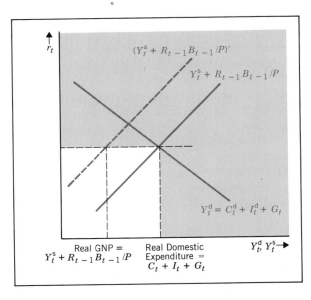

FIGURE 15.2 *Effect of a Temporary Supply Shock on a Small, Open Economy*
The supply shock lowers the domestic residents' aggregate supply of goods but has a negligible effect on demand. At the going world real interest rate, there is a fall in real GNP relative to real domestic expenditure. Consequently, the home country runs a current-account deficit, which corresponds to an inflow of capital from abroad.

r_t, the quantity of goods demanded by domestic residents now exceeds the quantity supplied. In the world economy this imbalance can be accommodated by the home country's borrowing from abroad. Then real domestic expenditure, $C_t + I_t + G_t$, equals the quantity of goods demanded, Y_t^d; real GNP equals the quantity of goods supplied, $Y_t^s + R_{t-1}B_{t-1}/P$; and the difference between the two is the real deficit on current account (see equation 15.2). If there is no change in the home country's holding of international currency, equation 15.2 says that the current-account deficit corresponds to a capital inflow from abroad—that is, to a negative value for the change in earning assets, $B_t^f - B_{t-1}^f$. Hence, a temporary supply shock induces the home country to borrow from abroad to avoid a cutback in current spending.

Notice that a worldwide supply shock would be different. In this case, the construction shown in Figure 15.2 applies to each country and therefore to the world aggregates of goods demanded and supplied. Consequently, the world real interest rate has to rise to clear the international credit market—that is, to equate the quantities of goods demanded and supplied in the world. Then the typical country ends up at the point where the new supply curve intersects the demand curve in Figure 15.2. At this point, there is a zero balance on the current account— that is, as must always be the case, the typical country does not borrow from abroad.[3] Notice that this treatment of a worldwide disturbance—including the determination of the world real interest rate—corresponds to the type of analysis that we carried out before for a closed economy.

International borrowing can also arise from shifts to the aggregate demand for goods. We represent this case in Figure 15.3 by shifting the demand curve rightward while keeping the supply curve in place. One example of this kind of shift would be an increase in domestic investment demand, resulting from an upward shift to the marginal product of capital, MPK.

As before, if the disturbance applies only to the home country, it is appropriate to hold fixed the world real interest rate, r_t. At this given value of r_t, Figure 15.3 shows no change in real GNP but an increase in real domestic expenditure. In this case, the home country borrows from abroad (runs a current-account deficit) to finance its higher level of investment. The ability to borrow from foreigners means that a small country with a favorable investment opportunity can pay for the investment boom without having to raise current production (real GNP) and without having to curtail current consumption or government purchases.

As with a supply shock, the results differ if the disturbance applies globally rather than just to the home country. For example, suppose that some technical innovation leads to an increase in investment demand for all countries. Then the construction shown in Figure 15.3 applies to the world aggregates of supply and demand. In this case the real interest rate, r_t, rises to ensure balance between the

---

[3]It is important to remember that the world as a whole, and hence the typical country, cannot run a current-account deficit. Despite this basic constraint on the world economy, it turns out that errors and omissions in the international accounts make it difficult to verify this condition with actual data. The reported numbers show a world current-account deficit of $76 billion in 1982 and $23 billion in 1986 (see World Bank, 1987, Table 2.2). These discrepancies are not fully understood but apparently relate to underreporting biases that affect exports more than imports. In addition, a few countries—such as Taiwan—are not included in the World Bank's concept of the world.

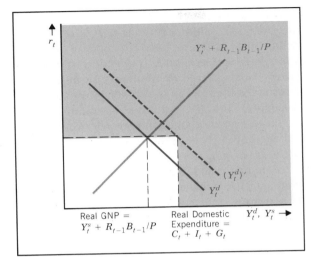

FIGURE 15.3 *Effect of a Shift in Demand on a Small, Open Economy*
The positive shock to demand leads to an excess of real domestic expenditure over real GNP. Hence the home country runs a current-account deficit.

world totals of real GNP and real expenditure on goods and services. For the world as a whole, it is not possible to finance an investment boom by borrowing from abroad. As in the case of a closed economy, the expansion of world investment must come from either an increase in production (the movement along the supply curve in Figure 15.3) or a decrease in the sum of consumption and government purchases.

EXAMPLES OF INTERNATIONAL BORROWING AND LENDING

We can identify various situations in which a country borrows heavily on the world credit market. Consider Poland from 1978 to 1981, when harvest failures and labor-force problems meant that output fell well below the anticipated average level of future output. An estimate of real product for Poland shows a decline of 14% from 1978 to 1981 (see Robert Summers and Alan Heston, 1988). Thus, the situation resembles that shown in Figure 15.2, where external borrowing avoids a sharp decline in current real spending. The gross foreign debt of Poland reached $25 billion in 1981, about half of the country's annual output of goods and services. (The centrally planned economies of Eastern Europe report a concept called "net material product," which is analogous to net national product.)

For a second situation where a country borrows heavily, consider Mexico. In this case, there was a major discovery of a natural resource, oil, which promised large amounts of income in future periods. By 1974, Mexico's oil prospects were great, but a significant volume of production had not yet appeared. In this situation, the increase in prospective income motivates an increase in consumption (and an expansion of marvelous government projects) before most of the oil revenue materializes. In addition, the oil discoveries motivated an increase in investment in oil-related industries. Thus, the case corresponds to an increase in the aggregate demand for goods, as shown in Figure 15.3. The conclusion is that Mexico would borrow from abroad to finance its increase in current expenditures. In fact, Mexico's gross external debt rose from $3.5 billion or 9% of GDP in 1971 to $61 billion or 26% of GDP in 1981.[4] Of course, this type of foreign borrowing runs into trouble when, as in 1982–86, the relative price of oil falls unexpectedly, so that Mexico's income turns out to be lower than predicted. (Whether the trouble applies mainly to Mexico or to Mexico's international creditors is another question.)

As another example, consider a developing country that has a high marginal product of capital. This type of country borrows abroad to finance large amounts of investment and thereby high growth rates of output. The potential to borrow abroad means that a developing country's level of consumption (plus government purchases) need not be depressed drastically during the period of high investment.

A recent example of this behavior is Brazil, which sustained an average growth rate of per capita real gross domestic product of about 5% per year from 1971 to 1980. Over this period, Brazil's gross external debt grew from $6 billion, or 11% of GDP, to $55 billion, or 22% of GDP.

For an earlier example of a rapidly developing country that borrowed heavily abroad, consider the United States. In 1890 the level of net foreign debt reached $2.9 billion, which amounted to 21% of GNP (see U.S. Department of Commerce, 1975, p. 869). Recall from Figure 15.1 that the United States was an international borrower for most years prior to 1890. Thus the situation of the United States in the late nineteenth century was roughly comparable to that for Brazil in the 1970s.

Recall that borrowing from abroad reflects a shortfall of national saving, S, from domestic investment, I. For Poland and Mexico, the borrowing reflected a drop in saving, which resulted from a decline in current income (Poland) or an increase in prospective income (Mexico). For Brazil and the nineteenth-century United States (and also for Mexico), the borrowing reflected the high value of investment demand.

By contrast, the countries that lend internationally are those with high desired saving—where current income is high relative to long-run income—or with relatively low investment demand. Included in the category of international lenders are the mature industrialized countries, such as the United States through 1983 and Switzerland. For example, the net international investment position of the United States (U.S. assets held abroad including international reserves less foreign assets held in the United States) was estimated to be $137 billion at the end of 1982 but then fell to −$264 billion at the end of 1986.[5] The reduction in this net asset position reflected the U.S. current-account deficits after 1982.

---

[4]The data on gross domestic product for Mexico and Brazil (mentioned below) are from *International Financial Statistics* (1982 Yearbook, April 1983). The data on external debt for Mexico and Brazil are from Organization of American States, *Statistical Bulletin of the OAS*, vol. 4, nos. 1–2 (January–June 1982): Table SA-5, p. 30; and Morgan Guaranty Trust, *World Financial Markets* (February 1983): Table 2, p. 5.

[5]See *Economic Report of the President* (1988, Table B-106). The estimates are very rough because of incomplete coverage and because the assets are typically carried at book value rather than market value. Although the figures show the United States with a negative net international investment position in 1986 and 1987, the net flow of investment income from abroad had roughly a zero balance in 1987. Thus, a more accurate measure of the U.S. net international investment position would probably be close to zero in 1987.

Another example of an important international creditor is Saudi Arabia, whose flow of oil income through 1981 was high relative to the long-term prospective flow. The estimate for the net international investment position of Saudi Arabia (including international reserves) was about $145 billion in 1982 but declined to about $99 billion in 1986 because of the drop in oil revenues (see Economist Intelligence Unit, 1987).

One important point is that—just as in the case of a credit market in a closed economy—the existence of an international credit market tends to be advantageous for both borrowers and lenders. Obviously this market enables borrowing countries to spend more than their current income, which is warranted in the cases mentioned above. But the potential to lend abroad also allows countries that have a relatively large amount of desired saving to achieve higher rates of return than would be available domestically. Therefore, although there have been significant recent troubles with foreign loans, we should not conclude that the existence of the international credit market is a bad idea overall.

Notice that throughout this analysis we assumed a "perfect" world credit market, where the real interest rate was the same for each country. However, as the residents of a country increase their borrowing—with the government of the country often doing the borrowing or guaranteeing the loans—there may be an increasing risk of default. When a government borrows abroad, we particularly have to consider that "sovereignty" makes it difficult for foreign creditors to enforce loans. (Governments are sovereign in that they are above any meaningful international law; in particular, it is difficult for a creditor to foreclose on government property.) The increasing default risk implies that the real interest rate paid by a country tends to rise as the amount borrowed increases.[6] Consequently, a country (or an individual) has difficulty in using the credit market to smooth out spending when there are major fluctuations in income.

When we take account of this effect, we find that the results are a composite of those that we found before for a closed economy with those discussed in this chapter for a perfect world credit market. For example, a temporary disturbance to a country's income shows up partly as a change in that country's real interest rate and level of real expenditure and partly in the amount of borrowing from abroad. International borrowing then buffers only a portion of the variations in a country's income.

FISCAL POLICY IN THE WORLD ECONOMY

GOVERNMENT PURCHASES

We considered in Figure 15.3 the effect on a small open economy from a shift in the demand for goods. We know from Chapter 12 that one important source of an

---

[6]For a discussion of these issues, see Jonathan Eaton, Mark Gersovitz, and Joseph Stiglitz (1986) and Jeremy Bulow and Ken Rogoff (1988).

increase in demand is a temporary expansion of government purchases, perhaps related to wartime. Because government purchases are high only temporarily, the present value of government purchases changes little. Therefore, the disturbance has only a small negative effect on wealth and, hence, only a minor impact on consumer demand. Given the small effect on consumer demand, the aggregate demand for goods rises on net relative to the supply, as shown in Figure 15.3. Consequently, the home country borrows from abroad to finance its temporary increase in government purchases. By borrowing, the country smooths out the reductions in private spending that are needed to pay for the extra government spending. A small part of the reduction occurs while the government's expenditure is temporarily high. The rest of the cutback arises in the future and corresponds to the payment of interest and principal on the accumulated foreign debt.

Suppose that the temporary government expenditures represent outlays during wartime. Then the international credit market allows the combatant countries to borrow from neutrals and thereby moderate the short-run changes in consumption, investment, and leisure. Examples of this borrowing were the large loans from the United States to its allies during World Wars I and II, especially before the United States entered the wars. Shaghil Ahmed (1987*b*) studied these kinds of effects in the context of the long-term British history of wartime spending and trade balances. (Recall that we examined the data on British military spending in Chapter 12.) In line with the theory, Ahmed found a positive effect of temporary government expenditures on the trade deficit, especially over the period from 1732 to 1830, which includes the major fluctuations in expenditures (see Figure 12.4).

The wartime context also demonstrates some further limitations on the use of the world credit market. The possibility of a country's wartime defeat raises the probability of default and thereby drives up the real interest rate paid on loans. Consequently, a combatant country would find it more difficult to pay for government expenditures without simultaneously cutting back on private spending or raising aggregate production.

It is also clear from wartime that the loan market is helpful only if combatants have noncombatants to borrow from. As in some examples that we considered before, a worldwide disturbance differs from a localized shock. In the case of a world war, there is no one abroad to borrow from. Then the worldwide incentive to borrow drives up real interest rates (if international loan markets remain open) but leaves the typical country with a zero balance on the current account. In Figure 15.3 this outcome corresponds to the intersection of the supply curve with the new demand curve at a higher value of r_t.

Recall from Chapter 12 that a permanent expansion of government purchases differs from a temporary increase. A permanent increase in purchases leads to a roughly one-to-one cutback in consumption demand and therefore has little effect on the aggregate demand for goods. It follows that permanent changes in government purchases do not lead to significant changes in the current-account balance. Countries tend to pay for permanent increases in the size of government by lowering private spending rather than by borrowing from foreigners.

The result seems reasonable if we think of borrowing from abroad as a way for a country to smooth out its adjustment to a temporary disturbance, such as a surge in government spending. The country pays for the spending partly through small reductions in current private spending but mostly through cutbacks in private spending at later times. This process makes sense if the increase in government spending is temporary but does not work if the increase is permanent. In the latter case the balanced adjustment to the disturbance is a one-to-one reduction of private spending at each date. Since current private spending falls by as much as current government spending rises, the country does not borrow from abroad. A country that borrows to finance a permanent expansion of government purchases would find itself in even greater stress later. That is, since the interest and principal on the debt must be repaid, private spending in future periods would have to decline by even more than the increase in government expenditures. (The assumption here is that the home country cannot continually surprise its foreign creditors by defaulting on its debts.)

TAX RATES

Recall that the current-account balance is the difference between national saving and domestic investment, $S - I$. Changes in tax rates matter for the current-account balance if they influence desired national saving relative to domestic investment demand.

Effects on investment demand arise if the government changes the tax rate on income from capital. For example, the Reagan tax cuts between 1981 and 1984 involved more favorable depreciation allowances and other changes that reduced the tax rate on income from capital. In Figure 13.5, these effects show up as a reduction in the ratio of corporate profits taxes to corporate profits from 0.41 in 1980 to an average of 0.31 from 1982 to 1986.[7] The predicted response is an expansion of investment demand and—given the behavior of national saving—a move toward deficit on the current account. In fact, the ratio of real business, nonresidential investment to real GNP rose from 0.117 in 1980 to 0.139 in 1984. Including residential investment, the increase was from 0.160 in 1980 to 0.188 in 1984.[8] At the same time, the ratio of net foreign investment to GNP went from 0.005 in 1980 to -0.024 in 1984. Thus, the movement toward deficit on the current account corresponds roughly to the increase in domestic investment. When viewed this way, the shift toward a current-account deficit is not necessarily a symptom of adverse events.

Permanent changes in marginal tax rates on labor income have little impact on desired national saving, S. Therefore, these types of tax changes have little effect on

[7]Some of the cuts in corporate taxes were undone by the legislation of 1986. For example, the investment-tax credit was eliminated, depreciation allowances were made less generous, and the tax rate on capital gains was increased. On the other hand, the federal tax rates on corporate taxable income were reduced. Note that the ratio of corporate profits taxes to corporate profits (Figure 13.5) rose from 0.31 in 1986 to 0.39 in 1987.

[8]Purchases of consumer durables—another form of investment—also boomed at this time. As a ratio to real GNP, these real purchases rose from 0.077 in 1980 to 0.092 in 1984.

the current-account balance. For example, a permanent cut in marginal tax rates stimulates labor supply but raises consumer demand by an amount similar to the increase in labor income. Therefore, desired saving changes little. It follows, for a given behavior of investment demand, that the current-account balance does not change.

As stressed in previous analyses, desired saving responds mainly to changes that affect the present relative to the future. For example, a temporary cut in the marginal tax rate on labor income would increase desired saving. That is, current labor supply and the supply of goods rise, but current consumption demand increases by only a small amount. Therefore, this kind of change in tax rates tends to create a surplus on the current account.

BUDGET DEFICITS

In Chapter 14 we spent a lot of time considering whether a deficit-financed cut in lump-sum taxes affects consumer demand. (For present purposes, think of lump-sum taxes, which do not affect the incentive to work today rather than tomorrow.) In the Ricardian view, as long as the present value of government purchases does not change, households do not feel wealthier if current taxes decline. Therefore, consumer demand does not change, and desired private saving rises one-to-one with the budget deficit. Equivalently the increase in private saving exactly offsets the decrease in public saving, so that desired national saving, S, does not change. With no change in national saving—and no effect on investment demand—it follows that the current-account balance, $S - I$, does not change.

To understand this result, recall that the Ricardian view implies that the households in the home country absorb all of the government's additional debt. Therefore the budget deficit does not induce residents of the home country to borrow more from foreigners, and the current-account balance does not change.

The standard view of budget deficits—which we also discussed in Chapter 14—starts with the assumption that a deficit-financed tax cut leads to an increase in consumer demand. That is, desired private saving rises by less than one-to-one with the budget deficit, so that desired national saving, S, declines. One rationale for the increase in consumption demand is that finite-lived individuals feel wealthier when the government uses its budget deficit to shift tax obligations toward future generations.

In a closed economy the boost to the aggregate demand for goods leads to an increase in the real interest rate and to a fall of domestic investment. But an open economy can borrow from foreigners to pay for its increased demand for goods. We can again use Figure 15.3 to assess the effects. At the given value of the world real interest rate, r_t, real domestic expenditure rises because of the increase in consumer demand. On the production side, real GNP does not change. The gap between expenditure and GNP is the current-account deficit. Thus, when applied to an open economy, the standard analysis predicts that a budget deficit leads to a current-account deficit.

Many economists (and even more journalists) attribute the large U.S. current-account deficits since 1983 to the effects of excessive budget deficits. (Recall that the current-account deficit averaged 3.2% of GNP from 1984 to 1987 and equaled 2.1% in 1988.) Despite this consensus of opinion, a careful look at the evidence does not provide much support for a linkage between budget and current-account deficits. One point is that, over the longer history, the main movements in U.S. budget and current-account deficits have been independent. For example, from 1948 to 1982, the ratio of the current-account deficit to GNP was uncorrelated with various measures of the budget deficit, also expressed as ratios to GNP. The U.S. data since World War II reveal a single incident—the period from 1983–88—when budget and current-account deficits were high at the same time.

Paul Evans (1988) carried out a careful statistical study of the relation between budget and current-account deficits in the post–World War II period in the United States, Canada, France, Germany, and the United Kingdom. His main conclusion was that the data were consistent with the Ricardian view that budget deficits did not cause current-account deficits. However, Evans's study leaves unexplained the recent surge in U.S. borrowing from abroad.

In an earlier discussion, we noted that a possible cause for the recent U.S. current-account deficits was the decline from 1981 to 1984 in marginal tax rates on the income from capital. This argument is attractive—although by no means a settled issue—because it explains not only the movement toward a current-account deficit since 1983 but also the boom over the same period in U.S. investment spending. From another perspective, the approach that stresses marginal tax rates does assign some weight to budget deficits. Budget deficits would matter if they were the necessary counterpart of the cuts in marginal tax rates on income from capital. Note, however, that the argument relies on an impact of tax-rate cuts on investment demand rather than a direct wealth effect on consumption.

THE TERMS OF TRADE

Up to now we have assumed that the home country and the rest of the world produced goods that were physically identical. Also, by neglecting transport costs, we assumed that all goods were **tradable** across countries. Continue to assume for now that all goods are tradable, but suppose that countries specialize in the production of goods. For example, Chile produces a substantial fraction of the world's copper, whereas Brazil produces a large share of the world's coffee. Under these circumstances countries are affected significantly when the prices of their principal products change relative to the prices of other goods.

To keep things simple, pretend that the home country produces a single good (or market basket of goods) that sells at the dollar price P, while the rest of the world produces another good (or market basket of goods) that sells at the price $\overline{P}$. Then we want to study changes in the ratio, $P/\overline{P}$. If the ratio increases, the home country's **terms of trade** improve. That is, for each unit of goods that a home country produces and sells abroad (exports), it can now purchase more units of foreign goods (imports).

We have to modify the condition for the current-account balance to allow for differences between domestic and foreign prices of goods. To simplify the analysis, without affecting the main results, pretend that the entire gross domestic product, Y_t^s, is sold at price P and exported, while all of domestic expenditure (on consumption, investment, and government purchases) is on goods produced abroad (imports) and bought at price $\bar{P}$. Then the current-account balance is

$$PY_t^s + R_{t-1}B_{t-1} - \bar{P} \cdot (C_t^d + I_t^d + G_t). \qquad (15.6)$$

The current-account balance is still the difference between national saving and domestic investment. But national saving is now given by $PY_t^s + R_{t-1}B_{t-1} - \bar{P}(C_t^d + G_t)$, which depends on the two prices P and $\bar{P}$. For the purposes of discussion, assume that the current account has a zero balance at the initial values of P and $\bar{P}$.

Consider an improvement in the terms of trade—say an increase in P for a given value of $\bar{P}$—that reflects a disturbance in the rest of the world. For example, Chile may face an increase in the relative price of copper, or Brazil may experience a rise in the relative price of coffee. But since the disturbance originates from the rest of the world, Chile's capacity to produce copper or Brazil's to produce coffee does not change. We also assume, as is likely for the case of changes in coffee and copper prices, that people view the shift in P as temporary.

Suppose that the home country did not change its supply of goods, Y_t^s, or its demand for goods $C_t^d + I_t^d + G_t$. Then equation 15.6 implies that the improvement in the terms of trade leads to a surplus on the current account. With an increase in P, the unchanged volume of real exports—corresponding here to total domestic production Y_t^s—leads to a rise of export revenues, PY_t^s. Since import expenditures, $\bar{P}(C_t^d + I_t^d + G_t)$, are unchanged, the current account moves into surplus. (This result still holds if not all production is exported and if some of the expenditures are on domestic goods at price P rather than on imports at price $\bar{P}$.)

The improvement in the terms of trade motivates some changes in goods supplied and demanded. Since the disturbance is temporary, wealth effects are minor. The main responses that we have to consider involve substitution effects. For the moment let's neglect any effects on investment demand, I_t^d.

In deciding on work effort and production, households (in their role as workers and producers) looked before at the marginal product of labor, MPL. The difference now is that producers sell all of their output at the domestic price, P, but buy goods for consumption at the foreign price, $\bar{P}$. (The nature of the results would not change if, as is more realistic, households buy some goods at price P and others at price $\bar{P}$.) An increase in $P/\bar{P}$ means that households obtain more in consumption (of foreign goods) for each unit of work and production. Therefore, just as in the case of an improvement in the schedule for labor's marginal product, the substitution effect from an increase in $P/\bar{P}$ motivates an expansion of work effort and a corresponding rise in the supply of domestic goods, Y_t^s. This expansion in the physical volume of production (and exports) reinforces the movement toward surplus in the current account.

An increase in $P/\bar{P}$ also motivates some increase in consumer demand. However, if the price change is temporary, this response is relatively small. That is because households would spread their temporarily high current income over more consumption in many periods. Therefore, we still have the prediction that a temporary improvement of the terms of trade leads to a surplus on the current account.

Suppose now that the improvement in the terms of trade is permanent. In this case there is a strong wealth effect, which motivates an increase in consumption demand. In fact, there would now be little change in the home country's desired national saving, $PY_t^s + R_{t-1}B_{t-1} - \overline{P}(C_t^d + G_t)$. Hence, for given expenditure on investment, $\overline{P}I_t^d$, the current-account balance does not change. In this situation, the expenditures on imports rise along with the receipts from exports. Thus a surplus on the current account accompanies a temporary improvement in the terms of trade but not a permanent improvement.

Consider now the effects on investment demand. Producers pay the price $\overline{P}$ for new capital goods (purchased as imports) but receive the price P for each unit of output. Given the schedule for the marginal product of capital, MPK, an increase in $P/\overline{P}$ makes investment more attractive. It follows that an improvement in the terms of trade stimulates investment demand.

The effect of an improvement in the terms of trade on investment demand depends on how long producers expect the improvement to last. If the change is temporary, producers will not find it worthwhile to make much alteration to their investment plans. Because of adjustment costs for changing the stock of capital, investment demand will respond mainly to long-lasting shifts in the terms of trade.[9] Thus, we predict that investment demand will react little to a temporary improvement in the terms of trade but will respond positively to a permanent improvement. Consider, as an example, an increase in the price of oil. Oil producers would invest in new capacity if they expected the higher oil price to persist. But little investment would take place if producers thought that the price change was transitory.

We can now modify the previous analysis to include the responses of investment. A temporary improvement in the terms of trade raises desired national saving but has little effect on investment demand. Therefore, as before, the current account moves toward surplus. A permanent improvement in the terms of trade has little effect on desired national saving but raises investment demand. Therefore we now predict that a permanent improvement of the terms of trade leads to a deficit on the current account. If we consider intermediate cases—where the improvement in the terms of trade lasts for awhile but not forever—desired national saving and investment demand would both increase. Therefore, the effect on the current-account balance would be ambiguous.[10]

As an empirical example of effects from changes in the terms of trade, consider the current-account balance for the Organization of Petroleum-Exporting Countries

[9]We mentioned the effects of adjustment costs on investment demand in Chapter 9. These costs were not crucial for the analysis in that chapter but are significant for distinguishing the responses of investment to temporary versus permanent changes in the terms of trade.

[10]For further analysis of effects from changes in the terms of trade, see Jeffrey Sachs (1981) and Jeremy Greenwood (1983).

TABLE 15.1 *Current-Account Balance of Oil-Exporting Countries (OPEC)*

Year	Current-Account Balance ($ Billion)
1972	1
1974	60
1976	37
1978	−3
1980	104
1982	−10
1984	−7
1986	−28

Source: OECD, *OECD Economic Outlook* (June 1988, July 1983, July 1979).

(OPEC). Table 15.1 shows that OPEC's current account was nearly balanced in 1972. Then the sharp increases in oil prices during 1973–74 led to a current-account surplus of $60 billion in 1974. From 1974 to 1978, the relative price of oil fell somewhat. But more important, the growing perception that the relative price of oil would remain high motivated the OPEC countries to adjust their expenditures to their higher long-run incomes. By 1978 the current account of OPEC was again nearly balanced but at much higher dollar levels of exports and imports. Then the surprise increases in oil prices in 1979–80 led again to a large surplus on the current account ($104 billion in 1980). In this case the upward adjustment of expenditures moved the current account to a small deficit by 1982. Then the sharp decline in the price of oil in 1986 led to a current-account deficit of $28 billion.

NONTRADED GOODS

Thus far we assumed that all goods were tradable across countries. But some items, such as services and real estate, are difficult to transport across national borders. Economists account for this phenomenon by including **nontraded goods** in the analysis.[11] Recall that the terms of trade refers to the price of tradables produced in the home country relative to the price of tradables produced in the rest of the world. Given the terms of trade, it is possible for the price of the home country's nontradables to change relative to the price of its tradables. In particular, since the nontradables do not enter into international commerce (by definition), the home

[11]There are problems in implementing this idea since considerations such as transport costs mean that tradability is a relative matter. Although some goods enter more easily than others into international trade, with enough incentive, almost anything—including the services of workers—becomes a tradable good.

country's relative price of nontradables and tradables tends to be more sensitive than the terms of trade to disturbances that originate at home. (In the extreme case of a closed economy, none of its goods enters into international trade and only the domestic disturbances matter.)

Consider how the presence of nontraded goods affects the analysis of a change in the terms of trade. The main consideration is that an improvement in the terms of trade raises the price of the home country's tradables relative to its nontradables. This change motivates the home country to shift production, employment, and investment away from the nontradables sector and toward the tradables sector. Hence, the existence of nontradables reinforces the positive effect of the terms of trade on the production of tradables. However, the expansion in the tradables sector may go along with a contraction of production and employment in the nontradables sector. Despite these new effects, it is important to note that the existence of nontradables does not affect our main predictions about the relation between the terms of trade and the current-account balance.

SUMMARY

We began by introducing international trade in goods and credit. These possibilities allow for the efficient specialization of production across countries and for an individual country's spending to diverge temporarily from its income.

The current-account balance equals national saving less domestic investment. A temporary supply shock in one country reduces desired saving and thereby leads to a deficit on the current account. Similarly, a surge in one country's investment demand generates a current-account deficit. If the shocks apply to the entire world, there is no one abroad to borrow from. Therefore, the world real interest rate adjusts to equate the world aggregates of saving and investment. In this situation the typical country does not (and cannot) run a deficit on the current account. We showed that this type of analysis could account for some observed behavior of international borrowers and lenders.

We used the framework to analyze various fiscal policies. A temporary increase in one country's government purchases, as in wartime, leads to a cutback in national saving and therefore to a current-account deficit. In contrast, a permanent change in a country's government purchases has little effect on national saving and the current-account balance. Even if temporary, an increase in government purchases does not cause a current-account deficit if the shift applies to all countries (as in a world war). The absence of potential lenders implies that the typical country maintains a zero balance on the current account.

A cut in the tax rate on capital income stimulates investment demand and thereby leads to a current-account deficit. This mechanism may explain some aspects of the recent U.S. experience. In contrast, permanent reductions in marginal tax rates on labor income have little influence on desired national saving and the current-account balance. If these shifts in tax rates were temporary, they would have some impact on desired saving and the current account.

Budget deficits affect the current-account balance if these deficits alter desired national saving. In the Ricardian case, budget deficits do not affect desired national saving and therefore do not influence the current account. In some other approaches, a budget deficit lowers desired national saving and thereby leads to a deficit on the current account.

A temporary improvement in the terms of trade raises desired national saving and has little effect on investment demand. Therefore, the current account moves toward surplus. In contrast, a permanent improvement in the terms of trade stimulates investment demand and has little effect on desired national saving. Therefore, the current account moves toward a deficit. Some evidence of the predicted linkages between the terms of trade and the current-account balance comes from the recent experience of the OPEC countries.

IMPORTANT TERMS AND CONCEPTS

common currency
law of one price
international currency
direct investment abroad
net factor income from abroad
net foreign investment
balance on capital account

outflow (inflow) of capital
current-account balance
surplus (deficit) on current account
tradable goods
terms of trade
nontraded goods

QUESTIONS AND PROBLEMS

15.1   Equation 15.2 states that the current account balance is identically equal to net foreign investment. If GNP or domestic expenditure changes, why is there a change in net foreign investment rather than a change in the real interest rate? What is the accompanying change in net exports?

15.2   Explain why an improvement in the terms of trade need not be associated with an increase in net exports.

15.3   Why is it infeasible for all countries to run a current-account deficit at the same time?

15.4   If a country runs a budget deficit must it also run a current-account deficit? How does the linkage between the two deficits depend on the relation between budget deficits and national saving?

PROBLEMS FOR DISCUSSION

15.5 *Wealth Effects from Changes in the Real Interest Rate*

Consider the wealth effects from a change in the world real interest rate.

a. What is the effect for a single country?
b. What is the aggregate effect for the world?
c. How do these results compare with our earlier findings for a closed economy?

15.6 *Supply Shocks for a Single Country*

Consider a supply shock that adversely affects the home country's production of tradable goods. Assume that the shock is temporary and that no significant change occurs in the terms of trade.

a. If the country can borrow from abroad at the world real interest rate, what happens to the home country's consumption and current-account balance?
b. How do the results differ if the home country cannot borrow from abroad?
c. Assume now that the domestic industries are owned primarily by foreigners. (In other words, domestic residents had diversified their ownership of assets internationally so as not to be too susceptible to local supply shocks.) How does this change affect the answers?

15.7 *Effects of Tax Changes on the Current-Account Balance*

Discuss the effects on a country's current-account balance from the following changes in tax rates.

a. A permanent increase in the marginal tax rate on labor income.
b. A temporary increase in the marginal tax rate on labor income.
c. A permanent increase in the tax rate on consumption (say a general sales tax on consumables).
d. A temporary increase in the tax rate on consumption.
e. A permanent cut in the tax rate on income from capital.
f. A temporary cut in the tax rate on income from capital.

15.8 *A Change in the Terms of Trade*

In the text we considered a change in the terms of trade that reflected a disturbance from the rest of the world. Suppose instead that a supply shock at home leads to an increase in the relative price of the home country's tradable goods. For example, a harvest failure in Brazil would raise the relative price of coffee. What are the effects from this type of disturbance on the home country's:

a. wealth and consumption of various goods, and
b. current-account balance?

 (*Hint:* Did you assume that the disturbance was temporary or permanent?)

15.9 *Tariffs (optional)*

Suppose that a small country levies a tariff on imports of a tradable good from abroad. If the good sells at price $\bar{P}$ abroad and if the rate of tariff is 10%, domestic residents pay $1.1 \cdot P$ for each unit of the good. Assuming that the tariff is permanent, what are its effects on the home country's:

a. consumption of the various tradable and nontradable goods,
b. production of tradables and nontradables, and
c. balance on current account?

(*Hint:* What did you assume happened to the revenue collected from the tariff?) Redo the analysis for the case where the tariff is temporary.

CHAPTER 16

EXCHANGE RATES

n the previous chapter we discussed international markets for goods and credit but said nothing about exchange rates. We could not discuss exchange rates because we assumed that all countries used a common currency, such as the U.S. dollar, and that all prices were quoted in units of this currency. To analyze exchange rates, we have to introduce different types of currency (dollars, yen, marks, etc.), and allow for prices to be quoted in these different currency units. This chapter makes the necessary extensions to consider these matters.

It is important to note that, even without discussing exchange rates, the previous chapter brought out various factors that influenced the current-account balance, including variations in the terms of trade. The extensions to include exchange rates do not invalidate any of these results. We shall find that some of the forces that affect the current-account balance lead also to movements in exchange rates. But the underlying shocks that cause countries to borrow or lend internationally will be the same as those that we studied before.

INTERNATIONAL FLOWS OF MONEY

Suppose, as in the previous chapter, that the world's supply of international currency is fixed at the amount $\bar{H}$. We still assume that this currency is denominated in some nominal unit, such as the U.S. dollar, and that the nominal interest rate on international currency is zero.

Before we introduce different currencies for each country, let's consider how the world price level is determined in the common-currency model from Chapter 15. In this model each country expresses its price level, P, in the same units, say, as U.S. dollars per unit of goods. Since goods sell for the same price in each country, the price level of every country and, hence, the world price level, is also equal to P. To determine this price level, start by considering the demand for international currency by central banks.

Recall that the domestic central bank holds the real quantity, H_t/P, of international currency to facilitate transactions between domestic residents (including the home government) and foreigners. The demand for money by the central bank is analogous to the demand for real money balances by households.[1] In particular, a greater amount of real transactions with foreigners increases the real demand for international currency, whereas a higher nominal interest rate, R_t, reduces this demand.

We also found before that the change in a country's holdings of international currency, $H_t - H_{t-1}$, is one component of the current-account balance in equation 15.2. For a given price level, P, anything that increases a country's real demand for international currency—such as a rise in that country's real income—shows up as a positive value for $H_t - H_{t-1}$. A country can finance this increase in international currency either by running a current-account surplus—that is, exporting more than it imports—or by borrowing from abroad.

In each period, the world's aggregate demand for international currency must equal the given supply, $\overline{H}$. This situation is analogous to the one that we worked out previously for a closed economy, where the nominal quantity of money, M, was a given number. In that situation the domestic price level adjusted so that the real quantity of money, M/P, equalled the real amount demanded. The same idea applies to the world economy; that is, the world price level, P, adjusts so that the real value of international currency, $\overline{H}/P$, equals the real quantity demanded. It follows that the world price level depends positively on the world's money supply, $\overline{H}$, and negatively on the world's real demand for money. These results parallel those from our previous study of a closed economy.

DIFFERENT MONIES AND EXCHANGE RATES

In the real world, each country issues and uses currency in its own unit—whether dollars, pounds, yen, or whatever—instead of using a common currency. To allow

---

[1]Many researchers have studied the demand for **international reserves** by central banks. These reserves include the currency that our model considers but consist largely of interest-bearing assets, such as U.S. Treasury bills. In practice, there is considerable ambiguity about which assets to include as part of a country's international reserves and which to exclude. For a survey of the demand for international reserves, see Stanley Black (1985). Two interesting studies of the demand for international reserves are by Nasser Saidi (1981) and Sebastian Edwards (1985).

for this fact, let M^i be the quantity of domestic currency for country i. We measure this money in domestic currency units, such as Japanese yen. A typical setup is that the central bank of country i holds international currency, H^i, and then issues the domestic currency, M^i. Thus we would have the simplified balance sheet for a central bank as shown in Table 16.1. The central bank's assets include international currency, H^i, foreign interest-bearing assets, and domestic interest-bearing assets, which include bonds issued by the home government. The holdings of domestic earning assets are called the central bank's **domestic credit.** The central bank's liabilities consist of domestic currency, M^i. (In practice, the liabilities also include deposits of financial institutions held at the central bank. We discuss these deposits in Chapter 17.)

The domestic price level in country i, P^i, now expresses the number of local currency units, say yen, that exchange for a unit of goods. To start, think again of a case where the goods produced in all countries are physically identical. Then the same product sells for P^i units of one currency (yen) in country i and for P^j units of another currency (say, German marks) in country j.

We now must introduce a new market, called an *exchange market,* on which people trade the currency of one country for that of another. For example, traders might exchange Japanese yen for U.S. dollars or for German marks. The exchange market establishes exchange rates among the various currencies. For convenience, we express all exchange rates in terms of the number of units of domestic currency that trade for $1.00 (U.S.). For example, on March 13, 1989, 130 Japanese yen exchanged for $1.00, so that each yen was worth about 0.8 cent. Similarly, 1.87 German marks exchanged for $1.00, so that a German mark was worth about 53 cents.

The exchange rates for Japanese yen and German marks in terms of U.S. dollars determine the exchange rate between yen and marks. That is, 130 Japanese yen could buy $1.00, which could then be converted into 1.87 German marks. Hence, $130/1.87 = 70$ Japanese yen could buy one German mark. Thus, the exchange rate between yen and marks was 70 yen per mark. (In practice, traders can make these exchanges directly rather than going through U.S. dollars.)

Let ε^i (the Greek letter epsilon) be the exchange rate for country i. In other words, ε^i units of country i's currency (say, yen) exchange for $1.00. Alternatively, we see that the dollar value of one unit of country i's currency (1 yen) is $1/\varepsilon^i$. Notice that a *higher* value of the exchange rate, ε^i, means that country i's currency is *less* valuable in terms of dollars because it takes more of country i's currency to buy $1.00.

For any two countries, i and j, we observe the exchange rates, ε^i and ε^j. These rates prescribe the number of units of each currency that trade for $1.00. Hence,

TABLE 16.1 *Simplified Balance Sheet of a Central Bank*

Assets	Liabilities
International currency, H^i	Domestic currency, M^i
Foreign interest-bearing assets	
Domestic interest-bearing assets (domestic credit)	

ε^i units of currency i (say, 130 Japanese yen) can buy ε^j units of currency j (say, 1.87 German marks). Therefore, the exchange rate between currencies i and j—that is, the number of units of currency i needed to buy one unit of currency j—equals $\varepsilon^i/\varepsilon^j$ (130/1.87 = 70 yen per mark). Alternatively, for one unit of currency i, people can get $\varepsilon^j/\varepsilon^i$ units of currency j.

Figures 16.1 and 16.2 show the exchange rates between six major currencies (those for France, Germany, Italy, Canada, Japan, and the United Kingdom) and the U.S. dollar from 1950 to 1987. The figures show the proportionate deviation of the exchange rate for each year from the value that prevailed for the particular country in 1950. For example, in 1950, 1.09 Canadian dollars exchanged for $1.00 (U.S.). In 1987, it took 1.33 Canadian dollars to buy $1.00 (U.S.)—that is, as shown in Figure 16.2, the Canadian dollar exchange rate rose by about 20% from 1950 to 1987. (Remember that the rise in the exchange rate means that the Canadian dollar became less valuable relative to the U.S. dollar.)

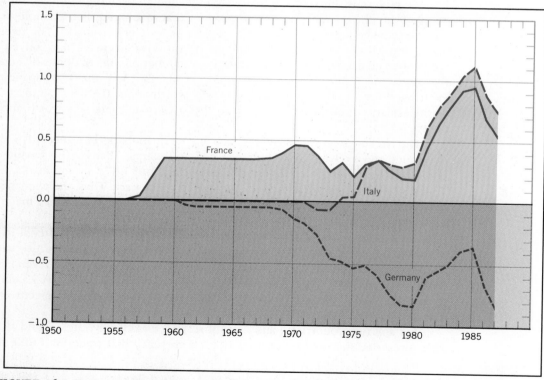

FIGURE 16.1 *Exchange Rates for France, Germany, and Italy*
We show the proportionate (logarithmic) deviation of the exchange rate from the value that prevailed for each country in 1950. The exchange rates for 1950 were: France, 3.5 francs per dollar; Germany, 4.2 marks per dollar; Italy, 625 lira per dollar. Data for Figures 16.1–16.6 are from International Monetary Fund, International Financial Statistics, Yearbook, *various years.*

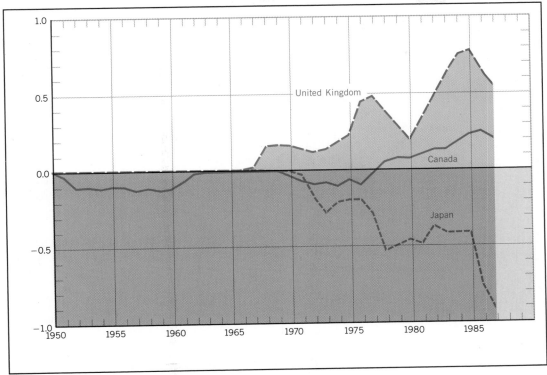

FIGURE 16.2 *Exchange Rates for Canada, Japan, and the United Kingdom*
See the note to Figure 16.1. The exchange rates for 1950 were: Canada, $1.09 (Ca.) per dollar (U.S.); Japan, 361 yen per dollar; United Kingdom, .357 pounds per dollar.

PURCHASING-POWER PARITY

We are now ready to derive the central theoretical proposition of international finance. This result connects the exchange rate between two currencies to the price levels that prevail in the two countries.

Suppose again that we can think of all goods as tradable and physically identical. Then a resident of country i can choose between, first, using local currency to buy goods domestically at the price P^i, or, second, exchanging money into the currency of country j to buy goods at the price P^j. For each unit of currency i, a person gets $1/P^i$ units of goods domestically. In the exchange market, he or she gets $\varepsilon^j/\varepsilon^i$ units of currency j for each unit of currency i. Then, buying at the price P^j, the person gets $(\varepsilon^j/\varepsilon^i) \cdot (1/P^j)$ units of goods. But for things to make sense, the two options *must* result in the same amount of goods. Otherwise everyone would want to buy goods in the cheap country and sell goods in the expensive country. This idea is a version of the law of one price, which we used before. Thus we must have that

$1/P^i = (\varepsilon^j/\varepsilon^i) \cdot (1/P^j)$, or, after rearranging terms,

$$\frac{\varepsilon^j}{\varepsilon^i} = \frac{P^j}{P^i}. \tag{16.1}$$

Equation 16.1 says that the ratio of the exchange rates for any two currencies, $\varepsilon^j/\varepsilon^i$, equals the ratio of the prices of goods in the two countries, P^j/P^i. This condition is called **purchasing-power parity (PPP).** It ensures that the purchasing power in terms of goods for each currency is the same regardless of where someone uses the currency to buy goods.

Define the rate of change of country i's exchange rate to be $\Delta\varepsilon^i$—that is, $\varepsilon^i_{t+1} = (1 + \Delta\varepsilon^i)\varepsilon^i_t$. Note that a positive value for $\Delta\varepsilon^i$ means that country i's currency becomes *less* valuable over time in terms of dollars; that is, it takes more of country i's currency to buy one dollar. Alternatively we can say that country i's currency *depreciates* in value relative to the dollar. Conversely, if $\Delta\varepsilon^i$ is negative, country i's currency *appreciates* over time relative to the dollar.

The PPP condition implies that the rates of change of any two exchange rates, $\Delta\varepsilon^j$ and $\Delta\varepsilon^i$, are related to the inflation rates in the two countries. Specifically, equation 16.1 implies

$$\Delta\varepsilon^j - \Delta\varepsilon^i \simeq \pi^j - \pi^i, \tag{16.2}$$

where π^j and π^i are the respective inflation rates. Equation 16.2 says that the higher a country's inflation rate, π^j, the higher the rate of depreciation of that country's currency, $\Delta\varepsilon^j$. This equation is called the **relative form of PPP,** whereas equation 16.1 is called the **absolute form of PPP** (in the sense of involving levels of prices and exchange rates rather than changes).

Equations 16.1 and 16.2 apply when the prices, P^i and P^j, refer to the same tradable goods. But since we are often interested in the general levels of prices in different countries, let us try to think of P^i and P^j as the prices of market baskets of goods produced or consumed in countries i and j, respectively. (In practice, we might measure these prices by the deflators for the GDP or by consumer or wholesale price indexes.) When we think of prices in this way, the PPP conditions need not hold exactly. One reason is that countries specialize in the production of different tradable goods, whose relative prices can change. Another reason is that countries produce and consume nontradable goods and services. Since nontradables cannot move from one country to another, the purchasing power of a currency in terms of nontradables may depend on where one buys them. For instance, the dollar cost of a hotel room in London may differ substantially from that in Pittsburgh. These considerations mean that equation 16.1 need not hold if P^i and P^j include prices of nontradables.

Suppose, as an example, that country j's terms of trade improve. That is, the prices of tradables produced in country j rise relative to the prices of tradables produced elsewhere. If P^i and P^j refer to market baskets of produced goods, P^j/P^i must rise for a given ratio of the exchange rates, $\varepsilon^j/\varepsilon^i$, because, by assumption, the goods produced in country j have become more expensive relative to those produced in country i. The general point is that various real disturbances can shift the

PPP condition in equation 16.1. Aside from changes in the terms of trade, some other factors that can affect this condition are changes in trade restrictions or transport costs, some aspects of tax policies, and various disturbances that shift the relative prices of traded and nontraded goods.

INTEREST-RATE PARITY

Suppose that there is a market-determined nominal interest rate in each country. The nominal rate in country i, R^i, will be expressed in units of its own currency—for example, as yen paid per year per yen lent out today. Think about this interest rate from the standpoint of U.S. dollars. At date t, a person can exchange \$1 (U.S.) for ε_t^i units of country i's currency (say Japanese yen). By lending at the interest rate R^i, the person receives $\varepsilon_t^i(1 + R^i)$ units of country i's currency (yen) at date $t + 1$. If he or she converts back to dollars using period $t + 1$'s exchange rate, ε_{t+1}^i, the amount of dollars obtained is

$$\frac{\varepsilon_t^i(1 + R^i)}{\varepsilon_{t+1}^i} = \frac{(1 + R^i)}{(1 + \Delta\varepsilon^i)},$$

where $\Delta\varepsilon^i$ is the rate of change of country i's (Japan's) exchange rate with the U.S. dollar. If the exchange rate rises at a faster rate over time, the dollar value of next period's holdings falls for a given value of country i's nominal interest rate R^i.

If there are no restrictions on the flows of assets across national borders (that is, no *capital controls*), people can hold assets in any country. If a person chooses country i, the dollar value of his or her holdings next period is $(1 + R^i)/(1 + \Delta\varepsilon^i)$. But if this amount is not the same for all countries, everyone would want to lend where the amount was largest and borrow where it was smallest. Thus, as another implication of the law of one price—applied here to the returns on assets—the amounts must be the same for all countries,

$$\frac{(1 + R^j)}{(1 + \Delta\varepsilon^j)} = \frac{(1 + R^i)}{(1 + \Delta\varepsilon^i)}.$$

We can use this result to derive a condition that is called **interest-rate parity**—namely,[2]

$$R^j - R^i \simeq \Delta\varepsilon^j - \Delta\varepsilon^i. \qquad (16.3)$$

The higher the rate of change of a country's exchange rate, $\Delta\varepsilon^j$—that is, the faster the depreciation in value relative to the U.S. dollar—the higher must be that country's nominal interest rate, R^j.

In practice, the changes in the exchange rates would not be known in advance. Then, as a first-order approximation, we would replace the variables $\Delta\varepsilon^j$ and $\Delta\varepsilon^i$ by

---

[2]Multiply through by the term $(1 + \Delta\varepsilon^i) \cdot (1 + \Delta\varepsilon^j)$. Then we get the interest-rate parity condition in equation 16.3 if we neglect the terms $R^i \cdot \Delta\varepsilon^j$ and $R^j \cdot \Delta\varepsilon^i$. As the length of the period diminishes, the approximation becomes more accurate.

their expectations.[3] With this modification, equation 16.3 says that a higher expected rate of change of the exchange rate, $(\Delta\varepsilon^j)^e$, implies a correspondingly higher nominal interest rate, R^j.

There are a number of real-world considerations that prevent interest-rate parity from holding exactly. These include varying tax treatments of interest income across countries, effects from uncertainties about asset returns and exchange-rate movements, and government restrictions on international borrowing and lending. For the industrialized countries, the departures from interest-rate parity tend to be small.

If purchasing power parity holds in relative form, equation 16.2 implies that the difference in the growth rates of the exchange rates, $\Delta\varepsilon^j - \Delta\varepsilon^i$, equals the difference in the inflation rates, $\pi^j - \pi^i$. Then the interest-rate parity condition from equation 16.3 implies that real interest rates are the same in all countries. More precisely, if we allow for uncertainty about changes in exchange rates and price levels, the equality applies to expected real interest rates.

Recall that the PPP conditions need not hold when the price levels, P^i and P^j, refer to market baskets of goods produced or consumed in the two countries. If relative PPP from equation 16.2 does not hold, expected real interest rates can differ across countries. There is some evidence of systematic differences across countries in expected real interest rates (as discussed by Robert Cumby and Maurice Obstfeld, 1984). For the industrialized countries, however, these differences tend to be small.

FIXED EXCHANGE RATES

Until the early 1970s and except during major wars, most countries typically maintained **fixed exchange rates** among their currencies. Figures 16.1 and 16.2 show that, from 1950 to the early 1970s, the exchange rates between six major currencies and the U.S. dollar moved infrequently and by small amounts compared to what came later. For the countries considered, the main exceptions to fixed exchange rates in this period were the fluctuations in the Canadian dollar rate until the early 1960s and some step adjustments in the rates for the French franc, German mark, and British pound.

We explored a simple but unrealistic system of fixed exchange rates in the previous chapter. In that setting all countries used a common currency, so the fixity of exchange rates held trivially. The fixed-rate regime that actually applied to the major industrialized countries from World War II until the early 1970s is called the

---

[3]This result is an approximation because holders of assets would worry also about the degree of uncertainty attached to changes in exchange rates. For the major currencies, individuals can protect themselves, or *hedge,* against this uncertainty. Suppose, for example, that a U.S. resident holds a one-period bond denominated in German marks. Assume that the holder wants to know the dollar value of this asset one period from now. There is uncertainty about this value because no one knows today the next period's exchange rate between marks and dollars. A trader can eliminate this risk with a one-period *futures contract* on the German mark. The appropriate contract in this case (corresponding to going *short* on the mark) is one that guarantees the holder the price at which he or she will be able to sell marks for dollars next period.

Bretton Woods System.[4] Under this system, the participating countries established narrow bands within which they pegged the exchange rate, ε^i, between their currency and the U.S. dollar. Country i's central bank stood ready to buy or sell its currency at the rate of ε^i units per dollar. For example, the German central bank (Bundesbank) provided dollars for marks when people wanted to reduce their holdings of marks, and vice-versa when people wished to increase their holdings of marks. To manage these exchanges, each central bank maintained a stock of assets in the form of U.S. currency or, more likely, in interest-bearing assets such as U.S. Treasury bills that could be readily converted into U.S. currency. Then the United States stood ready to exchange dollars for gold (on the request of foreign official institutions) at a fixed price, which happened to be $35 per ounce. Thus, by maintaining a fixed exchange rate with the U.S. dollar, each country indirectly pegged its currency to gold. (This setup is sometimes called a *gold-exchange standard.*)

Another example of a system of fixed exchange rates is the classical **gold standard.** Britain was effectively on the gold standard from the early eighteenth century until World War I, except for a period of suspension because of the Napoleonic wars from 1797 to 1821. Britain returned to the gold standard in 1926 but departed from the system during the Great Depression in 1931. The United States was on the gold standard from 1879 until the trough of the Great Depression in 1933, when the dollar price of gold was increased from $20.67 to $35.00 per ounce. Earlier periods in the United States involved a greater role for silver in the context of a *bimetallic standard.* From an international perspective, the gold standard reached its high point from 1890 to 1914.

Under a gold standard, each country pegs its currency directly to gold instead of to a central currency, such as the U.S. dollar. For example, an ounce of gold might be set at $20 in New York and at £4 in London (roughly the values prevailing in 1914). Then the exchange rate between U.S. dollars and British pounds would have to be close to $5 per pound. Otherwise (subject to the costs of shipping gold), it would be profitable for people to buy gold in one country and sell it in the other. As with the Bretton Woods System, the classical gold standard would—if adhered to by the participants—maintain fixed exchange rates among the various currencies.

It is possible for countries to maintain fixed exchange rates in a regime that has no role for gold or some other commodity. For example, since 1979, eight European countries in the **European Monetary System (EMS)** have kept the exchange rates among their currencies fixed within fairly narrow ranges. The countries in this system are Belgium (including Luxembourg, which lacks its own currency), Denmark, France, Germany, Ireland, Italy, and the Netherlands. Notice from Figure 16.1 for the period from 1979 to 1987 that the U.S. dollar exchange rates for France, Germany, and Italy varied but by similar proportionate amounts. Therefore, the exchange rates among these three currencies changed relatively little. Instead of using gold or U.S. dollars, the European Monetary System uses as an international currency unit the *European currency unit (ECU)*, which is a basket containing specified amounts of various European currencies.

---

[4]The system is named in honor of the meeting site, Bretton Woods, New Hampshire, where the regime was set up. For the details of this system, see James Ingram (1983, Chap. 9).

To see the workings of a system with fixed exchange rates, start by letting P represent the dollar price of goods in the United States. Then, if the absolute PPP condition from equation 16.1 holds, country i's price level is

$$P^i = \varepsilon^i \cdot P. \qquad (16.4)$$

(Note in equation 16.1 that the U.S. dollar exchange rate with itself is unity.) If country i's exchange rate with the U.S. dollar, ε^i, is fixed, the price level in country i, P^i, must maintain a constant ratio to the U.S. price level, P.

We can genealize the result by introducing deviations from absolute purchasing-power parity. As mentioned before, the reasons for these deviations include shifts in the terms of trade and a variety of other real disturbances. But we would retain the basic result—namely, a country cannot choose independently its exchange rate, ε^i, and its general price level, P^i. Given the variety of real factors mentioned above, a fixed exchange rate means that a country's price level must maintain a given relation to the U.S. price level.

If the U.S. price level, P, changes, equation 16.4 says that country i's price level, P^i, changes in the same proportion. In other words, any country that maintains a fixed exchange rate with the U.S. dollar experiences roughly the same inflation rate, π^i, as the U.S. rate, π.

Given fixed exchange rates, the interest-rate-parity condition from equation 16.3 implies that country's i's nominal interest rate, R^i, equals the U.S. rate, R. Thus, under fixed exchange rates, there is a single nominal interest rate in the world. (Again, differences in taxes and in riskiness of returns mean that this result does not hold exactly.)

THE QUANTITY OF MONEY UNDER FIXED EXCHANGE RATES

Before, when considering a closed economy, we stressed the relation between a country's quantity of money, M^i, and its price level, P^i. Yet we have determined a country's price level in equation 16.4 without saying anything about that country's quantity of domestic currency. Let us now investigate the relation between domestic money and prices in an open economy under fixed exchange rates.

It is still the case that the residents of country i demand a quantity of real money, M^i/P^i, which depends on variables like domestic output, Y^i, and the world nominal interest rate, R. (We assume here that the residents of country i use and hold their own currency rather than that of other countries.) The condition that all domestic money in country i be willingly held is

$$M^i = P^i \cdot L(Y^i, \quad R, \cdots).$$
$$(+)(-) \qquad (16.5)$$

If absolute purchasing-power parity holds, we can substitute in equation 16.5 for the domestic price level as $P^i = \varepsilon^i \cdot P$ from equation 16.4. Then we get the condition for the domestic quantity of money,

$$M^i = \varepsilon^i \cdot P \cdot L(Y^i, R, \cdots). \qquad (16.6)$$

Given the exchange rate, ε^i, the U.S. price level, P, and the determinants of the real demand for money in country $i, L(\cdot)$, equation 16.6 determines the nominal quantity of money, M^i, that must be present in country i. Hence, the quantity of domestic money *cannot* be regarded as a free element of choice by country i's central bank. If the central bank pegs the exchange rate at the value ε^i, there is a specific quantity of money, M^i, that is consistent with this exchange rate.

To understand these findings, assume that the domestic price level, P^i, accords initially with absolute purchasing-power parity, as specified in equation 16.4 and that the quantity of domestic money, M^i, is the amount prescribed by equation 16.6. Then the quantity of money equals the amount demanded.

Now suppose that the monetary authority increases the quantity of domestic money, M^i, say, by an open-market purchase of government securities. In Table 16.2 we illustrate this case in step 1 by assuming that the domestic currency and the central bank's holdings of interest-bearing domestic assets each rise by $1 million.

Our previous analysis of a closed economy suggests that the increase in the quantity of domestic currency would raise the domestic price level, P^i. But then the price level in country i would exceed the value dictated by purchasing-power parity in equation 16.4. Hence, for a given exchange rate, goods bought in country i would become more expensive relative to goods bought elsewhere. In response, households and firms would move away from buying goods in country i and toward buying goods in other countries (or toward goods imported from other countries). This reaction tends to keep the domestic price level P^i from rising; that is, the domestic price level stays in line with the prices prevailing in the rest of the world. But at this price level, domestic residents would be unwilling to hold the additional $1 million of domestic money, M^i. Accordingly, people would return their excess domestic currency to the central bank to obtain U.S. dollars or other currencies. (Since the central bank pegs the exchange rate, ε^i, it stands willing to make these exchanges at a fixed conversion ratio.) Thus, in step 2 of Table 16.2, we show that the quantity of domestic currency and the central bank's holdings of international currency each decline by $1 million.

Instead of reducing its holdings of international currency, the central bank could sell off other assets to get the international currency that people were de-

TABLE 16.2 *Effects of Open-Market Operations on the Central Bank's Balance Sheet*

	Assets	Liabilities
Step 1	Domestic interest-bearing assets: + $1 million	Domestic currency, M^i: + $1 million
Step 2	Assets International currency: − $1 million	Liabilities Domestic currency, M^i: − $1 million

Note: In step 1 the open-market purchase raises domestic currency by $1 million. But in step 2, the loss of international currency means that domestic currency declines by $1 million.

manding. Therefore, the more general point is that the return of domestic currency to the central bank causes the bank to lose some type of asset.

To complete the story, we must assess the central bank's reaction to its loss of international currency or other assets. As one possibility, the bank allows the domestic quantity of money, M^i, to decline. Then, as people return money to the bank, the domestic quantity of money falls back toward the level that is consistent with purchasing-power parity in equation 16.6. This automatic response of domestic money is a central element of the gold standard or other systems of fixed exchange rates.

On the other hand, when the automatic mechanism tends to reduce the quantity of domestic money, M^i, the central bank might offset this tendency, for example, by further open-market purchases of securities. When the bank acts this way, economists say that it attempts to **sterilize** the flow of international currency. By sterilization, economists mean that the central bank tries to insulate the quantity of domestic money, M^i, from changes in the bank's holdings of international currency or other assets. Eventually this type of policy can lead to a sufficient drain on assets so that the central bank becomes unwilling or unable to maintain the exchange rate. That is, the central bank may no longer provide dollars at the fixed rate of ε^i units of domestic currency per dollar. Instead, there may be a **devaluation,** which means that the exchange rate rises above ε^i units of domestic currency per dollar. Thus the tendency of central banks to sterilize the flows of international currency threatens the viability of fixed exchange rates.[5] (We shall discuss these matters further in a later section.)

We should mention another possible reaction of government policy to the loss of central bank assets. Recall that this drain results in the present case from the central bank's excessive monetary creation, which tends to make domestic goods more expensive relative to foreign goods. To counter this tendency, the home government might impose trade restrictions, which artificially raise the cost of foreign goods for domestic residents. Alternatively, the government might subsidize exports to make these goods cheaper for foreigners. The main point is that the government can interfere with free trade across national borders to prevent purchasing-power parity from holding. Thus there are two types of potential ill effects from excessive monetary expansion under fixed exchange rates. One is the loss of international currency, which leads eventually to devaluation. To avoid either this outcome or domestic monetary contraction, governments may interfere with free trade. In fact, the frequency of these interferences during the post–World War II period was a major argument used by opponents of fixed exchange rates (see Milton Friedman, 1968a, Chap. 9).

---

[5]The discussion in this and the following sections follows a viewpoint that is often called the **monetary approach to the balance of payments.** This approach was developed by Robert Mundell (1968, Part II; 1971, Part II). The early origins of this theory are in the eighteenth-century writings of David Hume; see Eugene Rotwein (1970).

WORLD PRICES UNDER FIXED EXCHANGE RATES

A system of fixed exchange rates, centered on the U.S. dollar, determines each country's price level, P^i, as a ratio to the U.S. price level, P (see equation 16.4). To complete the picture, we have to determine the U.S. price level. The analysis is similar to our earlier determination of the world price level; that is, we have to equate the demand for international currency to the supply.

Suppose that all countries hold their international currency in the form of U.S. dollars (as was reasonably accurate under the Bretton Woods System). Then the total real demand for U.S. currency includes the holdings of U.S. residents plus the holdings of foreigners in the form of international currency. Given the dollar quantity of U.S. currency, M, we can determine the U.S. price level, P, in the manner of our closed-economy analysis. Specifically, a greater amount of money, M, means a higher U.S. price level, P, and a correspondingly higher price level, P^i, in each other country. Conversely, an increase in the real demand for U.S. currency—whether by U.S. residents or by foreigners—lowers the U.S. price level, P, and correspondingly reduces the price level, P^i, in each other country.

Under the international regime that prevailed after World War II, there were a number of factors that constrained the Federal Reserve's choice of the quantity of U.S. money, M. First, if the Federal Reserve pursued a monetary policy that was inconsistent with stabilization of the U.S. price level, P, U.S. currency would become less attractive as an international medium of exchange. That is, other countries would not like it if their price levels—which were constrained to follow the path of the U.S. price level— grew too fast or fluctuated a great deal. Consequently, these countries might no longer find it desirable to peg their exchange rates to the U.S. dollar or to hold dollars as a form of international currency. This element constrained the expansion of U.S. money to the extent that the U.S. monetary authority wished to maintain the role of the U.S. dollar as the centerpiece of the international monetary system.

More important, the United States had a commitment to exchange U.S. dollars for gold at the rate of $35 per ounce. If the U.S. price level rose substantially—as it did during the late 1960s—it would become attractive for foreign central banks to trade their dollars for gold. As it lost more and more gold, the United States would become unable to maintain the dollar price of gold. Eventually the system would break down, as it did at the beginning of the 1970s.

DEVALUATION

Return now to the situation of a typical country in a regime of exchange rates tied to the U.S. dollar. As suggested before, a country that typically pegs its exchange rate, ε^i, occasionally faces pressures to shift this rate. In particular, any force that tends to increase the domestic price level, P^i, relative to the U.S. price, P, leads to losses of international currency or other assets by the central bank. These pressures could arise, for example, from rapid expansion of the domestic currency, M^i, or from a decrease in the demand for country i's real money, M^i/P^i. (The decline in real money demanded might reflect a domestic supply shock, which reduces output in country i.) In response to its loss of assets, the central bank has an incentive to raise the exchange rate, ε^i, which implies a devaluation of the domestic currency in terms of the U.S. dollar. Conversely, any pressure toward reduction in the domestic price level, P^i, relative to the U.S. price, P, implies gains in the central bank's assets, which may motivate a reduction in the exchange rate, ε^i. Since the domestic currency then becomes more valuable in terms of the dollar, there is an appreciation of the currency, which economists call a **revaluation.**

Typically devaluations and revaluations do not involve long periods during which the central bank gradually loses or gains international currency. That is because the expectation of a shift in the exchange rate leads to **speculation,** which tends to hasten the central bank's actions. If people anticipate a devaluation, they have an incentive to act in advance to exchange their domestic money at the central bank for international currency, which might be U.S. dollars. People react this way because they expect the domestic money to become less valuable relative to other moneys. But since this decline in the demand for domestic money leads to further losses of international currency by the central bank, the devaluation tends to occur sooner.

Figures 16.1 and 16.2 provide some examples of sudden devaluation and revaluation during the mainly fixed-rate period before the early 1970s. France devalued the franc by a total of 40% in 1957–58, Germany revalued the mark by 4% in 1961, and Britain devalued the pound by 14% in 1967.

Consider now the effects of a devaluation—that is, an increase in the exchange rate, ε^i. As noted before, this change may be a symptom of pressure for inflation in the devaluing country, such as excessive expansion of the domestic currency, M^i. But let's consider here the effects of an autonomous devaluation—that is, a devaluation that comes out of the blue rather than as a response to changes in domestic money supply or demand.

If the domestic price level P^i (measured, say, in terms of yen per unit of goods) did not change, an increase in the exchange rate ε^i (yen per dollar) means that goods in country i would become cheaper in terms of dollars. Therefore, for a given U.S. price level, P, there would be an increase in the demand for goods sold in country i. This increase in demand suggests that the price level, P^i, would rise. This response accords with the PPP condition, equation 16.4, which shows that a devaluation (a higher value of ε^i) leads to a higher domestic price level, $P^i = \varepsilon^i \cdot P$.

Suppose that we treat the devaluation and the rise in the domestic price level as one-time events. Then the higher domestic price level means a greater demand for domestic money in nominal terms (see equation 16.5). The rise in the nominal quantity of money, M^i, can come about in two ways. First, the central bank may create more money through open-market operations or other means. Second, if the central bank does not act, individuals would bring international currency to the central bank to get more domestic currency. As the bank exchanges domestic for international currency, the quantity of domestic money, M^i, rises. Thus, a one-time devaluation can lead to an expansion of the central bank's international currency, which accompanies the increase in the quantity of domestic money, M^i.

Notice that there is a two-way direction of association between devaluations and the behavior of domestic prices and money. First, expansionary monetary policy creates pressure for devaluation. In this sense, domestic inflation causes devaluation. Second a devaluation tends to raise domestic prices and money. In this sense, devaluation is itself inflationary.

The analysis treats the changes in the exchange rate, ε^i, and the domestic price level, P^i, as one-time happenings. But, in practice, countries that devalue once tend to devalue again. This outcome makes sense if we think of devaluation as primarily a symptom of pressure for domestic inflation, in particular, as an indication that the domestic central bank is increasing the quantity of money at a rapid rate. Countries that act this way today are likely to continue this behavior later. Hence, a devaluation can create expectations of future increases in the exchange rate, ε^i. Then the interest-rate parity condition from equation 16.3 implies that the domestic nominal interest rate, R^i, would rise above that in the United States. But this change reduces the real demand for country i's money, M^i/P^i. As a consequence, a devaluation of country i's currency may no longer generate an increase in country i's holdings of international currency.

FLEXIBLE EXCHANGE RATES

The international system of fixed exchange rates, centered on the U.S. dollar, broke down in the early 1970s. One reason for the breakdown was the excessive creation of U.S. dollars and the consequent rise in the U.S. price level after the mid-1960s. Thereby, it became difficult for the United States to maintain convertibility of the dollar into gold at the rate of $35 per ounce. Finally, President Nixon acted in 1971 to raise the dollar price of gold. This action signaled the end of the Bretton Woods System, where currencies were linked to gold through the U.S. dollar.

Since the early 1970s, many countries have allowed their exchange rates to vary or float more or less freely to clear the markets for foreign exchange. As is clear from a glance at Figures 16.1 and 16.2, the exchange rates of six major currencies with the U.S. dollar have fluctuated substantially over this period. Groups of countries, such as the European Monetary System since 1979, have maintained relatively fixed exchange rates among their currencies. Nevertheless, the important development since the early 1970s has been the increased reliance on **flexible exchange rates.** To study events in this period, we have to extend the analysis to consider the determination of exchange rates in a flexible-rate environment.

If the goods produced in various countires are physically identical, the condition for absolute purchasing-power parity, $P^i = \varepsilon^i P$ from equation 16.4, still holds under flexible exchange rates. That is, the purchasing power of any currency in terms of goods is still the same regardless of where someone uses the currency to buy goods. Also, deviations from purchasing-power parity can still arise from various disturbances, such as shifts in the terms of trade, changes in trade restrictions or transport costs, and so on.

A new result under flexible exchange rates is that country i's price level, P^i, is no longer tied to the U.S. price, P. Hence, country i's inflation rate, π^i, can also depart from the U.S. rate, π. The monetary authority of country i can now independently determine its domestic money supply, M^i, through open-market operations or other means. Given the quantity of domestic money, the domestic price level, P^i, is determined to ensure that this money is willingly held. In other words, using equation 16.5 and rearranging terms,

$$P^i = \frac{M^i}{L(Y^i, R^i, \cdots)}. \tag{16.7}$$

Note that since country i's inflation rate can differ from the U.S. rate, country i's nominal interest rate, R^i, can also differ from the U.S. rate, R. It is now the real interest rates, $R^i - \pi^i = r$, that will be the same in all countries.

Since the PPP condition, $P^i = \varepsilon^i \cdot P$, still holds, country i's exchange rate can be determined by substituting for P^i in equation 16.7 to get

$$\varepsilon^i = \frac{P^i}{P} = \frac{M^i}{P \cdot L(Y^i, R^i, \cdots)}. \tag{16.8}$$

Equation 16.8 shows how the exchange rate, ε^i, is determined by the monetary authority's choice of M^i and the values of Y^i, P (the U.S. price level), and R^i. (Note that R^i equals $r + \pi^i$, and π^i is the growth rate of P^i, which is determined from equation 16.7.)

Since $\varepsilon^i = P^i/P$, we also know that the rate of change of country i's exchange rate with the U.S. dollar, $\Delta\varepsilon^i$, must equal the difference between country i's inflation rate and the U.S. rate, $\pi^i - \pi$ (see equation 16.2). This proposition turns out to fit the data well for countries with high average rates of inflation. Not surprisingly, these countries turn out also to be the ones that have maintained flexible exchange rates with the U.S. dollar over most years, even before the 1970s. Table 16.3 reports the relative inflation rates (based on GDP deflators) and growth rates of the exchange rate for some high inflation countries, mainly over the period 1955–86. (The table covers the high-inflation countries for which data are available.) Notice that the difference between each country's average inflation rate and the U.S. rate, $\pi^i - \pi$, matches up closely with the average percentage change per year in the exchange rate, $\Delta\varepsilon^i$. Thus the relative form of PPP works well here.

Although each country can make independent choices about the quantity of money, it is important to recognize that flexible exchange rates do not isolate a country economically from the rest of the world. As long as an exchange rate system allows free trade in goods and assets, the precise nature of the system does not have a great deal to do with the extent of international trade in goods and services or with the amount of international borrowing and lending. (We did, however, discuss the possibility that countries would resort to trade restrictions to defend a fixed exchange rate without having to undergo domestic monetary contraction.) The main results about international trade in goods and assets apply as well to a setting of flexible exchange rates as to one with fixed rates. In fact, the results would also apply if all countries used a common currency—that is, in the unrealistic system of fixed exchange rates that we assumed in Chapter 15.

TABLE 16.3 *A Comparison of Inflation Rates with Changes in Exchange Rates for Some High-Inflation Countries*

	(% per year over 1955–86)	
	$\pi^i - \pi$	$\Delta \varepsilon^i$
Argentina	57.6	59.9
Brazil	38.4	38.6
Chile	40.5	40.9
Colombia	11.1	14.1
Iceland	17.6	16.9
Indonesia[a]	13.4	11.0
Israel	28.5	27.7
Peru[b]	23.5	24.3
South Korea	9.5	8.9
Uruguay	33.9	34.6
Zaire	17.7	23.2

[a]1967–85.
[b]1960–85.

Note: The table shows each country's average inflation rate, π^i, less the average U.S. rate, π. These values match up closely with the average percentage change per year in the exchange rate with the U.S. dollar, $\Delta \varepsilon^i$.

Sources: The data on price levels (deflators for the gross domestic product) and exchange rates are from IMF, *International Financial Statistics.*

PURCHASING-POWER PARITY UNDER FLEXIBLE AND FIXED EXCHANGE RATES

Many economists have noted that purchasing-power parity seems to hold less well under the flexible exchange rates that have prevailed since the early 1970s than under the fixed rates that prevailed earlier for most countries. We already looked in Figures 16.1 and 16.2 at the behavior of exchange rates for six of the major industrialized countries. To see the implications for PPP, we have to adjust these exchange rates to take account of the divergent movements in domestic price levels.

Figures 16.3 and 16.4 show the price levels (deflators for the GDP or GNP) for the six countries from 1950 to 1987. Each price level is expressed as a ratio to

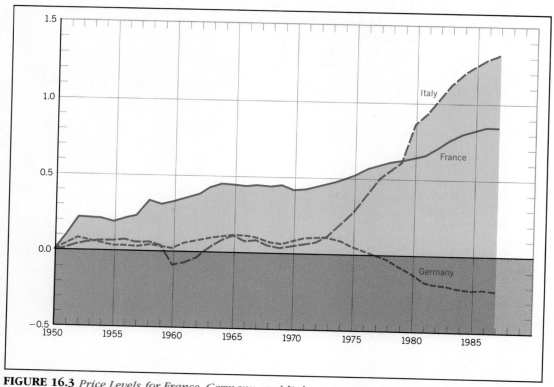

FIGURE 16.3 *Price Levels for France, Germany, and Italy*
Each price level is expressed as a ratio to the U.S. price level. The values shown are the proportionate
(logarithmic) deviations from the value prevailing for each country in 1950. For sources, see the note to Figure
16.1.

the U.S. price level—that is, the values correspond to P^i/P from our previous discussion. The figures show for each year the proportionate deviation of the price ratio from the value that prevailed in 1950. For example, for Germany in Figure 16.3, the value for 1987 was 20% below that in 1950 because the average German inflation rate from 1950 to 1987 was lower than that in the United States. In periods where a country's inflation rate exceeded the U.S. value, the lines shown in Figures 16.3 and 16.4 rise over time.

Figures 16.5 and 16.6 show the ratio of the exchange rate, ε^i, to the relative price, P^i/P. As in previous figures, the numbers plotted represent the proportionate deviation from the value that prevailed in each country in 1950. Under relative purchasing-power parity, the numbers would all equal zero. Therefore, deviations in relative PPP show up as movements above or below zero in Figures 16.5 and 16.6.

Economists often call the ratio of ε^i to P^i/P (which equals $\varepsilon^i \cdot P/P^i$) the real **exchange rate**. This ratio indicates the quantity of goods produced in country i that exchanges for one unit of goods produced in the United States. (A person can sell one unit of U.S. goods for P dollars, which can then be exchanged for $\varepsilon^i P$ units of country i's currency. This much currency buys $(1/P^i) \cdot \varepsilon^i P = \varepsilon^i \cdot P/P^i$ units of country i's goods. This last term equals the real exchange rate.) A rise in the real exchange rate means that goods produced in country i have become cheaper relative to those produced in the United States. Or, to put it the other way, U.S. goods have become relatively more expensive. In order to distinguish it from the real exchange, economists sometimes refer to the ordinary exchange rate—that is, ε^i—as the **nominal exchange rate**.

As an example, for Japan in Figure 16.6, the value of .70 for the real exchange rate in 1970 means that U.S. goods could be exchanged for only about 70% as much goods in Japan, as compared to the situation that prevailed in 1950. Thus Japanese goods became substantially more expensive relative to U.S. goods from 1950 to 1970. Recall that the nominal exchange rate was essentially fixed at this time (see Figure 16.2). Therefore, the fall in the real exchange rate reflected a *higher* average inflation rate in Japan (4.5% per year from 1950 to 1970) than in the United States (2.8% per year)—see Figure 16.4.

The real exchange rate for Japan continued to fall after 1970 (so that Japanese goods exchanged for more and more U.S. goods), until reaching the value 0.37 in

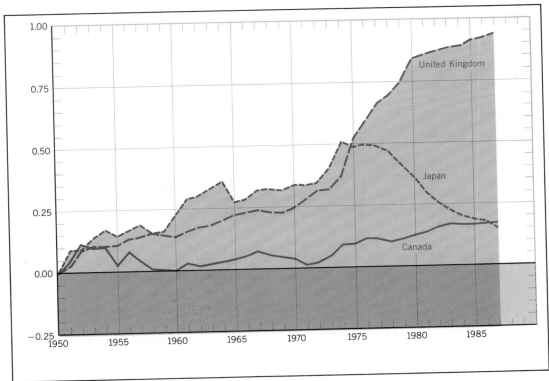

FIGURE 16.4 *Price Levels for Canada, Japan, and the United Kingdom*
See the note to Figure 16.3.

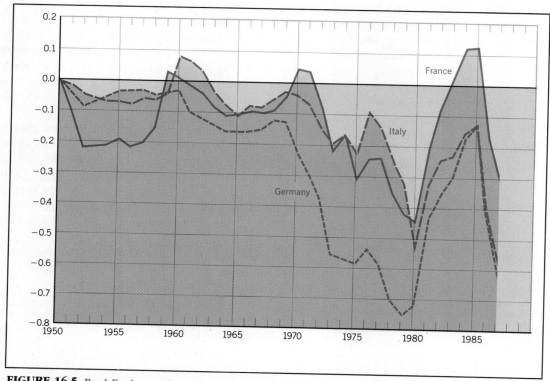

FIGURE 16.5 *Real Exchange Rates for France, Germany, and Italy*
The real exchange rate equals the nominal exchange rate, ε', divided by the ratio of GDP deflators, P'/P. The values shown are the proportionate (logarithmic) deviations from the value prevailing in each country in 1950. For the sources, see the note to Figure 16.1.

1978. Then the rate rose back to 0.55 in 1985, before falling to 0.35 in 1987. Since the mid-1970s the Japanese inflation rate has been *lower* than that in the United States (see Figure 16.4). Therefore, the periods of decline in the real exchange rate reflected decreases in the nominal exchange rate (Figure 16.2). The Japanese yen appreciated at an especially rapid rate from 1971 to 1973, 1976 to 1978, and 1985 to 1987.

The European countries—France, Germany, and Italy in Figure 16.5 and the United Kingdom in Figure 16.6—experienced broadly similar patterns of real exchange rates. In particular, each currency showed strong real appreciation from 1970 to 1980, followed by real depreciation until 1985, and a return to real appreciation from 1985 to 1987.

One interesting point, brought out by a comparison of Germany and Italy, is that the real exchange rates behaved similarly even when the domestic price levels and nominal exchange rates moved in very different ways. From 1970 to 1980, the Italian inflation rate averaged 8% per year more than that in the United States (Figure 16.3), and the Italian nominal exchange rate depreciated at an average rate of 3%

per year (Figure 16.1). Thus, the real exchange rate for Italy *appreciated* by 5% per year (Figure 16.5). Over the same period, the average German inflation rate was 2% per year below that in the United States (Figure 16.3), and the German nominal exchange rate appreciated at an average rate of 7% per year (Figure 16.1). Thus, as with Italy, the real exchange rate for Germany appreciated by 5% per year (Figure 16.5).

The lesson from the comparison between Germany and Italy is that very different patterns for nominal variables—domestic price levels, nominal exchange rates, and, it turns out, underlying rates of monetary growth—can coexist with similar patterns for real exchange rates. That is because the nominal exchange rates, which were flexible in the 1970s, behaved sufficiently differently in Germany and Italy so as to offset the divergent trends in domestic price levels. Although the real exchange rates between each country and the United States have changed substantially since the early 1970s, the suggestion is that some real disturbances—rather than the nominal policies that differed substantially between Germany and Italy—were at work. Unfortunately, economists have not been so successful in isolating the important real disturbances.

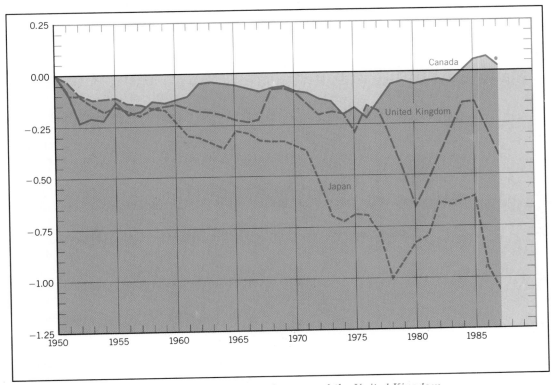

FIGURE 16.6 *Real Exchange Rates for Canada, Japan, and the United Kingdom*
See the note to Figure 16.5.

We know for high-inflation countries, such as those studied before in Table 16.3, that differences in inflation rates explain most of the divergent movements in nominal exchange rates. For the six industrialized countries that we have been considering, the inflation rates are relatively moderate, and the fluctuations of inflation account for only a small part of the year-to-year variations in nominal exchange rates. Nevertheless, over the longer term, the differing behavior of domestic price levels does explain a large fraction of the movements in nominal exchange rates. For example, from 1973 to 1987 for the six industrialized countries, the different movements in domestic price levels (shown in Figures 16.3 and 16.4) turn out to explain about 70% of the divergences in nominal exchange rates (Figures 16.1 and 16.2).

Finally, note for Canada that the shifts in the real exchange rate were relatively small (Figure 16.6). This outcome probably reflects the ease of moving goods and factors of production between Canada and the United States, as well as similarities in the types of goods produced. Figure 16.4 shows that the average Canadian inflation rate from 1950 to 1987 (4.8% per year) exceeded that in the United States (4.3%). Therefore, the Canadian dollar depreciated by a moderate amount over this period (Figure 16.2).

Let us try to summarize some of the major facts about real exchange rates in the post–World War II period.[6] Some of these observations follow directly from Figures 16.1–16.6, and others come from more detailed statistical analysis of these and other data.

1. Real exchange rates, calculated by means of GNP or GDP deflators, have not been constant. The extent of year-to-year fluctuations during the flexible-exchange-rate period from 1973 to 1987 turns out to be roughly two and a half times as great as that from 1951 to 1972, when most nominal exchange rates were fixed.[7] Therefore, departures from relative PPP have been important, especially since the early 1970s. There were, however, some substantial movements in real exchange rates in the earlier period when nominal exchange rates were fixed. Thus, fixed exchange rates do not guarantee stability in real exchange rates.

2. The real exchange rates for Canada remained relatively stable even under flexible exchange rates. Thus flexible rates do not lead necessarily to large fluctuations in real exchange rates.

3. It turns out that we cannot use the past experience of movements in real exchange rates to get very accurate predictions of future changes. For example, the real depreciation of the U.S. dollar against the European and Japanese currencies from 1970 to 1975 (Figures 16.5 and 16.6) would not have allowed us to predict the continuation of real depreciations from 1975 to 1980 (1975 to 1978 for Japan). Similarly, the real appreciation of the U.S. dollar from 1980 to 1985 would not have allowed us to predict the depreciations from 1985 to 1987. People who state

[6]For a related discussion, see Michael Mussa (1979, pp. 10–27).

[7]More precisely, the standard deviation of year-to-year changes from 1973 to 1987 is two and a half times as large as that from 1951 to 1972. The standard deviation is the square root of the variance. The variance is the average value of the squared deviation from the mean.

confidently that the U.S. dollar will rise or fall over some short-run horizon should not be taken seriously.

4. There is no clear connection between the behavior of real exchange rates and a country's experience with inflation or monetary growth. As an example, recall our comparison of Germany and Italy. Probably we can think of the movements in real exchange rates as reflecting primarily real changes, involving the terms of trade, the relative prices of traded and nontraded goods, trade restrictions and tax policies, and so on. But the details of the links between these real variables and the real exchange rates have not been worked out empirically.

5. Supply shocks, such as the changes in oil prices, have been unusually large since the early 1970s. These shocks imply shifts in the terms of trade and thereby in real exchange rates. Hence, the change to flexible exchange rates is not responsible for all of the increased variability of real exchange rates since the early 1970s. (The increased importance of real shocks may make flexible exchange rates more attractive. In this sense, the volatility of real exchange rates helps to explain why we have flexible exchange rates, rather than vice-versa.)

6. Fluctuations in real exchange rates reflect market forces that no economist (or politician!) understands very well. With flexible exchange rates, these forces show up as variations in nominal exchange rates. Under fixed exchange rates, the forces exert pressures for change in domestic price levels and money stocks. Policymakers may resist these tendencies by carrying out offsetting monetary policies, which may lead to restrictions on trade in goods and assets. Because of these restrictions, it may turn out that real exchange rates are less volatile under fixed exchange rates than under flexible rates. But because of the interferences with trade, the volume of international commerce would also be smaller. Note that although real exchange rates have been volatile since the early 1970s, it is also true that the volume of world trade increased substantially in comparison with the pre-1970 period. For example, we already mentioned that in relation to GNP, the volume of U.S. international trade from 1972 to 1987 was roughly double that from 1948 to 1971.

EXCHANGE RATES AND THE CURRENT-ACCOUNT BALANCE

The large U.S. current-account deficits since 1983 have received a lot of attention from economists and journalists. Discussions of these deficits often go along with analyses of U.S. dollar exchange rates. For example, a common argument in 1989 was that, to eliminate the current-account deficit, the U.S. dollar would have to depreciate further relative to the other major currencies. This type of analysis generally refers to real exchange rates—that is, the argument is that U.S. goods would have to become cheaper relative to foreign goods to eliminate the excess of imports over exports.

On one level it seems plausible that a real depreciation of the dollar would deter imports and encourage exports. But suppose for the moment that the physical quantities of goods imported and exported did not change. Then a depreciation of the dollar means that the dollar revenues from exports would not change, while the dollar expenses on imports would rise. As a result, the current account would show an even larger deficit! The problem is that importers now pay more in terms of dollars (or in terms of goods produced in the United States) for each unit of foreign goods.

The offsetting force is that the physical quantity of goods imported would tend to decline, while the physical quantity of goods exported would tend to rise. The current-account balance moves toward surplus if this force more than offsets the adverse effect from having to pay more for each unit of goods imported.

To think about the net effect from a real depreciation of the dollar, recall that the current-account balance is the difference between national saving and domestic investment. The current-account balance moves toward surplus if national saving rises relative to domestic investment. To go further, we have to say something about where a shift in the real exchange rate came from.

To take a case that we considered before, suppose that a real depreciation of the U.S. dollar reflects an adverse shift in the U.S. terms of trade. That is, the tradable goods produced in the United States become less valuable relative to the tradable goods produced elsewhere. We discussed in Chapter 15 the response of the current-account balance to this kind of disturbance. If the shift in the terms of trade is temporary, national saving tends to fall while domestic investment demand changes little. Therefore, the current account moves toward deficit. If the shift is permanent, national saving changes little, but investment demand tends to decline. Hence, the current account moves toward surplus. The important point is that the real exchange rate depreciates in both cases, while the current account moves toward a deficit in one situation and toward a surplus in the other.

We could think of other reasons for a real depreciation of the dollar, such as a shift in the price of U.S. nontradables relative to U.S. tradables. Then we would find again that the current-account balance could move toward surplus or deficit. The general lesson is that a real depreciation of the U.S. dollar may go along with a move in either direction in the current-account balance; the results depend on the details of the disturbances that led to the decline in the dollar.

The U.S. data do not reveal any clear pattern in the relation between current-account balances and real exchange rates. For example, from 1970 to 1980, the U.S. dollar depreciated dramatically in real terms relative to most other major currencies (see Figures 16.5 and 16.6). Over this period, the U.S. current-account balance (Figure 15.1) averaged roughly zero (0.02% of GNP) and showed no regular pattern over time. From 1980 to 1985, the U.S. dollar appreciated in real terms, and the current-account balance moved toward a substantial deficit (from zero in 1980 to 2.9% of GNP in 1985). Then the U.S. dollar fell sharply in real terms from 1985 to 1987, while the current-account deficit remained at about 3% of GNP. The overall indication is that movements in real exchange rates provide little or no information about what the current account is doing. This empirical observation is consistent with our theoretical reasoning because different underlying disturbances would lead to different patterns of association between the real exchange rate and the current-account balance.

Another point is that the real exchange rate is not a variable that is very amenable to government policy. The nominal exchange rate can readily be influenced by governments, for example, by changing the growth rate of money in a setting of flexible exchange rates. Governments also choose whether to have a system with fixed or flexible exchange rates. But we should think of the real exchange rate as a relative price, specifically, as the price of U.S. goods relative to the price of foreign goods. Governments can influence the real exchange rate in the same way that they can affect other relative prices, for example, by restricting international trade in goods and assets or by tax policies (including tariffs and subsidies). If an economist urges the U.S. government to make the U.S. dollar rise or fall in real terms, he or she is really advocating this kind of interference with market forces. Unfortunately, such advice is rarely accompanied by a rationale for the necessary form of government intervention.

SUMMARY

Purchasing-power parity (PPP) connects a country's exchange rate with, say, the U.S. dollar to the ratio of the country's price level to the U.S. price level. In relative form, the PPP condition relates changes in exchange rates to differences in inflation rates. A variety of real factors, including changes in the terms of trade, shifts in the relative prices of traded and nontraded goods, and variations in trade restrictions and tax policies, can lead to deviations from PPP. Such deviations—corresponding to variations in real exchange rates—have been especially important since the early 1970s.

Interest-rate parity implies that differences in nominal interest rates across countries correspond to differences in expected rates of change of exchange rates. Differences in taxes and in riskiness of returns can lead to violations of interest-rate parity. If purchasing-power parity holds in relative form, interest-rate parity implies that expected real interest rates are equal across countries.

Examples of regimes with fixed exchange rates are the classical gold standard, the Bretton Woods System, the European Monetary System, and a world with a common currency. When the exchange rate is fixed to the U.S. dollar, a country's price level is determined mainly by the U.S. price level. Then, to satisfy the PPP condition, there is a specific quantity of money that is consistent with a country's chosen exchange rate. The flows of international currency tend to generate this quantity of money automatically. However, countries sometimes sterilize the flows of international currency to maintain a higher quantity of domestic money. These actions tend to lead to devaluation of the currency or to trade restrictions. Overall, there is a two-way association, where domestic inflation tends to cause devaluation but where an autonomous devaluation is itself inflationary.

Flexible exchange rates have been prevalent since the early 1970s. The flexibility of exchange rates leaves intact the main results about international trade in goods and credit. In particular, the conditions for purchasing-power parity and interest-rate parity apply in the same manner as before. However, under flexible exchange rates, each central bank can make an independent choice of monetary growth and, hence, inflation.

We noted that U.S. real exchange rates do not have a regular pattern of association with the U.S. current-account balance. On theoretical grounds, the relationship depends on the underlying disturbance that causes the real exchange rate to change.

IMPORTANT TERMS AND CONCEPTS

international reserves

domestic credit

purchasing-power parity (PPP)

relative form of PPP

absolute form of PPP

interest-rate parity

fixed exchange rate

Bretton Woods System

gold standard

European Monetary System (EMS)

sterilization

devaluation

monetary approach to the balance of payments

revaluation

speculation (on exchange rate)

flexible exchange rate

real exchange rate

nominal exchange rate

QUESTIONS AND PROBLEMS

Mainly for Review

16.1 Explain how the real exchange rate differs from the nominal exchange rate. Which rate is pegged in a system of fixed exchange rates? Can the government readily influence both rates?

16.2 Explain the conditions for absolute and relative purchasing-power parity in equations 16.1 and 16.2. How do these conditions relate to the behavior of real exchange rates?

16.3 Under fixed exchange rates, does the central bank have discretion over the money supply? Show how an attempt to exercise an independent monetary policy may result in devaluation or revaluation. Why might the attempt lead to trade restrictions?

16.4 Under flexible exchange rates, a country that has a persistently high rate of inflation will experience a steady increase in its exchange rate. Explain why this happens. Why might the central bank like this system?

16.5 We mentioned that examples of regimes with fixed exchange rates were the classical gold standard, the Bretton Woods System, and a setup with a common currency. Explain how each of these regimes would ensure fixed exchange rates.

PROBLEMS FOR DISCUSSION

16.6 **Shifts in the Demand for Money**
Consider an increase in the real demand for money in country *i*.

    a. Under a fixed exchange rate, what happens to country *i*'s price level, P^i, and quantity of money, M^i? What happens to the country's quantity of international currency, H^i?

    b. Under a flexible exchange rate—with a fixed quantity of domestic money, M^i— what happens to the country's price level, P^i, and exchange rate, ε^i?

16.7 **Monetary Growth under Flexible Exchange Rates**
Equation 16.8 relates a country's exchange rate with the U.S. dollar, ε^i, to domestic money supply and demand. Suppose that a country raises its growth rate of money, μ^i, once and for all. Describe the effect of this change on the path of ε^i. (Assume here that the U.S. price level, P, the world real interest rate, r, and the path of domestic output, Y^i, do not change.)

16.8 **Flexible Exchange Rates and Inflation Rates**

    a. Show, by using the condition for relative purchasing-power parity in equation 16.2, that the percentage change in the exchange rate, $\Delta\varepsilon^i$, equals the difference between country *i*'s inflation rate, π^i, and the U.S. inflation rate, π.

    b. Using the IMF's *International Financial Statistics* (yearbook issue), calculate the values of $\Delta\varepsilon^i$ and $\pi^i - \pi$ for some countries in the post–World War II period. (Pick some other than those appearing in Table 16.3) What conclusions emerge?

16.9 **Nixon's Departure from Gold in 1971**
Under the Bretton Woods System, the United States pegged the price of gold at $35 per ounce.

    a. Why did trouble about the gold price arise in 1971?

    b. Was President Nixon right in eliminating the U.S. commitment to buy and sell gold (from and to foreign official institutions) at a fixed price? What other alternatives were there—in particular,

        i. What was the classical prescription of the gold standard?

        ii. The French suggested a doubling in the price of gold. Would that have helped?

16.10 **Shipping Gold under the Gold Standard**
Suppose that the price of gold is $5 per ounce in New York and £1 per ounce in London.

    a. Assume that the exchange rate is $6 per pound. If a person starts with dollars in New York, what can he or she do to make a profit. If the cost of transporting gold is 1% of the amount shipped, how high does the exchange rate have to go above $5 per pound to make this action profitable?

    b. Make the same calculations when the exchange rate is below $5 per pound
(The results determine a range of exchange rates around $5 per pound for which it is unprofitable to ship gold in either direction. The upper and lower limits

of this range are called *gold points.* If the exchange rate goes beyond these points, it becomes profitable to ship an unlimited amount of gold. Can you show that the potential to ship gold guarantees that the acutual exchange rate will remain within the gold points?)

16.11 *Futures Contracts on Foreign Exchange*

If a person buys a one-month futures contract on the German mark, he or she agrees to purchase marks next month at a dollar exchange rate that is set today. The buyer of this contract goes "long" on the mark and does well if the mark appreciates (more than the amount expected) over the month. Similarly, the seller of a one-month futures contract agrees to sell marks next month at a dollar exchange rate that is agreed on today. The seller goes "short" on the mark and does well if the mark depreciates (more than expected) over the month.

Consider a German bond with a maturity of one month. This bond sells for a specified number of marks today and will pay out a stated amount of marks in one month. How can a person use the futures market to guarantee the dollar rate of return from buying the German bond and holding it for one month?

16.12 *Changes in the Quantity of International Currency (optional)*

Our analysis treated the quantity of international currency as the constant, *H*. What modifications have to be made to allow for changes over time in this quantity? In answering, consider the following regimes:

a. International currency consists of U.S. dollar bills.
b. International currency is a pure bookkeeping entry, such as the European currency unit used by the European Monetary System.
c. International currency is gold.

16.13 *Alternative Systems of Exchange Rates (optional)*

In Chapter 15 we assumed a system with a common world currency. In this chapter we found that fixed exchange rates could be obtained by other means, such as a gold standard or an arrangement like the European Monetary System. We also found that exchange rates could be flexible rather than fixed. What seem to be the benefits and costs from the different setups? In particular,

a. Is it better to have fixed or flexible exchange rates?
b. Is it a good or bad idea for all countries to use a single form of currency?

(*Note:* This question is very difficult, and economists would not agree about the answer. In thinking about the issues involved, you might consider the following. Are there transaction benefits from having just one type of currency and just one unit for quoting prices? Do governments want to have independent monetary policies and perhaps to get revenue from printing money? Is it costly for governments or individuals to hold stocks of gold? Can we be sure that central banks will stick to their announced policies of fixed exchange rates? Is it useful in some respects for different countries to use different units for quoting prices? Is it true that real exchange rates have become more volatile since the early 1970s because of the move toward flexible exchange rates?)

16.14 *Nontraded Goods and Real Exchange Rates (optional)*

Suppose that each country produces some goods and services (such as haircuts and rents on buildings) that are not traded internationally. Assume that the price of nontraded goods in country i rises relative to the price of traded goods, but no change occurs in the relative price of nontraded and traded goods in the United States. What happens to country i's real exchange rate, $\varepsilon^i/(P^i/P)$? (Assume that P^i and P are the GDP deflators for country i and the United States, respectively.)

In answering, note that the general price levels, P^i and P, include the prices of traded and nontraded goods. The law of one price says that the purchasing power of any currency should be the same for traded goods, regardless of where they are produced, but the same may not hold for nontraded goods.

Can you use the result to suggest an explanation for the movement in Japan's real exchange rate from 1950 to 1970 (see Figure 16.6)?

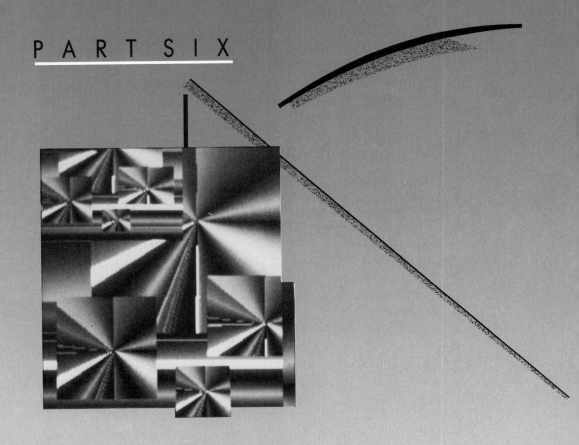

PART SIX

INTERACTIONS BETWEEN THE MONETARY SECTOR AND THE REAL SECTOR

*T*hus far, our analysis has stressed real factors, such as supply shocks, as sources of business fluctuations. The government can affect real variables by changing its purchases of goods and services or its tax rates, but there is little evidence that these fiscal actions have been major sources of business cycles in U.S. history. On the other hand, many economists believe that monetary fluctuations—created mainly by governmental actions—have been a principal cause of these cycles. In this part of the book, we examine the theoretical and empirical foundations for these beliefs.

Chapter 17 studies commercial banks and other financial institutions that intermediate between lenders and borrowers. These financial intermediaries create deposits, which can be good alternatives to currency as means of payments. Through the effects on the demand for currency, changes in the nature of financial intermediation have an effect on the price level. We show also that financial intermediation can aid in the allocation of credit and thereby improve the economy's performance. Accordingly, changes in the amount of financial intermediation—including those caused by shifts in governmental regulations—are nonneutral. We still conclude, however, that purely monetary disturbances—such as those generated by open-market operations—are neutral.

In Chapter 18 we survey the various pieces of empirical evidence that concern the relation between nominal and real variables. We find that the theory can explain some of the evidence as reactions to supply shocks or to changes in the nature of financial intermediation. One observation that conflicts with our theory is the apparent sensitivity of real variables to purely nominal disturbances. That is, there is some indication that money is nonneutral and plays a significant role in business fluctuations. Therefore, it is worthwhile to extend the theory to explain why monetary nonneutrality can be important.

Chapter 19 carries out this extension by introducing incomplete information about prices. We retain the setting of cleared markets and assume that people form rational expectations about prices and other variables. In this framework monetary surprises can lead to confusions between nominal and real disturbances and thereby to changes in real variables. In this way we explain some, but not all, of the observed linkages between money and business cycles. We go on to explore, first, the implications for monetary policy and, second, the possible empirical limitations of the approach.

Chapter 20 develops the Keynesian theory of business fluctuations. This approach is another extension of the basic framework—in this case, we replace the assumption of cleared markets with the alternative of sticky prices and rationed quantities. As in Chapter 19, where people have incomplete information about prices, the Keynesian theory can explain some nonneutralities of money. The two kinds of theories differ, however, in other respects, especially in regard to their implications for government policy. The discussion in Chapter 20 deals with the relative theoretical and empirical merits of the theories, although a final verdict is not yet available.

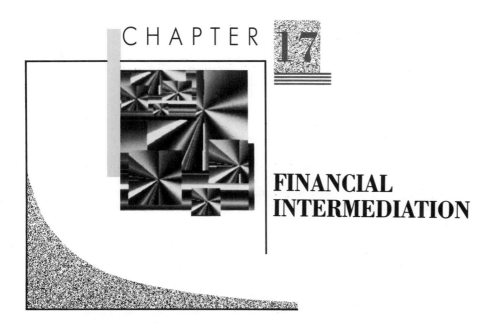

CHAPTER 17

FINANCIAL INTERMEDIATION

p to now the model treats money as currency—that is, as noninterest-bearing pieces of paper issued by the government. When we studied the demand for money in Chapter 4, we focused on the role of money as a medium of exchange. Households held money because they used it for purchases or sales of goods, bonds, or labor services. To reduce their average real money balance, households had to incur extra transaction costs, which might involve going more often to the bank or the store.

CHECKABLE DEPOSITS AND M1

We mentioned in Chapter 4 that currency is not the only medium of exchange in the real world. Typically, the most important alternative is checkable deposits. These deposits are now issued in the United States by various financial institutions, such as commercial banks and savings and loan associations. The holder of a deposit can purchase goods, bonds, or labor services by writing a check on his or her account. The check instructs the financial institution to transfer funds from the account of the check writer to that of another person. The important point is that checkable deposits are often preferable to currency as a medium of exchange.

The most popular definition of money, M1, attempts to classify together the assets that serve commonly as media of exchange. Thus, M1 is the sum of currency

INDEXES OF MONEY

*S*ome economists have used an index-number approach to measure the money supply. The general idea is to construct an aggregate that weights different assets according to their "degree of moneyness." One approach, used by William Barnett, Edward Offenbacher, and Paul Spindt (1984), begins with the observation that people hold currency although it bears zero interest. Other assets, such as various kinds of deposits, provide fewer monetary services and therefore must pay positive interest rates to induce people to hold them. Then the general idea is to weigh the quantities of various assets inversely to their interest rates (which are observable) and hence in direct relation to their amounts of monetary services (which are unobservable). Thus, currency counts one-to-one as money, checkable deposits (which bear low but positive interest rates) count somewhat less than one-to-one, time deposits (which bear higher interest rates) count still less, and so on. Using this technique, Barnett et al. have constructed a time series of a weighted monetary aggregate, which behaves somewhat differently from M1 or other concepts.

One difficulty with the approach is that differences in interest rates among assets reflect characteristics other than monetary services. Also it is sometimes hard to measure the implicit interest rate from free services to holders of deposits. To get around these problems, Paul Spindt (1985) took a different approach. He made direct estimates of monetary services by observing how frequently the various kinds of assets were used in exchanges. Thus, currency and checkable deposits—which have high velocities—received a high weight for monetary services. In contrast, time deposits—which have low velocity—received a low weight as money. Using this procedure, Spindt calculated a time series for another weighted monetary aggregate, which showed somewhat different behavior from the one described above. It is likely that economists will make increasing use of these weighted monetary aggregates in future research.

held by the public and checkable deposits. In the United States and most other countries today, checkable deposits account for the bulk of M1. For example, in 1987, checkable deposits were 74% of M1 in the United States, 85% of M1 in the United Kingdom, and 80% of M1 in Canada (see Table 4.1).

Some economists have argued that "money" should also include deposits that are not checkable but can be converted readily into checkable form or into currency. Thus, the broader aggregate M2 includes consumer time deposits at various financial institutions, money-market deposit accounts, and some other items. Still broader monetary aggregates, such as M3, include additional types of financial assets. The problem is that once we go beyond the definition of money as common media of exchange, there is no clear place to draw the line. In the boxed section, we consider some interesting attempts to solve this problem by constructing indexes of monetary aggregates.

For our purposes, it is unimportant to settle on a precise definition of money. But we do want to extend the model to assess the economic consequences from the existence of various types of deposits and various kinds of financial institutions.

Let's begin by noting that deposits in the United States differ in the following ways:

- Whether they can be withdrawn on demand at face value. This privilege applies to **demand deposits** and usually to **savings deposits,** which often have passbooks and legally allow for 30-days' notice of withdrawal. In contrast, **time deposits** have a stated maturity date, with some penalties typically attached to premature withdrawals.

- Whether people can write checks that instruct the financial intermediary to make payments to a third party. In the United States, all demand deposits are checkable.

- Whether they pay interest and at what rate.

- Whether they are insured by the federal government. Since 1980 this insurance applies to deposits up to $100,000 at most commercial banks, savings and loan associations, and mutual savings banks.

Households and firms decide how much to hold of the various deposits by considering the above characteristics as well as the interest rate paid. The main point is that these deposits are often more attractive than either currency or bonds. By bonds, we mean interest-bearing obligations of governments, businesses, or households. By holding a bond, a household or firm lends funds directly to governments or to other households or firms. In contrast, deposits are liablities of financial institutions. By holding a deposit, a household or firm lends funds to a financial institution. As we shall see, the financial institution then acts as an intermediary by lending its funds to governments or to other households or firms.

We want to understand why households and firms typically use the services of financial intermediaries rather than making loans directly. Then we can also see how the existence of financial intermediaries and the amount of financial intermediation affect the performance of the economy.

FINANCIAL INTERMEDIARIES AND THE CREDIT MARKET

Thus far in our model, the people who hold bonds make direct loans to others. For example, a lender may hold a mortgage on someone's house, a loan collateralized by someone's car, or a loan to a business for investment purposes. But this type of direct lending is often inefficient. First, it requires households and firms to evaluate the credit-worthiness of borrowers, which is usually difficult. Second, unless individual households and firms hold portions of many different types of loans, they may have substantial risks of losing a large part of their assets when a single loan goes bad. But it is hard for a single household or business to diversify by holding lots of different loans. Finally, the form of claim that someone holds—say, a home mortgage—must match the form of the loan in terms of its maturity. In the case of a 20-year loan to a home owner, the lender can cash in this claim only by selling it to someone else or by convincing the borower to pay it off.

Financial intermediaries, such as commercial banks, can solve these problems.[1] First, these institutions are in a good position to evaluate and collect on loans and to assemble a variety of loans by type and maturity. The credit market works better when loans are evaluated and administered by financial specialists rather than by households and nonfinancial firms. Second, as we already noted, financial institutions can attract funds by offering deposits, which are desirable forms of assets for households and businesses. In normal times, where financial institutions hold a sound, well-diversified portfolio of assets, the deposits are safe and easy to understand.

THE BALANCE SHEET OF A FINANCIAL INTERMEDIARY

A financial institution's deposits appear on the liablities side of its balance sheet, and various loans appear on the assets side. Table 17.1 shows a typical balance sheet. To be concrete, the figures apply in 1987 to an actual small commercial bank—The First National Bank of Rochester—which had total assets of about $160 million.

Let's look first at the main items on the asset side of the balance sheet. Here we have

- Cash of $12.7 million. This item includes currency (often called **vault cash**), deposits held on the books of the Federal Reserve, and deposits held at other financial institutions. The total of currency and deposits held at the Fed is called **reserves.**

- Loans of $108.8 million. The principal items are commercial loans, mortgages, and installment loans. Most large banks also have substantial foreign loans.[2]

- Securities of $29.4 million. This category includes government bonds and short-term money-market instruments (such as commercial paper and certificates of deposit issued by other financial institutions).

- Federal Funds of $10.9 million. These are short-term (often overnight) loans to other financial intermediaries through the **Federal Funds market.** The interest rate charged on these loans is called the **Federal Funds rate.** Typ-

[1]Others are savings and loan associations, money-market funds, mutual savings banks, pension funds, investment companies, insurance companies, and the government's mortgage associations.

[2]In the United States there are legal restrictions on the types of earning assets that financial intermediaries can hold. For example, commercial banks cannot hold corporate stock.

TABLE 17.1 *Balance Sheet of First National Bank of Rochester, December 31, 1987 (in millions of dollars)*

Assets		Liabilities	
Cash (includes deposits held at Fed and other financial institutions)	12.7	Demand deposits	22.3
Loans (net of loss reserve)	108.8	Time deposits	128.0
		Borrowing from Federal Funds market	0
Securities	29.4		
Federal funds	10.9	Borrowing from Fed	0
Other assets	4.3	Other liabilities	4.7
		Shareholders' equity	11.1
Total	166.1	Total	166.1

ically, smaller institutions—like the First National Bank of Rochester—lend funds on this market, while the large commercial banks are the main borrowers.

Now let's look at the liability side of the ledger. The principle items are

- Demand deposits of $22.3 million.
- Time deposits of $128.0 million.
- Borrowings from the Federal Funds market of $0. (First National is a lender of federal funds.)
- Borrowings from the Federal Reserve (also called the *Fed*), which are nil in this case. The Federal Reserve lends to financial institutions— principally commercial banks that are members of the Federal Reserve System—at the *discount window*. The interest rate charged on these loans is the Fed's **discount rate.**
- Shareholders' equity of $11.1 million. This "book value" is the sum of paid-in capital plus accumulated profits (as measured by accountants).

Reserves—Required and Excess. Financial intermediaries hold earning assets—by which we mean loans and securities—to obtain a flow of interest income. They hold physical capital and deposits at other financial institutions to carry out their business efficiently. Wht about cash? Since banks and some other depository institutions stand ready to convert their deposits into currency on demand, they keep some currency to meet the possible withdrawals of depositors. But in the United States in the post–World War II period, the main determinant of cash holdings by these institutions is the **reserve requirement** imposed by the Federal Reserve. (We shall discuss the Federal Reserve System later.) The Fed specifies the quantity of reserves that must be held against various categories of deposits. Legally the reserves can be held either as currency (vault cash) or as noninterest-bearing deposits on the books of the Federal Reserve. Before 1980, the Fed's requirements

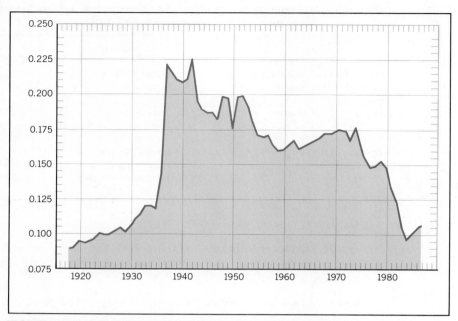

FIGURE 17.1 *Ratio of Required Reserves to Checkable Deposits*
Data for Figure 17.1 and subsequent figures are from Board of Governors of the Federal
Reserve System, Banking and Monetary Statistics, 1941–1970; Annual Statistical Digest,
1970–1979, and *Federal Reserve Bulletin,* various issues.

applied only to commercial banks that were members of the Federal Reserve System. However, the Monetary Control Act of 1980 extended the reserve requirements to all depository institutions (not including money-market funds) but at lower average percentages than before. The requirements in 1988 were 12% of checkable deposits[3] and 3% of business time deposits of maturity less than one and a half years. The Fed retains authority to change these requirements.

Figure 17.1 shows how the ratio of required reserves to checkable deposits behaved from 1918 to 1987. The main source of change in this ratio is shifts in legal requirements. But some requirements attach also to time and savings deposits, which do not enter into the total of checkable deposits. Also, the requirements depend on the total volume of deposits of the financial institution. Therefore, some changes in the ratio of required reserves to checkable deposits reflect shifts in the composition of deposits (between checkable and time or savings and among the categories of financial institutions). We shall discuss later some details and implications of shifts in the required-reserve ratio.

Instead of keeping noninterest-bearing cash, financial institutions prefer to hold assets that bear interest. Since these institutions can shift rapidly in and out of short-

---

[3]The requirement was only 3% of an institution's checkable deposits up to a total of $40.5 million. For further discussion of the Monetary Control Act, see Robert Auerbach (1985, Chaps. 6–8).

term securities or the Federal Funds market, even a moderate interest rate induces them to keep very little reserves above the required amount. Economists use the term **excess reserves** for the difference between total and required reserves. Figure 17.2 shows that excess reserves were less than 1% of total reserves from 1969 to 1982, when interest rates were especially high, and were between 1 and 2% of total reserves from 1983 to 1987. However, at the lower interest rates that prevailed earlier durng the post–World War II period, excess reserves were as much as 5% of the total. Notice also the large holdings of excess reserves from 1933 to 1941. Here, the ratio of excess reserves to the total averaged 37%. This behavior reflects the financial crises of the Great Depression, as well as the extremely low interest rates on safe assets. (We shall discuss this period in detail later.)

Excess reserves provide funds that a financial institution can dip into during emergencies. By contrast, required reserves do not serve this purpose. For a given amount of deposits, a depository institution is not permitted to let its reserves fall below the required amount.

Deposits and Earning Assets.   Suppose that a depository institution attracts an additional $100 of deposits. For concreteness, think about a checkable deposit for

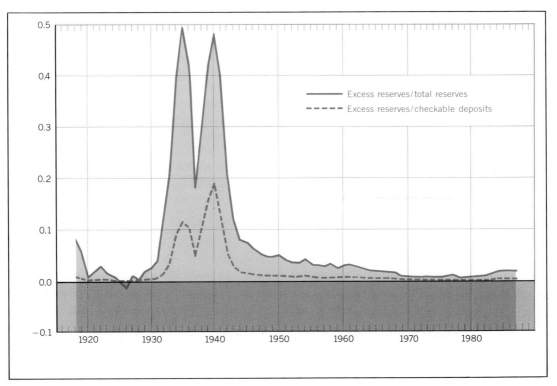

FIGURE 17.2 *Behavior of Excess Reserves*

which the required-reserve ratio is 12%. Then the institution holds $12 out of the extra $100 as required-reserves. The rest of the $100 may be divided as the institution chooses between loans and securities (which bear interest) or excess reserves (which do not bear interest).

The change in the institution's net earnings equals the interest on the additional earning assets, less the added costs of evaluating and collecting on loans or dealing in securities, less any extra costs of servicing the deposits (if no separate fees are charged), less the interest paid on the new deposits. For the institution to profit from this enterprise, it must be that the interest rate on deposits, call it R^d, is less than that on loans and securities, which we still call R. In particular, the spread, $R - R^d$, must cover the cost of the funds that the intermediary holds in noninterest-bearing form, the transaction costs associated with deposits and earnings assets, and some return on the capital invested in the business of being an intermediary. Let's call the total of these items the **costs of intermediation.** Competition among intermediaries would drive the interest rate on deposits high enough so that the spread, $R - R^d$, just covered the costs of intermediation.[4] It follows that the interest rate paid on deposits, R^d, would rise with the interest rate on loans and securities, R. However, the rate R^d would decline with an increase in the costs of intermediation, such as a rise in the required-reserve ratio.

Deposit Interest Rates and Financial Intermediation. The amount of deposits that households and firms want to hold—and hence the amount of funds that financial intermediaries have to loan out—depends on the interest rate on deposits, R^d. Deposits become more attractive relative to currency if R^d increases. (Note that the nominal interest rate on currency is fixed at zero.) On the other hand, deposits become less attractive relative to bonds if the spread, $R - R^d$, rises.

Suppose, for example, that the required-reserve ratio declines as it did from 1980 to 1984 (see Figure 17.1). For a given value of R, our analysis of competition among financial intermediaries predicts that the deposit interest rate, R^d, would rise. Therefore, households and firms would hold more deposits at the expense of currency and bonds. The increase in deposits means that financial intermediaries would expand their holdings of assets. Thus overall, we find that a lower reserve requirement leads, first, to more of M1 held as deposits rather than currency and, second, to more financial intermediation.

Regulation of Interest Rates on Deposits. From the 1930s until the early 1980s, the federal government regulated the interest rates that banks and other financial intermediaries could pay on deposits. With the Banking Acts of 1933 and 1935, the government prohibited interest payments on demand deposits. This restriction stayed in force until the middle and late 1970s, when interest-bearing checking accounts began to develop. These mainly took the form of negotiable-order-of-withdrawal (or N.O.W.) accounts. Of course, a negotiable order of withdrawal is just another name for a check. These types of accounts, which bear interest,

[4]For further discussion, see Benjamin Klein (1974).

began in New England in the mid-1970s and became available nationwide with the Monetary Control Act of 1980.

The Federal Reserve limited interest rates on time deposits through its **Regulation Q.** The ceiling rates on time deposits were high enough not to be binding at least until the 1950s. But the regulations were a significant constraint in the late 1960s, in much of the 1970s, and especially from 1979 to 1982. However, effective October 1983, the government removed the restrictions on the interest rates that institutions could pay on most time deposits.

What happens when the legal limit on deposits is below the interest rate that would otherwise be paid? One point is that the limits apply only to explicit interest. Institutions often compete for profitable deposits by providing services at below cost. The services that people receive by holding deposits amount to implicit interest, which substitutes for the explicit interest that the government prohibits. But despite the possibilities for evading restrictions on interest rates, we should not conclude that legal restrictions are irrelevant. Basically the implicit methods of paying interest tend to be less efficient than the explicit ones. That is because there are limits to the services that banks can conveniently provide as close substitutes for explicit interest. (However, an offsetting consideration is that explicit interest is taxable, whereas free services typically are not.) As market interest rates rose since the 1950s, the ceiling rates on deposits made it increasingly difficult for the regulated institutions to compete for funds. In this case the regulation of interest payments meant that the deposit interest rate, R^d, offered by these intermediaries was lower than otherwise. Our previous analysis of deposit interest rates predicts some of the outcomes:

- People moved away from deposits and toward direct holding of assets such as bonds and mortgages. This process, which is the reverse of intermediation, is called **disintermediation.**

- New types of unregulated financial intermediaries arose, which attracted funds away from banks and other institutions. In recent years, the primary example was money-market funds.

- The government eventually changed its regulations on deposit interest rates so that banks and other depository intermediaries could again compete effectively for funds. However, according to the regulations established through 1988, there are two remaining distinctions between money-market funds and other depository institutions. First, there are no reserve requirements on the money-market funds. But second, unlike the deposits at banks and some other intermediaries, the shares in money-market funds are not insured by the federal government.

Borrowing from the Federal Reserve. From the start of the Federal Reserve System in 1914 until 1980, banks that were members of the system could borrow short-term funds at the discount rate from a Federal Reserve bank. With the Monetary Control Act of 1980, all depository institutions with checkable deposits can borrow from the Fed.

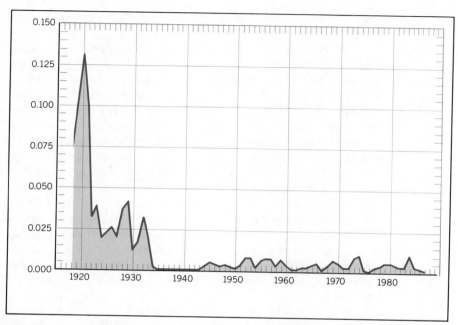

FIGURE 17.3 *Borrowings from the Federal Reserve as a Ratio to Checkable Deposits*

Borrowing from the Federal Reserve can be advantageous if the Fed's discount rate is below the rates at which financial institutions can otherwise borrow. Such borrowing may not always be desirable, however, even if the discount rate is relatively low. That is because, first, the Fed examines banks more carefully when they borrow frequently at the discount window and, second, the Fed can refuse to lend to banks that ask "too often." In any case, the lower the discount rate is, relative to market interest rates, the greater is the incentive for banks to borrow from the Fed.

Figure 17.3 shows the loans outstanding from the Fed to financial institutions. Notice that these borrowings were important during World War I and through the 1920s. The amount outstanding peaked at 13% of checkable deposits in 1920[5] and still amounted to 4% of these deposits in 1929, 3% in 1932 and 2% in 1933. However, borrowings fell to near zero for 1935–43. During the post–World War II period, some borrowing occurred, but the ratio of the amount outstanding to checkable deposits never exceeded 1%. For these years, the peaks in the ratio occurred in 1974 and 1984. For 1974, the average amount outstanding of $2.0 billion constituted about 1% of checkable deposits. Most of these loans were to the Franklin National Bank of Long Island, a large bank that engaged in questionable speculations and subsequently failed. For 1984, the average amount of $3.7 billion was again

[5]The borrowings of member banks actually exceeded their total reserves for 1919–21. For example, the average debt outstanding during 1920 was $2.5 billion, while the average amount of reserves was $1.8 billion.

about 1% of checkable deposits. Most of these loans went to the Continental Illinois National Bank, also a large bank in trouble.

Figure 17.4 shows how the annual average discount rate at the New York Fed compares to the interest rate on four to six-month maturity prime commercial paper. Although the two interest rates tended to move together, the discount rate typically has been lower than the commercial paper rate since World War II. Therefore, in these years the loans from the Fed usually involved a subsidy to the borrower. In some years—1966–67, 1969–70, 1973–74, 1981, 1984, and 1987—the discount rate was more than a full percentage point below the commercial paper rate. Looking at the earlier years, we see that the discount rate exceeded the commercial paper rate from 1932 to 1946 but was lower than the commercial paper rate during the 1920s and especially for 1918–20.

THE FEDERAL RESERVE SYSTEM

Since 1914 the Federal Reserve System has functioned as the central bank in the United States. There are 12 regional Federal Reserve banks, each of which was set

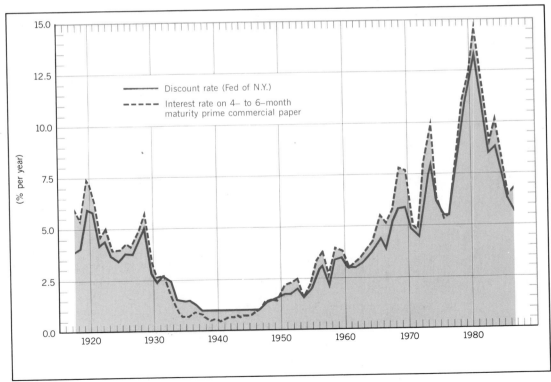

FIGURE 17.4 *The Fed's Discount Rate and Commercial Paper Rates*

up as a separate, quasi-private corporation. In the early days of the system, the 12 presidents of the regional banks served on the Governors' Conference, which had substantial influence over the Fed's policies. However, following the Great Depression and the Banking Act of 1935, the Governors' Conference was abolished, and the Fed's power was centralized in Washington, D.C. Since 1935 the main authority has resided with the **Board of Governors of the Federal Reserve System**. The seven members of this board are appointed by the President (and confirmed by the Senate) for staggered 14-year terms. The board is often dominated by its chairman—currently Alan Greenspan—who is appointed by the President for a four-year term.

The Fed carries out its open-market operations—purchases or sales of government securities in the open market—through the **Federal Open Market Committee (or FOMC)**. This important committee consists of the seven members of the Board of Governors plus the presidents of five of the regional banks (including the president of the New York bank and rotating memership among the other 11 banks). (We shall discuss the FOMC when we deal later with open-market operations.)

We have already mentioned some of the Fed's activities, which include the setting of reserve requirements, the regulation of interest rates on deposits, and the lending to financial institutions at the discount window.[6] Now we want to focus on the Fed's instruments for controlling the quantity of money. We begin by looking at the balance sheet of the Federal Reserve System.

Table 17.2 shows the balance sheet at the end of 1987. The main items on the asset side are the following:

- Gold account of $11.1 billion (carried at the official price of $42.22 per ounce). The Fed holds this gold on behalf of the U.S. Treasury. In past years, when the United States was on the gold standard, variations in the quantity of gold resulted mainly from dealing with foreign central banks. Now there are changes if the Treasury auctions off gold or if there are adjustments in the official price of gold. (These changes in price occurred in 1933 and a few times in the 1970s.)

- Loans to depository institutions of $3.8 billion. These are borrowings of depository intermediaries at the discount rate, which we mentioned before.

- U.S. government and agency securities of $231.4 billion. As the balance sheet makes clear, the bulk of the Fed's assets are held in this form.

The sum of loans to depository institutions, U.S. government and agency securities, and some miscellaneous assets is called **Federal Reserve credit.** This amount represents the total of the Fed's claims on the government and the private sector. Note that the great bulk of Federal Reserve credit takes the form of U.S. government securities. That is, unlike the central banks of many other countries, the Fed engages in little direct lending to the private sector.

---

[6]For discussions of the Federal Reserve System and its policy instruments, see Robert Auerbach (1985, Chaps. 14–16) and Milton Friedman (1960, Chap. 2).

TABLE 17.2 *Balance Sheet of All Federal Reserve Banks, December 31, 1987 (in billions of dollars)*

Assets		Liabilities and Capital Account	
Gold account	11.1	Federal Reserve notes (currency)	212.9
Loans to depository institutions	3.8	Deposits of depository institutions	41.8
U.S. government and agency securities	231.4	U.S. Treasury deposits	5.3
Other assets[a]	29.3	Other deposits and liabilities	11.5
		Paid-in capital and surplus	4.1
Total	275.6	Total	275.6

[a]Consists of special drawing rights at the International Monetary Fund ($5.0 billion), amounts due from the Federal Deposit Insurance Corporation (FDIC) ($2.6 billion), assets denominated in foreign currency ($7.8 billion), coin ($0.4 billion), accrued interest ($2.6 billion), physical capital ($0.8 billion), and some other items.

Source: U.S. Board of Governors of the Federal Reserve System, *Annual Report* (1987, pp. 218–19).

On the liability side of the Fed's ledger, we have the following main items:

▪ Federal Reserve notes (currency) of $212.9 billion. At present these notes are the only significant form of currency outstanding. But at earlier dates, currency was issued by the U.S. Treasury and—even earlier—by private banks.

▪ Deposits of depository institutions of $41.8 billion. These are the noninterest-bearing reserves of depository intermediaries, which we mentioned before.

▪ U.S. Treasury deposits of $5.3 billion. Essentially these deposits are the federal government's checking account, which is held at the Federal Reserve.

The total of federal reserve notes and deposits of depository institutions ($254.7 billion) is called the **monetary base** or **high-powered money** (or sometimes **M0**). This sum represents the total of the Fed's monetary liabilities (aside from those held by the U.S. Treasury or as foreign deposits). Note that in 1987, about 84% of the monetary base took the form of currency, while only 16% consisted of deposits of depository institutions.

CONTROL OF THE MONETARY BASE

Open Market Operations   In its early years of operation, the Federal Reserve focused on the discount window, which we shall discuss below, rather than on open-market operations. However, since the 1930s, open-market operations have become the principal instrument for controlling the monetary base.

Since 1935, decisions on open-market operations have been made by the Federal Open Market Committee (FOMC), which we mentioned earlier. The directives of this committee are carried out by the trading desk of the New York Federal Reserve Bank. Although the directives to the trading desk are explicit in terms of quantities of government bonds to buy or sell, the FOMC's reports on its policy stance are often vague. Typically, these reports mention the "condition of the market" or targets for the interest rate on Federal Funds. But it is unclear how to relate these targets to the volume of open-market operations, which is what the FOMC actually determines.

In the early 1980s, the targets of Federal Reserve policy were expressed more in terms of monetary aggregates, such as M1 or M2, and less in terms of interest rates. As we shall see later, we can relate the behavior of monetary aggregates to changes in the monetary base and hence to open-market operations. Therefore, it would be meaningful to guide open-market operations by a target for a specified monetary aggregate. But there is not much evidence that the Federal Reserve has actually paid much attention to its announced targets (which it began to release in 1978 at the insistence of Congress).

It is interesting to note that the FOMC delays for 30–60 days the publication of its statements on open-market policy. The Fed believes that this secrecy helps it to maintain "orderly" securities markets. Anybody who can explain this reasoning deserves at least an A in the course![7]

Let's consider how open-market operations affect the monetary base. In the case of an open-market purchase, the Fed writes a check to buy, say, $1 million of U.S. government securities. Suppose that the seller of the bonds is a commercial bank, which we call People's Bank. (We would end up with the same results if the seller were a household or, more likely, a large corporation.) The Fed credits this bank with $1 million more of reserves in the form of book-entry deposits at the Fed. At this point, the balance sheets of the Fed and People's Bank change as shown in Table 17.3. Notice that the Fed has $1 million more of assets in the form of government bonds. This amount balances the extra $1 million of liabilities, which show up as more deposits of depository institutions (in this case of People's Bank). Correspondingly, People's Bank has $1 million more of assets in the form of deposits held at the Fed but $1 million less of government bonds, which are part of the bank's portfolio of loans and securities.

The balance sheets shown in Table 17.3 are not the end of the story because People's Bank probably does not want to keep $1 million more of noninterest-bearing reserves at the Fed. But let's hold off on this matter for now to focus on the behavior of the monetary base. The open-market purchase of securities shown in Table 17.3 raises the monetary base by $1 million, which shows up initially as an extra $1 million in reserves held by depository institutions at the Fed. Note also that an open-market sale of securities would just reverse the process. If the Fed sells $1 million of U.S. government bonds, the monetary base declines by $1 million.

---

[7]The FOMC's secrecy has been challenged under the Freedom-of-Information Act, but the Supreme Court decided in favor of the FOMC. For a discussion, including the FOMC's defense of secrecy, see Marvin Goodfriend (1986).

TABLE 17.3 *Effects on the Balance Sheets of the Fed and Depository Institutions from an Open-Market Purchase of Government Bonds*

Assets	Liabilities
Federal Reserve	
U.S. Government securities: + $1 million	Deposits of depository institutions: + $1 million
People's Bank	
Loans and securities: − $1 million Deposits at Fed: + $1 million	

In the United States, open-market operations involve government bonds rather than private bonds, mortgages, shares in General Motors, and so on. That is because the Fed does not hold these types of private obligations. In fact, it would make little difference (except perhaps on political grounds) if the Fed switched from holdings of the public debt to holdings of private bonds. If this switch were made, the private sector would end up holding more of the public debt but would owe correspondingly more to the Fed. The Fed would have more claims on the private sector but less on the U.S. Treasury. Overall, there would be no changes in the net positions of the private sector, the Federal Reserve, and the U.S. Treasury.

Loans to Depository Institutions The Fed can also control the monetary base by varying the quantity of loans to depository institutions. Here, the Fed can change either the discount rate or other aspects of its lending policies to induce depository institutions to borrow more or less at the discount window. Suppose, for example, that People's Bank decides to borrow an additional $1 million from the Fed. Then the Fed records a loan of $1 million to People's Bank and also credits this bank with an extra $1 million of deposits. If People's Bank just holds these deposits at the Fed (perhaps because it would otherwise have fallen short of its reserve requirement), the balance sheets of the Fed and People's Bank change as shown in Table 17.4.

Notice that the borrowings show up as $1 million more in loans to depository institutions on the asset side of the Fed's books. Simultaneously, on the liability side,

TABLE 17.4 *Effects on the Balance Sheets of the Fed and Depository Institutions from Fed Lending at the Discount Window*

Assets	Liabilities
Federal Reserve	
Loans to depository institutions: + $1 million	Deposits of depository institutions: + $1 million
People's Bank	
Deposits at Fed: + $1 million	Borrowing from Fed: + $1 million

there is an increase by $1 million in the deposits of depository institutions. There are corresponding changes on the books of People's Bank. The main point is that, as before, the monetary base rises by $1 million.

It is important to recognize that an increase in borrowings by depository institutions at the discount window is essentially the same as an open-market purchase of securities by the Fed. In both cases the monetary base increases. The only difference is that in one case (the open-market purchase) the Fed ends up holding more U.S. government bonds, while in the other (lending at the discount window), the Fed ends up with more loans to depository institutions. Correspondingly, People's Bank ends up holding fewer government bonds in the first case and more debt to the Fed in the second. Overall, the difference amounts to a shift from the Fed's holding U.S. government bonds to the Fed's holding obligations on a private bank. But as mentioned before, these types of changes have no major consequences. The only significant difference concerns the subsidy that the Fed provides to depository institutions because the discount rate is typically set below the competitive interest rate.

Economists often say that a shift in the discount rate is significant not for its direct impact on borrowings but rather as an announcement of the Fed's intentions. Over the longer term, the Fed moves the discount rate to match changes in market interest rates (see Figure 17.4). Hence, most of the movements in the discount rate are reactions to changes in the economy rather than vice-versa. But the timing and sometimes the amount of a shift in the discount rate are at the Fed's discretion. It is possible that some of these changes are a useful signal about the future behavior of the monetary base. However, no one has yet shown that changes in the discount rate can actually help to predict the future quantity of the monetary base or other economic variables. So the suggestion that shifts in the discount rate have an "announcement effect" amounts to an interesting idea, which has not been proved.

Many economists think that the Fed should stop subsidizing borrowers—that is, it should set the discount rate at a penalty level above market interest rates. Of course, if the discount rate were actually a penalty rate, it would have to be above the rate at which an individual institution could otherwise borrow. For example, for a risky bank like Continental Illinois in 1984, the penalty rate would be well above the interest rate on commercial paper. But then, no institution would ever borrow from the Fed, so the suggestion for a penalty discount rate amounts to a proposal for closing the discount window.

From the standpoint of controlling the monetary base, the existence of the discount window adds nothing to open-market operations. Thus, the argument for the Fed's lending to depository institutions comes down to the desirability of subsidizing selected financial institutions—presumably mainly institutions that are in trouble. So far, no one has come up with good arguments to justify this policy.

THE MONETARY BASE AND MONETARY AGGREGATES

Thus far, our discussion shows how the Fed can control the monetary base. But we already mentioned that the Fed might adjust the base to achieve a target value for a monetary aggregate, such as M1 or M2. Recall that these aggregates add various categories of deposits to the amount of currency held by the public. Therefore, to study the relation between the monetary base and monetary aggregates, we have to understand the behavior of deposits.

Let's return to the case shown in Table 17.3 where the open-market purchase of government bonds raised the monetary base by $1 million. Instead of thinking of a single bank, consider now the effects on financial intermediaries as a whole. Table 17.5 shows that in step 1 these intermediaries have $1 million more of deposits at the Fed and $1 million less of loans and securities.

Suppose that the extra $1 million of deposits at the Fed are excess reserves, which the financial intermediaries do not wish to hold. Rather, these institutions place these funds into earning assets. To be concrete, assume that they make an additional $1 million of loans to households. However, the results would be the same if the intermediaries bought more securities. In any event, the recipients of the loans have an extra $1 million, which we suppose that they keep initially as deposits at a financial intermediary. Thus the balance sheet of these intermediaries changes as shown in step 2 of Table 17.5. On the asset side there is an additional $1 million of loans and securities, which offsets the initial decline by this amount. On the liability side, there is an added $1 million of customer deposits.

The recipients of the loan probably do not want to hold an extra $1 million of deposits. But as they spend these funds, they are transferred to the accounts of others. Ultimately people are either induced[8] to hold an extra $1 million of deposits at financial intermediaries, or they are motivated to redeem all or part of this $1

TABLE 17.5 *Effect of Open-Market Purchases of Bonds on the Financial System*

| | Financial Intermediaries (FIs) | | Households | | The Fed | |
	Assets	Liabilities	Assets	Liabilities	Assets	Liabilities
Step 1	Loans and securities: − $1 million Deposits at Fed: + $1 million				U.S. government bonds: + $1 million	Deposits of FIs: + $1 million
Step 2	Loans and securities: + $1 million	Customer deposits: + $1 million	Deposits at FIs: + $1 million	Loans from FIs: + $1 million		
Step 3	Loans and securities: + $880,000	Customer deposits: + $880,000	Deposits at FIs: + $880,000	Loans from FIs: + $880,000		

[8]As we show in the following section, the inducement derives in the present case from a higher price level.

million for currency (which the intermediaries stand ready to provide to depositors). For the moment, we will ignore this important possibility of moving into currency. Then we eventually reach the situation shown as step 2 in Table 17.5.

The extra $1 million in customer deposits raises the required reserves of the financial intermediaries. For illustrative purposes, assume a reserve ratio of 12%, which applies currently to most checkable deposits. Thus, required reserves rise by $120,000. But then the financial institutions still have $880,000 ($1 million less the $120,000) of excess reserves. Therefore, they again place these funds into earning assets, which we assume take the form of loans. When people are motivated to hold these additional funds as deposits we arrive at step 3 in Table 17.5. Here, the intermediaries' loans and securities and deposits each rise by another $880,000.

If we continue to work through this process, we find that the deposits held at financial institutions rise by a large multiple of the expansion in the monetary base. Specifically, the deposits increase eventually by the amount $1 million · $(1/0.12)$ = $8.33 million. In other words, the increase by $1 million in base money leads to an increase by $8.33 million in deposits. At this point, the intermediaries' required reserves are up by $0.12 · $8.33 million = $1 million—that is, the additional base money is all held as required reserves.

An important amendment to this **multiple expansion of deposits** concerns the household's demand for currency. Figure 17.5 shows the ratio of currency to checkable deposits since 1918. For the 1980s the ratio averaged 0.38, while for 1987, the ratio was 0.34. Using the value 0.4 for this ratio and assuming no changes

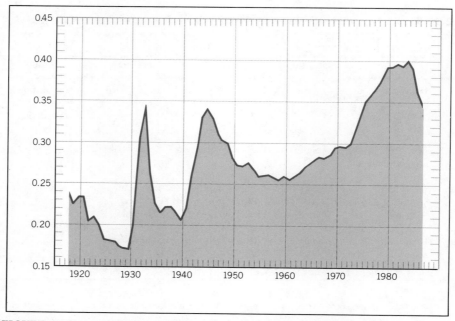

FIGURE 17.5 *The Ratio of the Public's Currency to Checkable Deposits*

in the relative attractiveness of currency and deposits, we predict that people will hold an additional 40 cents of currency along with each extra dollar of deposits.

Table 17.6 modifies the analysis to take account of currency. Now, with an extra $1 million· of funds in step 2a, the public is eventually motivated to hold (approximately) $700,000 more in deposits and $300,000 more in currency (assuming that the ratio of currency to deposits remains at 0.4). As the public redeems deposits to obtain this extra currency, the financial intermediaries must get this currency by running down their deposits at the Fed. Thus, in step 2a, the liabilities of financial institutions show $700,000 more in customer deposits, while their assets show $300,000 less in deposits at the Fed. Notice that required reserves are now up by $84,000 (0.12 · $700,000 of deposits) rather than the $120,000 in the previous step 2. But actual reserves are higher by only $700,000 rather than the previous $1 million. Thus, excess reserves are higher by $616,000 ($700,000 less $84,000) instead of the previous $880,000 ($1 million less $120,000). The "leakage" of funds into currency means that the financial intermediaries end up with less excess reserves than otherwise.

For the Fed, the additional currency outstanding of $300,000 corresponds to an equivalent reduction in the book-entry deposits of financial institutions. As shown in step 2a of Table 17.6, there is no change in the monetary base, which consists

TABLE 17.6 *Effect of Open-Market Purchases of Bonds on the Financial System, Including the Responses of Currency*

	Financial Intermediaries (FIs)		Households		The Fed	
	Assets	Liabilities	Assets	Liabilities	Assets	Liabilities
Step 1a	Loans and securities: − $1 million				U.S. government bonds: + $1 million	Deposits of FIs: + $1 million
	Deposits at Fed: + $1 million					
Step 2a	Loans and securities: + $1 million	Customer deposits: + $700,000	Deposits at FIs: + $700,000	Loans from FIs: + $1 million		Deposits of FIs: − $300,000
	Deposits at Fed: − $300,000		Currency: + $300,000			Currency: + $300,000
Step 3a	Loans and securities + $616,000	Customer deposits: + $440,000	Deposits at FIs: + $440,000	Loans from FIs: + $616,000		Deposits of FIs: − $176,000
	Deposits at Fed: − $176,000		Currency: + $176,000			Currency: + $176,000

of currency plus the deposits of the financial institutions at the Fed. Thus, the monetary base remains higher by $1 million.

The rest of the analysis proceeds as before, except that some funds leak out to currency at each stage. We can find the ultimate position from the following set of equations, where the symbol Δ represents the change in the associated variable:

$$\Delta \text{ (monetary base)} = \Delta \text{ (required reserves)} + \Delta \text{ (currency)} = \$1 \text{ million}$$

$$\Delta \text{ (required reserves)} = 0.12 \cdot \Delta \text{ (deposits)}$$

$$\Delta \text{ (currency)} = 0.4 \cdot \Delta \text{ (deposits)}$$

Substituting the second and third conditions into the first leads to

$$0.12 \cdot \Delta \text{ (deposits)} + 0.4 \cdot \Delta \text{ (deposits)} = \$1 \text{ million.}$$

Solving for the change in deposits, we get the results

$$\Delta \text{ (deposits)} = \$1 \text{ million}/0.52 = \$1,920,000$$

$$\Delta \text{ (currency)} = 0.4 \cdot \Delta \text{ (deposits)} = \$770,000$$

$$\Delta \text{ (required reserves)} = 0.12 \cdot \Delta \text{ (deposits)} = \$230,000$$

Thus, the incorporation of currency has a dramatic effect on the results. Instead of rising by $8.33 million, the deposits held at financial intermediaries end up increasing by only $1.92 million. Generally the ultimate expansion of deposits is larger the smaller is the ratio of reserves to deposits (fixed at 0.12 above) and the smaller is the ratio of currency to deposits (0.4 above).

Given the changes in deposits and currency, we can calculate how an open-market operation affects various monetary aggregates. If we limit attention to checkable deposits (with a required-reserve ratio of 0.12), the change in M1 is the sum of the changes in deposits and currency, or $2,690,000 above. Since an increase by $1,000,000 in high-powered money leads to an expansion by $2,690,000 in M1, we can say that the **money multiplier** (the ratio of M1 to the base) is 2.69. Generally the money multiplier is higher the lower are the ratios of reserves and currency to deposits.

Figure 17.6 shows the behavior of the money multiplier from 1918 to 1987. This multiplier has been relatively stable since World War II, with a range of 2.4 to 2.9. However, this stability reflects some long-term changes that happened to cancel. First, as shown in Figures 17.1 and 17.2, the ratios of required and excess reserves to checkable deposits declined from a total of 0.22 in 1950 to 0.11 in 1987. This change tended to raise the money multiplier. But second, as shown in Figure 17.5, the ratio of currency to checkable deposits rose from 0.26 in 1960 to 0.34 in 1987. This factor tended to lower the money multiplier.

The other striking feature of Figure 17.6 is the dramatic drop in the money multiplier from 3.9 in 1930 to 1.9 in 1940. This change reflected increases in the ratios of reserves and currency to checkable deposits. (We shall discuss the details of these changes later.)

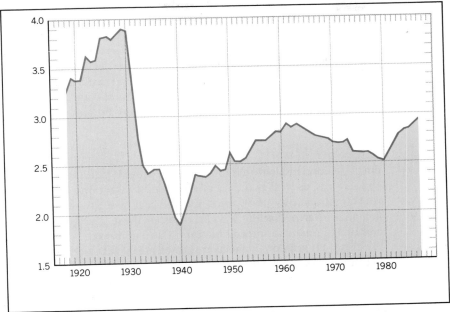

FIGURE 17.6 *Ratio of M1 to the Monetary Base (the Money Multiplier)*

EFFECTS OF FEDERAL RESERVE ACTIONS

THE NEUTRALITY OF OPEN-MARKET OPERATIONS

For a closed economy, we found in Chapter 14 that open-market operations were neutral. In particular, a one-time shift in the monetary base led only to proportional responses in the price level and other nominal variables (except for the quantity of public debt). This result applies also to an open economy under flexible exchange rates, as studied in Chapter 16, except that the nominal exchange rate moves along with the other nominal variables.

These results do not change when we introduce financial intermediation. But we have to include as nominal variables the dollar quantities of the various deposits and reserves. Then we find that these nominal magnitudes rise along with the other nominal variables in proportion to the change in the monetary base. An open-market operation leaves unchanged the real quantities of deposits and reserves, the ratio of deposits to currency, the ratio of reserves to deposits, and so on.

Among the variables that do not change when there is a one-time open-market operation are the nominal interest rate on earning assets, R, and the nominal interest rate, R^d, paid on deposits. Since these interest rates are unchanged, households and firms would not alter their desired holdings of currency and deposits in real terms. Thus, the results are consistent with the unchanged real quantities of currency and deposits, which we mentioned above.

The financial intermediaries also end up in the same real position as before the open-market operation. Specifically, there are no changes in the intermediaries' real quantities of deposits, reserves, and loans and securities. If these institutions held reserves initially only because of requirement—say, 12% of deposits—the final holdings of reserves again equal the required amount.

THE AMOUNT OF FINANCIAL INTERMEDIATION

Financial intermediation is important because it facilitates the matching of borrowers and lenders, as well as the carrying out of transactions. The reflection of this process is the real quantity of deposits and the real quantity of loans and securities held by financial intermediaries. We can think of these real quantities as a measure of the amount of financial intermediation in an economy.

The amount of financial intermediation that occurs depends on the benefits and costs. As mentioned before, the benefits relate to the efficient evaluation of loans, the diversification of assets by risk and maturity, and the convenience of deposits. The costs include the expenses of servicing deposits and loans, the return to capital in the intermediary business, reserve requirements, and the costs of evading restrictions for paying interest on deposits. If these costs of intermediation rise, we predict that less intermediation would occur.

As an example, suppose that the Fed increases reserve requirements. Since financial intermediaries must hold more noninterest-bearing reserves for each dollar of deposits, these institutions end up paying a lower interest rate, R^d, on deposits. Consequently, households switch from deposits to currency or earning assets, and financial institutions end up with smaller real quantities of deposits and assets. That is, there is less financial intermediation. Note that we would reach the same conclusion if, instead of assuming an increase in reserve requirements, we postulated a higher cost for financial intermediaries to service deposits or police loans. Again, we would end up with less financial intermediation.

When there is less financial intermediation, it becomes harder for resources to flow toward investors whose projects have the greatest marginal products or toward consumers who have the greatest desires to consume now rather than later. On both counts, the economy operates less efficiently. Typically this loss of efficiency shows up as smaller aggregates of the capital stock and output. But the principal conclusion is that less financial intermediation means a poorer match of resources to their ultimate uses.

To some extent, the costs of intermediation reflect the underlying expenses of policing borrowers and servicing deposits. We can think of these elements as part of the technology or production function that generates intermediating services. Then the amount of intermediation that results tends to be optimal, given this technology. But, as already noted, reserve requirements, government regulation of interest rates on deposits, and so on artificially raise the cost of intermediation. More restrictive policies—such as higher reserve requirements—tend to discourage intermediation, which leads to a less efficient allocation of resources.[9]

Financial Intermediation and the Price Level   The degree of financial intermediation may also interact with the determination of the price level. To see how this works, let's use our analysis of price level determination for a closed economy from previous chapters. (The results would be the same for an open economy under flexible exchange rates.) We now identify money with the monetary base—that is, as the sum of currency in circulation plus the reserves held by financial institutions at the Fed. Suppose that the Fed controls the dollar quantity of base money, M, through open-market operations, as discussed above. Then the process of financial intermediation influences the price level because it affects the real demand for base money, M^d/P. For a given dollar quantity of base money, anything that raises the real demand leads to a fall in the price level. Note that this effect works just like the various increases in the real demand for money that we considered in previous chapters.

As an example, suppose again that the Fed raises the required-reserve ratio on deposits. For a given quantity of deposits, there is an increase in the demand for reserves by depository institutions. Hence, on this count, there is an increase in the real demand for the monetary base.

There are some additional effects because, as noted before, the higher reserve ratio tends to reduce the interest rate paid on deposits. To the extent that households shift out of deposits and into currency, there is a further increase in the real demand for the monetary base. (That is because the demand for base money varies one-to-one with the demand for currency but varies only fractionally with the amount of deposits.) But to the extent that people move away from deposits and into earning assets, the real demand for base money tends to decline. (That is because the reduction in deposits reduces the real demand for reserves by financial institutions.) Thus, the shifting of households' assets among deposits, currency, and earning assets has an ambiguous overall effect on the real demand for the monetary base.[10]

Because of the direct positive effect on the demand for reserves, we can be pretty sure that the overall effect of an increase in the required-reserve ratio is to raise the real demand for base money. Therefore, for a given nominal quantity of base money, the rise in the real demand for base money means that the price level falls.

Historically, the main examples of large short-term variations in the real demand for base money involve banking panics and an experiment with changes in reserve requirements in 1936–37. Therefore, we now consider some details of these episodes.

Banking Panics   Banks and other financial intermediaries promise to convert their demand deposits into currency immediately at face value. Typically these

---

[9]For the argument that the financial industry should be fully deregulated, see Fischer Black (1970) and Eugene Fama (1983).

[10]For further discussion of these types of effects, see James Tobin (1971a, 1971b).

institutions also extend this instantaneous conversion privilege to savings deposits, for which some notice of withdrawal (usually 30 days) can legally be required. However, intermediaries do not hold nearly enough cash or liquid securities to allow for the simultaneous conversion of all deposits into currency at face value.[11] Even if the underlying loans and securities are sound, financial institutions can get into trouble if too many customers want their cash at the same time. If people become concerned about a bank's ability to convert its deposits into currency at face value, each individual has an incentive to get into line first to cash in. This incentive is especially great when the deposits are not insured by the government, as was the case in the United States until 1934. When many people attempt to cash in their deposits simultaneously, there is a "run on the bank." Sometimes a bank responds by temporarily *suspending* the privilege of converting demand deposits into currency. When this happens simultaneously at many banks or other financial institutions, we say that a **banking panic** occurs.

The hallmark of a banking panic is a sudden increase in the demand for currency rather than deposits. As a response, banks and other intermediaries tend to increase their demands for excess reserves and other liquid assets to meet their customers' possible demands for cash. Overall, the banking panic leads to increases in the real demand for base money—partly in the form of the public's currency and partly as reserves of financial institutions. Hence, from the previous analysis, a banking panic has two types of effects. First, it makes financial intermediation more difficult, which has adverse consequences for the efficient allocation of resources. Specifically, real output and investment are likely to decline. Then second, unless there is substantial increase in the nominal quantity of base money, the sharp increase in the real demand for base money puts strong downward pressure on the price level.

Banking panics occurred fairly often in the United States before the Federal Reserve began operations in 1914. There were 12 episodes between 1800 and 1914 that are generally called banking panics. For the period after the Civil War, where better data are available, the most severe crises were those in 1873, 1893, and 1907. Typically the panics exhibited increases in the ratios of the public's currency and banks' excess reserves to deposits. They also tended to show decreases in prices and in real economic activity. It is, however, hard to sort out the independent influence of the banking panics on output and other real variables. That is because, under the monetary system that was in place before the establishment of the Federal Reserve, poor economic conditions tended automatically to generate financial crises.[12] Economists think that these crises also made real economic conditions worse, but it is not easy to prove this proposition through statistical analysis.

A major reason for the creation of the Federal Reserve was the desire to mod-

---

[11]By *liquid,* we mean that little cost attaches to the quick sale of an asset. Thus, government bonds are liquid, but real estate is relatively illiquid. Loans that are costly to evaluate—such as those to local businesses and consumers—may also be illiquid.

[12]Phillip Cagan (1965, pp. 265ff.) argues that the banking panics have major elements that are independent of changes in business conditions. But Gary Gorton (1986) finds a close relationship between business failures and banking panics.

erate financial crises. One way that the founders of the Fed sought to promote financial stability was through the accommodation of seasonal demands for money. In this objective the Fed has been successful. In particular, there is evidence that the Fed's accommodation of seasonal variations in money demand eliminated the seasonal pattern in nominal interest rates that applied before 1914 (see Jeffrey Miron, 1986). Whether this success helped to eliminate banking panics is unclear.

A more controversial idea—related to views on the role played by the Bank of England (see Walter Bagehot, 1873)—was that the Fed would serve as the **lender of last resort** through the operation of its discount window. When a financial crisis threatened, the lender of last resort would lend liberally to financial institutions at the discount rate, which would be set below market interest rates. In practice, direct lending by the Fed through the discount window was important during World War I and in the 1920s but has since become less significant.

During the 1920s, the Fed was successful in averting banking panics. In particular, it is likely that the sharp economic contraction of 1921 would have resulted in a banking panic under the pre–World War I monetary regime. The worst banking panics in U.S. history occurred, however, from 1930 to 1933 during the Great Depression. Milton Friedman and Anna Schwartz (1963, chap. 7) argue convincingly that this financial crisis would have been much less severe if the Fed had not existed. That is because, under the earlier environment, the banks would not have relied on corrective measures from the Fed, which turned out not to materialize. In particular, the Fed failed to act as a lender of last resort.

Between 1930 and 1933 there was an unprecedented number of bank suspensions—roughly 9000 out of about 25,000 banks that existed at the end of 1929. Then in March 1933, President Roosevelt proclaimed a "banking holiday," which temporarily closed all of the banks. About one-third of those that had existed in 1929 never reopened.

Because of the banking panics from 1930 to 1933, there were sharp increases in the public's holdings of currency relative to deposits. Figure 17.5 shows that the ratio of currency to checkable deposits rose from 0.17 in 1930 to 0.34 in 1933. Similarly, the banking panics increased the ratio of excess reserves to checkable deposits from near zero in 1930 to 0.04 in 1933 and 0.12 in 1935 (see Figure 17.2). As mentioned before, these types of increases in the real demand for base money depress the price level if the nominal quantity of base money does not change.[13] In fact, base money increased from an average of \$6.6 billion in 1930 to \$7.9 billion in 1933. Yet the price level, as measured by the GNP deflator, fell at an annual rate of 7.9% over this period.

The reaction to the banking panics of the Great Depression was a substantial amount of banking legislation. The various regulations on deposit interest rates began at this time. Also, the Fed obtained the power to change reserve requirements. However, the principal innovation in 1934 was the creation of the Federal Deposit

---

[13]The costs of financial intermediation also rise. Ben Bernanke (1983b) stresses this feature of banking panics during the Great Depression.

Insurance Corporation (FDIC), which insures deposits at banks.[14] When the government guarantees the redemption of deposits, people lose most of their incentive to withdraw their funds when they are unsure about an institution's financial position. Therefore, it becomes harder for a bank run to start or for one bank's problems to spread to others. In fact, there have been no major banking panics since 1933. Accordingly, we no longer have this major source of instability in the real demand for base money and, hence, in the price level. We can be reasonably confident that this dramatic change from the earlier experience derives from the implementation of federal deposit insurance.

On the other hand, the presence of federal deposit insurance reduces the incentives of financial institutions to use caution in accepting risky loans. (This effect arises because an institution's insurance premium does not depend on the riskiness of that institution's portfolio of loans.) Some economists argue that this incautious attitude accounts for the high incidence of problems in lending to real estate developers, oil explorers, and foreign governments. In the end, the federal government (and the U.S. taxpayer) will have to pay through the FDIC (and the parallel agency for savings and loan associations, FSLIC) for much of this problem lending. Thus, federal deposit insurance may replace the problem of banking panics with the problem of greater incidence of insolvency for financial institutions.

Changes in Reserve Requirements in 1936–1937   There were no changes in legal reserve requirements from 1917 until 1936. Then, mindful of the large quantity of banks' excess reserves (49% of total reserves and 12% of checkable deposits in 1935), the Fed decided to "mop them up" by sharply raising reserve requirements. For example, the required-reserve ratio for member commercial banks in major cities other than New York and Chicago went from 10% of net demand deposits in 1935 to 15% in August 1936, 17.5% in March 1937, and 20% in May 1937. Overall, the ratio of required reserves to checkable deposits rose from an average of 12% in 1935 to 22% in 1937 (see Figure 17.1).

Apparently the Fed believed that banks would hold required reserves instead of excess reserves, with no major change occurring in total reserves. But the massive holdings of excess reserves after 1933 (see Figure 17.2) reflected the banks' precuations in order to avoid the kinds of banking panics that occurred from 1930 to 1933. Thus, although the ratio of excess reserves to checkable deposits fell from 12% in 1935 to 5% in 1937, the banks then rebuilt this ratio to 10% in 1938 and 16% in 1939. Accordingly, while the monetary base grew at an annual rate of 13% from 1937 to 1939, the GNP deflator declined over this period at an annual rate of 1.5%. We can attribute this behavior of prices to the growing demand for reserves by banks, which followed from the steep rise in required reserves during 1936–37.

Many economists also attribute the recession of 1936–38 to the Fed's steep increase in reserve requirements. Starting from the trough of the Great Depression

---

[14]The funds for this purpose come from a levy on the deposits of the insured banks. Formally, there is a ceiling for the size of insured deposits, which is $100,000. But in practice the government seems to guarantee even the larger deposits. This practice was made explicit for the depositors of the Continental Illinois National Bank in 1984.

in 1933, real GNP grew rapidly at the average rate of 9.6% per year until 1936. But the average growth rate was near zero between 1936 and 1938 (before rising strongly at the average rate of 7.3% per year from 1938 to 1940). At this point, our theory predicts a real effect from the increase in reserve requirements only because of the adverse effect on financial intermediation—that is, on the matching of lenders and borrowers. In particular, we do not predict real effects because of the depressing influence of higher reserve requirements on prices and other nominal variables. We shall, however, reexamine the important issue of linkages between nominal and real variables in Chapters 18–20.

Probably because of the economy's poor performance in 1936–38, the Fed has never again engineered a sharp short-run increase in reserve requirements. Although the legal requirements shifted many times—most of them downward—between 1938 and 1980, Figure 17.1 does not show any short-run movements in the required-reserve ratio that rival those of 1936–37. One notable development is the decline in the ratio from 15% in 1979 to less than 10% in 1984 (and 11% in 1987). This change reflected the spread of checkable deposits outside commercial banks and the reduced reserve requirements under the banking legislation of 1980.

SUMMARY

Financial institutions use the funds generated from deposits to make loans to house-holds, businesses, and the government. The intermediation between deposit holders and borrowers is useful because it allows financial specialists to evaluate and collect loans. In addition, the process creates various types of deposits, which are convenient as stores of value and as media of exchange. The conventional definition of money, M1, adds those deposits that are checkable to the public's holding of currency. Thus, M1 attempts to measure the assets that serve as common media of exchange.

The amount of financial intermediation depends on the costs of intermediating, which include expenses for servicing deposits and loans, returns to capital in the intermediary business, requirements to hold noninterest-bearing reserves, and costs of avoiding restrictions on the payments of interest on deposits. An increase in these costs—such as a rise in reserve requirements on deposits—leads to less financial intermediation. Consequently there are adverse real effects, which include a greater difficulty of matching borrowers and lenders. These effects tend to show up as reductions in the quantities of investment and output.

The Federal Reserve controls the size of the monetary base (the sum of the public's currency and the reserves of financial institutions) mainly through open-market operations. In the United States these operations typically involve exchanges between base money and U.S. government bonds. However, the Fed's loans to financial institutions at the discount window affect the monetary base in a similar manner.

An increase in the monetary base leads to a multiplicative expansion of deposits and of monetary aggregates, such as M1. The money mulitplier, which is the ratio of M1 to the base, is greater the smaller are the ratios of reserves and currency to deposits. The money multiplier has been reasonably stable since World War II, but fell sharply in the 1930s.

Open-market operations are still neutral in the model. That is, they affect the price level and other nominal variables but do not change any real variables (aside from the private sector's holdings of real government bonds). Among the real variables that do not change are the ratios of deposits to currency and of deposits to reserves.

Given the quantity of base money, the price level depends inversely on the real demand for the monetary base. Historically for the United States, the major short-term movements in this demand stemmed from banking panics. These panics featured sharp increases in the public's demand for currency and in banks' demands for excess reserves. The implementation of deposit insurance in 1934 apparently eliminated banking panics but also increased the tendency for financial institutions to make risky loans.

IMPORTANT TERMS AND CONCEPTS

demand deposits	Regulation Q
savings deposits	disintermediation
time deposits	Board of Governors of the Federal Reserve System
financial intermediaries	
vault cash	Federal Open Market Committee (FOMC)
reserves (of depository institutions)	Federal Reserve credit
Federal Funds market	monetary base
Federal Funds rate	high-powered money
discount rate (of Fed)	multiple expansion of deposits
reserve requirement	money multiplier
excess reserves	banking panic
costs of intermediation	lender of last resort

QUESTIONS AND PROBLEMS

Mainly for Review

17.1 What considerations limit the amount of excess reserves held by financial institutions? Explain how the volume of reserves can be less than the volume of deposits.

17.2 What factors account for the spread between the interest rate on earning assets and the interest rate on checkable deposits? Is an increase in the spread associated with a lower volume of deposits?

17.3 Show that for an increase in the monetary base to be matched by an equivalent increase in reserves and currency held by the public, there must be a multiplicative expansion of deposits. How much would deposits expand if the reverse requirement were 100%?

17.4 Why does the expectation of a bank failure give individuals an incentive to cash in their deposits? Show that this expectation can be a self-fulfilling prophecy. How does the provision of deposit insurance reduce the likelihood of this event?

17.5 Explain why a shift by households away from currency and toward demand deposits would raise the price level.

PROBLEMS FOR DISCUSSION

17.6 *The Fed's Discount Rate and Borrowing at the Fed*
How does the volume of borrowing at the Fed depend on the discount rate and the interest rate on earning assets? Do the data shown in Figures 17.3 and 17.4 support the answer?

Suppose that the Fed lowers the discount rate so that borrowings increase. Are the effects on the economy the same as those from an open-market purchase of bonds?

17.7 *Reserve Requirements*
Suppose that the Fed increases the required-reserve ratio on checkable deposits.
a. How does this change affect the real demand for base money?
b. How does it affect the price level?
c. How does it affect the nominal quantity of M1?
d. What real effects occur from the increase in reserve requirements?

Let's pretend now that the government imposes reserve requirements on something that has nothing to do with "money." For example, the requirement could be on refrigerators—anyone who owns a refrigerator must hold $10 of noninterest-bearing reserves at the Fed.

How does this new policy affect the real demand for base money and the price level? What other effects arise (for example, on the number of refrigerators)? In what ways do the answers differ from those above, where the requirements apply to checkable deposits?

17.8 *Vault Cash and Reserve Requirements*
From 1917 until December 1959, vault cash did not count toward satisfying the Fed's reserve requirements. Part of it counted until November 1960, after which all of vault cash counted toward the requirements. Just before the change in 1959–60, vault cash at banks that were members of the Federal Reserve System was $2.2 billion, which amounted to about 2% of all checkable deposits.

If the monetary base did not change for 1960–61, how would the new treatment of vault cash affect the price level? (In fact, base money declined from an average of $50.4 billion in 1959 to $50.0 billion in 1960 and $49.1 billion in 1961.)

17.9 *Interest on Reserves Held at the Fed*

At present, reserves held at the Federal Reserve bear no interest. Suppose that reserves were paid interest at a rate that was some fraction of the interest rate on commercial paper. If the quantity of base money stayed the same, how would this change affect the following:

a. the interest rate paid on checkable deposits?
b. the dollar amount of checkable deposits?
c. the price level?
d. the amount of intermediation in the economy?
e. the profits of the Federal Reserve (which go to the U.S. Treasury)?

17.10 *Gold and the Monetary Base*

Suppose that the U.S. Treasury receives $1 billion of gold from abroad. Then the Treasury deposits the gold at the Fed, so that the Fed's gold account and the Treasury's deposits at the Fed each rise by $1 billion.

a. What happens to the monetary base if the Treasury holds the extra $1 billion in deposits?
b. What happens if the Treasury spends the extra $1 billion and thereby restores its deposits to their initial level?
c. How can the Fed offset the effect of the gold inflow on the monetary base? (If it takes this action, the Fed is said to "sterilize" the inflow of gold.)
d. Suppose that the government raises the official price of gold from $42.22 per ounce to the market price of around $418 (at the end of 1988). Then the capital gain on the Fed's gold holdings (valued at $11.1 billion at the end of 1988, using the official price of $42.22) is credited to the Treasury's deposits at the Fed. What might this action do to the monetary base (which was $283 billion at the end of 1988)? What could the Fed do to keep the monetary base from changing?

17.11 *Membership in the Federal Reserve System*

Until 1980 only commercial banks that were members of the Federal Reserve System were subject to the Fed's reserve requirements. (There were also some services, such as check clearing and access to the discount window, that were provided free to members.) Membership was optional for banks with state charters but required for those with federal charters. (In 1980 only 30% of all commercial banks had national charters. But these institutions accounted for 55% of the deposits at commercial banks.)

The fraction of state banks that were members of the Federal Reserve System declined from 21% in 1948 to 10% in 1980. Why do you think this happened?

17.12 *Runs on Financial Institutions*

In the text we discussed runs on banks. How does the analysis differ if the run applies to other financial intermediaries, which do not offer checkable deposits? (For example, this description would apply unitl recently to savings and loan associations.)

17.13 *Deposit Insurance* (*optional*)

We discussed the role of federal deposit insurance, which has apparently prevented banking panics since 1933. A number of unsolved questions arise here, which you might want to think about.

a. Could private companies satisfactorily provide insurance on deposits? In particular, would the private sector end up providing the "right" amount of insurance? Would private companies also charge for this insurance in accordance with the riskiness of an institution's earnings? What problems can arise if the government provides the insurance but does not take proper account of risk? More generally, why is deposit insurance an area where the government should be involved?

b. Is there a reason for the government to be in the insurance business for deposits but not for other things, such as corporate obligations? (In fact, the federal government has gotten into the business of insuring the debt of doubtful borrowers—such as New York City and the Chrysler Corporation—as well as pension obligations and accounts at stockbrokers.)

CHAPTER

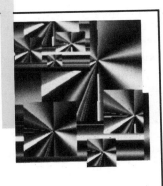

THE INTERPLAY BETWEEN NOMINAL AND REAL VARIABLES—WHAT IS THE EVIDENCE?

o far, our analysis has not stressed monetary variables as a source of fluctuations in real economic activity. Yet many economists think that movements in money and prices—that is, nominal disturbances—have a great deal to do with the short-term behavior of real variables, such as aggregate output and employment. In this chapter we concern ourselves primarily with the empirical evidence on this important issue. But first, let's summarize what our theory says so far about the interaction between nominal and real variables.

The theory predicts that changes in the monetary base are neutral. In particular, a one-time shift in the quantity of base money leads to proportional changes in the nominal variables but no changes in the real variables. For example, in a closed economy, we would get responses in the price level, the nominal wage rate, and the dollar values of output, investment, and so on. In an open economy with flexible exchange rates, we would see a corresponding change in the nominal exchange rate. But the important point is that there are no changes in the quantities of output and employment, the real interest rate, the real exchange rate, and so on.

We can also consider complicated monetary disturbances, where the changes do not occur entirely at the present time. Then the anticipations of future monetary changes lead to complicated responses of the price level, as well as to shifts in the nominal interest rate. But the model still predicts no changes in the real variables. At least, the only exception in the theory concerns the transaction costs for moving between money and either goods or interest-bearing assets. Since changes in the nominal interest rate affect the real demand for money, we get some real effects through this channel. But these influences are insufficient to account for sizable fluctuations in aggregate real economic activity.

The results differ if monetary fluctuations reflect shifts in the cost of intermediation rather than changes in the quantity of base money. As examples, increases in reserve requirements or restrictions on the payment of interest on deposits raise the cost of intermediation, and a banking panic lowers households' willingness to hold deposits.[1] In these cases, as with reductions of the monetary base, the price level and other nominal variables decline. But the higher cost of intermediation leads also to contractions of investment and output. Therefore, these types of disturbances move nominal and real variables in the same direction.

There are also real disturbances, such as the oil crises of 1973–74 and 1979–80, which we can represent as shifts to production functions.[2] An adverse shock reduces output, which lowers the quantity of real money demanded. For a given amount of base money, the price level rises. Hence the price level moves in the opposite direction of output in this case.

In an open economy with fixed exchange rates, we found in Chapter 16 that it was not easy for the monetary authority to determine the quantity of base money once the exchange rate had been chosen. To sustain an increase in the monetary base (which did not reflect a prior increase in the real demand for the base), governments tend to restrict trade in goods or assets. Then it is not surprising that these restrictions—even if not the increase in base money itself—would have real effects.

Overall, the theory does allow for some relationships between nominal and real variables, although the sign of the interaction depends on the nature of the underlying disturbance. However, let's stress the key theoretical proposition, which concerns monetary neutrality. Purely monetary disturbances—in the sense of changes in the monetary base—have no real effects. Although these monetary disturbances can create substantial variations in prices and other nominal variables, we still predict no response in the aggregates of output, employment, and so on.[3]

Most economists regard the proposition of monetary neutrality as incorrect, at least in some short-run contexts. In fact, many researchers attribute a large portion of aggregate business fluctuations to monetary disturbances, which the theory says have no important real effects. The common view is that monetary expansion

---

[1]Banking panics are typically not independent of prior changes in business conditions. However, the potential for panics does depend on some features of the financial structure. In particular, as discussed in Chapter 17, the implementation of federal deposit insurance in 1934 has apparently prevented panics since that time.

[2]For most purposes, we can also include here changes in government purchases and shifts in taxes and transfers. For example, an increase in marginal tax rates is analogous to an adverse shift of the production function.

[3]The variations in prices lead to changes in the distribution of real assets. Specifically, nominal debtors gain from surprise inflation, and nominal creditors lose. But the theory does not allow for effects of these types of distributional shifts on the aggregates of output and employment. One possibility would be to extend the theory so that these distributional changes do have aggregate consequences.

tends to stimulate real economic activity and monetary contraction tends to cause recessions.

THE PHILLIPS CURVE

Economists often express their ideas about the relation between real and nominal variables in terms of the **Phillips curve** (named after the British economist A. W. Phillips). This curve is intended to summarize the relation between a measure of real economic activity—such as the unemployment rate or the level or growth rate of output—and a nominal variable—such as the rate of change of prices or nominal wages or the stock of money. The basic notion behind the Phillips curve is that more inflation (and more monetary growth underlying this inflation) brings about an economic boom, which shows up as lower unemployment and a higher growth rate of real GNP. Initially this idea was presented as an empirical, inverse relation between the unemployment rate and the rate of growth of nominal wages. But subsequently, researchers have often replaced the rate of wage change by the growth rate of either prices or money. Figure 18.1 shows a simple version of the Phillips curve. In this figure, a lower inflation rate, π, is associated with a higher unemployment rate, u.

Economists sometimes argue that more inflation or more monetary growth results in lower unemployment and a higher growth of output only in the short run. The economy adjusts eventually to any established rate of inflation, so that the real variables no longer depend on the behavior of the nominal variables. Suppose that we think of the expected rate of inflation, π^e, as the rate of inflation to which the economy has adjusted itself. Then, as shown in Figure 18.2, it is only the surprise

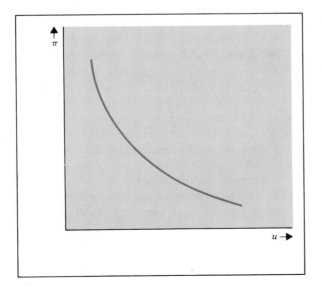

FIGURE 18.1 *A Simple Phillips Curve*
The Phillips curve associates a lower value of the inflation rate, π, with a higher unemployment rate, u.

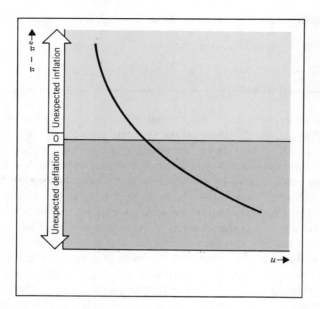

FIGURE 18.2 *An Expectational Phillips Curve*
The expectational Phillips curve associates a lower value of unexpected inflation, $\pi - \pi^e$, with a higher unemployment rate, u. Thus, a given unemployment rate (say 6%) can coexist with any rate of inflation.

part of inflation, $\pi - \pi^e$, that would relate systematically (and presumably negatively) to the unemployment rate. This type of relation is called an **expectational Phillips curve** because the inflation rate enters relative to the amount of expected inflation. One important property of this curve is that a given unemployment rate can coexist with any amount of inflation. For example, an unemployment rate of 6% is consistent with an inflation rate of 0%, 10%, 20%, and so on. If the inflation rate rises from 0% to 10% but the expected inflation rate rises by the same amount, unexpected inflation, $\pi - \pi^e$, does not change. Therefore, if the expectational Phillips curve is correct, this kind of increase in expected inflation has no significance for the unemployment rate. Equivalently we can say that the simple Phillips curve in Figure 18.1 applies for a fixed value of the expected inflation rate, π^e. When π^e changes, the curve in this figure shifts. Specifically, a higher value of π^e means that a higher inflation rate is associated with any given value of the unemployment rate.

We can view much of the macrotheorizing since the 1930s as attempts to explain versions of the Phillips curve and, as a related matter, the absence of monetary neutrality. This perspective applies as much to the Keynesian theory as to the more recent monetary theories of business fluctuations. But before we explore these theories, we should understand the nature of the facts that they are trying to explain. In particular, we want to know to what extent the Phillips curve—either the simple one or the expectational variety—and monetary nonneutrality are "facts." In this chapter we bring out the major pieces of empirical evidence that concern the interplay between nominal and real variables. Throughout this discussion, we look especially for findings that demonstrate the existence of the Phillips curve and the nonneutrality of money.

THE RELATIONSHIP BETWEEN UNEMPLOYMENT AND THE RATES OF CHANGE OF WAGES, PRICES, AND MONEY—LONG TERM EVIDENCE FOR THE UNITED KINGDOM AND THE UNITED STATES

The term *Phillips curve* derives from studies of the relationship between unemployment and the growth rate of nominal wages carried out by A. W. Phillips (1958) and Richard Lipsey (1960). Lipsey's statistical analysis documented a significant inverse relationship between the unemployment rate and the growth rate of nominal wages in the United Kingdom in the late nineteenth and early twentieth centuries. The nature of his findings shows up in Figure 18.3, which plots the British data from 1863 to 1913. The growth rate of the nominal wage, Δw, appears on the vertical axis, while the unemployment rate, u, is on the horizontal. The curve shows a clear negative relationship, which excited Lipsey and many subsequent researchers.

The inverse relation between unemployment and the growth rate of nominal wages does not hold up after World War I. The interwar period, 1923–39, exhibited exceptionally high unemployment rates; the average value of 14.3% contrasts with that of 4.7% from 1862 to 1913. But Figure 18.4 shows that there is no significant correlation between the unemployment rate and the rate of change of wages over the period 1923–39.

A different pattern of association between wage-rate changes and unemployment arises in the post–World War II period. For the years 1947–87, the relation between the unemployment rate and the rate of change of wages is significantly positive, as shown in Figure 18.5. In other words, the Phillips curve for the United Kingdom slopes in the "wrong" direction since World War II! The most notable change, however, from the pre–World War I period is the higher average growth rate of nominal wages: 7.9% per year for 1947–87 versus 0.8% for 1862–1913 (and −0.1% for 1923–39). In comparison with the period before World War I, the recent years involve mainly an increase in the average rate of wage change, with no significant difference in the average unemployment rate.

The results for the United Kingdom look basically similar if we replace the growth rate of nominal wages by the growth rate of either prices or the M1 definition of money. The only indication of an inverse relation between unemployment and the growth rate of a nominal variable—wages, prices, or M1—appears in the years before World War I. Also, for any of the nominal variables, the slope of the Phillips curve has the wrong sign in the recent period.

The pattern of results for the United States resembles that for the United Kingdom.[4] Figure 18.6 shows a significantly negative association between the unem-

---

[4]Irving Fisher (1926) carried out an early statistical study of this type of relationship for the United States, although he used price changes instead of wage changes. This study is reprinted (under the cute title, "I Discovered the Phillips Curve") in the *Journal of Political Economy*, April 1973.

ployment rate and the growth rate of wages from 1890 to 1913. Figure 18.7 shows the relationship over the interwar period, 1923–39. Although the slope is negative, this relation is not statistically significant. Unlike the United Kingdom, the unemployment rates in the United States were low during most of the 1920s. But for the 1930s, the unemployment rates were similar in the two countries.

Figure 18.8 shows the absence of a significant correlation between the unemployment rate and the growth rate of nominal wages for the United States in the post–World War II period, 1947–87. Some weak indication of a positive relationship—that is, of a wrongly sloped Phillips curve—shows up for the United States from 1947 to 1987 if we replace the growth rate of wages by that of either prices or a monetary aggregate, such as M1.

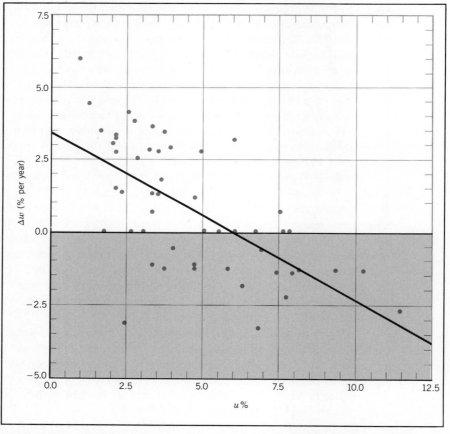

FIGURE 18.3 *The Unemployment Rate and the Rate of Change of Wages in the United Kingdom, 1863–1913*
Sources of data for figures 18.3–18.5. The unemployment rate is from B. R. Mitchell and P. Deane (1962), B. R. Mitchell (1980), and Monthly Digest of Statistics, *various issues. The wage rate index is from B. R. Mitchell (1980), Department of Employment and Productivity (1971), and* Monthly Digest of Statistics, *various issues.*

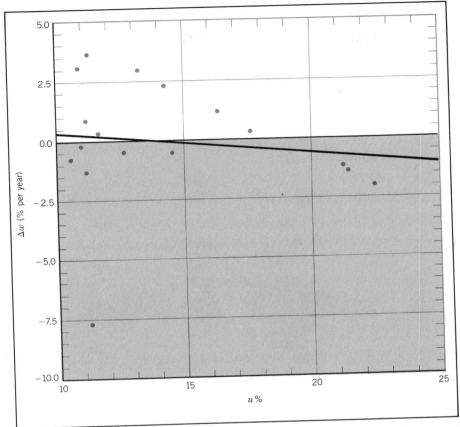

FIGURE 18.4 *The Unemployment Rate and the Rate of Change of Wage Rates in the United Kingdom, 1923–39*

What conclusions can we draw from the long-period relationships between the unemployment rate and the growth rates of the nominal variables? First, there is no stable relation between the unemployment rate—or, it turns out, real economic activity more generally—and the growth rates of nominal wages, prices, or money.[5] Thus, the sharply higher growth rates of the nominal variables since World War II, as compared with those before World War I, correspond to little change in the average rate of unemployment (or in average growth rates of real GNP). Hence, we can firmly reject the notion of a Phillips curve, such as that shown in Figure 18.1, which is stable over the long term. At least in the long run, it is not true that more inflation leads to a lower unemployment rate or that to have low inflation a country must accept a high unemployment rate.

What about the negative relation between unemployment and the growth rates of the nominal variables before World War I? One important consideration is that

[5]Formal statistical support for this proposition appears in Robert Lucas (1980) and John Geweke (1986).

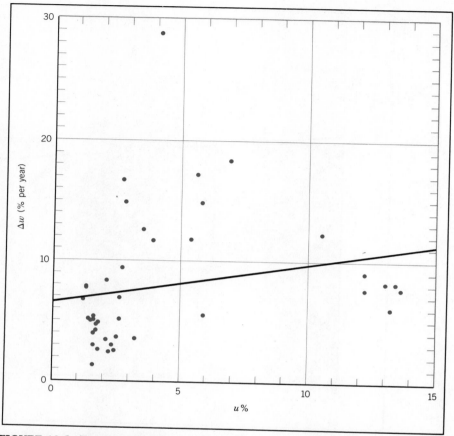

FIGURE 18.5 *The Unemployment Rate and the Rate of Change of Wages in the United Kingdom, 1947–87*

the United Kingdom and the United States (after 1879) were on the gold standard during these years. Under this regime (discussed in Chapter 16), the monetary policy in each country had to conform to a fixed nominal price of gold. Accordingly, the long-term average rates of change of nominal wages and prices were small. For example, in the United Kingdom, the average rate of change of nominal wages from 1863 to 1913 was 0.8% per year, while that for prices was −0.4% per year. For the United States from 1890 to 1913, the average growth rate of nominal wages was 1.5% per year, while that for prices was 0.9% per year.

Under the gold standard, high rates of inflation represented rates that were high relative to the long-term average rate of inflation, which was close to zero. If we think of zero as the expected rate of inflation (at least over long periods), the results from Figures 18.3 and 18.6 suggest an inverse relation between unexpected inflation, $\pi - \pi^e \simeq \pi$, and the unemployment rate, that is, an expectational Phillips curve of the form shown in Figure 18.2. Note that this form of the Phillips curve is also consistent with the breakdown of the relationship over the longer term. Once countries moved off the gold standard—as happened in part around World War I and more so in the 1930s and around World War II—the inflation rates no longer average close to zero. Rather, inflation rates tend to be high and unstable. But the general rise in actual and expected rates of inflation—which shows up especially after World War II—does not mean that unexpected inflation, $\pi - \pi^e$, is systematically high or low. Therefore, the data would no longer show an inverse association between the rate of inflation and the unemployment rate.

What about the positive relation between unemployment and the growth rates

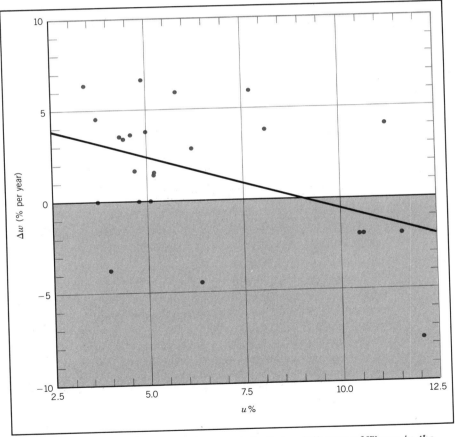

FIGURE 18.6 *The Unemployment Rate and the Rate of Change of Wages in the United States, 1890–1913*
Sources of data for Figures 18.6–18.8. The unemployment rate is from Figure 1.3. The wage-rate index is from Albert Rees (1959) and Economic Report of the President, *various issues. The recent data include an adjustment for overtime pay.*

of the nominal variables, as shown in some of the data since World War II? There are two elements that explain at least part of this behavior. First, as noted before, disturbances to production functions tend to generate this pattern. Second, any tendency of governments to raise monetary growth during recessions reinforces this outcome. That is, lower output triggers more money, which raises the price level. This pattern of active monetary policy applies to the United States and the United Kingdom since World War II but not during the earlier years under the gold standard.

Overall, the main phenomenon that our theory does not yet explain is the tendency for higher-than-expected growth rates of the nominal variables to accompany low rates of unemployment. So far, the data indicate the presence of this type of expectational Phillips curve for the period before World War I.

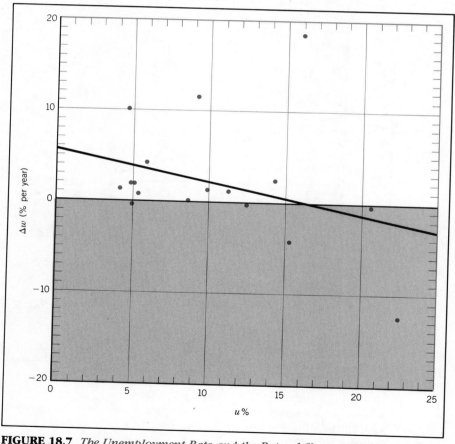

FIGURE 18.7 *The Unemployment Rate and the Rate of Change of Wages in the United States, 1923–39*

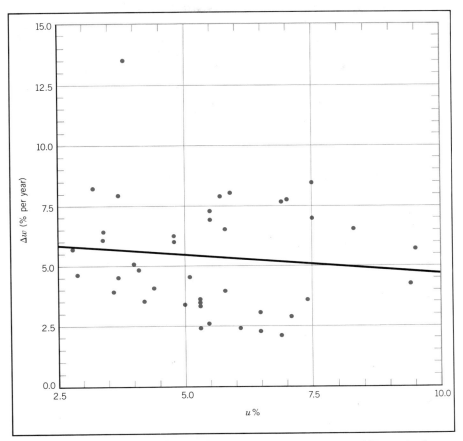

FIGURE 18.8 *The Unemployment Rate and the Rate of Change of Wages in the United States, 1947–87*

CROSS-COUNTRY RELATIONS BETWEEN NOMINAL AND REAL VARIABLES

Suppose that we look at average growth rates of real GNP for various countries[6] and compare these with the average growth rates of prices, money, and so on. If we look at averages over one or more decades, the main variations across countries reflect differences in the long-term average growth rates of real GNP, prices, money, and so forth. Hence, the relations among these variables should indicate how dif-

---

[6]Because of differences in concepts and lack of data, it is hard to compare unemployment rates across countries.

ferences in the growth rates of the nominal variables associate in the long run with differences in the real growth rates.

Figure 18.9 uses data from 78 countries to relate the average growth rate of real GNP (over intervals of one to three decades since World War II) to the average rate of inflation. (Recall that we looked at these data before in Chapter 7.) There is no apparent relation between the two variables in the figure, as can be verified from a formal statistical analysis. Similar conclusions arise if we relate the average growth rate of real GNP to either the average growth rate of currency or the average growth rate of M1. Again, there is no significant long-term relation between real growth and the rate of change of the nominal variables.

Roger Kormendi and Phillip Meguire (1984, p. 147) carried out a detailed statistical analysis of the growth experience of 46 countries in the post–World War

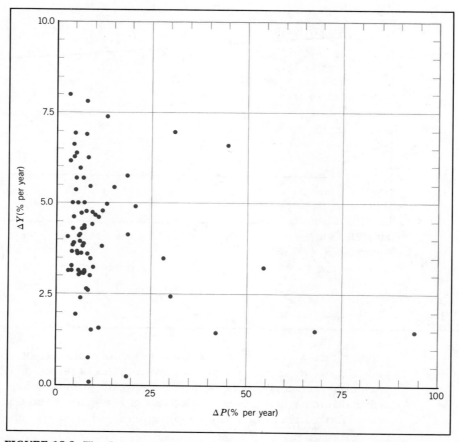

FIGURE 18.9 *The Cross-Country Relation between the Growth Rate of Real GNP and Inflation*
Looking at 79 countries, there is no significant relation between the average growth rate of real GNP, ΔY, and the average rate of inflation, ΔP.

II period. One of their findings was that *increases* in inflation rates were associated with lower average growth rates of real output. This result suggests that a higher rate of inflation leads to a lower *level* of output. Thus there is some indication of a form of Phillips curve with the "wrong" sign. One possibility is that the transaction costs associated with higher inflation reduce the incentive for people to engage in market activity.

THE RELATION BETWEEN REAL AND NOMINAL VARIABLES DURING THE MAJOR RECESSIONS BEFORE WORLD WAR II

Some of the evidence already presented suggests that the main short-term interplay between nominal and real variables arises when the nominal variables behave in an unusual or surprising manner. Hence, we should focus on shocks or surprises to money and prices to find interesting short-run interactions with the real variables. Table 18.1 brings out this type of relationship for the five principal U.S. recessions between 1890 and 1940. Three of these—1892–94, 1906–8, and 1929–33—contained banking panics. Another one, 1937–38, involved the Fed's steep increase in reserve requirements. The fifth episode, 1920–21, occurred along with a dramatic fall in money and prices after World War I.

The first section of Table 18.1 shows the estimated shortfall of real GNP for each recession. Aside from the Great Depression of 1929–33, where the shortfall was 37%, the values are similar to the most severe of the post–World War II recessions, those of 1980–82 and 1974–75. (See Table 9.1.)

The second section of the table shows the monetary base, M,[7] along with an estimate of the "normal" or expected amount of the base, which we call M^0. For example, M = \$1.57 billion in 1894. To calculate M^0, consider what the quantity of base money would have been in 1894 if it had grown at a normal or expected rate from the benchmark year, 1892. By a normal rate, we mean the rate that someone would have predicted in 1892 for monetary growth over the next two years (pretending that people were thinking about such matters!). Operationally, we can estimate this rate as the average value, 3.4% per year, that applied over the five years prior to 1892. Then the corresponding estimate for the normal amount of base money, M^0, in 1894 is \$1.65 billion. The actual stock, M, was 4.8% below this normal value. Although the result depends somewhat on the procedure for estimating the normal growth rate of money, we can satisfactorily use a value of 5% to gauge the rough size of the shortfall in base money for 1892–94.

A similar procedure applied to the other recessions reveals that base money

---

[7]Gold and silver coins and certificates accounted for roughly half of the monetary base through World War I and still retained a substantial role until 1933. The reserves held at the Fed appear in the monetary base after the start of the Federal Reserve System in 1914.

TABLE 18.1 *Real and Nominal Variables during Five Major Recessions before World War II*

Final Year of Recession Benchmark Year for Comparison	1894 1892	1908 1906	1921 1920	1933 1929	1938 1937
Y	200.8	346.8	486.4	498.5	664.2
Y^0	216.9	373.2	513.3	796.8	716.5
$Y^0 - Y$	16.1	26.4	26.9	298.3	52.3
% shortfall	7.4	7.1	5.2	37.4	7.3
M	1.57	3.09	6.33	7.92	14.4
M^0	1.65	2.89	7.15	7.03	14.9
$M^0 - M$	0.08	−0.20	0.82	−0.89	0.5
% shortfall	4.8	−6.9	11.5	−12.7	3.4
P	0.0660	0.0814	0.151	0.112	0.129
P^0	0.0689	0.0810	0.180	0.145	0.130
$P^0 - P$	0.0029	−0.0004	0.029	0.033	0.001
% shortfall	4.2	−0.5	16.1	22.8	0.8
% change in $M1/M$	−5.4	−12.0	0.3	−32.9	−8.6

Note: Y is real GNP, M is the monetary base, P is the GNP deflator, and $M1$ is the M1 definition of the money stock. (For the two earliest cases, the estimate of M1 comes from the available data on M2.) The normal or expected values, Y^0, M^0, and P^0, equal the values from the benchmark year, adjusted by the normal growth rates. For real GNP, we use the long-term average growth rate of 2.9% per year. For the monetary base and the price level, we use the average growth rates over the five years prior to the benchmark year. An exception is 1921, where we generate the normal values, M^0 and P^0, by using the average growth rates of these variables for 1909–14. We then apply these rates to the values for 1920.

Sources: See Figures 1.1 and 1.4 and Table 7.2. For the monetary base and M1, Friedman and Schwartz (1963).

exceeded the normal amount for two cases—by 6.9% in 1906–8 and 12.7% in 1929–33. But for the 1937–38 recession, the shortfall of base money was 3.4%.

We have some difficulties in generating the normal growth rate of money for 1920–21. The five years prior to 1920 featured the rapid growth of money during World War I. But people would have had no reason to expect these high rates of expansion to continue after 1920. So to get a rough estimate, we can use the growth rate of the monetary base that applied before World War I from 1909 to 1914; this value was 2.7% per year. Using this number, we find that the shortfall in the monetary base for 1920–21 was 11.5%. Although this number is imprecise, there is no doubt that the sharp drop in base money during 1921 represented a substantial decline relative to anyone's predictions.

Overall, the five major recessions between 1890 and 1940 do not suggest a close association between contractions of output and shortfalls in the monetary base. In fact, for two of the cases—1929–33 and 1906–8—the movements in base money were expansionary. Only in the case of the post–World War I contraction, 1920–21, do the figures suggest a dominant role for the shortfall in base money. (The percentage shortfall in output, 5.2%, for this case turns out to be the smallest of those considered in Table 18.1.) It is also interesting that, for this episode, the fall in the monetary base reflected mostly a sharp decline in borrowing from the Fed. This decline stemmed at least in part from a dramatic increase in the Fed's discount rate—that is, from a reduction in the subsidy to borrowing by banks.

Conceivably a focus on the episodes of major economic contraction would mislead us about the overall role of shortfalls in base money. But the notion that this role is minor is confirmed by the more thorough analysis of Mark Rush (1985). His study, which uses all the data from 1885 to 1913, employs more sophisticated techniques for measuring the normal growth rate of the monetary base. In addition, he allows for lagged effects of changes in the monetary base on real variables. But his basic finding is that unusual movements in the monetary base played at most a minor role in influencing output and employment over this period.

The third section of Table 18.1 makes calculations for the price level. The procedure here parallels that for the monetary base. We find shortfalls in prices relative to the normal or expected level, P^0, by less than 5% for three cases—1892–94, 1906–8, and 1937–38—by 16% for 1920–21 and by 23% for 1929–33.

Given the earlier results, we know that, except for 1920–21, the shortfalls in prices cannot be explained by contractions in base money. That is, increases in the real demand for base money must be important during some of these recessions. But we expect this behavior during banking panics—which occurred in 1893, 1907, and 1930–33—or in response to the sharp increase in reserve requirements in 1936–37.

We can get some idea about the size of the change in the real demand for base money by examining the relation between base money, M, and a broader monetary aggregate, such as $M1$. The ratio of $M1$ to M reflects the amount of financial inter-mediation in the economy. The previous analysis implies that this ratio declines when the real demand for base money expands, as in a banking panic.[8] The fourth section of Table 18.1 shows that the ratio $M1/M$ declined substantially for four of the five cases. The declines by 5% for 1892–94, 12% for 1906–8, and 33% for 1929–33 reflected the impacts of the banking panics. The reduction by 9% for 1937–38 stemmed from the increase in reserve requirements. But for 1920–21, the ratio of $M1$ to the monetary base was virtually unchanged.

The results suggest a positive relation between changes in financial interme-diation—as proxied by the ratio of $M1$ to the monetary base—and real economic activity. Further, this indication from the major recessions that we considered is reinforced by the more detailed analysis of Mark Rush (1985, 1986). Over the period 1885–1913 and again for the 1930s, he finds an important linkage between shifts in the ratio of $M1$ to the monetary base and subsequent changes in output and employment.

The evidence from before World War II indicates important real effects from changes in financial intermediation, especially when these shifts reflect banking

---

[8]Before 1914, data on M1 are unavailable because we cannot separate banks' time deposits from their demand deposits. But we can estimate M1 by looking at a broader monetary aggregate, which includes the banks' time deposits. This aggregate used to be called M2, although this concept now encompasses some additional assets.

panics and changes in reserve requirements. Further, the movements in the ratio of *M1* to the monetary base serve as a rough proxy for these effects. But there is not much connection between shifts to the monetary base—even when they are surprisingly large—and changes in real economic activity. The one suggestion of this linkage comes from the relatively mild contraction of 1920–21. But even here, the dramatic reduction in the monetary base reflects a major decrease in the Fed's subsidy for borrowing at the discount window. Thus, this episode does not decisively demonstrate important real effects from a pure reduction in the monetary base (when generated, for example, through open-market sales of bonds).

THE RELATION BETWEEN REAL AND NOMINAL VARIABLES SINCE WORLD WAR II

For the post–World War II period, there are many detailed studies that attempt to isolate the effects on real variables from unusual movements in the nominal variables. Let's consider first some research that deals with shocks to the price level and then some work that focuses on monetary disturbances.

EFFECTS FROM CHANGES IN PRICES

An econometric study by Ray Fair (1979) analyzes the relation between surprise movements in the price level and the amount of real economic activity in the post–World War II United States. He focuses on the unemployment rate, u_t, as the measure of real economic performance. The statistical procedure seeks to estimate the effect on unemployment from surprises in prices, $P_t - P_t^e$, where P_t is the actual price level and P_t^e is the price that the typical person expected for period t. In other words, the study estimates an expectational Phillips curve. Operationally, Fair interprets the expected price, P_t^e, as the best forecast for the actual price, P_t, that people could have made with the data available through the previous period, $t - 1$. In practice, the periods are treated as quarters of years. Fair uses statistical techniques to obtain a best fit between the actual price level, P_t, and the lagged values of a group of explanatory variables. Then he uses the fitted value from this relationship to proxy for the expected price, P_t^e—that is, for the best prediction of prices that could have been made from the assumed list of explanatory variables, when observed up to date $t - 1$.

Fair finds no significant relationship between the unemployment rate and the price surprise over the period 1954–73. Moreover, when he adds data from 1974 to 1977, the estimated effect of price shocks on unemployment becomes positive. That is, the expectational Phillips curve has the wrong sign.

Recall that the analysis in previous chapters implies that the relation between a real variable, such as the unemployment rate or the level of output, and surprise movements in the price level depends on the nature of the underlying disturbance.

Specifically, shifts to production functions can generate a negative relation between movements in output and movements in prices. Hence, this element can account for the positive relation between price shocks and unemployment that Fair reports when he adds the data for 1974–77. Recall that these years include the effects from the first oil crisis of 1973–74, which we can interpret as a major supply shock. For this reason, the expectational Phillips curve, which is the relation between unemployment and price surprises, tends to confound two types of effects. First, there would be the positive relation caused by supply shocks. Second, if monetary disturbances raise prices and lower unemployment, the expectational Phillips curve would tend to have a negative slope. Thus, even if money is nonneutral, the slope of the Phillips curve could have the wrong (positive) sign.

MONETARY SHOCKS AND REAL ECONOMIC ACTIVITY IN THE POST–WORLD WAR II UNITED STATES

I have analyzed the real effects of monetary shocks in a number of papers (see Barro, 1981). The starting point is the division of monetary growth into anticipated and unanticipated components. Conceptually, I identified the anticipated part with the prediction that could have been made by exploiting the historical relation between money and a specified set of explanatory variables. Using the M1 definition of money over the period since World War II, I found that monetary growth for year t depends positively on three variables: last year's monetary growth, last year's unemployment rate, and this year's level of federal expenditure relative to a measure of normal spending. The positive relation to past unemployment may reflect the Fed's desire to expand money during a recession, which is a form of "countercyclical" or "activist" monetary policy. The positive effect of federal spending may involve the incentive for inflationary finance.

I used the estimated relation of monetary growth to the explanatory variables to construct a series labeled **anticipated money growth.** Then I took the difference between actual and anticipated monetary change as the empirical counterpart of **unanticipated money.** Essentially this procedure does for money what Fair did for prices in the study discussed above.

I estimated equations for real GNP and the unemployment rate over the post–World War II period to ascertain the real effects of anticipated and unanticipated changes in money. I found that unanticipated money had expansionary real effects that lasted over a one- to two-year period. Conversely, the anticipated parts of monetary change did not have important real effects. Quantitatively, I estimated that a 1% rise in money above expectations raises next year's output by about 1% and lowers next year's unemployment rate by about six-tenths of a percentage point. Thus, unlike the price shocks that Fair studied, positive monetary surprises seemed to have important expansionary effects on real economic activity.[9]

[9]Empirical analysis of anticipated versus unanticipated money has become popular in recent years. Some of the contributions are C. L. F. Attfield, et. al. (1981), Roger Kormendi and Phillip Meguire (1984), and Frederic Mishkin (1982).

The results just mentioned pertain to the monetary aggregate, M1. But we can think of disturbances to M1 as composed partly of shocks to the monetary base, M, and partly to the ratio of M1 to the base. Remember that the ratio of M1 to the monetary base tends to proxy for the state of financial intermediation. We found before that this ratio—but not the movements in the monetary base—was associated with business fluctuations prior to World War I. If we look just at the monetary base since World War II, the association with real variables is weaker than that for M1. However, Mark Rush (1986) reports that shocks to the base do have a significantly positive association with U.S. real economic activity in the annual data since World War II (as well as for the 1920s).

DOES MONEY AFFECT THE ECONOMY OR IS IT THE ECONOMY THAT AFFECTS MONEY?

The evidence that money (the monetary base or M1) affects output comes, first, from the observation that money and output are positively correlated, and, second, from the observation (which is harder to document) that movements in money precede those in output. An important question is whether these observations imply that money affects output or instead that money responds to changes in economic conditions. Economists often refer to the latter situation as one of **endogenous money**—that is, a situation where the quantity of money is determined by economic forces rather than being set (*exogenously*) from outside.

We have already discussed some cases where the positive association between M1 and real economic activity seems to reflect mainly the response of money to the economy. For example, for a given quantity of base money, a banking panic tends to contract the economy and also to lower the amount of M1. Moreover, since the response of M1 may be quicker than that of real GNP, the movement in M1 could precede the change in output. In any event, the change in the quantity of money is not the underlying causal element in this example.

In many previous cases we considered changes in the real demand for base money while holding fixed the nominal quantity of base money. For example, a temporary supply shock reduces output and the real quantity of base money demanded. If the nominal quantity of base money does not change, the price level would rise. But under some monetary systems, the monetary base would change automatically in these circumstances. Suppose, for example, that the monetary authority followed a rule where it tried to offset disturbances by reducing the monetary base whenever the price level tended to increase, and vice versa. Then a supply shock would result in lower output and also smaller quantities of the monetary base and M1. In the data we would find positive associations between output and the monetary base and between output and M1. But these associations would reflect endogenous responses of money rather than the impact of money on the economy.

The last example is important historically because monetary authorities tended

SEASONAL FLUCTUATIONS IN MONEY

One straightforward example of endogenous money is the regular seasonal movements in the monetary base and M1. Before the founding of the Federal Reserve in 1914, there was a seasonal pattern in nominal interest rates; in particular, rates tended to be higher than average in the fall of each year. One of the reasons given for the creation of the Fed was that it would eliminate this pattern by allowing the amount of currency outstanding to vary seasonally to accommodate the regular variations over the year in the real demand for money (see Carter Glass, 1927, p. 387). The Federal Reserve has, in fact, been successful in this respect. Almost since the Fed's inception, and especially since the end of World War II, there has been no important seasonal pattern in nominal interest rates.[10]

The counterpart of the elimination of the seasonal pattern in nominal interest rates was the introduction of substantial seasonal variation into the monetary base and M1. Robert Barsky and Jeffrey Miron (1988) document these seasonal patterns for the post–World War II period. They also show that the seasonal movements in the monetary base and M1 are positively correlated with the seasonal variations of real GNP; the most dramatic instances are the increases in all variables around Christmas and the reductions in all variables after Christmas. Probably all macroeconomists would accept the proposition that this seasonal behavior is an example of endogenous money. Money is high around Christmas because real activity is high and because the Fed allows the monetary base to expand at such times. Real activity is not high in December because the Fed capriciously expands the quantity of money at this time every year.

The seasonal evidence makes it clear that a positive association between money and output is not concrete evidence that money affects output. Some macroeconomists (such as Robert King and Charles Plosser, 1984) go further. They argue that the pattern of endogenous money that is so clear for seasonals applies also to the patterns that show up in business cycles. The reasoning is that, as with the Christmas season, the increase in the real demand for money during a boom induces the accommodating monetary authority to raise the nominal quantity of money at such times.

It is hard to evaluate this argument empirically. Without some additional information (such as knowledge about the effects of Christmas), it is hard to tell

[10]For recent discussions, see Jeffrey Miron (1986), Truman Clark (1986), and Greg Mankiw, Jeffrey Miron, and David Weil (1987).

statistically whether the positive association between money and output reflects the influence of money on output, or vice-versa. In fact, this problem of sorting out the direction of causation among variables is the most difficult problem empirical economists face.

to behave in the assumed manner under the gold standard, or more generally, in regimes where the authorities attempted to fix the exchange rates between domestic and foreign currencies. (See the discussion in Chapter 16.) For present purposes the important point is that these systems make money endogenous; in particular, they create a pattern where the nominal quantity of money moves automatically in the same direction as the real demand for money. Since movements in output have positive effects on the real demand for money, the movements in output and nominal money would be positively correlated.[11]

The gold standard and fixed exchange rates have become less important in recent years, but monetary authorities still follow rules of behavior that make money (the monetary base and M1) endogenous. Specifically, the nominal quantity of money still tends to move in the same direction as the real demand for money; or, to put it another way, the variations in money tend to *accommodate* the movements in the demand for money. The point of this **monetary accommodation** is that it avoids changes that would otherwise have to occur in variables, such as the price level and the nominal interest rate, that influence the real demand for money.

Suppose that the monetary authority has some objectives or targets for the path of the price level or the nominal interest rate. (**Interest-rate targeting** has, in fact, been an important part of the Federal Reserve's operating policy at least since World War II; see Marvin Goodfriend, 1987.) If the quantity of base money did not vary, shifts in the real demand for money would tend to affect prices and nominal interest rates. To avoid or dampen these effects, the monetary authority could adjust the amount of base money to accommodate the shifts in the demand. But, as with the gold standard, this pattern of endogenous money generates a positive association between money and real economic activity. Again, the existence of this association does not demonstrate that money affects the real economy.

IMPLICATIONS OF THE EVIDENCE

If shocks to the monetary base matter for business fluctuations, this observation would conflict with our theory. Remember that the theory predicts that changes in the monetary base would be neutral, at least if we neglect transaction costs and

[11]It is possible, but not inevitable, that the movements in nominal money would precede those in output. This timing depends on the precise specifications for the demand for money and the determination of output.

distributional effects. In the next chapter we explore some extensions of the theory that allow for nonneutral effects from changes in the monetary base. In evaluating these extensions, we should keep in mind the empirical evidence. There is some suggestion that monetary nonneutrality is significant, but the evidence is not very strong.

SUMMARY

Much of the macrotheorizing since the 1930s can be viewed as attempts to rationalize a strong interplay between nominal and real variables, which shows up in various versions of the Phillips curve. We can view the Keynesian theory and more recent monetary theories of business fluctuations in this context. But before considering these theories, we should think about how much evidence there is to explain.

Neither the long-period evidence nor that from across countries suggests important effects on real variables from differences in the average growth rates of money, prices, or wages. That is, in the long run there is no systematic relation between real variables and nominal variables.

Before World War II, the evidence suggests important real effects from banking panics and changes in reserve requirements, which show up as fluctuations in the ratio of M1 to the monetary base. Also, these episodes typically involve some surprise decreases in prices (and nominal wages). But there is not much evidence for real effects from changes in the monetary base.

After World War II, there is an indication that monetary shocks—but not price surprises—are positively associated with real economic activity. The strongest indication of this association shows up when we consider a broad aggregate like M1. But there is also some evidence of positive association between real economic activity and shocks to the monetary base.

A positive association between money and output may indicate that money responds to the economy (endogenous money), rather than the reverse. In particular, a positive association between money and output arises when the monetary authority accommodates variations in the real demand for money with movements in the nominal quantity of money. This monetary behavior arises under the gold standard and also in systems where the monetary authority targets the price level or the nominal interest rate. At this point it is unclear how much of the empirical association between money (the monetary base or M1) and real economic activity can be explained by endogenous money rather than as effects of money on the economy.

If changes in the monetary base were nonneutral and quantitatively important, our theory would be seriously incomplete. At this point the empirical evidence suggests that money is nonneutral, but the evidence is not very strong. Therefore, although the nonneutrality of money deserves some attention, it is likely that economists have given it too much weight. The interplay between nominal and real variables is neither as large nor as pervasive as most people believe.

IMPORTANT TERMS AND CONCEPTS

Phillips curve

expectational Phillips curve

anticipated money growth

unanticipated money growth

endogenous money

monetary accommodation

interest-rate targeting

QUESTIONS AND PROBLEMS

Mainly for Review

18.1 What is the theoretical link between the price level and real variables? the inflation rate and real variables? Why do you think it might be important to distinguish between expected and unexpected inflation?

18.2 Consider the statement, "Makers of economic policy face a cruel choice between unemployment and inflation." Explain why this statement is not supported by either (a) theoretical results or (b) empirical findings on the Phillips curve.

18.3 How does the expectational Phillips curve explain the negative association between inflation and unemployment rates in the United States prior to World War I? Could the absence of this negative association in subsequent years be "explained" by shifts in the Phillips curve?

18.4 To what extent was the Great Depression (1929–33) accompanied by a change in the nominal quantity of money? in the real quantity of money?

18.5 Explain why it is important to distinguish between shifts in the nominal quantity of money and shifts in money demand. What association would we expect between the price level and real output in periods where both types of shifts occur?

18.6 What is the meaning of the term *endogenous money?* Under what circumstances would endogenous money generate a pattern where money and output were positively correlated?

PROBLEMS FOR DISCUSSION

18.7 ***The Timing of Money and Output***
Suppose that the data show that movements in money (say, the monetary base) are positively correlated with subsequent movements in output. Does this finding imply

that money affects the economy, rather than the reverse? If not, give some examples of endogenous money in which the movements of money precede those of output.

18.8 **Seasonal Variations in Money**

Suppose that the quantity of real money demanded is relatively high in the fourth quarter of the year and relatively low in the first quarter. Assume that there is no seasonal pattern in the expected real interest rate.

a. Suppose there were no seasonal variations in the monetary base. What would be the seasonal pattern for the price level and the nominal interest rate?

b. What seasonal behavior for the monetary base would eliminate the seasonal pattern in the nominal interest rate? Is there still a seasonal pattern in the price level?

c. Suppose there is a seasonal pattern for the expected real interest rate. Can the monetary authority affect this pattern? If not, can the monetary authority eliminate the seasonal behavior of the nominal interest rate? Is there still a seasonal pattern in the price level in this case?

18.9 **Interest-Rate Targeting (optional)**

Suppose that the Fed wants to keep the nominal interest rate constant. Assume that the expected real interest rate is constant, but the real demand for money shifts around (perhaps because of changes in output).

a. What should the Fed do to the quantity of money if the real demand for money increases temporarily? What if the real demand increases permanently?

b. How does the price level behave in the answers to part **a**? What should the Fed do if it wants to dampen the fluctuations of the price level?

c. In the real world, the nominal interest rate moves around a lot. How can we incorporate this fact into the analysis?

CHAPTER 19

MONEY AND BUSINESS FLUCTUATIONS IN THE MARKET CLEARING MODEL

n recent years, some macroeconomists have developed a new line of theory to explain the role of money in business fluctuations. The new approach is sometimes called *rational expectations macroeconomics*, but we shall refer to it—somewhat more descriptively—as the *market-clearing model with incomplete information about prices.*[1]

It is important to stress that the theory developed in this chapter applies mainly to the interaction between monetary and real phenomena. Thus, the evidence surveyed in Chapter 18 indicates the potential scope for the theory. That evidence suggests something interesting to explain but does not imply that monetary shocks are the most important source of business fluctuations.

As with the previous analysis, this chapter relies on the conditions for general market clearing as its central analytical device. The approach also retains the assumption that households and firms behave rationally, even including the manner in which they form expectations of inflation and other variables. However, we introduce an important source of "friction" by allowing for incomplete information about prices. An important way in which people receive information—and thereby make their allocative decisions—is by observing prices of various goods. But it

---

[1]For a survey of the research, see Ben McCallum (1979). See also the papers collected in Robert Lucas (1981). Two early papers that stimulated much of the subsequent work are Milton Friedman (1968c) and Edmund Phelps (1970).

would be prohibitively expensive for individuals to observe all prices instantly. Therefore, households and firms typically make do with partial knowledge about the prices of different goods, about wage rates in alternative jobs, and so on. In this situation, decisions often differ from those that they would make with full information.

Variations in money and the general price level make it difficult for households and businesses to interpret the limited set of prices that they observe. Hence, when there is an increase in the general price level, a household or firm may mistakenly think that the price of its output has increased *relative* to other prices. Consequently, the household or firm tends to produce more goods than it would under full information. Because of these responses, we shall find that surprise increases in money and the general price level can lead to expansions in the aggregate level of real economic activity.

In this chapter we work out the details of a representative model from this new line of macroeconomic theory. To bring out the role of incomplete information, we have to move away from the simplified model with an economy-wide market for commodities. Now we make things more realistic by including a variety of local markets on which households and firms buy and sell goods and services.

THE STRUCTURE OF A MODEL WITH LOCAL MARKETS

Consider again the model of a closed economy where households produce goods and sell them on a commodity market. Instead of assuming that all goods are the same, let's now imagine products that differ by physical characteristics, location, and so on. Accordingly, we now index commodities by the symbol z, which takes on the possible values 1, 2, . . . , q, where q is a large number. To be concrete and to simplify matters, we usually think of z as a location—that is, a "local market." But more generally, we could identify this index with various characteristics of goods, occupations, methods of production, and so on. So the value $z = 1$ might signify the automobile industry, $z = 2$ the computer industry, and so on.

Since changes in job location or type of product entail substantial costs, people do not move too often from one place or line of work to another. To capture this idea in a workable model, we assume that each household produces and sells goods in only one location during each period. But there is mobility in the sense that people may change locations at some cost from one period to the next.

We now distinguish prices by location of product and by date, so that $P_t(z)$ is the price of goods of type z during period t. Thus, $P_t(1)$ might be the dollar price of a market basket of goods in Detroit and $P_t(2)$ the price of the same market basket in Pittsburgh. Correspondingly, the ratio, $P_t(1)/P_t(2)$, is the price of goods in location 1 relative to that in location 2. It is important to distinguish this concept of a *relative price* from the general price level, which we have stressed in previous chapters. By the general price level P_t we mean an average of the individual prices at date t.

To keep things manageable, we neglect any long-lasting differences across lo-cations. That is, we ignore a variety of things that make goods permanently more or less expensive in different places. (For example, a market basket of goods always costs more in Alaska than in New York.) So in our model, if the "local price," $P_t(z)$, exceeds the average price, P_t, market z looks relatively favorable for sellers during period t. This situation attracts producers from elsewhere, and the expansion of goods supplied to market z tends to drive down the local price toward the general level of prices. Similarly, if the local price is lower than the average price, producers move to other territory, and this process tends to bring the local price up to the general price level. Thus, there is a process of entry to and exit from local markets that keeps each local price reasonably close to the average price. Because of this tendency for prices to converge, the long-range forecast of the price in any local market equals that for the average of the markets.

SUPPLY OF GOODS IN A LOCAL MARKET

At the beginning of period t, a producer in market z has the stock of capital $k_{t-1}(z)$. Correspondingly, the amount of goods that he or she produces at location z during period t is given from the production function as

$$y_t(z) = f[k_{t-1}(z), n_t(z)] \tag{19.1}$$

where $n_t(z)$ is the producer's work effort. Note that we again think of each household as working on its own production process, although we could extend things to include firms and hired workers. Also, we think of last period's capital, $k_{t-1}(z)$, as stuck in market z rather than movable across locations.

The dollar revenue from sales equals output, $y_t(z)$, multiplied by the local price, $P_t(z)$. But households buy goods from many locations. As an approximation, the typical household pays the average price, P_t, for its purchases of consumables and capital goods. In this case, a producer calculates the real value of the revenue from local sales—that is, the value in terms of the goods purchased—by dividing the dollar amount by the general price level, P_t. Hence the real revenue from production is

$$\left[\frac{P_t(z)}{P_t}\right] \cdot y_t(z) = \left[\frac{P_t(z)}{P_t}\right] \cdot f[k_{t-1}(z), n_t(z)]. \tag{19.2}$$

The term $P_t(z)/P_t$ is the price of goods sold in market z relative to the average price of goods. Notice that for a given amount of physical product, $y_t(z)$, an increase in the relative price, $P_t(z)/P_t$, means a greater real value of sales. (An increase in $P_t(z)/P_t$ looks like an improvement in the terms of trade from the model of international trade in Chapter 15.)

When deciding how much to work during period t, producers (and workers) looked before at the physical marginal product of labor, $MPL_t(z)$. (Here, the index z means that the marginal product applies to additional work and output in market z). Now to compute the effect on real sales revenue, producers multiply the change in physical product by the relative price, $P_t(z)/P_t$. Hence, the real value of labor's marginal product is $[P(z)/P_t] \cdot MPL_t(z)$.[2] An increase in the relative price looks to the producer just like a proportional upward shift in the schedule for labor's physical marginal product. Therefore, producers respond to changes in the relative price, $P_t(z)/P_t$, just as they did before to changes in the schedule for labor's marginal product.

Consider the response to an increase in the relative price, $P_t(z)/P_t$. Suppose that this increase is temporary, so that households do not anticipate a higher relative price for subsequent periods. Then the change amounts to an upward shift in the schedule for labor's marginal product during period t but not for later periods. Therefore, producers increase work effort, $n_t(z)$, and the supply of goods, $y_t^s(z)$. Recall that these responses involve two types of substitution effects: first, a shift away from leisure and toward consumption and second, a shift away from today's leisure and toward tomorrow's leisure. The second channel, which is an intertemporal-substitution effect, suggests that the current responses of work and production will be large.[3] As an example, we can think of the strong response of labor supply to the unusually high wages that firms offer during overtime periods.

Consider now the determination of investment demand. We can use the approach developed in Chapter 9 but amended for a model with local markets. Suppose first that producers in market z buy capital goods from other markets at the *general* price level, P_t. If capital, $k_t(z)$, rises by one unit, next period's output, $y_{t+1}(z)$, increases by the marginal product of capital, $MPK_t(z)$. Since this output will sell at the *local* price, $P_{t+1}(z)$, revenues next period will rise by the amount $P_{t+1}(z) \cdot MPK_t(z)$. As before, we can pretend that producers sell their used capital at the *general* price, P_{t+1}.

If we neglect depreciation for simplicity, the nominal rate of return to investment is $[P_{t+1}(z) \cdot MPK_t(z) + P_{t+1}]/P_t - 1$. Letting π_t be the inflation rate (for the general price level), this expression becomes $(1 + \pi_t)[(P_{t+1}(z)/P_{t+1})MPK_t(z) + 1] - 1$. As in Chapter 9, producers would invest enough to equate this rate of return to the nominal interest rate, R_t. (We still treat R_t as determined on an economywide market for credit.) Writing out this equation and simplifying leads to the condition for investment demand,

$$\left[\frac{P_{t+1}(z)}{P_{t+1}}\right] \cdot MPK_t(z) = r_t, \tag{19.3}$$

---

[2] With separate labor markets, a worker would look at the local dollar wage rate, $w_t(z)$, divided by the average price of commodities, P_t. The real wage rate, $w_t(z)/P_t$, is the value of the local wage in terms of the goods that it buys on the average commodity market. Firms would hire labor until the local marginal product, $MPL_t(z)$, equaled the local cost of labor, $w_t(z)$, expressed relative to the price of the firm's product, $P_t(z)$. That is, firms would operate where $MPL_t(z) = w_t(z)/P_t(z)$. Substituting for $MPL_t(z)$, we find that $[P_t(z)/P_t] \cdot MPL_t(z) = w_t(z)/P_t$. Thus, by responding to $w_t(z)/P_t$, labor suppliers ultimately react to the term $[P_t(z)/P_t] \cdot MPL_t(z)$, which we used in the text. Since the answer is the same, we again simplify by not introducing firms or separate labor markets.

[3] The higher relative price, $P_t(z)/P_t$, increases wealth for sellers in market z but reduces wealth for buyers. Since the changes in relative prices are temporary, the wealth effects will be small in any case. In order to focus on the main points, we neglect these wealth effects.

where r_t is the economy-wide real interest rate (as defined by $1 + r_t = (1 + R_t)/(1 + \pi_t)$). The condition for investment demand in equation 19.3 is the same as the one in Chapter 9, except that capital's marginal product, $MPK_t(z)$, is multiplied by the prospective relative price, $P_{t+1}(z)/P_{t+1}$. Thus, investment demand for period t rises with either an upward shift in the schedule for capital's marginal product or an increase in $P_{t+1}(z)/P_{t+1}$. Also, as before, investment demand falls with an increase in r_t.

To carry out investment projects, producers typically have to buy some goods and labor services locally at the price $P_t(z)$. (Think of a gold rush, where the prospectors have to pay high local prices for labor and shovels.) In this case the main change to our formal analysis is that the purchase price of capital becomes $P_t(z)$ rather than P_t. The result of this modification is that, other things equal, investment demand falls with an increase in the current relative price, $P_t(z)/P_t$. However, if the prospective relative price, $P_{t+1}(z)/P_{t+1}$, increases at the same time, demand for local goods could rise despite an increase in the current relative price, $P_t(z)/P_t$.

CONSUMER DEMAND

Thus far, we have examined the behavior of producers. Now we consider the incentives of consumers, who may come from elsewhere to purchase goods. The important point is that a higher relative price, $P_t(z)/P_t$, reduces consumption demand, $c_t^d(z)$. (Note that the index z refers to goods bought in market z, although the buyers may use the goods in other locations.)

CLEARING OF THE LOCAL MARKET

If we put the pieces of the analysis together, the condition for clearing the local market is

$$Y_t^s(z) \underbrace{\left[\frac{P_t(z)}{P_t}, r_t, \cdots \right]}_{(+)(+)} = C_t^d(z) \underbrace{\left[\frac{P_t(z)}{P_t}, r_t, \cdots \right]}_{(-)\ (-)}$$
$$+ I_t^d(z) \underbrace{\left[\frac{P_t(z)}{P_t}, \frac{P_{t+1}(z)}{P_{t+1}}, r_t, \cdots \right]}_{(-)\ (+)\ (-)}. \quad (19.4)$$

Here, we use capital letters to denote the quantity of goods supplied or demanded in market z. Notice that a higher current relative price, $P_t(z)/P_t$, raises the supply of goods but lowers consumption and investment demand. Also, a higher prospective relative price, $P_{t+1}(z)/P_{t+1}$, increases investment demand.

We also include in the supply and demand functions the real interest rate, r_t. As before, an increase in r_t raises the supply of goods, $Y_t^s(z)$, but lowers the demands, $C_t^d(z)$ and $I_t^d(z)$.

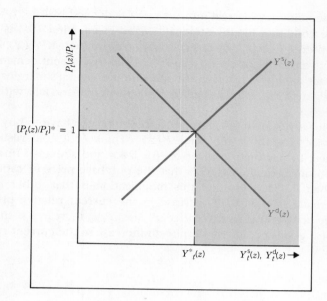

FIGURE 19.1 *The Clearing of a Local Commodity Market* We show the dependence of commodity supply and demand on the relative price, $P_t(z)/P_t$. Here we hold fixed the effects of other variables, including the real interest rate, r_t, and the prospective relative price, $P_{t+1}(z)/P_{t+1}$. Note that, for the average market, the market-clearing relative price is one.

Figure 19.1 depicts the clearing of a local commodity market. We put the current relative price, $P_t(z)/P_t$, on the vertical axis. The supply and demand curves in the figure assume given values for the prospective relative price, $P_{t+1}(z)/P_{t+1}$, and the real interest rate, r_t. (We also hold fixed the initial stock of capital in the local market, $K_{t-1}(z)$, and the forms of production functions.) Notice that the intersection of the curves determines the market-clearing values of the relative price, $[P_t(z)/P_t]^*$, and local output, $Y_t^*(z)$. Also, for the average market—which, by definition, has not experienced unusual changes in its supply and demand curves—the market-clearing relative price must equal one. That is, in the average market, the local price, $P_t^*(z)$, equals the average price, P_t^*.

DISTURBANCES TO LOCAL MARKETS

We can imagine a variety of changes in tastes and technology that affect the clearing of a local market for goods. For example, there may be shifts in the numbers of producers, in production functions, in the numbers of demanders, and so on. Let's think of an increase in local consumption demand, $C_t^d(z)$, which might reflect an increase in the number of shoppers in market z. Alternatively, we can think of an increase in demand that reflects the popularity of some new or improved product, such as CD players or personal computers.

Figure 19.2 shows the effect on a local commodity market from the increase in consumer demand. The solid lines reproduce the supply and demand curves from Figure 19.1. The new demand curve is the dashed line, labeled $Y^d(z)'$, which lies to the right of the original curve. Note that we hold constant the real interest rate, r_t, and the prospective relative price, $P_{t+1}(z)/P_{t+1}$. Since the disturbance applies only to the local market, it is reasonable to hold fixed the real interest rate. That is, this economy-wide variable responds to movements in the aggregates of supply and demand rather than to changes in a single location. We consider in a moment the behavior of the prospective relative price.

Figure 19.2 shows that the current relative price and local output increase. Notice that the rise in the relative price motivates producers to work more and supply more goods. Thus, we can think of the high relative price as the signal that generates the unusually large volume of work and production. The higher relative price means, however, that investment falls. Since total output is higher, consumption, $C_t(z)$, must be up on net. Finally, if the market-clearing relative price were initially equal to one—as is true for the average market—the new relative price must exceed one.

PROSPECTIVE RELATIVE PRICES

The increase in consumer demand tends also to raise the prospective relative price, $P_{t+1}(z)/P_{t+1}$. The reason is that the disturbance—in our case, an upward shift in demand—tends to persist. Although the high relative price stimulates entry, we assume that this process is too slow to return the relative price to unity within a single period.

An increase in the prospective relative price raises investment demand, $I_t^d(z)$. Therefore, we modify the analysis from Figure 19.2 to include a larger rightward shift of demand. The main point of this modification is that investment may now increase. This increase is likely if it is crucial for investors to move aggressively to capitalize on opportunities for high prospective relative prices.

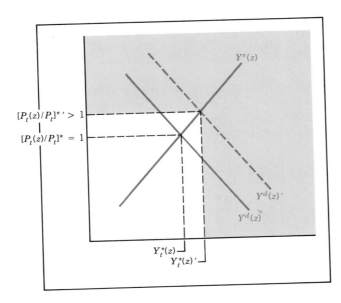

FIGURE 19.2 *The Responses to an Increase in Local Demand The change in consumer demand shows up as a positive shift to the local demand curve. Hence, the relative price and local output increase. Notice that the suppliers respond to the higher relative price by producing more goods (and by working harder). Also, if the market-clearing relative price is initially one (which holds for the average market), the new value exceeds one.*

Note that, so far, we have considered only the response of a local market to a local disturbance. Hence, we have not yet explained movements in the economy-wide totals of output and investment. In later sections we show how a monetary disturbance may look, in each market, like a shift to local demand. Then producers in each market change output and investment, just as they do in response to a shift in local demand. When all producers act in this way, we end up with movements in the aggregate variables.

CHANGES IN THE STOCK OF MONEY

Consider a once-and-for-all increase in the quantity of base money, M_t. As in some cases that we explored before, this change might involve an open-market purchase of bonds by the Fed.

Previously, we found for a closed economy that an increase in the quantity of money raises the general price level proportionately but leaves unchanged real variables like aggregate output and employment. This conclusion still holds when there are a variety of locations in which households produce and trade goods. As in previous analyses, we can think of households as attempting to spend their excess real money balances on the goods in various markets. Then the price in each market, $P_t(z)$, ends up rising by the same proportion as the increase in money. It follows that the general or average price level, P_t, also moves one-to-one with the quantity of money. Therefore, the relative price, $P_t(z)/P_t$, does not change. There is also no change in the level of output, $Y_t(z)$, in each market. At this point, we still lack any connection between money and real variables, which include the quantities of output and the relative prices of the different goods.

IMPERFECT INFORMATION ABOUT MONEY AND THE GENERAL PRICE LEVEL

Now we make a crucial change in the setup to remove some information that individuals have about money and prices. The basic idea is that people know the prices of things that they recently bought or sold. So they know the wage rate for their labor services (at least on the present job), the price of groceries at the local market, the rent on their apartment, and so on. Similarly, producers know a good deal about the costs of labor and other inputs, as well as the price of their own product (at least in a local market). People have much poorer knowledge, however, about the prices of objects that they shopped for last year or perhaps have not yet examined.

We can model these general ideas by assuming that sellers and buyers know the local price of goods, $P_t(z)$, but are less sure about the general or average price, P_t. So the local goods correspond to the items that people have dealt with recently and for which they know the current price. The general price applies to other goods, which are potential alternatives to local product but for which people have a blurrier notion of the price.

As before, sellers and buyers in market z respond to their perception of the relative price, $P_t(z)/P_t$. But although they know the local price, $P_t(z)$, they no longer are sure about the general price level, P_t. Therefore, we have to analyze how people compute expectations of this average price under incomplete information. Here, we use the idea of rational expectations, which we mentioned in Chapter 7. This approach says that if people do not observe something directly—such as the current price level—they form the best possible estimate of this variable given the information that they possess. In other words people make efficient use of their limited data so as not to commit avoidable errors.[4]

Consider the expectations that people have about prices for period t. For simplicity, imagine that all markets look the same beforehand. That is, before period t, people cannot predict whether the price in market z, $P_t(z)$, will be higher or lower than the average price P_t. Then, regardless of which market a person chooses to enter, we can focus on expectations of the general price level, P_t. To keep things manageable, pretend that everyone has the same information beforehand and therefore calculates the same expectation, which we denote by P_t^e.

Generally the expectation of prices depends on past information and on knowledge about the workings of the economy. We can think of this expectation as incorporating information about the quantity of money and about variables that influence the aggregate real demand for money. Often people will get useful information about these variables from lagged values of money and prices, from interest rates, and possibly from the government's announcements about monetary and fiscal policy. Therefore, the expectation, P_t^e, incorporates all of these elements.

CLEARING OF A LOCAL COMMODITY MARKET WHEN INFORMATION IS INCOMPLETE

Given the expected general price level, P_t^e, people compute the **perceived relative price** for market z as $P_t(z)/P_t^e$. We assume that sellers and buyers react to this price ratio just as they did to the actual ratio, $P_t(z)/P_t$, in the model with complete information. That is, an increase in the perceived relative price, $P_t(z)/P_t^e$, raises the supply of local goods, $Y_t^s(z)$, but lowers the demands, $C_t^d(z)$ and $I_t^d(z)$.

Figure 19.3 shows the supply and demand in a local market when people do not observe the general price level. We plot the perceived relative price, $P_t(z)/P_t^e$, on the vertical axis. For the moment, we hold fixed the prospective relative price, $P_{t+1}(z)/P_{t+1}$, and the real interest rate, r_t. Notice that the local market clears when the price ratio, $P_t(z)/P_t^e$, equals one. This result applies to the average market, which, by definition, has not experienced unusual recent changes in local supply and demand. For the typical market, supply equals demand when the local price, $P_t(z)$, equals the expected price elsewhere, P_t^e.

Prospective Relative Prices   So far, we have neglected the prospective relative price, $P_{t+1}(z)/P_{t+1}$. Before, when people had full information about the general price

---

[4]The basic idea of rational expectations comes from John Muth (1961). For a discussion of applications to macroeconomics, see Robert Lucas (1976).

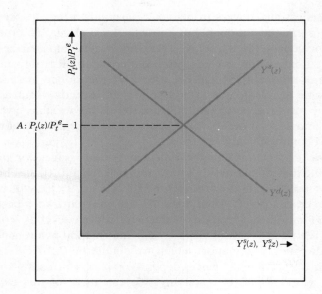

FIGURE 19.3 *Response of a Local Market to the Perceived Relative Price*
A higher perceived relative price, $P_t(z)/P_t^c$, raises supply and lowers demand. The typical market clears when $P_t(z)/P_t^c = 1$.

level, there was a tendency for high relative prices to persist. These effects still arise when sellers and buyers do not observe the current general price level. In particular, an increase in the perceived relative price, $P_t(z)/P_t^e$, tends to raise expectations of the relative price in market z for the next period. Then this expectation raises today's investment demand, $I_t^d(z)$.

We add this effect to the supply and demand curves in Figure 19.4. As $P_t(z)/P_t^e$ increases, the higher prospective relative price raises $I_t^d(z)$. Therefore, the demand curve is more nearly vertical than before—that is, the quantity demanded falls by less on net when today's perceived relative price rises. Note that the demand curve now combines two types of effects: first, the effect from an increase in $P_t(z)/P_t^e$ (which lowers consumption and investment demand) and, second the effect from the accompanying change in expectations of $P_{t+1}(z)/P_{t+1}$ (which raises investment demand). For now, the main point to note from Figure 19.4 is that the typical local market still clears at the point where $P_t(z)/P_t^e = 1$.

CHANGES IN MONEY WHEN THERE IS INCOMPLETE INFORMATION

Now let's reconsider the effects of a once-and-for-all increase in the stock of money, M_t. Here, we deal with a surprise increase in money—one that people did not anticipate when they formed their expectation of prices, P_t^e. Although this expectation was rational, it could not incorporate the effects from unanticipated changes in money.

Suppose, as before, that the local price, $P_t(z)$, rises in the typical market. (As usual, we can think of people attempting to spend their excess money balances, which tends to bid up prices.) Then, since the expectation P_t^e is given, there must be an increase in $P_t(z)/P_t^e$. In other words the typical person now thinks that he or she is located in a market where the relative price is high. Of course, this belief must be incorrect, since the average across markets of the local prices, $P_t(z)$, always equals the general price level, P_t. But the surprise increase in money and prices—together with the lack of direct information about either the average price, P_t, or the quantity of money, M_t—means that the typical person underestimates the rise in the general price level. Thus, this person overestimates the relative price that he or she faces and reacts by raising goods supply and lowering consumption demand. The net impact on investment demand is ambiguous. The direct effect from an increase in $P_t(z)/P_t^e$ is negative, but the higher expectation of $P_{t+1}(z)/P_{t+1}$ offsets this effect.

Point A in Figure 19.5 shows the price ratio, $P_t(z)/P_t^e = 1$, that would clear the typical local market. The surprise increase in money means, however, that the price in a typical market, $P_t(z)$, must exceed the expectation, P_t^e, as shown at point B in the figure. Then the supply of goods would exceed the demand in the typical market. So something else has to happen for this market to clear.

Effects on the Real Interest Rate   Recall that the real interest rate, r_t, still equals the nominal rate R_t—which everyone observes on the economy-wide credit market—less the general rate of inflation, π_t. The expected real interest rate, r_t^e—which matters for supply and demand decisions—equals the nominal rate, R_t, less the expected inflation rate, π_t^e.

So far, we have not allowed for any effects of the monetary disturbance on the expected real interest rate. But for a given value of r_t^e, Figure 19.5 shows that the

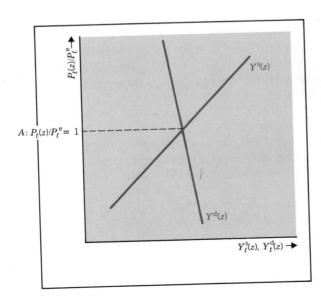

FIGURE 19.4 *Response of a Local Market to the Perceived Relative Price, Including the Response of the Prospective Relative Price*
As the price ratio, $P_t(z)/P_t^e$, *rises, the higher prospective relative price stimulates investment demand. Hence, as compared with Figure 19.3, the demand curve is more nearly vertical.*

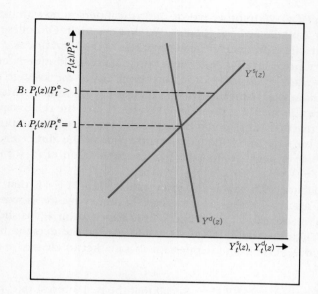

FIGURE 19.5 *Effect of a Surprise Increase in Money on the Typical Commodity Market For given values of prospective relative prices and the real interest rate, the typical market would clear at point A, where $P_t(z)/P_t^e = 1$. But the surprise increase in money and prices means that the ratio, $P_t(z)/P_t^e$, exceeds one, as shown at point B. Here, the supply of goods, $Y_t^s(z)$, exceeds the demand, $Y_t^d(z)$.*

supply of goods would exceed the demand in the typical market. We know from previous analyses that the real interest rate must decline in this situation.

Here we pretend that everyone has the same expectation, r_t^e. In fact, these can differ because of differences in expected inflation rates, π_t^e. However, the basic results would not change if we added this complication.

Let's consider the results from the perspective of the typical commodity market. First, we reproduce the supply and demand curves from Figure 19.5 as the solid lines in Figure 19.6. Then, as r_t^e declines, the demand curve shifts rightward, while the supply curve shifts leftward. That is, the fall in r_t^e motivates people to consume and invest more but to work and produce less. We show the new curves as dashed lines in the figure. Notice that these curves intersect along the line labeled B, where $P_t(z)/P_t^e$ exceeds one. Thus, although people still perceive a high relative price in the typical commodity market, the reduction in the expected real interest rate allows the market to clear.

Monetary Effects on Output, Work, and Investment   Figure 19.6 shows an increase in local output, $Y_t(z)$, although the sign of this change is generally ambiguous. Let's consider the various forces that affect output in the typical market. (By typical, we mean that no unusual shifts in local supply or demand apply to this market.)

First, the high price ratio, $P_t(z)/P_t^e$, stimulates supply but deters consumption and investment demand. Second, the anticipation of a high future relative price, $P_{t+1}(z)/P_{t+1}$, encourages investment. Finally, the decrease in the expected real interest rate, r_t^e, boosts investment and consumption demand but discourages supply.

The presumption that output increases in the typical market depends on a strong positive effect from the prospective relative price, $P_{t+1}(z)/P_{t+1}$, on local investment demand. Given this property, the monetary disturbance tends to raise local investment, output, and work effort. Further, since this result applies to the *typical* market, it shows up also in the *aggregates* of investment, output, and work.

Let's review the process by which a surprise increase in money and prices can lead to higher work, output, and investment. First, the general rise in prices looks to local suppliers like an increase in their relative price. Therefore, they work more and increase production, just as they would in the case of a true expansion of local demand. In other words, the suppliers confuse the change in the general price level with the type of local disturbance that warrants an expansion of their real activity. (Recall that we considered this type of local disturbance in Figure 19.2.)

Second, since the increase in $P_t(z)/P_t^e$ makes people think that the local market will remain favorable to sellers for awhile, people raise their expectations of the future relative price, $P_{t+1}(z)/P_{t+1}$. Then, just as in the case of a true increase in local demand, this belief stimulates investment. Further, the investment shows up currently as purchases of goods and services at the local price, which people perceive to be relatively high. Investors make these purchases to position themselves for the expected high returns later.

Finally, since the disturbance causes an excess supply of goods in the typical commodity market, the expected real interest rate, r_t^e, must decline. This response clears the typical market by raising the demand for goods and lowering the supply. Moreover, our previous analysis (from Chapter 9) suggests that investment demand would be especially responsive to the reduction in the real interest rate. Therefore, the model predicts a strong positive response of investment to a surprise increase in money.

Overall, the expansion of work, output, and investment occurs because the typical household confuses a high general price level for a high relative price in its

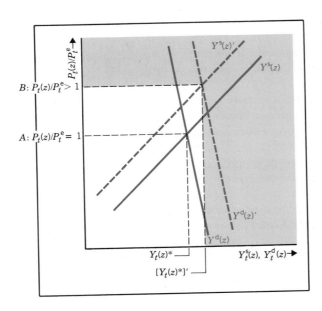

FIGURE 19.6 *Clearing of the Typical Commodity Market after a Surprise Increase in Money*
The solid lines for supply and demand come from Figure 19.5. The decline in the expected real interest rate shifts the demand curve rightward and the supply curve leftward. Hence, the typical commodity market clears where $P_t(z)/P_t^e$ exceeds one.

location. Although households strive to avoid these kinds of mistakes, the available information does not allow them to distinguish all changes in general prices from those in relative prices. Also, households have to weigh their mistaken reactions to changes in general prices against the potential errors from not responding to true shifts in relative prices. In most instances the local price, $P_t(z)$, accurately signals the reward for local production and investment. An overly cautious producer who fails to react to these signals—in order to avoid the mistaken responses to changes in the general price level—will also fail to exploit a variety of true opportunities for profit.

To summarize, the theory shows how surprise injections of money can be nonneutral. Moreover, unanticipated changes in money can generate the responses in quantities that typify aggregate business fluctuations. For example, the theory explains how a surprise contraction in the monetary base can cause a recession, in which output, employment, and investment decline. Recall that, at least for the post–World War II period, there is some evidence that movements in the monetary base have these sorts of effects.

PERSISTING EFFECTS OF MONEY ON REAL VARIABLES

During recessions, variables like output, employment, and investment tend to be depressed for periods of a year or more. Therefore, we want to know whether the theory can account for persisting effects of monetary disturbances on real variables. One possibility is that misperceptions about the general price level persist for a long time, such as a year or more. Then any real effects from these misperceptions would also persist. But this argument is implausible. Earlier we argued that households have incomplete information about prices in other markets and about monetary developments, which means that they can be ignorant for awhile about shifts in the general price level. But households presumably receive enough information about prices so that they would not make the same mistake in estimating the general price level for very long. Thus, it seems unlikely that the persistence in these errors would be as long as the persistence of booms and recessions.

The theory does not require a persistence of confusions about prices in order to explain the persistence in the responses of quantities. For example, we showed that the confusions from a monetary disturbance can lead to more investment. Then, perhaps a few months later, investors recognize that they confused an increase in the general price level for an increase in their relative price. But once producers have incurred the initial costs to initiate a project, it often does not pay to terminate the project (even if the producers regret the start-up decision). Hence, investment demand may remain high even after the confusion about prices disappears. Further, the higher level of investment shows up later as more productive capacity, which tends to raise output and employment even after people learn the truth about past money and prices. Through this type of mechanism, a monetary disturbance can have a long-lasting influence on output and employment.

THE NEUTRALITY OF PERCEIVED CHANGES IN MONEY

The analysis in the previous sections applies to surprise changes in money and the general price level. It is important to recognize that the confusion between general and relative prices cannot arise if households and firms understand fully the movements in money and prices. To see this, suppose that everyone accurately anticipates a once-and-for-all increase in the quantity of money between dates $t - 1$ and t. Then the higher value of the money stock, M_t, shows up one-to-one as a higher rational expectation of prices, P_t^e. Hence, the increase of the price level in a typical market, $P_t(z)$, no longer represents a shift relative to people's expectations. Rather, actual and expected prices end up increasing in the same proportion, so that the perceived relative price, $P_t(z)/P_t^e$, does not change. In this case there are no effects on commodity supply and demand in the typical market, which means no effects on the quantities of output and work or on the real interest rate. Fully understood movements in money and prices are neutral, just as in our earlier models.

Changes in the long-run averages of monetary growth and inflation would be accompanied by corresponding changes in expectations of monetary growth and inflation. The theory predicts no effect from these long-term changes on real variables, such as the growth rate of output or the rate of unemployment. Therefore, the theory is consistent with the long-term evidence for the United States and the United Kingdom and with the data across countries for the post–World War II period. Remember that this evidence indicates that the average rate of monetary growth or inflation bears no relation to the unemployment rate or the growth rate of output.

IMPLICATIONS FOR MONETARY POLICY

If changes in money can have real effects, it is natural to think about a systematic policy of varying the money supply to stabilize the economy. Specifically, economists often advise the Federal Reserve to accelerate money—for example, through open-market purchases of bonds—to bring the economy out of a recession. The theory developed in this chapter does not support this view of monetary policy.

We can think of monetary policy as a regular procedure for adjusting the quantity of money, M_t, in relation to the state of the economy. For example, the monetary authority may expand money more rapidly than usual in response to a recession but hold down the growth rate of money in response to a boom. As noted before, there is some evidence that the Federal Reserve has pursued this sort of countercyclical monetary policy since World War II.

What does the theory predict for the real effects of this type of policy? Given that the policy is in place, a reasonable guess is that people take it into account when they formulate expectations of prices. In particular, if everyone knows that the Fed tends to inflate the economy in response to a recession, households and firms raise their forecasts of money and prices accordingly. Hence, the expectation of prices, P_t^e, incorporates the typical response of the Fed to the observed state of the economy. But this adjustment of expectations means that the Fed changes money and prices relative to people's perceptions only when it departs from its usual practice. It follows that only the erratic part of the Fed's behavior has real effects. The systematic part of monetary policy—which is the predictable acceleration of money in response to a recession and the contraction in response to a boom—does not create any confusions between general and relative prices. Therefore, these monetary changes are neutral in the model. Sometimes economists call this finding the **irrelevance result for systematic monetary policy.**[5]

A great deal of actual fluctuations in money is unpredictable, and the irrelevance result does not apply to these types of monetary movements. But we also cannot think of this erratic behavior as representing useful policy. Rather, sometimes the changes are expansionary and sometimes contractionary but not in a way that systematically improves the workings of the economy.

STAGFLATION

Economists use the term **stagflation** to describe a situation where inflation is either high or rising during a recession. For example, during the recession of 1974–75, the civilian unemployment rate reached a peak of 9.0% in May 1975, while the annual rate of change of the GNP deflator increased from about 4% in 1972 to 9% in 1975. Similarly, during 1979–80, the unemployment rate peaked at 7.8% in July 1980, and the inflation rate rose from about 7% in 1978 to 9% in 1980.

Although stagflation is a big problem for analyses based on the Phillips curve, this phenomenon poses no difficulty for the model developed in this chapter. First, there is no relation in the theory between the perceived parts of monetary growth or inflation and the real variables. So the increase in the average growth rates of money and prices from the late 1960s to the early 1980s, which were presumably perceived by everyone, give us no reason to predict low unemployment rates. Second, the oil crises of 1973–74 and 1979–81 constituted supply shocks, which tend to raise the general price level for a given behavior of the money stock. Thus, we predict in these cases that a burst of inflation would accompany the shortfalls in output.

CURRENT INFORMATION ON PRICES

Thus far, expectations of prices, P_t^e, depend only on information available before period t. Now we develop some interesting new results by allowing people to adjust their beliefs based on current information.

Recall that, during period t, producers find that goods sell locally at the price $P_t(z)$. If this price differs from P_t^e, there are two possibilities. First, some local condition—such as a shift to demand in market z—may make the relative price of goods in this market either high or low. Second, the forecast of general prices may be inaccurate. That is, the general price level, P_t, may turn out to be either higher or lower than P_t^e. But, by assumption, people cannot check things out directly by immediately sampling lots of prices in other markets or by observing a useful pub-

[5]For discussions of this result, see Thomas Sargent and Neil Wallace (1975) and Ben McCallum (1979).

lished index of current prices. Because the process of obtaining information is costly, sellers and buyers make do with incomplete knowledge about the prices of alternative goods. But the observation of the local price, $P_t(z)$, does convey some information about the current general price level, P_t. It is this information that we want to consider now.

Suppose first that people can predict the general price level, P_t, with a high degree of accuracy, as would be true if the monetary authority pursued a policy that usually provided for overall price stability. To carry out such a policy, the authority would have to avoid large random changes in the quantity of money, M_t. In this kind of stable environment, people would not make significant adjustments to their expectations, P_t^e, when they observed the local price, $P_t(z)$. Rather, they would be confident that movements of $P_t(z)$ signaled changes in relative prices, $P_t(z)/P_t$, rather than movements in P_t. Of course, this high degree of confidence implies that people get fooled substantially on the rare occasions when monetary surprises do generate large movements in the overall price level. Even so, knowing they are right in the great majority of cases, suppliers and demanders will respond a lot when they observe changes in $P_t(z)$. Thus, an increase in prices caused by a surprise increase in money will create a large increase in output.

In contrast, consider an economy where money is volatile and the general price level, P_t, often departs substantially from the forecast, P_t^e. In this setting people would be much less confident that a movement in $P_t(z)$ reflected a change in the relative price, $P_t(z)/P_t$. To a significant extent they would believe that a high value of $P_t(z)$ signals a higher than expected value of P_t. It follows that perceptions of the relative price, $P_t(z)/P_t$, become less responsive to observed changes in $P_t(z)$. That is because people adjust P_t^e in the same direction as the movement in $P_t(z)$.

Recall that the response of perceived relative prices is the mechanism whereby surprise movements in money have real effects. Since people are now less willing to believe that relative prices have changed, we find that monetary shocks have smaller real effects than before. The general result is that *the greater the historical volatility of money, the smaller the real effect of a monetary shock.* This conclusion follows because a greater volatility of money makes people more inclined to associate observed increases in local prices with unexpectedly high general price levels. Therefore, it is harder for monetary shocks to fool people into thinking that relative prices have changed.

These propositions receive empirical support from some studies of various countries during the post–World War II period.[6] First, it turns out that monetary disturbances (measured by surprise movements in M1) have a positive relation to real GNP for most countries. As the theory predicts, however, the strength of this relation diminishes as a country's rate of monetary growth becomes less predictable. Countries such as the United States that display relative stability of money turn out to be the ones where monetary shocks (for M1) have a strong positive relation to real GNP. In places like Argentina and Brazil where monetary growth fluctuates

---

[6]See Roger Kormendi and Phillip Meguire (1984) and C. L. F. Attfield and N. W. Duck (1983).

unpredictably, there is essentially no connection between monetary disturbances and real GNP.

Let's return now to the theory to derive another result. We already noted that greater fluctuations in money mean that perceived relative prices become less responsive to changes in local prices. On the one hand, this means that people make fewer mistakes when the changes in prices reflect surprises in money and the general price level. But it implies also that people make *more* mistakes when there actually are shifts in relative prices. Overall, more uncertainty about money and the overall price level means that observed prices become less useful as signals of changes in relative prices. Thus, in a general sense, the price system becomes less effective as a mechanism for channeling resources. For example, the economy becomes less responsive to shifts in the composition of tastes and technology, which require resources to shift from one place to another.[7] Note especially that—in contrast to variations in the average growth rate of money—changes in the predictability of money are nonneutral in this model. From this standpoint the best monetary policy is the one that is the most predictable.

SOME PROBLEMS WITH THE THEORY

We have shown how the market-clearing model with incomplete information about prices generates some results that compare favorably with empirical evidence. But before we accept the theory and its intriguing implications for monetary policy, we should investigate more of its properties. Here, we consider some serious criticisms of the theory.

THE BEHAVIOR OF PRICES AND REAL INTEREST RATES

According to the theory, the real effects of monetary disturbances operate through the channels of price surprises and movements in the real interest rate. But the empirical evidence does not verify these channels of effect. For example, as discussed in Chapter 18, the post–World War II data do not indicate much of a connection between price surprises and fluctuations in real economic activity.[8] Also, some studies for the post–World War II period do not find much connection between monetary disturbances and real interest rates.[9]

Overall, the theory gets mixed reviews for its predictions about monetary disturbances. On the one hand, the analysis neatly accommodates the positive re-

[7]For discussions of these types of adverse consequences of monetary uncertainty, see Friedrich Hayek (1945) and Henry Simons (1948).

[8]As noted in Chapter 18, it is possible that supply shocks obscure this relation. Since these shocks lead to an inverse relation between prices and output, the available studies may not isolate the positive relation that results from monetary shocks.

[9]See, for example, Robert Litterman and Laurence Weiss (1985).

sponses of production, employment, and investment to monetary shocks. But on the other hand, the available evidence does not support the model's story about the channels of transmission from monetary changes to the real variables.

INCOMPLETE INFORMATION ABOUT PRICES AND MONEY

A central element in the theory is that people do not observe immediately the general price level or the quantity of money. For instance, if people always know the general level of prices—perhaps because they look regularly at a useful index, such as the CPI or the deflator for the GNP—they cannot confuse shifts in the general price level with changes in relative prices. Alternatively, suppose that people observe quickly the quantity of money but not the general price level. Then—at least if they understand the economics taught in this book!—they can figure out the implications of the monetary movements for the general price level. Therefore, they would not confuse at least the monetary-induced parts of changes in general prices with shifts in relative prices. But then the model predicts that the monetary changes would be neutral.

In fact, it is not difficult for people to observe quickly an index of prices (with a one-month lag for the CPI) or measures of monetary aggregates (with a one-week lag for M1). Also, if people read the *Wall Street Journal,* they can observe the value of each week's monetary base. Of course, most people do not bother to collect and interpret these types of data. But presumably, that is because the information is of minor value to them.

Let's think about the usefulness of the available indexes of prices. One reason that they may not be very helpful is that each individual cares about a market basket of goods that differs substantially from the one used in the index. Also, the indexes sometimes have conceptual problems, which limit their value. (The CPI's treatment of mortgage interest costs until the recent change in procedures was an example.) Then, in order to keep well informed about prices, people would have to take detailed samples from a variety of markets. But this process is costly. Hence, this viewpoint suggests that people would sometimes make significant errors in their interpetations of observed prices.

A similar argument is that the data on monetary aggregates provide little useful information. Possibly because of seasonal adjustments and the arbitrariness in defining money, the reported measures bear little relation to the concept of money that matters in the theory. However, this argument leads to a puzzle. Namely, it is the reported figures—on M1 and perhaps on the monetary base—that seem to have a positive relation to real economic activity in the post–World War II period. If the data are meaningless, it is hard to explain this relation. Alternatively, if the reported measures are important, why would people not bother to observe them?

To put the various points together, it seems reasonable that ignorance about the general price level and the quantity of money can account for small and short-lived confusions about relative prices. That is because people would find it too costly to monitor continuously and interpret the behavior of general prices and the quantity

RULES VERSUS DISCRETION

*A*n exciting recent development in macroeconomics is the application of models of strategic behavior to the study of government policy. The initial inspiration for these ideas came from the distinction between anticipated and unanticipated monetary and price changes in the kinds of models that we have considered in this chapter. If only unanticipated money and unexpected changes in the price level matter for real variables, policymakers who wish to affect real variables have an incentive to surprise people. But if individuals form expectations rationally, it is difficult to fool people systematically.[10] The resolution of these conflicting objectives involves the strategic interplay between the policymakers and the individuals in the economy. The nature of this interaction can be illustrated by working through a simple example about monetary policy.

Suppose that the monetary authority can use its instruments to achieve any desired rate of inflation, π. It would be more realistic to assume some error between the desired and actual inflation rate, but that change would not affect the basic results. The policymaker wants to reduce unemployment (or raise employment or output) but can do so only by creating a positive amount of unexpected inflation, $\pi - \pi^e$. This surprise inflation would correspond to a positive amount of unanticipated money growth. For a given expected rate of inflation, π^e, the unemployment rate decreases with π. (This result holds in the expectational Phillips curve shown in Figure 18.2 and the model worked out earlier in this chapter.)

Assume that the monetary authority does not like inflation for its own sake. In particular, aside from its effect on unemployment, assume that the policymaker prefers an inflation rate of zero. Then, for given π^e, an increase in π above zero entails a trade-off between the benefits of lower unemployment (or higher output) and the costs of higher inflation. The resolution of this trade-off determines the inflation rate, denoted by $\hat{\pi}$, that the policymaker selects.

Generally, the value $\hat{\pi}$ depends on people's expectations, π^e. Write this dependence as the function, ψ (the Greek letter psi)—that is,

$$\hat{\pi} = \psi(\pi^e) \qquad (19.5)$$
$$(+)$$

If π^e is higher, the monetary authority would have to set a correspondingly higher value of π to maintain the surprise, $\pi - \pi^e$. For this reason, the policymaker's choice,

---

[10]Abraham Lincoln had a somewhat different view: "you may fool all of the people some of the time; you can even fool some of the people all of the time" (see Alexander McClure, 1901, p. 124).

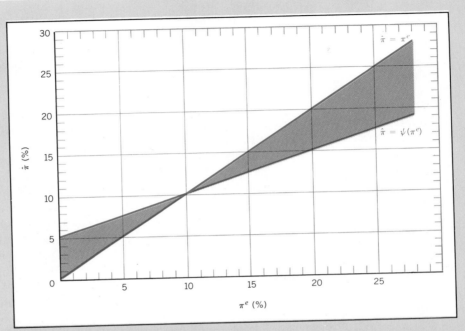

FIGURE 19.7 *Inflation in a Discretionary Regime*
The line with the flatter slope shows the policymaker's choice of inflation rate, $\hat{\pi}$, as a function of the expected rate of inflation, π^e. The 45-degree line shows points where $\hat{\pi}$ corresponds to π^e.

$\hat{\pi}$, tends to increase with π^e, as shown in equation 19.5. The graph of $\hat{\pi} = \psi(\pi^e)$ in Figure 19.7 makes two additional assumptions. First, $\pi > 0$ holds if $\pi^e = 0$; that is, the policymaker finds it worthwhile to inflate if people expect zero inflation. Second, the slope of the function, $\psi(\pi^e)$, is flatter than that of a 45-degree line—that is, an increase in π^e raises $\hat{\pi}$ by less than one-to-one.[11]

Consider how an individual would form a rational expectation of inflation in this model. Suppose that each person knows everyone else's expectation, π^e, and also knows what the government is trying to do: set $\pi = \hat{\pi}$ to achieve a desired trade-off between unemployment and inflation. Then each individual can figure out the policymaker's choice, $\hat{\pi}$, and compute the rational expectation, $\pi^e = \hat{\pi}$. Thus, rational formation of expectations corresponds to the 45-degree line shown in Figure 19.7.

The intersection of the two lines in the figure determines the equilibrium inflation rate, $\pi^* = (\pi^e)^*$. This value satisfies two conditions. First, if $\pi^e = \pi^*$, the policymaker—who is trading off the benefits of lower unemployment against the

---

[11]It is possible to show that this property holds if the cost attached at the margin to more inflation rises as the inflation rate increases.

costs of higher inflation for a given value of π^e—will select the value $\hat{\pi} = \pi^*$, because this point lies on the line, $\hat{\pi} = \psi(\pi^e)$. Second, the expectation $\pi^e = \pi^*$ is rational because it is the best possible forecast of inflation. (In this model—but not in some extended versions—the forecast error is zero; that is, people have **perfect foresight.**)

We can clarify the nature of the results by thinking about some (made-up) numbers. Conjecture that $\pi^e = 0$. Facing this belief, the policymaker finds that the optimal choice for $\hat{\pi}$ is, say, 5%. But any individual can figure out (by knowing what the government is up to) that the policymaker would pick 5% inflation if everyone expected zero inflation. More generally, everyone knows that the government will engineer high inflation if people expect low inflation. Hence $\pi^e = 0$ is an irrational expectation, and each individual would switch to $\pi^e = 5\%$. But if everyone expects 5% inflation, the government would set $\hat{\pi}$ to be, say, 7%. Then everyone would switch to $\pi^e = 7\%$, which motivates the government to pick $\hat{\pi} = 8\%$, and so on. In the equilibrium, perhaps at 10% inflation, the government is motivated to pick $\hat{\pi} = \psi(10\%) = 10\%$, and people also expect inflation to be 10%. This result applies when the two lines intersect in Figure 19.7. At this point the government attaches such a high cost to additional inflation that it is not motivated to surprise people by choosing a still higher inflation rate. Hence people regard 10% inflation as credible.

The nasty aspect of the equilibrium is that it entails a high inflation rate, $\pi = \pi^*$ in Figure 19.7, without any benefits from *surprisingly* high inflation. Since π^e is as high as π, the inflation surprise, $\pi - \pi^e$, is zero. Therefore employment and output receive no stimulus.

The economy would perform better with zero actual and expected inflation because the costs associated with inflation would be lower. In that case the inflation surprise, $\pi - \pi^e$, is again zero, but at least the inflation rate is low. It is clear, however, from Figure 19.7 that $\pi = \pi^e = 0$ is not an equilibrium in the model. If $\pi^e = 0$, the policymaker picks $\hat{\pi} > 0$, and—since people know that the policymaker would behave in this way—$\pi^e = 0$ is inconsistent with rational expectations.

The high inflation result, $\pi = \pi^e = \pi^* > 0$, is often referred to as the outcome under **discretionary policy.** This outcome results if the policymaker can make no commitments or binding promises about future actions. In contrast, a policymaker who can make such commitments is thought of as operating subject to a **policy rule.** One simple form of rule specifies a constant rate of monetary growth or a constant rate of inflation (so-called **constant-growth-rate rules**). In the present setting, where inflation is costly, the best thing that the monetary authority could do is to commit to zero inflation. (In other models the optimal rule would be more complicated.) With this commitment, the outcome $\pi = \pi^e = 0$ would be attainable and also superior to the discretionary result, where $\pi = \pi^e > 0$.

Figure 19.7 illustrates the tension in a rule with low inflation. At $\pi^e = 0$, the policymaker really wants to renege on commitments and set $\pi = \hat{\pi} > 0$.[12] If this repudiation is feasible, individuals presumably would have known it in advance and would not have maintained expectations of zero inflation. Then the equilibrium tends toward the discretionary one worked out before in Figure 19.7. To avoid this outcome, it is crucial that commitments be well enforced. They have to be strong enough so that policymakers cannot overturn them later, even if they want to. To the extent that the government's "sovereign power" makes such commitments infeasible, the outcomes tend to look more like the high inflation under discretion and less like the low inflation under rules.

An important point is that the high inflation result under discretion can arise even if the policymaker is well meaning and competent. The force that drives the result is the benefit from the inflation surprise. In the example just considered, this benefit arises if, first, an increase in surprise inflation reduces unemployment and, second, if the decrease in unemployment is desirable. The last property holds if the private economy tends to generate unemployment rates that are typically too high. Two possible reasons for this market failure are the existence of income taxes and the availability of unemployment-insurance benefits. (The Keynesian model, discussed in the next chapter, suggests that price or wage stickiness may be another reason that unemployment might be too high on average.)

Similar results about policy come up in many areas in which the policymaker would benefit by surprising people after the fact. For example, debtor countries may surprise creditors by defaulting on foreign debts, governments may surprise owners of capital by assessing high tax rates on existing capital (so-called *capital levies*), tax collectors may surprise people by announcing tax amnesties, governments may fail to honor patents after inventions have been made, and so on. In all of these areas, the surprise is tempting after the fact. But if people understand the government's incentives, expectations before the fact will take account of the likelihood of subsequent policy actions. Then the equilibria have undesirable properties, as in the case of high inflation under discretion. In particular, the equilibria may exhibit little foreign borrowing, low investment, poor tax compliance, and a low volume of inventions. To avoid these outcomes, governments would like to promise that they will resist the temptation to surprise people later. But the credibility of these commitments is a major question.

There has been a lot of recent research on the applications of strategic behavior to government policy. A pioneering paper in this area was written by Finn Kydland and Ed Prescott (1977). More recent developments, especially in applications to macroeconomics and monetary policy, are surveyed by Ken Rogoff (1989).

---

[12]The outcome, $\pi > \pi^e = 0$, is preferred to the rules solution, $\pi = \pi^e = 0$, as well as to the discretionary result, $\pi = \pi^e > 0$. However, $\pi > \pi^e$ is inconsistent with rational expectations in this model. Generally, this result is not something that the policymaker can achieve because it is infeasible to fool people consistently.

of money. But it is unlikely that large or long-lasting confusions would arise. The costs of being misinformed about relative prices—and therefore making incorrect decisons about production, work, and investment—seem excessive relative to the costs of gathering the necessary information. Hence, this view suggests that monetary-induced confusions of general for relative prices can account for only small fluctuations in the aggregate economy. We cannot use this line of theory to explain massive contractions of output and employment.

In terms of the U.S. history, the theory has promise for explaining a role for money in relatively mild recessions. Recall that, if we identify money with the monetary base, there is some evidence that this role has been significant since World War II. But it is unlikely that the approach can account for a major portion of a severe contraction, such as the Great Depression of 1929–33. On the other hand, we also suggested before that this episode—and some others from before World War I that featured banking panics—involved a cutback in financial intermediation rather than a contraction of the monetary base. So we probably do not need to rely on incomplete information about money and prices to understand these experiences.

SUMMARY

A new line of macroeconomic theory attempts to explain the role of money in business fluctuations. This approach retains the framework of market clearing and rational behavior but introduces incomplete information about prices to explain some real effects from monetary disturbances. In this model surprise increases in money and the general price level make producers in local markets think that the relative price of their output has risen. Thereby, monetary injections can induce people to expand the quantitites of production, work, and investment. In this respect the theory accords with some evidence, which suggests that surprise variations in the quantity of base money may be nonneutral.

Perceived changes in money and the general price level do not lead to confusions about relative prices. Therefore, the perceived parts of monetary changes are still neutral. This result is consistent with the absence of a long-term relation of real variables to either monetary growth or inflation.

The systematic part of monetary policy causes no confusions about relative prices. Therefore, the theory predicts that this part of policy has no significance for real variables. An increase in monetary uncertainty is nonneutral, however, because it alters the information that people receive by observing local prices. Since people recognize that monetary shocks are often large, the real variables become less sensitive to monetary disturbances. But because the observed prices become less useful as allocative signals, there is also a worsening in the allocation of resources. Specifically, the economy becomes less responsive to variations in the composition of tastes and technology. Thus, the model's main lesson is that monetary policy should be predictable rather than erratic.

Although the theory accords with some empirical evidence, it also has some problems. For example, the data do not support the role of price shocks during recessions or the prediction that monetary disturbances depress the real interest rate. Also, since the costs of obtaining information about money and prices are not very large, the theory cannot explain major business contractions such as the Great Depression. But the theory may help to understand some aspects of mild recessions, such as those experienced since World War II.

IMPORTANT TERMS AND CONCEPTS

perceived relative price

irrelevance result for systematic monetary policy

stagflation

perfect foresight

discretionary policy

policy rule

constant-growth-rate rule

QUESTIONS AND PROBLEMS

Mainly for Review

19.1 Explain why it is reasonable to assume that individuals have imperfect information about the general price level. What are the costs of collecting information about prices?

19.2 Explain what a relative price is. Is the real wage an example of a relative price? Show how a proportional increase in $P_t(z)$ and P_t^e leaves buyers and sellers unaffected.

19.3 What are the factors that might cause the relative price in a market to remain high for many periods of time? What are the factors that cause changes in the relative price to be offset in later periods? (Consider in your answer the changes in the capital stock and in the numbers of buyers and sellers in a market.)

19.4 Can there be unexpected changes in the quantity of money when expectations are rational? If so, does a policymaker have the option of counteracting business cycles through surprise increases in money?

19.5 When expectations are rational, any errors made in estimating the price level will not persist. How then can we explain persistent deviations of aggregate output from trend?

PROBLEMS FOR DISCUSSION

19.6 *Investment Demand in a Local Market*

a. Suppose that producers in market z buy capital at the price P_t. What is the condition that determines investment demand if old capital sells next period at the price P_{t+1}?

b. What is the condition for investment demand if producers in market z buy capital locally at the price $P_t(z)$? How does the result depend on whether old capital sells the next period at price $P_{t+1}(z)$ or P_{t+1}?

19.7 *Changes in the Predictability of Money*

Suppose that the fluctuations of money become less predictable from year to year. What happens to the following:

a. The responsiveness of the perceived relative price, $P_t(z)/P_t$, to the observed local price, $P_t(z)$?

b. The effect of a given size monetary disturbance on output?

c. The allocation of resources?

19.8 *Money and the Dispersion of Relative Prices (optional)*

The local price, $P_t(z)$, differs across locations because each market experiences local shocks to supply and demand. (Think here of changes in the composition of tastes and technology.) Thus, the model generates a dispersion of relative prices across markets at each point in time. Now suppose, as in problem 19.7, that the fluctuations in money become less predictable from year to year. Then what happens to the dispersion of relative prices across markets at a point in time?

(There is evidence that this effect is important during extreme inflations, such as the German hyperinflation, but not for the U.S. experience. See Zvi Hercowitz, 1982. For a survey of the related literature on price dispersion, see Alex Cukierman, 1983.)

19.9 *Monetary Effects on Consumption (optional)*

In the text we noted some shortcomings of the market-clearing model with incomplete information on prices. Here, we explore another problem, which concerns the behavior of consumption.

We argued that a positive monetary shock could increase output, employment, and investment. Suppose, in fact, that work effort increases, so that leisure declines.

a. What must be the effect on consumption? (*Hint:* Does the monetary shock alter the terms on which people can substitute today's leisure for today's consumption?)

b. Would the results change if the monetary disturbance raised perceived wealth?

c. How do the theoretical results about consumption conform with the data on U.S. recessions?

19.10 *Monetary Effects on Real Wage Rates (optional)*

Another problem with the theory concerns the behavior of real wage rates. We explore this problem here.

Suppose that we allow each locality to have a labor market, on which the wage rate is $w_t(z)$. How would a surprise increase in money affect the real wage, $w_t(z)/P_t(z)$, in the typical market? (See note 2 for a suggestion on how to proceed.) How does the result compare with empirical evidence on real wage rates during recessions and booms?

19.11 *Revisions of the Monetary Data*

a. Suppose that people observe the monetary base as it is reported from week to week. Then what does the theory predict about the effects of changes in base money on real variables?

b. The Federal Reserve often revises its data on money—especially M1—several months after the initial reports. (Mostly, these revisions arise because the Fed has to estimate the monthly figures on checkable deposits for nonmember banks and some other financial institutions.) What does the theory say about the economic effects of these revisions in the monetary figures? (Empirically, the revisions bear no relation to real economic activity.)

19.12 *The Effects of Anticipated Policy*

a. What is the irrelevance result for systematic monetary policy?

b. Does the result mean that the unpredictable parts of money do not matter?

c. Does the result mean that the systematic parts of all government policies are irrelevant? Consider, as examples, the following:

i. The unemployment-insurance program.

ii. A policy of raising government purchases during a recession.

iii. A policy of cutting income-tax rates during a recession.

19.13 *The Fed's Information and Monetary Policy*

Suppose that the Fed has a regular policy of accelerating money during a recession.

a. Why does the theory say that this policy does not matter?

b. If the Fed observes the recession before others do, does the policy still not matter?

c. Suppose that the Fed knows no more about recessions than anyone else does. But the Fed also knows that real activity expands when monetary growth is surprisingly high. Thus, when the economy is in a recession, the Fed attempts to expand money by more than the amount people expect. What problems arise here? (*Hint:* Suppose that people understand that the Fed is pursuing this type of policy. What then is the rational expectation of monetary growth and inflation?)

19.14 *Rules versus Discretion (optional)*

Assume that the monetary authority's preferred inflation rate is zero, but the authority also wants to reduce unemployment by making inflation surprisingly high.

a. Show how the equilibrium inflation rate can be high. Is the rate surprisingly high? Does the result depend on the authority's having the "wrong" objective or on being incompetent?

b. Can the results improve if the policymaker has the power to bind himself or herself in advance to a specified inflation rate? If so, explain why this constraint (or rule) can improve matters.

c. Do you think that the policymaker's reputation may be a satisfactory substitute for a formal rule that prescribes future policies?

d. Can you think of some reasons aside from possibly reducing unemployment that a policymaker might like surprisingly high inflation?

CHAPTER 20

THE KEYNESIAN THEORY OF BUSINESS FLUCTUATIONS

he Keynesian theory was developed to understand the tendency of private enterprise economies to experience fluctuations in aggregate business activity. More specifically, Keynes's (1935) analysis sought to explain and suggest policy remedies for the prolonged depressions that occurred in the United States during the 1930s and in the United Kingdom during the 1920s and 1930s.

The Keynesian theory focuses on the process by which private markets match up suppliers and demanders. Notably, the theory assumes that prices on some markets do not adjust perfectly to ensure continual balance between the quantities supplied and demanded. Hence, unlike our previous models, some markets do not always clear. (The imbalance between supply and demand is often referred to as "disequilibrium," but we shall avoid that ambiguous term.) Because of the absence of general market clearing, output and employment typically end up below the efficient amounts. Although everyone could be made better off by an expansion of economic activity, the private market sometimes fails to generate this higher level of activity.

Keynesian models assume, at least implicitly, that there are constraints on the flexibility of some prices. For example, the models assume that the nominal wage rate or the dollar price of commodities responds only sluggishly to changes in market conditions. In extreme cases the wage rate or price level is rigid—or at least fully determined from the past. Then current market forces have no influence on these prices. But economists' willingness to accept this type of assumption as reasonable has diminished with the advent of high and variable inflation in the United States and other industrialized countries. Thus we shall also consider the possibilities for introducing some flexibility of prices into the Keynesian model.

A SIMPLE KEYNESIAN MODEL

Keynes's analysis and some subsequent treatments[1] focused on "sticky" nominal wage rates and the resultant lack of balance between labor supply and demand. Prices for commodities were sometimes assumed to be perfectly flexible (leading to the so-called **complete Keynesian model**) but were more often treated also as sticky. In our framework, we can generate the basic Keynesian results without explicitly considering a separate labor market. Here, we treat as sticky the dollar price, P_t, for goods and services that people exchange on the commodity market. (We return now to the case of an economy-wide market for goods and also assume a closed economy.) We should stress that the neglect of the labor market is purely a simplification. The same sorts of conclusions emerge if we choose instead to examine this market and postulate a sticky nominal wage rate.

Some early analyses assumed that prices were rigid. This assumption turns out to be unnecessary because the Keynesian framework can accommodate nonzero inflation rates. The crucial feature is not completely fixed prices but rather the failure of prices to clear all markets instantly. It is convenient, however, to begin with a model in which the price level is fixed. After we develop this model, we can introduce a nonzero inflation rate.

Start by writing down the standard conditions for general market clearing. For the commodity market, the condition for period t is

$$Y^S(r_t, \; G_t, \; \cdots) = C^d(r_t, \; G_t, \; \cdots) + I^d(r_t, \; \cdots) + G_t. \qquad (20.1)$$
$$(+)(+) \qquad\quad (-)(-) \qquad\quad (-)$$

Recall that a higher quantity of government purchases, G_t, means a larger amount of goods supplied (because public services are productive) but a smaller amount of consumer goods demanded. We assume lump-sum taxes, although an income tax could also be considered. Equation 20.1 takes as given the stock of capital, K_{t-1}, and the characteristics of the production function.

Next we have the condition that money be willingly held,

$$M_t = P_t \cdot L(Y_t, \; r_t, \; \cdots), \qquad (20.2)$$
$$(+)(-)$$

where M_t is the nominal quantity of money for period t. As usual, the aggregate real demand for money depends positively on output, Y_t, and negatively on the interest rate, r_t. We enter the real interest rate, r_t, because with a fixed price level—and hence, zero inflation—the nominal interest rate equals the real rate.

---

[1]See Don Patinkin (1956, Chap. 13) and Barro and Grossman (1976).

Equations 20.1 and 20.2 determine the general-market-clearing values of the interest rate r_t^* and the price level P_t^*. Correspondingly, we denote the general-market-clearing level of output by Y_t^*.

The departure for Keynesian analysis is that the fixed price level, P_t, differs from the general-market-clearing value, P_t^*. The standard Keynesian results emerge when the price level is excessive; that is, $P_t > P_t^*$. In this situation it will generally be impossible for the economy to attain full market clearing, as specified in equations 20.1 and 20.2. Consequently, we have to search for some concept other than supply equals demand to determine the interest rate and the level of output.

Think of starting from a position of general market clearing and then arbitrarily raising the price level above its market-clearing value. In this case, equation 20.2 can no longer hold at the general-market-clearing values of output, Y_t^*, and the interest rate, r_t^*. The excessive price level means that the quantity of money, M_t, would fall short of the aggregate quantity demanded. We can think of individuals as attempting to replenish their money balances, partly by selling bonds and partly by reducing consumer demand and leisure. The first channel suggests upward pressure on the interest rate. Since a higher interest rate raises Y_t^s and lowers $C_t^d + I_t^d$, an excess supply of commodities results. The second channel—whereby consumer demand and leisure decline—reinforces this outcome. Thus, the excessive price level leads to an excess supply of goods.

THE RATIONING OF SALES

How does the commodity market operate under conditions of excess supply? That is, what happens when—at the going price P_t—the total of offers to sell goods exceeds the overall willingness to buy? Normally, we expect a decline in the price level, but that mechanism is ruled out by assumption. Therefore, we have to study the commodity market when excess supply prevails but the price level cannot fall.

Some type of rationing rule must allocate sales when there is an imbalance between the quantities supplied and demanded. The usual mechanism assumes two properties. First, no supplier or demander can be forced to sell or buy more than he or she desires, a condition that follows from the principle of *voluntary exchange.* Second, trade proceeds as long as some seller and some buyer are both made better off—that is, the market ensures the execution of all mutually advantageous exchanges, given that the fixed price P_t applies to all trades. The first condition means that the total quantity of goods sold, Y_t, cannot exceed the smaller of aggregate supply and demand; otherwise, some involuntary sales or purchases would occur. The second condition guarantees that the amount sold is at least as great as the minimum of aggregate supply and demand; if not, some mutually advantageous trades at price P_t would be missed. Thus, the combination of the two properties ensures that output is determined by the **short side** of the market—that is, by the condition

$$Y_t = \text{MIN.}(Y_t^s, Y_t^d) \tag{20.3}$$

where MIN. denotes the minimum of the variables in the parentheses. Note that we deal here with the rationing of sales on the commodity market. In a more general

Keynesian framework, we would include also the rationing of jobs—that is, sales of labor services—on a separate labor market. Then the people who seek jobs but cannot find them are considered to be **involuntarily unemployed.**

Under conditions of excess supply—that is, $Y_t^s > Y_t^d$—output is determined by aggregate demand, Y_t^d, which defines the short side of the commodity market. Therefore, the typical demander experiences no difficulty in finding goods to purchase from the eager suppliers. However, the representative supplier faces an insufficiency of buyers for the products that he or she offers for sale at the price P_t.[2] Thus, we have to reconsider households' decisions in the presence of this constraint. These modifications play an essential role in Keynesian analysis.

In the standard model of a competitive market, individual sellers and buyers are able to transact any amount desired at the going price. But this condition cannot hold for all suppliers when an excess supply of goods prevails. Here, we want to specify the constraint that confronts an individual supplier of goods. We assume that the total quantity of real sales available, Y_t, is somehow apportioned by a nonprice mechanism among the sellers, who offer the larger quantity, Y_t^s. In other words, there is a rationing process, which assigns each producer the quantity of real sales, y_t. Notice that we consider a ration on sales rather than on purchases. A ration on purchases would arise if goods were in excess demand.

We assume that each producer regards his or her real sales limit, y_t, as a given, in the same way that they take as given the price level, P_t, and the interest rate, r_t. We do not allow an individual to take any actions that would influence the size of his or her ration. That is, we exclude such possibilities as greater search for buyers, black-market activities that could involve price cutting, overstatement of the true sales offers to secure a larger individual ration, and so on. Basically, the allowance for these features would amount to relaxing the constraint of the fixed price, P_t.

THE CHOICE OF WORK EFFORT

The production function implies

$$y_t = f(k_{t-1}, \ n_t, \ G_t). \tag{20.4}$$
$$(+) \quad (+)(+)$$

We assume that the ration is an effective constraint on sales—that is, $y_t < y_t^s$ applies for the typical producer.[3] Therefore, the level of output, y_t, is now a given to the producer rather than something that he or she can choose.

Given the quantity of capital, k_{t-1}, and the level of government purchases, G_t, the amount of work, n_t, is the minimum amount necessary to produce the assigned level of output, y_t. Therefore, the production function from equation 20.4 determines

[2] In a disaggregated setup, excess supply could appear in some markets and excess demand in others. The standard Keynesian model applies when the great majority of markets experience excess supply.

[3] Note that we do not allow producers to store up excess output as inventories. This option becomes especially important if people perceive the state of excess supply to be temporary. For extensions of the Keynesian model to include inventories, see Ajit Chaudhury (1979) and Alan Blinder (1980).

n_t for given values of y_t, k_{t-1}, and G_t. We can write the quantity of work as the function

$$n_t = n(y_t, \ k_{t-1}, G_t). \qquad (20.5)$$
$$(+)(-)(-)$$

For given values of the other inputs, n_t varies directly with y_t, as shown by the graph of the production function in Figure 20.1. For any value of y_t on the vertical axis, we can read off n_t on the horizontal. Note that more output means more labor input. With the labor market included, more work also means less involuntary unemployment.

Increases in either of the other inputs, k_{t-1} and G_t, mean that less work is needed to produce a given amount of output. Therefore, n_t declines in equation 20.5. (In Figure 20.1 we can verify these results by shifting the production function upward.)

In the model without sales constraints, households set the level of work to equate the marginal product of labor to the value placed on an extra unit of leisure time. But an effective restraint on sales means that work effort is smaller than otherwise. Because of diminishing marginal productivity, labor's marginal product now exceeds the value placed on an extra unit of leisure. Households would like to work and produce more, if only the goods could be sold at the going price. But the constraint on sales prevents the expansion of work and production. We can also say that the constraint on sales means that the economy operates inefficiently. Everyone could be made better off if work and production were higher—as they would be if all markets cleared. But in the Keynesian model, where the commodity market (and the labor market) do not clear, these efficient adjustments are assumed not to occur.

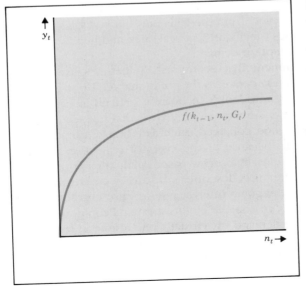

FIGURE 20.1 *The Determination of Labor Input The graph of the production function shows the effect on output of more labor input, given the quantities of capital and government purchases. For a given level of output on the vertical axis, the graph determines the quantity of work on the horizontal. Notice that more output means more labor input.*

THE KEYNESIAN CONSUMPTION FUNCTION

The restraint on sales means that households receive less real income than otherwise. In our model, where the households are also the producers, each household's current real receipts from the commodity market equal the real sales ration, y_t. If prospective real sales equal the current value, variations in y_t have a one-to-one effect on future real incomes. Then the effect on consumption demand would also be roughly one-to-one. If the constraint on sales is temporary, the effect of y_t on consumption demand is weaker.

In the more realistic case where workers are employed by firms, an imposed limit on sales implies that firms have lower employment than otherwise. Thus, movements in households' total income reflect partly changes in wage income and partly changes in profit income (since some households own the businesses). Overall, we would find that shifts in total income lead to adjustments in consumption demand, as in our simpler model where firms and households are not distinguished.

The main point is that an increase in current output, y_t, has a positive effect on consumer demand. Hence, the consumption function, now denoted by $\hat{c}^d$, takes the form

$$c_t^d = \hat{c}^d(y_t, \ r_t, \ \cdots). \tag{20.6}$$
$$(+)(-)$$

Notice that the interest rate, r_t, still has a negative intertemporal-substitution effect on current consumer demand.

The expression in equation 20.6 is called the **Keynesian consumption function.** The distinctive feature of this function is the presence of the quantity of real sales or real income, y_t. In our previous analysis, households chose consumption by considering wealth effects, the real interest rate, the possibilities for substituting between consumption and leisure, and the nature of their preferences. But now there is a separate effect from the given level of real sales in the commodity market. Anything that raises the quantity of real sales, and hence, real income, y_t, spills over to increase consumption demand.

Another argument that economists sometimes use to derive the Keynesian consumption function concerns the credit market. Up to now we have assumed that this market allows households to borrow or lend any amount they desire at the going interest rate r_t. An alternative view is that households cannot borrow readily unless they have good collateral, such as a house, car, or business, to secure the loan. In particular, because of the costs of collection and customer evaluation, households cannot usually borrow based solely on a promise to repay out of future labor income. Economists describe as **liquidity constrained** a person who would like to borrow at the going interest rate to raise current consumption but cannot obtain a loan (at a "reasonable" interest rate). People in this situation would alter their consumption demand, c_t^d, virtually one-to-one in response to changes in their current income, y_t. Therefore, this viewpoint can also explain why the variable y_t appears on the right side of equation 20.6 for some consumers. We shall try to evaluate the importance of liquidity constraints later on.

DETERMINATION OF OUTPUT IN THE KEYNESIAN MODEL

Putting together the results thus far, we can write the level of aggregate demand in the form

$$Y_t^d = \hat{C}^d(Y_t, \ r_t, \ \cdots) + I^d(r_t, \ \cdots) + G_t$$
$$(+)(-) \qquad\qquad (-)$$

where $\hat{C}^d$ is an aggregate version of the Keynesian consumption function and I^d is the investment demand function, which we have studied previously. Recall that the price level exceeds the general-market-clearing value—that is, $P_t > P_t^*$—which means that goods are in excess supply. Consequently, output is demand determined, as follows:

$$Y_t = Y_t^d = \hat{C}^d(Y_t, \ r_t, \ \cdots) + I^d(r_t, \ \cdots) + G_t. \qquad (20.7)$$
$$(+)(-) \qquad\qquad (-)$$

Equation 20.7 is the key relation in the Keynesian model. It says that output, Y_t, equals aggregate demand, Y_t^d. But the tricky aspect is that the consumption part of aggregate demand is itself a function of output. Thus, equation 20.7 says that the level of output (and hence, income), Y_t, determines a level of demand, Y_t^d, which is, in turn, equal to output.

An important element in the determination of output is the responsiveness of aggregate consumer demand to variations in output—that is, the aggregate marginal propensity to consume out of changes in current real income, Y_t. Typically, the marginal propensity is between zero and one, with the value approximating one when people view a change in output as permanent. We denote the marginal propensity to consume by v (the Greek letter nu).

For now, let's consider an extreme version of the Keynesian model, where the interest rate, as well as the price level, is fixed. Later we shall allow the interest rate to be flexible. Figure 20.2, which is called the **Keynesian-cross diagram,** shows how equation 20.7 determines the level of output for a given interest rate, r_t. First, the line labeled Y_t^d indicates the dependence of aggregate demand on the level of output. Note that I_t^d and G_t in equation 20.7 do not depend on Y_t. Therefore, the slope of the Y_t^d line reflects only the positive effect of Y_t on C_t^d. The slope of the line equals the marginal propensity to consume, v, which is positive but less than one. (We show Y_t^d as a straight line only for convenience.)

The 45-degree line in Figure 20.2 indicates positions where output, Y_t, equals the level of demand, Y_t^d. Therefore, equation 20.7 holds when the aggregate demand curve intersects the 45-degree line. We denote the level of output at this intersection by $\hat{Y}_t$. The Keynesian model with a given interest rate predicts that the economy's output will be this quantity $\hat{Y}_t$.

The Multiplier. To illustrate the determination of output, consider an increase in aggregate demand, Y_t^d. This increase could apply to either consumption demand or investment demand. However, the Keynesian model usually focuses on shifts to

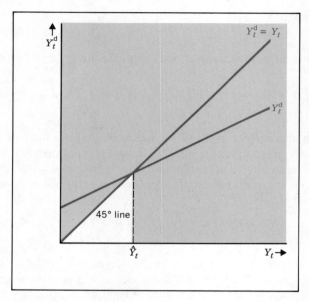

FIGURE 20.2 *Determination of Output via the Keynesian-Cross Diagram*
The line denoted Y_t^d *shows the response of aggregate demand to changes in output,* Y_t. *But output equals demand only along the 45-degree line. Therefore, we determine the level of output at the intersection of the curves as the value* $\hat{Y}_t$.

investment demand that reflect changing beliefs about the marginal product of capital.[4]

The increase in aggregate demand leads to an increase in output, Y_t. (Recall that with excess supply of goods, output is demand determined.) The increase in output means more real income and hence a *further* increase in aggregate demand. This leads to another rise in output, and thereby to more demand, and so on. Because each successive increase in output is smaller than the one before, the process does not lead to an infinite expansion of output. Rather, the ultimate rise in output is a finite multiple of the initial expansion of demand. To calculate the exact change, we can use the Keynesian-cross diagram.

In Figure 20.3, the aggregate demand curve is initially the one labeled Y_t^d. The intersection with the 45-degree line determines the level of output, $\hat{Y}_t$. Then an **autonomous increase in demand** of size A shifts the aggregate demand curve upward to the one labeled $Y_t^{d\prime}$. (By autonomous, we mean that the change comes from outside of the model rather than being explained by the theory.) Accordingly, the level of output, $\hat{Y}_t'$, corresponds to the new intersection with the 45-degree line.

The geometry of the Keynesian-cross diagram in Figure 20.3 reveals the relation between the initial and final levels of output, $\hat{Y}_t$ and $\hat{Y}_t'$. Let $\Delta \hat{Y}$ be the change in output, $\hat{Y}_t' - \hat{Y}_t$, and observe the smaller right-angle triangle with base $\Delta \hat{Y}$. Note that the slope of the line marked with an arrow equals the marginal propensity to

---

[4]Keynes attributed a large part of these disturbances to *animal spirits,* by which he meant spontaneous shifts in optimism or pessimism. These shifts caused businesses to alter their expectations for the profitability of investment. See Keynes (1935, Chap. 12).

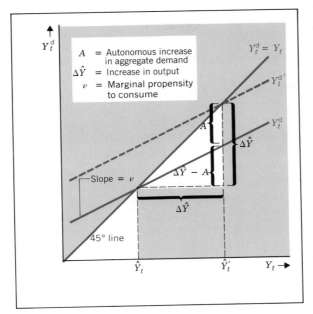

FIGURE 20.3 *The Multiplier*
Aggregate demand increases by the amount A. *The figure shows that the response of output,* $\Delta \hat{Y}$, *exceeds the initial expansion of demand. The geometry implies that* $(\Delta \hat{Y} - A)/\Delta \hat{Y}$ $= v$, *so that* $\Delta \hat{Y} = A/(1 - v)$. *The term* $1/(1 - v)$ *is the multiplier.*

consume, v. Since the vertical side of the triangle is of length $\Delta \hat{Y} - A$, the slope satisfies the relation

$$v = \frac{(\Delta \hat{Y} - A)}{\Delta \hat{Y}}.$$

It follows that the change in output is given by

$$\Delta \hat{Y} = \frac{A}{(1 - v)}. \tag{20.8}$$

Thus, output changes by a multiple of the autonomous shift in demand, A. The **multiplier** is the term $1/(1 - v)$, which is positive and greater than one. Note that the higher is the marginal propensity to consume, v, the larger is the multiplier. Also, for the analysis to make sense—that is, for the ultimate expansion of output to remain finite—the marginal propensity to consume must be less than one, as we have assumed.

We can better understand the source of the multiplier by deriving equation 20.8 in an alternative manner. The autonomous increase in demand leads initially to an increase in output by the amount A. Then the rise in real income by the amount A leads to an increase in aggregate demand by the quantity $v \cdot A$. The additional increase in output of size $v \cdot A$ causes demand to rise further by the amount $v \cdot vA$. In other words, there is a continuing sequence where each round's increase in output is the amount v multiplied by the previous round's increase. It follows that the full increase in output comes from summing up all the rounds—[5]

$$\Delta \hat{Y} = A + vA + v^2A + \cdots = A(1 + v + v^2 + \cdots) = A/(1 - v). \quad (20.9)$$

Notice that the result coincides with the one in equation 20.8.

We should stress two points about the derivation of the change in output, $\Delta \hat{Y}$. First, we assume that excess supply of goods prevails throughout, so producers never hesitate to meet extra demand with more output. Second, the discussion mentions a sequence of rounds only for the purpose of exposition. In the basic model, we do not allow any time to elapse while households adjust demand or production. Therefore, an autonomous increase in demand leads immediately to the full multiplicative response of output, as shown in equation 20.9. More generally, we could include some dynamics, whereby output adjusts gradually toward the value dictated by the Keynesian-cross diagram in Figure 20.3.

Before going on, let's work out a third way to look at the multiplier. We can rewrite the condition for determining output from equation 20.7 as

$$Y_t - \hat{C}^d(Y_t, \quad r_t, \quad \cdots) = I^d(r_t, \cdots) + G_t. \quad (20.10)$$
$$\quad (+)(-) \qquad\qquad (-)$$

The left side is the sum of desired private saving plus taxes. Hence equation 20.10 says that the level of output is such that desired private saving plus taxes equals investment demand plus government purchases. (Equivalently, if we moved G_t to the left side of equation 20.10, the equality would be between desired national saving and investment demand.)

Suppose that an autonomous increase in demand means that the right side of equation 20.10 rises by the amount A. (Equivalently, part of this change could show up as an increase in consumer demand and, hence, as a decrease in the left side of the equation.) If taxes do not change, output must rise enough to generate a matching expansion of desired saving on the left side of the equation. Since the marginal propensity to consume is v, the marginal propensity to save is $1 - v$. Hence the change in saving is the amount $(1 - v)\Delta \hat{Y}$. Since this extra saving, $(1 - v)\Delta \hat{Y}$, must balance the autonomous increase in demand, A, it follows that $\Delta \hat{Y} = A/(1 - v)$. This answer for the change in output coincides with those in equations 20.8 and 20.9.

The multiplier is a distinctive feature of the Keynesian model and would not arise under conditions of general market clearing. To see this, assume an autonomous increase in aggregate demand, Y_t^d, with no shift in aggregate supply, Y_t^s. In a market-clearing setting, as in Chapter 5, we know that the real interest rate, r_t, rises to clear the commodity market. Since the increase in r_t reduces Y_t^d, output must rise by less than the autonomous increase in demand. (Remember that consumer demand does not depend directly on output in the market-clearing model.) Thus, the market-clearing model features a *dampener* rather than a multiplier. The general point is that a well-functioning economy—with cleared markets—typically operates to buffer disturbances rather than to magnify them. The presence of a multiplier in the

---

[5]The formula for a geometric series implies that $1 + v + v^2 + \ldots = 1/(1 - v)$ if $-1 < v < 1$. See note 13 of Chapter 4.

Keynesian model reflects the assumption that private markets fail to clear and therefore operate inefficiently.

THE DETERMINATION OF EMPLOYMENT

For a given level of output, Y_t, the amount of work, N_t, is the minimum amount necessary to produce this quantity of goods. That is, using an aggregate version of equation 20.5, we have

$$N_t = N(Y_t, K_{t-1}, G_t).$$
$$(+)(-)\ (-)$$

$$(20.11)$$

For given values of the capital stock and government purchases and for a given form of the production function, anything that leads to a change in output leads to a change of the same sign for employment. For example, the previous discussion showed that an autonomous increase in aggregate demand led to a multiplicative expansion of output. Now we find that an increase in employment accompanies this rise in output.

Recall that the analysis applies in the range where goods are in excess supply. Since the marginal product of labor exceeds the value attached to leisure time, people eagerly work more whenever it becomes feasible to sell more goods. With a separate labor market with a sticky nominal wage, we would find that suppliers of labor—who face rationing of jobs—readily accept more work whenever the employers raise their demands. In this setting, the amount of involuntary unemployment corresponds to the gap between the aggregate supply of labor, N_t^s, and the quantity of work. Thus, increases in employment show up as decreases in involuntary unemployment.

THE KEYNESIAN INVESTMENT FUNCTION

Because of the multiplier, small disturbances to the aggregate demand for goods can be magnified into sizable fluctuations in aggregate output. For example, a small cutback in investment demand could generate a recession where real GNP and consumption fell significantly below trend. On the other hand, typical recessions feature large shortfalls in investment with relatively small contractions in consumer expenditures on nondurables and services. Recessions do not usually involve small reductions of investment that are accompanied by major declines in consumption. To explain these aspects of the data, we have to modify the Keynesian model to include a direct effect of economic conditions on investment demand.

Recall that, with excess supply of goods, producers reduce their inputs of labor services. Thereby the marginal product of labor exceeds the value of leisure time. Similar reasoning suggests that producers would cut back on their inputs of capital services. That is, when sales are rationed, producers reduce their desired stocks of capital. Thereby the marginal product of capital (less the depreciation rate) exceeds the real interest rate. The main point is that a reduction in the available real sales leads to a smaller desired stock of capital and hence to less investment demand.

THE INVESTMENT ACCELERATOR

*T*he Keynesian investment function is related to the **investment accelerator,** which was discussed frequently in earlier literature on business cycles. The main difference is that the accelerator relates investment demand to the change in output, whereas the investment demand function in equation 20.12 involves the level of output—more precisely, the prospective amount of output, y_{t+1}. Recall that the level of the capital stock, k_{t-1}, appears with a negative sign among the omitted terms of the investment demand function in equation 20.12. If we allowed for changes over time in the quantity of capital, we could generate a dynamic relation for investment. This relation turns out to resemble the accelerator. For an analysis of a model with an accelerator and a multiplier, see Paul Samuelson (1939).

We can write the **Keynesian investment function** as

$$i_t^d = i^d(y_t, \quad r_t, \quad \cdots).$$

$$(+)(-)$$

(20.12)

Notice that by including the level of output, y_t, the Keynesian investment function looks similar to the Keynesian consumption function, which we introduced in equation 20.6. Actually, what matters for desired capital and therefore for investment demand is the prospective quantity of real sales and output, y_{t+1}. Therefore, a cutback in current output, y_t, reduces investment demand, i_t^d, to the extent that prospective output, y_{t+1}, also declines.

The formal analysis of the determination of output and employment does not change when we introduce the Keynesian investment function. The only difference is that we have to redefine the parameter v to be the **marginal propensity to spend**—that is, the total effect of a change in current output, y_t, on the demand for goods, y_t^d. This total effect is the sum of the marginal propensity to consume and the **marginal propensity to invest.** The latter term is the impact of a change in output, y_t, on investment demand in equation 20.12. For the analysis to go through, the marginal propensity to spend, v, must be less than one.

Recall that the multiplier in equation 20.8 is the expression $1/(1 - v)$. The term $1 - v$ is now one minus the marginal propensity to spend rather than the marginal propensity to save. Note that if the marginal propensity to spend, v, is less than one, the term $1 - v$ is positive.

The new results concern the composition of output during business fluctuations. The Keynesian investment function implies that an autonomous contraction of demand can lead to a major decline of investment. At least this response follows if the contraction lasts long enough for prospective output, y_{t+1}, to decline.

On the other hand, the recession may not persist so long that it has a major effect on the present value of income. In this case the cutback in current output, y_t, has only a minor impact on consumer demand, c_t^d. Therefore, most of the shortfall in output could show up as less investment rather than less consumption. In other words, the Keynesian model can now be consistent with this important feature of recessions in the real world.

We mentioned before that liquidity constraints, where some people cannot borrow readily at the going interest rate, could be a basis for the Keynesian consumption function. But if such constraints were important, we would expect recessions to exhibit major shortfalls in consumer expenditures on nondurables and services. In fact, the data show relatively little fluctuation in these categories of spending. The components that decline proportionately more during recessions are—aside from business investment—the purchases of consumer durables, including residential housing, automobiles, and appliances. These goods are relatively easy to buy on credit because durables serve as good collateral for loans. Therefore, this observation does not support the idea that liquidity constraints play a key role in U.S. business fluctuations.

IS/LM ANALYSIS AND THE ROLE OF THE INTEREST RATE

Our previous analysis, which includes the multiplier, shows how to determine the level of output for a given interest rate. As long as there is excess supply of goods, the condition for determining output is, repeating equation 20.7,

$$Y_t = Y_t^d = \hat{C}^d(Y_t, r_t, \cdots) + \hat{I}^d(Y_t, r_t, \cdots) + G_t. \qquad (20.13)$$
$$(+)(-) \qquad\qquad (+)(-)$$

However, our assumption to this point that the interest rate is a given means that the analysis is seriously incomplete. Therefore, we now want to go further to consider the determination of the interest rate, r_t, in the Keynesian model. To carry out this analysis, we have to reintroduce the condition that all money be willingly held. This condition is, repeating equation 20.2,

$$M_t = P_t \cdot L(Y_t, r_t, \cdots). \qquad (20.14)$$
$$(+)(-)$$

Given that the price level, P_t, is fixed by assumption, equations 20.13 and 20.14 determine the interest rate and the level of output. (Recall that, with no inflation, the real and nominal interest rates coincide.) Notice that equation 20.13 determines Y_t for a given value of r_t. But a change in r_t would affect aggregate demand, Y_t^d, and thereby the level of output. What we want to do now is figure out the value of Y_t

that corresponds to each value of r_t. That is, we want to trace out the combinations of r_t and Y_t that are consistent with the equality between output and aggregate demand, as specified in equation 20.13.

An increase in the interest rate lowers aggregate demand on the right side of equation 20.13. As with any decline in demand, the level of output falls. Therefore, if we map out the combinations of r_t and Y_t that satisfy equation 20.13, we determine a downward-sloping relationship. Following standard notation, we label as **IS** the curve in Figure 20.4 that shows this relation.[6] Along the IS curve, the interest rate and the level of output are consistent with the equality between output and aggregate demand.

Consider now the condition that money be willingly held, as specified in equation 20.14. Given the quantity of money, M_t, and the price level, P_t, this condition defines another array of combinations for the interest rate and output. We want to trace out the pairs of r_t and Y_t that are consistent with this condition. Note that a higher value of Y_t raises the demand for money on the right side of equation 20.14. Therefore, r_t must rise to lower the demand for money back to the given level, M_t. Hence, when we map out the combinations of r_t and Y_t that satisfy equation 20.14, we determine an upward-sloping relationship. Again following the conventional notation, the curve designated **LM** in Figure 20.4 shows this relation. Along the LM curve, the interest rate and the level of output are consistent with the condition that all money be willingly held.

The intersection of the LS and LM curves in Figure 20.4 picks out the combination of output and the interest rate—labeled $\hat{Y}_t$ and $\hat{r}_t$—that satisfies the two necessary conditions: output equals aggregate demand, and all money is willingly held. As long as the price level is fixed, the Keynesian model predicts that the level of output will be the amount $\hat{Y}_t$ and the interest rate will be the value $\hat{r}_t$. Hence, we can use the IS/LM apparatus to analyze the determination of output and the interest rate in the Keynesian model. Because of the popularity of the Keynesian model, the IS/LM diagram has been the principal analytical tool for many macroeconomists in the last four decades.

VARIATIONS IN OUTPUT AND THE INTEREST RATE

To bring out the role of the interest rate, consider again an autonomous increase in aggregate demand. If the interest rate did not change, output would rise multiplicatively. However, the expansion of output increases the demand for money above the given quantity M_t. Households' attempts to move out of bonds and into money imply that the interest rate must increase to restore balance on the credit market. This increase in the interest rate reduces the demand for money, but it also decreases aggregate demand. Hence, the overall effect on output is less than the full multi-

---

[6]The terminology IS refers to the equation of investment demand to desired saving. Recall from equation 20.10 that the condition, $Y_t = Y_t^d$, is equivalent to an equality between desired private saving (plus taxes) and investment demand (plus government purchases). The apparatus in Figure 20.4 comes from John Hicks (1937).

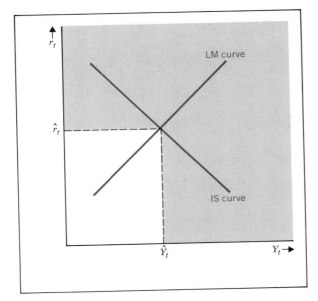

FIGURE 20.4 *Use of IS/LM Curves to Determine Output and the Interest Rate*
The IS curve shows the combinations of Y_t and r_t that satisfy the condition, $Y_t = Y_t^d$. The LM curve shows the combinations that induce people to hold all the existing money, M_t. Thus, the levels of output and the interest rate correspond to the intersection of the two curves.

plicative amount. In fact, the increase in output may fall short of the autonomous expansion of demand. In other words, the increase in the interest rate may make the multiplier be less than one in the Keynesian model (as it is for sure in the market-clearing model).

Figure 20.5 uses the IS/LM apparatus to show the results. We reproduce the solid lines from Figure 20.4. The boost to aggregate demand appears as a rightward shift in the IS curve—that is, output increases for a given value of the interest rate. The size of this shift is the change in aggregate demand, A, times the multiplier, $1/(1 - v)$. Since the LM curve does not shift in this example, the figure shows that output and the interest rate rise. But the increase in output is less than the full multiplier amount, which equals the rightward shift of the IS curve.

For a given amount of government purchases, it is clear that total private spending for consumption and investment increases. But because of the rise in the interest rate, it is possible that one of these components would decline. For example, suppose that the autonomous disturbance is an increase in investment demand. The rise in output stimulates consumer demand, but the increase in the interest rate depresses this demand. Thus, consumption may fall along with the expansion of output and investment. Similarly, if the autonomous change applies to consumer demand, investment may decline.

FISCAL POLICY IN THE KEYNESIAN MODEL

The government can influence aggregate demand directly by changing the level of its purchases, G_t. Suppose that the government raises its purchases by one unit and finances this extra spending with lump-sum taxes. Consider the case where the rise

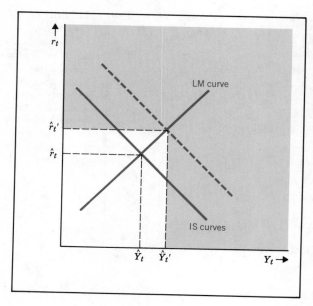

FIGURE 20.5 *Keynesian Analysis of the Effect of an Increase in Aggregate Demand on Output and the Interest Rate The increase in aggregate demand shifts the IS curve rightward. The size of the shift is the autonomous rise in demand, A, times the multiplier, $1/(1 - v)$. We find that output and the interest rate increase. But the rise in output falls short of the full multiplier amount, $A/(1 - v)$*

in purchases is temporary, so that wealth effects are small. As in the analysis from Chapter 12, consumer demand falls by a fraction of the increase in purchases.[7] Thus, aggregate demand expands, but by less than one unit. In terms of the IS/LM diagram, the disturbance can again be represented by Figure 20.5.[8] Now the rightward shift of the IS curve equals some fraction of the increase in government purchases, times the multiplier, $1/(1 - v)$. Notice that output and the interest rate increase. But the increase in output is again less than the full multiplier amount.

The effects of more government purchases on private spending are uncertain. The expansion of output stimulates private demands, but the higher interest rate reduces these demands. In addition, there is the direct negative effect of government purchases on consumer spending. Recall that empirically for the United States, a temporary burst of wartime expenditure tends to crowd out investment but has little effect on consumer expenditures for nondurables and services.

Another type of fiscal policy is a reduction in taxes, financed by more issue of government bonds. Economists often argue that this policy is expansionary in the Keynesian model. But to get this answer, we have to assume that deficit-financed tax cuts make people feel wealthier. Then the stimulus to consumer demand shifts the IS curve rightward, as shown in Figure 20.5. Given this shift, there would again be increases in output and the interest rate.

Because of the higher future taxes, it can still be true (as in Chapter 14) that a deficit-financed tax cut has no aggregate wealth effect on consumer demand. Since

---

[7]Remember that public services substitute for α units of private consumer spending, where α is a positive fraction.

[8]This diagram applies if the change in government purchases has no direct effect on the demand for money. Otherwise, there is also a shift of the LM curve.

the IS curve does not shift, output and the interest rate would not change. In other words, the Ricardian theorem—which states that taxes and deficits are equivalent—can remain valid within the Keynesian model.

If households treat a tax cut as a signal of more wealth, the Keynesian model predicts an expansion of output. Since production and employment are constrained initially by lack of demand, the typical household ends up better off in the situation. Thus, households actually do end up being wealthier. But this result has nothing to do with tax cuts as such. In the Keynesian model, *anything* that makes people feel wealthier generates the increases in output and employment that actually make them wealthier. (Think about what would happen in this model if we assumed that households felt poorer when they saw a tax cut.)

CHANGES IN THE PRICE LEVEL

Recall that the starting point for the Keynesian model was the excessive price level, $P_t > P_t^*$. If the price level declines toward the general-market-clearing value, P_t^*, the basic constraint on the economy relaxes. Therefore, we anticipate that the level of output, $\hat{Y}_t$, would rise toward the general-market-value, Y_t^*. To see how this works, we can use the IS/LM diagram.

Recall from equation 20.14 that the LM curve shows the combinations of r_t and Y_t that equate the amount of money demanded to the given quantity of money, M_t. A decline in the price level lowers the nominal demand for money, $M_t^d = P_t \cdot L(r_t, Y_t, \ldots)$. To restore equality with the given supply of money, we need changes in r_t or Y_t that raise the real demand for money, $L(r_t, Y_t, \ldots)$. Hence the LM curve shifts rightward, as shown in Figure 20.6.

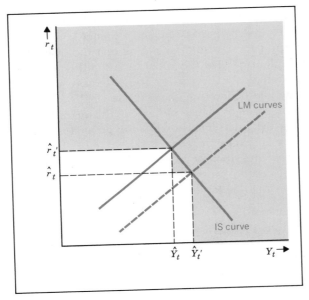

FIGURE 20.6 *Keynesian Analysis of the Effect of a Decrease in the Price Level on Output and the Interest Rate*
A decrease in the price level shifts the LM curve rightward. Therefore, the interest rate falls and the level of output rises.

Notice that the new LM curve intersects the unchanged IS curve at a lower interest rate—$(\hat{r}_t)' < \hat{r}_t$—and a higher level of output—$(\hat{Y}_t)' > \hat{Y}_t$. We can understand these changes by recalling that a lower price level reduces the nominal demand for money, $M_t^d = P_t \cdot L(r_t, Y_t, \dots)$. Households' attempts to exchange their excess money for bonds tends to depress the interest rate, which leads to greater aggregate demand for goods and hence higher output.

Consider a sequence of reductions in the price level from its initial value toward the general-market-clearing value, P_t^*. Each reduction in the price level shifts the LM curve rightward as shown in Figure 20.7. Correspondingly, the interest rate falls and the level of output rises. When the price level falls to the value P_t^*, the interest rate will have fallen to its general-market-clearing value, r_t^*, and output will have risen to its general-market-clearing value, Y_t^*.

Once the price level reaches P_t^*, further reductions in the price level would not generate more increases in output. That is because the commodity market shifts at this point to excess demand, $Y_t^d > Y_t^s$, rather than excess supply. Then the suppliers no longer produce the quantity demanded but rather produce the lesser amount, Y_t^s. Recall that the IS curve assumes that producers accommodate demand fully—that is, $Y_t = Y_t^d$. Therefore, we cannot use this curve to determine output when there is excess demand for goods.[9]

CHANGES IN THE QUANTITY OF MONEY

Assume again that the price level is fixed above the general-market-clearing value—that is, $P_t > P_t^*$. Consider an increase in the quantity of money, M_t, perhaps resulting from an open-market purchase of bonds. Since P_t is fixed, equation 20.14 implies that the real amount of money demanded, $L(r_t, Y_t, \dots)$, must go up for the additional money to be willingly held. Therefore, the increase in M_t works just like a reduction in P_t. We can again use Figure 20.6 to analyze the effects. The rightward shift of the LM curve leads to a lower interest rate and a higher level of output.

We can interpret these results by noting that the quantity of money, M_t, rises above the amount demanded at the initial values of the interest rate, $\hat{r}_t$, and output, $\hat{Y}_t$. As before, households' efforts to exchange excess money for bonds lead to a lower interest rate and hence to higher output.

The important finding is that an increase in the quantity of money is a substitute for a reduction in the price level toward the general-market-clearing value. One way to correct for an excessive price level, $P_t > P_t^*$, is for prices to fall. But an alternative is to raise the stock of money and thereby increase the general-market-clearing level of prices, P_t^*. Monetary expansion closes the gap between P_t and P_t^* by raising P_t^* rather than by lowering P_t.

---

[9]Under excess demand it is purchases of goods and services, rather than sales, that have to be rationed. For a theoretical discussion, see Barro and Grossman (1976). For empirical applications to the centrally planned economies of Eastern Europe, see David Howard (1976) and Richard Portes and David Winter (1980).

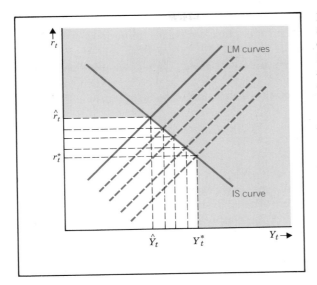

FIGURE 20.7 *Effects of Declines in the Price Level to the General-Market-Clearing Value,* P_t^*

Each decrease in the price level shifts the LM curve rightward. Therefore, the interest rate falls, and the level of output rises. When the price level reaches its general market-clearing value, P_t^*, *the interest rate and output attain their general market-clearing values,* r_t^* *and* Y_t^*.

SHIFTS IN THE DEMAND FOR MONEY

Notice from equation 20.14 that a reduction in the real demand for money, $L(r, Y, \ldots)$, works exactly like a decrease in the price level. Both changes lead to an excess of money, M_t, over the amount demanded, M_t^d. If the demand for money falls—for example, because of a financial innovation—the LM curve shifts rightward, as shown in Figure 20.6. Therefore, we again have a decrease in the interest rate and an expansion of output.

These results follow because the decline in the demand for money raises the general-market-clearing value of the price level, P_t^*. From this perspective, a decrease in the real demand for money works in the same way as an increase in M_t. Both changes reduce the spread between P_t and P_t^* by raising the value of P_t^*.

IS/LM ANALYSIS AND GENERAL MARKET CLEARING

The IS/LM framework is designed to bring out the interaction between monetary phenomena (the LM curve) and real phenomena (the IS curve). In the Keynesian model, the main source of this interaction is the stickiness of the general price level (or the nominal wage rate). That is why the IS/LM apparatus was helpful when we studied various disturbances in the context of a fixed price level.

Suppose that we return to a setting of general market clearing, where the price level is flexible. Then Figure 20.7 shows how we could use the IS/LM diagram to find the general-market-clearing values of the interest rate, r_t^*, and output, Y_t^*. However, the apparatus would be cumbersome because disturbances typically imply shifts of the IS and LM curves, as well as changes in the market-clearing price level, P_t^*.

When we allow the price level to be flexible, we eliminate the main source of interaction between monetary and real phenomena in the model.[10] Therefore, we also lose the main point of the IS/LM diagram—namely, to study the interplay between monetary and real factors. If we want to analyze the economy under conditions of general market clearing, we can return to the framework developed in Chapter 5. Although we could get the same answers from the IS/LM model, the earlier framework is more convenient.

THE SUPPLY SIDE IN THE KEYNESIAN MODEL

The Keynesian model—whether the simple version we have been studying or more sophisticated versions—views aggregate demand as the central determinant of output and employment. The analysis pays little attention to aggregate supply. In formal terms, the neglect of the supply side arises because the postulated excessive price level, $P_t > P_t^*$, means that excess supply of goods and services prevails. Thereby the model assumes that productive capacity and the willingness to work do not represent effective constraints on output. Only the willingness to spend limits the extent of economic activity in this model. This perspective explains why Keynesian analyses typically pay little attention to some matters that are important in a market-clearing framework. Among these are shifts to the production function, variations in the stock of capital, effects of the tax system on the willingness to work, and so on.[11] The neglect of these elements became embarrassing with the supply shocks of the 1970s. In fact, the failure to handle supply shocks was one of the major elements that led many economists to look for alternatives to the Keynesian model. In any case, let's examine some Keynesian predictions about business cycles.

KEYNESIAN PREDICTIONS ABOUT BUSINESS FLUCTUATIONS

As we developed the market-clearing model in previous chapters, one of our major concerns was the identification of types of disturbances that have been important in real-world business fluctuations. The possibilities include supply shocks, shifts to investment demand (which could reflect supply shocks), autonomous changes in consumption demand or labor supply, monetary disturbances, and variations in the

---

[10]The interaction can arise also if transaction costs or the level of real money balances influence the amounts of commodities supplied and demanded. Recall that the neglect of transaction costs is only an approximation but probably a good one in most circumstances. Another source of interaction between monetary and real phenomena involves incomplete information about prices, as studied in Chapter 19. But since the IS/LM model assumes an economy-wide market for commodities, it is not helpful in this context.

[11]The Keynesian model considers these factors to the extent that they influence investment or consumption demand. Also, the supply of labor services matters when computing the amount of involuntary unemployment.

government's expenditures or tax rates. The Keynesian model does not enlarge the set of possibilities. Rather, it narrows the list by limiting attention to disturbances that impinge on aggregate demand. This neglect of the supply side is a basic weakness of the Keynesian model.

Decreases in aggregate demand may reflect autonomous declines in investment and consumption demand or reductions in government purchases. In the Keynesian model, these changes tend to produce a recession, whereby output, employment, investment, and consumption decline. Although the model does not explain the initial disturbance, it does show why the aggregate variables tend to move together during recessions and booms. By including the Keynesian investment function, the model can explain why the shortfall of output during a recession shows up mostly as less investment.

The presence of the multiplier suggests that small disturbances can be magnified into significant fluctuations in aggregate activity. However, empirical evidence on the effects of government purchases (discussed in Chapter 12) suggests that there is no multiplier. The Keynesian model is consistent with the absence of a multiplier if we extend it, as in the IS/LM model, to include the determination of the interest rate. But the loss of the multiplier eliminates a distinctive feature of Keynesian analysis. In particular, a model without a multiplier requires large shocks to trigger a recession.

The Keynesian model predicts an expansionary effect from an increase in the quantity of money (relative to the given price level). This effect operates via a reduction in the interest rate. However, this prediction tends to explain too much since the empirical evidence indicates no long-term connection between monetary growth and real variables. To reconcile the model with this observation, we have to introduce some flexibility of prices (see below). But there is another problem since the data do not suggest even a short-run relation between monetary fluctuations and changes in real interest rates. Recall that this last finding also caused difficulties for the market-clearing model in the previous chapter.

Notice that shifts to aggregate demand, which affect the IS curve, change the real interest rate in the same direction. But movements in the quantity of money (or shifts to velocity), which affect the LM curve, cause inverse movements in the real interest rate. Therefore, the Keynesian model does not predict a definite cyclical pattern for the real interest rate. (Remember that the data also reveal no definite pattern.) In the Keynesian model, the behavior of the real interest rate depends on whether the dominant disturbance is to aggregate demand or to the supply and demand for money.

INFLATION IN THE KEYNESIAN MODEL

Thus far, we have assumed in this chapter that the price level was fixed. This assumption is unsatisfactory, especially for present-day economies, where inflation rates are typically positive and often highly variable over time. Since the Keynesian model does not rely on market-clearing conditions to determine the price level, we need some other mechanism to replace the assumption that prices are rigid. The usual device is an ad hoc adjustment relationship, whereby the price level moves gradually toward the general-market-clearing value, P_t^*. Recall that the condition $P_t > P_t^*$ corresponds to an excess supply of commodities. Therefore, an adjustment of the price level toward the market-clearing value, P_t^*, means that prices decline when goods are in excess supply and rise when goods are in excess demand.

One simple form of a price-adjustment rule is

$$\pi_t = \lambda(Y_t^d - Y_t^s) \tag{20.15}$$

where λ (the Greek letter lambda) is positive. Note that the higher the parameter λ, the more rapidly prices adjust to an imbalance between supply and demand. Sometimes economists regard the reaction of prices to excess demand as different from that to excess supply. Prices are thought to rise quickly in the face of excess demand but to fall sluggishly when there is excess supply. This asymmetry would support the Keynesian focus on cases where the price level exceeds its market-clearing value. But the reason for this asymmetry in the price-adjustment relation has not been explained.

As it stands, the price-adjustment formula in equation 20.15 has some problems. First, inflation is nonzero only if the commodity market does not clear—that is, if $Y_t^d \neq Y_t^s$. But the theory should allow inflation and cleared markets to coexist. Second, as a related matter, inflation is negative in the Keynesian case where goods are in excess supply. Thus, we cannot use equation 20.15 to incorporate positive inflation into the Keynesian analysis.

Recall that equation 20.15 implies that the price level, P_t, moves toward the general-market-clearing price, P_t^*. But monetary growth or some other factors can lead to continuing changes in P_t^*. Intuitively, P_t would respond to the gap between P_t and P_t^*, which relates to the amount of excess demand for goods, and to the change over time in P_t^*. Call this last element π_t^*—that is, π_t^* is the expected rate of change of P_t^*. Using this concept, we might modify equation 20.15 to the form

$$\pi_t = \lambda(Y_t^d - Y_t^s) + \pi_t^* \tag{20.16}$$

Equation 20.16 says that actual inflation, π_t, exceeds the anticipated rate of change of the market-clearing price, π_t^*, when there is excess demand, and vice-versa for excess supply. Thus, the actual price level, P_t, tends to approach the target, P_t^*, even when the target moves over time.

Note that equation 20.16 is consistent with nonzero inflation when the commodity market clears. For example, a high rate of anticipated monetary growth would imply a high value for π_t^*, and hence for π_t. If π_t^* is positive, π_t can be positive even when goods are in excess supply. Hence, positive inflation can appear in the Keynesian model.

We now have the following general description of a recession. First, there is some adverse shock to aggregate demand, perhaps stemming from an autonomous decline in firms' desires to invest. Then output, employment, and investment (and probably consumption) fall below their general-market-clearing values. Correspondingly, there is an increase in unemployment.

The shortfalls in quantities persist because prices (and wages) do not adjust downward immediately to reestablish general market clearing. That is, although prices are no longer rigid, they are still sticky. But equation 20.16 says that the inflation rate, π_t, falls below the rate of change of the market-clearing price, π_t^*. Therefore, P_t tends to fall relative to P_t^*. The resulting increases in real money balances[12] lead to decreases in interest rates, and hence to expansions of aggregate demand and output. In this way, the economy tends to return gradually to a position of general market clearing.

The role for active policy in the Keynesian model appears as a substitute for the economy's automatic, but sluggish, reaction through price adjustment. Expansions in the growth rate of money (monetary policy) or increases in government purchases (fiscal policy) can spur aggregate demand. Thereby, the model says that the recovery from a recession can be quickened.

STICKY PRICES IN THE KEYNESIAN MODEL

All of the novel features in the Keynesian analysis derive from the assumption that prices (or wages) are sticky. The key postulate is that prices do not fall quickly when there is excess supply of goods. Among other things, this assumption delivers the following results:

- Output is determined by aggregate demand; supply-side elements play no important role.
- There may be a multiplier connecting autonomous shifts in aggregate demand to the responses of output.
- Whenever people feel wealthier and raise consumer demand, the expansions of output and employment actually make them wealthier.
- There are real effects from changes in the quantity of money.
- There is a desirable role for active monetary and fiscal policies.

Given all the results that follow from sticky prices, we should look further into the meaning of this assumption. Presumably the stickiness of prices does not to a significant degree reflect the costs of changing prices as such.[13] (In fact, the costs of changing production and employment—which Keynesian models usually ignore—are clearly much more important.) Instead, most macroeconomists use sluggish price adjustment as a proxy for other problems that make it difficult for the

---

[12]The discussion assumes that the growth rate of the market-clearing price, π_t^*, reflects an equal growth rate for the quantity of money. Therefore, the growth rate of money exceeds that of prices.

[13]Until recently most macroeconomists seemed to agree that the direct costs of adjusting prices were unimportant for understanding macroeconomic phenomena. Yet a recent literature relies on **menu costs** for changing prices. For a discussion, see Lawrence Ball, Greg Mankiw, and David Romer (1988).

private sector to operate efficiently. For example, there are costs of obtaining various kinds of information, costs of moving from one job to another, costs of changing methods of production, and so on. These types of coordination problems mean that the economy does not always react appropriately to changes in the composition of tastes and technology or to shifts in the levels of aggregate demand and supply.

There is no question that the elements just mentioned are important for explaining variations in the aggregates of output and employment and for understanding unemployment. But it is unclear that we can represent these matters by the Keynesian device of imposing an excessive price level on the trades that the private sector can carry out. For example, incomplete information does not imply that aggregate demand is more important than aggregate supply. Also, the gaps in people's knowledge do not necessarily imply a desirable role for activist monetary and fiscal policies.

When we allow for incomplete information and adjustment costs, we find that the allocation of resources is a hard problem for the private sector to solve. There are often mistakes, which sometimes show up as unemployment and underproduction. But the challenge to Keynesian analysis is to explain why these problems are eased if the government occasionally throws in a lot of money or steps up its purchases of goods. In the type of model that we are exploring in this chapter, these policy actions look good because the assumption of an excessive price level forces the private economy to commit easily correctable mistakes. Namely, output and employment fall short of the levels at which labor's marginal product equals the value of workers' time. Similarly, the marginal product of capital (less the rate of depreciation) exceeds the real interest rate. But these types of problems are transparent and easy for the private sector to solve without governmental assistance. What has not been shown is that activist governmental policies can assist when the economy has to deal with incomplete information or other serious problems.

LONG-TERM CONTRACTS

It has long been recognized that the weak link in Keynesian analysis is the absence of a theory of sticky prices. One interesting attempt to explain this behavior involves **long-term contracts.** This approach recognizes that buyers and sellers often form long-term relationships rather than dealing exclusively on auction markets, such as wholesale markets for agricultural commodities, organized securities markets, and so on. For example, the associations between employers and workers or between firms and their suppliers often extend over many years. Frequently these types of continuing interchanges involve formal—though more often implicit—contractual obligations between the parties. Some presetting of prices—or, more likely, of wages—may be one feature of these contracts.[14]

Prior agreement on prices or wages may allow one party, which might be a

---

[14]Some major papers in this area are Donald Gordon (1974), Costas Azariadis (1975), Martin Baily (1974), and Herschel Grossman (1979).

group of workers, to shift some risk from themselves to the other party, say a large corporation. For example, an automobile company may shield its workers from some of the fluctuations in the demand for cars. This setup is desirable if the company is in a better position than the workers to assume risks, perhaps because the company has better access to insurance and other financial markets.

The presetting of some prices may also prevent one person from demanding "unreasonable" terms, ex post. For example, a firm might lower the wage rate after an employee had incurred significant costs in moving to a job. Similarly, a builder might raise the price for a construction project at a time when delays become prohibitively expensive. In these cases the market—for builders, workers, and employers—may be competitive beforehand but more like a monopoly later. Some of these problems can be avoided by entering into prior contractual arrangements about prices and other considerations.

Some economists have used the contracting approach to rationalize the stickiness of prices or wages in Keynesian models.[15] For example, suppose that two parties agree on a price, P, over the life of a contract.[16] In some cases the chosen price will be the best estimate of the average market-clearing price during the contract, P^*, given the information available at the outset. But unanticipated events—such as monetary disturbances—create departures of the price from its market-clearing value. When the contract expires, the parties will agree to a new price, which equals the anticipated market-clearing price over the next period.

At any point in time, there is an array of existing contracts, which specify prices that likely depart somewhat from market-clearing values. In particular, if there has been a recent monetary contraction, the typical price will be above its market-clearing value (and vice versa for monetary expansion). As more people renegotiate contracts, the average price adjusts gradually toward the average market-clearing value. In other words, we can use this model to rationalize a price-adjustment relation like that in equation 20.16:

$$\pi_t = \lambda(Y_t^d - Y_t^s) + \pi_t^*.$$

The gradual response of the average price to excess demand corresponds to the process of recontracting, while the anticipated rate of change of the market-clearing price, π_t^*, reflects the known factors that negotiators take into account when setting prices or wages at the start of contracts. Note that an excessive price—that is, excess supply of goods and services—is no more likely than too low a price. Since the price-adjustment relation would be symmetric, this approach does not support the Keynesian stress on cases where the average price level is too high.

Although the contracting viewpoint may rationalize a process of gradual price

---

[15]See, for example, Jo Anna Gray (1976), Stanley Fischer (1977), and John Taylor (1980).

[16]Actually the contracting theory motivates the presetting of a relative price or a real wage rate rather than dollar prices or wages. Yet most contracts in the United States are not explicitly "indexed"—that is, do not contain automatic adjustments of nominal prices or wages for changes in the general cost of living. Apparently firms and workers find it convenient to frame their contracts in terms of the standard unit of account—the dollar—even when inflation is moderately high and variable. But inflation does tend to produce contracts with shorter durations.

SOME EMPIRICAL EVIDENCE ON THE CONTRACTING APPROACH

*T*wo recent studies provide some direct empirical evidence about the contracting approach. Shaghil Ahmed (1987a) used a data set for 19 industries in Canada over the period 1961–74. He used these data because an earlier study by David Card (1980) calculated the amount of indexation—that is, automatic adjustment of wages for general inflation—in each industry's labor contracts. (Indexation ranged across the industries from zero to roughly 100%.) According to theories in which contracts are the basis for the Keynesian model, industries with little indexation should show substantial responses of real wages, and hence of employment and output, to nominal disturbances. On the other hand, those with lots of indexation would be affected little by nominal disturbances.

Ahmed found that nominal shocks—based on unanticipated changes in money or some other nominal variables—had positive effects on hours worked in most of the 19 industries. These results are consistent with some other findings that we discussed in Chapter 18 for the United States and other countries. The important point for present purposes, however, is that the extent of an industry's response to nominal disturbances bore no relation to the amount of indexation in that industry. Those with lots of indexation were as likely as those with little indexation to respond to nominal disturbances. This finding is damaging to theories that use long-term contracts as the basis for the Keynesian model.

Mark Bils (1989) studied labor contracts for 12 manufacturing industries in the United States. He reasoned that if the signing of new contracts was important, he should find unusual behavior of employment and real wages just after these signings. His results were mixed. On the one hand, some industries—especially motor vehicles—turned out to exhibit important changes in employment subsequent to new labor agreements. In particular, there was some tendency for prior changes in employment to be reversed just after a new contract. These results, although applying only to a few industries, provide some support for the contracting approach. On the other hand, Bils did not find any corresponding types of changes in real wage rates after new labor contracts were signed. Since these changes in wage rates are central to the contracting approach, it is difficult to reconcile this part of Bils's findings with that approach.

adjustment, there are difficulties in using this analysis to explain Keynesian unemployment and underproduction. The Keynesian results emerge when prices or wages are above market-clearing values *and* when the quantities of output and employment equal the smaller of supply and demand. Recall that this short-side rule for determining quantities accords with voluntary exchange on an impersonal market. But the rule is not generally sensible in a long-term contract, which is now the theoretical basis for sluggish price adjustment.

In an enduring relationship, where long-term contracts arise, firms and households do not have to change prices or wages every instant to get the "right" behavior of quantities. For example, workers can agree in advance that they will work harder when there is more work to do—that is, when the demand for a firm's product is high—and vice versa when there is little work. Unlike in an auction market, these efficient adjustments in work and production can occur even if wages do not change from day to day. (For large short-term increases in work, contracts may prescribe overtime premiums or other types of bonuses.) The important point is that stickiness of wages does not necessarily imply mistakes in determining the levels of employment and production.

Similarly, suppose that inflation is sometimes higher than expected and sometimes lower. Firms and workers know that inflation—if not accompanied by some real changes—does not alter the efficient levels of work and production. Therefore, it is reasonable to agree on a contract that insulates the choices of quantities from the rate of inflation. Over many periods—where the effects of unanticipated inflation on real wage rates tend to average out—both parties to a labor contract would benefit from this type of provision. (However, when inflation gets very high and unpredictable, firms and workers prefer either to index wages to the price level or to renegotiate contracts more frequently.)

One important lesson from the contracting viewpoint is that stickiness of prices or wages need not lead to underproduction and unemployment. Within a long-term agreement, it is unnecessary for prices and wages to move all the time to attain the general-market-clearing values of output and employment. Thus, stickiness in prices and wages no longer tends to generate Keynesian results. Rather than supporting the Keynesian model, the perspective of long-term contracting demonstrates that output and employment can be determined efficiently—as if prices and wages always adjusted to clear markets—even if prices and wages are sticky.

SUMMARY

In the Keynesian model the price level (or the nominal wage rate) exceeds the market-clearing value. The resulting excess supply of goods and services means that output is determined by aggregate demand. Correspondingly, there is underproduction and unemployment.

In the simplest Keynesian model, where the interest rate is given, an increase in aggregate demand leads to a multiplicative expansion of output. The increase in demand could reflect an autonomous shift to investment or consumption demand or could come from an increase in government purchases. Along with the expansion of output, there tend to be increases in employment, investment, and consumption. If we include the Keynesian investment function and the dependence of consumption on long-run income, the model can match the empirical observation that investment is more volatile than consumption.

The IS/LM analysis shows how to determine the interest rate along with the level of output. In this model, an increase in aggregate demand may no longer have a multiplicative effect on output. That is because the increase in the interest rate crowds out the demands for consumption and investment.

In the Keynesian model, a decrease in the price level implies more real money balances and a lower interest rate. The fall in the interest rate stimulates consumption and investment demand, and this increase in demand leads to an expansion of output and employment. Similarly, an increase in the quantity of money or a cutback in the demand for money leads to a lower interest rate, and thereby to higher levels of output and employment.

We can incorporate inflation into the Keynesian model by using a price-adjustment formula, which says that inflation responds positively to excess demand for goods and negatively to excess supply. When the commodity market clears, the inflation rate equals the anticipated rate of change of the market-clearing price. This mechanism allows the price level to fall, relative to the market-clearing value, during a recession. The resulting increases in real money balances lead to decreases in the interest rate and to increases in aggregate demand. Thus, the economy adjusts automatically toward the market-clearing levels of output and employment. In the Keynesian model, active monetary and fiscal policies can speed up this gradual process of automatic adjustment.

Some novel features of the Keynesian analysis are the following:

- Output is determined by aggregate demand; supply-side elements play no important role.

- There may be a multiplier connecting autonomous shifts in aggregate demand to the reponses of output.

- Whenever households feel wealthier and raise consumer demand, the expansions of output and employment actually make them wealthier.

- There are real effects from changes in the quantity of money.

- There is a desirable role for active monetary and fiscal policies.

These features follow from the assumption that prices are sticky downward. Most macroeconomists use sticky prices as a proxy for the coordination problems that characterize the private sector's reaction to fluctuations in aggregate supply and demand and to shifts in the composition of tastes and technology. But when economists model these problems in terms of incomplete information, costs of moving, and so on, the Keynesian features noted above do not tend to emerge.

An interesting rationale for sticky prices concerns long-term contracts. Each (explicit or implicit) contract specifies a wage or price over an interval of time.

Then the gradual process of recontracting means that the average wage or price adjusts gradually toward the average market-clearing value. Although this perspective may account for sticky prices, it is less successful in explaining the Keynesian predictions about quantities. That is because sensible agreements would allow for efficient adjustments of work and production even if wages or prices do not change from day to day. Thus, the existence of long-term contracts does not explain the type of unemployment and underproduction that arises in Keynesian models.

IMPORTANT TERMS AND CONCEPTS

complete Keynesian model

short-side rule (for determining quantities)

involuntary unemployment

Keynesian consumption function

liqudity constraint

Keynesian-cross diagram

autonomous change in demand

multiplier

Keynesian investment function

investment accelerator

marginal propensity to spend

marginal propensity to invest

IS curve

LM curve

menu costs

long-term contracts

QUESTIONS AND PROBLEMS

Mainly for Review

20.1 **a.** Contrast the form of consumption demand in the Keynesian model with that in Chapter 5. Why does a change in current income not affect consumption demand in the market-clearing model?
b. Make the same comparisons for investment demand.

20.2 What is involuntary unemployment? Are the temporary layoffs of workers on long-term contracts an example of involuntary unemployment?

20.3 How does output adjust to ensure the aggregate-consistency condition for the commodity market (equation 20.7)? Would this result apply if goods were not in excess supply?

20.4 Explain how an increase in the quantity of money reduces the real interest rate in the Keynesian model. Why does this effect not arise in the market-clearing model?

20.5 What is the output multiplier for an increase in government purchases? Discuss how the size of the multiplier is affected by:
a. Whether government purchases are tax financed or deficit financed.
b. Any increases in the interest rate.
c. Whether government purchases are temporary or permanent.

20.6 If the price level is fixed at a level that is "too high," show that the interest rate and output must adjust to ensure the condition that all money be willingly held. Can the interest rate be too high as a result? How does a downward adjustment of the price level bring down the interest rate and eliminate excess supply of commodities?

PROBLEMS FOR DISCUSSION

20.7 **The Paradox of Thrift**
Suppose that people become "thriftier" and thereby decide to save more and consume less.

  a. For a given interest rate, what happens to the quantities of output and employment? What happens to the amount of private saving? (*Hint:* What happens to the quantity of investment?) If the amount of private saving falls when people become thriftier, there is said to be a *paradox of thrift.*
  b. Redo the analysis when the interest rate is allowed to adjust. What happens now to the amount of saving? Is there a paradox of thrift?
  c. Can there be a paradox of thrift in the market-clearing model, where the price level is also allowed to adjust? What accounts for the differences in results?

20.8 **The Multiplier**
Consider an autonomous increase in investment demand.

  a. Why is there a multiplicative effect on output if we hold fixed the interest rate?
  b. Is there still a multiplier when the interest rate adjusts? In particular, how does this answer depend on the magnitudes of the following:
    i. The sensitivity of aggregate demand to the interest rate?
    ii. The sensitivity of money demand to output?
    iii. The sensitivity of money demand to the interest rate?

20.9 **Perceived Wealth in the Keynesian Model**
Suppose that the president makes a speech and announces that we are all wealthier than we previously thought. If we all believe the president, what does the Keynesian model predict for the changes in output, employment, and "wealth"? Explain these results and contrast them with the predictions from the market-clearing model.

20.10 **A Change in Inflationary Expectations**
Consider an (unexplained) increase in inflationary expectations, π^e.

  a. How does this change affect the IS curve?
  b. How does it affect the LM curve? (Recall that money demand depends on the nominal interest rate, $R = r + \pi^e$.)
  c. What happens to the level of output, the real interest rate, and the nominal interest rate? Explain these results and contrast them with those from the market-clearing model. (*Hint:* How does the change in inflationary expectations compare to an autonomous shift in the demand for money?)

20.11 ***Extreme Cases in the IS/LM Analysis***

Consider the following extreme cases (which have sometimes been suggested, but have not been supported empirically).

a. Suppose that money demand is insensitive to the interest rate. What does the LM curve look like? In this case, what is the effect on output and the interest rate from a disturbance that shifts the IS curve?

b. Suppose that money demand is extremely sensitive to the interest rate (sometimes called a *liquidity trap*). How does the LM curve look in this case? What is the effect now from a shift in the IS curve?

c. Suppose that the interest rate has a negligible effect on aggregate demand. How does the IS curve look in this situation? What are the effects from a shift in the LM curve?

d. Finally, suppose that aggregate demand is extremely sensitive to the interest rate. Draw the IS curve and describe the effects from a shift in the LM curve.

20.12 ***Stagflation in the Keynesian Model***

Suppose that we define stagflation as an increase in inflation during a recession.

a. Assume that a recession stems from an autonomous decline in aggregate demand. Can we get stagflation from this disturbance in the Keynesian model?

b. Is there some other way to generate stagflation in the Keynesian model?

BIBLIOGRAPHY

Aaron, Henry J. "Symposium on Tax Reform." *Journal of Economic Perspectives* 1, Summer 1987, 7–119.

Abraham, Katharine G., and Lawrence F. Katz. "Cyclical Unemployment: Sectoral Shifts or Aggregate Disturbances." *Journal of Political Economy* 94, June 1986, 507–522.

Ahmed, Shaghil. "Wage Stickiness and the Non-neutrality of Money: A Cross-Industry Analysis." *Journal of Monetary Economics* 20, July 1987a, 25–50.

———. "Government Spending, the Balance of Trade and the Terms of Trade in British History." *Journal of Monetary Economics* 20, September 1987b, 195–220.

Alchian, Armen A., and Harold Demsetz. "Production, Information Costs, and Economic Organization." *American Economic Review* 62, December 1972, 777–795.

Alogoskoufis, George S. "Aggregate Employment and Intertemporal Substitution in the U.K." *Economic Journal* 97, June 1987a, 403–415.

———. "On Intertemporal Substitution and Aggregate Labor Supply." *Journal of Political Economy* 95, October 1987b, 938–960.

Ando, Albert, and Franco Modigliani. "The 'Life-Cycle' Hypothesis of Saving: Aggregate Implications and Tests." *American Economic Review* 53, March 1963, 55–84.

Aschauer, David A. "Fiscal Policy and Aggregate Demand." *American Economic Review* 75, March 1985, 117–127.

———. "Is Public Expenditure Productive?" Presented at conference of National Bureau of Economic Research, Cambridge Mass., July 1988.

Attfield, C. L. F., and N. W. Duck. "The Influence of Unanticipated Money Growth on Real Output: Some Cross-Country Estimates." *Journal of Money, Credit and Banking* 15, November 1983, 442–454.

Attfield, C. L. F., D. Demery, and N. W. Duck. "A Quarterly Model of Unanticipated Monetary Growth, Output and the Price Level in the U.K." *Journal of Monetary Economics* 8, November 1981, 331–350.

Auerbach, Robert D. *Money, Banking and Financial Markets.* 2d ed. New York: Macmillan, 1985.

Azariadis, Costas. "Implicit Contracts and Underemployment Equilibria." *Journal of Political Economy* 83, December 1975, 1183–1202.

Bagehot, Walter. *Lombard Street.* New York: Scribner Armstrong & Company, 1873.

Bailey, Martin J. *National Income and the Price Level.* 2d ed. New York: McGraw-Hill, 1971.

Baily, Martin N., "Wages and Employment under Uncertain Demand." *Review of Economic Studies* 33, January 1974, 37–50.

Ball, Laurence, N. Gregory Mankiw, and David Romer. "The New Keynesian Economics and the Output-Inflation Tradeoff." *Brookings Papers on Economic Activity,* 1988.

Bank of England. *Quarterly Bulletin.* Various issues.

Barnett, William A., Edward K. Offenbacher, and Paul A. Spindt. "The New Divisia Monetary Aggregates." *Journal of Political Economy* 92, December 1984, 1049–1085.

Barro, Robert J. "Are Government Bonds Net Wealth?" *Journal of Political Economy* 82, November–December 1974, 1095–1118.

———. "Comment from an Unreconstructed Ricardian." *Journal of Monetary Economics* 4, August 1978a, 569–581.

———. "Unanticipated Money, Output and the Price Level in the United States." *Journal of Political Economy* 86, August 1978b, 548–580.

———. "On the Determination of the Public Debt." *Journal of Political Economy* 87, October 1979, 940–971.

———. "Output Effects of Government Purchases." *Journal of Political Economy* 89, December 1981, 1086–1121.

———. "Government Spending, Interest Rates, Prices and Budget Deficits in the United Kingdom, 1730–1918." *Journal of Monetary Economics* 20, September 1987, 221–247.

———. "The Ricardian Approach to Budget Deficits." *Journal of Economic Perspectives* 3, Spring 1989, 37–54.

Barro, Robert J., and Chaipat Sahasakul. "Average Marginal Tax Rates from Social Security and the Individual Income Tax." *Journal of Business* 59, October 1986, 555–566.

Barro, Robert J., and Herschel I. Grossman. *Money, Employment and Inflation.* Cambridge: Cambridge, University Press, 1976.

Barsky, Robert B., and Jeffrey A. Miron. "The Seasonal Cycle and the Business Cycle." Unpublished, University of Michigan, July 1988.

Baumol, William J. "The Transactions Demand for Cash: An Inventory Theoretic Approach." *Quarterly Journal of Economics* 66, November 1952, 545–556.

Becker, Gary S. "The Demand for Children." In *A Treatise on the Family.* Cambridge, MA: Harvard University Press, 1981.

Becker, Gary S., and Robert J. Barro. "A Reformulation of the Economic Theory of Fertility." *Quarterly Journal of Economics* 103, February 1988, 1–25.

Benjamin, Daniel K., and Levis A. Kochin. "War, Prices and Interest Rates: Gibson's Paradox Revisited." In Michael D. Bordo and Anna J. Schwartz, eds., *A Retrospective on the Classical Gold Standard, 1821–1931.* Chicago: University of Chicago Press, 1984.

Bernanke, Ben S. "Irreversibility, Uncertainty, and Cyclical Investment." *Quarterly Journal of Economics* 98, February 1983a, 85–106.

———. "Non-Monetary Effects of the Financial Collapse in the Propagation of the Great Depression." *American Economic Review* 73, June 1983b, 257–276.

Berndt, Ernst R., and David O. Wood. "Engineering and Econometric Interpretations of Energy-Capital Complementarity." *American Economic Review* 69, June 1979, 342–354.

Bernheim, B. Douglas, Andrei Shleifer, and Lawrence H. Summers. "The Strategic Bequest Motive." *Journal of Political Economy* 93, December 1985, 1045–1076.

Bienefeld, M. A. *Working Hours in British Industry.* London: Weidenfeld and Nicolson, 1972.

Bils, Mark. "Testing for Contracting Effects on Employment." Rochester Center for Economic Research. Working paper no. 174, January 1989.

Bird, Roger C., and Ronald G. Bodkin. "The National Service Life Insurance Dividend of 1950 and Consumption: A Further Test of the 'Strict' Permanent Income Hypothesis." *Journal of Political Economy* 73, October 1965, 499–515.

Black, Fischer. "Banking and Interest Rates in a World without Money." *Journal of Bank Research,* Autumn 1970, 9–20.

Black, Stanley W. "International Money and International Monetary Arrangements." In Ronald W. Jones and Peter B. Kenen eds., *Handbook of International Economics,* vol. 2. Amsterdam: North-Holland, 1985.

Blinder, Alan S. "Inventories in the Keynesian Macro Model." *Kyklos* 33, no. 4, 1980, 585–614.

Bloom, Murray T. *The Man Who Stole Portugal.* New York: Charles Scribner's Sons, 1966.

Board of Governors of the Federal Reserve System. *Annual Report,* 1984.

———. *Annual Statistical Digest 1970–1979.* Washington, D.C., 1981.

———. *Banking and Monetary Statistics, 1941–1970.* Washington, D.C., 1976.

Board of Governors of the Federal Reserve System. *Federal Reserve Bulletin.* Various issues.

Bomberger, William A., and Gail E. Makinen. "The Hungarian Hyperinflation and Stabilization of 1945–1946." *Journal of Political Economy* 91, October 1983, 801–824.

Bordo, Michael D., and Lars Jonung. "The Long-Run Behavior of the Income Velocity of Money in Five Advanced Countries, 1870–1975: An Institutional Approach." *Economic Inquiry* 19, January 1981, 96–116.

Boskin, Michael J. "Social Security and Retirement Decisions." *Economic Inquiry* 15, January 1977, 1–25.

———, ed. *The Crisis in Social Security.* San Francisco: Institute for Contemporary Studies, 1977.

Boskin, Michael J., Laurence J. Kotlikoff, Douglas J. Poffert, and John B. Shoven. "Social Security: A Financial Appraisal across and within Generations." *National Tax Journal* 40, March 1987, 19–34.

Bresciani-Turroni, Costantino. *The Economics of Inflation.* London: Allen and Unwin, 1937.

Brown, Charles, Curtis Gilroy, and Andrew Koehn. "The Effect of the Minimum Wage on Employment and Unemployment: A Survey." *Journal of Economic Literature* 20, June 1982, 487–528.

Brown, E. Cary. "Fiscal Policy in the Thirties: A Reappraisal." *American Economic Review* 46, December 1956, 857–879.

Brunner, Karl. "The Role of Money and Monetary Policy." Federal Reserve Bank of St. Louis, *Review,* July 1968, 9–24.

Buchanan, James M. *Public Principles of Public Debt.* Homewood, Ill.: Irwin, 1958.

Buckmaster and Moore. *Index-Linked Gilt Book.* London, May 1985.

Bulow, Jeremy, and Kenneth S. Rogoff. "Sovereign Debt: Is to Forgive to Forget?" Unpublished, Stanford University, February 1988.

Burda, Michael. "Reflections on 'Wait Unemployment' in Europe." Economic Policy Panel, London, April 1988.

Burtless, Gary. "Jobless Pay and High European Unemployment." In Robert Lawrence and Charles Schultze, eds., *Barriers to European Economic Growth.* Washington, D.C.: Brookings Institution, 1987.

Cagan, Phillip D. "The Monetary Dynamics of Hyperinflation." In Milton Friedman, ed., *Studies in the Quantity Theory of Money.* Chicago: University of Chicago Press, 1956.

———. "The Demand for Currency Relative to the Total Money Supply." *Journal of Political Economy* 66, August 1958, 303–328.

———. *Determinants and Effects of Changes in the Stock of Money. 1875–1960.* New York: Columbia University Press, 1965.

Campbell, Colin D. "Introduction." In *Controlling the Cost of Social Security.* Lexington, Mass.: Lexington Books, 1984.

Card, David. "Determinants of the Form of Long-Term Contracts." Princeton University. Working paper no. 135, June 1980.

Carlson, John A. "A Study of Price Forecasts." *Annals of Economic and Social Measurement* 6, winter 1977, 27–56.

Carroll, Chris, and Lawrence H. Summers. "Why Have Private Savings Rates in the United States and Canada Diverged?" *Journal of Monetary Economics* 20, September 1987, 249–279.

Caskey, John. "Modeling the Formation of Price Expectations: A Bayesian Approach." *American Economic Review* 75, September 1985, 768–776.

Central Statistical Office. *Annual Abstract of Statistics.* London. Various issues.

———. *Monthly Digest of Statistics.* London. Various issues.

Chaudhury, Ajit K. "Output, Employment and Inventories under General Excess Supply." *Journal of Monetary Economics* 5, October 1979, 505–514.

Clark, Kim B., and Lawrence H. Summers. "Labor Market Dynamics and Unemployment: A Reconsideration." *Brookings Papers on Economic Activity,* no. 1, 1979, 13–60.

———. "Unemployment Insurance and Labor Market Transitions." In Martin N. Baily, ed., *Workers, Jobs and Inflation.* Washington, D.C.: Brookings Institution, 1982.

Clark, Truman A. "Interest Rate Seasonals and the Federal Reserve." *Journal of Political Economy* 94, February 1986, 76–125.

Coase, Ronald H. "The Nature of the Firm." *Economica* 4, November 1937, 386–405.

Cukierman, Alex. "Relative Price Variability and Inflation, a Survey and Further Results." *Carnegie-Rochester Conference Series on Public Policy* 19, Autumn 1983, 103–158.

Cumby, Robert, and Maurice Obstfeld. "International Interest Rate and Price Level Linkages under Flexible Exchange Rates: A Review of Recent Evidence." In John F. O. Bilson and Richard C. Marston, eds., *Exchange Rate Theory and Practice.* Chicago: University of Chicago Press, 1984.

Darby, Michael R. "Three-and-a-Half Million U.S. Employees Have Been Mislaid: Or an Explanation of Unemployment, 1934–1941." *Journal of Political Economy* 84, February 1976, 1–16.

Darby, Michael R., John C. Haltiwanger, Jr., and Mark W. Plant. "Unemployment Rate Dynamics and Persistent Unemployment under Rational Expectations." *American Economic Review* 75, September 1985, 614–637.

David, Paul A. "The Growth of Real Product in the United States since 1840." *Journal of Economic History* 27, June 1967, 151–197.

Deane, P., and W. A. Cole. *British Economic Growth, 1688–1959.* 2d ed. Cambridge: Cambridge University Press, 1969.

Denslow, David A., and Mark Rush. "Supply Shocks and the Interest Rate." Unpublished, University of Florida, 1989.

Department of Employment and Productivity. *British Labour Statistics, Historical Abstract 1886–1968.* London, 1971.

Dewey, Davis R. *Financial History of the United States.* 11th ed. New York: Longmans, Green, 1931.

Dotsey, Michael. "The Use of Electronic Funds Transfers to Capture the Effect of Cash Management Practices on the Demand for Demand Deposits." *Journal of Finance* 40, December 1985, 1493–1503.

Easterlin, Richard A. *Population, Labor Force, and Long Swings in Economic Growth.* New York: Columbia University Press, 1968.

Eaton, Jonathan, Mark Gersovitz, and Joseph E. Stiglitz. "The Pure Theory of Country Risk." *European Economic Review* 30, June 1986, 481–513.

Economic Report of the President. Washington, D.C.: U.S. Government Printing Office. Various issues.

Economist Intelligence Unit, Ltd. (U.K.). *Quarterly Economic Review of Saudi Arabia.* Annual Supplement 1985.

————. *Country Profile, Saudi Arabia, 1987–88.* London, 1987.

Edwards, Sebastian. "On the Interest Rate Elasticity of the Demand for International Reserves: Some Evidence from Developing Countries." *Journal of International Money and Finance* 4, August 1985, 287–295.

Eisner, Robert, and Robert H. Strotz. "Determinants of Business Investment." In Commission on Money and Credit: *Impacts of Monetary Policy.* Englewood Cliffs, N.J.: Prenctice-Hall, 1963.

Eisner, Robert, and Paul Pieper. "A New View of the Federal Debt and Budget Deficits." *American Economic Review* 74, March 1984, 11–29.

Emerson, Michael. *What Model for Europe?* Cambridge MA: MIT Press, 1988.

Esposito, Louis. "Effect of Social Security on Saving: Review of Studies Using U.S. Time Series Data." *Social Security Bulletin* 41, May 1978, 9–17.

Evans, Paul. "Interest Rates and Expected Future Budget Deficits in the United States." *Journal of Political Economy* 95, February 1987a, 34–58.

————. "Do Budget Deficits Raise Nominal Interest Rates? Evidence from Six Industrial Countries." *Journal of Monetary Economics* 20, September 1987b, 281–300.

————. "Do Budget Deficits Affect the Current Account?" Unpublished, Ohio State University, August 1988.

Fair, Ray C. "An Analysis of the Accuracy of Four Macroeconometric Models." *Journal of Political Economy* 87, August 1979, 701–718.

Fama, Eugene F. "Short-Term Interest Rates as Predictors of Inflation." *American Economic Review* 65, June 1975, 269–282.

————. "Financial Intermediation and Price Level Control." *Journal of Monetary Economics* 12, July 1983, 7–28.

Fay, Jon A., and James L. Medoff. "Labor and Output over the Business Cycle: Some Direct Evidence." *American Economic Review* 75, September 1985, 638–655.

Feinstein, C. H. *National Income, Expenditures and Output of the United Kingdom, 1855–1965.* Cambridge: Cambridge University Press, 1972.

Feldstein, Martin S. "Social Security, Induced Retirement, and Aggregate Capital Accumulation." *Journal of Political Economy* 82, September–October 1974, 905–928.

Ferguson, James M., ed. *Public Debt and Future Generations.* Chapel Hill: University of North Carolina Press, 1964.

Fisher, Irving. "A Statistical Relation between Unemployment and Price Changes." *International Labor Review* 13, June 1926, 785–792. Reprinted as "I Discovered the Phillips Curve." *Journal of Political Economy* 81, March–April 1973, 496–502.

————. *The Theory of Interest.* New York: Macmillan, 1930.

————. *The Purchasing Power of Money.* 2d ed. 1922. New York: Augustus Kelley, 1971.

Fischer, Stanley. "Long-Term Contracts, Rational Expectations and the Optimal Money Supply Rule. *Journal of Political Economy* 85, February 1977, 191–206.

————. "Seigniorage and the Case for a National Money." *Journal of Political Economy* 90, April 1982, 295–313.

Fleisher, Belton M., and Thomas J. Kniesner. *Labor Economics: Theory, Evidence and Policy.* 3d ed. Englewood Cliffs, N.J.: Prentice Hall, 1984.

Flood, Robert P., and Peter M. Garber. "An Economic Theory of Monetary Reform." *Journal of Political Economy* 88, February 1980, 24–58.

Foley, Duncan K., and Miguel Sidrauski. *Monetary and Fiscal Policy in a Growing Economy.* New York: Macmillan, 1971.

Friedman, Milton. "The Quantity of Money—A Restatement." In *Studies in the Quantity Theory of Money.* Chicago: University of Chicago Press, 1956.

——. *A Theory of the Consumption Function.* Princeton: Princeton University Press, 1957.

——. *A Program for Monetary Stability.* New York: Fordham University Press, 1960.

——. "Free Exchange Rates." In *Dollars and Deficits.* Englewood Cliffs, N.J.: Prentice-Hall, 1968a.

——. "Inflation: Causes and Consequences." In *Dollars and Deficits.* Englewood Cliffs, N.J.: Prentice-Hall, 1968b.

——. "The Role of Monetary Policy." *American Economic Review* 58, March 1968c, 1–17.

——. *The Optimum Quantity of Money and Other Essays.* Chicago: Aldine, 1969.

Friedman, Milton, and Anna J. Schwartz. *A Monetary History of the United States, 1867–1960.* Princeton: Princeton University Press, 1963.

——. *Monetary Statistics of the United States.* New York: Columbia University Press, 1970.

Fullerton, Don. "On the Possibility of an Inverse Relationship between Tax Rates and Government Revenues." *Journal of Public Economics* 19, October 1982, 3–22.

Garber, Peter M. "Transition from Inflation to Price Stability." *Carnegie-Rochester Conference Series on Public Policy* 16, Spring 1982, 11–42.

Geweke, John. "The Superneutrality of Money in the United States: An Interpretation of the Evidence." *Econometrica* 54, January 1986, 1–22.

Glass, Carter. *An Adventure in Constructive Finance.* New York: Doubleday, Page, 1927.

Goldfeld, Steven M. "The Demand for Money Revisited." *Brookings Papers on Economic Activity,* no. 3, 1973, 577–638.

——. "The Case of the Missing Money." *Brookings Papers on Economic Activity,* no. 3, 1976, 683–730.

Goodfriend, Marvin. "Monetary Mystique: Secrecy and Central Banking." *Journal of Monetary Economics* 17, January 1986, 63–92.

——. "Interest Rate Smoothing and Price Level Trend Stationarity." *Journal of Monetary Economics* 19, May 1987, 335–348.

Gordon, Donald F. "A Neo-Classical Theory of Keynesian Unemployment." *Economic Inquiry* 12, December 1974, 431–459.

Gorton, Gary. "Banking Panics and Business Cycles." Unpublished. Federal Reserve Bank of Philadelphia, February 1986.

Gray, Jo Anna. "Wage Indexation: A Macroeconomic Approach." *Journal of Monetary Economics* 2, April 1976, 221–236.

Greenwood, Jeremy. "Expectations, the Exchange Rate and the Current Account." *Journal of Monetary Economics* 12, November 1983, 543–570.

Grossman, Herschel I. "Risk Shifting, Layoffs and Seniority." *Journal of Monetary Economics* 4, November 1979, 661–686.

Haberler, Gottfried. *Prosperity and Depression.* 2d ed. Geneva: League of Nations, 1939.

Hall, Robert E. "Investment, Interest Rates, and the Effects of Stabilization Policies." *Brookings Papers on Economic Activity,* no. 1, 1977, 61–103.

——. "A Theory of the Natural Unemployment Rate and the Duration of Unemployment." *Journal of Monetary Economics* 5, April 1979, 153–170.

——. "Employment Fluctuations and Wage Rigidity." *Brookings Papers on Economic Activity,* no. 1, 1980a, 91–123.

——. "Labor Supply and Aggregate Fluctuations." *Carnegie-Rochester Conference on Public Policy* 12, Spring 1980b, 7–33.

——. "The Importance of Lifetime Jobs in the U.S. Economy." *American Economic Review* 72, September 1982, 716–724.

——. "Consumption." In Robert J. Barro, ed., *Modern Business Cycle Theory.* Cambridge: Harvard University Press, 1989.

Hamermesh, Daniel. *Jobless Pay and the Economy.* Baltimore: Johns Hopkins University Press, 1977.

Hamilton, James D. "Oil and the Macroeconomy since World War II." *Journal of Political Economy* 91, April 1983, 228–248.

———. "Uncovering Financial Market Expectations of Inflation." *Journal of Political Economy* 93, December 1985, 1224–1241.

Hawtrey, Ralph G. "The Portuguese Bank Notes Case." *Economic Journal* 42, September 1932, 391–398.

Hayashi, Fumio. "Why Is Japan's Saving Rate So Apparently High?" *NBER Macroeconomics Annual 1986.* Cambridge MA: MIT Press, 1986.

Hayek, Friedrich A. "The Use of Knowledge in Society." *American Economic Review* 35, September 1945, 519–530.

Hercowitz, Zvi. "Money and the Dispersion of Relative Prices." *Journal of Political Economy* 89, April 1981, 328–356.

———. "Money and Price Dispersion in the United States." *Journal of Monetary Economics* 10, July 1982, 25–38.

Hicks, John. "Mr. Keynes and the 'Classics.'" *Econometrica* 5, April 1937, 147–159.

———. *Value and Capital.* 2d ed. Oxford: Oxford University Press, 1946.

Howard, David H. "The Disequilibrium Model in a Controlled Economy: An Empirical Test of the Barro-Grossman Model." *American Economic Review* 66, December 1976, 871–879.

Ingram, James C. *International Economics.* New York: Wiley, 1983.

International Monetary Fund. *International Financial Statistics.* Various issues.

Jevons, W. Stanley. *Money and the Mechanism of Exchange.* New York: D. Appleton, 1896.

Jones, Alice H. *Wealth of a Nation to Be.* New York: Columbia University Press, 1980.

Jones, Robert A. "The Origin and Development of Media of Exchange." *Journal of Political Economy* 84, August 1976, 757–776.

Judd, John P., and John L. Scadding. "The Search for a Stable Money Demand Function." *Journal of Economic Literature* 20, September 1982, 993–1023.

Katz, Lawrence F., and Bruce D. Meyer. "The Impact of the Potential Duration of Unemployment Benefits on the Duration of Unemployment." Unpublished. Harvard University, May 1988.

Kendrick, John W. *Productivity Trends in the United States.* Princeton: Princeton University Press, 1961.

Kenny, Lawrence W. "Cross-Country Estimates of the Demand for Money and Its Components." Unpublished. University of Florida, 1988.

Keynes, John Maynard. *The General Theory of Employment, Interest and Money.* New York: Harcourt Brace, 1935.

King, Robert G., and Charles I. Plosser. "Money, Credit and Prices in a Real Business Cycle." *American Economic Review* 74, June 1984, 363–380.

Klein, Ben. "Competitive Interest Payments on Bank Deposits and the Long-Run Demand for Money." *American Economic Review* 64, December 1974, 931–949.

Kormendi, Roger C. "Government Debt, Government Spending, and Private Sector Behavior." *American Economic Review* 73, December 1983, 994–1010.

Kormendi, Roger C., and Phillip G. Meguire. "Cross-Regime Evidence of Macroeconomic Rationality." *Journal of Political Economy* 92, October 1984, 875–908.

Kreinin, Mordechai E. "Windfall Income and Consumption—Additional Evidence." *American Economic Review* 51, June 1961, 388–390.

Kuznets, Simon. "Discussion of the New Department of Commerce Income Series." *Review of Economics and Statistics* 30, August 1948, 151–179.

Kydland, Finn E., and Edward C. Prescott. "Rules Rather than Discretion: The Inconsistency of Optimal Plans." *Journal of Political Economy* 85, June 1977, 473–491.

Lahaye, Laura. "Inflation and Currency Reform." *Journal of Political Economy* 93, June 1985, 537–560.

Laidler, David E. *The Demand for Money: Theories and Evidence.* 3d ed. New York: Harper and Row, 1985.

Landsberger, Michael. "Restitution Receipts, Household Savings and Consumption Behavior in Israel." Unpublished. Research Department, Bank of Israel, 1970.

Law, John. *Money and Trade Considered.* 1705. New York: Augustus Kelley, 1966.

Leimer, Dean, and Selig Lesnoy. "Social Security and Private Saving: New Time Series Evidence." *Journal of Political Economy* 90, June 1982, 606–629.

Lilien, David M. "Sectoral Shifts and Cyclical Unemployment." *Journal of Political Economy* 90, August 1982, 777–793.

Lindsey, Lawrence B. "Individual Taxpayer Response to Tax Cuts: 1982–1984." *Journal of Public Economics* 33, July 1987, 173–206.

Lipsey, Richard E. "The Relation between Unemployment and the Rate of Change of Money Wage Rates in the United Kingdom, 1862–1957: A Further Analysis." *Economica* 27, February 1960, 1–31.

Litterman, Robert B., and Laurence Weiss. "Money, Real Interest Rates, and Output: A Reinterpretation of Postwar U.S. Data." *Econometrica* 53, January 1985, 129–156.

Long, John B., Jr., and Charles I. Plosser. "Real Business Cycles." *Journal of Political Economy* 91, February 1983, 39–69.

Loungani, Prakash. "Oil Price Shocks and the Dispersion Hypothesis." Rochester Center for Economic Research. Working paper no. 33, January 1986.

Lucas, Robert E., Jr. "Adjustment Costs and the Theory of Supply." *Journal of Political Economy* 75, August 1967, 321–334.

———. "Understanding Business Cycles." *Carnegie-Rochester Conference on Public Policy* 5, 1976, 77–29.

———. "Two Illustrations of the Quantity Theory of Money." *American Economic Review* 70, December 1980, 1005–1014.

———. *Studies in Business-Cycle Theory.* Cambridge MA: MIT Press, 1981.

McCallum, Ben T. "The Current State of the Policy-Ineffectiveness Debate." *American Economic Review* 69, proceedings, May 1979, 240–245.

Macaulay, Frederick R. *The Movement of Interest Rates, Bond Yields and Stock Prices in the United States since 1856.* New York: National Bureau of Economic Reseach, 1938.

McClure, Alexander K. *Abe Lincoln's Yarns and Stories.* New York: W. W. Wilson, 1901.

McCulloch, J. Huston. "The Ban on Indexed Bonds, 1933–77." *American Economic Review* 70, December 1980, 1018–1021.

MaCurdy, Thomas E. "An Empirical Model of Labor Supply in a Life-Cycle Setting." *Journal of Political Economy* 89, December 1981, 1059–1085.

Mankiw, N. Gregory, and Jeffrey A. Miron. "The Changing Behavior of the Term Structure of Interest Rates." *Quarterly Journal of Economics* 101, May 1986, 211–228.

Mankiw, N. Gregory, Jeffrey A. Miron, and David N. Weil. "The Adjustment of Expectations to a Change in Regime: A Study of the Founding of the Federal Reserve." *American Economic Review* 77, June 1987, 358–374.

Mansfield, Edwin. *Microeconomics.* 5th ed. New York: Norton, 1985.

Marston, Stephen T. "Employment Stability and High Unemployment." *Brookings Papers on Economic Activity,* no. 1, 1976, 169–203.

Miron, Jeffrey A. "Financial Panics, the Seasonality of the Nominal Interest Rate, and the Founding of the Fed." *American Economic Review* 76, March 1986, 125–140.

———. "A Cross-Country Comparison of Seasonal Cycles and Business Cycles." Unpublished. University of Michigan, October 1988.

Mishkin, Frederic S. "Does Anticipated Monetary Policy Matter?" *Journal of Political Economy* 90, February 1982, 22–51.

Mitchell, B. R. *European Historical Statistics, 1750–1975.* 2d ed. London: Macmillan, 1980.

Mitchell, B. R., and H. G. Jones. *Second Abstract of British Historical Statistics.* Cambridge: Cambridge University Press, 1971.

Mitchell, B. R., and P. Deane. *Abstract of British Historical Statistics.* Cambridge: Cambridge University Press, 1962.

Modigliani, Franco. "Long-Run Implications of Alternative Fiscal Policies and the Burden of the National Debt." In James M. Ferguson, ed., *Public Debt and Future Generations.* Chapel Hill: University of North Carolina Press, 1964.

Modigliani, Franco, and Richard Brumberg. "Utility Analysis and the Consumption Function: an Interpretation of Cross-Section Data." In Kenneth Kurihara, ed., *Post-Keynesian Economics.* New Brunswick, N.J.: Rutgers University Press, 1954.

Morgan Guaranty Trust. *World Financial Markets.* New York, February 1983.

Mundell, Robert A. *International Economics.* New York: Macmillan, 1968.

———. *Monetary Theory.* Pacific Palisades, Calif.: Goodyear, 1971.

Musgrave, Richard. *Theory of Public Finance.* New York: McGraw-Hill, 1959.

Mussa, Michael. "Empirical Regularities in the Behavior of Exchange Rates and Theories of the Foreign Exchange Market." *Carnegie-Rochester Conference Series on Public Policy* 11, 1979, 9–58.

Muth, John F. "Rational Expectations and the Theory of Price Movements." *Econometrica* 29, July 1961, 315–335.

Nelson, Charles R., and G. William Schwert. "Short-Term Interest Rates as Predictors of Inflation: On Testing the Hypothesis that the Real Rate of Interest Is Constant." *American Economic Review* 67, June 1977, 478–486.

Ochs, Jack, and Mark Rush. "The Persistence of Interest Rate Effects on the Demand for Currency." *Journal of Money, Credit and Banking* 15, November 1983, 499–505.

O'Driscoll, Gerald P., Jr. "The Ricardian Nonequivalence Theorem." *Journal of Political Economy* 85, February 1977, 207–210.

Organization of American States. *Statistical Bulletin of the OAS.* Various issues.

Organization for Economic Cooperation and Development. *Main Economic Indicators.* Paris. Various issues.

———. *National Accounts, Main Aggregates.* vol. 1, 1952–1981. Paris, 1983.

———. *National Accounts of OECD Countries.* Paris. Various issues.

———. *OECD Economic Outlook.* Paris, September 1987.

Patinkin, Don. "Price Flexibility and Full Employment." *American Economic Review* 38, September 1948, 543–564.

———. *Money, Interest and Prices.* New York: Harper & Row, 1956.

Phelps, Edmund S. "The New Microeconomics in Employment and Inflation Theory." In *Microeconomic Foundations of Employment and Inflation Theory.* New York: Norton, 1970.

Phillips, A. W. "The Relation between Unemployment and the Rate of Change of Money Wage Rates in the United Kingdom, 1861–1959." *Economica* 25, November 1958, 283–299.

Pigou, Arthur C. "Economic Progress in a Stable Environment." *Economica* 14, August 1947, 180–188.

Plosser, Charles I. "The Effects of Government Financing Decisions on Asset Returns." *Journal of Monetary Economics* 9, May 1982, 325–352.

———. "Fiscal Policy and the Term Structure." *Journal of Monetary Economics* 20, September 1987, 343–367.

Portes, Richard, and David Winter. "Disequilibrium Estimates for Consumption Good Markets in Centrally Planned Economies." *Review of Economic Studies* 47, January 1980, 137–159.

Protopapadakis, Aris A., and Jeremy J. Siegel. "Are Money Growth and Inflation Related to Government Deficits? Evidence from Ten Industrialized Economies." *Journal of International Money and Finance* 6, 1987, 31–48.

Ramaswami, Chitra. "Equilibrium Unemployment and the Efficient Job-Finding Rate." *Journal of Labor Economics* 1, April 1983, 171–196.

Ramsey, Frank P. "A Mathematical Theory of Saving." *Economic Journal* 38, December 1928, 543–549.

Rees, Albert E. "Patterns of Wages, Prices and Productivity." In Charles Myers, ed., *Wages, Prices, Profits and Productivity.* New York: Columbia University Press, 1959.

Ricardo, David. "Funding System." In P. Sraffa, ed., *The Works and Correspondence of David Ricardo.* Cambridge: Cambridge University Press, 1957.

Rogoff, Kenneth S. "Reputation, Coordination, and Monetary Policy." In Robert J. Barro, ed., *Modern Business Cycle Theory.* Cambridge MA: Harvard University Press, 1989.

Romer, Christina D. "Spurious Volatility in Historical Unemployment Data." *Journal of Political Economy* 94, February 1986, 1–37.

———. "Gross National Product, 1909–1928: Existing Estimates, New Estimates, and New Interpretations of World War I and Its Aftermath." National Bureau of Economic Research. Working paper no. 2187, March 1987.

———. "The Prewar Business Cycle Reconsidered: New Estimates of Gross National Product, 1869–1908." Unpublished. University of California, Berkeley, June 1988.

Romer, Paul M. "Capital Accumulation in the Theory of Long Run Growth." In Robert J. Barro, ed., *Modern Business Cycle Theory.* Cambridge MA: Harvard University Press, 1989.

Rotwein, Eugene, ed. *David Hume—Writings on Economics.* Madison: University of Wisconsin Press, 1970.

Runkle, David E. "Liquidity Constraints and the Permanent Income Hypothesis: Evidence from Panel Data." Unpublished. Federal Reserve Bank of Minneapolis, November 1988.

Rush, Mark. "Unexpected Monetary Disturbances during the Gold Standard Era." *Journal of Monetary Economics* 15, May 1985, 309–322.

———. "Unexpected Money and Unemployment." Unpublished. University of Florida, September 1986.

Sachs, Jeffrey D. "The Current Account and Macroeconomic Adjustment in the 1970s." *Brookings Papers on Economic Activity,* no. 1, 1981, 201–268.

Saidi, Nasser. "The Square-Root Law, Uncertainty and International Reserves under Alternative Regimes: Canadian Experience, 1950–1976." *Journal of Monetary Economics* 7, May 1981, 271–290.

Samuelson, Paul A. "A Synthesis of the Principle of Acceleration and the Multiplier." *Journal of Political Economy* 47, December 1939, 786–797.

Sargent, Thomas J. "The Ends of Four Big Inflations." In Robert E. Hall, ed., *Inflation: Causes and Effects.* Chicago: University of Chicago Press, 1982.

Sargent, Thomas J., and Neil Wallace. "Rational Expectations, the Optimal Monetary Instrument, and the Optimal Money Supply Rule." *Journal of Political Economy* 83, April 1975, 241–254.

———. "Some Unpleasant Monetarist Arithmetic." Federal Reserve Bank of Minneapolis, *Quarterly Review,* Fall 1981, 1–17.

Siegel, Jeremy J. "Inflation-Induced Distortions in Government and Private Saving Statistics." *Review of Economics and Statistics* 61, April 1979, 83–90.

Simons, Henry C. "Rules versus Authorities in Monetary Policy." In *Economic Policy for a Free Society.* Chicago: University of Chicago Press, 1948.

Solon, Gary. "Work Incentive Effects of Taxing Unemployment Benefits." *Econometrica* 53, March 1985, 295–306.

Spindt, Paul A. "Money Is What Money Does: Monetary Aggregation and the Equation of Exchange." *Journal of Political Economy* 93, February 1985, 175–204.

Stuart, Charles E. "Swedish Tax Rates, Labor Supply and Tax Revenues." *Journal of Political Economy* 89, October 1981, 1020–1038.

Summers, Robert, and Alan Heston. "A New Set of International Comparisons of Real Product and Price Levels, Estimates for 130 Countries, 1950–1985." *The Review of Income and Wealth* 34, March 1988, 1–25.

Taylor, John B. "Aggregate Dynamics and Staggered Contracts." *Journal of Political Economy* 88, February 1980, 1–23.

Thornton, Henry. *An Enquiry into the Nature and Effects of the Paper Credit of Great Britain (1802).* Fairfield, N.J.: Augustus Kelly, 1978.

Timberlake, Richard H., Jr. *The Origins of Central Banking in the United States.* Cambridge MA: Harvard University Press, 1978.

Tobin, James. "The Interest-Elasticity of Transactions Demand for Cash." *Review of Economics and Statistics* 38, August 1956, 241–247.

———. "A General Equilibrium Approach to Monetary Theory." In *Essays in Economics,* vol. 1, *Macroeconomics.* Chicago: Markham, 1971a.

———. "Deposit Interest Ceilings as a Monetary Control." In *Essays in Economics,* vol. 1, *Macroeconomics.* Chicago: Markham, 1971b.

Topel, Robert, and Finis Welch. "Unemployment Insurance: Survey and Extensions." *Economica* 47, August 1980, 351–379.

United Nations. *Statistical Yearbook.* Various issues.

U.S. Bureau of Labor Statistics. *Employment and Earnings.* Various issues.

U.S. Department of Commerce. *Fixed Reproducible Tangible Wealth in the United States, 1925–85.* Washington, D.C., 1987.

———. *Historical Statistics of the U.S., Colonial Times to 1970.* Washington, D.C., 1975.

———. *National Income and Product Accounts of the U.S., 1929–1982.* Washington, D.C., 1986.

———. *Statistical Abstract of the United States.* Various issues.

———. *Survey of Current Business.* Various issues.

Van Ravestein, A., and H. Vijlbrief. "Welfare Cost of Higher Tax Rates: An Empirical Laffer Curve for the Netherlands." *De Economist* 136, 1988, 205–219.

Varian, Hal R. *Intermediate Microeconomics.* New York: Norton, 1987.

Walre de Bordes, J. van. *The Austrian Crown.* London: King, 1927.

Winston, Gordon C. "An International Comparison of Income and Hours of Work." *Review of Economics and Statistics* 48, February 1966, 28–39.

World Bank. *World Development Report 1987.* New York: Oxford University Press, 1987.

GLOSSARY

absolute form of PPP The version of purchasing-power parity that involves levels of exchange rates and prices.

adjusted gross income Gross income less adjustments for tax purposes, such as business and moving expenses and deferred compensation through pension plans.

after-tax marginal product of labor The marginal product of labor less the tax levied on the resulting increase in product.

after-tax rate of return to investment The real rate of return from investment less the tax levied on the resulting increase in net product.

after-tax real interest rate The real interest rate less the tax paid on the interest earnings.

aggregate-consistency conditions Conditions on quantities that must hold when we add up the actions of all participants in a market—for example, the total of goods sold equals the total bought, and the total of funds lent equals the total borrowed. In the basic model, we use market-clearing conditions to ensure that the aggregate-consistency conditions are satisfied.

anticipated money growth The public's forecast of the rate of monetary growth, based on the historical relationship between the quantity of money and economic variables.

autonomous change in demand An unexplained shift in the aggregate demand for commodities.

average tax rate The ratio of taxes to a measure of income. *See* **marginal tax rate.**

balance on capital account The net acquisition of interest-bearing assets from abroad.

balance of international payments The summary statement of a country's international trade in commodities, bonds, and international currency.

balanced budget A situation in which there is no change in the real amount of money and bonds issued by government; zero real saving by government.

banking panic Simultaneous runs on many banks and financial institutions, where depositors attempt to convert their deposits into currency.

barter Direct exchange of one good for another, without the use of money. *See* **medium of exchange.**

Board of Governors of the Federal Reserve System The seven-member group, appointed by the U.S. president, that makes most decisions of the Federal Reserve System.

bond A contract that gives the holder (lender) a claim to a specified stream of payments from the issuer (borrower).

boom A period in which aggregate economic activity or real gross national product is high and rising.

Bretton Woods System A system of international payments established after World War II in which each country pegged the exchange rate between its currency and the U.S. dollar. The United States exchanged dollars for gold at a fixed price ($35 per ounce), thus pegging the value of each country's currency to gold.

budget constraint The equation relating the sources of funds in a period, such as income from the commodity market and initial assets, to the uses of funds in that period, such as consumption and end-of-period assets.

budget line A graph of the combinations of consumptions over two periods that satisfy the two-period budget constraint.

burden of the public debt The possible negative effect of the public debt on saving and investment, and hence on the stock of capital available later.

closed economy An economy isolated from the rest of the world.

common currency A regime where all countries use the same currency and quote prices in units of this currency.

complete Keynesian model A version of the Keynesian theory that assumes sticky nominal wage rates but a perfectly flexible general price level.

constant-growth-rate rule A rule for monetary policy where a specified monetary aggregate grows at a constant rate.

constant returns to scale The property of some production functions that a proportionate increase in all inputs results in an equi-proportionate increase in output.

consumer durables Consumable commodities purchased by households that last for a long time, such as homes, automobiles, and appliances.

consumer nondurables and services Consumable commodities purchased by households that last for a short time.

consumer price index (CPI) A weighted average of prices of consumer goods relative to a base year.

costs of intermediation The total cost of operating a financial intermediary.

crowding out (from government deficits) The decline in private investment that may result from a tax cut financed by a government budget deficit.

crowding out (from government purchases) The decrease in consumption and investment that accompanies an increase in government purchases.

currency Noninterest-bearing paper money issued by the government.

current-account balance The value of goods produced by domestic residents (including the net factor income from abroad) plus net transfers from abroad, less the expenditure by domestic residents on goods; if the current-account balance is positive (negative), there is a surplus (deficit) on current account.

deflation A sustained decrease in the general price level over time. See **inflation.**

demand deposits Deposits held at a financial institution that can be withdrawn at face value without restrictions.

demand for money The amount of money that someone desires to hold, expressed as a function of the volume of spending, the interest rate, transaction costs, and other variables.

depreciation The wearing out of capital goods over time; often expressed as a fraction of the stock of capital.

desired stock of capital The stock of capital chosen by a producer, depending on factors such as the marginal product of capital, the real interest rate, and the depreciation rate.

devaluation An action by the central bank of a country that raises the number of units of its currency that exchange for other currencies; a rise in the exchange rate.

diminishing marginal productivity A characteristic of the production function by which successive increments of an input yield progressively smaller increments in output.

direct investment abroad Purchase of capital goods that are located in foreign countries.

discount factor The relative value of a dollar in different periods of time; for example, between one period and the next, the nominal discount factor is one plus the nominal interest rate.

discount rate of Fed   The interest rate charged on loans from the Federal Reserve to financial institutions.

discouraged workers   Workers who leave the labor force following a period of unemployment.

discretionary policy   A setup where government policy is not restricted by prior commitments.

disintermediation   The decline in the use of the services of financial intermediaries that results when the public moves away from holding deposits toward direct holding of bonds and mortgages.

disposable personal income   Personal income less taxes.

distributional effects   Shifts in the distribution of resources across households, with no change in the aggregate of resources; changes such that some sectors in the economy gain at the expense of others.

domestic credit   The total of the central bank's claims on the domestic economy. In the United States, the bulk of domestic credit takes the form of U.S. government securities held by the Federal Reserve. See **Federal Reserve credit.**

double coincidence of wants   The situation required for barter to take place, in which the type and quantity of goods offered by one trader match those desired by the other trader.

duration of jobs   The average length of time that a job is expected to last. The duration of jobs is inversely related to the job-separation rate.

duration of unemployment   The length of time that a spell of unemployment is expected to last. The duration of unemployment is inversely related to the job-finding rate.

economies of scale in the demand for money   The property of the demand for money that the desired average real money holding increases less than proportionately with a rise in real income.

employment   The number of persons working at jobs in the market sector.

endogenous money   The automatic response of the quantity of money to changes in the economy. Money is endogenous under the gold standard or in regimes where the monetary authority targets interest rates or the price level.

European Monetary System (EMS)   Arrangement since 1979 whereby eight European countries have maintained nearly fixed exchange rates among their currencies. The countries are Belgium (including Luxembourg), Denmark, France, Germany, Ireland, Italy, and the Netherlands.

excess demand   A situation in a market where, at the prevailing price, the quantity demanded exceeds the quantity supplied.

excess reserves   The difference between the total reserves held by financial institutions and the amount required to be held under the reserve requirement of the Federal Reserve.

excess supply   A situation in a market where, at the prevailing price, the quantity supplied exceeds the quantity demanded.

exchange rate   The number of units of the currency of a country that trade for one unit of another currency, such as the U.S. dollar.

expectation of inflation   The public's forecast of the inflation rate.

expectational Phillips curve   The relation between unexpected inflation and the unemployment rate. According to this curve, an unexpected increase in the inflation rate has a negative effect on the unemployment rate.

expected real interest rate   The real interest rate that is expected to be earned (or paid) after adjusting the nominal interest rate by the expectation of inflation.

experience rating (for unemployment insurance)   The feature of the U.S. program of unemployment insurance that taxes employers more heavily if they have a history of a higher job-separation rate.

exports   Goods that are produced by the residents of a country but are sold to foreigners.

Federal Funds market   The market for very short-term borrowing and lending between financial institutions, primarily commercial banks.

Federal Funds rate   The interest rate on loans made in the Federal Funds market.

Federal Open-Market Committee (FOMC)   A committee of the Federal Reserve that has responsibility for open-market operations.

Federal Reserve credit   The sum of the Fed's holdings of loans to depository institutions, U.S. government securities, and miscellaneous assets. The total of the Fed's claims on the government and the private sector. See **domestic credit.**

financial intermediaries   Institutions that obtain funds from deposits made by individuals and make loans to households and businesses. Examples are banks, savings and loan associations, and money-market funds.

firm   An economic organization that employs and supervises various factors of production and then sells its products to consumers or other firms.

fiscal policy   The choice of levels of government spending, taxation, and borrowing to influence the level of aggregate economic activity.

fixed exchange rate   A system in which countries peg the exchange rate between their currency and other currencies, such as the U.S. dollar. Examples of fixed-exchange rate regimes are the gold standard, the Bretton Woods System, the European Monetary System, and a setup with a common currency.

flat-rate tax   A kind of income tax in which the amount of tax is a constant fraction of taxable income. See **graduated-rate tax.**

flexible exchange rate   The system of international payments, prevalent since the early 1970s, in which countries allow the exchange rates for their currencies to fluctuate so as to clear the exchange market.

full-employment deficit   The government deficit after adjusting for the automatic response of government spending and taxes to recession or boom; an estimate of what the deficit would be if the economy were operating at a full-employment level.

fully funded system (for social security)   A system in which each individual's payments accumulate in a trust fund and retirement benefits are paid out of the accumulated funds. See **social security; pay-as-you-go system.**

general market clearing   Simultaneous clearing of all markets. See **market-clearing approach; Walras' Law of Markets.**

general price level   The dollar price per unit of a (physically uniform) aggregate of commodities.

gold standard   A system of international pyaments under which countries agree to buy or sell gold for a fixed amount of their currencies. The high point of this system was from 1890 to 1914.

government budget deficit (or surplus)   In real terms, the increase (or decrease) in the real value of the government's obligations to the private sector in the forms of money and bonds.

government purchases of goods and services   Expenditures by government on commodities and services produced by the private sector.

governmental budget constraint The equation showing the balance between total expenditures and total revenues of the government.

government's revenue from printing money The real income that government obtains by increasing the quantity of high-powered money. In the United States this revenue accrues to the Federal Reserve and is subsequently transferred to the U.S. Treasury. See **inflation tax.**

graduated-rate tax A kind of income tax in which the marginal tax rate rises with taxable income. See **flat-rate tax.**

Great Depression The decline in the aggregate economic activity in the United States that occurred from 1929 to 1933.

gross domestic product (GDP) The market value of an economy's domestically produced goods and services over a specified period of time.

gross investment The purchases of capital goods.

gross national product (GNP) The total market value of the goods and services produced by the residents of a country over a specified period of time; GNP equals gross domestic product plus the net factor income from abroad.

gross private domestic investment Total private expenditure on investment goods, including business spending on plant and equipment, the net change in business inventories, and residential construction.

high-powered money The total amount of Federal Reserve Notes (currency) and non-interest-bearing deposits (reserves) held at the Fed by depository institutions; the monetary base.

human capital Skills and training that are embodied in workers and add to productivity.

hyperinflation A period with an extraordinarily high inflation rate, such as that in Germany after World War I.

implicit GNP price deflator The price index that relates the gross national product, measured in nominal terms, to real GNP.

imports Goods that are produced in foreign countries and purchased by the domestic residents of a country.

income effect Another term for a wealth effect.

increasing (or decreasing) returns to scale A characteristic of the production function such that a proportionate increase in all inputs results in a more than (or less than) proportionate increase in output.

indexation A system of contracts in which payments are revised upward or downward according to increases or decreases in the general price level so as to keep the real value of payments independent of inflation; **inflation correction.**

indifference curve A graph showing the combinations of two items, such as consumption and work effort, that yield the same level of utility.

inferior goods Goods for which the wealth effect is negative.

infinite horizon The household's planning horizon when plans extend into the indefinite future; used in models that stress the role of intergenerational transfers.

inflation A sustained increase in the general price level over time.

inflation correction Another term for **indexation.**

inflation rate The percentage change in the price level between two periods of time.

inflation tax The revenue that the government gets by printing money at a faster rate (and thereby causing more inflation). See **government's revenue from printing money.**

interest rate The ratio of the interest payment per period to the amount borrowed; the return to lending or the cost of borrowing.

interest-rate parity   The equalization of interest rates across countries, taking account of an adjustment for prospective changes in exchange rates.

interest-rate targeting   A setup where the monetary authority attempts to keep a designated nominal interest rate close to a target value. In this regime, the quantity of money is endogenous.

intermediate goods   Commodities that are purchased for resale or for use in the production and sale of other commodities.

international currency   International media of exchange, such as gold or U.S. currency, held by central banks.

international reserves   The total quantity of liquid assets, including international currency, that central banks use for international transactions.

intertemporal-substitution effect   The effect on current consumption (leisure) when the cost of future consumption (leisure) changes relative to that of current consumption (leisure).

inventories   Stores of commodities held by businesses either for sale or for use in production.

investment accelerator   The positive effect of changes in output on investment demand. See **Keynesian investment function.**

investment demand   The quantity of investment that is desired by firms and households, expressed as a function of the real interest rate, the depreciation rate, and the existing stock of capital.

involuntary employment   The inability of workers to obtain employment at the prevailing market wage; a feature of Keynesian theory.

irrelevance result for systematic monetary policy   The theoretical finding that a policy of changing the quantity of money in response to the state of economy is predictable and therefore powerless to affect the economy.

irreversible investment   The property that, once output has been used to form new capital goods, the process cannot be reversed by consuming the capital. Because investment is irreversible, uncertainty about the returns to investment can substantially reduce or delay investment spending.

IS curve   A graph used in Keynesian theory showing the combinations of aggregate output and the interest rate that satisfy the condition that aggregate output equals the aggregate demand for commodities.

IS/LM model   The analytical tool used in Keynesian theory to study the simultaneous determination of aggregate output and the interest rate.

job-finding rate   The rate at which workers move from being unemployed or outside of the labor force to being employed.

job-separation rate   The rate at which workers move from being employed to being unemployed or outside of the labor force.

Keynesian consumption function   The dependence of consumption demand on income and the interest rate; a central element of Keynesian theory.

Keynesian cross diagram   The graph depicting the determination of the level of aggregate output for a given interest rate.

Keynesian investment function   The dependence of investment demand on output and the interest rate; an important element of Keynesian theory.

Keynesian model   The theory developed by John Maynard Keynes that sought to explain aggregate business fluctuations.

labor force   The total number of employed workers plus the number of unemployed.

Laffer curve   A graph showing that tax revenues initially rise as the marginal tax rate rises but eventually reach a maximum and decline with further increases in the marginal tax rate.

Law of one price The condition that identical goods in different countries must sell at the same dollar price.

legal tender A characteristic of money, whereby its use as a medium of exchange is reinforced by government statute.

lender of last resort The role of the central bank as a provider of loans to financial institutions during crises.

life-cycle model The theory of the choices of consumption and leisure that are made when the planning horizon is equal to the individual's expected remaining lifetime; it predicts that an individual will build up savings during working years and exhaust them during retirement years. See **infinite horizon.**

liquidity constraint The negative effect on consumer demand from the inability to borrow at the "going" interest rate.

LM curve A graph used in Keynesian theory showing the combinations of aggregate output and the interest rate that satisfy the condition that the demand for money equals the given quantity of money.

long-term contracts Aggreements between buyers and sellers or between firms and workers that specify the terms of exchange over a number of periods.

lump-sum taxes Taxes paid to the government so that the amount paid does not depend on any characteristic of the individual, such as income or wealth.

lump-sum transfer A transfer payment from government to an individual in which the amount paid does not depend on any characteristic of the recipient, such as income or wealth.

M1 The definition of money as the sum of currency plus checkable deposits plus travelers' checks; a measure of the volume of assets that serve regularly as media of exchange.

marginal product of capital (MPK) The increment of output obtained per unit increment in the input of physical capital, while holding fixed any other inputs.

marginal product of labor (MPL) The increment of output obtained per unit increment in labor input while holding fixed any other inputs; the slope of the graph of the production function relating output to labor input.

marginal propensity to consume The effect of a change in income on consumption demand.

marginal propensity to invest The effect of a change in output on investment demand.

marginal propensity to save The effect of a change in income on desired saving.

marginal propensity to spend The effect of a change in income (or output) on the total demand for goods, whether for consumption or investment.

marginal tax rate The fraction of an additional dollar of income that must be paid as tax. This rate varies according to the level of adjusted gross income. See **average tax rate.**

market-clearing approach The viewpoint that prices, such as the interest rate and the general price level, are determined to clear all markets, such as those for credit and commodities; that is, supply equals demand in each market.

medium of exchange The commodity or other item that people use as a means of paying for purchases; money.

menu costs Costs of a lump-sum type that must be paid to adjust a nominal price or wage. Some Keynesian models rely on these costs to rationalize the sluggish adjustment of prices or wages.

microeconomic foundations The theoretical analysis of individual behavior that underlies the macroeconomic model of the economy.

minimum wage   The amount below which the wage rate paid by a firm cannot legally fall.

monetarism   A school of thought, based on the quantity theory of money, that changes in the nominal quantity of money primarily account for movements in the price level in the long run and for fluctuations in real gross national product in the short run.

monetary accommodation   The response of the nominal quantity of money to a change in the nominal amount demanded. Accommodation tends to occur in regimes where the monetary authority targets nominal interest rates or in some other setups where money is endogenous.

monetary approach to the balance of payments   Analyses of the balance of international payments and exchange rates that stress the quantity of money and the demand for money in each country.

monetary base   See **high-powered money.**

monetary reform   A fundamental change in the monetary system or in the formulation of monetary policy.

monetize the deficit   Raise revenue to meet interest payments on government debt by increasing the quantity of money.

money multiplier   The ratio of M1 to the monetary base.

multiple expansion of deposits   The effect of an increase in the monetary base on the volume of deposits held at financial institutions.

multiplier   The change in aggregate output per dollar autonomous increase in aggregate demand; assumed in simple Keynesian models to be positive and greater than one.

national income   The income earned from aggreate production; gross national product adjusted for depreciation and sales and excise taxes.

national-income accounts   The summary statement of gross national product and its components during a year.

national saving   The total saving carried out by the residents of a country; the sum of private and public saving.

natural unemployment rate   The average unemployment rate that prevails in the economy, depending on the average rates of job separation and job finding.

net exports   The difference between the value of exports and the value of imports.

net factor income from abroad   Income earned by the residents of a country from labor supplied to foreign countries or from net claims on foreign assets.

net foreign investment   The change in a country's net holdings of interest-bearing assets from abroad plus the change in its international currency.

net investment   The change in the capital stock; gross investment minus the amount of depreciation.

net national product (NNP)   Gross national product minus the depreciation of capital.

neutrality of money   The theoretical finding that once-and-for-all changes in the nominal quantity of money affect nominal variables such as the general price level but leave real variables such as real gross national product unaffected.

nominal   Measured in current dollar magnitudes; valued at current dollar prices; unadjusted for changes in the general price level.

nominal deficit   The current dollar value of the government's **real deficit.**

nominal exchange rate   The customary exchange rate between one currency and another. The term emphasizes the distinction from the real exchange rate, which adjusts the nominal exchange rate for differences in national price levels.

nominal interest rate   The amount paid as interest per dollar borrowed for one period; the rate at which the nominal value of assets that are held as bonds grows over time.

nominal saving   The current dollar value of real saving, calculated by multiplying real saving by a price index.

nontraded goods Goods, such as services and real estate, that do not enter readily into international commerce.

open economy An economy that conducts trade with the rest of the world.

open-market operations The purchase or sale of government securities by the Federal Reserve in exchange for newly created high-powered money.

outflow (inflow) of capital The positive (negative) balance on capital account for a country.

outside of the labor force The classification of a person who is neither employed nor currently looking for a job.

pay-as-you-go system (for social security) A system in which benefits to retired persons are financed by taxes on the current working generation.

perceived relative price The ratio of the observed price in a local market to the perceived general price level.

perfect competition The assumption that individuals participating in a market each view themselves as sufficiently small that they can buy or sell any amount without affecting the established price.

perfect foresight A situation where expectations of inflation or of other variables are accurate, so that there are no forecast errors.

permanent income The hypothetical amount of real income that, when received constantly throughout the individual's planning horizon, has the same real present value as the actual flow of income; the per-period equivalent of the total present value of income. A temporary change in income entails a less than equivalent change in permanent income.

personal consumption expenditure Purchases of goods and services by households for use in consumption.

personal income Income received directly by persons; national income adjusted for undistributed corporate profits, social security contributions, transfer payments, and some other items.

Phillips curve The relationship between nominal variables such as the inflation rate and real variables such as the unemployment rate or growth rate of aggregate output.

physical capital Capital inputs into production, such as machinery and buildings.

planning horizon The number of future periods that enter the household's budget constraint; the length of time for which the household plans consumption and leisure choices.

policy rule A rule or commitment for governmental actions with regard to money or other variables.

present value The value of future dollar amounts, after dividing by the discount factor.

principal of bond The amount borrowed, to be repaid at maturity.

private fixed capital The sum of producers' durable equipment and structures and residential structures; a measure of the private capital stock that excludes business inventories and consumer durables other than homes.

producer price index (PPI) A weighted average of prices of raw materials and semifinished goods, relative to base-year prices.

producers' durable equipment and structures The measure of physical capital that includes machinery and buildings used in production.

production function The relationship between the quantity of output obtained and the quantities of inputs into production, such as labor and capital.

profit The difference between revenues and costs for a firm.

public debt The volume of interest-bearing governement obligations to the public.

public goods Goods that are enjoyed jointly by many people, such as the space program and national defense.

puchasing-power parity (PPP) The condition that the ratio of the exchange rates for the currencies of any two countries must equal the ratio of the prices of goods in each country.

quantity theory of money   The theory that changes in the nominal quantity of money account for the majority of long-run movements in the general price level.

rate of monetary growth   The percentage increase in the nominal quantity of money between two periods.

rate of time preference   The parameter that determines the relative weights applied to utility in different periods. The higher the rate of time preference, the higher the discount applied to future utility.

rational expectations   The viewpoint that individuals make forecasts or estimates of unknown variables, such as the general price level, in the best possible manner, utilizing all information currently available.

real-balance effect   The effect of a change in wealth resulting from a change in the general price level; the wealth effect of a rise in the real value of money balances.

real business cycle theory   A theory of business fluctuations that relies on real disturbances rather than monetary shocks. This theory emphasizes shifts to the production function, and usually assumes full market clearing and rational behavior of individuals.

real deficit   The change in the real value of the government's obligations to the public in the form of money and bonds.

real exchange rate   The exchange rate between two currencies divided by the ratio of the price levels in the two countries.

real gross national product   The gross national product (GNP) divided by a price index to adjust for changes in the average level of market prices; GNP in constant dollars.

real interest rate   The rate at which the real value of dollar assets that are held as bonds grows over time; the interest rate on an asset after adjusting for inflation.

real rate of return from investment   The net real proceeds from investment over one period expressed relative to the real cost of the investment.

real saving   The change in the real value of assets of a household or of the economy as a whole.

real terms   Measured in units of commodities; valued at base-year prices; dollar magnitudes that are adjusted for inflation by deflating by a price index.

real wage rate   The value in real terms of the dollar amount paid for an hour of labor services.

recession   A period of decline in the level of aggregate economic activity or real gross national product.

Regulation Q   The legal limit (applicable in previous years) imposed by the Federal Reserve on the interest rate payable on time deposits and savings deposits held at banks.

relative form of PPP   The version of purchasing-power parity that involves changes in exchange rates and prices.

replacement ratio (for unemployment insurance)   The ratio of unemployment benefits to the prior wage earnings of a worker.

reservation wage   The wage rate that is just high enough to induce someone to accept a job.

reserve requirement   The requirement imposed by the Federal Reserve that depository institutions must hold a certain quantity of reserves. For each category of deposits, the requirement is specified as a fraction of the amount of deposits.

reserves (of depository institutions)   The total amount of currency and noninterest-bearing deposits at the Fed held by banks and other depository institutions.

revaluation   An increase in the value of a country's currency in terms of another currency, such as the U.S. dollar.

Ricardian Equivalence Theorem The theoretical finding that, given the amounts of government purchases, an increase in current taxes has the same effect on the economy as an equal increase in the government budget deficit.

saving The change in an individual's assets during a period of time.

savings deposits Deposits held at banks that usually allow funds to be withdrawn without penalty with a 30-day notice of withdrawal.

seasonally adjusted data Adjustment of quantities for normal seasonal variations. Seasonal adjustments are important for most national-accounts variables, such as real gross national product and its components, and also for monetary aggregates.

short-side rule (for determining quantities) The condition that the quantity of output or sales in a situation of excess demand or excess supply is determined by the lesser of the quantity demanded and the quantity supplied.

social security Transfer payments made by government to households through social insurance programs such as old age and survivors' insurance and disability insurance.

speculation (on exchange rates) Sale (or purchase) of a currency in exchange for another currency whenever a devaluation (or revaluation) is expected.

stagflation A stituation where a recession is accompanied by high and rising inflation.

steady state A situation where the rate of growth of the economy is zero so that output, consumption, gross investment, and work effort are all constant.

steady-state growth A situation where output, the stock of physical capital, consumption, and work effort all grow at the same rate as population so that the amounts per person are constant.

steady-state per capita growth A situation where the amounts of output, capital stock, and consumption per person all grow at some constant rate.

sterilization An action by the central bank of a country that prevents increases (decreases) in the amount of international currency from increasing (decreasing) the quantity of money in the country.

stock market A market where people trade shares of ownership in firms. The owners of stock receive the dividends paid out by firms.

substitution effects The response of households to changes in the relative cost of obtaining any two goods such as consumption and leisure.

superior goods (or normal goods) Goods for which the wealth effect is positive.

superneutrality of money The theoretical finding that a change in the pattern over time of monetary growth does not affect real variables such as aggregate output and the real interest rate. See **neutrality of money.**

supply shock Changes that alter the production function, that is, raise or lower the output obtainable from given inputs or alter the marginal products of the inputs. Examples are harvest failures and technological changes.

supply-side economics The study of the causes and effects of changes in the supply and productivity of factors of production. This approach emphasizes the negative effect of income taxes on the incentive to work.

surplus (deficit) on current account A positive (negative) current-account balance.

taxable income Adjusted gross income minus the value of tax exemptions.

tax-exempt income Income from production, interest earnings, or government transfers that is not liable for income taxes.

technological change Improved knowledge about methods of production that shifts the production function upward.

temporary layoffs Job separations where the worker is usually rehired within a few months.

terms of trade The price of a country's tradable goods expressed relative to the price of a market basket of the world's tradable goods; often approximated by the ratio of a country's export prices to its import prices.

time deposits   Deposits at banks and other depository institutions that have a stated maturity date and carry penalties for early withdrawal.

tradable goods   Goods that are actually exchanged or could potentially be exchanged with foreign countries.

transaction costs   Costs incurred in the process of making sales or purchases, such as brokerage fees or the cost of the time involved.

transfer payments   Transfers of funds from government to individuals, such as welfare payments, that do not constitute payments for goods and services.

unanticipated money growth   The difference between the actual amount of monetary growth and anticipated money growth.

underground economy   The collection of economic activities from which the income earned is not reported and therefore not taxed.

unemployment   The situation of a worker who has no job and is looking for work.

unemployment insurance   The government program of providing temporary benefits to workers who have lost their jobs and are currently unemployed.

unemployment rate   The ratio of the number of unemployed workers to the total number of employed and unemployed workers; the fraction of the labor force that is unemployed.

unexpected inflation   The difference between the actual rate of inflation and the expectation of inflation; the forecast error made in predicting inflation.

utility   The level of happiness of a household, measured in units called utils. Utility increases with increases in either consumption or leisure. See **utility function.**

utility function   The relationship between the amount of utility obtained and the amounts of consumption and labor chosen by the household.

utilization rate   The percentage of time that capital is used in production; for example, an increase in the number of shifts per day in a factory increases the utilization rate of machinery.

vacancies   The difference between the number of job openings at firms and the level of employment.

value added   The increase in value of product at a particular stage of production.

vault cash   Currency held by a depository institution.

velocity of money   The ratio of the dollar volume of transactions per period to the average money holding; the number of times per period that the average dollar turns over in making transactions.

wage rate   The dollar amount paid to a worker in exchange for an hour of labor services.

Walras' Law of Markets   The finding that if all but one of the conditions for general market clearing hold, the final one must hold as well; this result follows because households' budget constraints must be satisfied.

wealth effects   The response of consumption and leisure (or labor) to changes in the household's opportunities for increasing utility. An increase (decrease) in wealth occurs when the household can raise (must reduce) consumption while leisure remains unchanged.

AUTHOR INDEX

SUBJECT INDEX